AI, Policy, and the Future of Human-Centered Education

Andi Asrifan
Universitas Negeri Makassar, Indonesia

IGI Global
Scientific Publishing
Publishing Tomorrow's Research Today

Vice President of Editorial	Melissa Wagner
Director of Acquisitions	Mikaela Felty
Director of Book Development	Jocelynn Hessler
Production Manager	Mike Brehm
Cover Design	Jose Rosado

Published in the United States of America by
IGI Global Scientific Publishing
701 East Chocolate Avenue
Hershey, PA, 17033, USA
Tel: 717-533-8845
Fax: 717-533-7115
Website: https://www.igi-global.com E-mail: cust@igi-global.com

Library of Congress Cataloging-in-Publication Data

Names: Asrifan, Andi, 1985- editor
Title: AI, policy, and the future of human-centered education / Edited by Andi Asrifan.
Description: Hershey : IGI Global Scientific Publishing, [2026] | Includes bibliographical references and index. | Summary: "The book discusses using AI to customize and modify learning settings, improve critical thinking and problem-solving, and encourage multidisciplinary education"-- Provided by publisher.
Identifiers: LCCN 2025029117 (print) | LCCN 2025029118 (ebook) | ISBN 9798337357812 hardcover | ISBN 9798337357829 paperback | ISBN 9798337357836 ebook
Subjects: LCSH: Artificial intelligence--Educational applications | Education and state | Student-centered learning
Classification: LCC LB1028.43 .A3974 2026 (print) | LCC LB1028.43 (ebook)
LC record available at https://lccn.loc.gov/2025029117
LC ebook record available at https://lccn.loc.gov/2025029118
British Cataloguing in Publication Data
A Cataloguing in Publication record for this book is available from the British Library.

Table of Contents

Detailed Table of Contents

and systemic inequalities. By integrating modern tools like telehealth, mobile applications, and remote monitoring, midwives may provide more individualized, accessible, and culturally attuned care. Human-centered design principles guarantee that these technologies are intuitive, empathic, and customized to women's distinct experiences. Case studies from several nations illustrate effective integration, leading to enhanced prenatal care, patient empowerment, and health literacy. The document also examines ethical issues, including data protection and informed consent, and emphasizes the necessity of equipping midwives with digital skills. This interdisciplinary approach offers a possible avenue for achieving more equitable and effective maternity healthcare systems.

Artificial intelligence technology has transformed the world of education and the way students learn. Artificial intelligence has become a highly valuable partner in the field of education due to its ability to analyze data on a large scale and provide interactive learning tools. An educational policy that supports the use of artificial intelligence as a medium in the learning process is necessary. In addition, it is important to conduct ongoing evaluations to ensure that students' learning outcomes have a positive impact. Using artificial intelligence provides the opportunity to implement innovative teaching methods, customize the curriculum, and tailor learning individually. Therefore, educational institutions must have a deep understanding of how to optimally utilize artificial intelligence and prepare the skills of educators and learners. The education curriculum is crucial for producing graduates who are competitive and can contribute in an increasingly complex and interconnected era of artificial intelligence.

AI and education appear to share a synergy, let alone stretching the sustainable goals way beyond their logical limit. One of them is SDG 4, specifically that concerns availability and access to quality education. The autonomy in learning is made possible by the AI systems where the application will provide lessons that are ideal and within the capability of the student. Consequently, learners' learning engagement as well as learning success rates increase continuously. This chapter

networks for knowledge sharing, resource access, and culturally and socioeconomically adapted learning. Virtual learning environments, multilingual translation, and AI-powered coaching enable real-time communication and understanding between global learners and instructors. These technologies provide underrepresented communities with customized content and high-quality education. Data privacy, digital infrastructure, and culturally sensitive algorithms are practical and ethical challenges with AI products. Global successes demonstrate how such gadgets reduce achievement gaps and promote educational justice. The global education network can alter if AI-supported collaboration tools erase trocational boundaries, promote inclusivity, and build a more connected and fair learning ecosystem for future generations.

This chapter examines various funding strategies crucial for the sustainable incorporation of Artificial Intelligence (AI) in education. While AI revolutionizes education via adaptive systems, data analytics, and personalized learning tools, sustainable financing continues to be a significant obstacle. The study examines conventional funding sources including government grants and philanthropy, alongside innovative forms such as venture capital, social impact bonds, and subscription-based frameworks. Case studies demonstrate both successful and unsuccessful AI applications, emphasizing lessons about stakeholder participation, equity, and quantifiable impact. Focus is directed towards synchronizing financial strategies with educational objectives, utilizing data to illustrate value, and establishing partnerships for sustained viability. The results support the implementation of innovative, inclusive, and performance-oriented funding mechanisms to guarantee that AI technologies improve educational outcomes broadly.

This study examines the crucial function of public-private partnerships (PPPs) in promoting educational technology to mitigate gaps in access, innovation, and quality. Given the issues in education stemming from the digital divide, antiquated infrastructure, and constrained resources, public-private partnerships present a

Preface

INTRODUCTION

We are at the cusp of a transformative era where artificial intelligence (AI) intersects with education, policy, and the pursuit of a human-centered society. As we shift from the Internet-of-Things-driven Society 4.0 to the vision of Society 5.0, our mission is no longer solely to innovate technologically, but to ensure that such advancements enhance human well-being, inclusivity, and purpose. *AI, Policy, and the Future of Human-Centered Education* is an edited volume that responds directly to this shift by reimagining educational systems for a world increasingly shaped by intelligent technologies.

This book brings together a multidisciplinary cohort of scholars, educators, and innovators who share a unified vision: to align AI integration in education with the principles of equity, personalization, ethics, and lifelong learning. As AI reshapes industries and redefines skillsets, traditional curricula struggle to keep pace. This volume proposes forward-looking strategies and tools to bridge that gap, showcasing how curriculum design can evolve to prepare learners—not just to survive, but to thrive—in AI-enhanced societies.

The chapters explore the intersections of AI with pedagogical innovation, digital ethics, and access equity. Real-world case studies, theoretical models, and evidence-based approaches reveal how educators and decision-makers can adopt AI technologies without compromising the human element that defines transformative learning. This book targets educators at all levels, policymakers developing inclusive and ethical AI regulations, curriculum designers rethinking instructional models, and researchers exploring the societal implications of AI in education. It is equally essential for edtech entrepreneurs and innovators seeking to responsibly integrate AI into learning environments.

Ultimately, this volume is more than an academic contribution; it is a call to action. We must collectively embrace AI not only as a tool of efficiency but as a catalyst for sustainable, human-centered advancement. By doing so, we can build educational systems that nurture critical thinking, creativity, empathy, and social responsibility—essential attributes in a rapidly evolving global society.

It is our hope that this book equips its readers with the insights, frameworks, and inspiration to lead the next wave of educational transformation—one that empowers individuals, strengthens communities, and shapes a more equitable Society 5.0.

ORGANIZATION OF THE BOOK

Chapter 1: Real-Time Feedback Loops: Utilizing Big Data for Continuous Curriculum Improvement

This chapter initiates our discussion with a compelling vision for curriculum innovation grounded in real-time feedback mechanisms and big data analytics. The authors detail how modern educational ecosystems—spanning K-12 to higher education—can employ learning management systems, visualization tools, and assessment technologies to continuously adapt and enhance pedagogy. Drawing upon well-established educational theories and curriculum design frameworks, the chapter makes a persuasive case for a systemic shift toward collaborative, adaptive, and individualized learning. Through illuminating case studies and a thoughtful treatment of ethical concerns such as data privacy and equity, the chapter underscores the evolving role of educators in a data-rich educational landscape. This foundational piece sets the stage for understanding how data and digital feedback can be key instruments in the evolution of human-centered education.

Chapter 2: Empowering Maternal Health: Integrating Human-Centric Technology in Midwifery Practices

Here, the conversation expands beyond traditional classrooms to explore how human-centered technologies can revolutionize maternal health education and midwifery. This interdisciplinary chapter showcases how midwives across diverse global contexts are leveraging tools such as telehealth, mobile apps, and remote monitoring systems to offer personalized, culturally competent care. Anchored in human-centered design, the chapter illuminates how empathy, usability, and digital literacy come together to foster better maternal outcomes. Ethical considerations, particularly regarding consent and data protection, are addressed with nuance. The chapter ultimately advocates for policy and training investments that empower healthcare educators and providers to champion equitable maternal care through digital innovation.

Chapter 3: Education Reform in the Application of Artificial Intelligence in Supporting Learning Media: AI and Education for Sustainable Development Goals (SDGs)

Focusing on the intersection of AI and curriculum reform, this chapter emphasizes the need for educational policies that proactively integrate AI as both a medium and catalyst for learning. The authors argue that AI offers dynamic opportunities to customize instruction, enhance engagement, and develop globally competitive graduates. Ongoing evaluation of student outcomes is highlighted as essential to ensuring these AI-driven methods fulfill their promise. As educational institutions prepare students for an AI-driven world, this chapter provides valuable guidance for curriculum developers and administrators seeking to implement pedagogical change aligned with the broader Sustainable Development Goals.

Chapter 4: AI and Education for Sustainable Development Goals (SDGs)

This chapter deepens the focus on Sustainable Development Goal 4—quality education—by examining AI's capacity to personalize instruction and foster autonomous learning. With AI systems that adapt to learners' strengths and limitations, the chapter explores how educational equity can be improved through data-informed teaching and learning. Ethical dimensions, including the moral implications of delegating pedagogical authority to algorithms, are critically evaluated. The chapter concludes by reinforcing AI's potential not only to enhance educational outcomes but also to cultivate global citizenship and environmental stewardship, expanding the scope of what quality education can accomplish in a sustainable society.

Chapter 5: Artificial Intelligence in Education: A Pathway to Achieving SDG 4

Continuing the thread of SDG-aligned education, this chapter examines how AI can serve as a catalyst for achieving SDG 4 by enabling more inclusive, personalized, and collaborative learning environments. The authors explore the use of adaptive learning technologies and intelligent tutoring systems, showcasing how AI can tailor content to meet each student's needs while promoting equity and accessibility. Additionally, the chapter delves into the potential for AI to enhance teacher support systems and global educational collaboration. Through concrete examples, the chapter illustrates how AI not only expands access but also enriches the quality and relevance of education worldwide.

Chapter 6: Lifelong Learning Systems in the Age of AI: Effectiveness, Challenges, and Strategies

As the workforce continues to evolve alongside technological advancements, this chapter highlights the urgency of building effective lifelong learning systems enhanced by AI. The authors present compelling arguments for how AI facilitates personalized, flexible, and skills-focused adult education. From professional training to upskilling initiatives, the chapter discusses the capacity of AI to improve access, accommodate diverse learning styles, and sustain learner engagement. Addressing both the opportunities and challenges of integrating AI in adult education, this chapter offers strategic insights for educational institutions, employers, and policymakers tasked with preparing citizens for lifelong adaptability in an AI-infused society.

Chapter 7: AI Policy Framework in Education for Advancing Society 5.0 with Safe AI Implementation

Concluding this collection is a comprehensive policy framework aimed at guiding ethical and effective AI deployment in education. In alignment with the human-centered ideals of Society 5.0, this chapter emphasizes the need for transparent governance, AI literacy, algorithmic accountability, and equitable digital access. The authors argue that educational institutions must adopt clear, adaptive policies that safeguard students' and educators' digital rights while maximizing the transformative benefits of AI. By integrating cross-sector collaboration among policymakers, educators, and technologists, the chapter sets forth a roadmap for responsible innovation. It provides essential policy considerations to ensure that AI serves as a force for good in advancing inclusive, safe, and forward-looking education systems.

Chapter 8: Bridging Educational Gaps Across Nations with AI-Supported Collaboration Tools

This chapter addresses one of the most critical goals of human-centered education—closing global educational disparities—through the lens of AI-powered collaboration tools. By leveraging AI to foster interconnected networks among educators, institutions, and governments, this chapter demonstrates how resource sharing, multilingual communication, and culturally responsive learning can be enabled on a global scale. Virtual learning environments, AI-driven translation, and coaching tools serve as bridges across linguistic, geographic, and economic divides. Case studies highlight the success of these tools in delivering high-quality, customized education to underserved populations. Ethical considerations—such as data privacy and culturally sensitive algorithm design—are thoughtfully examined. This chapter makes a strong case for the transformative power of AI in creating an inclusive global education ecosystem that transcends traditional barriers.

Chapter 9: Funding Models for AI in Education: Ensuring Sustainability and Impact

The ninth chapter explores a critical but often underrepresented component of education innovation: sustainable funding. As AI technologies become more embedded in educational practices, the challenge of financing such integration is paramount. This chapter evaluates traditional and emerging funding models—including public grants, philanthropic investments, venture capital, and social impact bonds—and their role in scaling and sustaining AI-based learning solutions. Through a series of case studies, readers gain insight into what makes funding models effective or problematic, particularly when equity and measurable impact are considered. The chapter advocates for strategic alignment between financial mechanisms and educational goals, providing essential guidance for stakeholders seeking long-term, inclusive, and performance-oriented investment in educational AI.

Chapter 10: Bridging the Gap: The Role of Public-Private Partnerships in Educational Technology

Chapter 10 delves into the strategic role of public-private partnerships (PPPs) in deploying educational technologies that reduce inequity and accelerate innovation. As educational systems worldwide grapple with outdated infrastructure and digital divides, PPPs offer a collaborative solution to bridge these challenges. This chapter categorizes different partnership models—ranging from joint ventures to strategic alliances—and evaluates their success across primary, secondary, and higher education sectors. Emphasis is placed on the importance of shared objectives, stakeholder trust, and continuous evaluation. The chapter also explores the promise of frontier technologies such as AI and virtual reality, calling for clear policy frameworks and cooperative models that ensure sustainability, scalability, and ethical deployment.

Chapter 11: Building a Culture of Accountability: Best Practices for Credential Management in Educational Institutions

In an age where digital credentials influence academic credibility and career mobility, this chapter presents a comprehensive approach to responsible credential management. Focusing on leadership, compliance, and stakeholder engagement, it outlines best practices for ensuring the transparency, accuracy, and security of academic records. Technological innovations such as blockchain, encrypted credentialing systems, and micro-credentials are discussed as tools for institutional trust-building. Through real-world examples and practical insights, this chapter empowers institutions to foster a culture of accountability that upholds both academic integrity and learner trust.

Chapter 12: Language and Digital Rights: Fostering Communication Skills for Responsible Online Engagement

This chapter offers a rich exploration of the nexus between language, communication ethics, and digital rights, urging educators and policymakers to consider linguistic identity and equity in digital spaces. As online platforms become key venues for global discourse, communication skills rooted in empathy, inclusivity, and multilingual awareness are paramount. The chapter examines how language shapes digital identities and calls for proactive promotion of media literacy, privacy rights, and ethical expression. Drawing from multidisciplinary perspectives, the authors propose strategies for fostering responsible digital citizenship through language education, emphasizing the critical role of inclusive communication in building equitable digital communities.

Chapter 13: Empowering Citizens: Integrating Digital Citizenship Skills into Public Policy and Governance

Chapter 13 extends the conversation to civic life, examining how digital citizenship skills can be embedded within public policy to strengthen democratic participation. It underscores key competencies—digital literacy, online safety, and collaboration—as foundational to active and ethical civic engagement in the digital era. Through analysis of policies and educational programs, the chapter highlights how governments and institutions can bridge digital divides, counter misinformation, and foster lifelong learning. Case studies illustrate the benefits of inclusive access and community-centered governance models. Ultimately, the chapter presents a visionary policy agenda for cultivating digitally empowered citizens equipped to navigate and influence tomorrow's interconnected societies.

Chapter 14: Technology Literacy in Empowering University Students' Extrinsic Motivation in Language Learning

Concluding this set of chapters is a focused study on the role of technology literacy in enhancing university students' extrinsic motivation for language learning. Using quantitative data from 102 Indonesian language learners, the chapter reveals a strong correlation between technological proficiency and motivation, particularly when learning environments are rich with interactive tools, rewards, and real-world relevance. Students responded positively to gamified content, mobile learning apps, and digital platforms that reinforced confidence and skill mastery. This chapter highlights how digital literacy not only supports language acquisition but also fosters motivation through personalized, practical, and engaging educational experiences. It affirms the value of integrating digital fluency into curriculum design to better align with learners' evolving expectations and technological realities.

CONCLUSION

As we draw this volume to a close, it becomes clear that artificial intelligence is not merely a tool—it is a catalyst reshaping the very foundation of education. The chapters within this book have illuminated a critical truth: for education to remain relevant and impactful in the age of Society 5.0, it must evolve beyond traditional boundaries. We must embrace AI not as a replacement for human connection, but as a means to deepen it—enhancing personalization, expanding access, and supporting equity on a global scale.

From real-time feedback loops and curriculum innovation to AI-supported global collaboration, maternal health education, and digital citizenship, this book has explored how AI can serve both as a mirror and a bridge. It reflects the challenges we face—inequities, outdated systems, fragmented policies—and offers pathways to cross into a more just, responsive, and inclusive educational future. Crucially, it reminds us that technology must always be guided by ethical stewardship, cultural sensitivity, and a steadfast commitment to human dignity.

As educators, researchers, policymakers, and technologists, we share a collective responsibility: to shape learning environments that prepare individuals not just for economic participation, but for thoughtful citizenship in a rapidly evolving world. We hope this volume serves as both a roadmap and a call to action—empowering readers to lead with innovation, grounded in empathy, ethics, and equity. Together, we can transform education not only to keep pace with change, but to shape a more sustainable, human-centered future for generations to come.

Andi Asrifan
Universitas Negeri Makassar, Indonesia

Chapter 1
Real-Time Feedback Loops:
Utilizing Big Data for Continuous Curriculum Improvement

Saprina Mamase
https://orcid.org/0009-0005-0454-4587
Universitas Gorontalo, Indonesia

Irwan Karim
Universitas Gorontalo, Indonesia

Nurhayati Doda
Universitas Gorontalo, Indonesia

Andi Asrifan
https://orcid.org/0000-0002-9934-6129
Universitas Negeri, Makassar, Indonesia

ABSTRACT

This chapter examines the transformative capacity of real-time feedback loops, facilitated by big data analytics, in improving curriculum design and teaching methodologies. Utilizing educational theories and curriculum creation frameworks, it emphasizes how prompt, data-driven decisions empower educators to more effectively meet student needs. The amalgamation of learning management systems, assessment instruments, and visualization technologies enables the ongoing collecting and analysis of both quantitative and qualitative data. Case studies from K-12 and higher education contexts demonstrate the practical applications and beneficial results of employing data-driven feedback systems. The chapter discusses ethical

DOI: 10.4018/979-8-3373-5781-2.ch001

considerations, including data privacy and equity, and highlights the changing role of educators in a data-intensive learning environment. It ultimately promotes a systemic transition towards ongoing curriculum enhancement via collaborative, adaptive, and individualized learning methodologies.

INTRODUCTION

Understanding Feedback Loops

Feedback loops are essential elements in education, functioning as systems for the collection, analysis, and application of data regarding student performance and learning outcomes (Weber et al. 2025). Feedback loops fundamentally comprise a cyclical process that initiates with data collection, advances through analysis, and concludes with the execution of modifications intended to enhance educational methods. In the realm of education, these loops are crucial for cultivating a culture of continuous improvement, allowing instructors to adapt responsively to student demands.

Historically, educational feedback techniques have undergone substantial evolution. Conventional approaches frequently depended on end-of-term evaluations, such as final examinations or standardized assessments, which offered restricted insights into student learning and advancement (Bulut et al. 2025). These examinations generally provided a retroactive perspective, emphasizing what pupils had acquired post hoc, rather than guiding current instructional methodologies. This deferred feedback strategy frequently led to lost possibilities for prompt interventions that could improve student learning.

Furthermore, the incorporation of big data into educational methodologies has transformed the functioning of feedback loops. By utilizing extensive data from diverse sources—such as learning management systems, attendance records, and formative assessments—educators can acquire profound insights about student behavior and learning patterns (Yoon et al., 2021). This data-driven methodology enables instructors to make informed judgments, customizing their instructional tactics to address the varied requirements of their students.

In conclusion, comprehending feedback loops is essential for educators aiming to improve the efficacy of their teaching methodologies. The historical transition from conventional evaluation methods to real-time, data-driven feedback systems highlights the necessity of adjusting to the evolving educational environment. This book examines real-time feedback loops and how utilizing big data can facilitate ongoing curriculum enhancement, eventually benefiting both students and educators.

The Role of Big Data in Education

Big data denotes the extensive quantities of organized and unstructured data produced continuously across diverse platforms and devices (El-Afifi et al. 2024). In the realm of education, big data comprises a vast collection of information sourced from various platforms, including learning management systems, student information systems, online examinations, and social media interactions. The capacity to analyze and comprehend this data could revolutionize educational methods, enabling more informed decision-making and tailored learning experiences.

The three core characteristics of big data are volume, velocity, and variety. The volume denotes the substantial quantity of data produced, encompassing student grades, attendance records, and engagement metrics from online learning platforms. Velocity emphasizes the rapidity with which this data is produced and processed, facilitating real-time analysis and feedback (Jin et al. 2024). Ultimately, variety refers to the diverse categories of data, encompassing quantitative data (e.g., test scores) and qualitative data (e.g., student feedback), which can be utilized to achieve a thorough comprehension of student learning.

In educational contexts, diverse data kinds are gathered to enhance teaching and learning methodologies (Çetin, 2021). These encompass:

1. Academic Performance Data: This includes grades, test scores, and assessment outcomes, offering insights into student accomplishment and areas requiring enhancement. Such data can be compiled over time to monitor progress and discern trends.
2. Engagement Metrics: Data obtained from learning management systems can indicate the frequency of student interactions with course materials, participation in discussions, and completion of tasks. Comprehending engagement levels enables educators to customize their methodologies to sustain pupil motivation and involvement.
3. Demographic and Socioeconomic Data: Data regarding students' backgrounds, encompassing socioeconomic level, ethnicity, and previous educational experiences, helps contextualize their performance and involvement. This data is essential for identifying achievement disparities and executing targeted interventions.
4. Behavioral Data: Monitoring student behavior, including attendance trends and involvement in extracurricular activities, can provide insights into elements affecting academic achievement. Behavioral data can assist instructors in comprehending the comprehensive context of a student's educational experience.

5. Feedback Data: Surveys and course evaluations offer qualitative insights into student attitudes regarding the curriculum and instructional methodologies. This input can be essential in enhancing pedagogical methods and curriculum development.

By utilizing these many data types, educators can establish real-time feedback mechanisms that facilitate ongoing curriculum enhancement. The incorporation of big data into educational methodologies improves the monitoring of student progress and cultivates a personalized learning environment tailored to the distinct needs of each learner. As we further investigate the significance of big data in education, we will reveal its capacity to effect significant change and enhance educational outcomes.

THE FRAMEWORK FOR CONTINUOUS CURRICULUM IMPROVEMENT

Theoretical Foundations

To successfully execute real-time feedback loops for ongoing curriculum enhancement, it is crucial to base our methods on recognized learning theories and solid curriculum development models (Brandenberger, 2023). Theoretical underpinnings establish the basis for comprehending the impact of feedback on learning and for designing and adapting courses to address the changing needs of students.

Constructivism is a fundamental learning theory pertinent to feedback. This theory asserts that learners develop their own comprehension and knowledge of the universe via experiences and reflection. In a constructivist classroom, feedback functions as an essential instrument for directing students' learning processes. Real-time feedback enables educators to deliver prompt replies to student questions and misconceptions, hence enhancing engagement with the topic (Rajaram & Rajaram 2021). Through the integration of big data analytics, educators can discern prevalent misconceptions within a cohort and modify their instructional tactics accordingly, so fostering a more effective learning environment.

A notable theory is Behaviorism, which highlights the importance of reward in influencing behavior. Feedback is seen as a mechanism of reinforcement that can incentivize pupils to enhance their performance (Chen, 2022). In this environment, real-time feedback can be utilized to reinforce positive actions and outcomes, motivating students to engage more profoundly with the curriculum. The strategic application of data enables educators to discern the most effective feedback forms for fostering desirable behaviors, hence enhancing their instructional methods.

Alongside learning theories, diverse curriculum development models guide the design and execution of feedback loops. The Tyler Rationale underscores the necessity of establishing explicit objectives, choosing suitable learning experiences, and evaluating outcomes (Tandiono, 2024). This model closely adheres to the concepts of continuous improvement, as it motivates educators to consistently assess and modify their curriculum based on student performance data. By employing big data to monitor advancement towards defined goals, instructors may guarantee that their curriculum remain pertinent and efficacious.

The Backward Design framework is another significant methodology that starts with the desired outcome (Levin, 2022). Educators initially ascertain the intended learning outcomes and subsequently design evaluations and learning activities that correspond with those objectives. This methodology intrinsically facilitates the establishment of feedback loops, promoting continuous evaluation and reflection on student learning. Integrating real-time data collecting into this process enables instructors to perpetually enhance their teaching tactics and curricular content to more effectively address the requirements of their pupils.

In conclusion, anchoring real-time feedback loops in recognized learning theories and curriculum creation frameworks is essential for their effective execution. By comprehending the impact of feedback on learning and utilizing systematic methods for curriculum development, educators can establish a dynamic and adaptive educational setting that promotes ongoing enhancement and improves student performance.

Designing Effective Feedback Loops

Creating efficient feedback loops is crucial for utilizing big data to enable ongoing curriculum enhancement (Song et al., 2024). Feedback loops are dynamic systems that iterate through data gathering, analysis, feedback delivery, and subsequent action. Comprehending the essential elements of these loops and following optimal implementation strategies can markedly improve the educational experience for both students and instructors (Franco et al. 2024). Essential Elements of Feedback Loops:

1. Data Collection: The initial phase in creating a feedback loop involves the methodical gathering of pertinent data. This may encompass quantitative data, such test scores and attendance records, with qualitative data, such as student feedback and observational notes. Employing many data sources guarantees a thorough comprehension of student performance and engagement.
2. Data Analysis: Following data collection, it is essential to examine the information to discern trends, patterns, and opportunities for enhancement. Educators can utilize data analytics technologies to quickly handle extensive datasets, allowing them to reveal insights that guide instructional practices. This analysis

must concentrate on both individual student performance and aggregate data to discern systemic flaws within the program.

3. Feedback Provision: Effective feedback should be prompt, precise, and actionable. Educators must convey insights obtained from data analysis to pupils in a straightforward and productive manner. Feedback must emphasize strengths while also identifying areas for enhancement, directing students towards their educational objectives.
4. Action and Adjustment: The concluding element of the feedback loop entails executing modifications in response to the feedback obtained. Educators want to utilize data insights to modify instructional methodologies, curricular material, and assessment techniques. This iterative process guarantees that the curriculum adapts to student demands and fosters continuous enhancement.

Best Practices for Implementation

1. Cultivate an input-Oriented Culture: Establishing an environment that prioritizes input is essential. Educators should promote the perception of feedback as a mechanism for development rather than as a form of criticism. This mentality cultivates resilience and an openness to constructive criticism.
2. Employ Technology: Utilizing technology can enhance the efficiency of the feedback process. Learning management systems and data analytics technologies can automate the gathering and analysis of data, enabling educators to concentrate on understanding outcomes and enacting modifications. Moreover, digital systems can provide real-time feedback, allowing for prompt replies to student performance.
3. cooperate and Exchange Insights: Educators ought to cooperate with peers to exchange insights and optimal methods for feedback implementation. Professional learning communities can function as venues for analyzing data discoveries, enhancing feedback methodologies, and collaboratively tackling difficulties.
4. Continuous Professional Development: Sustained training in data literacy and feedback approaches is crucial for educators. Professional development programs must furnish instructors with the competencies required to assess data proficiently and deliver substantive feedback.

By concentrating on these essential elements and optimal methods, educators may create efficient feedback loops that leverage big data for ongoing curriculum enhancement. This method not only improves student learning outcomes but also fosters a more flexible and responsive teaching environment.

Integrating Big Data into Curriculum Design

Incorporating big data into curriculum design is a revolutionary strategy that improves educational efficacy and adaptability (George & Wooden, 2023). By utilizing sophisticated tools and technology for data collecting, educators can synchronize their instructional tactics with learning objectives, thus promoting a more tailored and effective learning experience.

Tools and Technologies for Data Collection

A multitude of methods and technology exist for educators to collect data swiftly and effectively. Learning Management Systems (LMS) like Canvas, Moodle, and Google Classroom function as centralized platforms for administering course content, monitoring student progress, and collecting data on student interactions (Maslov et al. 2021). These tools enable educators to track engagement metrics, assignment completion rates, and assessment results in real time.

Furthermore, assessment instruments such as Kahoot!, Quizizz, and formative assessment platforms allow educators to develop interactive quizzes and polls that deliver instantaneous feedback on student comprehension (Tautz et al., 2021). These solutions not only streamline data gathering but also actively include students in the learning process, rendering exams more dynamic and less daunting.

Furthermore, data analytics software like Tableau, Power BI, and Google Data Studio can analyze and visualize extensive datasets, assisting instructors in seeing trends and patterns in student performance. By employing these tools, educators can acquire profound insights into student learning processes and identify areas of difficulty, facilitating prompt interventions (Lee et al. 2023).

Aligning Data with Learning Objectives

To successfully incorporate big data into curriculum design, it is crucial to link the gathered data with defined learning objectives. This connection guarantees that insights obtained from data analysis directly influence instructional methodologies and curricular modifications (Hailikari et al., 2022).

Initially, educators must explicitly delineate their learning objectives in accordance with educational standards and anticipated outcomes. These objectives must be specific, measurable, attainable, relevant, and time-bound (SMART). Upon establishing objectives, data gathering methodologies must be created to assess advancement towards these aims. Formative assessments can be connected with certain learning objectives to evaluate student comprehension at different phases of the educational process.

Subsequently, educators ought to evaluate data concerning these aims. By analyzing student performance data in relation to specified objectives, instructors can discern areas of student proficiency and those requiring further assistance. This data-driven methodology facilitates targeted interventions, including differentiated education and individualized learning plans, tailored to specific student requirements.

Moreover, continuous contemplation and modification are essential. Educators must consistently evaluate the alignment of their instructional tactics and curricular materials with learning objectives while gathering and analyzing data. This iterative process fosters a culture of perpetual enhancement, guaranteeing that the curriculum stays pertinent and efficacious in addressing the requirements of all learners.

In conclusion, the incorporation of big data into curriculum design via efficient tools and technology, aligned with learning objectives, enables educators to develop adaptive and significant learning environments. By adopting this methodology, instructors can improve student performance and cultivate a culture of ongoing enhancement in education.

DATA COLLECTION AND ANALYSIS

Types of Data in Education

In education, effective data collection and analysis are essential for informed decision-making and ongoing curriculum enhancement (Nadeem, 2024). Comprehending the many categories of data—quantitative and qualitative—and their corresponding sources is crucial for instructors seeking to improve student learning via real-time feedback mechanisms.

Quantitative vs. Qualitative Data

Quantitative data denotes numerical information that may be measured and subjected to statistical analysis (Taherdoost, 2022). This data is typically gathered via standardized assessments, quizzes, and examinations, yielding quantifiable indicators such as test scores, grades, and attendance rates. Quantitative data is essential for discerning trends, assessing progress, and facilitating comparisons among various student populations or cohorts (Müllensiefen et al. 2022). Analyzing test scores enables instructors to assess the efficacy of instructional initiatives and pinpoint areas where students may be experiencing difficulties.

Conversely, qualitative data includes non-numerical information that offers insights into students' thoughts, emotions, and experiences. This data is typically collected by open-ended questionnaires, interviews, classroom observations, and student reflections. Qualitative data is essential for comprehending the context underlying numerical data, providing a more profound insight into student involvement, motivation, and learning obstacles (Moore et al. 2021). Student feedback obtained via surveys can elucidate attitudes regarding the curriculum, instructional techniques, and classroom atmosphere, thereby guiding educators in improving the learning experience.

Sources of Data: Assessments, Surveys, and Learning Analytics

Multiple essential data sources enhance the understanding of student performance and learning outcomes.

1. Assessments: Formative and summative assessments serve as principal sources of quantitative data in education. Formative assessments, such quizzes and exit tickets, offer continuous feedback during the learning process, whereas summative assessments, such as final examinations, measure comprehensive understanding at the conclusion of a unit or course. Through the analysis of assessment data, educators can discover learning deficiencies and modify their instructional approaches accordingly.
2. Surveys serve as an effective instrument for gathering qualitative data from students, parents, and educators. They can be constructed to collect feedback on multiple facets of the educational experience, encompassing curriculum efficacy, pedagogical approaches, and student contentment. Surveys can evaluate students' self-assessments of their learning and engagement, offering insights that quantitative data alone may not provide.
3. Learning Analytics: Learning analytics entails the aggregation and examination of data produced by students' engagements with digital learning environments. This encompasses data from learning management systems, online debates, and educational applications. Through the analysis of learning analytics, instructors can monitor student engagement trends, recognize at-risk students, and customize interventions to address specific learning requirements.

The amalgamation of quantitative and qualitative data from various sources is crucial for a comprehensive picture of student learning. Through the efficient collection and analysis of this data, educators may make educated decisions that facilitate ongoing curriculum enhancement, thereby improving the educational experience for all students.

Techniques for Data Analysis

Data analysis is essential for utilizing big data in education, allowing educators to extract significant insights from the collected information (Vashishth et al. 2024). By implementing suitable statistical techniques and data visualization tools, educators can accurately analyze educational data and make informed decisions that promote ongoing curriculum enhancement.

Statistical Methods for Interpreting Educational Data

Statistical methodologies establish the basis for the analysis of quantitative data within educational contexts. These strategies enable instructors to summarize, compare, and infer conclusions from data sets (Fischer et al. 2023). Some commonly used statistical methods include:

1. Descriptive Statistics: This entails the summarization of data using metrics such as mean, median, mode, and standard deviation. Descriptive statistics offer an overview of student performance, enabling educators to comprehend major tendencies and variability in the data. Calculating the average test score enables instructors to assess overall student performance.
2. Inferential Statistics: These techniques allow instructors to draw predictions or inferences regarding a population from a sample. Methods such as hypothesis testing, t-tests, and ANOVA (Analysis of Variance) enable educators to ascertain whether the disparities in student performance are statistically significant. Comparing test scores from two distinct teaching approaches can determine which approach is more efficacious.
3. Correlation and Regression Analysis: These methodologies assist educators in examining relationships among variables. Correlation analysis determines the intensity and direction of the association between two variables, such as attendance and academic performance. Regression analysis extends to forecasting outcomes based on one or more independent variables, enabling educators to comprehend how various aspects affect student progress.

Data Visualization Tools and Their Applications

Data visualization tools are essential for rendering complex data more accessible and comprehensible. Educators can swiftly discern trends, patterns, and outliers by converting raw data into visual forms (Hassani & Silva, 2023). Notable data visualization tools comprise:

1. Tableau: This robust data visualization software enables schools to develop interactive dashboards and visualizations. Tableau accommodates extensive datasets and allows users to analyze data using filters and drill-down functionalities. Educators can utilize Tableau to illustrate trends in student performance over time or to compare several cohorts.
2. Microsoft Power BI: Power BI is a powerful data visualization tool that connects effortlessly with other Microsoft applications. It enables users to generate reports and dashboards that can be disseminated within teams. Educators can employ Power BI to assess key performance indicators (KPIs) and evaluate progress towards learning objectives.
3. Google Data Studio: This complimentary product enables instructors to generate bespoke reports and dashboards with data from diverse sources, including Google Sheets and Google Analytics. Its intuitive design renders it accessible for educators lacking considerable data analysis expertise. Google Data Studio is very effective for showing survey results and student evaluations.

In conclusion, utilizing statistical approaches for data analysis, along with proficient data visualization technologies, enables educators to analyze educational data effectively. Through data analysis and visualization, educators can reveal insights that guide instructional tactics and curricular modifications, thereby improving student learning outcomes and promoting a culture of continuous enhancement.

Ethical Considerations in Data Usage

As educational institutions increasingly utilize big data for real-time feedback and ongoing curriculum enhancement, ethical questions about data exploitation become critical (Saxena and Parivara 2025). Two key concerns are privacy and data security, together with the assurance of justice and fairness in data interpretation. Resolving these difficulties is crucial for sustaining trust among students, parents, and instructors, as well as for promoting an inclusive educational atmosphere.

Privacy Concerns and Data Security

Privacy issues dominate conversations around data utilization in education. The collecting and preservation of student data, encompassing academic performance, behavioral indicators, and personal information, require rigorous privacy safeguards. Educational institutions are required to adhere to rules and regulations, including the Family Educational Rights and Privacy Act (FERPA) in the United States, which protects student educational data and provides parents and qualifying students the ability to access and modify these records (Krutka et al., 2021).

Institutions must adopt stringent cybersecurity protocols to safeguard sensitive information from illegal access and breaches (Sharma, 2024). This include the utilization of encryption, robust user authentication, and periodic security assessments. Furthermore, data anonymization methods can be employed to exclude personally identifiable information from datasets, thereby mitigating the danger of privacy breaches while still facilitating significant analysis. Educators and administrators must formulate explicit data governance policies delineating processes for data collection, storage, and utilization (Alam and Mohanty 2023). Transparency in data collection and usage cultivates confidence among stakeholders and guarantees that students and parents are aware of their rights concerning data privacy.

Ensuring Equity and Fairness in Data Interpretation

Equity and fairness are essential factors in the analysis of educational data (Marras et al. 2022). In data analysis, it is crucial to acknowledge the potential existence of systemic biases, which may result in inequitable outcomes for specific student populations. If data analysis unduly emphasizes the performance of specific demographic groups while overlooking others, it may perpetuate existing inequities in educational opportunity.

To foster equity, educators must employ a culturally responsive methodology for data interpretation (Banwo et al., 2022). This entails acknowledging the varied backgrounds and experiences of students throughout data analysis and understanding that standardized measures may inadequately reflect the intricacies of individual learning trajectories. Utilizing disaggregated data analysis enables educators to discern certain trends and requirements among various student groups, facilitating tailored interventions to rectify inequities.

Furthermore, including a variety of stakeholders in the data interpretation process helps improve equity. Involving students, parents, and community members in dialogues with data findings guarantees the consideration of diverse perspectives, leading to equitable and inclusive measures.

In conclusion, ethical issues in data utilization are essential for promoting a responsible and equitable educational environment. By emphasizing privacy and data security while guaranteeing equality and fairness in data analysis, educators may effectively leverage big data for ongoing curriculum enhancement, eventually benefiting all students and fostering a culture of trust and inclusivity.

CASE STUDIES OF SUCCESSFUL IMPLEMENTATION

K-12 Education Examples

The incorporation of real-time feedback mechanisms in K-12 education has produced encouraging outcomes, illustrating the capacity of big data to augment student learning and refine curriculum efficacy (Song et al., 2024). Numerous educational institutions throughout the United States have effectively adopted these techniques, resulting in substantial outcomes and insightful lessons acquired.

A prominent instance is the Cleveland Metropolitan School District (CMSD) in Ohio (Coulton et al. 2023). The CMSD implemented a data-driven strategy to enhance student performance by utilizing real-time feedback mechanisms. The district established a comprehensive data management system to aggregate data from multiple sources, such as standardized exams, attendance records, and student engagement measures. Educators employed this data to identify at-risk pupils and customize interventions accordingly. Consequently, CMSD documented a significant enhancement in student performance and a reduction in dropout rates. The principal lesson derived from this program was the significance of cultivating a culture of data utilization among educators. Professional development sessions were essential in providing teachers with the skills necessary to analyze data effectively and implement insights into their instructional methods.

A further successful implementation is shown in Hillsborough County Public Schools, Florida. The district established a comprehensive data analytics platform that delivered real-time insights into student performance (Castro et al. 2024). Through the use of a centralized data dashboard, educators may track individual student development and modify their teaching tactics based on real-time feedback. This approach resulted in enhanced student results, especially among underachieving demographics. A notable result was the rise in the proportion of kids achieving grade-level proficiency in reading and maths. The district recognized that continuous communication and collaboration among educators, administrators, and data analysts were crucial for the effective deployment of feedback loops. Consistent meetings enabled educators to exchange insights, address challenges, and collaboratively formulate strategies for enhancement.

The Success Academy Charter Schools in New York City have demonstrated the effective implementation of feedback loops. The schools utilize a thorough evaluation system featuring regular formative assessments to collect data on student performance and engagement (Dudek et al. 2023). This data is examined to guide instructional choices and curricular modifications. The outcome has been a sustained history of elevated academic success among pupils, especially in traditionally marginalized communities. A fundamental lesson from Success Academy is the significance of cultivating a growth mentality in students (Yu et al., 2022). By highlighting the significance of feedback in the educational process, educators motivated students to perceive problems as chances for development, so augmenting their resilience and motivation.

The effective execution of real-time feedback loops in K-12 education has yielded substantial beneficial results, such as enhanced student performance and customized instructional approaches. The experiences of institutions such as CMSD, Hillsborough County, and Success Academy underscore the significance of cultivating a data-driven culture, enhancing cooperation among educators, and creating a growth mindset among students. These lessons can act as essential frameworks for other educational institutions aiming to leverage big data for ongoing curriculum enhancement.

Higher Education Initiatives

Numerous colleges have effectively utilized big data and real-time feedback mechanisms to refine their courses and better student performance (Saxena and Parivara2025). These programs exemplify diverse methodologies for incorporating data-driven decision-making in higher education, highlighting the potential for ongoing enhancement in teaching and learning.

A notable instance is Georgia State University. Confronted with a significant dropout rate, Georgia State instituted a comprehensive data analytics project to enhance student retention and achievement. The institution employed predictive analytics to identify at-risk students based on criteria including academic achievement, attendance, and demographic data (Gonzalez-Nucamendi et al. 2023). Through the implementation of focused interventions, such as tailored advising and academic support, Georgia State experienced a substantial rise in graduation rates, escalating from 32% to over 60% within a few years. This program underscored the need of prompt action and the necessity for institutions to cultivate a supportive atmosphere that addresses student needs.

Conversely, Arizona State University (ASU) implemented an alternative strategy by emphasizing course design and delivery via big data analytics (Saxena and Parivara 2025). ASU established a technology known as the "Intelligent Adaptive Learning" platform, which evaluates student engagement with course materials in real time. This approach enables instructors to customize information and teaching methods according to individual learning styles and speeds. Consequently, ASU has documented enhanced student engagement and performance, especially in large introductory classes that typically face elevated failure rates. The principal insight from ASU's program is the capacity of adaptive learning technology to customize education on a large scale, enhancing accessibility and efficacy for varied student demographics.

Another significant endeavor is at the University of California, Berkeley, which has utilized data analytics to improve its curriculum by emphasizing student feedback (Mani et al. 2021). The university created a portal named "Berkeley's Course Feedback System" that gathers real-time evaluations from students on their courses and instructors. Evaluating this input enables professors to implement prompt modifications to their instructional techniques and course material. This adaptive strategy has resulted in increased student satisfaction levels and enhanced educational achievements. Berkeley's experience highlights the importance of integrating student perspectives into curriculum creation, promoting a sense of ownership and involvement among learners.

In summary, institutions such as Georgia State, Arizona State, and UC Berkeley exhibit varied methodologies in utilizing big data for curriculum improvement. Georgia State promotes predictive analytics for student retention, ASU emphasizes adaptive learning technologies, and Berkeley focuses on real-time student input. Each effort underscores the transformative capacity of data-driven decision-making in higher education, providing significant insights for other institutions aiming to establish real-time feedback mechanisms for ongoing curriculum enhancement. By implementing these tactics, colleges can cultivate more adaptive and efficient educational experiences that address the needs of their students.

Challenges and Solutions

The incorporation of real-time feedback loops and big data in educational environments has shown considerable advantages, however numerous obstacles frequently emerge during execution (Ahmed et al., 2024). Comprehending these challenges and creating effective tactics to surmount them is crucial for guaranteeing the success of data-driven efforts in both K-12 and higher education.

A prevalent difficulty is the apprehension surrounding data privacy and security. As the volume of sensitive student data collected rises, educational institutions must contend with intricate legislation and ethical implications of data utilization (Liu et al. 2022). Stakeholders, including as students and parents, may be concerned about the storage and utilization of personal data. Institutions can develop stringent data governance policies to ensure compliance with standards such as FERPA and GDPR. Furthermore, ensuring honest communication regarding data collecting procedures and the safeguards implemented to preserve privacy helps foster confidence among stakeholders.

A notable challenge is the deficiency of data literacy among instructors. Numerous educators may lack the requisite abilities to assess and understand data effectively, hence constraining their capacity to leverage insights for instructional enhancement (Ghamrawi et al. 2024). Professional development programs centered on data literacy should be instituted to address this issue. These programs can provide educators with the competencies required to analyze data, understand results, and implement insights into their instructional methodologies. Promoting collaboration among educators, data analysts, and instructional leaders helps cultivate a culture of data-informed decision-making inside the institution.

Opposition to change is a common obstacle when instituting real-time feedback loops. Educators and administrators may exhibit reluctance to embrace new technologies or modify entrenched procedures, resulting in inertia (Wang et al., 2023). To mitigate this resistance, it is imperative to engage stakeholders in the decision-making process from the beginning. Involving educators in dialogues regarding the advantages of data-driven methodologies and offering opportunity for practical engagement with novel tools can foster acceptance. Furthermore, presenting success narratives from colleagues who have successfully established feedback loops might motivate others to adopt change.

Ultimately, technical obstacles associated with data system integration can hinder the establishment of feedback loops. Educational institutions frequently utilize various systems for data collecting, resulting in data silos and discrepancies (Nezami et al. 2022). To resolve this challenge, educational institutions should invest in interoperable technologies that enable smooth data sharing across platforms. Establishing a centralized data management system may optimize data gathering and analysis, guaranteeing that instructors possess full and precise information.

In conclusion, although challenges such as data privacy issues, insufficient data literacy, reluctance to change, and technical difficulties may impede the deployment of real-time feedback loops, strategic solutions are available. By emphasizing data governance, allocating resources for professional development, promoting stakeholder involvement, and improving technical infrastructure, educational institutions can effectively overcome these challenges. Ultimately, surmounting these hurdles is essential for fully leveraging big data to provide ongoing curriculum enhancement and improve student learning results.

FUTURE DIRECTIONS AND INNOVATIONS

Emerging Technologies in Education

As the educational landscape evolves, emerging technologies are crucial in improving the efficacy of real-time feedback mechanisms and the application of big data for ongoing curriculum enhancement (Bhimdiwala et al. 2022). Artificial intelligence (AI), machine learning (ML) applications, and predictive analytics are at the forefront of revolutionizing educational methods and enhancing student outcomes.

Artificial Intelligence and Machine Learning Applications

Artificial intelligence and machine learning are transforming the analysis and application of educational data (Yadav2025). These technologies facilitate the automation of data processing and the extraction of insights from extensive databases, permitting educators to concentrate on tailored instruction and student engagement. AI-driven tutoring systems may adjust to individual student learning styles and speeds, offering customized guidance and resources that improve comprehension. Platforms like Carnegie Learning and Knewton utilize adaptive learning algorithms to tailor instructional content according to real-time student performance metrics.

Furthermore, AI can enable the creation of sophisticated feedback systems that evaluate student assignments and deliver prompt, constructive critiques (Hooda et al. 2022). Applications such as Grammarly and Turnitin employ artificial intelligence to evaluate writing and provide enhancement recommendations, enabling students to perpetually hone their abilities. Integrating AI-driven tools in the classroom enables instructors to establish a more personalized and adaptive learning environment that addresses the varied needs of all pupils.

Predictive Analytics for Student Success

Predictive analytics represents a significant application of big data in education, enabling institutions to forecast student requirements and outcomes based on previous data trends (Umer et al. 2023). Through the examination of parameters including attendance, engagement, and academic achievement, predictive analytics can ascertain students who are at danger of underachieving or discontinuing their education. Georgia State University employs predictive analytics to proactively assist at-risk students, leading to enhanced retention and graduation rates.

Moreover, predictive analytics might enhance curriculum design by identifying areas where students frequently encounter difficulties. Educators can utilize this data to make educated judgments on instructional tactics, resource distribution, and curricular modifications (Grecu, 2023). If data indicates that many students are struggling with a specific idea, educators can adjust their teaching methods or offer supplementary resources to mitigate these difficulties.

With the growing integration of AI, machine learning, and predictive analytics in educational institutions, it is crucial to guarantee the ethical and equitable implementation of these technologies (Nguyen et al. 2023). This involves tackling data privacy issues and ensuring that algorithms do not reinforce prejudices or disparities in educational results.

In summary, the future of education is being influenced by developing technologies, including artificial intelligence, machine learning, and predictive analytics. These innovations possess the capacity to improve real-time feedback mechanisms, equipping educators with the necessary resources to develop individualized, data-informed learning experiences that promote student achievement. By using these technologies, educational institutions can enhance curricula and assist all learners in realizing their full potential.

The Evolving Role of Educators

The incorporation of real-time feedback mechanisms and big data in education is transforming the role of educators, requiring changes in teaching methods and an enhanced emphasis on professional development (Sharif & Atif, 2024). As educational methodologies progress, instructors must adjust to emerging expectations and duties associated with data-driven instruction and individualized learning settings.

Shifts in Teaching Methodologies with Feedback Loops

A notable transformation in pedagogical methods is the transition to a more student-centered approach (Soubra et al. 2022). Conventional pedagogical approaches frequently prioritize direct instruction, wherein educators present material to students uniformly. Conversely, real-time feedback loops enable instructors to implement differentiated instruction, customizing their teaching methods to address the distinct needs of each student. By employing data gathered from exams and learning analytics, educators can discern individual learning styles, capabilities, and areas needing enhancement, facilitating more precise interventions.

The implementation of collaborative learning methodologies is becoming more widespread. Feedback loops promote continuous communication among students, educators, and peers, establishing a culture of collaboration and collective accountability for learning (Zamiri & Esmaeili, 2024). Educators can provide peer feedback and group discussions, allowing students to learn collaboratively and enhance their critical thinking abilities. This transition to collaboration not only improves student engagement but also equips learners with the cooperation and communication skills vital for the contemporary workforce.

Professional Development and Training Needs

To adeptly manage these changes, educators must participate in ongoing professional development centered on data literacy and the strategic use of feedback loops (Zhao et al., 2024). Conventional training programs frequently prioritize topic knowledge and teaching methodologies; yet, the changing educational environment necessitates that educators cultivate competencies in data analysis, interpretation, and application.

Professional development programs must incorporate training on data analytics tools and platforms, empowering educators to leverage big data in their teaching methodologies (Hennessy et al. 2022). Workshops and seminars offer educators the opportunity to assess student performance data, extract meaningful insights, and execute data-driven interventions. Moreover, cultivating a collaborative culture among educators can improve professional learning communities, enabling instructors to exchange best practices, address issues, and jointly better their methodologies for utilizing data in the classroom.

Furthermore, continuous assistance and mentorship are essential for educators as they adjust to these novel techniques. Institutions ought to contemplate the establishment of mentorship programs that align seasoned educators with novices in data-driven methodologies, offering direction and support during this shift.

In conclusion, the changing role of educators regarding real-time feedback loops and big data requires substantial alterations in teaching approaches and a pronounced focus on professional development. By adopting student-centered methodologies and allocating resources for training, educators can proficiently utilize data to improve learning outcomes and cultivate a more adaptive and stimulating educational atmosphere. By adapting to these developments, educators will be more proficient in addressing the varied demands of their kids and preparing them for achievement in a progressively intricate globe.

Call to Action

In concluding our examination of real-time feedback loops and the application of big data for ongoing curriculum enhancement, it is crucial to contemplate the principal insights acquired during this discourse (Ahmadi et al., 2021). The use of data-driven methodologies in education signifies a fundamental transformation in educators' approaches to teaching and learning. By leveraging big data, educators may establish a more personalized, adaptive, and efficient teaching environment that addresses the varied requirements of all pupils.

A notable observation is the transformative capacity of real-time feedback loops (Kuppan et al. 2024). These loops facilitate the continuous collection and analysis of data by educators, permitting prompt actions that improve student learning results. The transition from conventional, retrospective evaluation techniques to real-time analytics promotes a proactive educational approach, guaranteeing that pupils have necessary help at critical moments.

A significant insight is the changing role of educators in this data-driven environment. As pedagogical methods evolve towards student-centered and collaborative frameworks, instructors must adopt their roles as facilitators of learning (Bhardwaj et al., 2025). This necessitates a dedication to continuous professional development, providing educators with the competencies need for efficient data analysis and the application of insights to their teaching methodologies.

The significance of ethical considerations in data utilization is paramount. As educational institutions increasingly depend on data, it is essential to consider privacy, security, and equity in data analysis. Educators must remain attentive to prevent data practices from unintentionally reinforcing prejudices or injustices, thereby cultivating an inclusive climate conducive to the success of all children (Wang, 2025).

In consideration of these findings, we urge educators, administrators, and policymakers to adopt data-driven decision-making as a fundamental component of the educational process (Mpofu and Chasokela2025). By emphasizing the adoption of real-time feedback mechanisms and big data analytics, educational institutions may foster a culture of continuous improvement that elevates teaching and learning. This dedication must be evident in strategy planning, resource distribution, and professional development programs.

Furthermore, we urge educators to participate in collaborative initiatives to exchange best practices, insights, and experiences concerning data exploitation (Ghamrawi et al. 2024). By cultivating a community of practice, educators can collaboratively enhance their methodologies, surmount obstacles, and acknowledge achievements.

In summary, the future of education depends on our capacity to leverage big data and real-time feedback mechanisms to cultivate significant learning experiences for all students. By adopting these technologies and dedicating themselves to data-driven methodologies, instructors may facilitate ongoing curriculum enhancement and enable students to realize their maximum potential. Let us together enact change, enhancing the educational landscape.

CONCLUSION

The incorporation of real-time feedback mechanisms and big data analytics into educational practices signifies a significant transformation in the design, implementation, and enhancement of curriculum. This chapter has illustrated that when feedback transforms into a continuous, data-driven process instead of a retrospective evaluation, educational systems can evolve to be more flexible, responsive, and focussed on students. Real-time feedback mechanisms enable educators to promptly respond to learning trends and student performance data, facilitating tailored interventions that address varied learning requirements.

By anchoring feedback mechanisms in known learning theories and integrating them with strategic curriculum design models like the Tyler Rationale and Backward Design, educators may guarantee that instructional decisions are pedagogically sound and data-driven. The proficient application of technology like Learning Management Systems, assessment instruments, and data visualization software facilitates a thorough understanding of both quantitative and qualitative student data.

The ethical and professional dimensions are equally crucial. Institutions must protect data privacy and security while fostering equity in interpretation. Educators require ongoing training in data literacy to effectively analyze patterns and convert insights into significant instructional practices. The success narratives from both K-12 and higher education emphasize that a collaborative and reflective culture about data utilization is essential.

In summary, real-time feedback mechanisms, driven by extensive data, provide a means for ongoing curriculum enhancement. They promote both instructional enhancement and institutional reform aimed at achieving more egalitarian, effective, and future-oriented education.

REFERENCES

Ahmadi, M. J., Fadil, M., & Miri, M. A. (2021). Feedback loops in teacher professional development: A qualitative study in Herat Province of Afghanistan. Cogent Education. tandfonline.com

Ahmed, I., Asif, M., Alhelou, H. H., & Khalid, M. (2024). A review on enhancing energy efficiency and adaptability through system integration for smart buildings. [HTML]. *Journal of Building Engineering*.

Alam, A., & Mohanty, A. (2023, January). From bricks to clicks: The potential of big data analytics for revolutionizing the information landscape in higher education sector. In International Conference on Data Management, Analytics & Innovation (pp. 721-732). Singapore: Springer Nature Singapore. [HTML] DOI: 10.1007/978-981-99-1414-2_51

Banwo, B. O., Khalifa, M., & Seashore Louis, K. (2022). Exploring trust: Culturally responsive and positive school leadership. [HTML]. *Journal of Educational Administration*, *60*(3), 323–339. DOI: 10.1108/JEA-03-2021-0065

Bhardwaj, V., Zhang, S., Tan, Y. Q., & Pandey, V. (2025). Redefining learning: student-centered strategies for academic and personal growth. Frontiers in Education. frontiersin.org

Bhimdiwala, A., Neri, R. C., & Gomez, L. M. (2022). Advancing the design and implementation of artificial intelligence in education through continuous improvement. [springer.com]. *International Journal of Artificial Intelligence in Education*, *32*(3), 1–27. DOI: 10.1007/s40593-021-00278-8

Brandenberger, J. W. (2023). Investigating personal development outcomes in service learning: Theory and research. Research on service learning. [HTML]

Bulut, O., Gorgun, G., & Yildirim-Erbasli, S. N. (2025). The impact of frequency and stakes of formative assessment on student achievement in higher education: A learning analytics study. [wiley.com]. *Journal of Computer Assisted Learning*, *41*(1), e13087.

Castro, A., Siegel-Hawley, G., Bridges, K., & Williams, S. E. (2024). Drawn into policy: A systematic review of school rezoning rationales, processes, and outcomes. [HTML]. *Review of Educational Research*, *94*(4), 539–583. DOI: 10.3102/00346543231195816

Çetin, E. (2021). Digital storytelling in teacher education and its effect on the digital literacy of pre-service teachers. [HTML]. *Thinking Skills and Creativity*.

Chen, C. Y. (2022). Immersive virtual reality to train preservice teachers in managing students' challenging behaviours: A pilot study. [HTML]. *British Journal of Educational Technology*, *53*(4), 998–1024. DOI: 10.1111/bjet.13181

Coulton, C., Richter, F. G. C., Cho, Y., Park, J., Jeon, J., & Fischer, R. L. (2023). Making the case for lead safe housing: Downstream effects of lead exposure on outcomes for children and youth. [HTML]. *Health & Place*, *84*, 103118. DOI: 10.1016/j.healthplace.2023.103118 PMID: 37839260

Dudek, C. M., Reddy, L. A., & Kettler, R. J. (2023). One size does not fit all: A concurrent analysis of the framework for teaching and the Classroom Strategies Assessment System. [HTML]. *Educational Assessment, Evaluation and Accountability*, *35*(3), 353–386. DOI: 10.1007/s11092-023-09405-6

El-Afifi, M. I., Sedhom, B. E., Eladl, A. A., & Padmanaban, S. (2024). Survey of technologies, techniques, and applications for big data analytics in smart energy hub. [sciencedirect.com]. *Energy Strategy Reviews*, *56*, 101582. DOI: 10.1016/j.esr.2024.101582

Fischer, H. E., Boone, W. J., & Neumann, K. (2023). Quantitative research designs and approaches. In *Handbook of research on science education* (pp. 28–59). Routledge. [HTML] DOI: 10.4324/9780367855758-3

Franco D'Souza, R., Mathew, M., Mishra, V., & Surapaneni, K. M. (2024). Twelve tips for addressing ethical concerns in the implementation of artificial intelligence in medical education. [tandfonline.com]. *Medical Education Online*, *29*(1), 2330250. DOI: 10.1080/10872981.2024.2330250 PMID: 38566608

George, B. & Wooden, O. (2023). Managing the strategic transformation of higher education through artificial intelligence. Administrative Sciences. mdpi.com

Ghamrawi, N., Shal, T., & Ghamrawi, N. A. (2024). Exploring the impact of AI on teacher leadership: Regressing or expanding? [springer.com]. *Education and Information Technologies*, *29*(7), 8415–8433. DOI: 10.1007/s10639-023-12174-w

Gonzalez-Nucamendi, A., Noguez, J., Neri, L., Robledo-Rella, V., & García-Castelán, R. M. G. (2023, October). Predictive analytics study to determine undergraduate students at risk of dropout. [). Frontiers Media SA. frontiersin.org]. *Frontiers in Education*, *8*, 1244686. DOI: 10.3389/feduc.2023.1244686

Grecu, Y. V. (2023). Differentiated instruction: Curriculum and resources provide a roadmap to help English teachers meet students' needs. [HTML]. *Teaching and Teacher Education*, *125*, 104064. DOI: 10.1016/j.tate.2023.104064

Hailikari, T., Virtanen, V., Vesalainen, M., & Postareff, L. (2022). Student perspectives on how different elements of constructive alignment support active learning. [sagepub.com]. *Active Learning in Higher Education, 23*(3), 217–231. DOI: 10.1177/1469787421989160

Hassani, H. & Silva, E. S. (2023). The role of ChatGPT in data science: how ai-assisted conversational interfaces are revolutionizing the field. Big data and cognitive computing. mdpi.com

Hennessy, S., D'Angelo, S., McIntyre, N., Koomar, S., Kreimeia, A., Cao, L., Brugha, M., & Zubairi, A. (2022). Technology use for teacher professional development in low-and middle-income countries: A systematic review. [sciencedirect.com]. *Computers and Education Open, 3*, 100080. DOI: 10.1016/j.caeo.2022.100080

Hooda, M., Rana, C., Dahiya, O., Rizwan, A., & Hossain, M. S. (2022). Artificial intelligence for assessment and feedback to enhance student success in higher education. [wiley.com]. *Mathematical Problems in Engineering, 2022*(1), 5215722. DOI: 10.1155/2022/5215722

Jin, L., Zhai, X., Wang, K., Zhang, K., Wu, D., Nazir, A., Jiang, J., & Liao, W. H. (2024). Big data, machine learning, and digital twin assisted additive manufacturing: A review. [sciencedirect.com]. *Materials & Design, 244*, 113086. DOI: 10.1016/j.matdes.2024.113086

Krutka, D. G., Smits, R. M., & Willhelm, T. A. (2021). Don't be evil: Should we use Google in schools?. TechTrends. springer.com

Kuppan, N., Padman, M., Mahadeva, M., Srinivasan, S., & Devarajan, R. (2024). A comprehensive review of sustainable bioremediation techniques: Eco friendly solutions for waste and pollution management. Waste Management Bulletin. sciencedirect.com

Lee, H. Y., Lin, C. J., Wang, W. S., Chang, W. C., & Huang, Y. M. (2023). Precision education via timely intervention in K-12 computer programming course to enhance programming skill and affective-domain learning objectives. [springer.com]. *International Journal of STEM Education, 10*(1), 52. DOI: 10.1186/s40594-023-00444-5

Levin, M. (2022). Technological approach to mind everywhere: an experimentally-grounded framework for understanding diverse bodies and minds. Frontiers in systems neuroscience. frontiersin.org

Liu, B. F., Shi, D., Lim, J. R., Islam, K., Edwards, A. L., & Seeger, M. (2022). When crises hit home: How US higher education leaders navigate values during uncertain times. [springer.com]. *Journal of Business Ethics, 179*(2), 353–368. DOI: 10.1007/s10551-021-04820-5 PMID: 34002104

Mani, N. S., Cawley, M., Henley, A., Triumph, T., & Williams, J. M. (2021). Creating a data science framework: A model for academic research libraries. [tandfonline.com]. *Journal of Library Administration, 61*(3), 281–300. DOI: 10.1080/01930826.2021.1883366

Marras, M., Boratto, L., Ramos, G., & Fenu, G. (2022). Equality of learning opportunity via individual fairness in personalized recommendations. [springer.com]. *International Journal of Artificial Intelligence in Education, 32*(3), 636–684. DOI: 10.1007/s40593-021-00271-1

Maslov, I., Nikou, S., & Hansen, P. (2021). Exploring user experience of learning management system. [emerald.com]. *The International Journal of Information and Learning Technology, 38*(4), 344–363. DOI: 10.1108/IJILT-03-2021-0046

Moore, A., Nguyen, A., Rivas, S., Bany-Mohammed, A., Majeika, J., & Martinez, L. (2021). A qualitative examination of the impacts of financial stress on college students' well-being: Insights from a large, private institution. [sagepub.com]. *SAGE Open Medicine, 9*, 20503121211018122. DOI: 10.1177/20503121211018122 PMID: 34094560

Mpofu, S., & Chasokela, D. (2025). Data-Informed Decision-Making: Using Analytics to Drive Strategic Management in Higher Education. In Building Organizational Capacity and Strategic Management in Academia (pp. 103-138). IGI Global Scientific Publishing. [HTML]

Müllensiefen, D., Elvers, P., & Frieler, K. (2022). Musical development during adolescence: Perceptual skills, cognitive resources, and musical training. [wiley.com]. *Annals of the New York Academy of Sciences, 1518*(1), 264–281. DOI: 10.1111/nyas.14911 PMID: 36251356

Nadeem, M. (2024). Distributed leadership in educational contexts: A catalyst for school improvement. Social Sciences & Humanities Open. sciencedirect.com

Nezami, M. R., de Bruijne, M. L., Hertogh, M. J., & Bakker, H. L. (2022). Collaboration and data sharing in inter-organizational infrastructure construction projects. [mdpi.com]. *Sustainability (Basel), 14*(24), 16835. DOI: 10.3390/su142416835

Nguyen, A., Ngo, H. N., Hong, Y., Dang, B., & Nguyen, B. P. T. (2023). Ethical principles for artificial intelligence in education. [springer.com]. *Education and Information Technologies*, *28*(4), 4221–4241. DOI: 10.1007/s10639-022-11316-w PMID: 36254344

Rajaram, K., & Rajaram, K. (2021). Learning interventions: collaborative learning, critical thinking and assessing participation real-time. Evidence-Based Teaching for the 21st Century Classroom and Beyond: Innovation-Driven Learning Strategies, 77-120. [HTML]

Saxena, S., & Parivara, S. A. (2025). Leveraging Data Analytics for Enhanced Academic Outcomes: Strategies and Applications. In Impacts of AI on Students and Teachers in Education 5.0 (pp. 349-380). IGI Global Scientific Publishing. [HTML]

Sharif, H. & Atif, A. (2024). The evolving classroom: How learning analytics is shaping the future of education and feedback mechanisms. Education Sciences. mdpi.com

Sharma, B. P. (2024). Role of advanced cybersecurity frameworks in safeguarding data integrity and consumer trust in digital commerce and enterprise systems. researchgate.net

Song, C., Shin, S. Y., & Shin, K. S. (2024). Implementing the dynamic feedback-driven learning optimization framework: a machine learning approach to personalize educational pathways. Applied Sciences. mdpi.com

Soubra, L., Al-Ghouti, M. A., Abu-Dieyeh, M., Crovella, S., & Abou-Saleh, H. (2022). Impacts on student learning and skills and implementation challenges of two student-centered learning methods applied in online education. [mdpi.com]. *Sustainability (Basel)*, *14*(15), 9625. DOI: 10.3390/su14159625

Taherdoost, H. (2022). What are different research approaches? Comprehensive review of qualitative, quantitative, and mixed method research, their applications, types, and limitations. [hal.science]. *Journal of Management Science & Engineering Research*, *5*(1), 53–63. DOI: 10.30564/jmser.v5i1.4538

Tandiono, R. (2024). Gamifying online learning: An evaluation of Kahoot's effectiveness in promoting student engagement. [HTML]. *Education and Information Technologies*, *29*(18), 24005–24022. DOI: 10.1007/s10639-024-12800-1

Tautz, D., Sprenger, D. A., & Schwaninger, A. (2021). Evaluation of four digital tools and their perceived impact on active learning, repetition and feedback in a large university class. [HTML]. *Computers & Education*, *175*, 104338. DOI: 10.1016/j.compedu.2021.104338

Umer, R., Susnjak, T., Mathrani, A., & Suriadi, L. (2023). Current stance on predictive analytics in higher education: Opportunities, challenges and future directions. [HTML]. *Interactive Learning Environments, 31*(6), 3503–3528. DOI: 10.1080/10494820.2021.1933542

Vashishth, T. K., Sharma, V., Sharma, K. K., Kumar, B., Panwar, R., & Chaudhary, S. (2024). AI-driven learning analytics for personalized feedback and assessment in higher education. In *Using traditional design methods to enhance AI-driven decision making* (pp. 206–230). IGI Global Scientific Publishing. [HTML] DOI: 10.4018/979-8-3693-0639-0.ch009

Wang, R., Standfield, B., Dou, C., Law, A. C., & Kong, Z. J. (2023). Real-time process monitoring and closed-loop control on laser power via a customized laser powder bed fusion platform. Additive Manufacturing. sciencedirect.com

Wang, V. (2025). *Ethics and Equity in AI-Driven Education.* AI Integration Into Andragogical Education. [HTML] DOI: 10.4018/979-8-3373-0502-8.ch010

Weber, F., Wambsganss, T., & Söllner, M. (2025). Enhancing legal writing skills: The impact of formative feedback in a hybrid intelligence learning environment. British Journal of Educational Technology, 56(2), 650-677. wiley.com

Yadav, S. (2025). Leveraging AI to Enhance Teaching and Learning in Education: The Role of Artificial Intelligence in Modernizing Classroom Practices. In Optimizing Research Techniques and Learning Strategies With Digital Technologies (pp. 211-238). IGI Global Scientific Publishing. [HTML]

Yoon, M., Lee, J., & Jo, I. H. (2021). Video learning analytics: Investigating behavioral patterns and learner clusters in video-based online learning. [HTML]. *The Internet and Higher Education, 50,* 100806. DOI: 10.1016/j.iheduc.2021.100806

Yu, J., Kreijkes, P., & Salmela-Aro, K. (2022). Students' growth mindset: Relation to teacher beliefs, teaching practices, and school climate. Learning and Instruction. sciencedirect.com

Zamiri, M. & Esmaeili, A. (2024). Strategies, methods, and supports for developing skills within learning communities: A systematic review of the literature. Administrative Sciences. mdpi.com

Zhao, Y., Zhao, M., & Shi, F. (2024). Integrating moral education and educational information technology: A strategic approach to enhance rural teacher training in universities. [HTML]. *Journal of the Knowledge Economy.*

Chapter 2
Empowering Maternal Health:
Integrating Human-Centric Technology in Midwifery Practices

Yuli Setiawati
https://orcid.org/0000-0002-6102-5450
Universitas Muhammadiyah, Palopo, Indonesia

Israini Suriati
Universitas Muhammadiyah, Palopo, Indonesia

Asmawati Asmawati
Universitas Muhammadiyah, Palopo, Indonesia

Patmahwati Patmahwati
Universitas Muhammadiyah, Palopo, Indonesia

Ummi Kalsum Marwan
Universitas Muhammadiyah, Palopo, Indonesia

Nur Ainin Alfi
Universitas Muhammadiyah, Palopo, Indonesia

ABSTRACT

This research examines the potential of human-centric technology to transform midwifery practices and enhance maternal health outcomes. Maternal mortality continues to be a global issue, intensified by restricted access, financial obstacles, and systemic inequalities. By integrating modern tools like telehealth, mobile applications, and remote monitoring, midwives may provide more individualized, accessible, and culturally attuned care. Human-centered design principles guarantee that these technologies are intuitive, empathic, and customized to women's distinct experiences. Case studies from several nations illustrate effective integration, leading to enhanced prenatal care, patient empowerment, and health literacy. The document also examines ethical issues, including data protection and informed consent, and emphasizes the necessity of equipping midwives with digital skills. This

DOI: 10.4018/979-8-3373-5781-2.ch002

interdisciplinary approach offers a possible avenue for achieving more equitable and effective maternity healthcare systems.

INTRODUCTION: UNDERSTANDING MATERNAL HEALTH

The Importance of Maternal Health

Maternal health is an essential aspect of public health, involving the well-being of women throughout pregnancy, childbirth, and the postpartum phase (Madden et al., 2023). Disturbing figures highlight the importance of maternal health: the World Health Organization (WHO) reported that almost 295,000 women perished due to problems associated with pregnancy and childbirth in 2017 (Abadi & Mebratie, 2021). This alarming statistic emphasizes the critical necessity for efficient maternal health interventions and reinforces the significance of providing women with appropriate care during their reproductive years.

The ramifications of maternal health reach well beyond the individual female. A mother's health directly impacts the health and well-being of her offspring (Hannon et al., 2022). Maternal mortality and morbidity can profoundly impact families, frequently resulting in children lacking maternal care and support. Studies demonstrate that offspring of mothers who encounter problems during gestation or delivery face an elevated risk of adverse health outcomes, such as developmental delays, malnutrition, and heightened mortality rates. Consequently, enhancing maternal health is essential not just for women but also for future generations.

Communities also endure the consequences of maternal health issues. Elevated rates of maternal mortality and morbidity might burden healthcare systems and impede socioeconomic progress. Families impacted by maternal health complications may encounter heightened financial strains resulting from medical costs, income loss, and the necessity for supplementary support services. Moreover, the emotional impact on families can be significant, resulting in enduring psychological consequences for both couples and children.

Enhancing maternal health is crucial for attaining overarching health and development objectives. The United Nations' Sustainable Development Goals (SDGs) seek to decrease the worldwide maternal death ratio to below 70 per 100,000 live births by 2030 (Ayele et al., 2021). Attaining this objective necessitates a comprehensive strategy that encompasses augmenting access to quality healthcare, advancing education on maternal health, and incorporating innovative solutions that empower both women and healthcare providers.

The use of human-centric technology into midwifery practices is a promising opportunity for enhancing maternal health outcomes. Utilizing technology that emphasizes women's needs and experiences can improve access to care, enable timely interventions, and ultimately empower women to manage their health during a pivotal period in their life. Comprehending the significance of maternal health is the initial step in cultivating an environment conducive to women's flourishing, bolstered by efficient healthcare practices and innovative solutions.

Historical Context of Midwifery

The profession of midwifery has profound historical origins, extending back millennia to ancient civilizations (Ndasauka, 2024). Midwives frequently served as the principal caregivers for women throughout pregnancy and childbirth, offering vital support and counsel. In numerous cultures, midwifery constituted not merely a profession but also a revered position within the community, with midwives acting as trustworthy individuals endowed with specific expertise in childbirth and mother care. This historical context underscores the inherent significance attributed to women's health and the necessity of female-focused care.

In ancient Egypt, midwives were esteemed, and their knowledge was recorded in medical manuscripts. In ancient Greece, midwives, referred to as “maia,” were tasked with attending births and were acknowledged for their expertise (Yee, 2022). Nevertheless, when medical procedures advanced, especially in the 19th century, the prominence of midwives started to decline in numerous Western societies. The emergence of obstetrics and the medicalization of childbirth resulted in a departure from conventional midwifery practices, frequently marginalizing midwives in maternal care.

Cultural viewpoints on birthing have significantly influenced midwifery practices (El2021). In numerous indigenous cultures, childbirth is regarded as a natural and sacred event, profoundly connected to community and household relationships. Midwives in these cultures frequently integrate traditional rites and practices that acknowledge the spiritual dimensions of birthing, highlighting the significance of emotional and psychological assistance in conjunction with physical care. This comprehensive approach starkly contrasts with the clinical, frequently impersonal characteristics of contemporary obstetric treatment, which may result in feelings of disempowerment among women.

In recent decades, there has been a revival of interest in midwifery and an increasing acknowledgment of the significance of culturally responsive care. A growing number of women are pursuing alternatives to conventional hospital deliveries, choosing midwifery-led care that prioritizes individualized support and empowerment (Crepinsek et al., 2023). This transition signifies a wider cultural trend acknowledging the significance of women's experiences and the necessity for care that addresses their specific requirements.

The use of human-centric technology into midwifery practices offers a chance to respect historical context while tackling modern concerns. By utilizing technology that improves communication, education, and support, midwives can deliver care that honors cultural views on birthing while guaranteeing optimal results for women (Mantula et al. 2023). Comprehending the progression of midwifery practices and the cultural importance of birthing is crucial for cultivating a more inclusive and effective maternal healthcare system that empowers women and aids their experience during pregnancy and childbirth.

Current Challenges in Maternal Health

Notwithstanding progress in medical research and heightened awareness of maternal health concerns, considerable obstacles remain that impede access to effective care for pregnant women. A primary obstacle to care is the limited accessibility of healthcare services, especially in rural and underserved urban regions (Rizkianti et al. 2021). Numerous women have logistical obstacles, including considerable distances to healthcare facilities, restricted transportation alternatives, and insufficient access to healthcare providers. This geographical mismatch frequently results in postponed prenatal appointments, which are essential for assessing the health of both the mother and the infant.

Financial limitations significantly restrict access to maternity healthcare. In numerous areas, the expenses associated with prenatal care, labor, and postpartum services can be exorbitant, especially for low-income families. In nations with universal healthcare systems, concealed expenses like transportation, childcare, and lost income can dissuade women from pursuing essential care (Gomez-Roas et al. 2022). The apprehension of unforeseen medical costs may result in the avoidance of treatment, hence intensifying the hazards linked to pregnancy and childbirth.

Disparities in maternal health outcomes represent a significant concern. Racial and ethnic minorities frequently encounter markedly elevated rates of maternal illness and mortality in comparison to their white counterparts (Canty, 2022). In the United States, Black women are three to four times more susceptible to mortality from pregnancy-related problems compared to white women. These inequities result from a complex interaction of factors, including institutional racism, socioeconomic position, and variations in access to quality healthcare. Implicit biases in the healthcare system can adversely impact the quality of care provided to underrepresented populations, resulting in insufficient treatment and support.

Cultural considerations can impede access to care. Women from various origins may face linguistic obstacles, a deficiency of culturally competent healthcare personnel, and divergent ideas regarding delivery, which might impede their engagement with the healthcare system (DeSa et al., 2022). These obstacles may result in sentiments of alienation and mistrust, so hindering their access to essential services.

Overcoming these obstacles and inequalities necessitates a unified initiative to transform maternity healthcare provision. The incorporation of human-centric technology into midwifery practices presents a possible approach. Utilizing telehealth services, mobile health applications, and community-based support systems can expand access to care, promote health literacy, and empower women to actively participate in their maternal health journey (Gillie et al. 2022). Comprehending and tackling the prevailing issues in maternal health is crucial for establishing a more fair and efficient healthcare system that aids all women, irrespective of their situations.

THE ROLE OF TECHNOLOGY IN HEALTHCARE

Overview of Health Technology

Health technology includes a wide array of tools, systems, and technologies aimed at improving healthcare delivery, enhancing patient outcomes, and optimizing healthcare procedures. Health technology fundamentally aids in the diagnosis, treatment, and management of health issues, allowing healthcare providers to offer more effective and efficient care (Fan & Zhao, 2022). The World Health Organization (WHO) characterizes health technology as any intervention employing structured knowledge and skills through technologies, pharmaceuticals, vaccines, procedures, and systems to enhance health and elevate quality of life.

Various categories of health technology exist, each fulfilling a distinct function within the healthcare ecosystem (Viswanadham, 2021). This encompasses medical gadgets, including diagnostic imaging apparatus (e.g., MRI machines), surgical instruments, and wearable health monitors. Health information technology (HIT) includes electronic health records (EHRs), telemedicine platforms, and health information exchanges that enable the dissemination of patient data among clinicians. Moreover, mobile health (mHealth) technology, encompassing health-related applications and wearable devices, enable patients to track their health and participate actively in their care.

In recent years, there has been a notable increase in digital health solutions, propelled by technological improvements and a growing need for accessible healthcare. The surge of smartphones and the internet has enabled the development of innovative digital technologies that augment patient engagement, promote communication between patients and clinicians, and support remote health condition monitoring (Butcher & Hussain, 2022). Telehealth has surged in popularity, enabling people to consult healthcare professionals from home, thus diminishing access hurdles and enhancing convenience.

The COVID-19 pandemic expedited the implementation of digital health solutions, as global healthcare systems aimed to reduce in-person visits and ensure continuity of care (Getachew et al., 2023). This transition has resulted in increased acceptance of telemedicine, virtual consultations, and remote patient monitoring, underscoring technology's potential to revolutionize healthcare delivery.

Digital health solutions exhibit significant potential in the realm of maternal health. Mobile applications can furnish expectant moms with crucial information regarding their pregnancy, monitor symptoms, and enhance communication with healthcare professionals. Telehealth services can guarantee that women obtain prompt prenatal and postnatal care, irrespective of their geographical location. Integrating human-centric technology into midwifery practices can foster a more supportive and empowering healthcare environment that caters to the distinct needs of women throughout their maternal health journey (Cantor et al., 2022). Comprehending the health technology landscape is essential for utilizing these technologies to increase maternal health outcomes and improve the overall quality of treatment.

Human-Centric Design Principles

Human-centric design, or user-centered design, is a strategy that emphasizes the needs, preferences, and experiences of users during the development of a product or service. This design concept is essential in healthcare for developing technologies that effectively boost patient participation and improve health outcomes. By prioritizing end-users—patients, caregivers, and healthcare providers—human-centric design guarantees that solutions are not only functional but also intuitive, accessible, and accommodating to the users' distinct contexts and difficulties (Dakulagi et al. 2025).

The significance of user-centered design in healthcare is paramount. Conventional healthcare technology frequently neglect the varied needs of individuals, resulting in irritation, disengagement, and suboptimal use. Conversely, human-centric design cultivates empathy and comprehension, allowing developers to devise solutions that resonate with people (Ebadpour et al. 2024). When developing mobile health applications for expectant moms, it is crucial to address their issues, preferences, and technological proficiency. Engaging people in the design process via interviews, surveys, and usability testing enables developers to obtain critical insights that guide the development of solutions that are both effective and user-friendly.

Numerous case studies illustrate the efficacy of human-centric technologies in healthcare. A prominent instance is the "Maternity Care App" created by a consortium of healthcare experts and designers. This application was developed to furnish expectant moms with tailored information, reminders for prenatal appointments, and access to educational materials (Bedenkov et al. 2021). The development team identified essential features to increase user experience, including an interactive calendar, symptom monitoring, and a community forum for peer support, through focus groups with pregnant women. The application's intuitive UI and customized information enhanced user engagement, leading to better compliance with prenatal care guidelines.

A further persuasive example is the implementation of telehealth services tailored exclusively for maternal health. The platform "Maven" facilitates virtual consultations with healthcare providers, allowing women to access care without the impediments of travel and schedule problems (Brinson et al. 2023). Maven has established a friendly environment that prioritizes the needs of mothers by incorporating features such as chat options, video calls, and seamless health information sharing. The platform's user-focused design has enhanced satisfaction rates and facilitated access to care, especially for women in rural or underserved regions.

Integrating human-centric design concepts into healthcare technology development is crucial for empowering women throughout their maternal health journey (Prabhakar et al. 2025). By concentrating on the experiences and requirements of users, we can develop new solutions that optimize care delivery, promote engagement, and ultimately better maternal health outcomes.

Ethical Considerations in Health Technology

As healthcare increasingly incorporates technology, ethical issues are essential to safeguard patient rights and maintain compassionate and equitable healthcare delivery (Vaishya et al., 2024). Two key ethical concerns in health technology are privacy and data security, alongside informed permission, especially with digital health solutions.

Privacy and data security are crucial issues regarding health technology. The delicate nature of health information requires stringent procedures to safeguard patient data from unwanted access and breaches (Keshta & Odeh, 2021). The proliferation of electronic health records (EHRs), telehealth platforms, and mobile health applications has led to a significant increase in the collection and storage of personal health data. This data may encompass medical histories, treatment regimens, and personal identifiers. If insufficiently protected, such information may be misused, resulting in grave repercussions for patients, including identity theft and prejudice. Consequently, healthcare institutions must enforce rigorous data security measures, including encryption, secure access restrictions, and periodic audits, to guarantee the confidentiality and security of patient information.

Furthermore, patients should be informed about their rights concerning privacy and data management. Transparency regarding the collection, utilization, and dissemination of data is crucial for fostering confidence between patients and healthcare professionals (Khang et al. 2022). Patients are more inclined to engage with health technologies confidently when they comprehend the safeguards implemented.

Informed consent represents a vital ethical consideration within the domain of digital health. Informed permission transcends the basic acquisition of a signature on a document; it necessitates that patients comprehend the ramifications of utilizing health technologies (Gesualdo et al. 2021). This encompasses transparency on the data to be collected, its intended use, associated hazards, and the rights patients own respecting their information. In the realm of maternal health, where women may be especially susceptible, it is imperative that consent procedures are formulated to be transparent and comprehensible. Healthcare professionals ought to provide information in many languages and formats to cater to diverse populations, so guaranteeing that all women can make educated decisions regarding their care.

Moreover, given that digital health solutions frequently engage with artificial intelligence (AI) and algorithms, it is crucial to confront the potential biases embedded within these systems (Hanna et al. 2024). Designing AI systems with justice and inclusivity can reduce the danger of exacerbating current inequities in maternal health outcomes.

In conclusion, as we adopt technology in healthcare, ethical considerations of privacy, data security, and informed permission must be highlighted. Establishing an ethical framework for health technology can augment trust, facilitate patient empowerment, and cultivate a more equitable and effective maternity healthcare system.

INTEGRATING TECHNOLOGY IN MIDWIFERY PRACTICES

Telehealth and Remote Monitoring

The use of telehealth and remote monitoring into midwifery practices signifies a revolutionary method in maternal healthcare, providing multiple advantages for both prenatal and postnatal care (Hod et al. 2023). Telehealth, comprising various digital communication technologies, allows healthcare providers to offer remote care, hence enhancing access to vital services for expectant and new mothers. This innovation is notably important in overcoming obstacles to care, including geographical distance, transportation issues, and schedule conflicts.

A key advantage of telemedicine in prenatal care is the enhanced accessibility it offers. Expectant women may engage with their midwives or obstetricians through video calls, telephonic consultations, or secure messaging systems, facilitating the acquisition of prompt advice and assistance without necessitating in-person visits (Nelson & Holschuh, 2021). This is particularly beneficial for women residing in rural or underserved regions, where access to healthcare services may be restricted. Furthermore, telemedicine can alleviate the stress and worry linked to travel, especially for women facing problems or high-risk pregnancies.

Telehealth enables ongoing surveillance of maternal health, essential for early detection of potential complications (Atkinson et al., 2023). Midwives can utilize telehealth systems to perform routine check-ins, evaluate symptoms, and remotely monitor vital signs. This continuous connection facilitates proactive management of potential issues, guaranteeing that women receive prompt and suitable solutions.

Remote monitoring solutions are essential for improving maternal health outcomes. Wearable fitness trackers and blood pressure monitors can deliver real-time information regarding a woman's health condition. These instruments can monitor vital signs, including heart rate and blood pressure, along with physical activity levels and sleep patterns. Integrating this data into telehealth consultations enables midwives to acquire significant insights into their patients' well-being and make educated care decisions (Kissler et al. 2024).

Mobile health applications function as efficient instruments for remote monitoring. Numerous applications are specifically tailored for expectant mothers, providing functionalities such as symptom monitoring, appointment notifications, and instructional materials (Moulaei et al. 2021). These programs enable women to actively engage in their health management and enhance communication with their healthcare providers. By promoting self-monitoring and participation, these tools can enhance health literacy and yield superior overall outcomes.

The use of telehealth and remote monitoring into midwifery practices provides substantial advantages for prenatal and postnatal care. By improving accessibility, facilitating continuous monitoring, and empowering women through technology, we can provide a more responsive and supportive maternity healthcare framework. This method not only mitigates current obstacles to care but also cultivates a sense of rapport and collaboration between mothers and their healthcare practitioners, ultimately resulting in improved health outcomes for both mothers and their infants.

Mobile Applications for Expecting Mothers

Mobile applications have become significant instruments in maternal health, offering expectant moms access to essential information, services, and support during their prenatal journey (Babu et al. 2024). Efficient maternal health applications are developed with distinct functionalities that address the special requirements of expectant mothers, improving their experience and enabling them to manage their health proactively.

A key aspect of excellent maternal health applications is tailored content. These applications should provide customized information based on the user's due date, medical history, and personal preferences (Lee et al. 2023). This customization enables expectant women to obtain pertinent updates and information, including guidelines for each trimester, nutritional counsel, and exercise suggestions. Moreover, numerous applications feature symptom monitors that allow women to oversee their health and communicate any issues to their healthcare professionals.

A vital component is educational resources. Comprehensive maternal health applications offer access to papers, videos, and tutorials covering diverse areas of pregnancy, childbirth, and postpartum care. This information enables women to make informed health decisions and equips them for potential obstacles (Moise et al. 2023). Moreover, interactive instruments like contraction timers and kick counters assist moms in monitoring their advancement and identifying significant indicators of labor.

Community support constitutes an essential element of good maternal health applications. Numerous programs integrate social functionalities enabling users to interact with fellow expectant mothers, exchange experiences, and solicit guidance (Akdim et al. 2022). This sense of community helps mitigate feelings of loneliness and offer emotional support throughout pregnancy, enhancing the overall experience.

Case studies of prominent maternal health applications demonstrate the influence of these elements on user engagement and satisfaction. A notable instance is the "What to Expect" app, derived from the bestselling pregnancy book. The application provides customized daily updates, a symptom tracker, and a comprehensive community forum for mothers to engage and exchange their experiences. Its intuitive interface and extensive resources have established it as a preferred application for millions of expectant women.

Another successful application is "Ovia Pregnancy," which emphasizes individualized health monitoring and education. Ovia enables users to record symptoms, feelings, and many health parameters while delivering personalized material depending on their inputs (Ortiz et al. 2023). The application includes a community component, enabling users to engage with one another and exchange insights. Its focus on data-driven insights and community assistance has cultivated a dedicated user base.

In summary, mobile applications are essential in assisting expectant women by offering tailored content, instructional materials, and community interaction. By including these elements into maternal health applications, developers can produce essential tools that empower women throughout their pregnant experience. As technology advances, the capacity for mobile applications to improve maternal health outcomes will increase, rendering them a vital element of contemporary midwifery practices.

Training Midwives in Technology Use

As technology transforms maternal healthcare, it is imperative to provide midwives with the requisite skills and knowledge to adeptly incorporate new advances into their practice (Hod et al., 2023). Educating midwives in the utilization of technology is essential for enabling them to employ digital technologies to augment patient care, boost communication, and optimize workflows. Nonetheless, the implementation of effective training programs and the mitigation of opposition to technology adoption pose considerable hurdles.

Healthcare institutions can implement many techniques to integrate technological training for midwives. Initially, it is imperative to develop comprehensive training modules that encompass many facets of technology utilization (Al-Adwan et al. 2021). These modules must encompass practical workshops, online tutorials, and access to resources that concentrate on certain tools, like telehealth platforms, electronic health records (EHRs), and mobile health applications. A blended learning approach accommodates diverse learning styles and schedules, guaranteeing participation for all midwives.

Moreover, mentorship programs can significantly contribute to the facilitation of technology adoption. Pairing seasoned midwives proficient in technology with those less acquainted can foster a conducive learning environment (Shikuku et al. 2024). This peer-to-peer methodology promotes information exchange and cultivates confidence in utilizing novel tools. Moreover, integrating technology training into continuous professional development might assist midwives in remaining informed about the latest innovations and optimal practices in maternity healthcare.

Addressing resistance to technology adoption is a crucial element in training midwives. Numerous midwives may experience trepidation regarding the adoption of new technology, stemming from apprehensions about their efficacy, the possibility of heightened workload, or insufficient knowledge with digital instruments (Wakelin et al., 2023). To mitigate these worries, it is imperative to articulate the advantages of technology explicitly. Emphasizing the capacity of digital technologies to augment patient care, promote efficiency, and alleviate administrative responsibilities may encourage midwives to adopt these innovations.

Fostering a culture of transparency and support inside healthcare organizations is essential for mitigating opposition. Leadership ought to promote midwives in articulating their concerns and offering input regarding technology use (Van et al. 2022). By including midwives in the decision-making process for the implementation of new tools, companies may cultivate a feeling of ownership and teamwork.

Ultimately, delivering continuous technical support is essential for achieving effective technology integration. Creating specialized help desks or support teams can aid midwives in resolving issues and addressing inquiries as they occur (Theodorio, 2024). Ongoing assistance might mitigate anxiety related to technology utilization and promote midwives' comprehensive engagement with digital instruments.

In summary, educating midwives in the utilization of technology is crucial for improving maternal healthcare services. By employing thorough training tactics, mitigating resistance, and cultivating a supportive environment, healthcare organizations can enable midwives to proficiently incorporate technology into their practices. This will result in enhanced patient outcomes and a more efficient and responsive maternal healthcare system.

CASE STUDIES OF SUCCESSFUL INTEGRATION

Global Perspectives on Technology in Midwifery

The incorporation of technology in midwifery practices varies worldwide, mirroring distinct healthcare systems, cultural contexts, and technical progress (Ferguson et al. 2025). Analyzing successful case studies from many nations offers significant insights into effective tactics and practices that can improve maternal health outcomes.

In Sweden, the establishment of a nationwide telehealth program has markedly enhanced access to prenatal care for expectant moms. The program enables women to participate in virtual consultations with midwives, guaranteeing timely guidance and assistance irrespective of their geographical location (Bilal et al. 2022). This effort has demonstrated significant advantages for women in rural regions, where access to healthcare services may be restricted. The success of this initiative underscores the need of utilizing technology to address disparities in care and guarantee that all women have access to vital maternal health treatments.

In India, the "mMitra" initiative exemplifies the efficacy of mobile health technology in enhancing maternal health outcomes. This initiative employs automated voice calls and SMS messages to deliver essential information to pregnant women concerning prenatal care, vaccines, and nutrition (De & Pradhan, 2023). mMitra directly engages women via their mobile phones, thereby overcoming obstacles associated with health literacy and information accessibility. The campaign has heightened awareness and involvement among pregnant women, leading to enhanced attendance at antenatal check-ups and improved health outcomes for mothers and infants.

The "Pregnancy, Birth and Baby" app in Australia illustrates how technology can empower women throughout their pregnancy experience (Strazdins, 2024). This application provides tailored information, tools, and assistance for pregnant moms, including access to a 24/7 helpline manned by midwives. The software has cultivated confidence and empowerment among users by offering rapid access to professional guidance and a plethora of educational resources. This scenario highlights the necessity of developing user-centric, informative applications that prioritize the needs and experiences of women.

The insights gained from these global approaches highlight the importance of cultural sensitivity and community engagement in the effective incorporation of technology in midwifery. Involving local stakeholders, such as midwives, healthcare practitioners, and community organizations, is crucial for customizing technology solutions to meet the specific needs of the population (Lukita et al. 2024). Moreover, continuous assessment and feedback systems are essential for enhancing technology implementations and ensuring their relevance and efficacy.

In conclusion, international viewpoints on technology in midwifery demonstrate a plethora of creative methodologies that may be tailored and implemented across diverse situations. By analyzing these effective case studies, healthcare systems may augment maternal health services, boost access to treatment, and empower women during their pregnant experiences. The use of human-centric technology into midwifery practices has the potential to transform maternal healthcare and result in improved outcomes for mothers and their offspring.

Impact of Technology on Maternal Outcomes

The use of technology into midwifery practices has shown substantial beneficial effects on maternal health outcomes in several hospital environments (Hod et al. 2023). As digital solutions gain prominence, research reveals that these innovations are not only facilitating access to treatment but also augmenting the quality of maternal health services and results.

A multitude of studies has demonstrated the efficacy of telemedicine in enhancing prenatal and postnatal care. A systematic evaluation published in the Journal of Medical Internet Research indicated that women utilizing telehealth services exhibited increased prenatal care attendance and enhanced monitoring of pregnancy-related problems (McCoy et al. 2024). Specifically, remote monitoring instruments, including wearable gadgets that monitor vital indicators and fetal heart rates, have empowered healthcare professionals to detect possible problems early, facilitating prompt actions that can avert difficulties.

Alongside quantitative data, patient testimonials offer significant insights into the transforming impact of technology on maternal health experiences (Pulimamidi, 2024). For instance, Sarah, a novice mother from a rural locality, recounted her experience utilizing a telehealth platform during her pregnancy. “Residing at a considerable distance from a hospital, I felt apprehensive about obtaining medical care,” she recounted. Telehealth enabled me to communicate with my midwife anytime I had concerns. It provided me with a sense of support and reassurance, knowing I could obtain assistance without the anxiety of going considerable distances. Sarah's narrative exemplifies how technology can empower women by granting them prompt access to healthcare specialists and cultivating a sense of security throughout pregnancy.

A more persuasive illustration arises from the utilization of mobile health applications. A study on the “What to Expect” app indicated that users experienced enhanced knowledge on pregnancy and more self-efficacy in health management (Aslantekin et al. 2022). Numerous users observed that the app's functionalities, including symptom tracking and educational tools, enhanced their engagement in their care. A mother remarked, “The application was my primary resource.” It provided guidance throughout each week of my pregnancy and instilled a sense of preparedness for the forthcoming events.

Moreover, initiatives like as mMitra in India have had significant effects on maternal health outcomes. Data from the campaign revealed a substantial rise in antenatal care visits and immunization rates among women who received mobile health messages (Singh & Walters, 2024). Participants' testimonials emphasized that the program furnished critical information, enabling them to pursue care proactively.

In conclusion, the use of technology into midwifery practices has resulted in enhanced maternal health outcomes, as demonstrated by both empirical data and anecdotal evidence. Technology significantly empowers women during their pregnant journeys by improving access to treatment, delivering timely information, and promoting patient engagement. In our pursuit of advancing human-centric technology in maternal health, it is imperative to prioritize continuous assessment and modification to guarantee that these innovations adequately address the needs of mothers and their families.

Future Innovations in Midwifery Technology

The future of midwifery technology is set to witness significant breakthroughs that are expected to improve maternal health outcomes. Innovative technologies are being created to tackle current issues in maternal healthcare, enhance patient involvement, and optimize service delivery (Batani & Maharaj, 2022). Utilizing these improvements, midwifery practices can enhance their responsiveness and efficacy in addressing the needs of expectant moms.

A significant area of innovation is the application of artificial intelligence (AI) and machine learning in maternal health. These technologies can evaluate extensive data from electronic health records, wearable devices, and mobile applications to discern patterns and forecast results (Roberts et al., 2022). AI systems could evaluate a woman's risk factors and offer individualized prenatal care suggestions, allowing healthcare providers to customize interventions according to specific requirements. This predictive ability may facilitate the earlier detection of problems, hence enhancing maternal and newborn outcomes.

Another nascent technology is the application of virtual reality (VR) and augmented reality (AR) in prenatal education and training. Immersive technologies can offer expectant moms realistic simulations of labor and postpartum care, enhancing their comprehension of the linked procedures (Nurlaily et al., 2021). Furthermore, virtual reality can be employed for the training of midwives and healthcare professionals, enabling them to hone their abilities in a secure and regulated setting. By improving education and readiness, these technologies can empower both women and healthcare professionals.

Telehealth is anticipated to progress, driven by developments in remote monitoring technologies. Wearable technologies with sensors can incessantly monitor vital signs, fetal heart rates, and other health metrics, relaying real-time data to healthcare providers (Jegan & Nimi, 2024). This ongoing flow of information will empower midwives to make informed judgments and intervene proactively when required. As these technologies advance, the capacity for remote management of high-risk pregnancies will expand, guaranteeing that women receive prompt and suitable care.

Moreover, the incorporation of blockchain technology in maternal health has the potential to transform data security and patient confidentiality. Blockchain facilitates a decentralized and secure method for storing health information, enabling women to manage personal data while assuring accessibility for approved healthcare practitioners (Deepa et al. 2022). This degree of security can bolster confidence in digital health solutions and motivate more women to use technology for their maternity health requirements.

The future of midwifery technology is promising, with forthcoming breakthroughs set to revolutionize maternal healthcare. Utilizing AI, VR, remote monitoring, and blockchain technology, midwifery practices can augment patient involvement, refine care delivery, and eventually yield improved health outcomes for women and their infants. As we adopt these developments, it is crucial to prioritize human-centric design, ensuring that technology empowers and supports women during their pregnancy experiences.

CREATING A SUSTAINABLE FUTURE FOR MATERNAL HEALTH

Policy and Advocacy for Maternal Health Technology

The ongoing integration of technology into maternal health practices necessitates a pivotal role for policymakers in cultivating an environment that promotes innovation and guarantees equal access to care (Ticona et al. 2025). Policymakers must establish frameworks that promote the incorporation of human-centric technology in midwifery, thereby enhancing health outcomes for mothers and their children.

Policymakers primarily set laws and recommendations to ensure the safe and effective use of technology in maternity healthcare. This encompasses the establishment of standards for telehealth services, the assurance of data privacy and security, and the formulation of policies for the utilization of digital health instruments. Clear regulations can foster confidence between healthcare practitioners and patients, thereby promoting the integration of technology in midwifery practices. Moreover, supporting programs that facilitate the development and implementation of breakthrough technology might substantially improve access to care, especially in marginalized populations (Crossley & Baybutt, 2024).

Furthermore, politicians can promote the integration of maternal health technologies into national health agendas. By emphasizing maternal health in policy deliberations, they can guarantee that the integration of technology obtains the requisite attention and resources (Aruah et al., 2023). This entails promoting collaboration among government entities, healthcare institutions, and technology developers to establish a unified strategy for maternal health innovation.

Advocacy techniques are crucial for midwives and healthcare professionals to effect change and ensure their perspectives are acknowledged in the policy-making process. An effective technique involves grassroots activism, rallying communities to enhance knowledge on the significance of technology in maternal health (Bhuiyan & Haque, 2024). By disseminating personal narratives and empirical facts regarding the beneficial effects of technology, midwives can shape public perception and secure backing for governmental initiatives.

Moreover, establishing coalitions with other healthcare professionals and organizations might enhance advocacy initiatives. Collaborative relationships can present a cohesive approach to tackle mutual issues, exchange resources, and promote joint objectives (Abdeen et al. 2021). Collaboration between midwives and healthcare professionals can enhance their impact on legislators and advocate for the incorporation of technology in maternal health.

Education and training are essential elements of advocacy (Sanders & Scanlon, 2021). Midwives must possess the requisite knowledge and abilities to participate in policy discussions and advocate effectively for their patients. This encompasses comprehending the ramifications of technology on maternal health and articulating the advantages of digital technologies in enhancing care delivery.

In summary, establishing a sustainable future for maternal health technology necessitates the active involvement of both governments and healthcare practitioners. Through the implementation of supportive policies, promotion of technology integration, and cultivation of collaborative relationships, we can guarantee that human-centric technology is seamlessly included into midwifery practices. This joint initiative will ultimately improve maternal health outcomes, empower women, and provide a more equitable healthcare system that addresses the needs of all mothers and their families.

Building Community Support Systems

Community engagement is essential for improving maternal health outcomes, since it creates a friendly atmosphere where expectant moms may obtain information, exchange experiences, and receive encouragement during their pregnancies (Anyanwu et al. 2024). Establishing resilient community support systems not only empowers women but also enhances the overall well-being of families and communities.

The significance of community engagement in maternal health is paramount. When families and communities participate in maternal health efforts, they foster a supportive culture that promotes healthy behaviors and motivates women to pursue care. Community-based programs can meet particular local needs by offering customized services that align with the requirements of women and their families (Stover et al., 2024). Peer support groups, facilitated by trained community members or experienced mothers, provide emotional support, practical guidance, and shared experiences, assisting women in managing the challenges of pregnancy and childbirth.

To effectively involve families and communities in maternal health, various ways may be utilized. Initially, it is crucial to enhance knowledge regarding the significance of maternal health and the services accessible. Community workshops, instructional sessions, and outreach initiatives can enlighten families about the importance of prenatal and postnatal care, along with the advantages of employing technology in health management. Healthcare professionals may ensure that families are aware and empowered to engage in maternal health programs by disseminating information via local media, social networks, and community activities (Stelwagen et al. 2021).

Another efficacious technique is to engage community leaders and organizations in the planning and execution of maternal health programs. Engaging with local leaders, including religious authorities, educators, and health advocates, helps foster trust and credibility within the community (Lansing et al. 2023). These leaders can act as advocates for maternal health, promoting engagement and cultivating a feeling of responsibility among community members.

Moreover, utilizing technology to establish community support networks might augment engagement. Mobile applications and online platforms can enhance communication among expectant moms, healthcare practitioners, and community resources (Kangana et al. 2024). A mobile application could link women to local support groups, educational resources, and healthcare facilities, facilitating their access to necessary information and aid. This digital method can also mitigate obstacles associated with transportation and schedule, guaranteeing that assistance is readily accessible.

Ultimately, acknowledging and commemorating the ethnic customs and traditions associated with pregnancy and childbirth might augment community engagement. Integrating culturally pertinent practices into maternal health programs enables healthcare providers to foster a more inclusive atmosphere that acknowledges and respects the different cultures of families (Raj et al., 2024). This method cultivates trust and promotes active engagement in maternal health initiatives.

In conclusion, establishing community support systems is vital for fostering a sustainable future for maternal health. Through the engagement of families and communities via awareness, collaboration, technology, and cultural sensitivity, we can empower women and enhance health outcomes for mothers and their children. A robust community foundation will ultimately improve the efficacy of midwifery practices and foster a more fair and supportive maternal healthcare system.

A Vision for Empowered Maternal Health

In concluding our examination of the integration of human-centric technology in midwifery practices, it is crucial to reflect on the principal ideas that have arisen during this discourse. The incorporation of technology in maternal health improves both accessibility and quality of care while empowering women to actively participate in their health journeys. Utilizing telehealth, smartphone applications, and remote monitoring tools, midwives may deliver tailored, prompt assistance that caters to the specific need of expectant moms.

Furthermore, the significance of community engagement has been emphasized as a vital element in enhancing maternal health outcomes. Involving families and communities cultivates a supportive atmosphere that builds trust, promotes health-seeking behaviors, and improves the overall efficacy of maternal health programs. Establishing resilient community support structures helps guarantee that women obtain the necessary resources, information, and emotional assistance throughout pregnancy and thereafter.

The significance of policymakers and healthcare stakeholders in promoting and facilitating the integration of technology is paramount. By instituting explicit laws, financing new projects, and prioritizing maternal health in policy discourse, we may foster an atmosphere conducive to technological developments that benefit women and their families.

Given these observations, a call to action is imperative for midwives and healthcare stakeholders. Midwives are at the forefront of maternal care and must leverage technological advancements to improve their professions. This necessitates continuous training and education to ensure midwives possess the requisite skills to effectively employ digital tools. By championing technological integration, midwives can effect policy reforms and encourage the use of innovative solutions that enhance care delivery.

Healthcare stakeholders, comprising governments, healthcare organizations, and community leaders, must unite to establish a sustainable framework that facilitates the integration of human-centric technology in maternal health. This entails allocating funding to research, cultivating collaborations between technology developers and healthcare professionals, and guaranteeing access to these resources for underrepresented communities.

In conclusion, the vision for enhanced maternal health resides in the cooperative endeavors of midwives, healthcare stakeholders, and communities. By adopting technology and cultivating a supportive environment, we can improve maternal health outcomes and establish a more equal healthcare system. The pursuit of enhanced maternal health necessitates dedication, ingenuity, and cooperation, although the prospective advantages for women and their families are substantial. Collectively, we can establish a future in which every woman has access to the care, support, and resources necessary for her to flourish during pregnancy and thereafter.

CONCLUSION

The use of human-centric technology into midwifery practices signifies a pivotal advancement in tackling enduring issues in maternal health. This article has shown that by utilizing tools such as telehealth, mobile applications, remote monitoring, and AI-driven platforms, midwives may enhance the accessibility and quality of maternal care, especially in impoverished populations. These technologies not only improve service accessibility but also provide real-time monitoring, early identification of difficulties, and tailored advice during the prenatal and postnatal phases.

The advancement is fundamentally based on the principle of human-centric design, which guarantees that digital solutions are attuned to the needs, emotions, and cultural settings of expectant women. Technologies that emphasize usability, empathy, and inclusivity can enable women to engage more actively in their healthcare, thus enhancing health literacy, decision-making, and outcomes.

For technology to be both successful and ethical, it is imperative to rigorously uphold principles such as data privacy, informed consent, and digital equity. It is equally imperative to equip midwives with the requisite skills and training to proficiently utilize and advocate for these instruments. Moreover, supportive policies, community involvement, and intersectoral collaboration are essential for the sustainable scaling of these innovations.

In conclusion, human-centric technology provides an effective means to address deficiencies in maternal healthcare. By integrating innovation with compassion and fairness, midwifery may transform into a more adaptive, inclusive, and efficient practice—ultimately protecting the health and dignity of mothers and their families in an increasingly dynamic world.

REFERENCES

Abadi, T. & Mebratie, A. D. (2021). Cost of treating maternal complications and associated factors in Mekelle General Hospital, northern Ethiopia. Risk management and healthcare policy. tandfonline.com

Abdeen, F. N., Fernando, T., Kulatunga, U., Hettige, S., & Ranasinghe, K. A. (2021). Challenges in multi-agency collaboration in disaster management: A Sri Lankan perspective. [sciencedirect.com]. *International Journal of Disaster Risk Reduction, 62*, 102399. DOI: 10.1016/j.ijdrr.2021.102399

Akdim, K., Casaló, L. V., & Flavián, C. (2022). The role of utilitarian and hedonic aspects in the continuance intention to use social mobile apps. [sciencedirect.com]. *Journal of Retailing and Consumer Services, 66*, 102888. DOI: 10.1016/j.jretconser.2021.102888

Al-Adwan, A. S., Albelbisi, N. A., Hujran, O., Al-Rahmi, W. M., & Alkhalifah, A. (2021). Developing a holistic success model for sustainable e-learning: A structural equation modeling approach. [mdpi.com]. *Sustainability (Basel), 13*(16), 9453. DOI: 10.3390/su13169453

Anyanwu, E. C., Maduka, C. P., Ayo-Farai, O., Okongwu, C. C., & Daraojimba, A. I. (2024). Maternal and child health policy: A global review of current practices and future directions. [semanticscholar.org]. *World Journal of Advanced Research and Reviews, 21*(2), 1770–1781. DOI: 10.30574/wjarr.2024.21.2.0306

Aruah, D. E., Henshaw, Y., & Walsh-Childers, K. (2023). Tweets that matter: Exploring the solutions to maternal mortality in the United States discussed by advocacy organizations on twitter. [mdpi.com]. *International Journal of Environmental Research and Public Health, 20*(9), 5617. DOI: 10.3390/ijerph20095617 PMID: 37174137

Aslantekin Özçoban, F., Ergün, S., & Erkal Aksoy, Y. (2022). Effects of health literacy education on adaptation to pregnancy, self-efficacy, fear of childbirth and health literacy in Turkish pregnant women: A randomized, controlled trial. [HTML]. *Health & Social Care in the Community, 30*(2), e537–e549. DOI: 10.1111/hsc.13690 PMID: 34957621

Atkinson, J., Hastie, R., Walker, S., Lindquist, A., & Tong, S. (2023). Telehealth in antenatal care: recent insights and advances. BMC medicine. springer.com

Ayele, A. A., Tefera, Y. G., & East, L. (2021). Ethiopia's commitment towards achieving sustainable development goal on reduction of maternal mortality: There is a long way to go. Women's Health. sagepub.com

Babu, S., Park, N., Woodland, G., Garcia, N., Page, W., & Page, R. (2024). Maternal health applications: Qualitative findings of user needs. [sagepub.com]. *Digital Health, 10*, 20552076241285422. DOI: 10.1177/20552076241285422 PMID: 39347510

Batani, J. & Maharaj, M. S. (2022). Towards data-driven models for diverging emerging technologies for maternal, neonatal and child health services in Sub-Saharan Africa: a systematic review. Global Health Journal. sciencedirect.com

Bedenkov, A., Moreno, C., Agustin, L., Jain, N., Newman, A., Feng, L., & Kostello, G. (2021). Customer centricity in medical affairs needs human-centric artificial intelligence. [springer.com]. *Pharmaceutical Medicine, 35*(1), 21–29. DOI: 10.1007/s40290-020-00378-1 PMID: 33464482

Bhuiyan, M. I. & Haque, M. A. (2024). NGOs' initiatives and grassroots approach for accessing to health care services for the slum people in Dhaka. Frontiers in Health Services. frontiersin.org

Bilal, W., Mohanan, P., Rahmat, Z. S., Ahmed Gangat, S., Islam, Z., Essar, M. Y., Aborode, A. T., & Onyeaka, H. (2022). Improving access to maternal care in Africa through telemedicine and digital health. [HTML]. *The International Journal of Health Planning and Management, 37*(4), 2494–2500. DOI: 10.1002/hpm.3498 PMID: 35570361

Brinson, A. K., Jahnke, H. R., Rubin-Miller, L., Henrich, N., Challa, B., Moss, C., Shah, N., & Peahl, A. (2023). Trajectories of digital prenatal service utilization and pregnancy outcomes: A multitrajectory analysis. [sciencedirect.com]. *Mayo Clinic Proceedings. Digital Health, 1*(1), 13–24. DOI: 10.1016/j.mcpdig.2022.12.001 PMID: 40207144

Butcher, C. J. T. & Hussain, W. (2022). Digital healthcare: the future. Future healthcare journal. sciencedirect.com

Cantor, A. G., Jungbauer, R. M., Totten, A. M., Tilden, E. L., Holmes, R., Ahmed, A., Wagner, J., Hermesch, A. C., & McDonagh, M. S. (2022). Telehealth strategies for the delivery of maternal health care: A rapid review. [HTML]. *Annals of Internal Medicine, 175*(9), 1285–1297. DOI: 10.7326/M22-0737 PMID: 35878405

Canty, L. (2022). The lived experience of severe maternal morbidity among Black women. Nursing Inquiry. wiley.com

Crepinsek, M., Bell, R., Graham, I., & Coutts, R. (2023). A global review of the inferred meaning of woman centred care within midwifery professional standards. [HTML]. *Women and Birth; Journal of the Australian College of Midwives, 36*(1), e99–e105. DOI: 10.1016/j.wombi.2022.05.001 PMID: 35550121

Crossley, S., & Baybutt, M. (2024). Access to healthcare: Underserved communities. [tandfonline.com]. *International Journal of Health Promotion and Education, 62*(5), 341–342. DOI: 10.1080/14635240.2024.2403238

Dakulagi, V., Yeap, K. H., Nisar, H., Dakulagi, R., Basavaraj, G. N., & Galindo, M. V. (2025). An overview of techniques and best practices to create intuitive and user-friendly human-machine interfaces. Artificial Intelligence and Multimodal Signal Processing in Human-Machine Interaction, 63-77. [HTML]

De, P. & Pradhan, M. R. (2023). Effectiveness of mobile technology and utilization of maternal and neonatal healthcare in low and middle-income countries (LMICs): a systematic review. BMC Women's Health. springer.com

Deepa, N., Devi, T., Gayathri, N., & Kumar, S. R. (2022). Decentralized healthcare management system using blockchain to secure sensitive medical data for users. Blockchain security in cloud computing, 265-282. [HTML]

DeSa, S., Gebremeskel, A. T., Omonaiye, O., & Yaya, S. (2022). Barriers and facilitators to access mental health services among refugee women in high-income countries: a systematic review. Systematic reviews. springer.com

Ebadpour, Z., Nikghadam-Hojjati, S., & Barata, J. (2024, June). Human-Centric Principles for Computational Systems Supporting Collaborative Creativity. In Doctoral Conference on Computing, Electrical and Industrial Systems (pp. 61-81). Cham: Springer Nature Switzerland. [HTML] DOI: 10.1007/978-3-031-63851-0_4

El Kotni, M. (2021). Midwifery in cross-cultural perspectives. In *The Routledge Handbook of Anthropology and Reproduction* (pp. 454–467). Routledge. [HTML] DOI: 10.4324/9781003216452-36

Fan, K. & Zhao, Y. (2022). Mobile health technology: a novel tool in chronic disease management. Intelligent Medicine. sciencedirect.com

Ferguson, B., Baldwin, A., Harvey, C., & Henderson, A. (2025). Navigating Quality and Innovation: Actor-Network Theory and Hybrid Assemblages in Midwifery Practice, Implications of Maternity Early Warning Tools and Artificial Intelligence. [wiley.com]. *Nursing Inquiry, 32*(2), e70001. DOI: 10.1111/nin.70001 PMID: 40025864

Gesualdo, F., Daverio, M., Palazzani, L., Dimitriou, D., Diez-Domingo, J., Fons-Martinez, J., Jackson, S., Vignally, P., Rizzo, C., & Tozzi, A. E. (2021). Digital tools in the informed consent process: A systematic review. [springer.com]. *BMC Medical Ethics, 22*(1), 1–10. DOI: 10.1186/s12910-021-00585-8 PMID: 33639926

Getachew, E., Adebeta, T., Muzazu, S. G., Charlie, L., Said, B., Tesfahunei, H. A., Wanjiru, C. L., Acam, J., Kajogoo, V. D., Solomon, S., Atim, M. G., & Manyazewal, T. (2023). Digital health in the era of COVID-19: Reshaping the next generation of healthcare. [frontiersin.org]. *Frontiers in Public Health, 11*, 942703. DOI: 10.3389/fpubh.2023.942703 PMID: 36875401

Gillie, M., Ali, D., Vadlamuri, D., & Carstarphen, K. J. (2022). Telehealth literacy as a social determinant of health: A novel screening tool to support vulnerable patient equity. [sagepub.com]. *Journal of Alzheimer's Disease Reports*, *6*(1), 67–72. DOI: 10.3233/ADR-210024 PMID: 35360275

Gomez-Roas, M. V., Davis, K. D. M., Leziak, K., Jackson, J., Williams, B. R., Feinglass, J. M., Grobman, W. A., & Yee, L. M. (2022). Postpartum during a pandemic: Challenges of low-income individuals with healthcare interactions during COVID-19. [plos.org]. *PLoS One*, *17*(5), e0268698. DOI: 10.1371/journal.pone.0268698 PMID: 35609090

Hanna, M., Pantanowitz, L., Jackson, B., Palmer, O., Visweswaran, S., Pantanowitz, J., & Rashidi, H. (2024). Ethical and Bias considerations in artificial intelligence (AI)/machine learning. [sciencedirect.com]. *Modern Pathology*, •••, 100686. PMID: 39694331

Hannon, S., Newnham, E., Hannon, K., Wuytack, F., Johnson, L., McEvoy, E., & Daly, D. (2022). Positive postpartum well-being: What works for women. [wiley.com]. *Health Expectations*, *25*(6), 2971–2981. DOI: 10.1111/hex.13605 PMID: 36321376

Hod, M., Divakar, H., Kihara, A. B., & Geary, M. (2023). The femtech revolution—A new approach to pregnancy management: Digital transformation of maternity care—The hybrid e-health perinatal clinic addressing the unmet needs of low-and middle-income countries. [wiley.com]. *International Journal of Gynaecology and Obstetrics: the Official Organ of the International Federation of Gynaecology and Obstetrics*, *163*(1), 4–10. DOI: 10.1002/ijgo.15032 PMID: 37554042

Jegan, R. & Nimi, W. S. (2024). On the development of low power wearable devices for assessment of physiological vital parameters: a systematic review. Journal of Public Health. springer.com

Kangana, N., Kankanamge, N., De Silva, C., Goonetilleke, A., Mahamood, R., & Ranasinghe, D. (2024). Bridging Community Engagement and Technological Innovation for Creating Smart and Resilient Cities: A Systematic Literature Review. [mdpi.com]. *Smart Cities*, *7*(6), 3823–3852. DOI: 10.3390/smartcities7060147

Keshta, I. & Odeh, A. (2021). Security and privacy of electronic health records: Concerns and challenges. Egyptian Informatics Journal. sciencedirect.com

Khang, A., Ragimova, N. A., Hajimahmud, V. A., & Alyar, A. V. (2022). Advanced technologies and data management in the smart healthcare system. In *AI-Centric Smart City Ecosystems* (pp. 261–270). CRC Press. [HTML] DOI: 10.1201/9781003252542-16

Kissler, K., Thumm, E. B., Smith, D. C., Anderson, J. L., Wood, R. E., Johnson, R., Roberts, M., Carmitchel-Fifer, A., Patterson, N., Amura, C. R., Barton, A. J., & Jones, J. (2024). Perinatal telehealth: Meeting patients where they are. [wiley.com]. *Journal of Midwifery & Women's Health, 69*(1), 9–16. DOI: 10.1111/jmwh.13560 PMID: 37641584

Lansing, A. E., Romero, N. J., Siantz, E., Silva, V., Center, K., Casteel, D., & Gilmer, T. (2023). Building trust: Leadership reflections on community empowerment and engagement in a large urban initiative. [springer.com]. *BMC Public Health, 23*(1), 1252. DOI: 10.1186/s12889-023-15860-z PMID: 37380973

Lee, V. V., Vijayakumar, S., Ng, W. Y., Lau, N. Y., Leong, Q. Y., Ooi, D. S. Q., Su, L. L., Lee, Y. S., Chan, S.-Y., Blasiak, A., & Ho, D. (2023). Personalization and localization as key expectations of digital health intervention in women pre- to post-pregnancy. [nature.com]. *NPJ Digital Medicine, 6*(1), 183. DOI: 10.1038/s41746-023-00924-6 PMID: 37775533

Lukita, C., Lutfiani, N., Salam, R., Pangilinan, G. A., Rafika, A. S., & Ahsanitaqwim, R. (2024, August). Technology Integration in Cultural Heritage Preservation Enhancing Community Engagement and Effectiveness. In 2024 3rd International Conference on Creative Communication and Innovative Technology (ICCIT) (pp. 1-5). IEEE. [HTML] DOI: 10.1109/ICCIT62134.2024.10701088

Madden, S. K., Ahuja, K. D., Blewitt, C., Hill, B., Hills, A. P., & Skouteris, H. (2023). Understanding the pathway between work and health outcomes for women during the preconception, pregnancy, and postpartum periods through the framing of maternal obesity. [wiley.com]. *Obesity Reviews, 24*(12), e13637. DOI: 10.1111/obr.13637 PMID: 37655832

Mantula, F., Chamisa, J. A., Nunu, W. N., & Nyanhongo, P. S. (2023). Women's Perspectives on Cultural Sensitivity of Midwives During Intrapartum Care at a Maternity Ward in a National Referral Hospital in Zimbabwe. [sagepub.com]. *SAGE Open Nursing, 9*, 23779608231160476. DOI: 10.1177/23779608231160476 PMID: 36875792

McCoy, H. C., Allison, M. K., Hernandez, M., Ali, M. M., Stokes, M., Bogulski, C. A., & Eswaran, H. (2024). Assessment of pregnancy-related telehealth interventions in the United States: A 10-year scoping review. [HTML]. *Telemedicine Journal and e-Health, 30*(1), 36–46. PMID: 37256707

Moise, I. K., Ivanova, N., Wilson, C., Wilson, S., Halwindi, H., & Spika, V. M. (2023). Lessons from digital technology-enabled health interventions implemented during the coronavirus pandemic to improve maternal and birth outcomes: A global scoping review. [springer.com]. *BMC Pregnancy and Childbirth, 23*(1), 195. DOI: 10.1186/s12884-023-05454-3 PMID: 36941565

Moulaei, K., Sheikhtaheri, A., Ghafaripour, Z., & Bahaadinbeigy, K. (2021). The development and usability assessment of an mhealth application to encourage self-care in pregnant women against COVID-19. [wiley.com]. *Journal of Healthcare Engineering, 2021*(1), 9968451. DOI: 10.1155/2021/9968451 PMID: 34336175

Ndasauka, Y. (2024). Historical Origins of Technology in Africa. In African Mind, Culture, and Technology: Philosophical Perspectives (pp. 17-36). Cham: Springer Nature Switzerland. [HTML] DOI: 10.1007/978-3-031-62979-2_2

Nelson, G. A., & Holschuh, C. (2021). Evaluation of telehealth use in prenatal care for patient and provider satisfaction: A step toward reducing barriers to care. [HTML]. *The Journal for Nurse Practitioners, 17*(4), 481–484. DOI: 10.1016/j.nurpra.2020.12.026

Nurlaily, S., Ahmad, M., Syarif, S., & Idris, I. (2021). Effectiveness of Augmented Reality (AR) based learning media on increasing the physical examination system of pregnant women urinary system. Gaceta Sanitaria. sciencedirect.com

Ortiz Juarez-Paz, A. V., Doherty, E. F., Storch, S. L., Kallis, R. B., & Kleinman, S. B. (2023). "Anyone else? Is this normal?": Anonymously seeking information on the Ovia Pregnancy App. [HTML]. *Atlantic Journal of Communication, 31*(1), 30–51. DOI: 10.1080/15456870.2021.1984238

Prabhakar, P., Pati, P. B., & Parida, S. (2025). Navigating Legal and Ethical Dimensions in AI, IoT, and Cloud Solutions for Women's Safety. In Developing AI, IoT and Cloud Computing-based Tools and Applications for Women's Safety (pp. 155-191). Chapman and Hall/CRC. [HTML]

Pulimamidi, R. (2024). To enhance customer (or patient) experience based on IoT analytical study through technology (IT) transformation for E-healthcare. Measurement: Sensors. sciencedirect.com

Raj, M., Silva, L. Q., & Khan, N. (2024). Building an inclusive health care system requires offering culturally inclusive foods in health care environments. Journal of the Academy of Nutrition and Dietetics. sciencedirect.com

Rizkianti, A., Saptarini, I., & Rachmalina, R. (2021). Perceived barriers in accessing health care and the risk of pregnancy complications in Indonesia. [tandfonline.com]. *International Journal of Women's Health, 13*, 761–772. DOI: 10.2147/IJWH.S310850 PMID: 34429661

Roberts, J. M., Heider, D., Bergman, L., & Thornburg, K. L. (2022). Vision for improving pregnancy health: innovation and the future of pregnancy research. Reproductive Sciences. springer.com

Sanders, C. K. & Scanlon, E. (2021). The digital divide is a human rights issue: Advancing social inclusion through social work advocacy. Journal of human rights and social work. springer.com

Shikuku, D. N., Bar-Zeev, S., Ladur, A. N., Allott, H., Mwaura, C., Nandikove, P., Uyara, A., Tallam, E., Ndirangu, E., Waweru, L., Nyaga, L., Bashir, I., Bedwell, C., & Ameh, C. (2024). Experiences, barriers and perspectives of midwifery educators, mentors and students implementing the updated emergency obstetric and newborn care-enhanced pre-service midwifery curriculum in Kenya: A nested qualitative study. [springer.com]. *BMC Medical Education, 24*(1), 950. DOI: 10.1186/s12909-024-05872-7 PMID: 39217305

Singh, K. & Walters, M. R. (2024). Use of mHealth in promoting maternal and child health in "BIMARU" states of India "A health system strengthening strategy": Systematic literature review. PLOS Digital Health. plos.org

Stelwagen, M., van Kempen, A., Westmaas, A., Vet, E., & Scheele, F. (2021). Parents' experiences with a model of integrated maternity and neonatal care designed to empower parents. [sciencedirect.com]. *Journal of Obstetric, Gynecologic, and Neonatal Nursing : JOGNN, 50*(2), 181–192. DOI: 10.1016/j.jogn.2020.11.001 PMID: 33428875

Stover, J., Avadhanula, L., & Sood, S. (2024). A review of strategies and levels of community engagement in strengths-based and needs-based health communication interventions. Frontiers in Public Health. frontiersin.org

Strazdins, L. (2024). Action: Time to Change?. The Unequal Hour: How Time Is Shaping Health. [HTML]

Theodorio, A. O. (2024). Examining the support required by educators for successful technology integration in teacher professional development program. Cogent Education. tandfonline.com

Ticona Machaca, A., Cano Ccoa, D. M., Gutiérrez Castillo, F. H., Quispe Gomez, F., Arroyo Beltrán, M., Zirena Cano, M. G., Sánchez-Chávez-Arroyo, V., Manrique Chavez, C. P., Romualdo Rosario, A., Adauto-Medina, W. A., & Montes Salcedo, M. (2025). Public Policy for Human Capital: Fostering Sustainable Equity in Disadvantaged Communities. [mdpi.com]. *Sustainability (Basel), 17*(2), 535. DOI: 10.3390/su17020535

Vaishya, R., Scarlat, M. M., Bhadani, J. S., & Vaish, A. (2024). Ethics in orthopaedic surgery practice: balancing patient care and technological advances. International Orthopaedics. springer.com

Van Baarle, E., Hartman, L., Rooijakkers, S., Wallenburg, I., Weenink, J. W., Bal, R., & Widdershoven, G. (2022). Fostering a just culture in healthcare organizations: Experiences in practice. [springer.com]. *BMC Health Services Research, 22*(1), 1035. DOI: 10.1186/s12913-022-08418-z PMID: 35964117

Viswanadham, N. (2021). Ecosystem model for healthcare platform. Sādhanā. springer.com

Wakelin, K. J., McAra-Couper, J., Fleming, T., & Erlam, G. D. (2023). Communication technology practices used by midwives with pregnant women/people in Aotearoa New Zealand to ensure quality maternal and newborn care. Midwifery. sciencedirect.com

Yee, G. A. (2022). Midwives in Egypt, Mesopotamia, and Ancient Israel: An Intersectional Investigation. [HTML]. *Biblical Theology Bulletin, 52*(3), 146–159. DOI: 10.1177/01461079221102970

Chapter 3
Education Reform in the Application of Artificial Intelligence in Supporting Learning Media:
AI and Education for Sustainable Development Goals (SDGs)

Junaidi Junaidi
https://orcid.org/0000-0002-2948-696X
Sjakhyakirti University, Palembang, Indonesia

ABSTRACT

Artificial intelligence technology has transformed the world of education and the way students learn. Artificial intelligence has become a highly valuable partner in the field of education due to its ability to analyze data on a large scale and provide interactive learning tools. An educational policy that supports the use of artificial intelligence as a medium in the learning process is necessary. In addition, it is important to conduct ongoing evaluations to ensure that students' learning outcomes have a positive impact. Using artificial intelligence provides the opportunity to implement innovative teaching methods, customize the curriculum, and tailor learning individually. Therefore, educational institutions must have a deep understanding of how to optimally utilize artificial intelligence and prepare the skills of educators and learners. The education curriculum is crucial for producing graduates who are competitive and can contribute in an increasingly complex and interconnected era of artificial intelligence.

DOI: 10.4018/979-8-3373-5781-2.ch003

INTRODUCTION

Various aspects of human life have been influenced by the development of artificial intelligence, including education. Artificial intelligence is increasingly important to help students succeed in the modern technological era. In the field of education, artificial intelligence has made great advances in technology, enabling more effective and customised learning to suit individual needs. In education, the integration of artificial intelligence is considered a component that can significantly change the learning experience and prepare students for a technology-orientated world. In addition, Zawacki-Richter *et al.* (2019) suggests that artificial intelligence is one of the main components of emerging educational technologies in education. It emphasises that educators should adopt artificial intelligence technologies to drive innovation and customise their learning experiences.

Artificial intelligence has the ability to change the way teachers teach and the way students acquire information, which makes this phenomenon very significant, (Rifky, 2024). The incorporation and development of artificial intelligence in education systems and curricula has resulted in great progress. It has provided educators and academic institutions with the latest artificial intelligence-based tools and applications, (Zhang, Ruan, Fan, & Roychoudhury, 2024). According to Al-Ghonmein and Al-Moghrabi (2024), intelligent technology can help educators understand the unique learning needs of each student and provide appropriate teaching. For example, smart technology can help educators analyse information about students, create more effective learning environments, increase student engagement, and determine teaching objectives.

To create a better future, education is essential. Therefore, there is a high possibility that the utilisation of artificial intelligence technology in the field of education will improve the efficiency of the learning process. Artificial intelligence-powered learning tools are one of the ways this technology is being utilised in education. Artificial intelligence-based learning tools are designed to support students in their learning activities, provide suggestions that match their learning abilities and preferences, and provide feedback quickly.

Artificial intelligence-based algorithms allow teachers to design more personalised learning experiences for their students by reviewing and analysing huge amounts of data, (Aldosari, 2020). Artificial intelligence can modify learning materials according to each student's needs by recognising their unique potential, challenges and learning methods. This non-personalised approach can increase student participation, improve learning outcomes, and encourage a love of lifelong learning, (Arun, 2021).

It is important to remember that the use of artificial intelligence in higher education must be based on proper ethics and safe management. Ethical and management guidelines are essential to ensure that the use of artificial intelligence technologies is done in a moral, trustworthy, and fair manner, (Bozkurt et al., 2021). In the field of education, artificial intelligence is used as a tool and support in the teaching and learning process. By using it as a learning tool, teachers, educators, and mentors can help them convey information to students better and make lessons easier for students to understand, (Ardiansyah, 2022).

Artificial intelligence has the power to transform the world of education by changing the way students learn, using advanced technology to teach, and automating the process of creating course materials. Addressing ethical concerns, however, and ensuring that the use of artificial intelligence is done in a responsible and inclusive manner, is important. We can build an educational ecosystem that empowers students, enhances their critical thinking skills, and prepares them for future challenges by utilising artificial intelligence.

Research that discusses the variables of artificial intelligence (AI) technology, digital literacy, and learning evaluation include Supriyadi's (2023) research. The results of their research revealed that digital literacy has a positive effect on socio-emotional development, (Lewis, 2022). According to Muhamad Rizki Firdaus et al. (n.d.), Artificial Intelligence technology has a significant impact on the development of student education by expanding access, increasing efficiency, and presenting a variety of learning methods, (Sabella & Arrahimi, 2023). Another research was conducted by Almusharraf and Khahro in Ardiansyah (2022) who examined student satisfaction at Sultan University, Riyadh, Saudi Arabia. The findings showed that students were highly satisfied with Google Hangouts for lecture delivery, followed by Google Classroom and LMS (Moodle) for course management and assessment, (Wanli Xing, 2021).

There are many aspects that need further research in the context of student interaction with AI. Firstly, the application of artificial intelligence in the teaching and learning process can have an impact on students' drive and interest in learning. With the rapid advancement of technology, students can now access lessons in a more interactive and engaging way. In addition, artificial intelligence (AI) can provide immediate feedback, which can influence how students learn. Secondly, it is important to consider the social and moral consequences of implementing AI in education. In such a situation, questions of data privacy, equality of access, and the impact of replacing humans by technology become crucial. Students should also recognise how AI works, understand its limitations, and learn to use it wisely. Finally, research into how students interact with artificial intelligence can help us understand how prepared they are for an increasingly automated world of work. We need to know how students use artificial intelligence technology and how to use it to prepare themselves for future problems, (Cunningham-Nelson et al., 2019).

Therefore, the rapidly growing research and innovation in this field has the ability to transform the way we teach and learn. However, there are still many issues that need to be addressed. This study was conducted to find out how best to incorporate artificial intelligence into learning tools; this includes artificial intelligence-based apps and websites that can be used as learning tools. The research also aimed to see how the use of such technology impacts academic outcomes. In addition to this, the study also looked into what teachers and students should do when using such technologies.

RESEARCH METHODS

This research method is descriptive and uses a qualitative approach. According to descriptive research, research should be conducted based on existing facts or phenomena that can be observed practically in the real world. The purpose of this research is to gain a better understanding of the importance of descriptive qualitative research methods when using artificial intelligence as a learning aid. The sources of information in this research are books, local and international journals, and other literature. Furthermore, the data that has been researched is analysed with descriptive methods to evaluate the use of artificial intelligence as a learning tool based on mutual connections and data.

RESULTS AND DISCUSSION

Effectiveness of Artificial Intelligence Utilisation as Learning Media in Improving Learners' Ability

According to Musafa (2022), the era of education 5.0 begins with the use of the latest technologies such as the Internet of Things (IoT), machine learning, and artificial intelligence in the learning process. These methods can fulfil the needs of the 21st century by teaching student's skills and insights that are relevant to technological advancements, (Cotton, 2023). Technology-focused interventions in education will include designing, developing and implementing a range of products, services and processes utilising scientific knowledge with the aim of meeting needs, finding innovative solutions or increasing value. With these interventions, students will be introduced to digital devices and advanced technologies that can enrich their learning experiences, summarise and utilise scientific knowledge to achieve these goals, (Sopiansyah et al., 2021).

In education, the use of artificial intelligence technology has had a significant impact on the way students understand material and their engagement in the learning process. These artificial intelligence systems also support the creation of learning profiles for each student, allowing course materials to be customised to each student's abilities, learning styles and experiences. Customised digital learning content is also beginning to emerge as a result of the adoption of artificial intelligence and machine learning technologies, (Apriliani, 2024).

Interactive learning applications such as educational games and online exercises can be created with artificial intelligence to tailor the learning experience to each student's unique learning style. Adlawan stated that artificial intelligence helps produce more engaging and interactive learning methods, encouraging students to participate more actively in class. For example, an Indonesian-language chatbot helps students speak directly, increasing their participation in class, (Widdows et al., 2024). Artificial intelligence allows students to learn material according to their needs and in the way they learn, increasing student participation, (Rooein, 2019).

In education, artificial intelligence is a system designed to assist the teaching and learning process. The utilisation of artificial intelligence is becoming a major topic. ChatGPT's artificial intelligence tools increase student participation, co-operation, and ease of access, (Vázquez-Cano et al., 2021). They provide a means for communication that does not always take place simultaneously, which is a great advantage of artificial intelligence-based language models. Because they provide opportunities for students to ask questions and talk about various topics without having to be present at the same time, they have been shown to increase student participation and co-operation, (Evangelos Kapris, 2020). Another ChatGPT advantage is the ability to help students work together. ChatGPT can be used to organise groups of students so that they can work together on projects and assignments, (Liriwati, 2023).

Artificial intelligence also helps to customise learning content, which allows for a more tailored fit to each student's needs and abilities, (Graesser, 2016). Artificial intelligence algorithms use information from online activities, test results, and previous achievements to create a unique learning profile for each student, (Kim, Kim, & Cha, 2021). A study shows that using personalisation can help students learn better. For example, artificial intelligence-powered voice assistants allow students to find references and learning resources that suit their needs and offer exercises that match their level of understanding, (Nurhuda, 2022). This customisation improves students' overall understanding and learning outcomes by ensuring that the material presented matches each student's ability.

The main impact of implementing artificial intelligence on students is an increase in their enthusiasm and participation in learning, (Syarafudin, 2020). Artificial intelligence can also make learning environments more interactive by using specialised tools such as Smart Sparrow, which increases student participation with educational material, (Fitrianto & Saleh, 2024). Artificial intelligence technology support has shown great progress in academic performance, (bin Salem, 2024). Artificial intelligence significantly improves learning and student well-being, (Khan et al., 2021), in addition to optimising students' learning potential and achievement. According to Cunningham-Nelson et al. (2019), Supporting and enriching individual learning experiences is one component that may be driving this high level of motivation and achievement. Finally, ChatGPT can be used to support online education. This is particularly beneficial for students who are unable to attend classes due to physical or mental health issues, (Hill, Ford, & Fareras, 2015).

In addition, artificial intelligence improves the efficiency of the learning process and reduces the management responsibilities of teachers, allowing them to concentrate on more intensive teaching interactions, (Kamila et al., 2022). Artificial intelligence can reduce the burden of administrative tasks faced by teachers because it has the ability to manage learning materials and provide answers quickly and objectively, (Hong dan Kwihoon Kim, 2024). As the research shows, the use of artificial intelligence-based data analysis tools in teaching allows educators to change their learning approach based on student performance in real-time, which results in a more efficient learning process, (Muarif et al., 2023). For administrative and assessment tasks, artificial intelligence allows educators to focus more on the learning process and interact with students.

It also provides students with capabilities, such as innovating and analytical thinking, that support the measurement and evaluation of complex skills, (Afrita, 2023) and stimulate deeper thinking, (Gunawan et al., 2021). It also helps students interact with others and communicate better, (Salsabilla et al., 2023). This is due to the fact that artificial intelligence encourages collaborative learning and helps peers communicate better, (Sharma & Giannakos, 2020). These findings suggest that artificial intelligence can help students with learning difficulties to reach their full potential.

It is possible that the development of students' critical thinking skills will be influenced by the use of artificial intelligence in learning. The learning media used, word games and chatbots are examples of artificial intelligence learning tools that encourage students to think creatively and independently, (Mageira et al., 2022). Interactive games that utilise new vocabulary and the context in which terms are used can help students improve their critical thinking, (Chen & Lin, 2020). However, over-reliance on artificial intelligence can interfere with students' ability to act and think critically independently. Studies show that while artificial intelligence can help find solutions, it is important to align the use of artificial intelligence with activities that encourage critical thinking directly, (Tjahyanti, Saputra, & Gitakarma, 2022).

The use of artificial intelligence technology in the affective aspects of students is proven to increase student confidence in learning outcomes, (Lin & Chang, 2020). This is due to the ability of artificial intelligence technology to create an interesting and comfortable learning environment for students, (Pabubung, 2021), that can boost students' confidence and reduce their anxiety while learning. Human-robot interaction can make low-achieving students feel more confident, useful and less embarrassed. According to research conducted by Crompton, educational programmes using artificial intelligence have successfully lowered the anxiety levels of students in secondary schools. Therefore, artificial intelligence technology can help students reduce their feelings of anxiety and help them gain the confidence and skills they need to succeed, (Yahya & Hidayat, 2023).

In the learning process, artificial intelligence offers many advantages to students and teachers. Its ability to create customised and adaptive learning experiences is one of the main advantages of artificial intelligence. Artificial intelligence gives educators the opportunity to better alter their teaching strategies by assessing student learning data to identify weaknesses and strengths. For example, a study conducted by Ibnu Fitrianto found that by using a more flexible and well-rounded curriculum, the application of artificial intelligence can improve students' participation and enthusiasm as well as their academic results, (Firdaus et al., n.d.).

According to Aldosari, the application of artificial intelligence technology in management, learning and teaching processes has become a very beneficial tool for educators, (Cholilah et al., 2023). Educators have shown a positive response to the application of artificial intelligence in education. The main advantage of the application of artificial intelligence is the improvement of teaching ability, (Amanda, 2023), as well as improving teaching skills through encouragement and inspiration for self-reflection, which makes teaching approaches more flexible, (Muthmainnah & Faizin, 2024), as it can increase teachers' knowledge of the student learning process and offer strategies to support students, (Dehouche, 2021). Artificial intelligence acts responsively by observing students' feelings and behaviour, (Xia et al., 2022). In addition, artificial intelligence helps educators' career development by offering teaching assessment models and suggestions for better teaching methods, (Haristiani, 2019).

In addition, artificial intelligence has the potential to improve the effectiveness of learning and administrative tasks. By automating everyday tasks such as assessment and reporting, teachers can concentrate more on more important pedagogical aspects, such as interacting directly with students and designing more in-depth teaching strategies. A study conducted by Ibrahim bin Salem (2024) showed that using artificial intelligence for data-driven learning analytics can provide immediate feedback to teachers. This allows them to adjust teaching strategies according to how students behave in real-time, (Zawacki-Richter et al., 2019). As a result, it can improve the effectiveness and efficiency of the teaching and learning process.

Artificial intelligence technology enables the evaluation of students based on their abilities. A smart, automated system that helps teachers assess their students' learning abilities through the use of an artificial intelligence-based chatbot, (Winkler & Söllner, 2018). In addition, artificial intelligence can help gather information about students' learning and supervise their learning process, (Rachmi et al., 2024). To study students' complex understanding and make accurate predictions about their learning performance, various types of multimodal data, such as electroencephalography, physiological measurements, and eye movement tracking, have been used, (Winkler & Söllner, 2018). Artificial intelligence, such as speech recognition and pronunciation correction, can help learn foreign languages, (Luckin & Holmes, 2016).

Artificial intelligence enhances students' creativity and analytical thinking skills. Chatbots and interactive educational platforms are examples of artificial intelligence technologies that help students think critically and independently when facing problems or completing tasks. Learning tools powered by artificial intelligence, such as word games and interactive exercises, can enhance students' creativity and their problem-solving abilities, which are essential components of the learning process, (Rifky, 2024). Artificial intelligence enables faster and wider access to a variety of reference and learning resources. It can recognise subject matter that suits students' needs and learning styles, thereby increasing student interest and engagement in the learning process. Artificial intelligence helps enrich the learning content by customising the content to the student's liking and learning style. This improves students' understanding of the learning material.

The development of artificial intelligence technology has a positive impact by making it easier to get information and this has led to a decrease in students' interest in learning because they rely more on artificial intelligence. The use of artificial intelligence (AI) technology in the learning process carried out by students requires supervision from educators.

The use of these technologies has shaped a more personalised, efficient and focused learning experience. Firstly, AI enables personalisation in learning. AI systems can analyse students' individual learning styles and needs, provide appropriate materials, and design tailored learning strategies. This creates a more adaptive learning environment and reinforces understanding of the material. Secondly, AI contributes to the development of students' digital and technological skills. By interacting with AI technology, students not only gain knowledge on a particular subject but also hone abilities that are highly relevant in the digital age. Thirdly, AI applications can be a helpful tool in research and project development. With automated data analysis capabilities, students can explore ideas, conduct experiments, and expand their knowledge, (Ronsumbre & Rukmawati, 2023).

In addition, artificial intelligence has the ability to complete a number of repetitive tasks, thus easing the work of teachers and administrative officials. By assessing student work, giving grades, and providing feedback, chatbots help educators complete administrative tasks, (Kim et al., 2021). For example, AutoGradr and Repl. it automatically grades assignments and exams, saving teachers a lot of time. The time gained can be used for lesson planning, providing support to students, and professional development. Learning platforms based on artificial intelligence also offer many advantages to students and educators. Colleges and schools have started using chatbots to answer students' questions and assist them after teaching and learning hours are over. Chatbots are also being used in libraries, school canteens, student services, and educational programmes to provide customised learning experiences, assist students, and make tasks easier. In the future, more sophisticated learning management systems are expected to emerge due to advances in artificial intelligence.

In this case, the author argues that the implementation of artificial intelligence faces many challenges. The main problem is the possibility that students will become overly dependent on the technology, which may reduce their engagement in learning. In addition, educational inequity can be further exacerbated if students have differential access to advanced technology. The new study shows how important it is to have balanced access to technology and create strategies to reduce reliance on artificial intelligence to keep it effective and beneficial. Taking a rigorous approach to maximise the use of artificial intelligence to support and enrich students' learning experiences while maintaining their active engagement is needed to address these issues.

Personalisation of learning, artificial intelligence enables personalisation of learning by collecting and analysing data on students' individual learning preferences, needs and tendencies. AI systems can identify students' learning patterns and provide content, resources and learning strategies that match each student's unique characteristics. This helps improve learning effectiveness and ensures that students get relevant and engaging learning experiences, (Xu et al., 2023). Therefore, a teacher/lecturer must always adapt to the development of an increasingly sophisticated era in order to improve his professionalism, so that students can get better with innovative and adaptive learning created by professional teachers/lecturers, (Barber, 2021).

Adaptive learning with artificial intelligence, the learning system can adapt automatically by monitoring and analysing student performance. The AI system can recognise the difficulties students face and provide appropriate additional materials or exercises to help them overcome these obstacles. This enables personalised learning that is responsive to students' individual needs. Automatic evaluation, Artificial intelligence can also be used to automatically evaluate students' assignments and exams. AI systems can check students' answers, provide appropriate feedback, and generate evaluation results quickly and accurately. This helps reduce educators' workload in assessment and allows them to provide more effective and detailed feedback to students, (Vincent-Lancrin & van der Vlies, 2020).

Just like any other learning medium, the existence of artificial intelligence as a tool in the learning process is bound to have both positive and negative effects. Artificial intelligence in learning offers many advantages, such as making the learning process easier for students and teachers, reducing the number of tasks that teachers have to do, allowing storage and easy access to research, and improving productivity and quality of work. Meanwhile, the negative effect of using such media is the tendency for students and teachers to become lazier, which may lead to the neglect of some educators' tasks, especially administration. This is due to the fact that artificial intelligence operates only within a predefined programme. In addition, there is a high risk of hacking, and there is a possibility that the system will crash and lose data.

While artificial intelligence offers many benefits to the assessment process in learning, the author argues that learning tools such as ChatGPT and other artificial intelligence-based language models may face a number of major problems when it comes to evaluation in an academic environment. Potential plagiarism is one of the issues that arise when using GPT-3 for evaluation in higher education institutions. Essay writing systems powered by artificial intelligence are designed to create essays using certain parameters or prompts. As such, there is a possibility that this system will be used by students to make mistakes in completing assignments by submitting essays that are not created by themselves, (Nasution & Amalia, 2024).

According to the authors, artificial intelligence can produce biased results if the data used in training AI models contains unintentional biases. This can lead to unfairness and discrimination in decision-making regarding student learning. It is important to ensure that the data used is representative and free from bias so that the AI system can make fair and objective decisions. The application of artificial intelligence in education is changing the role of educators. Educators must adapt to these changes and develop new skills in using AI technologies. While AI can assist in the personalisation of learning and evaluation, the role of educators as facilitators, motivators and companions to students remains important to provide a holistic learning experience and support students' all-round development.

Therefore, it is imperative for educators and policy makers to make a wise and thorough approach to incorporating artificial intelligence into the learning process so that students can make the most of this technology while maintaining their critical thinking skills and independence. Thus, the application of artificial intelligence in learning can bring many benefits, (Akinwalere & Ivanov, 2022).

Transformation of Indonesia's Education System: Harnessing the Potential of Artificial Intelligence

In the era of artificial intelligence, the education curriculum has become more complex and faces significant challenges in various countries, including Indonesia, (Syanurdin, 2020). One of the biggest challenges is adapting curricula to keep pace with the rapid advancement of artificial intelligence technology and its impact on the world of work. Curricula must be designed to prepare students with the appropriate skills for an age where artificial intelligence is increasingly taking over high-quality and interesting jobs.

There are three perspectives in education: student-facing, teacher-facing, and system-facing, (Thomas et al., 2023). One of the main advantages of using artificial intelligence in education in Indonesia is its ability to provide learning experiences that are customised to individual needs. Unlike conventional classrooms that use generic methods, artificial intelligence technology has the ability to change learning materials according to each student's needs and preferences. Using machine learning algorithms, artificial intelligence is able to evaluate student performance and change learning materials according to each student's needs and preferences, (T. K. F. et al., 2023).

There are several things that will shape and influence future learning experiences due to the function and role of artificial intelligence in Education, including, (Zhang et al., 2023):

1) Artificial intelligence may be able to automate important tasks in education, such as conducting assessments.

Although teachers divide assignments and exams across a wide range of courses, grading assignments and exams can be a monotonous task in universities. Teachers in secondary schools often realise that the assessment process takes up a lot of time, which could otherwise be spent following professional development, interacting with students, or preparing lesson materials. While artificial intelligence may not be able to replace human assessment entirely, it comes pretty close. Educators can now automate grading for almost all types of multiple-choice questions and exams in fill-in-the-blank format. There may also be automated writing assessments for students. Software for essay grading is still in the development stage and is not widely used yet. However, it may improve as time goes by. This will allow teachers to concentrate more on classroom activities and interactions with students rather than conducting assessments.

2) Educational software can be customised to suit student needs.

Through the application of more personalised and customised learning, artificial intelligence is having a major influence on education, from kindergarten to postgraduate education. Many of these have emerged as a result of the increasing number of customised learning programs, games, and software applications. These systems cater to the needs of students by giving special attention to certain topics, repeating material that has not been mastered, and generally supporting the pace at which students learn. This type of customised education can use technology to help students with different skill levels work together in one class. Teachers act as learning facilitators in this case and help and support students when needed. Customisable learning has changed the world of education in many places. With the advancement of artificial intelligence in the next few decades, customisable programmes such as these are likely to increase and expand even more.

3) Artificial intelligence programmes can help both students and teachers.

Such artificial intelligence systems not only allow students to receive the help they need but also help teachers find students who may be having difficulty in lessons. These universities and schools do not only offer artificial intelligence programmes for specific courses. There are some people working to create a system that can help students choose a major that matches the areas in which they succeed and have difficulty. The recommendations can help prospective students choose a bold college major, even if they are not required to follow it.

4) Artificial intelligence technology may change the role of educators.

In education, the role of educators remains, but with new technologies, such as intelligent computing systems, the nature and function of educators may change. As explained earlier, artificial intelligence can take over tasks such as evaluation and assist students in improving their learning. In addition, artificial intelligence can be used as an alternative to real-world academic tutoring. Artificial intelligence systems can be designed to present knowledge, serve as a platform where students can ask questions and seek information, or serve as a platform where students can ask questions and seek information. However, artificial intelligence will change the role of educators to facilitators in some situations. Students will receive personalised experiences and direct interaction, artificial intelligence subject matter, and educator support. Many changes in education have been caused by technology, especially in schools that use online learning or blended learning methods such as the flipped classroom model.

5) Artificial intelligence can change the way schools support students, teach, and seek information.

High schools have changed the way they communicate with potential and active students due to intelligent data collection fuelled by computer technology. Intelligent computer systems serve to tailor every aspect of the college experience to students' needs and wants, from the recruitment process to helping students choose the best courses. While data mining systems have become an important part of higher education today, artificial intelligence might make an even bigger difference in this sector. Some educational institutions have started programmes that allow their students to get training with the help of artificial intelligence, which can help speed up their transition from high school to college. In the future, the college selection process will probably be similar to that of Amazon or Netflix, with systems suggesting programmes and schools that best suit students' interests.

6) Artificial intelligence technologies have the ability to transform students' learning environments, the teachers who instruct them, and basic skill development strategies.

The fact that artificial intelligence has the ability to significantly transform almost all aspects of education that we have taken for granted can be changed, although major transformations will probably occur in a few more decades. Students can gain knowledge from anywhere in the world by utilising artificial intelligence technology, software and support systems. With programmes like this replacing certain types of classroom teaching, artificial intelligence may only be able to take over the role of the teacher in some situations, which could make the student's learning experience better or otherwise. However, as these programmes progress and more developers get involved, artificial intelligence professionals around the world have developed artificial intelligence-powered educational programmes to help students learn basic skills.

The author argues that educational institutions can use artificial intelligence to modify their learning methods to meet the needs of each student. Artificial intelligence algorithms and techniques can be used to evaluate student learning data, find areas that are lacking, and provide customised feedback or direction. In addition, artificial intelligence has the potential to change the way students assess the education system in Indonesia. Standardised exams and other assessment methods can be supplemented or even replaced with artificial intelligence assessment tools. Artificial intelligence systems can assess students' writings, projects, and even oral responses through machine learning technology and natural language processing. The automated evaluation process not only reduces the amount of time spent by teachers but also provides fairer and more consistent feedback. In turn, this will improve the accuracy and reliability of assessment in the education system.

Along with the transition to the digital era, the impact of artificial intelligence advancements on curriculum and teaching methods in educational institutions is increasingly becoming a hot topic of discussion. Curriculum transformation, according to Liriwati (2023), means changing and improving the existing curriculum by adding new elements or changing the overall learning method. To adapt the curriculum to the advancement of artificial intelligence in the era of 5.0, a change is needed.

Using artificial intelligence, curriculum transformation allows each student to follow the learning process in a way that better suits their own interests, inclinations and learning rhythms. In addition, artificial intelligence allows the creation of teaching materials that can be customised to the individual needs of each student, making it easier to monitor and provide direct feedback to students. Learners will become more active during the learning process, which will lead to optimal results.

The method of incorporating artificial intelligence) into the curriculum is a key solution to overcome the challenges that arise in today's digital age, (Zhang et al., 2024). One key approach is to design curricula that are sensitive to advances in artificial intelligence technology. This means adjusting the curriculum to include an understanding of artificial intelligence, the ability to utilise it, and how to use artificial intelligence in the learning process. As a result, students will have the necessary understanding and skills to fit into an era where artificial intelligence is increasingly important in various areas of life.

According to the author, using artificial intelligence in the curriculum requires teacher training. Teachers should be trained on how to use artificial intelligence technology in learning activities. Utilisation of artificial intelligence-powered learning platforms, data processing to customise learning experiences, and implementation of creative artificial intelligence-assisted learning approaches are some examples of these training activities.

One important step towards incorporating artificial intelligence into the curriculum is to develop teaching materials that meet the demands of the times. The curriculum should include materials on artificial intelligence, such as an understanding of the basic principles of artificial intelligence, moral issues in using artificial intelligence, and how artificial intelligence is used in various industries. Thus, students can gain a better understanding of artificial intelligence technology. Students can improve their ability to solve problems, analyse and think critically in a real-world context by engaging in projects that utilise artificial intelligence technology. This allows them to apply their knowledge of artificial intelligence to the real world and deepen their understanding of complex artificial intelligence concepts.

Merdeka Curriculum was created with the aim of giving educators more freedom and flexibility in organising their learning process. It is the first step towards the integration of artificial intelligence into learning design, (dan Musafa, 2022)[1]. Merdeka Curriculum focuses on innovative, creative and technology-based learning. Students have the opportunity to learn various technologies, including artificial intelligence. The material on artificial intelligence includes understanding the concepts, technology, algorithms, and applications of artificial intelligence.

These artificial intelligence materials can be incorporated into appropriate subjects, such as informatics. A free curriculum with artificial intelligence is proven to simplify learning assessment and evaluation, discover additional needs of students, and optimise the use of educational resources (Shiddiq, 2020). All of this is expected to improve the overall quality of education and provide fairer opportunities for every student, in line with the objectives of the Merdeka Curriculum (Cholilah, Tatuwo, Komariah, Rosdiana, & Fatirul, 2023).

As educators in the age of society 5.0, educators must improve their digital skills and innovative thinking. According to Kamila, as educators in the era of artificial intelligence, teachers face challenges that require skills to guide future generations to become individuals who not only have high abilities and qualities but also have moral values[2]. According to the author, an educator can do 5 (five) things in integrating artificial intelligence: provide skills-focused education, identify and use the Internet of Things (IoT), use virtual or augmented reality technology, and implement and optimise artificial intelligence. Technology can be a very useful tool, especially for constructive purposes such as education, which makes it easier for educators to create more engaging teaching materials and strengthen students' ability to analyse various data.

The author argues that the advancement of artificial intelligence and its utilisation in the teaching-learning process must be matched by the skills of teachers. However, the skills of teachers in Indonesia are still uneven, especially in terms of technological skills. Many educators do not understand how to use artificial intelligence in education. Therefore, training programmes should include an understanding of artificial intelligence concepts, appropriate use of technology, and teaching methods that incorporate various disciplines. The government has an important role to play in providing sufficient training for teachers in this context.

The use of artificial intelligence technology can enhance students' learning experience by providing adaptive learning. This approach involves the implementation of artificial intelligence-powered learning systems, which can customise materials to suit each student's level of understanding and learning rhythm. With this customisation in the learning process, students can learn the material according to their individual learning needs and rhythms, thereby improving academic results. In addition, in an effort to incorporate artificial intelligence into the curriculum, it is necessary to improve the capabilities required in the 21st century. Capabilities such as digital skills, innovation, problem-solving and co-operation are increasingly important to deal with changes caused by advances in artificial intelligence technology. These capabilities should be facilitated in the curriculum by utilising technology and innovative learning approaches.

The way education is conducted in the era of computers and the internet has changed thanks to advancements in artificial intelligence. Smart chatbots and customizable learning platforms have paved the way for significant changes in the education sector. With artificial intelligence, learning is not only easier and more efficient, but also allows for a learning experience tailored to the needs of each student. The role of teachers in this situation shifts from merely conveying information to assisting and guiding the learning process. The future of education in the digital era is filled with various innovations that will help students reach their full potential and enhance their learning experience. The development of artificial intelligence technology is accelerating. As a continuously evolving community, it is very important for us to wisely harness the innovations of artificial intelligence. We must ensure that the transformation in the world of education caused by artificial intelligence will support the crucial role of teachers in shaping and motivating the future generation, not take over.

Artificial intelligence technology has caused many problems in education, economics and socio-politics. It also raises fundamental questions about how it will impact human beings (Pabubung, 2021a). Artificial intelligence has great potential, but it is not related to moral responsibility because the moral dimension is always related to humans who have knowledge, desire, and consciousness. The principles of ethics and responsibility should determine the use of artificial intelligence systems. Moreover, it is very important to consider moral values during each phase of its development (Pabubung, 2021b).

The author is of the opinion that it is very important to emphasise responsibility and morals in the utilisation of artificial intelligence technology in the curriculum. The social, legal and moral impacts of the utilisation of artificial intelligence as well as ethical principles in relation to artificial intelligence are discussed in this plan. In this way, students will not only learn about artificial intelligence, but they will also learn how important it is to use this technology responsibly. In addition, to incorporate artificial intelligence into the curriculum, this approach may also include collaboration with industry sectors and relevant organisations to ensure that the curriculum matches the demands of the job market. The curriculum should be adapted to the needs of industries that are increasingly using artificial intelligence, so that graduates are prepared to enter a world of work that is influenced by artificial intelligence. Cooperation with industry sectors and related organisations can also provide students with opportunities to gain hands-on work experience.

To incorporate artificial intelligence into the independent curriculum, strategic steps are needed. These steps are essential to equip students and educators with the necessary skills. Strategies that can be used to implement artificial intelligence in the Merdeka curriculum are:

1) Use of Chatbot

Chatbots that help and assist students can be created with artificial intelligence. These chatbots can help students by providing information about classes, lecture schedules, assignments, and more.

2) Automatic Evaluation

Artificial intelligence can be used to automatically evaluate student work, such as exams or assignments. To grade and provide immediate responses to students, these systems use natural language processing and machine learning. Not only does this reduce the time that teachers have to spend, but it also allows teachers to provide faster feedback to students and help them better understand what they are learning.

3) Simulation and Virtual Reality (VR)

Simulations and virtual experiences that support learning in vocational fields can be created with the help of artificial intelligence. Virtual reality (VR) technology gives students the opportunity to improve their practical skills in an organised and safe environment. In a mechanical engineering class, students can use VR to practice assembling or repairing machines without having to buy expensive physical tools.

4) Recommendation System

A recommendation system using artificial intelligence can be created to assist students in choosing a vocational education programme that suits their interests and abilities. The system uses algorithms and data to evaluate students' interests, abilities, and career goals, and then provides appropriate and individualised recommendations.

5) Analyse Educational Data

Artificial intelligence can be used to analyse educational data such as student data, test results, and curriculum. Using data analytics and machine learning methods, artificial intelligence can discover important patterns, trends, and insights that can be used to improve educational efficiency.

6) Training Teachers in Using Artificial Intelligence Technology

To improve the quality of human resources contributing to the field of education, particularly with regard to teachers and principals, continuous support and training is required, both at local and international levels. This is done to provide them with the ability to address various issues that arise in the industry and prepare them to face the modern era. Thus, teachers can implement more responsive learning approaches while motivating students to use information technology more wisely.

7) Development of Ethical Guidelines

Principles such as fairness, confidentiality, and openness should be a firm ethical basis for using artificial intelligence in education.

The author argues that although artificial intelligence can enhance creativity and learning development, there are several issues that need to be addressed, such as:

1) The asymmetry of access and technological infrastructure can be a problem, especially in remote areas that may lack facilities. Additionally, educators' competence in using artificial intelligence technology is also a concern because many educators may not yet be trained to utilize it effectively. Many educational institutions face significant challenges due to the cost of implementing artificial intelligence, especially for those lacking funds;
2) Another challenge is data security and privacy because artificial intelligence often collects students' personal data. This information must be carefully safeguarded to prevent leaks. Moreover, excessive reliance on artificial intelligence can diminish students' ability to think critically and independently and reduce their capacity for social interaction. Moreover, there is a possibility that there will be a greater disparity between students who have access to advanced technology and those who do not, which could exacerbate educational inequality;
3) The quality of education is still low. This is reflected in the low abilities of Indonesian students at the elementary and middle school levels in reading, mathematics, and science, according to PISA scores. The learning experiences of students at vocational and higher education levels are not sufficient to equip them with the skills they need to enter the job market. A curriculum that does not align with industry standards, excessive administrative burdens on faculty, and insufficient faculty capacity are the main causes of the above issues[3].

To incorporate artificial intelligence into the curriculum, many changes are also needed, and that might take time. Finally, developing artificial intelligence that can understand and adapt to the cultural diversity of Indonesia is a complex technical challenge. Careful planning, adequate training for educators, investment in technological infrastructure, and policies that ensure the security and privacy of student data are all necessary to address this issue and maximize the benefits of artificial intelligence for learning.

According to the author, the development of artificial intelligence must align with ethical education, which includes responsible use and special attention to components that support independence in the learning process. They also argue that the development of artificial intelligence in the field of education must consider the risk of dependency on artificial intelligence. By considering student responses, the development of integrating artificial intelligence in education can be directed to enhance the quality, availability, and learning experience of students while still paying attention to the challenges and risks that may arise as a result of its use.

The author argues that it is important to emphasise that the application of artificial intelligence in education should be based on strong ethical principles and safe regulation. Regulations and ethical management guidelines are essential to ensure that the application of artificial intelligence in higher education is done in a fair, ethical and trustworthy manner. In education, artificial intelligence is used as a tool and amplifier in the learning process. By utilising it as a learning aid, teachers, educators and mentors can help them deliver lessons to students in the most effective and optimal way. It will also help students understand the lessons.

CONCLUSION

Artificial intelligence technology has changed the world of education and the way students learn. Artificial intelligence has become an invaluable partner in the field of education because of its ability to analyse data on a large scale, make tailored suggestions, and provide interactive learning tools. With artificial intelligence, more personalised learning methods can be created. However, it must suit both educators and students and requires investment in technological infrastructure. In education, incorporation must be done carefully in order to achieve the best results without compromising the development of students' abilities and their critical thinking. An educational policy that supports the use of artificial intelligence as a medium in the learning process is needed. In addition, it is important to conduct continuous evaluation to ensure that the learning outcomes of learners have a positive impact.

The education sector is greatly influenced by advancements in artificial intelligence. Using artificial intelligence can enhance the efficiency of the free curriculum. Artificial intelligence provides the opportunity to implement innovative teaching methods, customize the curriculum, and tailor individual learning. Although there are benefits, there are challenges. This includes technical issues, a shortage of educators, and ethical concerns related to the responsible use of artificial intelligence. Therefore, educational institutions must have a deep understanding of how to optimally utilize artificial intelligence and prepare the skills of educators and learners. Indonesia has the capability to prepare its youth to succeed in an increasingly integrated and AI-dominated era by transforming its curriculum responsively and comprehensively, emphasizing the development of holistic, analytical, and innovative skills. The education curriculum in Indonesia is crucial for producing graduates who are ready to compete and contribute in an increasingly complex and interconnected era of artificial intelligence.

REFERENCES

Abdurrahman, A. B. S. (2020). the Application of «Nemo» Artificial Intelligence in Arabic Language Learning in the 4.0 Revolution Era At Al-Khalifah Islamic Boarding School Cibubur. learning, 6(1).

Akinwalere, S. N., & Ivanov, V. (2022). Artificial Intelligence in Higher Education: Challenges and Opportunities. *Border Crossing*, *12*(1), 1–15. Advance online publication. DOI: 10.33182/bc.v12i1.2015

Al-Ghonmein, A. M., & Al-Moghrabi, K. G. (2024). The potential of ChatGPT technology in education: advantages, obstacles and future growth. IAES International Journal of Artificial Intelligence (IJ-AI), 13(2), 1206-1213.

Aldosari, S. A. M. (2020). The Future of Higher Education in the Light of Artificial Intelligence Transformations. *International Journal of Higher Education*, *9*(3), 145. Advance online publication. DOI: 10.5430/ijhe.v9n3p145

Apriliani, D. (2024). *Penggunaan Artificial Intelligence dalam Pembelajaran Bahasa Indonesia*. DIKBASTRA: Jurnal Pendidikan Bahasa dan Sastra 7(1), DOI: 10.22437/dikbastra.v7i1.33262

Ardiansyah. (2022). VIRTUAL SYNCHRONOUS LEARNING AKUNTANSI MANUFAKTUR DALAM MENDORONG EFEKTIVITAS PEMBELAJARAN: Virtual Synchronous Learning of Manufacturing Accounting In Supporting Learning Effectiveness. Jurnal Teknodik, 49–68. https://doi.org/10.32550/teknodik.vi.871

Armanda, L. (2022). *Multimodal Large Language Models for Inclusive Collaboration Learning Tasks*. Proceedings of the 2022 Conference of the North American Chapter of the Association for Computational Linguistics: Human Language Technologies: Student Research Workshop, https://doi.org/ srw.26DOI: 10.18653/v1/2022.naacl

Bozkurt, A., Karadeniz, A., Baneres, D., Guerrero-Roldán, A. E., & Rodríguez, M. E. (2021). Artificial intelligence and reflections from educational landscape: A review of AI studies in half a century. *Sustainability (Basel)*, *13*(2), 800. DOI: 10.3390/su13020800

Chiu, T. K., Moorhouse, B. L., Chai, C. S., & Ismailov, M. (2024). Teacher support and student motivation to learn with Artificial Intelligence (AI) based chatbot. *Interactive Learning Environments*, *32*(7), 3240–3256.

Chiu, T. K. F., Xia, Q., Zhou, X., Chai, C. S., & Cheng, M. (2023). Systematic Literature Review on Opportunities, Challenges, And Future Research Recommendations of Artificial Intelligence in Education. *Computers and Education: Artificial Intelligence*, *4*, 100118. DOI: 10.1016/j.caeai.2022.100118

Cholilah, M., & Tatuwo, A. G. P., Komariah, Rosdiana, S. P., & Fatirul, A. N. (2023). Pengembangan Kurikulum Merdeka Dalam Satuan Pendidikan Serta Implementasi Kurikulum Merdeka Pada Pembelajaran Abad 21. *Sanskara Pendidikan Dan Pengajaran*, *1*(02), 56–67. DOI: 10.58812/spp.v1i02.110

Cotton, D. R., Cotton, P. A., & Shipway, J. R. (2024). Chatting and cheating: Ensuring academic integrity in the era of ChatGPT. *Innovations in Education and Teaching International*, *61*(2), 228–239. DOI: 10.1080/14703297.2023.2190148

Cunningham-Nelson, S., Boles, W., Trouton, L., & Margerison, E. (2019). A review of chatbots in education: practical steps forward. In 30th annual conference for the australasian association for engineering education (AAEE 2019): educators becoming agents of change: innovate, integrate, motivate (pp. 299-306). Engineers Australia.

Dehouche, N. (2021). Plagiarism in the age of massive Generative Pre-trained Transformers (GPT-3). *Ethics in Science and Environmental Politics*, *21*, 17–23. Advance online publication. DOI: 10.3354/esep00195

Durall, E., & Kapros, E. (2020). Co-design for a competency self-assessment chatbot and survey in science education. In Learning and Collaboration Technologies. Human and Technology Ecosystems: 7th International Conference, LCT 2020, Held as Part of the 22nd HCI International Conference, HCII 2020, Copenhagen, Denmark, July 19–24, 2020 [Springer International Publishing.]. *Proceedings*, *22*(Part II), 13–24.

Firdaus, M. R., Irawan, R. R., Mahardika, C. H. Y., Gaol, P. L., & Prinaryanto, B. A. (2024). Tantangan teknologi artificial intelligence pada kegiatan pembelajaran mahasiswa. *Indonesian Journal of Education and Development Research*, *2*(1), 379–384.

Fitrianto, I., Setyawan, C. E., & Saleh, M. (2024). Utilizing Artificial Intelligence for Personalized Arabic Language Learning Plans. International Journal of Post Axial: Futuristic Teaching and Learning, 30-40.

Graesser, A. C. (2016). Conversations with AutoTutor Help Students Learn. *International Journal of Artificial Intelligence in Education*, *26*(1), 124–132. Advance online publication. DOI: 10.1007/s40593-015-0086-4

Gunawan, K. D. H., Liliasari, L., Kaniawati, I., & Setiawan, W. (2021). Implementation of competency enhancement program for science teachers assisted by artificial intelligence in designing HOTS-based integrated science learning. *Jurnal Penelitian Dan Pembelajaran IPA*, *7*(1), 55–65. DOI: 10.30870/jppi.v7i1.8655

Haristiani, N. (2019). *Artificial Intelligence (AI) Chatbot as Language Learning Medium: An inquiry*. Journal of Physics: Conference Series, Volume 1387, International Conference on Education, Science and Technology 2019, Padang, Indonesia, https://doi.org/DOI: 10.1088/1742 6596/1387/1/012020

Hill, J., Ford, R., & Fareras, I. (2015). Real Conversations with Artificial Intelligence: A Comparison Between Human–Human Online Conversations and Human Chatbot Conversations. *Computers in Human Behavior, 49*, 245–250. Advance online publication. DOI: 10.1016/j.chb.2015.02.026

Hong, J., & Kim, K. (2025). Impact of AIoT education program on digital and AI literacy of elementary school students. *Education and Information Technologies, 30*(1), 107–130. DOI: 10.1007/s10639-024-12758-0

Hsieh, Y.-Z., Lin, S.-S., Luo, Y.-C., Jeng, Y.-L., Tan, S.-W., Chen, C.-R., & Chiang, P.-Y. (2020). ARCS-Assisted Teaching Robots Based on Anticipatory Computing and Emotional Big Data for Improving Sustainable Learning Efficiency and Motivation. *Sustainability (Basel)*, *12*(14), 5605. Advance online publication. DOI: 10.3390/su12145605

Juwika, A. (2023). Peran Artificial Intelligence dalam Meningkatkan Efisiensi dan Efektifitas Sistem Pendidikan. *COMSERVA: Jurnal Penelitian Dan Pengabdian Masyarakat*, *2*(12), 3181–3187. Advance online publication. DOI: 10.59141/comserva.v2i12.731

Kamila, J. T., Nurnazhiifa, K., Sati, L., & Setiawati, R. (2022). Pengembangan guru dalam menghadapi tantangan kebijakan pendidikan di era revolusi industri 4.0. *Jurnal Pendidikan Tambusai*, *6*(2), 10013–10018.

Khan, I., Ahmad, A. R., Jabeur, N., & Mahdi, M. N. (2021). An Artificial Intelligence Approach To Monitor Student Performance and Devise Preventive Measures. *Smart Learning Environments*, *8*(1), 17. Advance online publication. DOI: 10.1186/s40561-021-00161-y

Kim, H. S., Kim, N. Y., & Cha, Y. (2021). Is it beneficial to use AI chatbots to improve learners' speaking performance? *Journal of Asia TEFL*, *18*(1), 161–178. DOI: 10.18823/asiatefl.2021.18.1.10.161

Kim, S., Jang, Y., Kim, W., Choi, S., Jung, H., Kim, S., & Kim, H. (2021). Why and What to Teach: AI Curriculum for Elementary School. *Proceedings of the AAAI Conference on Artificial Intelligence*, *35*(17), 15569–15576. Advance online publication. DOI: 10.1609/aaai.v35i17.17833

Li, C., & Xing, W. (2021). Natural language generation using deep learning to support MOOC learners. *International Journal of Artificial Intelligence in Education*, *31*(2), 186–214. DOI: 10.1007/s40593-020-00235-x

Lin, M. P. C., & Chang, D. (2020). Enhancing post-secondary writers' writing skills with a chatbot. *Journal of Educational Technology & Society*, *23*(1), 78–92.

Liriwati, F. Y. (2023). Transformasi Kurikulum; Kecerdasan Buatan untuk Membangun Pendidikan yang Relevan di Masa Depan. *IHSAN: Jurnal Pendidikan Islam*, *1*(2), 62–71. DOI: 10.61104/ihsan.v1i2.61

Safii, M., & Amanda, A. (2023). Optimisasi Algoritma MOOSRA Pada Seleksi Penerima Beasiswa KIP Kuliah. [Jurnal Sains Manajemen Informatika dan Komputer]. *Jurnal SAINTIKOM*, *22*(2), 555–561.

Mageira, K., Pittou, D., Papasalouros, A., Kotis, K., Zangogianni, P., & Daradoumis, A. (2022). Educational AI Chatbots for Content and Language Integrated Learning. *Applied Sciences (Basel, Switzerland)*, *12*(7), 3239. Advance online publication. DOI: 10.3390/app12073239

Manongga, D., Rahardja, U., Sembiring, I., Lutfiani, N., & Yadila, A. B. (2022). Dampak Kecerdasan Buatan Bagi Pendidikan. *ADI: Bisnis Digital Interdisiplin Jurnal*, *3*(2), 41–55. Advance online publication. DOI: 10.34306/abdi.v3i2.792

Muarif, J. A., Jihad, F. A., Alfadli, M. I., & Setiabudi, D. I. (2023). Hubungan perkembangan teknologi AI terhadap pembelajaran mahasiswa. Jurnal Pendidikan. *SEROJA*, *2*(2), 53–60.

Muthmainnah, N., Rahmayanti, V. A., & Faizin, M. (2024). *Modernitas Alat Pendidikan Dalam Perspektif Artificial Intelligence Fenomena Kemajuan Zaman Pendidik Abad 21*. Pedagogi. *Jurnal Ilmu Pendidikan*, *24*(1), 46–55. Advance online publication. DOI: 10.24036/pedagogi.v24i1.1937

Nayze, L. S. A.. (2021). Smartpathk: A Platform for Teaching Glomerulopathies Using Machine Learning. *BMC Medical Education*, *21*(1), 248. Advance online publication. DOI: 10.1186/s12909-021-02680-1 PMID: 33926437

Nurhuda, H. (2022). *Masalah-masalah Pendidikan Nasional; Faktor-Faktor dan Solusi yang Ditawarkan*. Jurnal Pemikiran dan Pendidikan 5(2), https://doi.org/ https://doi.org/10.51476/dirasah.v5i2.406

Pabubung, M. R. (2021a). 'Human Dignity' dalam Pemikiran Yohanes Paulus II dan Relevansi untuk Dunia Masa Kini. [Journal of Theology]. *Jurnal Teknologi*, *10*(1), 49–70. http://dx.doi.org/10.24071/jt.v10i1.2905

Pabubung, M. R. (2021b). Epistemologi kecerdasan buatan (AI) dan pentingnya ilmu etika dalam pendidikan interdisipliner. *Jurnal Filsafat Indonesia*, *4*(2), 152–159. DOI: 10.23887/jfi.v4i2.34734

Rachmi, . (2024). Transformasi Pendidikan di Era Digital Tantangan dan Peluang. *Journal of International Multidisciplinary Research*, *2*(2). Advance online publication. DOI: 10.62504/6y4qb169

Rifky, S. (2024). Dampak Penggunaan Artificial Intelligence Bagi Pendidikan Tinggi. *Indonesian Journal of Multidisciplinary on Social and Technology*, *2*(1), 37–42. DOI: 10.31004/ijmst.v2i1.287

Rifky, S. (2024). Professionalism Of Educators In Learning Development. *International Journal of Teaching Learning*, *2*(2). https://injotel.org/index.php/12/article/view/93

Rooein, D. (2019). Data-Driven Edu Chatbots. Conference: Companion The 2019 World Wide Web Conference, DOI: 10.1145/3308560.3314191

Luckin, R., & Holmes, W. (2016). *Intelligence Unleashed: An argument for AI in Education*. UCL Knowledge Lab, University College London, https://www.researchgate.net/publication/299561597_Intelligence_Unleashed_An_argument_for_AI_in_Education

Sabella, B., Rhomadhona, H., & Arrahimi, A. R. (2023). Pelatihan pembuatan game sederhana sebagai media pembelajaran untuk pengajar smp berbasis artificial intelegent. Jurnal Widya Laksmi. *Jurnal Pengabdian Kepada Masyarakat*, *3*(2), 69–76.

Salem, I. (2024). Integrating Artificial Intelligence in Personalized Learning: A Future-Oriented Approach to Enhance Student Engagement and Achievement. *International Journal of Post Axial*, *2*(2). Advance online publication. DOI: 10.59944/postaxial.v2i2.299

Salsabilla, K. A. Z., Hadi, T. D. F., Pratiwi, W., & Mukaromah, S. (2023, November). Pengaruh penggunaan kecerdasan buatan terhadap mahasiswa di perguruan tinggi. In Prosiding Seminar Nasional Teknologi Dan Sistem Informasi (Vol. 3, No. 1, pp. 168-175). DOI: 10.33005/sitasi.v3i1.371

Ronsumbre, S., Rukmawati, T., Sumarsono, A., & Waremra, R. S. (2023). Pembelajaran digital dengan kecerdasan buatan (AI): Korelasi AI terhadap motivasi belajar siswa. *Jurnal Educatio Fkip Unma*, *9*(3), 1464–1474.

Sharma, K., & Giannakos, M. (2020). Multimodal data capabilities for learning: What can multimodal data tell us about learning? *British Journal of Educational Technology, 51*(5), 1450–1484. DOI: 10.1111/bjet.12993

Shiddiq, A. B. (2020). The Application of «Nemo» Artificial Intelegence in Arabic Language Learning in the 4.0 Revolution Era At Al-Khalifah Islamic Boarding School Cibubur. *IJLECR International Journal of Language Education and Cultural Review, 6*(1), 58–61. DOI: 10.21009/IJLECR.061.07

Sir Michel Barber. (2021). *Gravity assist: Propelling higher education towards a brighter future – Digital teaching and learning review.* https://blobofsproduks.blob.core.windows.net/files/Gravity%20assist/Gravity-assist-DTL-finalforweb.pdf

Soegiarto, I. (2023). *Inovasi Pembelajaran Berbasis Teknologi Artificial Intelligences (AI) pada Sekolah Kedinasan di Era Revolusi Industri 4.0 dan Society 5.0.* Innovative. *Journal of Social Science Research, 3*(5). https://j-innovative.org/index.php/Innovative/article/view/6132/4308

Sopiansyah, D., Masruroh, S., Zaqiah, Q. Y., & Erihadiana, M. (2022). Konsep dan implementasi kurikulum MBKM (merdeka belajar kampus merdeka). *Reslaj: Religion Education Social Laa Roiba Journal, 4*(1), 34–41. DOI: 10.47467/reslaj.v4i1.458

Vincent-Lancrin, S., & Van der Vlies, R. (2020). Trustworthy artificial intelligence (AI) in education: Promises and challenges. OECD education working papers, (218), 0_1-17.

Supriyadi, S., & Nasution, Z. (2024). Teknologi Artificial Intelligence (AI) dan Literasi Digital Mahasiswa terhadap Hasil Belajar Mata Kuliah Evaluasi Pembelajaran: Artificial Intelligence, Literasi Digital, Evaluasi Pembelajaran. Jurnal Teknodik, 113-118.

Supriyadi, S. M., & Maesyaroh, S. (2023). The Effect of Parenting Patterns and Digital Literacy on Social-Emotional Development in Early Children. *Jurnal Ilmiah Profesi Pendidikan, 8*(1b), 859–867. Advance online publication. DOI: 10.29303/jipp.v8i1b.1202

Syanurdin, S. (2020, October). Pembelajaran Bahasa Indonesia Berbasis Digital dalam Membina Karakter Siswa. In Seminar Nasional Pendidikan Bahasa dan Sastra (pp. 44-51).

Syarafudin, H. M., & Ikawati, H. D. (2020). Faktor-faktor yang mempengaruhi profesionalisme guru. Jurnal Cahaya Mandalika ISSN 2721-4796 (online), 1(2), 47-51.

Tjahyanti, L. P. A. S., Saputra, P. S., & Santo Gitakarma, M. (2022). Peran artificial intelligence (AI) untuk mendukung pembelajaran di masa pandemi Covid-19. Komteks, 1(1).

Vázquez-Cano, E., Mengual-Andrés, S., & López-Meneses, E. (2021). Chatbot To Improve Learning Punctuation in Spanish and To Enhance Open and Flexible Learning Environments. *International Journal of Educational Technology in Higher Education, 18*(33), 33. Advance online publication. DOI: 10.1186/s41239-021-00269-8

Widdows, D. (2024). *Natural Language, AI, and Quantum Computing 2024: Research.* Research Ingredients and Directions in QNLP, http://arxiv.org/abs/2403.19758

Winkler, R., & Soellner, M. (2018). Rainer Winkler dan Matthias Söllner. (2018). *Unleashing the Potential of Chatbots in Education: A State-Of-The-Art Analysis. Proceedings - Academy of Management, 2018*(1), 15903. Advance online publication. DOI: 10.5465/AMBPP.2018.15903abstract

Xia, Q., Chiu, T. K. F., Lee, M., Sanusi, I. T., Dai, Y., & Chai, C. S. (2022). A self-determination Theory (SDT) Design Approach for Inclusive and Diverse Artificial Intelligence (AI) Education. *Computers & Education, 189*, 104582. Advance online publication. DOI: 10.1016/j.compedu.2022.104582

Xu, S. (2023). Retracted: Design and Implementation of Intelligent Teaching System Based on Artificial Intelligence and Computer Technology. *Security and Communication Networks, 2023*, 1. Advance online publication. DOI: 10.1155/2023/9854971

Yahya, M., & Hidayat, A. (2023, July). Implementasi Artificial Intelligence (AI) di bidang pendidikan kejuruan pada era revolusi industri 4.0. In Seminar Nasional Dies Natalis 62 (Vol. 1, pp. 190-199).

Mufid, Z., & Musafa, M. (2022). Implementasi penggunaan Internet of Things (IoT) di dunia pendidikan selama masa pendemi COVID-19. *Jurnal Konseling Pendidikan Islam, 3*(2), 439–446.

Zawacki-Richter, O., Marín, V. I., Bond, M., & Gouverneur, F. (2019). Systematic Review of Research on Artificial Intelligence Applications in Higher Education-Where Are the Educators? *International Journal of Educational Technology in Higher Education, 16*(39), 39. Advance online publication. DOI: 10.1186/s41239-019-0171-0

Zhang, Y., Ruan, H., Fan, Z., & Roychoudhury, A. (2024, September). AutoCodeRover: Autonomous program improvement. In *Proceedings of the 33rd ACM SIGSOFT International Symposium on Software Testing and Analysis* (pp. 1592-1604). doi:DOI: 10.48550/arXiv.2404.0542

Zhang, Y., Pei, H., Zhen, S., Li, Q., & Liang, F. (2023). Chat Generative Pre-Trained Transformer (ChatGPT) Usage in Healthcare. *Gastroenterology & Endoscopy, 1*(3), 139–143. Advance online publication. DOI: 10.1016/j.gande.2023.07.002

ENDNOTES

1 Deni Sopiansyah, et.al. (2021). *Konsep dan Implementasi Kurikulum MBKM (Merdeka Belajar Kampus Merdeka).* RESLAJ: Religion Education Social Laa Roiba Journal 4(1), 34-41, https://doi.org/10.47467/reslaj.v4i1.458

2 Jenisa Tasya Kamila, et.al. (2022). *Pengembangan Guru dalam Menghadapi Tantangan Kebijakan Pendidikan di Era Revolusi Industri 4.0.* Jurnal Pendidikan Tambusai 6(2), 10013-10018, https://doi.org/10.31004/jptam. v6i2.4008

3 Hengki Nurhuda. (2022). *Masalah-masalah Pendidikan Nasional; Faktor-Faktor dan Solusi yang Ditawarkan.* Jurnal Pemikiran dan Pendidikan 5(2), 127-137 https://doi.org/https://doi.org/10.51476/dirasah.v5i2.406

Chapter 4
AI and Education for Sustainable Development Goals (SDGs)

Poornima Mahesh
https://orcid.org/0009-0004-9364-1866
N.R.B. College, University of Mumbai, India

A Saranya
Amity University, Mumbai, India

Rajiv Iyer
https://orcid.org/0000-0002-1136-2061
Amity University, Mumbai, India

Vedprakash Maralapalle
https://orcid.org/0000-0002-7770-1134
Amity University, Mumbai, India

ABSTRACT

AI and education appear to share a synergy, let alone stretching the sustainable goals way beyond their logical limit. One of them is SDG 4, specifically that concerns availability and access to quality education. The autonomy in learning is made possible by the AI systems where the application will provide lessons that are ideal and within the capability of the student. Consequently, learners' learning engagement as well as learning success rates increase continuously. This chapter focuses mainly on artificial intelligence in education and puts a lot of value on SDG 4 and how AI can support educators in administering and facilitating, by virtue of data analytics wisdom of the learner's character, studying strengths and limitations, and tailoring higher quality content for the learners. This chapter focuses on the

DOI: 10.4018/979-8-3373-5781-2.ch004

moral implication of the potential of AI in education. Finally, this chapter provides a multifaceted analysis of how AI technologies can be applied to enhance good education, environmental awareness and the 'Global Citizen.'

INTRODUCTION

In the contemporary world, where modern structures of learning are just a few decades old and the world is fast adopting the fourth industrial revolution, AI provide a solution for achieving the United Nations Sustainable Development Goal 4 (SDG4) on Quality Education. AI technologies are changing the paradigm in the delivery of educational service as it has the propensity to proactively deliver service that is suitable for each learner and which effectively narrows down the gap in educational penetration across the world. Modern ITSs and AI-based applications are now able to build the learning process for each student based on his/her skills, weaknesses, and learning-rates. Such technologies present great potential in addressing technological divide and expanding access to instruction and learning to remote areas, children at risk, and indigenous beneficiary groups who have not been well served by conventional learning interventions. Still, the application of AI is not limited for personalization. AI can thus analyze student performance data and pinpoint areas where students have had difficulties in learning; give suitable recommendations on how best to handle these issues and develop overall e-portfolios that will capture the academic and co-curricular activities of the students. Furthermore, AI-related interventions such as the adoption of augmented reality (AR) and virtual reality (VR) are enhancing learning and experiences in this realm in various contexts. But the incorporation of AI learning into the education sector must be done ethically and selectively, so that the enhanced technology enhances human learning rather than hinders and replaces the human ability to learn with supported artificial algorithms that castigate the virtues and shortcomings of algorithms and data privacy.

Overview of Sustainable Development Goals (SDGs)

The SDGs are an ambitious conventional plan of actions to meet the needs of humanity by the year 2030. Entered into force in January 2016, the SDGs encompass 17 goals, each of which links with the other, and covers the social, economic, and environmental spectrum of sustainable development. Comprehensive development is characteristic of the SDGs, as all of them are interconnected because the progress in one area impacts the others. They are blind to the country's level of development and hood to "leave no one behind". In contrast to the previous Millennium Development Goals, the SDGs address a wider threat threaten developed and developing countries include global partnerships combine social, economic, and environmental values (Popescu & González, 2024). The goals relate to highly relevant areas; eradicating poverty, ensuring sustainable access to quality education for all, promoting gender equality, acting on climate change. Most importantly, the achievement of the SDGs calls for multi-stakeholder engagement of governments, the private sector, non- state actors, and the world's people. They understand that these strident goals can only be met through innovation, the use of appropriate technology, and finances, along with interdisciplinary and international cooperation (Human-Centricity, Sustainability, & Resilience in Asia, n.d.). The SDGs are a progressive framework for developing a new sustainable development vision and a more just, sustainable, and prosperous future by the year 2030.

Importance of AI in Education

Artificial Intelligence (AI) plays a transformative role in advancing educational objectives aligned with Sustainable Development Goals (SDGs), particularly SDG 4: Quality Education. Advancements in AI technologies are changing the learning paradigm through development of flexible, tailored, and accessible learning models that respond to key issues in global education. In Figure 1, AI expands education and educational opportunities through the delivery of individual, targeted educational needs especially for students with special needs through such tools as the voice-to-text transcribers it provides 24 hours, any time and any place education solution which reduces the barriers to education through the provision of mass, affordable solutions (Rana, Bhambri, & Kautish, 2024). It has become possible to generate complex metrics for learning preferences detect learning paths, identify first signs of learning issues, manage non-instructional tasks to release staff for value-added activities. That is not to say that AI is not more than just technological engagement. It is a revolution in teaching method as it boosts the student engagement decreases the learning pressure avails digital skills training for the current emerging job market demands (Feroz & Stines, 2024). The use of AI in educational institutions can give them the ability to create even more relevant and effective schooling platforms as well as be part of progress towards sustainable development around the world when properly incorporated.

Figure 1. Role of artificial intelligence in education

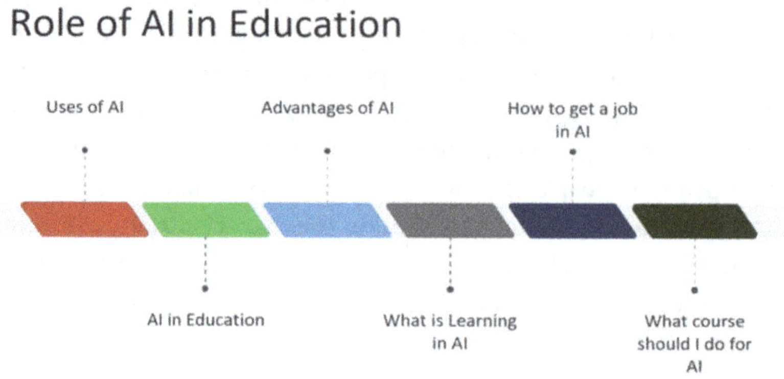

AI AND EDUCATION FOR SUSTAINABLE DEVELOPMENT GOALS (SDGS)

Artificial intelligence has come to be considered as a significant enabler for realizing the UN Sustainable Development Agenda 2030 goal number 4 that is quality education. Acting as a pioneer in the use of progression technologies, AI is evolving the possibilities regarding who and how may learn, where, and in what styles for future education, and, stations possesses unprecedented features that make it possible for learning to be customized to the learners' individual needs, methods that utilize intelligent tutors augmented with step-by-step instructions to learners depending on their abilities and learning deficiencies and performance analysis to discover the weaknesses of learners and what can be done to address them. Advanced AI technologies are driving the immersive and virtual learning space (Sematlane, 2022). Automated electronic portfolios reflecting academic and co-curricular activities, intelligent tutoring systems helping learners improve education dynamically. AI has been identified by the United Nations as a valuable means for reducing inequality in education and for promoting learning to disadvantaged groups supporting lifelong learning projects. Most crucially, AI goes deeper than an interventionist approach. It embodies unique changes in method of handling education whereby flexibility, inclusiveness and efficacy are primary means and ends which foster sustainable development of the globe (Jacques, 2020). If integrated thoughtfully, AI will open new possibilities of learning experiences at educational institutions in relation to improvement of society and empowering human beings.

AI as a Catalyst for Achieving SDGs

AI comes out as a significant enabler that helps The United Nations Sustainable Development Goals (UNSDG), especially on education-related changes and learning difficulties. AI technologies are making education more accessible and effective by delivering customized learning paths for every learner using the assessment of learner's academic data to determine where he or she requires improvement, offering instructional interventions through accurate learning systems designing learning environments that can address the needs of the disadvantaged groups. Some of the chief technological advancements are identified as follow: AI-based tutoring systems such as Alef, Squirrel AI, Byjus. Tracking academic accomplishments through AI supported e-portfolios and using the platform of Virtual Reality Learning Environment (Indrajaya, n.d.). Smart Cramer as an individual learning assistants helping clients in their ongoing learning processes. According to the analysis, AI has the capability of achieving 134 targets (79 percent) of SGD with the highest opportunity based on AI in education. UN acknowledges AI as a valuable mechanism in the fight against education930 disparities for promoting inclusive and equitable quality education for sustainable development for learning for a lifetime. However, when AI is used appropriately by educational institutions, they are thus able to impact learners worldwide positively and thus be able to support the Sustainable Development Goals.

Interlinkages Between AI and SDG Targets

AI can enhance the SEP practice for the SDGs with emphasis on, the fourth goal which aims at quality education for all. Currently educational systems can leverage using the AI technologies to help develop methods that are friendly to every learner as well as adapt to every individual learning rates. For example, the utilization of AI in tutoring can help the system understand thy performance metrics of learners and attempt to complement for knowledge deficiencies that need to be closed to improve the performance of the students. Furthermore, AI can support the idea of accessibility of education by using translation tools that helps to remove language barriers so that various people receive quality education (Aswani, Sajith, & Bhat, 2021). A simple but powerful illustration of how AI can provide individualized tutorials built on the students' abilities and areas that need improvement is faced by Intelligent tutoring systems like Alef and Squirrel AI. Nonetheless, integrating of the AI in the learning process must be done carefully. Potential risks regarding the use of data from their subjects, the bias presented by the algorithms, and the necessity of the subject to explain its decisions show the need for the ethical considerations in implementation of these technologies (Pineiro-Villaverde & García-Álvarez, 2020). For AI to effectively support education for sustainable development an integrated effort from all stakeholders needs to be made in establishing effective frameworks that will govern the usage of artificial intelligence in education while at the same time facilitating access to quality education to all learners across the world.

Challenges and Ethical Considerations

The integration of AI in education faces several challenges and have ethical issues that needs to be solved to advance the achievement of the Sustainable Development Goals (SDGs). The provincial health ministry has some critical issue, the first of which is data privacy (Wakiyama et al., 2019). Accumulation and scanning of large amounts of students' data and information lead to concerns regarding the use, storage, and sharing of such data, therefore, requiring good policies for people's rights protection and making AI systems more transparent. Equity and access can be considered another critical challenge that organizations have to think through. Over time, the innovations in the field of AI technologies surfaces critical issues with the cohesion of education for minority communities that predisposes existing disparities to worsen. It is thus the role of every educational system leadership to provide equal access to AI supported learning materials for students. Moreover, developing an issue related to the training of educators is discovered. Incorporation of AI in the classroom requires the teachers to possess certain sets of digital competencies (Nimbarte, 2024). This incubates technological precedence in professional education and support mechanisms that correspond adequately to the dynamics of education. Also, an important issue should be raised – ethical concerns related to algorithm bias. Preconceived notions inserted in the system by training are imposed on certain categories of students to favor or neglect them. Creating ethical guardrails for AI in the context of learning is necessarily to reduce these harms while preventing unfairness and bias in learning systems.

LEVERAGING AI TO ACHIEVE QUALITY EDUCATION (SDG 4)

AI possesses revolutionary capabilities for attaining Quality Education which is expressed by the SDG 4. AI technologies utilized in educational setting enable institutions to develop differentiated learning environment that meets the needs of the learners. Studying implies the use of a more traditional educational model which in most of the cases does not consider students' needs and abilities. On the other hand, the use of AI in curriculum enhances the design of personalized learning approaches suitable for learning style, speed, and aptitude. That is why Generative AI is one of the biggest use cases of AI in education – it is capable of processing great amounts of data to create individualized programs (Supriya et al., 2024). It also focuses of modifying content to meet state standards and benchmarks, making it not only practical, but also safe from non-compliance issues. For example, AI systems can analyze student performance data and find out the issues in patterns and recommend changes in curriculum on the go. Besides, AI increases involve the provision of resources that address different learning styles hence promote diversity. With institutions embracing AI - based solutions, there is the ability to scale up quality education across the institutions as the solutions reduce on the cost's aspect. In conclusion, the adoption and integration of artificial intelligence in education shift the process to a significant level toward achieving the sustainable developmental goal 4, Namely, provide quality education to all leaners around the globe.

Personalized Learning Environments

AI enhances the delivery of education through technology-based learning that is in support of the achievement of SDG 4. With help of AI, an educator can create individual approaches to learners' learning processes according to their abilities and preferences. Besides, this approach helps in creating more participation amongst learners and at the same time provides a method where learners are allowed to learn at their personal convenience hence minimizing on irritation and maximizing on productivity in learning (Holroyd, 2022). Current school AI systems allow them to manage data on each student's performance in classroom and other activities with real-time feedback. It also provides instant relief to students to adapt their learning needs and get the support process they deserve immediately. For example, it can give a student who performs well in mathematics even more challenging material in that area but assist the same student with language arts which will be a weak area for them, maximizing the benefit in learning. In addition, there are other effective approaches to the use of AI solutions, as well as intelligent tutoring systems that deliver learning and support on a personal level. These systems adjust content according to the continuous performance analysis; therefore, each learner gains proper support and challenges. Through such patterns of more individualized approach in learning, AI also contributes to enhancing both learning engagement and student retention and helps to accomplish SDGs concerning increasing access to quality education for all and providing it as diverse and adapted to people's needs as possible.

Data Analytics for Educational Improvement

This chapter has established that AI-driven data analytics is crucial in supporting educational improvement, in relation to the sustainable development goal four which is focused on quality education. Mined from Sch ELSSA data of students' interactions, formative, and summative assessments, and learning process, AI unlocks unprecedented understanding by teachers of the learner and group learning processes (Lytras et al., 2024). This capability helps to identify relative strengths and weaknesses in the context of instructional activities and to apply instruction techniques appropriate for meeting the needs of a diverse learner population. In Figure 2, the AI capability can predict performance and flag those students that are likely to underperforming in class. This prevents the students from dropping out and makes the educators conduct appropriate interventions that enhance the students' performance and success rates. For example, AI systems can identify students needing assistance based on their scores on tests and quizzes and the amount of engagement or recommend the next level of difficulty for good performers so all learners get the right level of support. Also, AI makes continuous formative feedback efficient and timely to support instantaneous alteration in teaching communication approaches. Such an iterative data feedback loop makes learning more learner-centered and allows for the calibration of instruction based on learner data. In conclusion, integrating AI in educational analytics not only enhances teaching learning practices but also fosters organizational learning and thus enhances the consideration of SDG 4 by making education qualitative and quantitative to learners vastly (Wu, Liu, & Liang, 2024).

Figure 2. AI data analysis technique

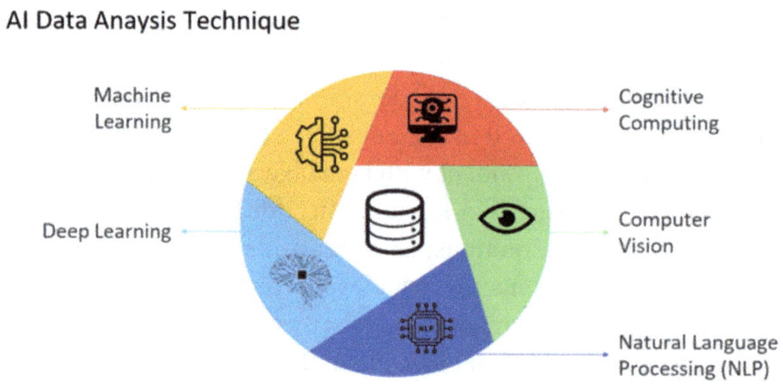

Access and Equity in Education

AI can help improve access and equality in learning which is essential for reaching SDG 4. In applying AI solutions, educational facilities can overcome previous disadvantages that hindered improving the quality of life for excluded groups. In this vein, it is crucial to support students' need diverse or special educational needs and AI-powered platforms offer unique experiences to students, making this is possible. In Figure 3, another crucial fantastic that AI has offered is the creation of virtual learning environments that are not limited by the geography locale (Bhutoria, 2022). Thus, with flexibility students from remote or in areas that are not adequately served can also get quality educations materials and instructions hence minimizing the effect of location on the students' achievement. Besides, it means that while creating the AI tools, much attention should be paid to the differences in the learning styles as well as the abilities of the students with disabilities and make the tools fit for use by the learners. However, AI must be used in the context of education carefully. Otherwise, there is a danger that current inequalities might are only magnified due to unequal distribution of technology and internet access (Di Vaio et al., 2020). AI infused institution need front and center approaches to address issues of discriminator access to AI tools and resources as well as needed framework for infrastructure put in place and recurrent professional development for educators on how to count for biases and improve fairness on the results. To this extent, the solution of these issues means that AI can become the driving force of change to promote a closer to a fair educational environmen

Figure 3. Digital equity framework

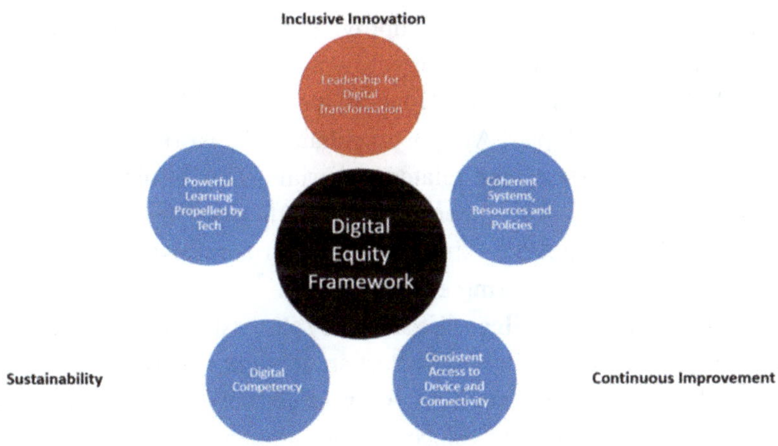

Case Studies of Successful AI Implementations

Previous studies in AI application to education have shown a lot of promises to improve quality of learning and learning access, which adds value to the bid for SDG 4. Here are notable case studies showcasing successful AI applications in educational settings:

a. **Georgia Institute of Technology (USA):** These issues included: Timely and efficient ways of handling the large mass of students and methods of giving feedback to the students as experienced by Georgia Tech. In response to this, they adopted artificial intelligence teaching assistant known as Jill Watson which is under the brand of IBM's Watson. Using over 40,000 previous forum posts, Jill was able to respond to typical student questions in an online Master's course. This not only enhanced students' participation but also enabled the instructors to attend to other students needs that were intense and complex illustrating how AI enhances the environment for learning (Son et al., 2023).
b. **The University of Sydney (Australia):** Smart Sparrow has been used by the University of Sydney to develop learning paths based on the learner's progress. Letting the professors create coursework with responsiveness based on how students perform helped increase engagement and better performance at the university. This case has shown that applying the AI system in combination with conventional teaching models can create a more sensitive learning environment.
c. **Oak National Academy (UK):** Opened during the COVID-19 outbreak, Oak National Academy adopted AI apps to enhance the work of educators by helping them develop lessons and related materials. This initiative intended to cut teachers' load tremendously in terms of contact hours with learners as educators. The use of AI made not only the procedures of administrative nature but also upped the quality of delivering education.
d. **Ivy Tech Community College (USA):** They study student data in the beginning of the semester to determine early alert students at Ivy Tech. Using data from over ten thousand course sections, they effectively prevent/reintervene with 3000 at risk students at a 98% success rate in terms of passing these students. It demonstrates how and to what extent the use of AI boosts the performance of students and aids timely corrective measures (Cath et al., 2018). These two projects demonstrate that the use of AI in education is important as it will help to improve the learner practice and make education more effective to the learners who are in marginalized and disadvantaged areas and thus help in the achievement of SDG 4.

PROMOTING ENVIRONMENTAL LITERACY AND GLOBAL CITIZENSHIP THROUGH AI-ENHANCED PROGRAMS

Such orientations of AI are crucial for environmental education and developing global citizens because of the support of SDG 4. It is shown that AI technologies can be implemented into educational frameworks to make students interact with the environment effectively. One of the informative applications is virtual and augmented reality that which is used to teach students about the different environments that exist and the impacts our actions have on them. These realistic and enjoyable experiences result in a range of environmental understandings that enhance the students of today to stewardship of the environment. Furthermore, AI can elicit a great amount of data concerning the environmental problems, including climate change and species extinction. In this manner, sharing such data in form of attractive visual tools and social applications which students can interact with, the educators can help the learners to understand such issues and offer solutions to similar challenges happening in their societies. For instance, an artificial intelligence that comes in applications for example; an application called i-naturalist get the students involved in citizen science making and hence improves their familiarity with natural environments and deepens their thinking abilities. Besides, artificial intelligence can also adapt learning to students' performance and preferences so that each learner will be actively studying environmental topics. Not only does it improve educational results and develop awareness of cultural and environmental issues around the world but also creates a local connection between students and numerous environmental projects (Singh, 2023). In conclusion, applying the AI effectiveness in learning has the following effects: pushing the environmental literacy and engendering student knowledge about the solutions of the vital global issues; thus, developing the generation, ritually focused on the sustainability.

Integrating Sustainability into Educational Curricula

The case for incorporating sustainability into educational contexts is crucial when it comes to building consciousness and practice concerning worldwide challenges, that align with SDG4. The cross-curricular approach to teaching and learning set out in this framework will enable educators to develop in students' sustainable ways of thinking about environmental and social questions. This integration is especially going beyond the luxury of compartmentalized teaching of subject areas such as science, economics, and social studies. AI can help to perform a tremendous function in integration with subject matters by offering learning experiences that are focused on sustainability concepts appropriate for each discipline. for example, it is possible to identify students' preferences and achievements to offer them, based on an AI system, interdisciplinary projects that incorporate the topic of sustainability, for instance, including ideas of renewable sources of energy or sustainable farming (Malia et al., 2024). More than just making the students interested this kind of approach helps them be active participants in the promotion of sustainability. Also, with the help of AI technologies, hands-on projects further impactful experiential learning. Students can engage in technical environments and policies, use AI technologies to solve various problems, analyze data on environmental effects, suggest creative approaches, outcomes, and solutions. Some of these experiences will foster the development of appalling problems solving skills that are necessary in tackling emergent or complex global problems. Finally, the development of sustainability integration and curricula through incorporation of AI innovation enables the creation of citizens' training relating to global challenges such as climate change and relative depletion of resources. This synchronization with the SDG 4 guarantees that education also embodies more than the dissemination of knowledge with a call to action towards a sustainable world.

Global Citizenship Education Through Technology

Technology should therefore be infused in education to support the implementation of GCE as postured under SDG 4. Technology applications enhance student learning through integrating them into responsible global citizens. With AI tools, educators will have the best opportunities to develop lesson plans that will foster communication between students from different countries, achieving the goals to have better vision of current global issues including climate change, inequality, human rights, etc. In Figure 4, they provide a way of implementing joint projects that cutting across geographical regions. For instance, Empatico provides classrooms with opportunities to conversation with other classrooms through live video, to exchange stories and foster understanding of different needs and world views. Moreover, AI can capture student experience and feedback of their tutorial and in turn develop a content delivery system that fits well into different cultural setting. Furthermore, AI integrated analysis of learning condition can be used to evaluate effectiveness of GCE activities regarding the students' performance data which indicates their engagement level with learning process. This brings about the enhancement of curricula since it is in consistent with the current practices providing relevant education that suits the society in this globalization period (Mak, Wong, & Pichika, 2024). Finally, the use of AI in GCE benefits learners by improving their educational achievement and by developing skills that enable an informed active global citizenship in a globalized world. Education that uses technologies and AI, means critical thinking, creativity, and prompts ethical decision making which are the foundation for constructing a more just and sustainable society.

Figure 4. Benefits of global citizenship education

Collaborative Learning Platforms

Collaborative learning enabled by artificial intelligence is revolutionizing education by supporting group work, interacting, and sharing in effective training and education which supports SDG 4. These platforms use computing algorithms to design comprehensive learning facilities in which students could easily share lessons across the country. Collaborative learning MN using AI has the major advantage of the capacity to foster dynamic group formation. With the help of some of the AI algorithms, grouping is done according to the student's capability, difficulty level, and interest in different subjects, to create a variety of group compositions that improve the learning environment. This way not only makes the discussions more diverse and includes more people into the conversation but is also effective. Further, AI gives students an immediate response to their inputs and thus, students are always able to learn from their mistakes. Of the platforms we are discussing here 360Learning and EdApp can serve as an example of how AI can help avoid problems when creating courses complicated and stimulate discussions between learners. These tools enable one to incorporate some of the principles of gamification and microlearning into facilitation of collaborative tasks. Also, AI can help in the moderation of the discussions to make certain that all the participants in any discussion are courteous and constructive. Through integration of AI in collaborative learning environments, educational organizations can develop beneficial twenty-first century competencies including interpersonal skills, problem solving competencies and versatility. Besides making learning fun, it makes the student competent in interrelated world hence achieving the SDG4 by improving on educational practices.

Examples of AI Programs Promoting Environmental Literacy

Currently, AI programs are being adopted to enhance environmental literacy in line with the Sustainable development goal 4 (SDG4), to proactively build a generation capable of addressing environmental issues. Here are some notable examples:

a. **i-Naturalist**: This is an application developed to help people interface with plants and animals using images, through artificial intelligence. I-Naturalist achieves effective learning because it enables students to contribute to citizen science projects hence develops an appreciation of nature and observational skills. People can record and share information on the presence of different species in their areas to raise the public understanding of ecosystems and resulting initiatives.
b. **Seek by i-Naturalist**: Like i-Naturalist, the application called Seek relies on computer vision to help users to get more engaged with the outdoors. It makes learning more enjoyable since the users are rewarded for the correct identification of different species in the process, students are encouraged to be active in their environment as well as putting into practice the problem solving and inquiry skills in relation to environmental science.
c. **Virtual Reality (VR) and Augmented Reality (AR):** AI improves VR and AR environment that puts student into an environment of their choice like a reef or a forest. These technologies make the learners understand how their activities affect these environments, which enhances their appreciations for ecological conservation.
d. **AI Teaching Systems:** Several studies show that through AI teaching systems, students' learning processes in environmental education could be enriched and improved. For example, a cross-sectional survey in college students demonstrated that the AI-based courses increased environmental knowledge and promotion of positive behavioral intentions toward environmental sustainability.
e. **Eco-education Platforms**: Several educational processes connect AI with eco-education, for instance, the Pedagogical Synergy with AI (PSAI). This approach follows the model of inclusiveness and sustainability of curricula to enable students to produce the needed results for stewardship of the environment. These examples demonstrate that and helping students acquire knowledge about the environment, AI programs enable them to begin to practice environmental responsibility.

FUTURE DIRECTIONS AND RECOMMENDATIONS

AI has a great potential and risks in education for achieving sustainable development objectives especially the SDG 4 – Quality Education. To effectively harness AI's potential, several recommendations can be made:

a. **Develop Comprehensive Policies:** AI technologies will have to be regulated to improve the different educational institutions in the future and that is why organizations need to set standards which have to do with the different technologies they will need to use. They MUST include ethical issues, data protection and the ability NOT to worsen existing disparities with such applications. The study by UNESCO also calls for a humanistic approach to AI which is sensitive to inclusion in education.
b. **Foster Collaboration Across Sectors:** There is a need for the governments and the companies with the educational technology institutions to come up with better and unique solutions that meet the regions' education requirements concerning AI. Efforts such as the Higher Education Sustainability Initiative (HESI) can help people exchange good practices and collaborate to build sustainability into education.
c. **Invest in Teacher Training:** Continuing education should be incorporated to teach educators how best to apply AI in their classrooms fruitfully should be incorporated. Training should be directed towards how to use AI tools to help make learning more effective, and help students develop critical thinking skills.
d. **Promote Research and Development:** Promoting the further studies concerning the outcomes of the usage of AI in education may help to understand the implementation of the technologies better. It also meant that institutions must conduct insights-based research to determine the effectiveness of AI technologies in enhancing learning outcomes to later cultivate environmental literacy.
e. **Ensure Accessibility and Equity**: There is a need to create an opportunity of using AI in delivering education to all the learners especially those in the minority groups. This comprises of enhancing public facilities in access and delivery of quality education equally. If educational stakeholders implement these recommendations, they can work with AI in achieving the SDGs through particularly fostering the inclusion, equity, and quality education to learn environments.

Innovative Approaches to AI in Education

New trends in adopting AI apply in enhancing learning processes to enhance the achievement of Quality Education for All, as posed by the Sustainable Development Goals 4 (SDG-4). AI technologies lead students to engage with courses in a more intensive manner, support educational administration with improved and efficient technologies, and enhance learning through smart content. One such example is Squirrel AI an intelligent system that humanizes education by individualizing learning processes in real time. Due to performance and learning behavior analysis, Squirrel AI periodically adapts the content and exercises to foster learning and ensure students acquire knowledge in subjects they find challenging at their own pace. This puts into force a more person-centered approach that, in addition to enhancing academic success, offers better appreciation of concepts. Another newfangled appearance is Quizlet which utilizes AI for creating study plans. Its Learn mode knows the student(s) performance level and adapts the level of questions it poses to the learner(s). This makes learners to concentrate on sectors which require help and boost the effectiveness, and the engagement level of learning sessions. Moreover, the company of Coursera that offers a wide range of courses applies the AI solutions for the recommendation of classes and learning paths. With accomplished user-friendly statistics and performance information, Coursera optimizes the online learning process, and guarantees students get content that meets their learning advancement. In addition, the applications of artificial intelligence that include VR and AR ensure students develop advantageous learning experiences through teamwork and effective thinking. These technologies enable learners to solve different scenarios like environmental issues or post in history, the formation of global citizenship and environmental concern. By adopting these novel AI applications, such learning institutions can forge agreeable learning environments that help enhance education results and enhance students' preparedness for the contemporary world to support the attainment of goal 4 of the sustainable development goals.

Policy Recommendations

Several policy recommendations will therefore be useful in order to apply AI in education to attain SDG 4 as mentioned below.

a. **Develop Inclusive AI Policies:** Local and global educational sectors and governments must take full responsibility and develop adequate measures that not only regulate and govern the usage of Artificial Intelligence, but also make sure the said regulation complies with the internationally accepted ethical principles. Such policies should consider data privacy, algorithmic bias, and addressing equitable access and use of technology, for all students, which means students from diverse populace such as marginalized groups.
b. **Foster Multi-Stakeholder Collaboration:** Co-operative efforts are required on part of the governments, educational establishments, and technology providers as well as the civil society. It may allow collaborative working by sharing of the

best practices, and other resources, and expertise in the usage of AI solutions for education. Involving multiple stakeholders ensures that AI solutions that are developed address the specific needs and environments of the area that they serve.

c. **Invest in Teacher Training:** There is the need to ensure implementation of professional development programs that is aimed at preparing professional to fit the aspect of AI technologies in their learning practices. Learning activities should be driven through AI technology to improve learners' experience and to develop their thinking skills.
d. **Promote Research and Innovation:** Supporting research on how the integration of AI will affect education will assist in the identification of best practice. Education organizations should conduct surveys that seek to identify how the use of AI technologies could help improve student learning outcomes and foster environ metrics literacy.
e. **Ensure Continuous Evaluation and Adaptation:** Measures and procedure need to be qualitatively integrated in policies to regularly check, review, and evaluate AI applications within education to identify whether they are having a positive effect for learners' achievement and progress. This is a cyclic process which helps to make correction after period of time to ensure that practices in place meet the needs of the current society. Through the adoption of the presented suggestions, actors with an interest in the learners' success can unleash the power of AI to help deliver environments that are conducive to effective learning for all learners in line with the fourth Sustainable Development Goal.

Call for Multi-Stakeholder Collaboration

Thus, using the call to involve multiple actors in the development and implementation of AI possibilities in education to promote SDG (especially the 4th one). Together with governments, educational institutions, tech companies and civil society organizations the current and future gaps in educational attainment must be closed and learning achievements optimized. Using a blend of technical, economic, pedagogical, and liberal arts knowledge, stakeholders can develop contextually appropriate AI-based educational aids. For instance, value creating relationships can help establish platforms that contribute to different learning environments that address learner needs. Further, partnering can help make certain risks associated with AI's use, including data privacy, algorithmic bias, and other and other considerations, a priority. In addition, such approaches as the United Nations Education, Scientific, and Cultural Organization's Global Education Coalition make it clear how multi-stakeholder can solve education-related problems through mobilization of various resources and authorities. Through collaboration, different stakeholders can be able to share the existing best practices on Digital literacy and work towards improving the information technology accessibility in parts of the world that are most unaffected. Finally, building a collective AI environment will not only help the AI improved teaching and learning environment, but also ensure all learners of different backgrounds have the same opportunities to embrace these innovations while creating a better future.

CONCLUSION

Therefore, the adoption of AI in education system heralds an innovation that has potential of supporting SDG 4 to enhance, inclusive and equitable quality education. AI technologies can be employed to deliver differentiated learning and instructions, improve students' consciousness about environment, and cultivate the values of global citizenship. Such potential, nevertheless, holds tightly linked with ethical concerns, data protection, and technology distribution to different stakeholders. There is need to have sustainable working relations between the government, education centers and technology suppliers as they come up with new methods to ensure equality in education. In addition, spending on such training and structures will enable teachers to transform AI instruments into action. By adopting these strategies, it becomes possible to seize the potential of AI for promoting velocity in learning processes so that education emerges as a key to success and effective learning for learners while powering sustainable and equitable learning as the future of learners' education.

Summary of Key Points

AI must be a catalyst in shaping the education system that will contribute to the fulfillment of Sustainable Development Goal 4 (SDG 4). Major points include the ability to make tutorials much more student-centered using AI based tutoring systems that take into consideration the needs of the student and his or her performance. AI also helps people to get educational materials regardless their choice language, which is an important step towards equality. More so, the AI technologies can promote environmental education since it can offer virtual and augmented reality learning environments and citizen science. AI integrated collaborative learning applications help in developing both team work and problem-solving skills. To fully benefit from these opportunities, there is the need to adopt the multi-stakeholder model that will avoid compromising ethics of the use of this technology while at the same time improving on equity stakes on the use of the same to Insights for the Future of Education with AIs the power of AI to create dynamic learning environments that not only improve educational outcomes but also contribute to a more sustainable and equitable future for all learners.

Vision for the Future of Education with AI

In particular, the vision of how education with AI will continue in the future belongs to the principle of sustainable development and was developed in accordance with Sustainable Development Goal 4 (SDG 4). AI technologies will help in creating personalized learning environment in which the content to be delivered to the students will be more relevant to their learning level and thereby assists them in having enhanced level of understanding of the material to be taught. In addition, AI can also create a global classroom and also an opportunity for learners from different parts of the world to come together and learn from one another by sharing cultural difference.

In the future, AI will become even more important for solving problems with education inequality, which means that the people who need the resources, will be provided with a quality base. This is the reason why decision-makers must pay attention to ethical issues and data protection to avoid aggravation of existing gaps due to the use of AI solutions in learning. Finally, incorporating AI in education seeks to equip learners with knowledge and skills that allow them respond adequately to the emerging challenges within the world over, produce a generation of well-informed global citizens for sustainable development.

REFERENCES

Aswani, R. S., Sajith, S., & Bhat, M. Y. (2021). Realigning India's Vietnam policy through cooperative sustainable development: A geostrategic counterbalancing to China in Indo-Pacific. *East Asia (Piscataway, N.J.)*, 1–19. PMID: 34276182

Bhutoria, A. (2022). Personalized education and artificial intelligence in the United States, China, and India: A systematic review using a human-in-the-loop model. *Computers and Education: Artificial Intelligence, 3*, 100068. DOI: 10.1016/j.caeai.2022.100068

Cath, C. (2018). Artificial intelligence and the 'good society': The US, EU, and UK approach. *Science and Engineering Ethics, 24*, 505–528. PMID: 28353045

Di Vaio, A., Palladino, R., Hassan, R., & Escobar, O. (2020). Artificial intelligence and business models in the sustainable development goals perspective: A systematic literature review. *Journal of Business Research, 121*, 283–314. DOI: 10.1016/j.jbusres.2020.08.019

Feroz, A. K., & Stines, A. (2024). Utilization of AI, big data, and internet of things (IoT) in sustainable innovation and their role in the emergence of novel business models. *Issues in Information Systems, 25*(1).

Holroyd, C. (2022). Technological innovation and building a 'super smart' society: Japan's vision of society 5.0. *Journal of Asian Public Policy, 15*(1), 18–31. DOI: 10.1080/17516234.2020.1749340

Indrajaya, A. N. (n.d.). Critical reflections on flourishing businesses through collaborative online international learning in the context of the UN Sustainable Development Goals.

Jacques, P. (2020). *Sustainability: The basics*. Routledge. DOI: 10.4324/9780429346613

Lytras, M. D. (2024). Transformative learning for future higher education: The artificial intelligence-enabled learning revolution 2035. In *Digital Transformation in Higher Education, Part B* (pp. 231–241). Emerald Publishing Limited.

Mak, K.-K., Wong, Y.-H., & Pichika, M. R. (2024). Artificial intelligence in drug discovery and development. In *Drug discovery and evaluation: Safety and pharmacokinetic assays* (pp. 1461–1498). DOI: 10.1007/978-3-031-35529-5_92

Malia, A. (2024). New opportunities for sustainable development in the tourism sector with the use of disruptive digital technologies. In *Sustainable Tourism, Part A* (pp. 67–86). Emerald Publishing Limited. DOI: 10.1108/978-1-83797-979-020241005

Nimbarte, N. (2024). Quantitative analysis of urban transformation using remote sensing data and machine learning approach. *Communications on Applied Nonlinear Analysis, 31*(2s), 388–401. DOI: 10.52783/cana.v31.656

Pineiro-Villaverde, G., & García-Álvarez, M. T. (2020). Sustainable consumption and production: Exploring the links with resources productivity in the EU-28. *Sustainability (Basel), 12*(21), 8760. DOI: 10.3390/su12218760

Popescu, C. R. G., & González, A. L. (2024). Exploring the synergies between environmental social governance and AI for business sustainability: Tackling climate adaptation, mitigating climate change efforts, and pursuing climate justice. In *Intersecting Environmental Social Governance and AI for Business Sustainability* (pp. 1–41). IGI Global. DOI: 10.4018/979-8-3693-1151-6.ch001

Rana, R., Bhambri, P., & Kautish, S. (2024). Responsible digital technologies: Shaping sustainable practices. In *Digital technologies to implement the UN Sustainable Development Goals* (pp. 399–411). Springer Nature Switzerland. DOI: 10.1007/978-3-031-68427-2_20

Sematlane, M. (2022). The universal language of sustaining quality peace and resilience: Enhancing learning and harmony across cultures. In *Handbook of Research on Teaching in Multicultural and Multilingual Contexts* (pp. 143–169). IGI Global. DOI: 10.4018/978-1-6684-5034-5.ch009

Singh, S. (Eds.). (2023). *Data-driven intelligent business sustainability*. IGI Global. DOI: 10.4018/979-8-3693-0049-7

Son, T. H., Weedon, Z., Yigitcanlar, T., Sanchez, T., Corchado, J. M., & Mehmood, R. (2023). Algorithmic urban planning for smart and sustainable development: Systematic review of the literature. *Sustainable Cities and Society, 94*, 104562. DOI: 10.1016/j.scs.2023.104562

Supriya, Y., Bhulakshmi, D., Bhattacharya, S., Gadekallu, T. R., Vyas, P., Kaluri, R., Sumathy, S., Koppu, S., Brown, D. J., & Mahmud, M. (2024). Industry 5.0 in smart education: Concepts, applications, challenges, opportunities, and future directions. *IEEE Access : Practical Innovations, Open Solutions, 12*, 81938–81967. DOI: 10.1109/ACCESS.2024.3401473

Wakiyama, T., Lenzen, M., Faturay, F., Geschke, A., Malik, A., Fry, J., & Nansai, K. (2019). Responsibility for food loss from a regional supply-chain perspective. *Resources, Conservation and Recycling, 146*, 373–383. DOI: 10.1016/j.resconrec.2019.04.003

Wu, H., Liu, J., & Liang, B. (2024). AI-driven supply chain transformation in Industry 5.0: Enhancing resilience and sustainability. *Journal of the Knowledge Economy*, *16*(1), 1–43. DOI: 10.1007/s13132-024-01999-6

Chapter 5
Artificial Intelligence in Education:
A Pathway to Achieving SDG 4

Priyam Rathi
Christ University, India

Jasmine Kaur
https://orcid.org/0000-0002-3683-0909
Christ University, India

ABSTRACT

Artificial Intelligence (AI) has emerged as a transformative force in education, offering innovative solutions to some of the most pressing challenges in the global education system. As the world strives to achieve the United Nations Sustainable Development Goals (SDGs), particularly SDG 4 (Quality Education), AI offers significant potential to enhance educational access, equity, and quality. This chapter explores the intersection of AI and education with a focus on how AI can contribute to the achievement of SDG 4. The chapter examines the role of AI in personalizing learning, promoting equity and inclusion, enhancing teacher effectiveness, and fostering global collaboration for sustainability. AI's ability to deliver personalized learning experiences is one of its most significant contributions to education. Through adaptive learning platforms and intelligent tutoring systems, AI can tailor educational content to meet the unique needs of individual students, ensuring that learning is accessible and engaging for all.

DOI: 10.4018/979-8-3373-5781-2.ch005

INTRODUCTION

AI and Education for Sustainable Development Goals (SDGs)

The rapid advancement of Artificial Intelligence (AI) technologies over recent decades has led to transformative shifts across numerous sectors, with education being one of the most significantly impacted. As AI technologies continue to evolve, they offer unprecedented opportunities for reimagining how education is delivered, accessed, and experienced. Education, a fundamental human right and essential foundation for advancing other goals, is central to the United Nations' Sustainable Development Goals (SDGs). Among the 17 SDGs, SDG 4 focuses on ensuring inclusive, equitable, and quality education, as well as promoting lifelong learning opportunities for all by 2030. In this context, AI is emerging as a key enabler of educational innovation, offering solutions that can help address the diverse challenges faced by educational systems worldwide and contribute to the broader global agenda of sustainable development.

AI holds the potential to revolutionize education by enabling personalized learning, improving access to resources, and enhancing the quality of teaching. Through adaptive learning platforms, AI systems can analyse students' learning patterns and adjust content delivery to meet individual needs, ensuring that every student has an opportunity to succeed. This personalized approach can be especially beneficial in addressing the disparities in learning outcomes that exist between different socioeconomic and geographical groups. By tailoring educational experiences to students' unique strengths, preferences, and pace of learning, AI can help close the achievement gaps that often exist in traditional education systems, thereby promoting more equitable access to education, which is a key focus of SDG 4.

AI's ability to automate administrative tasks and streamline processes can also improve the efficiency of educational institutions, allowing educators to focus more on teaching and less on administrative duties. Automated grading systems, for instance, can help reduce the time teachers spend on grading assignments, while AI-driven tools for curriculum planning and assessment can assist in designing more effective educational programs. By automating routine tasks, AI can free up valuable time for educators to engage with students on a more personalized level, fostering deeper learning and student engagement.

The role of AI in education extends beyond SDG 4 and has the potential to support the achievement of other interconnected SDGs as well. For instance, AI can contribute to SDG 3, which focuses on ensuring healthy lives and promoting well-being for all at all ages. AI-powered technologies can enhance health education, provide early diagnosis of health conditions, and enable access to critical health information, all of which can improve public health outcomes. AI systems that analyse large datasets can also support research on diseases and treatments, contributing to the overall goal of improving global health. Moreover, AI has the potential to support SDG 5, which advocates for gender equality, by creating educational opportunities for women and girls. AI-driven platforms can help bridge the gender gap in education by offering personalized learning experiences and addressing specific challenges that female learners may face, such as cultural barriers or limited access to resources.

This chapter aims to explore the intersection of AI and education in the context of the SDGs, examining how AI can contribute to the realization of the global education agenda. Through an exploration of relevant literature and case studies, this chapter will highlight the opportunities and challenges of integrating AI into education systems worldwide. Additionally, it will provide insights into the ethical, social, and technological considerations that must be addressed to ensure that AI serves the greater good of society, particularly in the pursuit of the SDGs. By the end of this chapter, readers will gain a comprehensive understanding of the potential of AI to drive sustainable educational development and its role in advancing the SDGs, with a particular focus on SDG 4.

Objectives: AI and Education for Sustainable Development Goals (SDGs)

The rapid integration of Artificial Intelligence (AI) into education presents a powerful tool for accelerating progress towards achieving the United Nations' Sustainable Development Goals (SDGs). SDG 4, which focuses on quality education, is particularly pivotal as it underpins the success of all other SDGs. Education is the means by which individuals and communities can be empowered to address the pressing global challenges of poverty, inequality, and environmental sustainability. In this context, AI has the potential to redefine education systems and contribute to sustainable development in ways that were previously unimaginable. The objectives of this chapter are to explore the multifaceted roles AI can play in education to advance SDG 4 and its interconnected relationship with other SDGs, as well as the challenges and ethical considerations that need to be addressed to fully leverage AI's potential.

Objective 1: Understanding the Role of AI in Enhancing Education Quality and Equity (SDG 4)

The first objective of this chapter is to explore how AI can contribute to enhancing the quality of education globally, particularly in terms of making it more inclusive and equitable. SDG 4 aims to ensure that all learners have access to high-quality education, regardless of their background or geographic location. Traditional educational systems often struggle to address the diverse needs of students, particularly in regions with limited resources. AI has the potential to bridge these gaps by personalizing learning experiences and providing targeted support to underserved populations.

AI technologies such as adaptive learning platforms, automated feedback systems, and virtual tutors can tailor educational content to the needs of individual students, ensuring that learners progress at their own pace and receive the support they need to succeed. For example, AI can analyse student data in real-time to identify areas where learners are struggling and suggest customized learning pathways. This individualized approach can significantly improve learning outcomes, particularly for students who may have previously been left behind due to the one-size-fits-all approach of traditional classrooms.

Objective 2: Investigating the Impact of AI on Education for Sustainable Development (SDGs 3, 5, and 13)

AI's impact on education extends far beyond SDG 4 and has the potential to support other critical SDGs. This objective seeks to explore how AI can contribute to the achievement of SDG 3 (Good Health and Well-Being), SDG 5 (Gender Equality), and SDG 13 (Climate Action) through educational initiatives.

SDG 3: Good Health and Well-Being

AI can enhance the quality and accessibility of health education, a vital component of promoting global health and well-being. Through AI-powered learning platforms, students can gain real-time access to reliable health information, including preventive measures for diseases, mental health resources, and wellness practices. AI also facilitates personalized health education, tailoring content based on a student's age, medical history, or health interests. For example, AI-driven applications can provide students with customized health advice or strategies for managing stress, thereby contributing to their well-being.

Moreover, AI can play a role in improving health outcomes through the use of health diagnostics and monitoring systems that are integrated into educational programs. Students in the fields of medicine, nursing, and public health can benefit from AI-driven simulations, which provide them with hands-on experience in diagnosing and treating conditions. By incorporating AI into medical curricula, institutions can better equip the next generation of healthcare professionals with the skills needed to address global health challenges.

SDG 5: Gender Equality

AI can also support gender equality by fostering more inclusive and empowering learning environments for girls and women. Historically, education systems have perpetuated gender disparities, especially in STEM (Science, Technology, Engineering, and Mathematics) fields. AI-driven platforms can help bridge these gaps by offering personalized learning experiences that encourage female students to pursue traditionally male-dominated fields, such as engineering and computer science. AI can also provide targeted resources for girls, ensuring they have access to educational opportunities that promote their empowerment and independence.

Additionally, AI-powered systems can be used to monitor and address issues of gender bias in educational materials and teaching practices. For example, AI can analyse textbooks, curricula, and assessments for gender bias, ensuring that content is inclusive and free from stereotypes. By promoting gender equality through education, AI can contribute to the realization of SDG 5 and empower women and girls to become agents of change in their communities.

SDG 13: Climate Action

AI can be an invaluable tool in addressing the challenges posed by climate change by enhancing education on environmental issues and promoting sustainable practices. AI technologies can be used to monitor and analyse environmental data, such as carbon emissions and deforestation rates, which can then be used in educational programs to raise awareness about climate change. AI-powered simulations can help students understand the complexities of climate change and its impact on ecosystems and communities, providing a more interactive and engaging learning experience.

Furthermore, AI can facilitate the integration of sustainability principles into various curricula, from primary school to higher education. AI tools can help design educational programs that teach students about renewable energy, waste reduction, and sustainable agriculture. By equipping learners with the knowledge and skills needed to address climate challenges, AI plays a crucial role in fostering a generation of environmentally conscious citizens.

Objective 3: Identifying Opportunities and Challenges in Implementing AI for Education in Diverse Contexts

An important objective of this chapter is to assess both the opportunities and challenges associated with implementing AI in education systems across diverse global contexts. While AI holds great promise, its integration into education is not without obstacles, particularly in low-income and rural areas where access to technology and the internet is limited. This objective will explore how AI can be adapted and implemented in these contexts, considering the technological, infrastructural, and social challenges that may arise.

One of the primary challenges is the digital divide, which refers to the gap between those who have access to digital technologies and those who do not. In many developing countries, inadequate infrastructure, such as unreliable electricity, limited internet access, and a lack of digital devices, hinders the widespread adoption of AI in education. For AI to contribute to SDG 4, it is crucial to address these infrastructural barriers by ensuring that all learners have access to the necessary technology.

Another challenge is the need for teachers to develop the skills required to effectively use AI in the classroom. Teacher training programs must be updated to include digital literacy and the effective use of AI tools in teaching. This requires investment in professional development and the creation of accessible resources for educators. Moreover, educators need to be equipped with knowledge of the ethical implications of AI in education, particularly regarding issues of data privacy and algorithmic bias.

Finally, it is important to consider the social and cultural contexts in which AI is being implemented. Education systems around the world are deeply influenced by local customs, beliefs, and practices. As such, AI technologies should be designed and implemented in ways that are culturally sensitive and aligned with the values of the communities they serve. Collaborating with local stakeholders, including governments, educational institutions, and community organizations, is essential to ensuring that AI solutions are effective, sustainable, and accepted by the wider society.

Objective 4: Exploring Ethical Considerations and Regulatory Frameworks for AI in Education

The ethical implications of AI in education are a significant area of concern and an essential objective of this chapter. As AI technologies become increasingly integrated into education systems, it is crucial to ensure that their use adheres to ethical principles, such as fairness, transparency, and accountability. This objective will examine the ethical challenges posed by AI in education and explore the regulatory frameworks needed to govern its use.

One of the most pressing ethical concerns is data privacy. AI systems rely on vast amounts of student data, which raises questions about how this data is collected, stored, and used. It is essential to ensure that student data is protected and that AI systems are designed with robust security measures in place. Additionally, consent must be obtained from students or their guardians before data is collected, and students must have the right to access, correct, or delete their data.

Another concern is the potential for algorithmic bias in AI systems. AI systems are trained on data, and if this data reflects existing biases or inequalities, the AI system may perpetuate these biases, leading to unfair outcomes. For example, AI algorithms used for admissions or grading may unintentionally disadvantage certain groups of students. It is essential to develop AI systems that are transparent, explainable, and regularly audited for bias to ensure that they promote equity and fairness.

Objective 5: Fostering Global Collaboration and Partnerships for AI in Education

The final objective is to explore how AI can be used as a catalyst for global collaboration and partnerships to advance education for sustainable development. Achieving the SDGs requires collective action, and AI can facilitate collaboration between governments, educational institutions, non-governmental organizations, and the private sector. By sharing resources, knowledge, and expertise, these stakeholders can create innovative solutions that leverage AI to address the global challenges of education.

AI has the potential to transform not only individual education systems but also the way countries collaborate on education at a global level. By promoting cross-border partnerships and information exchange, AI can help countries learn from each other's successes and challenges in implementing AI-driven educational solutions. Collaborative research, data sharing, and joint initiatives can create a global learning network that accelerates progress toward achieving SDG 4 and other SDGs.

THEORETICAL FRAMEWORK: AI AND EDUCATION FOR SUSTAINABLE DEVELOPMENT GOALS (SDGS)

The integration of Artificial Intelligence (AI) into education holds significant promise in advancing the United Nations' Sustainable Development Goals (SDGs), particularly SDG 4, which aims to ensure inclusive, equitable, and quality education for all. Understanding the role of AI in education for sustainable development requires a comprehensive theoretical framework that considers multiple perspectives from educational theory, technology adoption, and sustainability.

This framework draws on theories related to educational technology, learning theory, the diffusion of innovation, and sustainable development. It incorporates perspectives on personalized learning, equity, the digital divide, and the ethical implications of AI use in education. By bringing these diverse theories together, this framework provides a holistic view of how AI can contribute to the achievement of SDG 4 and other SDGs.

Constructivist Learning Theory

Constructivism, a widely recognized theory in educational psychology, is foundational in understanding how AI can enhance learning. The theory, championed by Piaget (1976) and Vygotsky (1978), emphasizes that learners construct their knowledge through active engagement with the environment, guided by their experiences and interactions with others. In a constructivist classroom, students are encouraged to explore, solve problems, and engage in collaborative learning processes.

AI technologies, such as adaptive learning platforms and intelligent tutoring systems, align well with the principles of constructivism. These AI-driven systems enable personalized learning by adjusting the difficulty and pace of content delivery according to individual student needs. By providing students with tailored resources and immediate feedback, AI supports learners in building their knowledge through inquiry-based and experiential learning. As learners interact with AI systems, they actively construct their understanding, making learning more relevant and context-specific. This aligns with SDG 4's goal of providing quality education that is inclusive, equitable, and responsive to the needs of all learners (UNESCO, 2015).

Technological Pedagogical Content Knowledge (TPACK)

The Technological Pedagogical Content Knowledge (TPACK) framework (Mishra & Koehler, 2006) is an essential lens for understanding the integration of AI in educational contexts. This framework proposes that effective technology integration in education requires the intersection of three critical components: content knowledge (CK), pedagogical knowledge (PK), and technological knowledge (TK).

Content Knowledge (CK) refers to the subject-specific knowledge that teachers and students must understand.

Pedagogical Knowledge (PK) is the understanding of how to teach, which involves strategies, methods, and techniques that promote effective learning.

Technological Knowledge (TK) is the understanding of how to integrate various technologies, such as AI, into teaching and learning processes.

AI offers significant opportunities to enhance all three areas. For example, AI-powered tools can help teachers develop content-rich educational experiences that are tailored to student needs (CK). These tools also enable teachers to use innovative pedagogical strategies, such as adaptive learning and real-time formative assessments, which improve the personalization of education (PK). Moreover, AI equips teachers with the technological skills required to implement digital tools effectively, fostering a more technology-savvy teaching force (TK).

The integration of AI through the TPACK framework aligns with SDG 4 by promoting high-quality education that leverages technology in ways that enrich the learning experience. As AI becomes more embedded in education systems, teachers must continue to develop their TPACK to maximize its potential in fostering learning environments that prepare students to engage with the challenges of sustainable development.

The Diffusion of Innovations Theory

The Diffusion of Innovations (DOI) theory, developed by Rogers (2003), provides a useful lens for understanding how new technologies, such as AI, are adopted in educational systems. The theory outlines five key factors that influence the adoption of an innovation:

Relative Advantage: The degree to which an innovation is perceived as better than its predecessor.
Compatibility: The degree to which an innovation aligns with the values, experiences, and needs of potential adopters.
Complexity: The ease or difficulty of understanding and using the innovation.
Trialability: The ability to experiment with an innovation before full adoption.
Observability: The degree to which the results of an innovation are visible to others.

In the context of AI and education, the DOI theory suggests that the adoption of AI technologies will be influenced by how educators and institutions perceive the advantages of AI in enhancing teaching and learning. For instance, if AI systems are seen as improving learning outcomes, increasing efficiency, and making education more accessible, they are more likely to be adopted. Furthermore, the compatibility of AI with existing teaching practices and curricula is crucial. AI systems must align with the pedagogical goals of educators and be easy to integrate into classrooms.

Sustainable Development Theory

The Sustainable Development Theory (WCED, 1987) emphasizes the importance of integrating environmental, social, and economic factors into development processes. This theory advocates for meeting the needs of the present without compromising the ability of future generations to meet their own needs. In the context of education, sustainable development involves preparing students to understand and address the complex challenges of sustainable living, environmental conservation, social justice, and global equity.

AI can play a crucial role in advancing sustainable development by promoting education that aligns with the SDGs, particularly SDG 4 (Quality Education). For instance, AI-driven learning tools can provide students with real-time data and simulations that help them understand environmental challenges, such as climate change or biodiversity loss. AI can also promote sustainability education by fostering critical thinking and problem-solving skills, which are necessary to develop solutions for global sustainability challenges.

Theories of Equity and the Digital Divide

As AI becomes more embedded in educational systems, issues of equity and access to technology become critical concerns. Theories of equity in education emphasize the importance of providing all students, regardless of their background, with equal opportunities to succeed. However, the digital divide the gap between those who have access to technology and those who do not remains a significant challenge.

Theories related to the digital divide (Norris, 2001) highlight the disparities in access to digital tools, the internet, and technological infrastructure between different socioeconomic groups, regions, and countries. AI's potential to enhance education can only be fully realized if these disparities are addressed. To align AI with SDG 4, policymakers and educators must ensure that technology is accessible to all learners, particularly those in underserved or remote areas.

The theoretical framework outlined in this chapter integrates various perspectives that provide a comprehensive understanding of AI's role in education for sustainable development. Drawing from constructivism, the TPACK framework, the diffusion of innovations theory, sustainable development theory, and theories of equity and the digital divide, this framework offers a nuanced approach to the integration of AI in education. By exploring how AI can support personalized learning, enhance accessibility, and promote sustainable development, this framework provides the conceptual foundations for understanding how AI can contribute to achieving SDG 4 and other SDGs.

Ultimately, the theoretical perspectives discussed here underscore the need for a thoughtful, ethical, and equitable approach to AI implementation in education. While AI holds the potential to revolutionize education and contribute to sustainable development, it is crucial to ensure that its adoption is inclusive, accessible, and aligned with the broader goals of social justice and sustainability. Through these lenses, AI can be a transformative force in advancing education and achieving the SDGs.

CONCEPTUAL DEVELOPMENT: AI AND EDUCATION FOR SUSTAINABLE DEVELOPMENT GOALS (SDGS)

The rapid evolution of Artificial Intelligence (AI) is fundamentally transforming education, offering innovative solutions to longstanding challenges. As countries and educational institutions strive to achieve the United Nations' Sustainable Development Goals (SDGs), AI presents unique opportunities to enhance the accessibility, inclusivity, and quality of education. Particularly, AI's role in achieving SDG 4: Quality Education is central to discussions on how AI can be leveraged to ensure equitable and inclusive education for all. However, AI's potential extends beyond SDG 4, encompassing other SDGs, such as SDG 3 (Good Health and Well-being), SDG 5 (Gender Equality), and SDG 13 (Climate Action), by providing scalable, adaptive solutions that address global challenges in education and beyond.

This conceptual development section explores the intersection between AI and education within the context of sustainable development. It highlights how AI reshapes educational practices, improves learning outcomes, and fosters the broader goals of sustainable development. Drawing on key concepts from educational theory, sustainability, and technological innovation, this section examines how AI can be positioned as a tool to support both individual learners and global sustainability objectives.

Personalized Learning and Inclusivity

One of the most significant contributions of AI in education is its ability to deliver personalized learning. This concept refers to tailoring the learning experience to meet the diverse needs, preferences, and abilities of each student. Traditionally, education systems have operated within a one-size-fits-all approach, where all students receive the same curriculum at the same pace. This approach often leaves certain groups behind, particularly those with learning disabilities, language barriers, or other contextual challenges. AI, through adaptive learning technologies, has the capacity to overcome these limitations by providing a customized learning journey for each student, making education more inclusive and equitable.

Personalized learning is supported by AI systems such as Intelligent Tutoring Systems (ITS) and Learning Management Systems (LMS), which use algorithms to adjust the pace, difficulty level, and type of content delivered to each student based on real-time performance data. AI-driven platforms like Knew ton and Dream Box adapt to students' progress, providing immediate feedback, targeted lessons, and continuous assessments that help students stay on track and receive the support they need. For instance, AI-based platforms can monitor student performance across different subjects and identify areas of difficulty, offering extra support in real-time.

By facilitating differentiated instruction, AI ensures that no learner is left behind, which directly aligns with SDG 4's goal to "ensure inclusive and equitable quality education and promote lifelong learning opportunities for all" (UNESCO, 2015).

Data-Driven Decision-Making for Educational Improvement

Another key concept in the development of AI for education is its capacity to support data-driven decision-making. Data analytics plays a crucial role in improving both teaching and learning by enabling educators to make informed decisions based on real-time insights into student performance and learning patterns. With AI's ability to process vast amounts of data, it can identify trends, measure student progress, and predict outcomes, which helps educators intervene proactively to address potential learning gaps.

The role of data-driven AI systems in education also extends to the institutional level. By using AI for institutional analytics, educational administrators can assess school-wide performance, identify systemic challenges, and optimize resource allocation. AI can provide insights into which teaching methods or programs are most effective, helping institutions align their curricula with the learning needs of students and the sustainability goals of the education system. This focus on data-based decision-making contributes to SDG 4 by ensuring that educational practices are continually improved, adaptive, and responsive to student needs.

AI and Education for Gender Equality (SDG 5)

Achieving gender equality is another critical aspect of sustainable development, and AI has the potential to play a transformative role in promoting gender-inclusive education. AI-powered educational platforms can help address gender disparities in learning opportunities by providing personalized support that encourages both girls and boys to pursue subjects that align with their interests and strengths, particularly in fields like Science, Technology, Engineering, and Mathematics (STEM), where girls have historically been underrepresented.

AI can also contribute to the eradication of gender biases in education by identifying and addressing stereotypes present in educational content. Through Natural Language Processing (NLP) algorithms, AI can analyse textbooks, reading materials, and assessments to detect gender bias or stereotypical portrayals, ensuring that content is fair and balanced. AI-driven gender-sensitive curricula can empower girls and boys to engage in educational experiences that promote equality and challenge traditional gender norms.

Additionally, AI technologies can help mitigate barriers faced by female students in rural or conflict-affected areas by providing access to educational resources through mobile learning platforms. These platforms can offer digital access to high-quality content, which can be critical in regions where access to traditional schooling is limited. For instance, AI-based learning apps provide personalized learning paths and resources for girls who may face constraints due to cultural, financial, or geographical factors, thus promoting the empowerment of women and girls in line with SDG 5.

Sustainability Education and Climate Action (SDG 13)

Education for sustainable development (ESD) is essential for achieving SDG 13: Climate Action. In the context of climate change, education plays a key role in raising awareness about environmental issues, promoting sustainable lifestyles, and preparing future generations to act on climate challenges. AI can significantly contribute to sustainability education by providing interactive simulations, virtual environments, and data analytics tools that enhance students' understanding of environmental challenges and the complexities of climate change.

AI-powered tools can simulate real-world environmental scenarios, allowing students to explore the effects of climate change, resource depletion, and ecosystem degradation. For example, AI-based simulations can model the impact of different policy interventions on carbon emissions, allowing students to explore and evaluate potential solutions for mitigating climate change. AI systems can also aggregate large-scale environmental data, providing real-time information on air quality, water scarcity, and deforestation, which can be incorporated into educational programs.

Ethical and Societal Implications of AI in Education

While AI presents tremendous opportunities for enhancing education and advancing the SDGs, its use in education also raises ethical and societal questions. AI systems operate based on algorithms that rely on data collected from students, teachers, and educational institutions. This data is often sensitive, raising concerns about data privacy and security. Ensuring the ethical use of AI in education requires transparent and responsible practices regarding data collection, storage, and use, as well as clear guidelines for safeguarding the rights of learners.

Another significant challenge is the potential bias in AI algorithms. Since AI systems are trained on existing datasets, they can perpetuate existing biases, including those related to gender, race, or socioeconomic status. This bias can manifest in discriminatory educational practices if not carefully monitored and addressed. For example, AI systems used for admissions or assessments could unintentionally Favor certain groups of students over others. To avoid these outcomes, it is critical to develop ethical AI frameworks that prioritize fairness, accountability, and transparency.

Finally, AI must be used in a way that complements, rather than replaces, human educators. While AI can provide personalized learning experiences and data insights, it cannot replace the essential human elements of teaching, such as empathy, mentorship, and social interaction. Education systems must therefore strike a balance between leveraging AI's potential and preserving the social, emotional, and interpersonal aspects of learning.

The integration of AI into education for sustainable development presents both exciting opportunities and complex challenges. From personalized learning and data-driven decision-making to promoting gender equality, climate action, and ethical AI practices, the potential of AI to contribute to the achievement of the SDGs is immense. As educational systems around the world seek to leverage AI to advance SDG 4 and other SDGs, it is critical to ensure that AI tools are designed and implemented in ways that are inclusive, ethical, and aligned with the values of sustainable development.

Through personalized learning, equitable access, and sustainability education, AI can be a transformative force in advancing global education and supporting the achievement of the SDGs. However, this potential can only be realized if we navigate the ethical, social, and technological challenges associated with AI integration. In the process, AI must be harnessed not just as a tool for educational enhancement but as a vehicle for advancing a more sustainable, equitable, and just global future.

CONTRIBUTION TO THE FIELD: AI AND EDUCATION FOR SUSTAINABLE DEVELOPMENT GOALS (SDGS)

Artificial Intelligence (AI) has emerged as a transformative force in the field of education, with the potential to fundamentally alter the way we approach teaching, learning, and educational policy. The integration of AI in education aligns with the United Nations' Sustainable Development Goals (SDGs), particularly SDG 4 (Quality Education), which aims to ensure inclusive, equitable, and high-quality education for all. AI's contribution to education goes beyond enhancing learning outcomes—it also plays a crucial role in addressing broader global challenges, such as gender equality, climate action, and social inclusion.

This section explores the contributions of AI to the field of education, focusing on its impact on educational theory, practice, and policy. It examines how AI supports personalized learning, promotes educational equity, fosters teacher development, and enhances global sustainability efforts. Additionally, it delves into AI's potential to address key challenges in education, such as the digital divide, and how it can help achieve the SDGs by empowering educators, students, and communities worldwide.

Enhancing Personalized Learning and Inclusivity

AI's most significant contribution to education lies in its ability to personalize learning, ensuring that each student receives instruction tailored to their unique needs, strengths, and learning styles. Personalized learning has long been a goal for educators, but it has often been difficult to achieve in traditional classroom settings due to time and resource constraints. AI-powered tools, such as Intelligent Tutoring Systems (ITS) and adaptive learning platforms, now offer solutions to this challenge by adjusting the learning experience in real-time based on students' individual progress and performance.

AI's contribution to personalized learning extends beyond individual tutoring. By continuously assessing students' knowledge and skills, AI systems can provide feedback and interventions when necessary, allowing for differentiated instruction. This is particularly valuable for students with diverse learning needs, including those with disabilities, language barriers, or socio-economic challenges. Personalized learning powered by AI fosters inclusive education, a key tenet of SDG 4, which seeks to provide quality education that caters to all learners, regardless of background or ability.

For instance, AI platforms like DreamBox and Knewton provide students with tailored learning experiences in subjects like mathematics and language arts. These platforms offer personalized lessons and activities that adjust the level of difficulty based on students' abilities, ensuring that learners are neither overwhelmed nor under-challenged. By offering personalized support, AI helps close achievement gaps, enabling students from underprivileged backgrounds to access high-quality education and fostering greater educational equity.

Addressing the Digital Divide and Expanding Access

AI also plays a critical role in addressing the digital divide, which remains a significant barrier to equitable education worldwide. The digital divide refers to disparities in access to digital technologies, such as the internet, computers, and AI-powered educational tools, between different regions, socio-economic groups, and countries. AI-powered platforms can bridge these gaps by providing educational resources that are accessible through mobile devices and low-bandwidth internet connections, enabling students in rural or underserved areas to benefit from high-quality education.

In regions where traditional education infrastructure is lacking, AI offers an alternative model for delivering content. Mobile learning apps, for instance, leverage AI to provide personalized learning experiences even in remote areas. Through these platforms, students can access educational content, receive personalized feedback, and track their progress without the need for a physical classroom or internet-connected computers. This is particularly important in low-income countries, where schools may lack the resources to provide traditional educational tools, and digital education is becoming an essential means of fostering learning opportunities.

AI also contributes to overcoming geographical and logistical barriers, particularly in areas affected by conflict or natural disasters. In such contexts, AI-driven platforms can offer continuity of education, ensuring that students in crisis-affected regions continue their learning without interruption. The ability of AI to provide accessible, flexible, and scalable educational resources makes it an essential tool for achieving the accessibility and equity goals of SDG 4.

Supporting Teachers and Facilitating Professional Development

In addition to benefiting students, AI contributes to teacher development by providing new tools and resources that enhance instructional practices. AI-powered systems help educators by offering insights into student performance, identifying learning gaps, and providing suggestions for instructional strategies. For example, AI-based Learning Analytics can analyse student data to pinpoint areas where students are struggling, enabling teachers to adjust their teaching methods or provide targeted interventions.

AI also facilitates professional development for educators. By using AI-driven tools, teachers can receive real-time feedback on their teaching practices, learn new instructional strategies, and improve their pedagogical techniques. AI can recommend personalized professional development resources based on a teacher's strengths and areas for growth, fostering continuous improvement. This is particularly valuable in the context of teacher shortages and the need for scalable, cost-effective professional development programs.

Furthermore, AI-powered platforms offer teachers more time to focus on higher-level tasks, such as mentoring students, collaborating with colleagues, and engaging in creative instructional design. By automating administrative tasks, such as grading and data entry, AI reduces the workload of teachers, allowing them to focus on the more human aspects of education, such as building relationships with students and fostering a positive learning environment.

Promoting Global Sustainability and Education for SDGs

AI's contribution to education also extends to global sustainability efforts, particularly in relation to SDG 13 (Climate Action) and SDG 12 (Responsible Consumption and Production). Through AI, educational platforms can raise awareness about pressing environmental issues and promote sustainable practices. AI can support sustainability education by providing students with tools to simulate environmental impacts, analyse data related to climate change, and explore potential solutions to global challenges.

For example, AI can be used to create interactive simulations that allow students to visualize the consequences of different environmental policies or behaviours, such as the impact of deforestation on biodiversity or the effects of renewable energy adoption on carbon emissions. By engaging students in these simulations, AI helps to foster a deeper understanding of the complex relationships between human activity and the environment.

AI can also support sustainable decision-making in education systems by helping institutions reduce their carbon footprint. AI-based systems can monitor and optimize the use of resources in schools, such as energy consumption, waste management, and water usage, contributing to the greening of educational institutions. In this way, AI not only supports sustainability education but also directly contributes to SDG 13 by promoting more sustainable practices within the education sector itself.

Fostering Collaboration and Global Connectivity

Another significant contribution of AI in education is its potential to foster global collaboration and connectivity. In today's interconnected world, learning is no longer confined to the local classroom. AI-powered tools can facilitate cross-border educational collaborations, allowing students from different parts of the world to work together on global challenges, share knowledge, and learn from diverse perspectives.

For example, AI platforms that offer real-time language translation enable students from different linguistic backgrounds to engage in collaborative learning activities. This opens up opportunities for international partnerships, where students from diverse cultural and geographical contexts can work together on projects related to sustainability, human rights, or social justice. By fostering global collaboration, AI helps students develop global competencies that are crucial for addressing the interconnected challenges outlined in the SDGs.

Addressing Ethical and Social Challenges in AI Education

As AI continues to transform education, it is essential to address the ethical and social challenges that come with its integration. One of the most pressing concerns is bias in AI algorithms, which can perpetuate inequalities and discrimination. AI systems often rely on large datasets to train algorithms, and if these datasets contain biases (e.g., gender, race, or socio-economic bias), the AI systems may inadvertently reinforce these biases in educational settings. Therefore, it is crucial for researchers, policymakers, and educators to develop AI technologies that are fair, transparent, and accountable.

Furthermore, as AI becomes more embedded in education, there is a need for ethical frameworks that ensure AI is used responsibly. This includes safeguarding data privacy, protecting student information, and ensuring that AI is used in ways that promote student well-being and equity. Ethical AI use in education is critical to achieving the inclusive, equitable, and high-quality education that is central to SDG 4.

AI's contributions to the field of education are vast and multifaceted, spanning from enhancing personalized learning and promoting inclusivity to supporting teacher development and fostering global collaboration. By addressing key challenges in education—such as the digital divide, resource allocation, and sustainability—AI helps create more equitable and effective educational systems that can contribute to the achievement of the SDGs. AI is not only transforming how education is delivered but is also enabling the global community to address some of the most pressing issues facing humanity, from climate change to social inequality.

As the field of AI in education continues to evolve, it is essential to ensure that AI is used ethically, transparently, and inclusively. By fostering responsible AI development and integration, we can harness its potential to create an education system that is sustainable, inclusive, and capable of empowering students to navigate the challenges of the 21st century. AI's contributions to education are not merely technological advancements—they are foundational to building a more sustainable, equitable, and just world.

FUTURE RESEARCH AND PROSPECTS: AI AND EDUCATION FOR SUSTAINABLE DEVELOPMENT GOALS (SDGS)

The integration of Artificial Intelligence (AI) in education is still in its early stages, yet it holds immense potential to transform educational systems worldwide. As AI technologies continue to evolve, they present both exciting opportunities and significant challenges. This section explores key areas where future research can expand AI's impact on education and how it can better align with the United Nations'

Sustainable Development Goals (SDGs), especially SDG 4 (Quality Education). By identifying emerging trends, challenges, and opportunities, we aim to provide a roadmap for future research that will enhance AI's contribution to education for sustainable development.

Personalized Learning at Scale

One of the most promising applications of AI in education is personalized learning. However, while AI has already demonstrated its ability to tailor learning experiences to individual students, scaling personalized learning across diverse educational contexts remains a significant challenge. Future research can explore how AI can be used to create scalable, adaptable models for personalized learning that can be implemented in different educational systems, particularly in low-resource settings where access to technology may be limited.

Research should focus on optimizing AI algorithms to better understand the diverse learning needs of students, especially those from underrepresented or marginalized communities. AI systems could be developed to not only personalize content but also adapt teaching methods to fit different cultural contexts and learning environments. For example, research could investigate the role of AI in supporting multilingual learning, ensuring that personalized learning tools can be accessible in a variety of languages and dialects, further promoting inclusivity and equity in education. As AI continues to evolve, the aim would be to ensure that personalized learning is not a luxury, but a universal right for all students.

Addressing Ethical and Social Implications of AI in Education

AI's increasing presence in educational contexts raises important ethical, social, and political questions. These concerns include data privacy, algorithmic bias, equity in access to AI tools, and the potential replacement of teachers with AI systems. Given the potential risks AI poses, future research must focus on the ethical use of AI in educational settings to ensure that AI enhances education in a responsible, equitable, and transparent manner.

Specifically, research can explore how AI algorithms can be made fairer, ensuring that biases in data are mitigated to prevent discriminatory practices. AI systems that make decisions about students, such as admissions, grading, and career guidance, must be carefully designed to avoid reinforcing existing social inequalities. Investigating algorithmic transparency, which allows educators and policymakers to understand how AI tools make decisions, will be crucial to building trust in AI systems.

Moreover, data privacy will continue to be a critical area for research. AI-powered educational platforms rely heavily on student data, and as such, it is vital to establish clear guidelines for how this data is collected, stored, and shared. Future research should explore how AI can be integrated into education systems while ensuring students' privacy rights are upheld and that their data is used ethically.

AI for Sustainable Education Systems

AI holds considerable promise for advancing sustainable development through education. However, to effectively contribute to the SDGs, particularly SDG 4, AI applications in education must align with the principles of sustainability. Future research could focus on the role of AI in promoting green education, whereby AI tools teach students about sustainability and encourage sustainable practices. For example, AI-based systems could simulate environmental systems, allowing students to explore topics such as climate change, resource depletion, and biodiversity conservation through interactive learning experiences.

Additionally, AI can play a role in the greening of educational institutions by optimizing resource use (energy, water, etc.) and reducing waste. Research could explore how AI can be leveraged to make schools, universities, and other educational institutions more resource-efficient and environmentally friendly. By reducing the environmental footprint of educational institutions, AI could contribute to SDG 12 (Responsible Consumption and Production) and SDG 13 (Climate Action). AI can enable institutions to monitor and optimize the use of resources, helping to create more sustainable educational practices and model responsible consumption behaviours for students.

Teacher Training and Professional Development with AI

AI can not only support student learning but also facilitate teacher development. Future research should investigate how AI can be utilized to provide teachers with personalized professional development. This could include AI-based platforms that assess teachers' strengths and areas for growth, suggesting customized learning modules or resources to enhance their teaching skills.

For instance, AI could support the creation of virtual learning communities, where educators can collaborate, share resources, and engage in peer learning. AI-powered tools can help teachers stay informed about the latest teaching methodologies and research, fostering a culture of lifelong learning for educators, which is essential to the achievement of SDG 4. Research could also examine how AI can support the development of pedagogical content knowledge, helping educators bridge the gap between subject expertise and effective teaching practices.

Moreover, AI can be used to assist in the development of pedagogical frameworks for inclusive and equitable education. As AI systems increasingly assist in data analysis, research can focus on how AI can support teachers in identifying learning gaps, particularly for students with special educational needs, and suggest appropriate interventions. This research could result in more effective professional development programs for teachers, better preparing them to implement inclusive education practices.

AI and Global Collaborative Learning for SDGs

AI offers the possibility of connecting students across the globe, enabling global collaborative learning focused on addressing complex global challenges such as climate change, poverty, and inequality. Research into the potential of AI to foster global learning communities can explore how AI-driven platforms can connect students from different countries to collaborate on SDG-related projects. These collaborations could empower students to become agents of change, equipping them with the knowledge and skills to solve pressing global problems.

AI-powered tools that enable real-time translation and cultural exchange could create new opportunities for students from diverse linguistic and cultural backgrounds to work together on common goals. Research could investigate the design and implementation of these tools to promote cross-cultural dialogue and global citizenship, encouraging students to engage in shared projects on sustainability, social justice, or humanitarian issues.

Additionally, AI can help address the global skills gap, which has become a growing concern as technology evolves at a rapid pace. Research could explore how AI can facilitate skills development programs that prepare students for the jobs of tomorrow, ensuring that they are equipped with the competencies required to thrive in the changing labour market. These initiatives could also be aligned with the SDGs, ensuring that future workers are capable of addressing issues like sustainable development and climate change.

AI in Assessment and Evaluation

AI has the potential to revolutionize assessment and evaluation in education. However, research into the future applications of AI in assessment is still in its early stages, and there are many unexplored possibilities. For example, AI can provide real-time feedback on student performance, offering a more continuous and dynamic evaluation system than traditional exams or tests.

Research could focus on developing formative assessment models that leverage AI to assess students on a continuous basis, providing timely feedback to guide further learning. This approach aligns with SDG 4's emphasis on lifelong learning and helping students develop a growth mindset. AI can also play a role in diagnostic assessments, identifying students' strengths and weaknesses early in their learning journey, thus enabling timely intervention and support.

Furthermore, AI could play a role in automatic essay scoring and peer assessment models. By ensuring fair, unbiased, and consistent evaluations, AI has the potential to make the assessment process more transparent and efficient. However, future research should explore how AI-based assessments can complement human evaluations, ensuring that AI does not replace the nuanced judgment and expertise of teachers but instead serves as a tool for enhancement.

Interdisciplinary Research on AI and Education

Finally, interdisciplinary research is essential for understanding and maximizing the potential of AI in education. The intersection of AI, education, ethics, policy, and sustainability requires collaboration between researchers from diverse fields, including education, computer science, sociology, psychology, and environmental studies. Future research must not only explore the technical aspects of AI but also investigate the socio-cultural and psychological implications of AI in education.

Researchers must also focus on policy frameworks that guide the ethical use of AI in education. Investigating policy models that encourage the responsible use of AI while ensuring equitable access, data privacy, and inclusivity will be essential for scaling AI in education. Collaboration between governments, technology developers, and educators will ensure that AI technologies are implemented in ways that align with the broader goals of sustainable development.

The future of AI in education holds immense promise, particularly in terms of its potential to contribute to the realization of the SDGs. While much has been achieved, significant research opportunities remain to ensure that AI technologies are used effectively, ethically, and inclusively. From personalized learning and teacher development to fostering global collaboration and promoting sustainability, AI can be a transformative force in education. As we continue to explore and expand the use of AI in education, it is essential to address the challenges and opportunities identified in this section, ensuring that AI contributes to a more equitable, inclusive, and sustainable future for all learners.

CONCLUSION: AI AND EDUCATION FOR SUSTAINABLE DEVELOPMENT GOALS (SDGS)

The transformative potential of Artificial Intelligence (AI) in education has become increasingly evident as nations around the world strive to meet the United Nations Sustainable Development Goals (SDGs). Of particular importance is SDG 4 (Quality Education), which advocates for inclusive, equitable, and quality education for all. AI's integration into education systems has the potential to reshape how we approach learning, teaching, and educational policy. With its capacity to address educational disparities, support teachers, and foster global collaboration, AI is positioned as a key enabler in the achievement of the SDGs.

This chapter has discussed the various roles AI plays in advancing education for sustainable development. From personalized learning and improved access to education, to enhancing teacher effectiveness and fostering global collaboration, AI offers transformative solutions to many of the challenges faced by modern education systems. However, as this chapter highlights, the widespread integration of AI into education also presents complex ethical, social, and technical challenges that must be addressed to ensure that AI is harnessed responsibly and equitably. This conclusion revisits the key themes of the chapter, emphasizing AI's promise and the challenges that need to be overcome, and offers a roadmap for how AI can contribute to realizing the SDGs and creating a more sustainable and equitable educational landscape.

AI as a Catalyst for Transforming Education

The most striking feature of AI in education is its ability to personalize learning, a key factor in achieving SDG 4. Traditional education systems often follow a one-size-fits-all model, which does not address the diverse learning needs of students. AI offers a scalable solution by adapting learning materials in real time to match individual learners' progress and needs. Intelligent tutoring systems (ITS) and AI-driven adaptive learning platforms are designed to cater to different learning styles, thus ensuring that students receive personalized instruction based on their unique capabilities and challenges (Woolf, 2020).

This ability to tailor educational experiences is critical for students from marginalized or disadvantaged backgrounds, as AI has the potential to bridge the digital divide. By making learning more individualized, AI promotes equity and supports the inclusion of students with diverse educational needs, thus advancing the SDG of providing universal access to quality education (Lucking et al., 2016). Moreover, AI-powered systems provide continuous feedback to students, fostering a growth mindset and encouraging lifelong learning—a key principle of SDG 4.

Promoting Educational Equity and Access

AI's role in promoting educational equity and access is of particular importance in low-resource settings where access to high-quality education remains a challenge. AI systems can break down barriers to education by providing affordable, scalable learning opportunities. For instance, mobile learning platforms powered by AI algorithms can offer personalized education experiences in areas where access to traditional schools or advanced technologies is limited (Ahuja & Sah, 2021). Such AI-based systems can help bridge gaps in access to education, particularly for girls, rural populations, and other underserved communities, directly contributing to the achievement of SDG 4.

The digital divide continues to be one of the most pressing issues in global education. However, AI can play a pivotal role in overcoming this challenge. Research by Pedro, Subosa, Rivas, and Valverde (2019) highlights that AI-powered educational tools, when appropriately designed, can be deployed in areas with limited infrastructure, offering a low-cost solution for education in resource-constrained environments. Furthermore, these tools can be designed to work in offline or low-bandwidth settings, ensuring that even students in rural or conflict-affected areas can access educational content.

Enhancing Teacher Effectiveness and Professional Development

While AI has been most prominently discussed in the context of student learning, its potential to enhance teacher effectiveness is equally significant. AI can support teachers in personalizing instruction, tracking student progress, and identifying learning gaps. AI-driven tools can offer real-time analytics, enabling teachers to make data-informed decisions that are tailored to each student's needs (Siemens, 2016). This is particularly valuable in large classrooms, where teachers may struggle to provide individualized attention to every student.

In addition, AI can support teacher professional development by offering personalized learning opportunities. AI platforms can assess teachers' strengths and areas for improvement, providing customized resources and strategies for enhancing teaching effectiveness. This aligns with the concept of lifelong learning, which is crucial in an age where teaching methodologies and technologies are constantly evolving (Fischer et al., 2019). By streamlining administrative tasks and allowing teachers to focus on pedagogical innovation, AI has the potential to address issues such as teacher burnout and shortages (Luckin et al., 2016).

Fostering Global Collaboration and Sustainability Education

AI also plays an important role in fostering global collaboration among students across the world. Given the increasingly interconnected nature of global challenges such as climate change, poverty, and inequality, AI-powered tools can facilitate cross-border educational collaborations. These collaborations enable students from diverse regions and backgrounds to work together on projects that directly align with the SDGs, particularly those related to sustainability and social justice (Selwyn, 2019).

For example, AI can enable real-time translation and collaboration across languages, allowing students from different linguistic backgrounds to engage in shared educational experiences. As AI-powered tools improve, they will create opportunities for global learning communities where students can solve complex challenges collaboratively, fostering a deeper understanding of global issues (UNESCO, 2020). This aligns with the SDG focus on fostering global citizenship and equipping students with the knowledge and skills to engage with and address global problems.

Moreover, AI can support sustainability education by providing simulations, modelling, and interactive learning experiences that expose students to the pressing challenges of climate change, resource depletion, and environmental conservation (Becker & Park, 2019). Through AI-powered platforms, students can explore scenarios and solutions that promote sustainability and learn the skills needed to navigate and mitigate global environmental issues.

Ethical Considerations and Challenges in AI Integration

While AI presents numerous opportunities, its integration into education raises significant ethical concerns. One of the most pressing issues is algorithmic bias. AI systems often rely on historical data to make predictions or decisions. If these data are biased or unrepresentative, the resulting AI systems may perpetuate existing inequalities, particularly in areas such as student assessment, admissions, and career guidance (O'Neil, 2016). Thus, future research must focus on the development of more fair, transparent, and accountable AI systems in education that mitigate bias and discrimination.

Moreover, the privacy of student data is a critical concern. As AI-powered platforms collect vast amounts of personal and behavioural data, it is essential that data privacy is prioritized. AI systems must adhere to ethical guidelines regarding the collection, storage, and use of student data, ensuring that students' rights are protected (Selwyn, 2019). Additionally, there is the issue of data ownership: who owns the data generated by AI-powered educational platforms, and how can it be used ethically?

Another significant ethical concern is the role of AI in replacing human teachers. While AI can undoubtedly enhance the learning experience, it is essential that it does not supplant the human elements of teaching, such as emotional support, mentorship, and social interaction. Teachers are not just instructors; they are facilitators of personal growth, mentors, and guides. Research should investigate ways to ensure that AI complements rather than replaces the role of teachers in the educational process (Luckin et al., 2016).

The Future of AI in Education: A Roadmap for the SDGs

Looking to the future, the integration of AI into education will continue to evolve. As AI technologies become more advanced, they will offer even greater opportunities to personalize learning, enhance teacher effectiveness, and foster global collaboration. However, to fully realize AI's potential in achieving the SDGs, several key areas must be addressed.

Future research should focus on developing AI systems that are inclusive and adaptive to different educational contexts. This includes making AI tools accessible to all students, particularly those in low-resource environments, and ensuring that AI platforms are culturally sensitive and adaptable to diverse learning contexts. Research could also explore the use of AI in sustainability education, ensuring that students develop the skills needed to address pressing global challenges such as climate change and resource depletion.

Moreover, AI-driven tools for lifelong learning are essential to equip individuals with the skills necessary to thrive in an increasingly dynamic world. AI platforms that offer personalized professional development can help adults continuously update their skills to meet evolving job market demands, contributing to the achievement of SDG 4's goal of lifelong learning for all (Becker & Park, 2019).

AI holds the promise of transforming education and contributing to the realization of the SDGs, particularly SDG 4. Through its ability to personalize learning, promote equity and access, support teachers, and foster global collaboration, AI is poised to address many of the challenges faced by education systems around the world. However, to ensure that AI's potential is fully realized, we must address the ethical and social challenges that come with its integration into education. By focusing on inclusivity, fairness, and data privacy, and ensuring that AI complements human teaching rather than replacing it, we can ensure that AI contributes to building a more equitable, sustainable, and prosperous world for all learners.

REFERENCES

Ahuja, A., & Sah, A. (2021). Artificial Intelligence in Education: Future Prospects and Challenges. *International Journal of Educational Technology, 15*(3), 101–115.

Becker, H., & Park, Y. (2019). Sustainability Education and AI Integration in Global Learning Systems. *Journal of Sustainability Education, 23*(2), 46–59.

Fischer, G., Klemmer, S. R., & Grudin, J. (2019). The Role of AI in Education: Insights and Prospects. *Journal of Educational Technology & Society, 22*(4), 40–50.

Holmes, W., Bialik, M., & Fadel, C. (2019). *Artificial intelligence in education: Promises and implications for teaching and learning*. Center for Curriculum Redesign.

Luckin, R., Holmes, W., Griffiths, M., & Forcier, L. B. (2016). *Intelligence Unleashed: An Argument for AI in Education*. Pearson Education.

Mishra, P., & Koehler, M. J. (2006). Technological pedagogical content knowledge: A framework for teacher knowledge. *Teachers College Record, 108*(6), 1017–1054. DOI: 10.1111/j.1467-9620.2006.00684.x

Norris, P. (2001). *Digital divide: Civic engagement, information poverty, and the internet worldwide*. Cambridge University Press. DOI: 10.1017/CBO9781139164887

O'neil, C. (2017). *Weapons of math destruction: How big data increases inequality and threatens democracy*. Crown.

Piaget, J. (1976). *The grasp of consciousness: Action and concept in the young child*. Harvard University Press.

Popenici, S. A. D., & Kerr, S. (2017). Exploring the impact of artificial intelligence on teaching and learning in higher education. *Research in Learning Technology, 25*, 1–13. DOI: 10.25304/rlt.v25.1941 PMID: 30595727

Rogers, E. M. (2003). *Diffusion of innovations* (5th ed.). Free Press.

Selwyn, N. (2019). Should Robots Replace Teachers? AI and the Future of Education. *British Journal of Educational Technology, 50*(5), 2126–2136.

Selwyn, N. (2019). Should robots replace teachers? AI in education. *Learning, Media and Technology, 44*(1), 1–17. DOI: 10.1080/17439884.2018.1532015

UNESCO. (2015). *Incheon Declaration and Framework for Action for the implementation of SDG 4*. UNESCO.

UNESCO. (2018). *ICT in Education: A Tool for Achieving SDG 4*. UNESCO.

UNESCO. (2019). *Education for sustainable development goals: Learning objectives.* https://www.unesco.org/en/articles/education-sustainable-development-goals-learning-objectives

UNESCO. (2019). *AI for education: Policy, challenges, and opportunities.* UNESCO.

UNESCO. (2020). *AI in education: A strategic overview.* UNESCO.

Pedro, F., Subosa, M., Rivas, A., & Valverde, P. (2019). *Artificial intelligence in education: Challenges and opportunities for sustainable development.* Working papers on education policy, 7. UNESCO. https://unesdoc.unesco.org/ark:/48223/pf0000366994?posInSet=7&queryId=N-EXPLORE-cff47795-58ac-43ec-9f45-b1acf2920b16

United Nations. (2015). *Transforming our world: The 2030 agenda for sustainable development.* United Nations. https://sdgs.un.org/2030agenda

Vygotsky, L. S. (1978). *Mind in society: The development of higher psychological processes.* Harvard University Press.

West, D. M. (2018). *Artificial intelligence: The implications for education.* Brookings Institution.

World Commission on Environment and Development (WCED). (1987). *Our common future.* Oxford University Press.

Chapter 6
Lifelong Learning Systems in the age of AI: Effectiveness, Challenges, and Strategies

Juvrianto Chrissunday Jakob
https://orcid.org/0000-0002-5267-3448
Politeknik Negeri Ambon, Indonesia

Maslan Abdin
https://orcid.org/0009-0006-9670-437X
Politeknik Negeri Ambon, Indonesia

Sri Ananda Pertiwi
https://orcid.org/0009-0009-6022-3066
Universitas Musamus, Indonesia

Nihla Afdaliah
https://orcid.org/0000-0002-9233-8513
STAIN Majene, Indonesia

ABSTRACT

The era of artificial intelligence, in which technological breakthroughs affect the dynamics of employment and education, has given rise to the notion that lifelong learning systems have become an essential necessity. Through the provision of a method that is individualized, adaptable, and effective, artificial intelligence technology makes a substantial contribution to the development of skills. The application of artificial intelligence in the field of professional training facilitates the creation of individualized learning experiences, improves access to a vast array of educational resources, and raises the level of training quality through the utilization of thorough

DOI: 10.4018/979-8-3373-5781-2.ch006

data analysis. Additionally, artificial intelligence improves adult education by providing a platform that accommodates a variety of learning styles and paces, speeds up the learning process, and increases student engagement throughout the process.

INTRODUCTION

The Concept of AI Learning

In today's world of quickly expanding artificial intelligence (AI), the need of continuous learning has grown exponentially for individuals striving to remain relevant and competitive. Lifelong learning, defined as the continuous practice of obtaining new knowledge, skills, and competencies throughout one's life, is no more a choice endeavor, but rather an essential mindset in the face of technological and societal developments. AI plays a critical role in transforming how education and skill development are conducted by breaking down traditional time and location constraints. Unlike traditional education models, which frequently require learners to be physically present at specified times and locations, AI-powered learning platforms provide unparalleled flexibility, allowing people to participate in educational activities whenever and wherever it fits into their personal schedule.

This accessibility guarantees that learning is no longer limited to formal institutions or time periods, but rather becomes an integrated, seamless aspect of daily life. Furthermore, AI technologies personalize learning experiences by tailoring content to each learner's specific needs, pace, and preferences, which boosts engagement and effectiveness. AI supports continuous self-improvement by providing real-time feedback and leveraging vast digital resources, not only in personal development (such as learning new hobbies or knowledge), but also in professional growth, where upskilling and reskilling are critical to navigate changing job markets and career demands (Gabriel et al., 2022). Finally, AI serves as a powerful enabler, promoting a culture of lifelong learning and empowering humans to adapt, prosper, and grow in an increasingly complicated and dynamic world.

AI not only facilitates information access but also customizes the educational experience. AI-driven educational systems may customize instructional resources and methodologies to suit individual learning preferences and requirements. The system evaluates student data, identifies their learning patterns, and modifies the difficulty level or pertinent subjects (Holmes et al., 2019). This approach enhances the learning process, making it more efficient and customized to the capabilities of each participant, a feat frequently challenging to accomplish in conventional education, which tends to be more generalized.

Moreover, AI facilitates data-driven learning and delivers real-time feedback. AI-driven learning facilitates immediate assessment of user progress, hence accelerating the learning process and expediting error correction. Immediate feedback is essential for skill development, particularly for individuals engaged in professional training or requiring rapid mastery of technical skills (Pedro et al., 2019). In conventional schooling, feedback frequently arrives tardily, complicating the process of implementing enhancements.

Holmes (2020) confirmed that AI-driven lifetime learning facilitates access to an extensive array of educational resources. This technology enables individuals to access resources from many internet platforms, enroll in online courses, or employ interactive learning tools without the constraints of a structured curriculum. This creates possibilities for individuals to acquire new skills, pursue current trends, and enhance their knowledge in response to shifts in the workforce. This flexibility enables continual learning, facilitating the development of skills pertinent to professional requirements or personal interests.

AI functions as a technology that facilitates lifelong learning, enhancing education's inclusivity, accessibility, and personalization. This technology facilitates learning at any time and place while offering a more efficient and focused educational experience. Thus, AI enables society to continually adapt to contemporary demands and enhance their quality of life through pertinent knowledge and abilities.

Lifelong learning is a concept that underscores the notion that the learning process extends beyond childhood and youth, persisting throughout an individual's life. This concept posits that every human, irrespective of age or life stage, possesses the right to perpetuate their learning and personal development (Camilleri, 2018). Lifelong learning encompasses diverse educational modalities, ranging from formal, organized instruction at academic institutions to informal learning derived from life events, social interactions, or self-directed discovery. Learning is now regarded as an ongoing aspect of human existence rather than a distinct phase in life.

In a progressively dynamic and swiftly evolving environment, lifelong learning is becoming vital. Due to the swift progression of technology, numerous businesses and professions necessitate the acquisition of new skills or alterations in work methodologies. The continual introduction of new technologies necessitates that individuals acquire digital and technical competencies, while numerous job sectors are undergoing automation, impacting conventional work practices. Lifelong learning enables individuals to consistently adapt to advancements, ensuring they remain competitive in the work market (Luo & Zhang, 2024).

The significance of lifelong learning pertains to the necessity of refreshing information and abilities. In some fields, particularly those associated with technology, pertinent knowledge can become outdated in a relatively brief period. Consequently, to maintain relevance in the employment, individuals must consistently enhance their knowledge, acquire the latest market trends, and refine their abilities to remain competitive. Lifelong learning facilitates adaptability to change and offers opportunities for professional advancement or career transition.

Moreover, the principle of lifelong learning enables individuals to pursue knowledge aligned with their personal interests. Informal learning, encompassing experiences from work, social contacts, or hobbies, frequently yields profound insights pertinent to daily life. This allows individuals the liberty to investigate subjects of personal interest beyond conventional academic routes (Berendt et al. 2020; Perrotta & Selwyn, 2019). An individual interested in art can acquire new abilities through online classes or by participating in a creative community, regardless of their formal background in the discipline.

Lifelong learning is a technique for cultivating individuals who are adaptable, innovative, and sustainable in their career advancement and personal lives. Amidst swift global transformations, conventional education alone is insufficient to equip individuals for impending difficulties. Consequently, by embracing the principle of lifelong learning, individuals can persist in their education, growth, and societal contributions. This education is essential for success and well-being in a period of perpetual change.

THE ROLE OF ARTIFICIAL INTELLIGENCE IN LIFELONG LEARNING

Customization in Education

Artificial intelligence facilitates a more individualized educational experience. Employing machine learning algorithms, AI can assess individual learning patterns and customize educational resources and methodologies to align with their specific learning styles and requirements (Gabriel et al., 2022; Jakob, 2023). For instance, if a student favors learning via videos and visuals, AI can deliver educational resources in the format of films or infographics. Conversely, for individuals who favor reading literature or engaging in activities, AI can recommend text-based resources or interactive quizzes. Educational systems such as Khan Academy and Duolingo employ artificial intelligence to deliver resources customized to the individual speed and comprehension levels of learners, thereby enhancing their motivation and educational efficacy.

Availability of Comprehensive Educational Materials

AI can curate and recommend educational resources pertinent to users' requirements, linking them to online courses, articles, videos, and further learning materials. For instance, AI can recommend pertinent materials or videos aligned with the subject a user is presently studying (Le & Metzger, 2024; Persulessy et al., 2024). AI accelerates information retrieval and filtering by delivering more precise recommendations, eliminating the need for personal search efforts. Platforms such as Coursera and Udemy employ artificial intelligence to suggest supplementary courses pertinent to users' interests and backgrounds, enabling them to enhance their knowledge or desired abilities without geographical constraints.

Data-Driven Learning and Analytics

AI facilitates the collecting and analysis of real-time educational data, which is crucial in comprehending learning patterns and the challenges encountered by pupils. These analytics enable educators and educational organizations to deliver more precise feedback and implement interventions more swiftly (Liu & Yushchik, 2024; Jakob et al., 2024). If AI identifies that a student consistently errs on a specific sort of problem, the system can notify the teacher to offer further support on that subject. Learning management systems such as Moodle or Google Classroom aggregate data regarding student engagement with the content and generate analytical reports to enhance targeted instruction addressing students' challenges.

Utilization of Chatbots and Virtual Assistants

Ciampa et al. (2024) explained that AI-driven chatbots and virtual assistants are progressively utilized in lifetime learning to offer assistance at any moment. Chatbots equipped with natural language processing (NLP) can respond to inquiries regarding the subject matter, offer supplementary explanations, or deliver motivational assistance to enhance engagement and excitement for learning. Virtual assistants can interactively coach users through content or challenges, similar to a human tutor. Duolingo employs chatbots to engage users in language learning sessions, offering conversational exercises with immediate feedback. Virtual assistants such as Siri or Google Assistant are used to respond to inquiries or assist in locating material pertinent to the subject under examination.

Adaptive Learning

AI-driven educational systems can adjust to a person's capabilities and learning speed. In an online course or training, AI can adjust the complexity of questions or instructional material based on the learner's proficiency (Wellner & Levin, 2023). Should the learner swiftly grasp the topic, AI can present further obstacles to sustain their involvement. If the learner encounters difficulties, AI will provide supplementary resources or tasks to enhance their comprehension. Platforms like as Smart Sparrow and DreamBox employ adaptive learning technology to modify content according to the learner's progress and proficiency, ensuring that they remain challenged without becoming overwhelmed by excessive complexity.

With these five points, it is clear that AI is bringing significant changes in the way we learn, enabling more effective, flexible and individualized learning experiences, and supporting lifelong learning processes.

CHALLENGES IN CONTINUOUS EDUCATION IN THE AGE OF ARTIFICIAL INTELLIGENCE

In the age of artificial intelligence (AI), lifelong learning presents significant opportunities for enhanced access to personalized, flexible, and cost-effective education. Nonetheless, although AI presents numerous advantages, its implementation in education is fraught with difficulties (Rahm, 2024). A significant concern is the disparity in access to technology. Not all persons possess equal access to the technology, software, or internet connectivity required to fully utilize AI-based technologies. In numerous regions, particularly in developing nations, these technical infrastructure challenges can intensify disparities in access to education and learning possibilities.

Moreover, issues exist concerning the competencies and preparedness of human resources, encompassing both educators and students. Zebua et al. (2023) conveyed that educators and learners utilizing AI in education must possess sufficient digital competencies to engage with AI-driven solutions. A significant number of educators remain untrained in the proper utilization of AI tools, hence impeding the technology's potential to enhance teaching and learning methodologies. Conversely, learners may encounter challenges in adjusting to technology-based learning methods, particularly those unaccustomed to self-directed learning or engagement with automated systems.

Ultimately, ethical and privacy concerns emerge with the implementation of AI in education. AI systems gather and assess user data to deliver enhanced personalized experiences; yet, this also prompts apprehensions over data security and privacy.

The accumulation of personal data without sufficient safeguards is susceptible to exploitation, necessitating meticulous management. Moreover, the utilization of AI may intensify pre-existing biases in algorithms, thereby affecting disparities within the education system. Consequently, although AI possesses significant promise, it is imperative to establish regulations and standards governing its application to guarantee that this technology is utilized equitably and securely.

Although AI brings many conveniences and great potential in lifelong learning, there are some challenges that need to be faced:

Disparity in Technological Access

The distribution of AI technology is uneven globally, resulting in inequities in educational possibilities. Numerous places, particularly in developing nations or isolated areas, continue to encounter inadequate infrastructure challenges (Rosid, 2022). This encompasses restricted internet access, insufficient technology, or an absence of software that facilitates AI-driven education. These gaps intensify the prevailing digital divide, preventing certain individuals or groups from leveraging AI technology for learning or skill development.

In numerous rural regions or poor nations, access to computers or cellphones capable of executing AI-based applications is restricted. Although AI possesses significant potential to enhance the learning process, insufficient infrastructure will result in many individuals being marginalized. In many regions of Indonesia, despite availability to online learning platforms, inadequate internet connectivity hinders many students and adult workers from effectively engaging in AI-based training.

Essential Technological Proficiencies

To employ AI technology in education, individuals must possess fundamental technological abilities (Pratiwi, 2024). AI-driven education depends on digital engagement and information administration, necessitating proficiency in the utilized software and applications. Nonetheless, not all individuals possess adequate digital competencies to properly employ AI technology, particularly those lacking foundational technological education.

A student utilizing an AI-driven platform, such as Khan Academy or Duolingo, must comprehend how to access the course, maneuver through the platform, and employ its functionalities. This learning process can provide a hurdle for individuals unfamiliar with technology. If the education system fails to deliver sufficient technological training, numerous students and working people may find it challenging to adjust to new AI-driven learning approaches, notwithstanding their potential for effective learning.

The Function of Educators and Community Engagement

Iqbal et al. (2024) explained that although AI can offer meticulously organized and individualized education, the function of the educator or mentor is essential in continuous learning. Learning encompasses not only the acquisition of knowledge and skills but also social development, the exchange of experiences, and interpersonal relationships that enhance the educational experience. AI can enhance and tailor learning, although it cannot substitute the social interactions inherent in a classroom or the collaborative and discursive processes of learning.

Platforms such as Coursera and Udemy enable learners to engage in self-directed study with customized content; yet, connection with instructors or peers is essential for enhancing comprehension and experience. Group conversations, direct feedback, and personal coaching are essential components of the learning process that AI cannot fully supplant. A professional enrolled in a skill development course utilizing AI still need a mentor to assist in cultivating soft skills and offering practical insights derived from real-world experiences.

Data Security and Privacy

AI-driven education entails the aggregation of substantial personal information, encompassing learning behaviors, preferences, and additional personal data. This elicits apprehensions regarding the utilization of data, the accessibility of such data, and the adequacy of user data protection. Data security and privacy should be paramount in the design of AI-driven learning systems to ensure users feel secure and safeguarded when engaging with the platform (Ohyver et al., 2024).

Illustration: Numerous online learning platforms, including Duolingo and EdX, gather data pertaining to user behavior, encompassing learning progress and course preferences. If this data is improperly accessed or exploited, it may jeopardize individual privacy. Consequently, AI-driven educational platforms must guarantee the safeguarding of personal data through robust encryption and adherence to data protection standards, including the GDPR in the European Union. This approach allows learners to feel at ease and concentrate on their growth without concerns regarding privacy infringements.

THE PROSPECTS OF CONTINUOUS EDUCATION IN THE ERA OF ARTIFICIAL INTELLIGENCE

In the future, artificial intelligence (AI) will progressively influence our learning and access to education. Lifelong learning, which underscores the notion of education unrestricted by age or temporal constraints, will increasingly be propelled by AI capable of real-time adaptation of curricula and learning resources. Ertel (2024) explained that AI will tailor learning experiences by identifying the distinct needs of each individual, so providing a more efficient and targeted approach. Education will become increasingly adaptive, tailored to the individual pace and learning style of each student. This approach will guarantee that all individuals, from young learners to working adults, receive pertinent and timely education.

One of the most significant effects of AI in education is the enhancement of accessibility. AI-driven educational platforms can streamline access to learning, diminishing dependence on conventional educational institutions that may not be universally accessible. Access to online courses, digital materials, and personalized learning modules enables individuals, regardless of location, to pursue their educational endeavors (Winston, 1984). This enables individuals constrained by geographic or economic limitations to gain new skills, enhance their knowledge, and cultivate personal development in previously inconceivable ways.

Furthermore, AI-driven education will increasingly facilitate dynamic interactions in the learning process. AI can deliver immediate feedback, identifying places where a learner requires assistance and supplying supplementary materials or targeted exercises. This accelerates the learning process, enhances interactivity, and fosters deeper engagement. In a technical skills development course, AI can offer practical exercises or simulations that enhance the learner's comprehension more efficiently than the conventional method that depends exclusively on theoretical instruction.

In the future, AI-driven educational systems will additionally promote international collaboration. Utilizing AI technology that facilitates interactions among users globally enables the real-time exchange of knowledge, experiences, and skills. This global learning platform will integrate diverse cultural and social viewpoints that enhance the educational experience. Lifelong learning will serve as a catalyst for personal growth and foster inclusive social relationships, enabling individuals to exchange knowledge irrespective of geographical constraints. This partnership will enhance a global social network that is primarily founded on knowledge and skills.

Nonetheless, although AI possesses significant potential in education, its integration must be executed judiciously. This technology ought to be employed to promote enhanced access and equity in education, rather than intensifying current disparities. Moreover, it is essential to guarantee that AI is employed ethically, with appropriate consideration for privacy and data security. In the future, through a meticulous and inclusive strategy, AI will significantly influence the development of a more adaptive, efficient, and sustainable educational ecosystem. In the future, platforms such as Coursera and edX may create courses that genuinely tailor the learning experience for each individual, informed by their progress, and engage with educators and students globally within a dynamic learning community (Mintz & Brodie, 2019).

Lifelong learning in the era of AI presents numerous options for individuals to persist in their growth and education within a constantly evolving landscape. Artificial intelligence enables education to be customized to the specific needs and learning preferences of each individual, resulting in a more personalized and effective experience. This education encompasses not only traditional schooling but also professional training, skills enhancement, and self-directed learning. An AI-based platform enables individuals to access pertinent information and courses at any time and from any location, which is crucial for addressing the difficulties of an increasingly dynamic period.

Nonetheless, although AI presents numerous advantages, there remain obstacles that must be confronted to provide equitable access to lifelong learning for everyone. A significant concern is the disparity in access to technology. In several impoverished nations or isolated regions, insufficient technology infrastructure can hinder persons from accessing AI-driven educational opportunities. Challenges exist with the digital competencies necessary for engaging with AI systems, which may not be accessible to all, particularly individuals lacking a technological educational background.

To maximize the benefits of lifelong learning, technology must be employed responsibly and inclusively. The implementation of AI in education must consider data privacy concerns and the safeguarding of personal information. Furthermore, measures must be implemented to guarantee that AI algorithms do not perpetuate bias or inequity in the provision of educational opportunities. By tackling these difficulties, AI-driven education can serve as a formidable instrument to equip individuals for a more intricate and dynamic environment, facilitating sustainable and inclusive self-improvement for everyone.

ARTIFICIAL INTELLIGENCE IN FACILITATING SKILLS DEVELOPMENT

Artificial intelligence (AI) has instigated a significant transformation in skill development and learning methodologies. In contrast to conventional educational approaches that are predominantly unidirectional and rigid, artificial intelligence can customize learning resources and techniques to suit an individual's requirements and capabilities. In skills training, AI may assess a learner's strengths and shortcomings in real-time and then modify exercises or materials for enhanced efficacy (Jackson, 2019). This personalizes the learning process, enabling learners to concentrate on areas requiring enhancement and progress at their own speed.

The learning process becomes increasingly adaptive with AI. Machine learning algorithms may evaluate individual learning habits and adapt information dynamically to maintain a balance between challenge and overwhelm for learners. For instance, if a student encounters difficulties with a specific problem or assignment, an AI-based system can offer a simpler problem or furnish supplementary explanations. Conversely, if a student is rapidly acquiring knowledge and successfully executing complex tasks, AI may present increased obstacles to sustain their engagement and skill enhancement.

Flasiński (2016) defined artificial intelligence is quite effective at delivering prompt feedback. In conventional schooling, feedback is typically provided post-completion of an assignment or examination, which may be several days or weeks. In AI-driven education, feedback is provided instantaneously, enabling learners to ascertain promptly their comprehension of the topic or identify areas requiring enhancement. This is particularly beneficial in the development of practical abilities, where prompt reflection on mistakes or deficiencies in comprehension is crucial for ongoing enhancement.

Furthermore, AI facilitates continual learning, as learners are no longer constrained by a fixed timetable or location. Learning can occur at any time and in any location, allowing individuals the autonomy to progress at their own pace and convenience (Ertel, 2024). An AI-driven learning platform enables individuals to enhance their skills independently of traditional classrooms or restricted in-person interactions. This is particularly significant for individuals with full-time employment or other limitations.

Nonetheless, although AI has numerous advantages in skill enhancement, its implementation necessitates careful consideration of various factors, including disparities in technological access. Access to the gadgets and internet connections necessary for utilizing AI-based learning is not uniform among individuals. Consequently, although AI provides a more efficient and adaptable learning method, it is crucial to guarantee that this technology is available to all demographics, even those in regions with inadequate infrastructure.

An authentic instance of AI in skill enhancement is evident in language acquisition applications such as Duolingo. The application uses artificial intelligence to calibrate question difficulty according to the user's proficiency, deliver immediate feedback, and facilitate additional practice contingent upon the user's performance (Finlay, 2020). Should a user err on a certain question, the AI will offer elucidations and supplementary practice to rectify the error. This enables users to persist in enhancing their language proficiency in a tailored and adaptive manner, eliminating the necessity for conventional language instruction.

Customization of Education

A primary benefit of AI in skill development is its capacity to deliver a tailored learning experience. Artificial intelligence can assess individual learning patterns, monitor progress, and customize educational resources and techniques to suit specific requirements and capabilities (Sajja & Sajja, 2021). In conventional education, instruction is typically standardized, with all pupils adhering to the same curriculum, without significant adaptation to individual capabilities or interests.

Instances of AI Application

Adaptive Learning Systems: Platforms such as Knewton or DreamBox employ artificial intelligence to modify the complexity of content according to the learner's comprehension. Should a learner encounter difficulty with a notion, the AI will supply further materials or tasks to enhance their comprehension. If the student has grasped the content, the AI will provide more challenging tasks.

Empirical Learning and Immediate Feedback

Wang et al. (2024) analyzed artificial intelligence facilitates immediate data acquisition and processing, offering prompt feedback that is highly beneficial for skill enhancement. In the realm of skill acquisition, particularly technical or professional competencies, AI can offer instantaneous feedback on executed activities, identify faults, and propose enhancements.

Instances of AI Application

Vocational Education and Professional Competencies: Platforms such as Duolingo for language acquisition and Codecademy for programming employ AI to deliver instantaneous feedback to users. Upon a user's error, the AI will promptly offer clarification and supplementary information to facilitate correction.

In conventional education, feedback frequently arrives tardily (such as post-assessment or assignment evaluation), which can impede the learning process and hinder students from rectifying their errors in a timely manner.

Access to Extensive and Diverse Educational Resources

Kalogirou (2007) clarified that AI can propose a broader and more varied array of educational resources, encompassing articles, videos, online courses, and other tools customized to individual need. This enables learners to access a broader array of instructional resources that may be unavailable in conventional academic environments.

Instances of AI Application

Artificial Intelligence-Driven Educational Platforms: Platforms such as Coursera and Udemy utilize artificial intelligence to suggest courses or resources tailored to the user's preferences and educational background. This enables individuals to acquire new skills in a highly flexible manner and at their own speed.

Conversely, conventional education frequently adheres to a curriculum and resources established by educational institutions, which may not consistently align with each student's own interests or requirements.

Adaptable and Cost-Effective Education

A significant advantage of AI is its capacity to facilitate learning at any time and in any location. Utilizing AI through technology-based learning applications or learning management systems (LMS) enables users to access educational content from their devices, thereby removing the temporal and spatial limitations inherent in conventional education (Plant, 2011).

Instances of AI Application

Online Courses with Adaptive Learning Options: Platforms such as EdX and LinkedIn Learning provide accessible learning opportunities at any time and from any location. This is particularly advantageous for cultivating competencies that necessitate ongoing practice, such as computer skills, languages, or other technical proficiencies.

Conventional education, although its significant benefit in facilitating direct engagement, is typically constrained by a rigid schedule and location, posing challenges for individuals with restricted time or access.

Simulation and Experiential Learning

AI can be utilized to develop simulations that enable users to hone skills in scenarios that closely resemble real-world conditions. In the realm of professional competencies such as medical, engineering, or business, AI facilitates the opportunity to engage in simulations devoid of any further risk or expense (Harrison et al., 2021).

Instances of AI Application

Artificial Intelligence Skill Simulations: In the medical domain, AI is utilized to develop simulations of medical operations, enabling medical students or healthcare professionals to practice without directly performing the process on a patient. In the corporate sector, AI-driven simulations can facilitate the training of decision-making and managerial competencies.

In traditional education, simulations and practical exercises are frequently useful techniques for aiding students in comprehending topics and honing skills. Nonetheless, the utilization of simulations is constrained by real-world scenarios that are occasionally challenging to recreate accurately in an educational setting. In fields such as medicine or aviation, although simulations can be utilized, the expenses and constraints of actual resources hinder the ability to deliver frequent and comprehensive encounters. This constrains pupils' opportunities to engage in authentic or quasi-authentic scenarios.

Resource limitations are a significant obstacle in conventional schooling. Numerous institutions or training programs lack access to the advanced equipment or resources necessary for delivering high-quality simulations. Moreover, constraints of time and faculty frequently hinder intensive or prolonged learning. Simulations frequently fail to encompass the complete range of scenarios or variations that may arise in reality. Consequently, although conventional education holds significant value, there are substantial limitations that hinder its efficacy in delivering an optimal learning experience.

Conversely, AI mitigates numerous restrictions by facilitating access to more realistic, frequent, and cost-effective simulations. This technology enables learners to engage in independent, hands-on training without the limitations of physical or resource constraints inherent in traditional schooling (Gamham, 2017). In the medical domain, AI can provide surgical or diagnostic simulations that can be frequently executed to refine abilities without requiring hospital facilities or the immediate guidance of an instructor. This facilitates a more immersive and uninterrupted learning experience, enabling students to persist in practicing and honing their abilities without the limitations of time and money.

In terms of customization, AI-powered education stands out by tailoring learning materials and processes to each student's individual abilities, enabling a more personalized learning experience. In contrast, traditional education typically follows a uniform approach with limited opportunities for customization, treating all students in a similar way regardless of their unique needs or pace.

Feedback mechanisms also differ significantly between the two models. AI-powered education provides immediate and data-driven feedback, allowing learners to quickly understand their progress and make improvements. Traditional education, however, tends to offer feedback only after assignments or exams have been completed, resulting in slower response times that may delay learning adjustments. Furthermore, AI-powered education enables easier access to a wide range of educational resources through multiple platforms and digital sources, whereas traditional education primarily depends on textbooks, classroom instruction, and institution-provided materials.

Flexibility and practical learning methods are additional areas of divergence. AI-based education offers temporal and spatial flexibility, allowing learners to study anytime and anywhere, breaking free from the fixed schedules and physical locations set by schools or universities. It also incorporates AI-driven simulations that provide safe, cost-effective practice environments for developing skills. Conversely, traditional education is constrained by physical infrastructure, making simulations more expensive and less accessible, and limiting learning to specific times and places defined by the institution. This comparison highlights how AI is transforming education by enhancing personalization, immediacy, resource availability, and flexibility.

Customized Learning: In AI-driven systems, education is extensively tailored as AI can modify instructional materials and techniques according to individual competencies and requirements (Ghosh & Thirugnanam, 2021). For instance, AI may assess a student's progress and provide assignments of varying difficulty tailored to their capabilities, so delivering a genuinely personalized experience. Conversely, traditional education typically employs a "one-size-fits-all" methodology, wherein instructional materials are standardized throughout the class, with minimal or no modifications to accommodate specific student requirements.

Feedback: In AI-driven education, feedback is delivered instantaneously, enabling students to promptly identify their errors or areas requiring enhancement. (Zhang et al., 2021) This enables them to promptly rectify their errors and persist in their learning without prolonged delays. Conversely, in conventional education, feedback is frequently delayed, occurring post-examination or assignment completion, so diminishing the efficacy of the correcting process. This squandered time can impede the learning process, particularly in abilities necessitating repetitive practice.

Access to Educational Resources: Qadir (2023) argued that AI facilitates seamless access to educational resources from many sources and platforms, allowing students the autonomy to select materials based on their preferences or requirements. Students can utilize the internet and digital platforms to access videos, articles, online courses, and additional resources. Conversely, conventional education typically relies on textbooks and resources supplied by educational institutions, which frequently impose restrictions on the quantity and variety of materials available to students.

Temporal and Spatial Flexibility: AI-driven education provides significant flexibility, enabling students to learn at any time and from any location, provided they possess a compatible device and internet access (Su & Yang, 2023). This is highly beneficial for individuals with demanding schedules or those situated in areas that are challenging to access by educational institutions. Conversely, conventional education is frequently bound by a timetable established by educational institutions, imposing constraints on the time and location of study, which may hinder individuals requiring greater flexibility.

Simulation and Practice: AI-driven education offers technology-enhanced simulations that enable students to hone their abilities without the associated risks or costs of medical or aviation training (Alasadi & Baiz, 2023). Through AI simulations, trainees can engage in repetitive practice inside near-realistic scenarios, devoid of the related expenses or hazards. Conversely, traditional education is generally constrained by physical facilities that entail significant expenses and restricted resources, such as aviation simulators or laboratory space, which may not be accessible to all students.

In general, artificial intelligence provides a number of distinct benefits, including the ability to personalize, provide quick feedback, access to materials, adaptability, and simulation. Artificial intelligence (AI) could be used in education in the future to broaden access to education and improve the quality of education for a greater number of people, thereby overcoming many of the obstacles that are inherent in traditional education.

Education has undergone a significant transformation as a result of artificial intelligence (AI), particularly in terms of the acquisition of skills. One of the most significant benefits of artificial intelligence is its capacity to tailor the educational experience. Learning can be made more effective and efficient with the use of artificial intelligence, which can analyze individual development and modify learning materials according to the requirements and capabilities of students (Mhlanga, 2023). The use of artificial intelligence enables each person to study at their own speed, address areas in which they are lacking, and improve their skills in a manner that is more targeted. This is made possible by real-time personalized learning. When compared to traditional schooling, which has a tendency to take an approach that is universally applicable, this is without a doubt a significant benefit.

Additionally, Renz et al. (2020) explained that artificial intelligence makes education more accessible to more people. Learners are able to access learning materials whenever and wherever they choose, which alleviates the constraints that are associated with traditional education, which is frequently bound to a certain time and location. With the help of an artificial intelligence-based learning platform, students are able to acquire knowledge from a wide variety of sources and delve into subjects that are of interest to them without being constrained by factors such as distance or expense. This is especially helpful for those who have physical constraints, restrict their access to educational institutions, or have a limited amount of time to commit to learning. In addition, artificial intelligence offers a variety of simulations and exercises that can assist learners in acquiring practical skills without the requirement of actual equipment or direct experience. This is particularly useful in the field of aviation and medical training.

The rapidity with which AI can deliver feedback is another of its many key advantages. Students are less likely to have the opportunity to immediately remedy their mistakes or enhance their comprehension when they are provided with feedback in traditional learning systems, which typically occurs after several days or weeks have passed. On the other hand, artificial intelligence (AI) offers instant feedback, which enables students to immediately remedy their errors and continue their education without having to wait for a significant amount of time. Students are able to learn from their mistakes in real time, which helps to speed up the learning process and develop practical abilities. This rapid feedback helps students acquire these skills (Giannakos et al., 2024).

In spite of the numerous benefits that artificial intelligence (AI) provides, traditional education continues to hold a significant amount of value, particularly in terms of the opportunities for social contact and practical experience. Not only is it important for students to be able to master the content, but it is also important for them to engage with their lecturers and other students (Rakuasa et al., 2024). The role of social contact that takes place in the classroom or in study groups cannot be replaced by learning that is based on artificial intelligence. When it comes to the development of social and emotional skills, education continues to be an essential component that includes activities such as discussion, collaboration, and the acquisition of experience through direct engagement with both teachers and fellow students.

Moreover, context-based learning is another essential component that artificial intelligence is not always capable of fulfilling. For students to have a good understanding of many topics, it is necessary for them to be able to apply such concepts to real-world experiences or practical situations. Hands-on experience with tools and situations in the field, for instance, provides a deeper understanding than simply simulations or theoretical material does in the field of engineering or medicine since it allows students to gain practical experience. Practicums, internships, and field experiences are all components of traditional education that cannot be totally replaced by technology. These components contribute to a more comprehensive and in-depth learning environment.

If all goes according to plan, the integration of AI and conventional education will produce a learning environment that is more comprehensive, efficient, and welcoming to all students. Traditional education can provide a solid foundation by means of direct engagement and learning based on context, whereas artificial intelligence has the potential to enhance that experience by enabling personalization, broader access, and in-depth simulations that involve hands-on practice (Helmiatin et al., 2024). Through this method, we are able to capitalize on the advantages of both methodologies in order to develop a learning environment that is more adaptable, flexible, and pertinent in this era of digital technology. In the future, education that combines traditional teaching methods with artificial intelligence will be a more comprehensive and efficient model for the development of abilities that are necessary in a world that is always changing.

ROLE OF ARTIFICIAL INTELLIGENCE IN VOCATIONAL EDUCATION AND ADULT LEARNING

Professional training and adult education are essential in the ever-evolving labor market. A multitude of individuals participate in lifelong learning to enhance their abilities, embrace new technology, or adjust to alterations in their professional environment. The necessity for upskilling is especially critical as numerous industries evolve and transform, presenting new difficulties that demand specific competencies. Artificial intelligence (AI) serves as an indispensable instrument, offering an innovative methodology for creating and administering more tailored, adaptable, and effective training (Chandra et al., 2023).

Artificial intelligence facilitates enhanced individualized education via comprehensive data analysis. By gathering and analyzing data regarding an individual's learning process, AI can customize training materials and content types to align with the learner's comprehension level and pace. This is particularly significant in adult education, as each individual possesses distinct experiences and histories that influence their information processing. AI can pinpoint areas for enhancement and offer customized supplementary resources or activities, resulting in a more pertinent and efficacious learning experience (Utina et al., 2024).

Besides customization, AI offers freedom regarding time and location, which is particularly significant for individuals with demanding schedules. Numerous professions encounter difficulties with conventional training that necessitates attendance at scheduled classes. An AI-driven platform enables training to be accessed at any time and from any location, facilitating learning outside work hours or during leisure time. This flexibility diminishes obstacles for individuals residing in remote areas or those with additional commitments, such as familial obligations, that hinder their ability to attend in-person seminars.

Efficiency represents an additional benefit provided by AI in adult education. AI-driven solutions can deliver quick feedback to learners, enabling them to promptly assess their progress and rectify errors. In contrast to conventional schooling, where feedback is frequently delayed, AI facilitates a more rapid and adaptive learning experience. This is particularly beneficial for training practical abilities that necessitate repetitive practice, such as technical skills or languages, where errors must be rectified promptly to ensure learners may advance without impediment.

The training process can be enhanced with more realistic simulations with AI. In disciplines like as medicine, engineering, or finance, where practical abilities are crucial, AI may generate computer-based simulations that replicate real-world scenarios. Trainees can practice in a secure, regulated setting devoid of real-world hazards, allowing them to refine their abilities repeatedly. In medical training, AI can offer simulations of medical procedures or disease diagnoses, enabling doctors and medical professionals to practice without requiring live patients. This enables students to enhance their talents more effectively and efficiently.

Mhlanga (2023) conveyed that although AI provides numerous advantages in professional training, issues have to be addressed. The disparity in technical access can hinder the efficacy of AI-driven education, particularly in nations or areas with insufficient technological infrastructure. Moreover, although AI can deliver exceptionally tailored learning experiences, some participants may perceive a deficiency in the necessary human involvement within the educational process. This indicates that although AI presents numerous advantages, the presence of a teacher or mentor capable of delivering direct assistance remains crucial for enhancing learning.

Companies such as LinkedIn Learning and Coursera have used AI into their training systems to provide more tailored and adaptable courses. LinkedIn Learning use artificial intelligence to suggest pertinent courses tailored to a user's profile, employment history, and competencies. This assists users in locating training that aligns with their requirements without the necessity of manual searching. Moreover, training applications such as Duolingo employ artificial intelligence to customize language exercises according to users' proficiency, offering immediate and continuous feedback, hence facilitating more effective learning without adherence to a strict curriculum. In this regard, AI enhances the development of professional abilities, expedites learning, and mitigates temporal and spatial limitations.

Customized Education for Professionals

Artificial intelligence facilitates tailored professional training by modifying the content, techniques, and learning speed according to the individual's profile, objectives, and competencies (Chandra et al., 2023). Each adult possesses a distinct learning style and varied work experiences, rendering a standardized method often ineffective. AI utilizes data gathered during the learning process to discern the learner's strengths and limitations, subsequently tailoring the course to address their individual requirements. This facilitates a more effective learning experience, as the content is customized to the learner's capabilities and objectives.

Instances of AI Application

Adaptive learning platforms such as LinkedIn Learning and Coursera for Business employ artificial intelligence to assess a learner's advancement and customize recommended courses accordingly. If a learner demonstrates significant interest in a subject such as data analytics, AI can suggest advanced courses or pertinent supplementary materials. If a learner is having difficulty grasping a specific topic, AI will offer further tasks or more accessible materials to enhance their comprehension. This approach renders training more individualized and efficacious.

Empirical Learning and Immediate Feedback

Artificial intelligence delivers immediate feedback derived from data gathered throughout the learning process. This is essential in professional training, as numerous abilities require continuous practice and refinement (Finlay, 2020). Utilizing data analytics, AI can offer a more precise understanding of learners' development, highlighting areas for correction or enhancement. This instantaneous feedback enables learners to promptly rectify errors and enhance their learning process.

Instances of AI Application

In technical skills training, such as programming or utilizing certain software, AI can offer automated feedback on the written code or the learner's application of the tool. Platforms such as Pluralsight and Udemy utilize artificial intelligence to deliver instantaneous feedback on the tasks or exercises undertaken by the learner. If a learner produces code containing syntax problems, the AI will promptly alert them and offer recommendations for rectification. This accelerates the learning process and facilitates more rapid enhancement compared to feedback provided post-task in conventional training.

Adaptive Learning and Universal Accessibility

For adults, time is a vital element in education. Numerous professionals possess demanding schedules, rendering them unable to consistently participate in training at a predetermined period (Flasiński, 2016). AI facilitates flexible learning, enabling learners to access educational resources at any time and from any location. AI-driven education may be customized to accommodate learners' schedules, allowing them the flexibility to study at their convenience, independent of conventional class timings.

Instances of AI Application

Platforms such as Skillshare and EdX enable professionals to select career-relevant courses and complete them at their convenience. AI can propose information that corresponds with a user's professional objectives and offer additional training that emphasizes abilities demanded by the job market. An individual employed in marketing may be recommended to pursue additional courses in data analytics or digital marketing, customized to align with industry trends and their particular preferences.

Practical Training and Simulation Utilizing Artificial Intelligence

Certain professional competencies necessitate comprehensive practical training. AI facilitates experiential training inside a secure, regulated setting, allowing humans to engage in repeated dialogues or simulations without the apprehension of committing a critical mistake (Ertel, 2024). This form of instruction is particularly crucial in fields like health, aviation, or engineering, where errors can have lethal consequences in real-world scenarios. Employing AI technology, this form of training can be conducted repeatedly and at a reduced expense.

Instances of AI Application

Artificial intelligence is utilized in medical training to develop simulations of medical operations, allowing experts to practice without endangering patients. Platforms such as Osso VR provide VR-based surgical simulations enabling physicians and surgeons to rehearse medical procedures within a wholly secure virtual setting. In domains like aviation and engineering, AI is employed to develop highly realistic simulations, including flight simulators and aircraft engine maintenance, enabling users to train in many settings that would be challenging to reproduce in a physical setting.

Enhancement of Interpersonal Skills

Alongside technical skills, cultivating soft skills, like communication, leadership, and emotional intelligence, is also a crucial aspect of professional training (Garnham, 2017). Artificial intelligence can assist individuals in cultivating these talents via interactive simulations and data-informed feedback. Competencies such as negotiation and public speaking are vital in the professional realm, and AI facilitates more pragmatic and pertinent training in scenarios that closely resemble reality.

Instances of AI Application

Platforms such as Youspeak and Mursion utilize artificial intelligence to generate simulated dialogues or managerial situations. In these simulations, learners can engage in speaking, negotiating, or conducting meetings utilizing an avatar or virtual assistant. The AI offers guidance on improving communication, emotional regulation, and leadership skills. For instance, if a participant demonstrates a deficiency in empathy during a simulated dialogue, the AI will offer recommendations for enhancing their communication abilities in more emotionally nuanced situations.

Ongoing Skill Enhancement

Professional occupations frequently necessitate ongoing skill enhancement due to the perpetual evolution of the labor market and technology. Artificial intelligence facilitates the creation of continuous learning pathways, enabling experts to remain pertinent by tracking industry trends and developments (Holmes, 2020). Through the utilization of AI, trainees receive recommendations for advanced courses and training derived from an assessment of their abilities and evolving market demands, ensuring they remain at the forefront of industry advancements.

Instances of AI Application

AI-driven platforms, like Coursera and LinkedIn Learning, enable users to enhance their abilities through courses that are perpetually revised in accordance with the most recent market trends. Artificial intelligence can pinpoint deficiencies in skills and suggest courses to enhance them, thereby establishing a continuous learning trajectory. For instance, if market trends reveal a high demand for artificial intelligence skills, AI would notify users of new AI-related courses that can assist them in preparing for career chances in this domain.

CONCLUSION

To make a long story short, artificial intelligence significantly transforms our approach to professional training and adult education. AI facilitates the customization of learning experiences according to individual requirements, resulting in more personalized and pertinent education. The system can assess learning data to customize training materials, offer more accurate recommendations, and develop learning pathways that align with the learner's objectives and capabilities. The primary advantage of this technique is its capacity to expedite the learning process, as learners acquire not just information but also experiences tailored to enhance areas requiring improvement as they advance.

Besides personalization, the adaptability provided by AI is also advantageous in the realm of adult education. Numerous professionals are impeded by temporal and geographical limitations when attempting to enhance their skills via conventional training methods. AI-based platforms enable learners to acquire knowledge at any time and from any location, enhancing accessibility to training, particularly for individuals with demanding schedules. This flexibility diminishes the physical and temporal constraints prevalent in conventional education, facilitating the adaptation of learning to one's daily life.

AI is highly proficient at delivering prompt feedback, enabling learners to rectify their errors swiftly. Prompt feedback is particularly crucial in technical skills training, as minor errors might impact the final result. In an AI-driven system, learners need not await the conclusion of a session or assessment to ascertain their progress. They can promptly identify areas for enhancement and implement immediate enhancements. This enhances the efficacy of the learning process and facilitates accelerated learning.

Furthermore, AI's capacity to deliver advanced simulations enables participants to hone practical skills within a secure, regulated setting. In fields necessitating extensive technical or practical expertise, such as medicine, aviation, or engineering, AI-driven simulations enable participants to engage in repetitive practice without incurring real-world dangers. AI-driven surgical simulations enable physicians to refine their abilities without the necessity of real patients, while flight simulators provide pilots with the expertise of managing emergency scenarios. This expedites the learning process and equips participants for practical scenarios in the field.

Nonetheless, despite the numerous benefits of AI, problems persist, including disparities in technological access and the significance of social interaction in the learning process. Conventional education holds significant significance in cultivating social and emotional competencies, which AI cannot entirely replicate. Engagement with educators and classmates offers a significant social dimension to the learning process. Consequently, although AI has numerous benefits regarding efficiency and customization, a balance must be maintained with aspects of traditional education grounded in human connection.

Practical instances of AI in professional training are evident on sites such as LinkedIn Learning and Udemy, which utilize AI to deliver tailored course recommendations to users. A professional seeking to enhance data analytics abilities can be offered courses customized to their competency level and areas for development, informed by their learning history. Moreover, systems such as Duolingo are utilizing AI to deliver adaptive language learning, wherein materials and exercises are customized to the user's proficiency, hence offering a more individualized and efficient experience. Such developments illustrate how AI may enhance the efficacy of professional training, expedite learning, and create additional chances for skill development in a rapidly evolving workplace.

REFERENCES

Alasadi, E. A., & Baiz, C. R. (2023). Generative AI in education and research: Opportunities, concerns, and solutions. *Journal of Chemical Education, 100*(8), 2965–2971. DOI: 10.1021/acs.jchemed.3c00323

Berendt, B., Littlejohn, A., & Blakemore, M. (2020). AI in education: Learner choice and fundamental rights. *Learning, Media and Technology*, *45*(3), 312–324. DOI: 10.1080/17439884.2020.1786399

Camilleri, P. (2018). Robot-proof: Higher education in the age of artificial intelligence. *Journal of Education for Teaching*, *44*(4), 519–520. DOI: 10.1080/02607476.2018.1500792

Chandra, M. J. A., Fernando, Z. J., & Wahyuni, P. M. (2023). The New Navigation of Education: Opportunities and Challenges for Artificial Intelligence (AI) Lecturers in Indonesia. In *Proceeding of the International Conference on Innovation in Open and Distance Learning* (Vol. 4, pp. 939-957).

Ciampa, K., Wolfe, Z., & Hensley, M. (2024). From entry to transformation: Exploring AI integration in teachers' K–12 assessment practices. *Technology, Pedagogy and Education*, •••, 1–20. DOI: 10.1080/1475939X.2024.2413378

Ertel, W. (2024). *Introduction to artificial intelligence.* Springer Nature., DOI: 10.1007/978-3-658-43102-0

Finlay, J. (2020). *An introduction to artificial intelligence.* Crc Press., DOI: 10.1201/9781003072485

Flasiński, M. (2016). *Introduction to artificial intelligence.* Springer., DOI: 10.1007/978-3-319-40022-8

Gabriel, F., Marrone, R., Van Sebille, Y., Kovanovic, V., & de Laat, M. (2022). Digital education strategies around the world: Practices and policies. *Irish Educational Studies*, *41*(1), 85–106. DOI: 10.1080/03323315.2021.2022513

Garnham, A. (2017). *Artificial intelligence: An introduction.* Routledge., DOI: 10.4324/9780203704394

Ghosh, M., & Thirugnanam, A. (2021). Introduction to Artificial Intelligence. In: Srinivasa, K.G., G. M., S., Sekhar, S.R.M. (eds) Artificial Intelligence for Information Management: A Healthcare Perspective. Studies in Big Data, vol 88. Springer, Singapore. https://doi.org/DOI: 10.1007/978-981-16-0415-7_2

Giannakos, M., Azevedo, R., Brusilovsky, P., Cukurova, M., Dimitriadis, Y., Hernandez-Leo, D., Järvelä, S., Mavrikis, M., & Rienties, B. (2024). The promise and challenges of generative AI in education. *Behaviour & Information Technology*, •••, 1–27. DOI: 10.1080/0144929X.2024.2394886

Harrison, J. H.Jr, Gilbertson, J. R., Hanna, M. G., Olson, N. H., Seheult, J. N., Sorace, J. M., & Stram, M. N. (2021). Introduction to artificial intelligence and machine learning for pathology. *Archives of Pathology & Laboratory Medicine, 145*(10), 1228–1254. DOI: 10.5858/arpa.2020-0541-CP PMID: 33493264

Helmiatin, H., Hidayat, A., & Kahar, M. R. (2024). Investigating the adoption of AI in higher education: A study of public universities in Indonesia. *Cogent Education, 11*(1), 2380175. Advance online publication. DOI: 10.1080/2331186X.2024.2380175

Holmes, W. (2020). Artificial intelligence in education. In *Encyclopedia of education and information technologies* (pp. 88–103). Springer International Publishing., DOI: 10.1007/978-3-030-10576-1_107

Holmes, W., Bialik, M., & Fadel, C. (2019). *Artificial intelligence in education promises and implications for teaching and learning*. Center for Curriculum Redesign.

Iqbal, M., Nasir, J., Supriyadi, A., Nurhayati, S., Hafidzah, H., Pernando, Y., & Purtiningrum, S. W. (2024). *Konsep Kecerdasan Buatan* (Vol. CV). Gita Lentera.

Jackson, P. C. (2019). *Introduction to artificial intelligence*. Courier Dover Publications.

Jakob, J. C. (2023). Exploring the Use of Flipped Classroom in Influencing Listening Comprehension of Civil Engineering Students. [Indonesian Journal of English Teaching]. *IJET, 12*(1), 48–56. DOI: 10.15642/ijet2.2023.12.1.48-56

Jakob, J. C., Sari, H. F. A., Wuarlela, M., Persulessy, S. I., Saptenno, S., Nussy, H., & Salawaney, V. S. (2024). How Does Technology-Assisted Language Learning (TALL) Influence Elementary School Students Learning? *IDEAS: Journal on English Language Teaching and Learning. Linguistics and Literature, 12*(2), 1633–1646. DOI: 10.24256/ideas.v12i2.5860

Kalogirou, S. A. (2007). Introduction to artificial intelligence technology. *Artificial intelligence in energy and renewable energy systems*, 1-46.

Le, A. V., & Metzger, W. (2024). Assessing the impact and challenges of AI-based language models on the education sector: A proposal for new assessment strategies and design. *Journal of Teaching in Travel & Tourism, 24*(2), 167–178. DOI: 10.1080/15313220.2024.2311907

Liu, Z., & Yushchik, E. (2024). Exploring the prospects of using artificial intelligence in education. *Cogent Education, 11*(1), 2353464. Advance online publication. DOI: 10.1080/2331186X.2024.2353464

Luo, Z., & Zhang, X. (2024). AI in education risk assessment mechanism analysis. *Applied Economics*, •••, 1–13. DOI: 10.1080/00036846.2024.2321835

Mhlanga, D. (2023). Open AI in Education, the Responsible and Ethical Use of ChatGPT Towards Lifelong Learning. In *FinTech and Artificial Intelligence for Sustainable Development*. Sustainable Development Goals Series. Palgrave Macmillan., DOI: 10.1007/978-3-031-37776-1_17

Mintz, Y., & Brodie, R. (2019). Introduction to artificial intelligence in medicine. *Minimally Invasive Therapy & Allied Technologies, 28*(2), 73–81. DOI: 10.1080/13645706.2019.1575882 PMID: 30810430

Ohyver, D. A., Junaidi, S., & Adawiyah, R. (2024). *Buku Ajar Kecerdasan Buatan*. PT. Sonpedia Publishing Indonesia.

Pedro, F., Subosa, M., Rivas, A., & Valverde, P. (2019). Artificial intelligence in education: Challenges and opportunities for sustainable development.

Perrotta, C., & Selwyn, N. (2019). Deep learning goes to school: Toward a relational understanding of AI in education. *Learning, Media and Technology, 45*(3), 251–269. DOI: 10.1080/17439884.2020.1686017

Persulessy, S. I., Nikijuluw, R. P. V., & Jakob, J. C. (2024). Utilizing Artificial Intelligence in Language Learning: What About Engineering Students' Perception? *Journal of English Education Program, 5*(1). Advance online publication. DOI: 10.26418/jeep.v5i1.71159

Plant, R. (2011). An introduction to artificial intelligence. In *32nd Aerospace Sciences Meeting and Exhibit* (p. 294).

Pratiwi, H. (2024). *Buku ajar kecerdasan buatan: disertai praktik baik pemanfaatannya*. Asadel Liamsindo Teknologi.

Qadir, J. (2023, May). Engineering education in the era of ChatGPT: Promise and pitfalls of generative AI for education. In *2023 IEEE Global Engineering Education Conference (EDUCON)* (pp. 1-9). IEEE. https://doi.org/DOI: 10.1109/EDUCON54358.2023.10125121

Rahm, L. (2024). 'Help!? My students created an evil AI': On the irony of speculative methods and design fiction. *Learning, Media and Technology*, •••, 1–15. DOI: 10.1080/17439884.2024.2367707

Rakuasa, H., Faris, D. A., & Hidayatullah, M. (2024). Transforming Education in the Age of Artificial Intelligence: Challenges and Opportunities in Indonesia, A Literature Review. [JEI]. *Journal Education Innovation*, *2*(1), 180–186.

Renz, A., Krishnaraja, S., & Gronau, E. (2020). Demystification of Artificial Intelligence in Education – How much AI is really in the Educational Technology? [iJAI]. *International Journal of Learning Analytics and Artificial Intelligence for Education*, *2*(1), 14–30. DOI: 10.3991/ijai.v2i1.12675

Rosid, M. A. (2022). Buku Ajar Kecerdasan Buatan/Artificial Intelegent (AI). *Umsida Press*, 1-197.

Sajja, P. S., & Sajja, P. S. (2021). Introduction to artificial intelligence. *Illustrated Computational Intelligence: Examples and Applications*, 1-25. https://doi.org/DOI: 10.1007/978-981-15-9589-9_1

Su, J., & Yang, W. (2023). Unlocking the power of ChatGPT: A framework for applying generative AI in education. *ECNU Review of Education*, *6*(3), 355–366. DOI: 10.1177/20965311231168423

Utina, S. S., Chusniyah, T., Inseachiangmai, J., Zahra, G. A., & Pambudi, K. S. (2024). A comparative study of artificial intelligence in education psychology: The cases of Indonesia and Thailand. *Bulletin of Social Informatics Theory and Application*, *8*(1), 70–85. DOI: 10.31763/businta.v8i1.663

Wang, Y., Fu, E. Y., Zhai, X., Yang, C., & Pei, F. (2024). Introduction of Artificial Intelligence. In Huang, X., & Tam, W. C. (Eds.), *Intelligent Building Fire Safety and Smart Firefighting. Digital Innovations in Architecture, Engineering and Construction*. Springer., DOI: 10.1007/978-3-031-48161-1_4

Wellner, G., & Levin, I. (2023). Ihde meets Papert: Combining postphenomenology and constructionism for a future agenda of philosophy of education in the era of digital technologies. *Learning, Media and Technology*, *49*(4), 656–669. DOI: 10.1080/17439884.2023.2251388

Winston, P. H. (1984). *Artificial intelligence*. Addison-Wesley Longman Publishing Co., Inc.

Zebua, R. S. Y., Khairunnisa, K., Hartatik, H., Pariyadi, P., Wahyuningtyas, D. P., Thantawi, A. M., ... & Kharisma, L. P. I. (2023). *Fenomena Artificial Intelligence (Ai)*. PT. Sonpedia Publishing Indonesia.

Zhang, L., Pan, Y., Wu, X., & Skibniewski, M. J. (2021). Introduction to Artificial Intelligence. In *Artificial Intelligence in Construction Engineering and Management. Lecture Notes in Civil Engineering* (Vol. 163). Springer., DOI: 10.1007/978-981-16-2842-9_1

Chapter 7
AI Policy Framework in Education for Advancing Society 5.0 with Safe AI Implementation

Muhammad Fachrurrazy
https://orcid.org/0000-0003-3742-4993
Institut Agama Islam Negeri Palopo, Indonesia

Firmansyah Firmansyah
https://orcid.org/0009-0004-1391-9718
Insititut Agama Islam Negeri Palopo, Indonesia

Rahmawati Beddu
https://orcid.org/0009-0006-6335-6698
Institut Agama Islam Negeri Palopo, Indonesia

Fitriani Jamaluddin
https://orcid.org/0000-0001-6923-8904
Institut Agama Islam Negeri Palopo, Indonesia

Erwatul Efendi
https://orcid.org/0009-0001-2002-6465
Insititut Agama Islam Negeri Palopo, Indonesia

Dirah Nurmila SIliwadi
https://orcid.org/0009-0002-6640-0544
Institut Agama Islam Negeri Palopo, Indonesia

ABSTRACT

Artificial intelligence in education can transform learning and enhance institutional efficiency. The rapid use of AI generates ethical, legal, and safety concerns, particularly for educational institutions and universities. This study delineates a comprehensive policy framework for the secure and ethical application of AI in education. The framework encompasses data privacy, algorithmic bias, equitable access, and the digital rights of students and educators, in accordance with the concepts of Society 5.0, which seeks to reconcile technological progress with societal well-being. Policymakers, educators, technologists, and legal experts should work

DOI: 10.4018/979-8-3373-5781-2.ch007

to design adaptive policies that balance innovation with risk mitigation. We support transparent governance of AI, systematic audits of AI technologies, and training in AI literacy for educators. The study emphasizes the importance of aligning these policies with global standards and local educational objectives to ensure an inclusive, safe, and progressive educational environment.

INTRODUCTION TO AI IN EDUCATIONAL SETTINGS

Background and Context

Evolution of AI in Education

Artificial Intelligence (AI) has swiftly advanced to become a fundamental component of various sectors, including education. AI fundamentally pertains to the creation of systems or machines capable of executing tasks that ordinarily necessitate human intelligence. (Gentili, 2022) In educational environments, AI covers diverse applications, such as automated grading systems, individualized learning platforms, AI-driven tutoring assistance, and administrative efficiency. The primary goal of AI in education is to enhance learning experiences, improve administrative efficiency, and provide personalized educational pathways for students.

The dimensions of AI in education span multiple facets, each contributing to the holistic development of teaching and learning environments. The use of AI in education is to enhance the learning experience, increase efficiency in administration, and provide personalized educational pathways for learners and students. The dimensions of AI in education cover various aspects, each of which contributes to the improvement of the teaching and learning environment. (Zhang & Aslan, 2023)

Importance of AI in Advancing Educational Goals

AI improves educational tools, AI education applications were grading and tutoring. AI improves learning. Machine learning algorithms find student performance trends in vast datasets, providing instructors and students with fast, accurate feedback. (Artificial Intelligence and the Future of Teaching and Learning, 2023) AI and Teaching and Learning Implications Recent AI integration includes adaptive learning systems that modify assignment difficulty based on a student's learning pace and virtual classrooms with AI-driven chatbots and virtual assistants for real-time support. (Tanjga, 2023) Textbooks and interactive learning materials are being made with AI, making education more accessible and inclusive.

Recent AI integration includes adaptive learning systems that match assignment complexity to a student's learning rate and virtual classrooms with chatbots and virtual assistants for rapid support. (Generative Artificial Intelligence for Education and Pedagogy, 2024)

Protecting data, ethical AI research, training educators, and managing AI-driven applications can reduce risks with a strong regulatory framework. The rules protect instructors and boost AI trust. Canada, Japan, and the EU's Ethical Guidelines for AI show education must balance innovation and accountability. In educational institutions, clear laws ensure ethical use of AI systems, encouraging technology to help improve human connection rather than replace it. (Artificial Intelligence and the Future of Teaching and Learning, 2023) Establishing trust among educators, students, and parents necessitates that regulations governing AI systems emphasize transparency and explainability.

Artificial intelligence is changing global education systems, requiring clear guidelines for its use. (Artificial Intelligence and the Future of Teaching and Learning, 2023) AI can improve education, but safety, equity, and inclusion must be prioritized to maximize its benefits and minimize its risks. Studied AI's rise in education and its impact on academics, as well as AI security policies.

Society 5.0 Concept

Defining Society 5.0 and its Relation to Education

Society 5.0 envisions a future centered on human well-being and sustainability, where advanced technologies, including AI, collaborate with human society to address the complex challenges of modern life. Japan pioneered the implementation of Society 5.0 within the framework of its fifth industrial revolution (Holroyd, 2023). Cyber-physical systems were used to transition from agrarian Society 1.0 to information-driven Society 4.0. Artificial intelligence, big data, and the Internet of Things work together to improve living standards, productivity, and sustainability (Radanliev et al., 2020).

Role of AI in Shaping a Future Society

AI helps Society 5.0 build a personalized, tech-savvy environment. Human and machine intelligence benefit cities, businesses, healthcare, and schools. This perspective uses technology to increase human well-being rather than profit and efficiency to transform societal processes' impact on future societies. To serve the knowledge society, Society 5.0 must incorporate AI into education (Ahmad et al., 2023; Onesi-Ozigagun, 2024). Education systems are increasingly recognized as crucial for developing communities that can survive in an age of advanced technology. Artificial intelligence enhances personalized learning, reducing educational inequities and offering high-quality education to varied demographics, especially those in remote or disadvantaged places (Kamalov & Gurrib, 2023). In Society 5.0, education emphasizes creativity, critical thinking, and collaborative problem-solving skills needed to navigate future difficulties.

Machine learning, natural language processing, and adaptive learning platforms provide personalized, scalable education. AI-driven systems can evaluate student learning and tailor training to providing timely feedback promotes student learning. This personalized approach helps all students succeed, regardless of background or ability. AI may help teachers with administrative tasks. Teachers would have more time with students and less scheduling and grading stress. Personalized education helps educators grow professionally (Kamalov et al., 2023), preparing pupils for future problems.

Artificial intelligence must be ethical, transparent, and secure, especially in education, to contribute to Society 5.0. Data privacy breaches, algorithmic prejudice, and incorrect AI use in education demand safe AI legislation. Safe AI rules are necessary to mitigate data privacy breaches, algorithmic prejudice, and incorrect AI use in education, (Huang, 2023) essential considerations must be considered when creating such policies.

1. **Data Privacy and Security:** The protection of data privacy and security is paramount, as it is essential to safeguard student privacy and to ensure secure management of educational data. Educational institutions are required to establish comprehensive data governance frameworks that adhere to international data protection regulations and safeguard personal information.
2. **Ethical Utilization of Artificial Intelligence:** AI systems within the educational sector must be developed with the intention of mitigating biases that may contribute to the perpetuation of inequality or discrimination. It is imperative that policies mandate the implementation of ethical practices in artificial intelligence, which encompass transparency in algorithmic decision-making processes and accountability for resultant outcomes.
3. **Training and Support for Teachers:** It is very important for teachers to keep learning about AI literacy so that they can use AI tools effectively in their lessons and also fully understand the systems' limitations and possible biases.
4. **Inclusive Education:** It is imperative that policies promote the inclusive application of artificial intelligence, thereby ensuring that all students (Tadimalla & Maher, 2024), regardless of their backgrounds or abilities, can derive benefits

from AI-enhanced educational resources. This encompasses the accommodation of diverse learning styles and the promotion of a collaborative learning environment, which is bolstered by AI-enhanced group dynamics.

Through the establishment of an environment that fosters the secure and equitable integration of AI, educational organizations can make substantial contributions to the progression of the objectives related to Society 5.0. This will establish a future in which artificial intelligence enhances educational outcomes while simultaneously contributing to the greater social good. Carefully crafted and thoughtfully structured policies possess the capability to enhance artificial intelligence in fostering a society that is more resilient, adaptive, and inclusive, thereby increasing its ability to address the challenges of the 21st century (Schiff et al., 2021).

Purpose and Scope of the Policy Framework

The rapid adoption of AI in education has pros and cons. AI can personalize education, improve administrative efficiency, and provide data-driven learning insights. This technology must be used ethically, safely, and fairly. The AI Policy Framework in Education addresses ethical, safety, and equity issues in education (Taddeo & Floridi, 2018; Tanveer et al., 2020).

The framework seeks to promote fairness, transparency, accountability, and inclusivity within educational AI systems. The framework prioritizes these core values to prepare for the responsible and effective use of AI in education, especially in Society 5.0. As AI transforms education, policymakers, educators, and other stakeholders must work together to design, implement, and refine policies to benefit all students and mitigate risks.

Ensuring Safe and Responsible AI Deployment

The implementation of AI technologies in educational settings must be approached with utmost caution to ensure the safety and well-being of students, educators, and institutions. To protect students, educators, and institutions, AI technologies in education must be implemented carefully. AI system security and misuse testing is essential to the policy framework (Smuha, 2020; Khosravi et al., 2022). For example, AI algorithms without oversight may reinforce biases, especially against under-represented or marginalized groups. To protect student's personal data, AI systems must follow strict data privacy regulations like the GDPR when collecting, storing, and processing data.

AI technologies must be transparent so educators, students, and regulators can monitor them. Grade-based and student assessment AI-driven decision-making systems should explain their decisions clearly. Transparency fosters trust and enables stakeholders to hold AI systems accountable (Chaudhry et al., 2022).

Emphasis on Ethics, Safety, and Equity in Education

The deployment of artificial intelligence for monitoring students must be conducted with caution to avoid infringing on their privacy or autonomy. The equity of AI deployment is a significant concern. Policies must guarantee that AI enhances education for all students, irrespective of socioeconomic status, geographical location, or special requirements.

Traditional educational systems may overlook students who may benefit from personalised learning resources from AI (Zawacki-Richter et al., 2019). AI-powered tools can adapt learning materials to different learning styles, provide real-time feedback, and help students who need it. To make AI truly equitable, schools must provide all students with the necessary technologies, training, and resources. AI must promote inclusive education. In Society 5.0, it is essential to ensure that AI tools are customised for the majority of users, including individuals with disabilities. AI-based tools for students with cognitive and limitations in language can facilitate equitable chances for education.

The AI policy framework covers curriculum design, teaching methods, student assessments, administrative functions, and student support systems (Holmes et al., 2021; Tanveer, 2020). It provides guidelines for AI tool development and implementation in K-12 and higher education. The policy framework should adapt to AI technology changes while upholding ethical, safety, and equity standards. The framework must facilitate collaboration among policymakers, educators, technology developers, and students to sustain the integration of AI in education. (Abdul et al. 2024) Educational policies that address the needs for the system and society must engage all society 5.0

In conclusion, the education AI policy framework increases the safe, ethical, and equitable deployment of AI, building a supportive and inclusive learning environment that enhances student outcomes and advances a human-centric future. The implementation of responsible AI can enhance educational outcomes and protect student rights.

THE NEED FOR AI POLICIES IN EDUCATION

Current Trends in AI Utilization in Education

AI has significantly altered the domains of teaching, administration, and learning within the educational sector. Artificial intelligence is streamlining administrative tasks and customising educational experiences, thereby influencing the future of education. The integration of AI in education necessitates thorough policy assessment to guarantee responsible and secure implementation. (Bittencourt et al. 2020) describe **Society 5.0** as a human-centric paradigm that integrates technology with human needs, influencing education AI policy.

Examples of AI Tools in Teaching, Administration, and Learning

AI applications in pedagogy, administration, and education show its classroom potential. The most common AI tools in education are intelligent tutoring systems (ITS), adaptive learning platforms, and AI-driven "Learning Management System". (Artificial Intelligence and the Future of Education, n.d.) To create personalised learning pathways, these systems evaluate student performance and adjust content and pacing. Example, Knewton and DreamBox personalise lectures in real time using AI. This customised approach can boost student engagement and performance by accommodating different learning styles.

Furthermore, AI-assisted content generation is progressively utilised in educational environments. AI-driven solutions, including ScribeSense and Quillionz, facilitate the quick generation of quizzes, assignments, and educational materials for educators (Ouyang & Jiao, 2021). These tools can optimise the curriculum preparation process, enabling educators to concentrate more on instruction and less on administrative duties. The advent of natural language processing (NLP) tools, such as Grammarly (Mozer et al., 2019) and ChatGPT (Khan et al., 2023), empowers students and educators to enhance writing, cultivate critical thinking, and participate in interactive dialogues, thereby improving the quality of communication and content creation.

AI in Administrative Functions

The function of AI extends beyond educational settings. AI is enhancing admissions processes, scheduling, grading, and resource allocation within educational institutions. Chatbots address student enquiries, thereby allowing administrative staff to focus on more complex responsibilities. AI solutions like Xenegrade automate gradebooks, enabling educators to manage student evaluations more efficiently and consistently. AI's ability to process large datasets also aids in student recruitment and retention by identifying patterns and predicting future needs (Artificial Intelligence in Higher Education: Applications, Promise and Perils, and Ethical Questions, 2019) thereby allowing institutions to allocate resources more efficiently.

Analytics tools powered by artificial intelligence are utilized to track student progress and effectively identify students at risk. Instruments like Civitas Learning and BrightBytes analyze student data to yield insights into learning outcomes and engagement, assisting administrators in making data-driven decisions to enhance institutional effectiveness.

Opportunities AI Offers for Personalized Education

AI can personalize education like never before. In contrast to traditional teaching methods, artificial intelligence allows large-scale personalized education. Chinese personal learning platforms like Squirrel AI use AI algorithms to track students' progress and provide tailored resources and feedback. (Cui et al. 2019) This allows students to learn at their own pace and gives them a chance to succeed. AI provides customized learning resources for disabled and special needs students, improving inclusive education. Microsoft's Seeing AI and speech recognition software for learning disabled students improve accessibility and inclusion.

Challenges in AI Implementation

The integration of AI in education offers transformative opportunities but also significant challenges. To establish comprehensive regulations ensuring equitable, safe, and ethical AI use in educational institutions, these issues must be addressed immediately. To promote the proper use of artificial intelligence in Society 5.0, a human-centric society using technology to solve problems, these issues must be addressed.

Data Privacy and Security Concerns

Student data privacy and security are major obstacles to AI in education. To provide personalized education, artificial intelligence systems need sensitive data like student performance metrics, behavioral patterns, and personal identifiers. Without proper security, this data can be compromised and misused. Educational platform data breaches, including cloud-based student record disclosures, highlight the risks of inadequate cybersecurity protocols. (Alamleh, 2020) Students and parents are unaware of how their data is collected, stored, and used, which raises privacy concerns.

The challenge is further exacerbated by regulations such as the General Data Protection Regulation (GDPR) and the Children's Online Privacy Protection Act (COPPA), which impose rigorous data protection standards. Although these regulations are designed to protect privacy, educational institutions (Lievens & Verdoodt, 2017; Legislation and Ethics, 2020) may encounter difficulties in achieving compliance as a result of constrained resources and insufficient technical expertise. Consequently, it is imperative that policies emphasise the importance of secure data management practices, transparency, and accountability within AI applications to effectively mitigate these risks.

Ethical Dilemmas and Biases in AI Systems

AI systems are not immune to biases, which can lead to ethical dilemmas in their implementation. These biases often stem from the datasets used to train AI models, which may reflect societal prejudices or lack diversity. In an educational context, biased AI algorithms can perpetuate inequalities, disadvantaging certain groups of students. (Chen, 2023)

If its training data disproportionately represents privileged demographics, an AI-powered admission system may unintentionally favor them. Language-processing AI tools may also struggle to accommodate dialect-speaking students, marginalizing underrepresented communities.

AI systems making educational decisions like grading or admissions raise ethical concerns. These decisions require nuanced judgment that AI systems may lack. To make AI tools fair, transparent, and less unequal, policies must be set.

Digital Divide and Access Inequalities

AI in education may widen the digital divide. While AI could democratize education, its benefits are not evenly distributed. Rural and low-income students may not have the gadgets, internet, or digital competence to employ AI-based learning tools.

Online learning during the COVID-19 epidemic revealed resource disparities, preventing millions of students from participating. Without deliberate efforts, AI integration could widen these gaps.

Additionally, institutions in developing regions may struggle to adopt AI due to limited infrastructure, funding, and technical expertise. To address these inequalities, policies must promote equitable access to AI technologies (Smith & Neupane, 2023; Alami et al., 2020) by investing in digital infrastructure, subsidizing resources for underserved communities, and fostering digital literacy programs.

The challenges of AI implementation in education—data privacy and security, ethical dilemmas and biases, and the digital divide underscore the need for a comprehensive policy framework. Such a framework should align with the principles of **Society 5.0**, emphasizing ethical, inclusive, and human-centered approaches to technology. By addressing these challenges proactively, educational institutions can harness the potential of AI while safeguarding the rights and interests of all stakeholders.

Global Policy Landscape

The global policy landscape for Artificial Intelligence (AI) in education is evolving, with countries adopting diverse approaches to balance innovation and regulation. (Chang et al., 2024) As AI technologies become integral to teaching, administration, and learning, a comparative analysis of existing international policies highlights critical areas for developing a robust framework that aligns with the principles of **Society 5.0**.

Existing AI Policies in Education Worldwide

Several countries have pioneered AI strategies that include education-specific components. For instance, China has invested heavily in AI-driven education, embedding AI tools into its classrooms and fostering partnerships between educational institutions and tech companies. (Liang, 2020) The Chinese government's Next Generation Artificial Intelligence Development Plan emphasizes AI literacy and talent cultivation from an early age.

Similarly, Singapore has integrated AI into its national education strategy through its AI Governance Framework and initiatives such as the AI in Education Roadmap. (Kim et al., 2021; Goode et al., 2023) These efforts focus on using AI for personalized learning while ensuring data privacy and ethical use.

The European Union has taken a human-centered approach, incorporating education into its broader Ethics Guidelines for Trustworthy AI. The EU emphasizes transparency, inclusivity, and alignment with fundamental rights, aiming to ensure that AI systems in education are fair and accountable.

Comparative Analysis of International Approaches

A key distinction in global approaches lies in balancing innovation with regulation. While countries like China prioritize technological advancement and large-scale implementation, European nations emphasize ethical considerations and privacy safeguards. The United States, meanwhile, follows a market-driven approach, with significant reliance on private sector innovation and limited federal regulation. (Buckley et al., 2019)

These variations reflect differing cultural, social, and economic priorities. A comparative analysis underscores the need for a balanced policy framework that incorporates the strengths of these approaches—ensuring ethical AI use, fostering innovation, and addressing global challenges such as the digital divide. Such policies are crucial for advancing the goals of a responsible Society 5.0.

KEY COMPONENTS OF A RESPONSIBLE AI POLICY FRAMEWORK

Ethical Guidelines for AI in Education

The implementation of Artificial Intelligence (AI) in education requires robust ethical guidelines to ensure fairness, transparency, and accountability. These principles are essential to fostering trust, promoting inclusivity, and ensuring that AI technologies are used responsibly in alignment with the vision of Society 5.0, a human-centered society leveraging technology for social good.

Fairness in AI Systems

Fairness underpins ethical AI in education. AI systems must treat students and stakeholders equally, without prejudice based on race, gender, socioeconomic background, or other protected characteristics. AI programs can accidentally introduce biases, making fairness difficult. Training AI models with uneven or non-representative datasets commonly causes these biases. A privileged demographic's history data may train an AI-powered admissions tool to perpetuate inequities. Ethical rules must require diverse and representative datasets. Regular AI system audits should be encouraged by policymakers to uncover and minimize biases and ensure equitable outcomes for all learners.

Transparency in AI Operations

AI transparency entails explaining AI processes to instructors, students, and parents. Many AI systems are "black boxes," with opaque decision-making. Lack of clarity can damage confidence and make error and bias correction difficult. Ethics must force AI developers to clarify how algorithms work, what data they use, and how judgments are made. Institutions should also allow stakeholders to challenge

AI-driven judgments. Transparency helps users critically evaluate AI systems, building trust and knowledge.

Accountability for AI Outcomes

Accountability ensures that developers, implementers, and institutions are responsible for the impacts of AI systems. Without clear accountability structures, it becomes difficult to address harm caused by AI-driven errors or biases. Ethical guidelines should define roles and responsibilities for all stakeholders involved in AI implementation.

For instance, if an AI tool misidentifies at-risk students, leading to inadequate intervention, the institution using the tool and the developer must be held accountable. This can be achieved by requiring clear agreements on liability, implementing regular impact assessments, and establishing oversight bodies to monitor AI use in education.

Ensuring Non-Bias and Inclusivity Ensuring Non-Bias and Inclusivity in AI Algorithms

Inclusivity is central to ethical AI in education, ensuring that systems are designed to accommodate the diverse needs of all learners. AI algorithms must be developed with inclusivity in mind, addressing the unique challenges faced by marginalized communities, students with disabilities, and those in underserved areas.

For example, AI-driven learning platforms should provide language support for students from diverse linguistic backgrounds and offer features like speech-to-text and text-to-speech to support students with disabilities. Ethical guidelines should encourage collaborative design processes involving educators, students, and experts from diverse fields to ensure that AI systems are truly inclusive.

Data Privacy and Security Measures

As Artificial Intelligence (AI) becomes an integral part of educational settings, the protection of students' personal data and the establishment of safe data-sharing protocols are paramount. With data being the backbone of AI applications, ensuring privacy and security is essential for fostering trust and safeguarding the rights of students, educators, and institutions. This focus aligns with the principles of **Society 5.0**, emphasizing a balance between technological advancement and human-centric values.

Protection of Students' Personal Data

AI applications in education rely on large volumes of data, including sensitive personal information such as academic records, behavioral patterns, and demographic details. Without robust protections, this data is vulnerable to breaches, unauthorized access, and misuse, posing risks to students' privacy and safety.

Ethical guidelines must mandate strict adherence to data protection laws such as the General Data Protection Regulation (GDPR) and Children's Online Privacy Protection Act (COPPA). These regulations provide frameworks for obtaining consent, limiting data collection to necessary information, and ensuring that data is stored securely. For instance, schools and institutions should implement encryption protocols to protect data during storage and transmission, minimizing the risk of unauthorized access.

Safe Data-Sharing Protocols for AI Applications

Effective AI applications often require data-sharing among various stakeholders, such as schools, technology providers, and researchers. However, this sharing must be conducted under strict protocols to prevent misuse and ensure compliance with privacy regulations.

One critical measure is the adoption of **data anonymization** techniques. By removing or encrypting personally identifiable information (PII), institutions can share data while minimizing privacy risks. For example, anonymized data can be used to train AI algorithms or conduct research without compromising individual students' identities.

Secure data-sharing agreements are another vital component. These agreements should outline the responsibilities of all parties involved, including data access limitations, permitted uses, and data retention policies. Educational institutions must work closely with AI developers and third-party providers to ensure that data-sharing practices align with ethical and legal standards.

To enhance security, institutions can also employ **blockchain technology** for data sharing. Blockchain offers a decentralized, tamper-proof ledger that records data transactions transparently and securely. This technology can ensure that all parties involved in data-sharing are accountable and that data integrity is maintained.

Building a Culture of Data Security

In addition to technical measures, fostering a culture of data security is essential. Institutions should provide regular training for educators and staff on data protection practices, including recognizing phishing attempts, using strong passwords, and managing access controls. Students and parents should also be educated about their role in maintaining data security and understanding their privacy rights.

Teacher and Student Involvement in Policy Development

The role of educators and students in shaping artificial intelligence (AI) policies for educational settings is critical to fostering a responsible AI ecosystem in schools and institutions.(Tanveer et al., 2020) As AI technologies are increasingly integrated into classrooms, it is essential to ensure that both teachers and students are actively involved in the development and implementation of AI policies. Their involvement helps ensure that these policies align with the needs of the educational community, promote digital literacy, and maintain ethical standards in AI usage. (Bulut & Beiting-Parrish, 2024)

Role of Educators in Shaping AI Policies

Teachers are crucial to integrating AI into education. As primary facilitators of learning, they ensure students can safely and effectively use AI tools. Teachers must be recognised as AI end-users and policy stakeholders. (Artificial Intelligence and the Future of Teaching and Learning, 2023) Their comprehension of pedagogical objectives and classroom interactions enables them to offer valuable insights into the utilisation of AI for the enhancement of teaching and learning.

Successful AI policies must align with the concerns and objectives of the educators responsible for their implementation. Educators understand the difficulties in preserving educational quality, equity, and inclusivity. Their insights are crucial in creating frameworks that reconcile technological advancement with educational integrity. Professional development programs must be structured to provide educators with the essential skills and knowledge required for involvement in policy development and critical engagement with AI tools. This encompasses an examination of the ethical implications of AI, its potential for bias, and the associated risks regarding data privacy. (Nguyen et al., 2022) Educators inform policymakers and students about AI technologies in education. Direct interactions with AI applications, such as adaptive learning platforms and AI-driven assessment tools, allow policy refinement by monitoring positive and negative outcomes.

Promoting Digital Literacy for Students and Teachers

Responsible AI use in education requires digital literacy. (JOYCE & Harris, 2018) Teachers and students must understand AI's mechanisms, applications, and implications. For ethical and effective AI adoption, a policy framework should prioritize digital literacy training for both groups. Digital literacy for educators requires critical analysis of AI's effects on education, society, and individual rights, not just AI tool use. Educators must understand AI biases and their effects on learning. This knowledge enables educators to make informed decisions regarding AI tools in their classrooms (Wang, 2020) and to advocate for policies that protect students' best interests.

Engaging educators and students in the formulation of AI policies ensures that these policies are grounded in practical experiences and empowers both groups to actively participate in shaping the future of AI in education. Educational institutions can prepare future learners and educators to navigate an AI-enhanced world responsibly by fostering a culture of digital literacy and ethical awareness (Bulut & Beiting-Parrish, 2024).

The involvement of both teachers and students in the formulation of AI policies is crucial for establishing a responsible AI framework within educational environments. The engagement of educators guarantees that policies align with pedagogical requirements, while the promotion of digital literacy provides both teachers and students with essential knowledge for the safe and ethical utilization of AI technologies. Educational institutions can establish a robust foundation for the responsible implementation of AI that benefits all stakeholders by promoting collaboration and continuous dialogue.

AI Governance and Accountability Structures

The integration of artificial intelligence (AI) into educational settings requires robust governance and accountability structures to ensure that its deployment aligns with ethical, legal, and educational standards.(Bulut & Beiting-Parrish, 2024) Establishing oversight bodies and regulatory frameworks, alongside effective accountability mechanisms for both AI developers and users, is essential to mitigate risks, foster transparency, and uphold the principles of fairness, privacy, and inclusivity. (Gevaert et al., 2021; Weber, 2019) This section outlines the importance of such governance structures in ensuring responsible AI implementation in schools and institutions.

Establishing Oversight Bodies and Regulatory Frameworks

Education needs oversight bodies to monitor and regulate AI use. Educational institutions, government agencies, and the public should be represented on these bodies, along with AI ethics, education policy, technology law, and data privacy experts. (Berendt et al., 2020) They set clear guidelines and standards for AI implementation in educational institutions to improve results while upholding ethics and student welfare. AI implementation requires algorithmic transparency and data protection in regulatory frameworks. Educational AI systems used for grading, student performance assessment, or behavioral observation may need audits under these frameworks. This guarantees AI system impartiality. (Kieslich et al., 2022) Frameworks should also include clear consent processes to inform students, parents, and educators about AI system data use and risks.

Oversight bodies must align AI policies with broader national and international standards. Collaborations with global organizations and governing bodies, including UNESCO, can ensure that AI in education aligns with internationally recognized principles of human rights, inclusivity, and equality. ("Guidance for Generative AI in Education and Research," 2023) National policies must embody these principles while remaining adaptable to local contexts and educational requirements, ensuring a balanced regulatory approach.

Accountability Mechanisms for AI Developers and Users

To maintain the integrity and responsible use of AI in education, it is crucial to establish clear accountability mechanisms for both AI developers and end-users. AI developers—whether companies, research institutions, or independent creators must be held accountable for ensuring that their systems adhere to ethical standards and regulatory guidelines throughout their development and deployment stages.(Gasser, 2023) To be accountable, AI developers must avoid algorithm bias, be transparent in decision-making, and protect user data. Developers must regularly evaluate AI system effects on students and teachers. Development must quickly fix negative effects by changing algorithms or compensating victims.

Schools, teachers, administrators, and students must also ensure ethical AI use. Educational institutions must have clear AI tool policies, including how to evaluate and choose ethical AI products. Teachers and administrators must be trained to use AI tools responsibly and safely by understanding their limitations and risks. (Wang, 2020) Schools must inform students and parents about AI tools and their privacy and learning effects.

Transparent reporting can encourage stakeholders to report AI issues. Schools could also assess and address AI's effects on educational equity, privacy, and inclusivity through "impact" reviews. These methods align AI deployment with education and social responsibility. (2024, Bulut & Beiting-Parrish)

POLICY DEVELOPMENT FOR THE SAFE IMPLEMENTATION OF AI

Policy Design and Stakeholder Engagement

Creating and enforcing rules for the safe use of artificial intelligence (AI) in schools requires the participation of many different groups to make sure the rules are complete, include everyone, and work. This collaborative approach enhances policy relevance and ensures that it meets the diverse needs of all stakeholders, including government bodies, educational institutions, AI developers, students, and educators. (Luan et al., 2020) A planned process for making policies increases participation, encourages openness, and helps people understand each other better. This leads to policies that are in line with everyone's goals and support smart AI use in schools.

Involvement of Government Bodies, Educational Institutions, and AI Developers

Governments must match AI policies with national, international, legal, and ethical standards. Governments set AI regulations, allocate resources, and ensure data privacy and human rights compliance. (Paunov et al. 2019) They must build public trust in AI and ensure that it does not harm kids or undermine educational goals.

Technically feasible and pedagogically successful policies should be developed by government and educational institutions. AI deployment greatly impacts educational institutions, making their contributions crucial to creating classroom-friendly regulations. Educational institutions, including schools and universities, should discuss AI uses in teaching, learning, and administration. This partnership ensures that rules manage AI technology while addressing practical issues like teacher training, curriculum creation, and data privacy when incorporating AI into educational systems (Ma & Jiang, 2023). Private firms, research groups, and independent innovators—including AI developers should influence policy.

Developers, as creators of AI technologies, possess essential knowledge regarding the capabilities, limitations, and risks inherent in AI systems. They offer essential insights into the technical dimensions of AI implementation in educational contexts, focusing on the fairness, transparency, and alignment of algorithms with educational objectives. (Balta 2023) AI developers should collaborate with educators and policymakers to ensure that their products adhere to ethical standards and enhance educational outcomes.

Collaborative Policy-Making Process

Effective and widely accepted AI policymaking requires collaboration. It must be inclusive, transparent, and iterative so all stakeholders can contribute their knowledge. Diverse group involvement ensures that policies address the needs and concerns of various communities, promoting ownership and accountability among all stakeholders. Stakeholder engagement initiates with the identification of principal actors, including government officials, educators, students, AI developers, parents, and associations for advocacy. Each group possesses distinct perspectives on the challenges and opportunities of AI in education, and their contributions should be solicited during the process of creating policies.

Government agencies may establish regulatory frameworks, while educators can contribute their experiences with AI tools and pinpoint potential areas for enhancement. (Artificial Intelligence and the Future of Teaching and Learning, 2023) Consultations, workshops, and forums serve as platforms for continuous dialogue among stakeholders. These interactions facilitate the exchange of ideas, the identification of common issues, and the formulation of collective solutions. Additionally, the policy-making process should incorporate feedback loops to facilitate adjustments in response to emerging technological advancements, educational requirements, and ethical considerations. Alongside public consultations, pilot programs or case studies within educational institutions can provide significant insights into the practical implementation of AI policies. (Iakovlev et al. 2023; The Impact of Artificial Intelligence on Learning 2018) The pilots can assess various AI applications, evaluate their effects on teaching and learning, and pinpoint potential issues that require attention in the final policy framework.

Legal and Regulatory Frameworks

The safe implementation of AI in educational settings requires a robust legal and regulatory framework that addresses both national and international laws governing AI use. These frameworks must ensure that AI technologies are used ethically, transparently, and in compliance with data privacy laws, human rights standards, and educational regulations.(NXP Ethical Framework for Artificial Intelligence, 2020) A clear understanding of these legal structures is critical to creating an environment in which AI can be safely integrated into schools and institutions without compromising students' rights or the integrity of educational processes.

National and International Laws for AI in Education

At the national level, AI policies must align with existing laws related to data protection, privacy, and digital rights. For instance, regulations such as the General Data Protection Regulation (GDPR) in the European Union set stringent rules regarding the collection and use of personal data, including data gathered through AI systems in schools.(Hadley, 2022; Mészáros et al., 2022) Similarly, in the U.S., laws like the Family Educational Rights and Privacy Act (FERPA) protect the privacy of student records, which must be adhered to when implementing AI technologies in education.

Internationally, AI policies should align with globally recognized ethical standards and frameworks. The UNESCO's "Recommendation on the Ethics of Artificial Intelligence" provides guidelines on ensuring that AI systems respect human dignity, avoid discrimination, and promote inclusivity. (Ethics of Artificial Intelligence, 2024) National policies should take these international standards into account to ensure that AI systems in education meet ethical and legal expectations on a global scale.

Aligning with Broader Technological and Ethical Regulations

AI policies in education should also be consistent with broader technological and ethical regulations. This includes promoting algorithmic transparency, ensuring accountability for AI developers and users, and addressing concerns related to bias and fairness in AI algorithms. Integrating ethical AI frameworks into educational policy ensures that AI systems not only comply with the law(Gevaert et al., 2021) but also align with societal values, fostering trust and acceptance in their use within schools and institutions.

Funding and Resource Allocation

The successful and equitable implementation of AI in educational settings hinges on effective funding and resource allocation. Schools and institutions must receive the necessary financial support to adopt AI technologies, while ensuring that resources are distributed fairly, addressing disparities between institutions and communities. Proper budgeting for AI adoption involves not only initial investments in technology but also long-term planning for infrastructure, teacher training, and maintenance.

Budgeting for AI Adoption and Infrastructure

Effective AI implementation requires good budgeting. Educational institutions should subsidise AI hardware, software, and infrastructure upgrades. AI development requires high-speed internet, cloud services, and secure data storage. Incorporate the costs associated with AI tools, such as adaptive learning platforms, automated grading systems, and AI-driven administrative functions, into the curriculum budget. (Joyce & Harris 2018; Mallik & Gangopadhyay (2023)

Long-term budgeting must include teacher and administrator AI training. AI-integrated instruction and classroom management require ongoing professional development for educators. Educational institutions must plan for AI system maintenance to ensure security, currency, and efficiency. (AI in Professional Learning: Navigating Opportunities and Challenges for Educators, n.d.)

Ensuring Equitable Distribution of Resources for AI Adoption

Equitable resource allocation is paramount to preventing the deepening of educational inequalities. Governments and educational institutions must ensure that AI technologies are accessible to all schools, regardless of their geographic location, economic status, or student demographics.(Gillani et al., 2023) This means prioritizing funding for underserved or underfunded schools, particularly those in rural or economically disadvantaged areas.

Equity in AI adoption involves providing the necessary support to bridge the digital divide, ensuring that all students have access to the educational benefits of AI. This could involve targeted grants, subsidies, or partnerships with private organizations to ensure that AI technologies are accessible to all schools.

FUTURE DIRECTIONS

The Future of AI in Education (e.g., AI Tutors, Learning Analytics)

The future of AI in education is expected to bring significant changes that will alter the processes of teaching, learning, and administration within educational institutions. As we progress toward Society 5.0, a society in which digital technologies align with human needs. AI will assume a progressively vital function in developing more personalized, efficient, and equitable educational settings. (Umamah et al., 2020) The emergence of new AI applications, including AI tutors and advanced learning analytics, will influence the evolution of educational practices, presenting both opportunities and challenges that necessitate careful policy and ethical considerations.

AI Tutors and Personalized Learning

Instructors using AI improve education. Intelligent systems reply to requests and provide personalized explanations based on student learning preferences, providing rapid, personalized support. (Hasse et al., 2019) AI instructors can customize feedback and alter difficulty levels in real time to pupil progress. This personalized approach can reduce learning gaps, especially for struggling students and those who want more advanced material. AI tutors can help teachers teach harder subjects while providing routine, customized training. Progress requires policies to ensure AI tutor development meets ethical, unbiased, and educational aims. (2024, Resnick)

Learning Analytics and Data-Driven Insights

Learning analytics signifies a significant area of progress in the utilization of AI in education. AI systems can analyze extensive student data to reveal patterns and trends, aiding educators in understanding student performance, predicting future outcomes, and identifying areas requiring additional support. Learning analytics can inform interventions and improve understanding of how teaching methods affect learning outcomes. As AI advances, it will enable more proactive and targeted education strategies, improving student success. (Zhai et al., 2021)

Innovations Shaping Society 5.0 and Education

As Society 5.0 approaches, advancements in AI will increasingly converge with other advanced technologies, including the Internet of Things (IoT), virtual reality (VR), augmented reality (AR), and blockchain. (Society 5.0, n.d.) These technologies possess the capacity to improve education by establishing immersive learning environments, safeguarding the confidentiality and privacy of academic data, and increasing collaborative learning experiences worldwide. Innovations in AI-powered content creation, such as automated curriculum development and customized educational materials, will greatly improve the learning experience.

Ensuring Long-Term Sustainability

Educational AI sustainability requires monitoring, policy change, and value alignment. AI is evolving swiftly, therefore schools must ensure relevance, efficiency, and ethics. (Iakovlev et al., 2023) This requires adaptive techniques that can adapt to new difficulties while retaining justice, openness, and social accountability. Aligning AI deployment with Society 5.0 goals of human-centric innovation and sustainable growth is key to education AI success.

Continuous Monitoring and Policy Adaptation

AI in education must be monitored to satisfy educational and societal goals. To improve learning outcomes and impact students, educators, and the educational environment, AI technologies are monitored. These assessments should inform legislative changes to keep AI systems efficient, ethical, and bias-free. (Zhang & Aslan, 2023)

Governments and educational institutions must establish frameworks for AI system reviews. Specialized oversight organizations should review performance, identify hazards, and advise improvements. This strategy allows decision-makers to quickly address emerging challenges including AI algorithm effects, privacy issues, and the possible replacement of human instructors. (Grabowicz et al., 2023) Policies must also be flexible enough to adapt to AI advances and social expectations. AI regulations must be updated to reflect ethical, legal, and technological advancements. This flexibility will ensure that AI continues to improve education rather than cause unintended harm or social instability.

Ensuring that AI Usage Remains Aligned with Evolving Societal Values

Education should reflect shifting social objectives and values with AI. Educational institutions and policymakers must update AI systems as social standards shift. We value fairness, inclusivity, privacy, and individuality. AI must be examined often to achieve Society 5.0's sustainable, egalitarian, and inclusive aims. (Botes & Townsend, 2023) Innovation and human-centered values must be balanced as AI is integrated into education. AI systems should enhance human engagement in education, not replace it. To address algorithmic biases, data security, and demeaning teaching, policies must be updated often. (Luan et al., 2020)

Our efforts long-term success depends on educators, students, parents, and governments working together to create AI ethical principles for education. This collaborative approach guarantees AI technology reflect social ideals, promoting trust, accountability, and responsibility.

CONCLUSION

The safe and responsible implementation of AI in educational settings requires a comprehensive policy framework that prioritizes ethical, technological, and social considerations. As the educational landscape increasingly integrates AI tools, the need for clear guidelines, continuous monitoring, and long-term sustainability becomes even more critical. In this context, advancing a responsible Society 5.0 through AI policy development not only enhances educational outcomes but also fosters a society where technological advancements benefit all members equitably.

Summary of Key Policy Recommendations

The key policy recommendations for advancing AI utilization in educational settings emphasize the need for:

1. **Ethical Guidelines and Oversight**: To ensure ethical usage of AI technologies, governments and educational institutions must establish clear guidelines and oversight to assure transparency, fairness, and responsibility. This encompasses data privacy, bias prevention, and inclusivity.
2. **Stakeholder Engagement**: Governments, educational institutions, AI developers, instructors, students, and parents must work together to create regulations that meet varied needs and expectations. Engagement with stakeholders ensures that AI tools meet educational and social aims.
3. **Continuous Monitoring and Adaptation**: To keep AI tools relevant and effective, policies should include procedures for constant monitoring and regular reviews. This guarantees that AI systems adapt to changing challenges, technologies, and social objectives.
4. **Equitable Resource Allocation**: Governments must deploy AI resources fairly, especially to underprivileged schools and communities, to prevent additional educational inequality. Infrastructure, teacher training, and equitable technology access are essential for inclusive AI implementation.
5. **Aligning AI with Societal Values**: AI in education must remain human-centered, prioritizing ethical considerations such as fairness, equity, and the well-being of students. Policies should ensure that AI usage aligns with the broader goals of Society 5.0—creating a sustainable, inclusive, and responsible society.

Final Thoughts on Advancing a Responsible Society 5.0 in Education

As we transition into Society 5.0, AI has the potential to revolutionize education, making it more personalized, efficient, and accessible. However, the integration of AI must be approached with caution and foresight to avoid negative consequences. (7 Principles on Responsible AI Use in Education, 2024) By adhering to responsible AI principles, fostering collaboration, and continuously adapting policies to meet evolving needs, we can ensure that AI in education serves as a positive force for societal change. Ultimately, the goal is to create an educational environment where technology enhances human potential, while upholding core values of fairness, justice, and equity.

REFERENCES

A Policy Agenda for Responsible Progress in Artificial Intelligence. (n.d.). Retrieved December 30, 2024, from https://storage.googleapis.com/gweb-uniblog-publish-prod/documents/A_Policy_Agenda_for_Responsible_Progress_in_Artificial_Intelligence.pdf

Abdul, R. K., Muhammad, I. H., & Zakki, Ah. F., M. Yunus, A. B., Muhaemin, M., & Arifuddin, A. (2024). Exploring The Rationality of Religious-Rational Islamic Thinkers Towards The Compatibility of The Islamic Education System (Vol. 13, Issue 2, p. 187). https://jurnal.uin-antasari.ac.id/index.php/jtjik/article/view/13638

Ahmad, S., Umirzakova, S., Mujtaba, G., Amin, M., & Whangbo, T. K. (2023). Education 5.0: Requirements, Enabling Technologies, and Future Directions. In arXiv (Cornell University). Cornell University. https://doi.org//arxiv.2307.15846DOI: 10.48550

Alami, H., Rivard, L., Lehoux, P., Hoffman, S. J., Cadeddu, S. B. M., Savoldelli, M., Samri, M., Ahmed, M. A. A., Fleet, R., & Fortin, J. (2020). Artificial intelligence in health care: laying the Foundation for Responsible, sustainable, and inclusive innovation in low- and middle-income countries. In Globalization and Health (Vol. 16, Issue 1). BioMed Central. https://doi.org/DOI: 10.1186/s12992-020-00584-1

Alamleh, H. (2020). Private and Secure Students' Data Sharing in Educational Systems (Vol. 71, p. 158). https://doi.org/DOI: 10.1109/econf51404.2020.9385450

Artificial Intelligence and the Future of Teaching and Learning. (2023). https://tech.ed.gov/files/2023/05/ai-future-of-teaching-and-learning-report.pdf

Artificial Intelligence and the Future of Teaching and Learning. (n.d.). Retrieved December 31, 2024, from https://www2.ed.gov/documents/ai-report/ai-report.pdf

Artificial Intelligence in Higher Education: Applications, Promise and Perils, and Ethical Questions. (2019). https://er.educause.edu/articles/2019/8/artificial-intelligence-in-higher-education-applications-promise-and-perils-and-ethical-questions

Balta, N. (2023). Embracing the Future: AI's Transformative Potential in Educational Research. In The European Educational Researcher (Vol. 6, Issue 2, p. 1). https://doi.org/DOI: 10.31757/euer.624

Berendt, B., Littlejohn, A., & Blakemore, M. (2020). *AI in education: learner choice and fundamental rights*. Taylor & Francis., DOI: 10.1080/17439884.2020.1786399

Bittencourt, I. I., Cukurova, M., Müldner, K., Luckin, R., & Millán, E. (2020). Artificial Intelligence in Education. In Lecture notes in computer science. Springer Science+Business Media. https://doi.org/DOI: 10.1007/978-3-030-52237-7

Botes, M., & Townsend, B. (2023). Bridging the regulatory gaps created by Smart and Connected technologies in South Africa. In South African Journal of Bioethics and Law (Vol. 16, Issue 2, p. 36). Health and Medical Publishing Group. https://doi.org/DOI: 10.7196/SAJBL.2023.v16i2.201

Buckley, R. P., Arner, D. W., Zetzsche, D. A., & Weber, R. H. (2019). The road to RegTech: the (astonishing) example of the European Union. In Journal of Banking Regulation (Vol. 21, Issue 1, p. 26). Palgrave Macmillan. https://doi.org/DOI: 10.1057/s41261-019-00104-1

Bulut, O., & Beiting-Parrish, M. (2024). The Rise of Artificial Intelligence in Educational Measurement: Opportunities and Ethical Challenges. In Chinese/English Journal of Educational Measurement and Evaluation (Vol. 5, Issue 3). https://doi.org/DOI: 10.59863/MIQL7785

Chang, S., Cheong, M., & Oliveira, E. (2024). Digital Environment and AI in International Education: The Gaps and Implications. In *International Higher Education*. Boston College Center for International Higher Education., DOI: 10.6017/895b9e0d.2b6eeadd

Chaudhry, M. A., Cukurova, M., & Luckin, R. (2022). A Transparency Index Framework for AI in Education. In arXiv (Cornell University). Cornell University. https://doi.org//arxiv.2206.03220DOI: 10.48550

Chen, Z. (2023). Ethics and discrimination in artificial intelligence-enabled recruitment practices. In Humanities and Social Sciences Communications (Vol. 10, Issue 1). Palgrave Macmillan. https://doi.org/DOI: 10.1057/s41599-023-02079-x

Cui, W., Xue, Z., & Thai, K.-P. (2019). Performance comparison of an AI-based Adaptive Learning System in China. In arXiv (Cornell University). Cornell University. https://doi.org/DOI: 10.48550/arxiv.1901.10268

Ethics of AI in Education. Towards a Community-Wide Framework. In International Journal of Artificial Intelligence in Education (Vol. 32, Issue 3, p. 504). Springer Science+Business Media. https://doi.org/DOI: 10.1007/s40593-021-00239-1

Ethics of Artificial Intelligence. (2024). https://www.unesco.org/en/artificial-intelligence/recommendation-ethics

Felix, J. R. B., & Webb, L. (2024). Use of artificial intelligence in education delivery and assessment. https://doi.org/DOI: 10.58248/PN712

Gasser, U. (2023). An EU landmark for AI governance. In Science (Vol. 380, Issue 6651, p. 1203). American Association for the Advancement of Science. https://doi.org/DOI: 10.1126/science.adj1627

Generative Artificial Intelligence for Education and Pedagogy. (2024). https://teaching.cornell.edu/generative-artificial-intelligence/cu-committee-report-generative-artificial-intelligence-education

Gentili, P. L. (2022). Photochromic and luminescent materials for the development of Chemical Artificial Intelligence. In *Dyes and Pigments* (Vol. 205, p. 110547). Elsevier BV., DOI: 10.1016/j.dyepig.2022.110547

Gevaert, C., Carman, M., Rosman, B., Georgiadou, Y., & Soden, R. (2021). Fairness and accountability of AI in disaster risk management: Opportunities and challenges [Review of Fairness and accountability of AI in disaster risk management: Opportunities and challenges]. Patterns, 2(11), 100363. Elsevier BV. https://doi.org/DOI: 10.1016/j.patter.2021.100363

Goode, K., Kim, H. M., & Deng, M. (2023). Examining Singapore's AI Progress. https://doi.org/DOI: 10.51593/2021CA014

Grabowicz, P. A., Perello, N., & Zick, Y. (2023). Towards an AI Accountability Policy. In arXiv (Cornell University). Cornell University. https://doi.org/DOI: 10.48550/arXiv.2307

Hadley, E. (2022). Prioritizing Policies for Furthering Responsible Artificial Intelligence in the United States. In arXiv (Cornell University). Cornell University. https://doi.org/DOI: 10.48550/arXiv.2212

Holroyd, C. (2023). Technological innovation and building a 'super smart' society: Japan's vision of society 5.0. https://www.tandfonline.com/doi/full/10.1080/17516234.2020.1749340

Huang, L. (2023). Ethics of Artificial Intelligence in Education: Student Privacy and Data Protection. In Science Insights Education Frontiers (Vol. 16, Issue 2, p. 2577). https://doi.org/DOI: 10.15354/sief.23.re202

Iakovlev, I., Kremleva, E. S., & Guzanov, R. (2023). Enterprise automation using artificial intelligence: Methods, technologies and prospects. In *E3S Web of Conferences* (Vol. 460, p. 4007). EDP Sciences., DOI: 10.1051/e3sconf/202346004007

JOYCE. J., & Harris, L. A. (2018). Artificial Intelligence (AI) and Education. https://digital.library.unt.edu/ark:/67531/metadc1228526/m2/1/high_res_d/IF10937_2018Aug01.pdf

Kamalov, F., Calonge, D. S., & Gurrib, I. (2023). New Era of Artificial Intelligence in Education: Towards a Sustainable Multifaceted Revolution. In Sustainability (Vol. 15, Issue 16, p. 12451). Multidisciplinary Digital Publishing Institute. https://doi.org/DOI: 10.3390/su151612451

Khan, R. A., Jawaid, M., Khan, A. R., & Sajjad, M. (2023). ChatGPT - Reshaping medical education and clinical management. In Pakistan Journal of Medical Sciences (Vol. 39, Issue 2). Professional Medical Publications. https://doi.org/DOI: 10.12669/pjms.39.2.7653

Khosravi, H., Shum, S. B., Chen, G., Conati, C., Tsai, Y., Kay, J., Knight, S., Martínez-Maldonado, R., Sadiq, S., & Gašević, D. (2022). Explainable Artificial Intelligence in education. In *Computers and Education Artificial Intelligence* (Vol. 3, p. 100074). Elsevier BV., DOI: 10.1016/j.caeai.2022.100074

Kieslich, K., Keller, B., & Starke, C. (2022). Artificial intelligence ethics by design. Evaluating public perception on the importance of ethical design principles of artificial intelligence. In Big Data & Society (Vol. 9, Issue 1). SAGE Publishing. https://doi.org/DOI: 10.1177/20539517221092956

Kim, S., Jang, Y., Kim, W., Choi, S., Jung, H., Kim, S.-H., & Kim, H. (2021). Why and What to Teach: AI Curriculum for Elementary School. In Proceedings of the AAAI Conference on Artificial Intelligence (Vol. 35, Issue 17, p. 15569). Association for the Advancement of Artificial Intelligence. https://doi.org/DOI: 10.1609/aaai.v35i17.17833

Legislation and Ethics. (2020). https://www.educause.edu/ecar/research-publications/the-evolving-landscape-of-data-privacy-in-higher-education/legislation-and-ethics

Liang, W. (2020). *Development Trend and Thinking of Artificial Intelligence in Education. In 2022 International Wireless Communications and Mobile Computing*. IWCMC., DOI: 10.1109/IWCMC48107.2020.9148078

Lievens, E., & Verdoodt, V. (2017). Looking for needles in a haystack: Key issues affecting children's rights in the General Data Protection Regulation. In Computer Law & Security Review (Vol. 34, Issue 2, p. 269). Elsevier BV. https://doi.org/DOI: 10.1016/j.clsr.2017.09.007

Luan, H., Géczy, P., Lai, H., Gobert, J. D., Yang, S. J. H., Ogata, H., Baltes, J., Guerra, R. da S., Li, P., & Tsai, C. (2020). *Challenges and Future Directions of Big Data and Artificial Intelligence in Education* [Review of Challenges and Future Directions of Big Data and Artificial Intelligence in Education]. Frontiers Media., DOI: 10.3389/fpsyg.2020.580820

Ma, X., & Jiang, C. (2023; Vol. 14). On the Ethical Risks of Artificial Intelligence Applications in Education and Its Avoidance Strategies. In Journal of Education Humanities and Social Sciences., DOI: 10.54097/ehss.v14i.8868

Mészáros, J., Minari, J., & Huys, I. (2022). The future regulation of artificial intelligence systems in healthcare services and medical research in the European Union. In *Frontiers in Genetics* (Vol. 13). Frontiers Media., DOI: 10.3389/fgene.2022.927721

Mozer, M. C., Wiseheart, M., & Novikoff, T. P. (2019, February 19). Artificial intelligence to support human instruction. In Proceedings of the National Academy of Sciences (Vol. 116, Issue 10, p. 3953). National Academy of Sciences. https://doi.org/DOI: 10.1073/pnas.1900370116

Nguyen, A., Ngo, H. N., Hong, Y., Dang, B., & Nguyen, B.-P. T. (2022). Ethical principles for artificial intelligence in education. In Education and Information Technologies (Vol. 28, Issue 4, p. 4221). Springer Science+Business Media. https://doi.org/DOI: 10.1007/s10639-022-11316-w

NXP Ethical Framework for Artificial Intelligence. (2020). https://www.nxp.com/docs/en/white-paper/AI-ETHICAL-FRAMEWORK-WP.pdf

Onesi-Ozigagun, O., Ololade, Y. J., Eyo-Udo, N. L., & Ogundipe, D. O. (2024). REVOLUTIONIZING EDUCATION THROUGH AI: A COMPREHENSIVE REVIEW OF ENHANCING LEARNING EXPERIENCES [Review of] ENHANCING LEARNING EXPERIENCES]. International Journal of Applied Research in Social Sciences, 6(4), 589. Fair East Publishers. https://doi.org/DOI: 10.51594/ijarss.v6i4.1011

Ouyang, F., & Jiao, P. (2021). Artificial intelligence in education: The three paradigms. In *Computers and Education Artificial Intelligence* (Vol. 2, p. 100020). Elsevier BV., DOI: 10.1016/j.caeai.2021.100020

Paunov, C., Planes-Satorra, S., & Ravelli, G. (2019). Review of national policy initiatives in support of digital and AI-driven innovation. In OECD science, technology and industry policy papers. https://doi.org/DOI: 10.1787/23074957

7. principles on responsible AI use in education. (2024). https://www.weforum.org/agenda/2024/01/ai-guidance-school-responsible-use-in-education/

Radanliev, P., Roure, D. D., Walton, R., Kleek, M. V., Montalvo, R. M., Maddox, L., Santos, O., Burnap, P., & Anthi, E. (2020). Artificial intelligence and machine learning in dynamic cyber risk analytics at the edge. In SN Applied Sciences (Vol. 2, Issue 11). Springer Nature. https://doi.org/DOI: 10.1007/s42452-020-03559-4

Reyer van der Vlies. (2020). Trustworthy artificial intelligence (AI) in education: Promises and challenges. https://www.oecd-ilibrary.org/education/trustworthy-artificial-intelligence-ai-in-education_a6c90fa9-en;jsessionid=dy2TD8yZnRd3pW9wSCpMWEPG.ip-10-240-5-70

Schiff, D., Rakova, B., Ayesh, A., Fanti, A., & Lennon, M. (2021). Explaining the Principles to Practices Gap in AI. In IEEE Technology and Society Magazine (Vol. 40, Issue 2, p. 81). Institute of Electrical and Electronics Engineers. https://doi.org/ DOI: 10.1109/MTS.2021.3056286

Smith, M., & Neupane, S. (2023). Artificial intelligence and human development. https://idl-bnc-idrc.dspacedirect.org/handle/10625/56949?show=full

Smuha, N. A. (2020). Trustworthy Artificial Intelligence in Education: Pitfalls and Pathways. In SSRN Electronic Journal. RELX Group (Netherlands). https://doi.org/ DOI: 10.2139/ssrn.3742421

Srivastava, S. (2023). The evolution of education: Navigating 21st-century challenges. *International Journal for Multidisciplinary Research*, *5*(5), 1–9.

Taddeo, M., & Floridi, L. (2018). How AI can be a force for good. In Science (Vol. 361, Issue 6404, p. 751). American Association for the Advancement of Science. https://doi.org/DOI: 10.1126/science.aat5991

Tadimalla, S. Y., & Maher, M. L. (2024). AI Literacy for All: Adjustable Interdisciplinary Socio-technical Curriculum. In arXiv (Cornell University). Cornell University. https://doi.org//arxiv.2409.10552DOI: 10.48550

Tanjga, M. (2023). E-learning and the Use of AI: A Review of Current Practices and Future Directions [Review of E-learning and the Use of AI: A Review of Current Practices and Future Directions]. https://doi.org/DOI: 10.32388/AP0208

Tanveer, M., Hassan, S., & Bhaumik, A. (2020). Academic Policy Regarding Sustainability and Artificial Intelligence (AI). In Sustainability (Vol. 12, Issue 22, p. 9435). Multidisciplinary Digital Publishing Institute. https://doi.org/DOI: 10.3390/su12229435

The Impact of Artificial Intelligence on Learning. (2018). https://publications.jrc.ec.europa.eu/repository/bitstream/JRC113226/jrc113226_jrcb4_the_impact_of_artificial_intelligence_on_learning_final_2.pdf

U.S. Department of Education. (n.d.). Artificial Intelligence and the Future of Teaching and Learning (PDF). Retrieved December 30, 2024, from https://www2.ed.gov/documents/ai-report/ai-report.pdf

Wang, Y. (2020). When artificial intelligence meets educational leaders' data-informed decision-making: A cautionary tale. In *Studies In Educational Evaluation* (Vol. 69, p. 100872). Elsevier BV., DOI: 10.1016/j.stueduc.2020.100872

Weber, R. H. (2019). Socio-ethical values and legal rules on automated platforms: The quest for a symbiotic relationship. In *Computer Law & Security Review* (Vol. 36, p. 105380). Elsevier BV., DOI: 10.1016/j.clsr.2019.105380

Zawacki-Richter, O., Marín, V. I., Bond, M., & Gouverneur, F. (2019). Systematic review of research on artificial intelligence applications in higher education – where are the educators? In International Journal of Educational Technology in Higher Education (Vol. 16, Issue 1). Springer Nature. https://doi.org/DOI: 10.1186/s41239-019-0171-0

Zhang, K., & Aslan, A. B. (2023). AI technologies for education: Recent research & future directions. https://www.sciencedirect.com/science/article/pii/S2666920X21000199

Chapter 8
Bridging Educational Gaps Across Nations with AI-Supported Collaboration Tools

Naidin Syamsuddin
https://orcid.org/0009-0002-4734-6239
Institut Agama Islam Negeri Palopo, Indonesia

Alfan Putra
https://orcid.org/0009-0005-1697-5368
Institut Agama Islam Negeri Palopo, Indonesia

Bustanul Iman
https://orcid.org/0000-0002-3130-0642
Institut Agama Islam Negeri Palopo, Indonesia

Midyan surya Ishak
https://orcid.org/0000-0001-6803-0087
Institut Agama Islam Negeri Pontianak, Indonesia

Mustafa Mustafa
https://orcid.org/0009-0003-6467-299X
Institut Agama Islam Negeri Palopo, Indonesia

ABSTRACT

High-quality education requires addressing global educational disparities. Explore how AI-supported cooperation can change global education in this chapter. Artificial intelligence can help teachers, institutions, and governments develop interconnected

DOI: 10.4018/979-8-3373-5781-2.ch008

networks for knowledge sharing, resource access, and culturally and socioeconomically adapted learning. Virtual learning environments, multilingual translation, and AI-powered coaching enable real-time communication and understanding between global learners and instructors. These technologies provide underrepresented communities with customized content and high-quality education. Data privacy, digital infrastructure, and culturally sensitive algorithms are practical and ethical challenges with AI products. Global successes demonstrate how such gadgets reduce achievement gaps and promote educational justice. The global education network can alter if AI-supported collaboration tools erase trocational boundaries, promote inclusivity, and build a more connected and fair learning ecosystem for future generations.

INTRODUCTION TO AI-DRIVEN EDUCATION AND CULTURAL SENSITIVITY

Overview of AI in Education

AI makes robots think and act like humans (Datta et al., 2024). AI provides machine learning algorithms, natural language processing technologies, and more to improve education (Welukar & Bajoria, 2021). AI can automate administrative tasks, create customized learning paths, give pupils immediate feedback, and adapt teaching methods (Bhutoria, 2022).

AI tools in classrooms have improved quickly in recent decades (Guan et al., 2020). AI in education initially consisted of tutoring systems that provided feedback and assisted students with certain courses (Núñez et al., 2023). Machine learning allows AI systems to perform more complex tasks like personalized learning algorithms that adapt in real-time to a student's progress, predictive analytics for identifying at-risk students, and virtual teaching assistants to help educators manage their classrooms (Tanjga, 2023).

Digital, internet, and traditional schools use AI (Yi et al., 2024; Zhang & Aslan, 2021). AI-powered systems can uncover patterns and trends in enormous student data sets to inform teacher education. AI can also improve inclusive learning by delivering speech-to-text and text-to-speech for disabled students (Toyokawa et al., 2023; Crompton & Burke, 2023).

The Importance of Cultural Sensitivity in Education

Cultural sensitivity in education considers students' backgrounds, attitudes, and beliefs (Etri, 2021; Samıer & ElKaleh, 2023). It acknowledges that social and cultural backgrounds affect learning. Inclusion and respect for all pupils require cultural understanding (Gurjar & Bai, 2023; Correa & Tulbert, 2023).

Globalized children encounter different cultures outside the classroom (Zhao, 2023). Teachers must address cultural differences and provide an inclusive and respectful curriculum, teaching techniques, and classroom atmosphere (Ober et al., 2023; Yefremtseva, 2021). Instructors must analyze how cultural values affect student involvement and topic understanding. Diversity includes accepting native languages, cultures, and learning styles that differ from Western education (Atif-nigar et al., 2023).

Cultural ignorance in education causes problems (Hyrynsalmi, 2024). Curricula may marginalize and distort culture. Culture-responsive teaching improves student engagement and learning (Idrus et al., 2023; Ober, 2023).

Purpose of the Study

This study investigates how AI-driven educational systems can incorporate cultural sensitivity to meet the different demands of students worldwide (Shams et al., 2023)(Adams et al., 2023)). AI can transform education, but it must be designed and used to respect and celebrate cultural diversity. The expanding global interconnection of learners, the necessity of inclusivity, and the role of education in social cohesion justify integrating cultural sensitivity into AI-based education systems (Lai, 2023)(Yu, 2021).

Technology and tradition must be combined to preserve culture and embrace innovation (Guo, 2021). Generations-old pedagogies emphasize community, teamwork, and respect for elders (Sima & Wu, 2022)(Adewumi, 2022). Adding cultural heritage and local knowledge to modern educational tools can enhance AI-driven learning (Yim & Su, 2024). This study combines technology and tradition to create a more inclusive, respectful, and successful educational environment that accommodates students' different cultural origins (Hwang & Lim, 2024)(Salazar & Guillaumier, 2024).

This work adds to the corpus of information on how AI may improve education while being culturally sensitive. The findings may help create AI-powered teaching tools that are efficient and culturally inclusive, improving learning outcomes for all students.

THE INTERSECTION OF TECHNOLOGY AND TRADITION IN EDUCATION

The Role of Technology in Modern Education

Technology transforms education, providing opportunities and problems (Vrabie, 2024; Dawadi et al., 2024). Technology makes education more accessible, flexible, and personalized (Bahja et al., 2021). Providing pupils with customized learning resources is a major benefit. Artificial intelligence-powered learning platforms can customize classes based on student success and learning styles (Bhutoria, 2022; Çelik, 2022). Technology also lets pupils access huge volumes of information, removing geographical and temporal constraints to education (Kerimbayev et al., 2023).

Additionally, technology aids collaborative learning. Video conferencing and collaborative documents enable global learning communities by connecting students and educators (Smith, 2023; Abdi et al., 2021). VR and AR technologies offer immersive learning experiences, allowing students to interact with complicated concepts in ways not conceivable in traditional classrooms (Gaol & Prasolova-Førland, 2021).

Technological integration in schooling has drawbacks. The digital gap is a major issue (Afzal et al., 2023; Vassilakopoulou & Hustad, 2021). Technology and high-speed internet connections vary by student, limiting educational potential. Overuse of technology can reduce face-to-face contact, which may affect social and emotional development (Matli & Wamba, 2023). Additionally, rapid technology advancement can leave instructors lacking in new tool use, requiring continual professional development (Lamptey et al., 2024).

Technology usage in education has varied globally (Mustapha et al., 2020; Blackwell, 2023). Many schools in industrialized countries invest extensively in digital platforms, online learning, and AI-based solutions. Due to infrastructure, economic, and teacher training issues, technology integration in developing nations is delayed (Woolf et al., 2011). International organizations and governments are contributing resources and support for educational technology adoption to bridge these gaps (Bizimana, 2018).

Traditional Educational Practices and Cultural Heritage

Traditional education and cultural legacy underpin many societies' learning systems (Sehgal, 2023; Zhao & Li, 2022; Xiuzhi & Yongtao, 2023). Local norms, values, and social systems often underpin these strategies. Numerous societies have relied on oral traditions, storytelling, and community-based learning for generations

(Ober et al., 2023). Relationships, elder respect, and knowledge-sharing are stressed in these practices.

Along with academics, traditional pedagogies value students' moral, social, and spiritual growth (Sullamo et al., 2023). Learning generally occurs in groups where teamwork, cooperation, and mutual support are valued over individual performance in collectivist cultures (Ye & Hu, 2023). Community, tribal, and religious schools use these methods (Rejeb, 2022).

Cultural traditions strongly influence learning methods and surroundings (Domoff et al., 2023; Atifnigar, 2023; Milne & Wotherspoon, 2023). Discipline, respect, and authority are valued in several Asian cultures, which can influence students' classroom behavior (Hu, 2022). Western education emphasizes critical thinking, individualism, and free debate (Sui, 2023). Different educational traditions can affect how students use content and technology in class.

The Need for a Hybrid Approach

Given the pros and cons of technology and traditional education, a hybrid approach is necessary for the future of education (Aleksandrova et al., 2023). This method combines AI and digital tools' tailored, scalable benefits with traditional pedagogies' cultural relevance and social-emotional strengths. A hybrid strategy protects empathy, connection, and cultural understanding from technology (Zhang & Aslan, 2021).

Combining traditional and AI-driven learning approaches makes learning more comprehensive and inclusive (Wang & Zhang, 2022). AI can automate administrative work, letting teachers focus on culturally appropriate material and student connections. To maintain social learning, digital classrooms can incorporate face-to-face learning, group discussions, and hands-on activities (Alharbi, 2023).

Global case examples demonstrate this hybrid approach's potential. In Finland, known for its innovative education system, inquiry-based learning, and student-centered instruction are enhanced by digital resources (Kallunki et al., 2023). Combining community-based education with mobile learning platforms has helped close educational disparities in rural India (Angrist et al., 2024). The case studies show that technology can complement conventional educational principles without compromising cultural integrity when applied properly.

Finally, combining technology with tradition in education can enhance learning. A hybrid approach that combines the best of both worlds can make education more accessible, engaging, and culturally responsive. By combining technology with traditional cultural practices, educators may build learning environments that honor the past and future, giving students a well-rounded education that prepares them for a globalized society.

INTEGRATING CULTURAL SENSITIVITY INTO AI EDUCATION SYSTEMS

AI Models and Cultural Adaptability

As AI transforms education, cultural flexibility is crucial (Dangol et al., 2024). To succeed in varied educational environments, AI technologies must comprehend and respect cultural norms, values, and languages (Adams et al., 2023). This demands a transition from universal models to localized, culturally appropriate ones.

Cultural norms affect how students interact with content, teachers, and peers (Ezeamuzie & Ezeamuzie, 2024). Some cultures value hierarchy and authority, while others value free speech and democracy. Cultural differences must be included in AI classroom management and individualized learning systems (Yam et al., 2023). Designing systems that respect these standards makes AI tools successful and culturally appropriate, promoting good learning experiences (Ober et al., 2023).

Language is also important for cultural adaptability (Millikin, 2023; Ge et al., 2024). Language processing is crucial to many AI tools, therefore models must recognize and respect linguistic variation (Hershcovich et al., 2022). To accommodate diverse learners, AI-driven educational platforms should support numerous languages and dialects. Google Translate and language learning apps have made progress, but AI must also recognize cultural nuances like colloquial expressions and culturally particular metaphors to give accurate and useful material (Benboujja et al., 2024).

AI techniques already incorporate cultural sensitivity. AI-powered educational platforms are being created to understand pupils' different linguistic and cultural backgrounds. Duolingo uses machine learning to adapt lessons based on users' competency, provide culturally relevant examples, and recognize second language learners' unique obstacles (Yundayani et al., 2023). Khan Academy and Coursera use adaptive learning algorithms to tailor information to student's learning styles and cultural contexts (Qaffas et al., 2020).

Personalizing Learning with Cultural Context

AI can transform customized learning, but it must adapt educational content to students' cultures (Kamalov & Gurrib, 2023; Ober et al., 2023). Beyond giving classes in several languages, culturally appropriate personalization entails knowing how students from different cultures learn, problem-solve, and collaborate (Maghsudi et al., 2021).

AI can tailor learning to students' cultural values, cognitive styles, and information consumption (Gligorea et al., 2023). Some cultures promote cooperation and learning, while others value individual success. Based on these inclinations, AI systems can teach collectivist cultures group-oriented activities and individualistic cultures autonomous tasks. Thus, AI can boost student achievement and engagement (Cukurova et al., 2023).

AI can also tailor difficulty, instructional methods, and information presentation to each learner through personalized learning paths (Maghsudi et al., 2021; Gligorea, 2023). Students in a multicultural classroom may have different backgrounds, learning styles, and cultural contexts. AI can track student progress and intervene when needed, ensuring no student is left behind (Mohammed & Watson, 2019). AI-driven platforms can provide new materials or viewpoints on a subject, taking into account cultural factors that may affect students' comprehension and approach.

Significant gains result from tailored learning in culturally diverse settings. Culturally relevant content makes students feel appreciated and understood. This can boost student motivation, learning results, and satisfaction (Ober et al., 2023). It also creates an inclusive learning environment where all students, regardless of culture, can succeed.

Overcoming Bias in AI Algorithms

AI has great potential to improve education, but biases can perpetuate inequality (Bulathwela et al., 2021; Holstein & Doroudi, 2021). If the data used to train AI algorithms is skewed or unrepresentative of varied cultural perspectives, the models may propagate prejudices, exclude minority groups, or favor specific cultural norms (Chen, 2023). This makes creating AI systems for education difficult since it can unintentionally discriminate against minority cultures.

Biases in AI models must be identified and addressed to make AI tools fair, inclusive, and useful for all learners (Ferrara, 2023). Linguistic, gender, social, and regional biases exist (Shams et al., 2023). An AI-driven evaluation tool trained on Western data may penalize non-Western students by not accounting for their various problem-solving, communication, and learning styles.

AI developers must actively assure fairness and inclusivity in their algorithms to overcome these biases (Nazer et al., 2023). Diverse datasets that reflect the intended user population's culture, language, and demographics are one approach. Engage cross-cultural experts to assess AI systems for biases from different perspectives (hÉigeartaigh et al., 2020). This will make AI models technically accurate and socially and culturally suitable.

AI-driven courses should also contain diverse cultural viewpoints (Kazimzade et al., 2019). Integrating culturally varied curricula, case studies, and examples from diverse students' lives can achieve this. AI systems can increase cultural awareness, equity, and inclusion in schools, making all students feel represented and empowered (Louie et al., 2022).

Finally, AI education systems must incorporate cultural sensitivity to create an inclusive, egalitarian, and successful learning environment. By creating AI models that respect cultural norms, personalizing learning with cultural context, and tackling algorithm biases, we can ensure that AI serves different students worldwide, improving learning outcomes and cultural comprehension.

PRACTICAL STRATEGIES FOR IMPLEMENTATION

Designing Culturally Inclusive Curricula

Educational designers must be deliberate when creating culturally inclusive AI-powered courses (Gaskins, 2022). It takes numerous steps to design a curriculum that incorporates varied cultural perspectives. A cultural audit of the curriculum is necessary first. Find gaps where specific cultural perspectives are underrepresented or distorted (Idrus et al., 2023). Educators can make the curriculum more inclusive and international by assessing content from many cultural perspectives.

Next, the AI-integrated curriculum should be flexible. AI can tailor student learning to their culture, learning style, and needs (Aliabadi et al., 2023). Based on the student's culture, AI systems can suggest movies, articles, or tasks. Localized information that reflects community cultures, histories, and customs can further boost engagement and relevance (Collins et al., 2020). Students can see themselves in literature, history, and social studies by including authors, leaders, and events from many cultures.

Education is essential for culturally sensitive AI integration (Tsai et al., 2022). Teachers must collaborate with AI systems to enhance education rather than replace it (Adams et al., 2023). Teachers could also lead talks regarding AI-generated content to enable students to critically evaluate and relate it to their own culture. Teachers mediate cultural awareness in the classroom to ensure technology promotes a diverse and inclusive learning environment (Bulathwela et al., 2021).

Teacher Training and Professional Development

Teachers need training and professional development to adopt AI-driven culturally sensitive curricula (Eguchi et al., 2021). Technologically and culturally competent teachers must negotiate AI-powered classrooms (Tadimalla & Maher, 2024). Teachers should be trained on how to use AI tools to respect and increase cultural diversity.

Professional development should focus on technical and cultural abilities (Gagné, 2023). Teachers must master AI technologies to tailor learning, track student progress, and facilitate varied classroom activities. They should also be culturally sensitive to how pupils from different backgrounds use technology (Zhu & Ren, 2022). Educators should learn how cultural variations affect communication, group work, and problem-solving.

Professional development is necessary to keep instructors abreast of AI technologies and pedagogical methods (Kim et al., 2022). Teachers should have regular workshops and training on AI technology and cultural competence (Michaeli et al., 2023). Cultural sensitivity in teacher training should be an ongoing process that changes with classroom dynamics and worldwide cultural trends. Integration of AI and cultural awareness into instruction requires ongoing support from educational leadership and institutions (Cassidy et al., 2023).

Collaboration with Cultural Experts

Cultural leaders and community members should be involved in curriculum development for culturally inclusive AI-powered curricula (Prabhakaran et al., 2022; Tsai, 2022). Schools and educational institutions can guarantee the content is representative and respectful of other cultures by working with cultural specialists (Luo, 2022). These specialists can help instructors produce information that connects with students from varied cultural settings by explaining how cultural norms, traditions, and values affect learning (Idrus et al., 2023).

Tech-cultural partnerships can improve this process (Louie et al., 2022). To ensure cultural sensitivity, tech businesses creating AI-powered educational systems must collaborate with cultural organizations, anthropologists, sociologists, and community leaders (Sandoval et al., 2023). Technology businesses may work with indigenous tribes to incorporate their traditions and knowledge into educational software. Schools in multicultural cities can work with local cultural groups to create community-specific material.

Collaborations can produce a more rich, culturally sensitive curriculum beyond tokenistic inclusion. Cultural experts can help schools avoid cultural biases and create respectful, relevant, and meaningful content for pupils by participating in curriculum and AI tool development (Solyst et al., 2023).

Policymakers and educational leaders should also collaborate to support cultural sensitivity in AI-driven education. This entails setting clear cultural inclusion requirements for AI tools and providing schools with financial and institutional support to deploy them (Aliabadi et al., 2023).

Finally, building culturally inclusive AI-powered curricula, training educators with cultural understanding, and cooperating with cultural specialists are crucial to integrating AI into education. By encouraging continual learning and collaboration, educators can create diverse, egalitarian classrooms for all children. These efforts ensure that AI technologies empower students, overcome cultural boundaries, and prepare them for a globalized society.

CHALLENGES AND FUTURE DIRECTIONS

Addressing Ethical Concerns and Cultural Integrity

AI in culturally sensitive education raises ethical issues (Holmes et al., 2021; Ma & Jiang, 2023). AI systems compromising cultural integrity is a major worry (Wang, 2020). AI can personalize and make learning more accessible, but it can also offer hazards if it doesn't respect cultural norms and customs (Prabhakaran et al., 2022). For instance, AI systems that use data from largely Western contexts may misrepresent non-Western values, customs, and worldviews. This could weaken cultural identities and encourage dominant cultural narratives at the expense of others (Wong, 2020).

Designing ethical AI development criteria is necessary to preserve cultural identity and customs in AI-driven educational systems (Nguyen et al., 2022). Developers must work with cultural experts, anthropologists, and community leaders to avoid stereotyping and missing cultural viewpoints in AI models. AI should be able to learn from multiple sources and not only reflect one culture. AI can improve educational institutions by recognizing and appreciating cultural variety and supporting cultural identities (Dutta & Pal, 2022).

Information privacy and exploitation are also ethical considerations (Holmes et al., 2021). Educational data collection in many regions may violate students' cultural context and privacy. AI data collection must comply with local cultural and ethical norms. AI systems must prioritize student privacy and be honest regarding data use, storage, and sharing (Huang, 2023).

Overcoming Technological Barriers in Diverse Regions

AI has the potential to transform education, but accessibility and equity issues, particularly in minority or low-resource groups, remain (Kamalov et al., 2023). Infrastructure shortages hinder AI adoption in varied places. Students in many countries lack access to high-speed internet, laptops, and mobile devices, making AI-powered learning tools difficult to use (KIEMDE & Kora, 2020).

In addition to infrastructural issues, AI resources and training are uneven. Students and teachers may lack the ability to apply AI technologies in the classroom in places with inadequate technology (Sundeen & Sundeen, 2013). The digital gap results from AI-driven education benefiting pupils in wealthier, technology-rich locations while leaving others behind (Carter et al., 2020).

To overcome these limitations, technology access must be egalitarian. Governments, NGOs, and commercial corporations must work together to make AI technologies inexpensive, accessible, and adaptive to varied groups (Gikunda, 2024). Lower-cost gadgets, internet access, and AI training for instructors in impoverished areas will help close the digital divide. AI technologies should also be built to function in low-resource situations so students and instructors worldwide may utilize them (Mitchell & D'Rozario, 2022).

Creating digital equality and AI in school policy is crucial to overcoming technical hurdles (Garcia & Wilson-Kennedy, 2024). By confronting these issues, we can ensure that AI serves all students, regardless of location or socioeconomic status (Owoc et al., 2021).

The Future of AI and Cultural Sensitivity in Education

Future education might benefit from AI and cultural awareness (Akgün & Greenhow, 2021; Eguchi et al., 2021). AI will get better at understanding and responding to cultural differences. AI in education will likely provide more tailored learning experiences that adapt to students' cultural backgrounds, learning methods, and language demands (Balta, 2023). Natural language processing innovations will let AI systems comprehend and respect linguistic variety, allowing students to study in their original languages or dialects (Liu, 2023).

AI trends suggest a more inclusive, culturally sensitive teaching style (Prabhakaran et al., 2022). AI technologies may include indigenous and non-Western perspectives and knowledge systems, which have been removed from mainstream education (Zhai et al., 2021). AI platforms can enhance learning for different pupils by incorporating local cultural practices, traditional knowledge, and narrative approaches (Salas-Pilco et al., 2022).

Additionally, AI will help instructors manage different classes. AI-powered technologies will let teachers track student progress, give real-time feedback, and recommend culturally relevant content (Chan & Tsi, 2023). Teachers may focus on relationships and critical thinking while AI handles administrative responsibilities and material delivery (Mozer et al., 2019).

A future of AI and cultural sensitivity in education includes balancing technology and tradition (Luckin & Holmes, 2016). AI should not replace conventional education but rather be used to combine the best of both (Aliabadi et al., 2023). AI may enhance education with individualized, data-driven insights and support and amplify learning's rich cultural traditions (Mello et al., 2023). Porayska-Pomsta

(2024) advocates for worldwide collaboration to enhance cultural understanding, equity, and inclusion using AI in education, educating students for a global society.

In conclusion, engineers, educators, cultural experts, and politicians must work together to solve ethical issues, overcome technological hurdles, and embrace AI in education. If AI-driven education respects cultural variety and encourages fair access, we may create a future where technology and tradition live happily, improving students' educational experiences globally.

REFERENCES

Abdi, A. W., Ridha, S., Yunus, M., Kamil, P. A., Safiah, I., & Gadeng, A. N. (2021). Assessing the Effectiveness of Geography-based Online Learning During the Covid-19 Pandemic in Higher Education. In Geosfera Indonesia (Vol. 6, Issue 3, p. 319). https://doi.org/DOI: 10.19184/geosi.v6i3.25811

Adams, C., Pente, P., Lemermeyer, G., & Rockwell, G. (2023). Ethical principles for artificial intelligence in K-12 education. In *Computers and Education Artificial Intelligence* (Vol. 4, p. 100131). Elsevier BV., DOI: 10.1016/j.caeai.2023.100131

Adewumi, A. (2022). Built heritage and planning laws in Africa: the Nigerian Experience. In Built Heritage (Vol. 6, Issue 1). Springer Nature. https://doi.org/DOI: 10.1186/s43238-022-00052-2

Afzal, A., Khan, S., Daud, S., Ahmad, Z., & Butt, A. (2023). Addressing the Digital Divide: Access and Use of Technology in Education. In journal of social sciences review (Vol. 3, Issue 2, p. 883). https://doi.org/DOI: 10.54183/jssr.v3i2.326

Akgün, S., & Greenhow, C. (2021). Artificial intelligence in education: Addressing ethical challenges in K-12 settings [Review of Artificial intelligence in education: Addressing ethical challenges in K-12 settings]. AI and Ethics, 2(3), 431. Springer Nature. https://doi.org/DOI: 10.1007/s43681-021-00096-7

Aleksandrova, A., Алексеева, М. Н., Лобанова, Е. Э., & Feoktistova, S. (2023). Application of hybrid educational technologies in the context of a personalized approach in adult education. In *E3S Web of Conferences* (Vol. 403, p. 8035). EDP Sciences., DOI: 10.1051/e3sconf/202340308035

Alharbi, L. A. (2023). A Systematic Literature Review on AI Algorithms and Techniques Adopted by e-Learning Platforms for Psychological and Emotional States. In International Journal of Advanced Computer Science and Applications (Vol. 14, Issue 2). Science and Information Organization. . 2023.0140254DOI: 10.14569/IJACSA.2023.0140254

Aliabadi, R., Singh, A., & Wilson, J. E. (2023). Transdisciplinary AI Education: The Confluence of Curricular and Community Needs in the Instruction of Artificial Intelligence. In Lecture notes on data engineering and communications technologies (p. 137). Springer International Publishing. DOI: 10.1007/978-981-99-7947-9_11

Angrist, N., Evans, D. K., Filmer, D., Glennerster, R., Rogers, H., & Sabarwal, S. (2024). How to improve education outcomes most efficiently? A review of the evidence using a unified metric [Review of How to improve education outcomes most efficiently? A review of the evidence using a unified metric]. Journal of Development Economics, 172, 103382. Elsevier BV. DOI: 10.1016/j.jdeveco.2024.103382

Atifnigar, H., Israr, S. W., Khanjar, I., & Hameed, S. A. B. A. (2023). Impacts of Culture on Classroom Participation Among Undergraduate EFL Learners in Afghanistan. In European Journal of Theoretical and Applied Sciences (Vol. 1, Issue 2, p. 291). https://doi.org/DOI: 10.59324/ejtas.2023.1(2).25

Bahja, M., Kuhail, M. A., & Hammad, R. (2021). Embracing Technological Change in Higher Education. In *IntechOpen eBooks*. IntechOpen., DOI: 10.5772/intechopen.100431

Balta, N. (2023). Embracing the Future: AI's Transformative Potential in Educational Research. In The European Educational Researcher (Vol. 6, Issue 2, p. 1). https://doi.org/DOI: 10.31757/euer.624

Benboujja, F., Hartnick, E., Zablah, E., Hersh, C., Callans, K., Villamor, P., Yager, P. H., & Hartnick, C. J. (2024). Overcoming language barriers in pediatric care: a multilingual, AI-driven curriculum for global healthcare education. In *Frontiers in Public Health* (Vol. 12). Frontiers Media., DOI: 10.3389/fpubh.2024.1337395

Bhutoria, A. (2022). Personalized education and Artificial Intelligence in the United States, China, and India: A systematic review using a Human-In-The-Loop model [Review of Personalized education and Artificial Intelligence in the United States, China, and India: A systematic review using a Human-In-The-Loop model]. Computers and Education Artificial Intelligence, 3, 100068. Elsevier BV. https://doi.org/DOI: 10.1016/j.caeai.2022.100068

Bizimana, B. (2018). Revolutionizing Education through Information Communication Technology: Progress and Challenges in Rwanda. In SSRN Electronic Journal. RELX Group (Netherlands). https://papers.ssrn.com/sol3/papers.cfm?abstract_id=3178209 DOI: 10.15580/GJER.2018.2.031018038

Blackwell, C. K., Lauricella, A. R., Wartella, E., Robb, M., & Schomburg, R. (2023). Adoption and use of technology in early education: The interplay of extrinsic barriers and teacher attitudes. https://www.sciencedirect.com/science/article/ pii/S0360131513001917

Bulathwela, S., Pérez-Ortiz, M., Holloway, C., & Shawe-Taylor, J. (2021). Could AI Democratise Education? Socio-Technical Imaginaries of an EdTech Revolution. In arXiv (Cornell University). Cornell University. https://doi.org/DOI: 10.48550/arXiv.2112

Cassidy, D., Borgne, Y. L., Bellas, F., Vuorikari, R., Rondin, E., Sharma, M., Niewint-Gori, J., Gröpler, J., Gilleran, A., & Kralj, L. (2023). Use Scenarios & Practical Examples of AI Use in Education. In arXiv (Cornell University). Cornell University. https://doi.org//arxiv.2309.12320DOI: 10.48550

Çelik, İ. (2022). Towards Intelligent-TPACK: An empirical study on teachers' professional knowledge to ethically integrate artificial intelligence (AI)-based tools into education. In Computers in Human Behavior (Vol. 138, p. 107468). Elsevier BV. https://doi.org/DOI: 10.1016/j.chb.2022.107468

Chan, C. K. Y., & Tsi, L. H. Y. (2023). The AI Revolution in Education: Will AI Replace or Assist Teachers in Higher Education? In arXiv (Cornell University). Cornell University. https://doi.org/DOI: 10.48550/arXiv.2305

Chen, Z. (2023). Ethics and discrimination in artificial intelligence-enabled recruitment practices. In Humanities and Social Sciences Communications (Vol. 10, Issue 1). Palgrave Macmillan. https://doi.org/DOI: 10.1057/s41599-023-02079-x

Collins, T. A., Heidelburg, K., & Scott, M. N. (2020). Using Technology to Teach Cultural Competence. In *Innovations in higher education teaching and learning* (p. 219). Emerald Publishing Limited., DOI: 10.1108/S2055-364120200000028021

Correa, V., & Tulbert, B. (2023). Teaching Culturally Diverse Students. https://www.tandfonline.com/doi/abs/10.1080/1045988X.1991.10871070

Crompton, H., & Burke, D. (2023). Artificial intelligence in higher education: the state of the field. In International Journal of Educational Technology in Higher Education (Vol. 20, Issue 1). Springer Nature. https://doi.org/DOI: 10.1186/s41239-023-00392-8

Cukurova, M., Miao, X., & Brooker, R. A. (2023). Adoption of Artificial Intelligence in Schools: Unveiling Factors Influencing Teachers Engagement. In arXiv (Cornell University). Cornell University. https://doi.org//arxiv.2304.00903DOI: 10.48550

Dangol, A., Newman, M., Wolfe, R., Lee, J. H., Kientz, J. A., Yip, J., & Pitt, C. (2024). Mediating Culture: Cultivating Socio-cultural Understanding of AI in Children through Participatory Design. In *Designing Interactive Systems Conference* (p. 1805). https://doi.org/DOI: 10.1145/3643834.3661515

Datta, S. D., Islam, M., Sobuz, Md. H. R., Ahmed, S., & Kar, M. (2024). Artificial intelligence and machine learning applications in the project lifecycle of the construction industry: A comprehensive review [Review of Artificial intelligence and machine learning applications in the project lifecycle of the construction industry: A comprehensive review]. Heliyon, 10(5). Elsevier BV. https://doi.org/. 2024. e26888DOI: 10.1016/j.heliyon

Dawadi, S., Goshtasbpour, F., & Kukulska-Hulme, A. (2024). Equitable Access to Higher Education Learning and Assessment: Perspectives from Low-Resource Contexts. In Journal of Interactive Media in Education (Vol. 2024, Issue 1). Ubiquity Press. https://doi.org/DOI: 10.5334/jime.832

Domoff, V. Ill., Pratt, Y. P., Drefs, M., & Wick, M. (2023). Challenging Definitions of Student Success Through Indigenous Involvement: An Opportunity to Inform School Psychology Practice. In Canadian Journal of School Psychology (Vol. 38, Issue 3, p. 191). SAGE Publishing. https://doi.org/DOI: 10.1177/08295735221149225

Dutta, D., & Pal, S. K. (2022). Interpretation of black box for short-term predictions of pre-monsoon cumulonimbus cloud events over Kolkata.

Eguchi, A., Okada, H., & Muto, Y. (2021). Contextualizing AI Education for K-12 Students to Enhance Their Learning of AI Literacy Through Culturally Responsive Approaches. In KI - Künstliche Intelligenz (Vol. 35, Issue 2, p. 153). Springer Science+Business Media. https://doi.org/DOI: 10.1007/s13218-021-00737-3

Etri, W. (2021). Intercultural sensitivity and its effects on ELT curricula – Teacher insights. In Higher Education Evaluation and Development (Vol. 16, Issue 1, p. 32). Emerald Publishing Limited. https://doi.org/DOI: 10.1108/HEED-03-2021-0027

Ezeamuzie, N. O., & Ezeamuzie, M. N. (2024). Multidimensional Framing of Environments Beyond Blocks and Texts in K–12 Programming. In *Review of Educational Research*. SAGE Publishing., DOI: 10.3102/00346543231216958

Ferrara, E. (2023). Fairness And Bias in Artificial Intelligence: A Brief Survey of Sources, Impacts, And Mitigation Strategies. In arXiv (Cornell University). Cornell University. https://doi.org/DOI: 10.48550/arXiv.2304

Gagné, J. C. D. (2023). The State of Artificial Intelligence in Nursing Education: Past, Present, and Future Directions. In International Journal of Environmental Research and Public Health (Vol. 20, Issue 6, p. 4884). Multidisciplinary Digital Publishing Institute. https://doi.org/DOI: 10.3390/ijerph20064884

Gaol, F. L., & Prasolova-Førland, E. (2021). Special section editorial: The frontiers of augmented and mixed reality in all levels of education. In Education and Information Technologies (Vol. 27, Issue 1, p. 611). Springer Science+Business Media. https://doi.org/DOI: 10.1007/s10639-021-10746-2

Gaskins, N. R. (2022). Interrogating Algorithmic Bias: From Speculative Fiction to Liberatory Design. In TechTrends (Vol. 67, Issue 3, p. 417). Springer Science+Business Media. https://doi.org/DOI: 10.1007/s11528-022-00783-0

Ge, X., Xu, C., Misaki, D., Markus, H. R., & Tsai, J. L. (2024). *How Culture Shapes What People Want From AI.*, DOI: 10.1145/3613904.3642660

Gligorea, I., Cioca, M., Oancea, R., Gorski, A.-T., Gorski, H., & Tudorache, P. (2023). Adaptive Learning Using Artificial Intelligence in e-Learning: A Literature Review [Review of Adaptive Learning Using Artificial Intelligence in e-Learning: A Literature Review]. Education Sciences, 13(12), 1216. Multidisciplinary Digital Publishing Institute. https://doi.org/DOI: 10.3390/educsci13121216

Guan, C., Mou, J., & Jiang, Z. (2020). Artificial intelligence innovation in education: A twenty-year data-driven historical analysis. In International Journal of Innovation Studies (Vol. 4, Issue 4, p. 134). Elsevier BV. DOI: 10.1016/j.ijis.2020.09.001

Guo, L. (2021). Research on the Main Strategies of Using Computer Technology to Inherit Traditional Culture. In Journal of Physics Conference Series (Vol. 1915, Issue 3, p. 32089). IOP Publishing. https://doi.org/DOI: 10.1088/1742-6596/1915/3/032089

Gurjar, N., & Bai, H. (2023). Assessing culturally inclusive instructional design in online learning. In Educational Technology Research and Development (Vol. 71, Issue 3, p. 1253). Springer Science+Business Media. DOI: 10.1007/s11423-023-10226-z

Hershcovich, D., Frank, S., Lent, H., de Lhoneux, M., Abdou, M., Brandl, S., Bugliarello, E., Piqueras, L. C., Chalkidis, I., Cui, R., Fierro, C., Margatina, K., Rust, P., & Søgaard, A. (2022). Challenges and Strategies in Cross-Cultural NLP. In *Proceedings of the 60th Annual Meeting of the Association for Computational Linguistics* (Volume 1: Long Papers). https://doi.org/DOI: 10.18653/v1/2022.acl-long.482

Holmes, W., Porayska-Pomsta, K., Holstein, K., Sutherland, E., Baker, T. T., Shum, S. B., Santos, O. C., & Rodrigo, Ma. M. T., Cukurova, M., Bittencourt, I. I., & Koedinger, K. R. (2021). Ethics of AI in Education: Towards a Community-Wide Framework. In International Journal of Artificial Intelligence in Education (Vol. 32, Issue 3, p. 504). Springer Science+Business Media. DOI: 10.1007/s40593-021-00239-1

Holstein, K., & Doroudi, S. (2021). Equity and Artificial Intelligence in Education: Will "AIEd" Amplify or Alleviate Inequities in Education? In arXiv (Cornell University). Cornell University. https://doi.org//arxiv.2104.12920DOI: 10.48550

Hu, C. (2022). A Comparative Study of Cultural and Traditional Education in Primary and Secondary Schools in Developed Countries Based on the MOPSO-CD-DNN Model. In *Computational Intelligence and Neuroscience* (Vol. 2022, p. 1). Hindawi Publishing Corporation., DOI: 10.1155/2022/3973763

Huang, L. (2023). Ethics of Artificial Intelligence in Education: Student Privacy and Data Protection. In Science Insights Education Frontiers (Vol. 16, Issue 2, p. 2577). https://doi.org/DOI: 10.15354/sief.23.re202

Hwang, Y., & Lim, C. (2024). Development of instructional design principles for using ICT in resource-limited learning environments: a case of Bangladesh. In Asia Pacific Education Review (Vol. 25, Issue 5, p. 1465). Springer Science+Business Media. https://doi.org/DOI: 10.1007/s12564-024-09996-9

Hyrynsalmi, S. M. (2024). Challenges and opportunities: Implementing diversity and inclusion in software engineering university level education in Finland. In *Journal of Systems and Software* (p. 112239). Elsevier BV., DOI: 10.1016/j.jss.2024.112239

Idrus, F., Ramli, L. N., & Habib, N. J. (2023). Exploring Preservice Teachers' Experiences of Implementing Culturally Responsive Teaching in the ESL Classrooms. In Theory and Practice in Language Studies (Vol. 13, Issue 3, p. 766). Academy Publication. https://doi.org/DOI: 10.17507/tpls.1303.26

Kallunki, V., Katajavuori, N., Kinnunen, P., Anttila, H., Tuononen, T., Haarala-Muhonen, A., Pyörälä, E., & Myyry, L. (2023). Comparison of voluntary and forced digital leaps in higher education – Teachers' experiences of the added value of using digital tools in teaching and learning. In Education and Information Technologies (Vol. 28, Issue 8, p. 10005). Springer Science+Business Media. https://doi.org/DOI: 10.1007/s10639-022-11559-7

Kamalov, F., & Gurrib, I. (2023). New Era of Artificial Intelligence in Education: Towards a Sustainable Multifaceted Revolution. In arXiv (Cornell University). Cornell University. https://doi.org//arxiv.2305.18303DOI: 10.48550

Kazimzade, G., Patzer, Y., & Pinkwart, N. (2019). Artificial Intelligence in Education Meets Inclusive Educational Technology—The Technical State-of-the-Art and Possible Directions. In *Perspectives on rethinking and reforming education* (p. 61). Springer Nature., DOI: 10.1007/978-981-13-8161-4_4

Kerimbayev, N., Umirzakova, Z., Shadiev, R., & Jotsov, V. (2023). A student-centered approach using modern technologies in distance learning: a systematic review of the literature [Review of A student-centered approach using modern technologies in distance learning: a systematic review of the literature]. Smart Learning Environments, 10(1). Springer Nature. DOI: 10.1186/s40561-023-00280-8

Kim, J., Lee, H.-K., & Cho, Y. H. (2022). Learning design to support student-AI collaboration: perspectives of leading teachers for AI in education. In Education and Information Technologies (Vol. 27, Issue 5, p. 6069). Springer Science+Business Media. https://doi.org/DOI: 10.1007/s10639-021-10831-6

Lai, Y.-H. (2023). Multi-ethnic computational thinking and cultural respect in unmanned aerial vehicle-assisted culturally responsive teaching. In *Frontiers in Psychology* (Vol. 14). Frontiers Media., DOI: 10.3389/fpsyg.2023.1098812

Lamptey, D., McIsaac, J. D., MacQuarrie, M., Cummings, R., Rossiter, M. D., Janus, M., & Turner, J. (2024). Relationship between Childhood Disability or Developmental Delay and COVID-19 Pandemic Impacts on Families across the Canadian Maritime Provinces. In Journal of Child and Family Studies (Vol. 33, Issue 2, p. 458). Springer Science+Business Media. DOI: 10.1007/s10826-023-02779-7

Liu, M. (2023). Exploring the Application of Artificial Intelligence in Foreign Language Teaching: Challenges and Future Development. In SHS Web of Conferences (Vol. 168, p. 3025). EDP Sciences. DOI: 10.1051/shsconf/202316803025

Louie, B., Björling, E. A., Kuo, A. C., & Alves-Oliveira, P. (2022). Designing for culturally responsive social robots: An application of a participatory framework. In *Frontiers in Robotics and AI* (Vol. 9). Frontiers Media., DOI: 10.3389/frobt.2022.983408

Luckin, R., & Holmes, W. (2016). Intelligence Unleashed: An argument for AI in Education. https://oro.open.ac.uk/50104/

Luo, S. (2022). The Optimization of Civic Education with the Assistance of Artificial Intelligence Devices. In *Wireless Communications and Mobile Computing* (Vol. 2022, p. 1). Wiley., DOI: 10.1155/2022/4144654

Ma, X., & Jiang, C. (2023; Vol. 14). On the Ethical Risks of Artificial Intelligence Applications in Education and Its Avoidance Strategies. In Journal of Education Humanities and Social Sciences., DOI: 10.54097/ehss.v14i.8868

Maghsudi, S., Lan, A., Xu, J., & van der Schaar, M. (2021). Personalized Education in the Artificial Intelligence Era: What to Expect Next. In IEEE Signal Processing Magazine (Vol. 38, Issue 3, p. 37). Institute of Electrical and Electronics Engineers. https://doi.org/DOI: 10.1109/MSP.2021.3055032

Matli, W., & Wamba, S. F. (2023). Work from anywhere: inequalities in technology infrastructure distribution for digit workers. In Digital Transformation and Society (Vol. 2, Issue 2, p. 149). https://doi.org/DOI: 10.1108/DTS-08-2022-0042

Mello, R. F., Freitas, E., Pereira, F. D., Cabral, L., Tedesco, P., & Ramalho, G. (2023). Education in the age of Generative AI: Context and Recent Developments. In arXiv (Cornell University). Cornell University. https://doi.org//arxiv. 2309.12332DOI: 10.48550

Michaeli, T., Seegerer, S., & Romeike, R. (2023). What Students Can Learn About Artificial Intelligence—Recommendations for K-12 Computing Education. In arXiv (Cornell University). Cornell University. https://doi.org// arxiv.2305.06450DOI: 10.48550

Millikin, C. C. (2023). Future-Proof your Instructional Design with Universal Design for Learning and Translanguaging. In Literacy Information and Computer Education Journal (Vol. 14, Issue 1, p. 3709). DOI: 10.20533/licej.2040.2589.2023.0488

Milne, E., & Wotherspoon, T. (2023). 'Success is different in our eyes': reconciling definitions of educational success among Indigenous families and education systems in Alberta, Canada. In Critical Studies in Education (Vol. 64, Issue 5, p. 428). Taylor & Francis. https://doi.org/DOI: 10.1080/17508487.2023.2173266

Mohammed, P., & Watson, E. (2019). Towards Inclusive Education in the Age of Artificial Intelligence: Perspectives, Challenges, and Opportunities. In Perspectives on rethinking and reforming education (p. 17). Springer Nature. https://doi.org/DOI: 10.1007/978-981-13-8161-4_2

Mozer, M. C., Wiseheart, M., & Novikoff, T. P. (2019, February 19). Artificial intelligence to support human instruction. In Proceedings of the National Academy of Sciences (Vol. 116, Issue 10, p. 3953). National Academy of Sciences. https://doi.org/DOI: 10.1073/pnas.1900370116

Mustapha, A., Mohammed, A., Egigogo, A. R., Kutiriko, A. A., & Dokoro, A. H. (2020). Factors Affecting the Utilization and Adoption of Technology in Education. In *IntechOpen eBooks*. IntechOpen., DOI: 10.5772/intechopen.85712

Nazer, L., Zatarah, R., Waldrip, S., Ke, J. X. C., Moukheiber, M., Khanna, A. K., Hicklen, R. S., Moukheiber, L., Moukheiber, D., Ma, H., & Mathur, P. (2023). Bias in artificial intelligence algorithms and recommendations for mitigation [Review of Bias in artificial intelligence algorithms and recommendations for mitigation]. PLOS Digital Health, 2(6). Public Library of Science. DOI: 10.1371/journal.pdig.0000278

Nguyen, A., Ngo, H. N., Hong, Y., Dang, B., & Nguyen, B.-P. T. (2022). Ethical principles for artificial intelligence in education. In Education and Information Technologies (Vol. 28, Issue 4, p. 4221). Springer Science+Business Media. https://doi.org/DOI: 10.1007/s10639-022-11316-w

Núñez, J. L. M., Harris, P., Fernández, R. P., Abbas, A., & Radovanović, D. (2023). Does intrinsic motivation mediate perceived artificial intelligence (AI) learning and computational thinking of students during the COVID-19 pandemic? In *Computers and Education Artificial Intelligence* (Vol. 4, p. 100128). Elsevier BV., DOI: 10.1016/j.caeai.2023.100128

Ober, T. M., Lehman, B., Gooch, R., Oluwalana, O., Solyst, J., Phelps, G., & Hamilton, L. S. (2023). Culturally Responsive Personalized Learning: Recommendations for a Working Definition and Framework. In ETS Research Report Series (Vol. 2023, Issue 1, p. 1). Wiley. DOI: 10.1002/ets2.12372

Porayska-Pomsta, K. (2024). From Algorithm Worship to the Art of Human Learning: Insights from 50-year journey of AI in Education. In arXiv (Cornell University). Cornell University. https://doi.org/DOI: 10.48550/arXiv.2403

Prabhakaran, V., Qadri, R., & Hutchinson, B. (2022). Cultural Incongruencies in Artificial Intelligence. In arXiv (Cornell University). Cornell University. https://doi.org//arxiv.2211.13069DOI: 10.48550

Qaffas, A. A., Kaabi, K., Shadiev, R., & Essalmi, F. (2020). Towards an optimal personalization strategy in MOOCs. In Smart Learning Environments (Vol. 7, Issue 1). Springer Nature. https://doi.org/DOI: 10.1186/s40561-020-0117-y

Rejeb, A. (2022). The Learning Situation in the Computer-Oriented Centers for Children in Tunisia, Interchangeability, and Interdependence: Contexts, Challenges and Experience's Building Ethnographic Approach. In Education and human development. https://doi.org/DOI: 10.5772/intechopen.101736

Salas-Pilco, S. Z., Xiao, K., & Oshima, J. (2022). Artificial Intelligence and New Technologies in Inclusive Education for Minority Students: A Systematic Review [Review of Artificial Intelligence and New Technologies in Inclusive Education for Minority Students: A Systematic Review]. Sustainability, 14(20), 13572. Multidisciplinary Digital Publishing Institute. DOI: 10.3390/su142013572

Salazar, D., & Guillaumier, C. (2024). *7. The Global Conservatoire*. In Open Book Publishers., DOI: 10.11647/obp.0353.07

Samıer, E. A., & ElKaleh, E. S. (2023). Culturally Sensitive Research Methods for Educational Administration and Leadership. In *Routledge eBooks*. Informa., DOI: 10.4324/9781003130666

Sandoval, J. C. B., de Santana, V. F., Berger, S., Thomas, L., & Hobson, S. (2023). Responsible and Inclusive Technology Framework: A Formative Framework to Promote Societal Considerations in Information Technology Contexts. In arXiv (Cornell University). Cornell University. https://doi.org/. 11565DOI: 10.48550/arxiv.2302

Sehgal, G. (2023). Refocusing Indian education system in the perspective of ancient Indian education system. In World Journal of Advanced Research and Reviews (Vol. 19, Issue 2, p. 861). GSC Online Press. https://doi.org/DOI: 10.30574/wjarr.2023.19.2.1673

Shams, R. A., Zowghi, D., & Bano, M. (2023). Challenges and Solutions in AI for All. In arXiv (Cornell University). Cornell University. https://doi.org/DOI: 10.48550/ arXiv.2307

Sima, Q., & Wu, S. (2022). The Acceptability of Traditional Culture under the Background of Deep Learning. In *Computational Intelligence and Neuroscience* (Vol. 2022, p. 1). Hindawi Publishing Corporation., DOI: 10.1155/2022/4010099

Smith, E. (2023). Challenges Encountered in the Implementation of Online Distance Learning in African Countries. In International Journal of Online and Distance Learning (Vol. 4, Issue 1, p. 1). https://doi.org/DOI: 10.47604/ijodl.1998

Solyst, J., Axon, A., Stewart, A., Eslami, M., & Ogan, A. (2023). Investigating Girls' Perspectives and Knowledge Gaps on Ethics and Fairness in Artificial Intelligence in a Lightweight Workshop. In arXiv (Cornell University). Cornell University. https://doi.org//arxiv.2302.13947DOI: 10.48550

Sui, J. (2023). Confucius Influence on Primary Education--- Research Based on Eastsouthern Asian Countries. In Lecture Notes in Education Psychology and Public Media (Vol. 2, Issue 1, p. 1049). https://doi.org/DOI: 10.54254/2753-7048/2/2022657

Sullamo, A. E., Mekonnen, E. A., & Mihirete, D. M. (2023). Teacher educators' views vis-à-vis their practices on facilitating learning to teach. In Pedagogical Research (Vol. 8, Issue 4). Lectito Journals. https://doi.org/DOI: 10.29333/pr/13477

Tadimalla, S. Y., & Maher, M. L. (2024). AI Literacy for All: Adjustable Interdisciplinary Socio-technical Curriculum. In arXiv (Cornell University). Cornell University. https://doi.org//arxiv.2409.10552DOI: 10.48550

Tanjga, M. (2023). E-learning and the Use of AI: A Review of Current Practices and Future Directions [Review of E-learning and the Use of AI: A Review of Current Practices and Future Directions]. https://doi.org/DOI: 10.32388/AP0208

Toyokawa, Y., Horikoshi, I., Majumdar, R., & Ogata, H. (2023). Challenges and opportunities of AI in inclusive education: a case study of data-enhanced active reading in Japan. In Smart Learning Environments (Vol. 10, Issue 1). Springer Nature. https://doi.org/DOI: 10.1186/s40561-023-00286-2

Tsai, C., Ma, Y., Chang, Y., & Lai, Y.-H. (2022). Integrating Multiculturalism Into Artificial Intelligence-Assisted Programming Lessons: Examining Inter-Ethnicity Differences in Learning Expectancy, Motivation, and Effectiveness. In Frontiers in Psychology (Vol. 13). Frontiers Media. https://doi.org/. 868698DOI: 10.3389/fpsyg.2022

Vassilakopoulou, P., & Hustad, E. (2021). Bridging Digital Divides: a Literature Review and Research Agenda for Information Systems Research [Review of Bridging Digital Divides: a Literature Review and Research Agenda for Information Systems Research]. Information Systems Frontiers, 25(3), 955. Springer Science+Business Media. https://doi.org/DOI: 10.1007/s10796-020-10096-3

Vrabie, C. (2024). Artificial Intelligence from Idea to Implementation. How Can AI Reshape the Education Landscape? In arXiv (Cornell University). Cornell University. https://doi.org//arxiv.2407.20236DOI: 10.48550

Wang, X., & Zhang, W. (2022). Improvement of Students' Autonomous Learning Behavior by Optimizing Foreign Language Blended Learning Mode. In Open, S. A. G. E. (Ed.), *Issue 1). SAGE Publishing* (Vol. 12)., DOI: 10.1177/21582440211071108

Wang, Y. (2020). When artificial intelligence meets educational leaders' data-informed decision-making: A cautionary tale. In Studies In Educational Evaluation (Vol. 69, p. 100872). Elsevier BV. https://doi.org/. 2020.100872DOI: 10.1016/j.stueduc

Welukar, J. N., & Bajoria, G. P. (2021). Artificial Intelligence in Cyber Security - A Review [Review of Artificial Intelligence in Cyber Security - A Review]. International Journal of Scientific Research in Science and Technology, 488. Technoscience Academy. https://doi.org/DOI: 10.32628/IJSRST218675

Wong, P. (2020). Cultural Differences as Excuses? Human Rights and Cultural Values in Global Ethics and Governance of AI. In Philosophy & Technology (Vol. 33, Issue 4, p. 705). Springer Nature (Netherlands). DOI: 10.1007/s13347-020-00413-8

Woolf, B. P., Arroyo, I., & Zualkernan, I. (2011). *Education Technology for the Developing World.*, DOI: 10.1109/GHTC.2011.69

Xiuzhi, F., & Yongtao, X. (2023). Excellent Traditional Culture Entering College Campus: Mechanism Innovation and Practical Strategies. In SHS Web of Conferences (Vol. 168, p. 1016). EDP Sciences. https://doi.org/DOI: 10.1051/shsconf/202316801016

Yam, K. C., Tan, T. C. Y., Jackson, J. C., Shariff, A., & Gray, K. (2023). Cultural Differences in People's Reactions and Applications of Robots, Algorithms, and Artificial Intelligence. In Management and Organization Review (Vol. 19, Issue 5, p. 859). Cambridge University Press. https://doi.org/DOI: 10.1017/mor.2023.21

Ye, Z., & Hu, D.-Y. (2023). Research on the Strategy of Integrating Chinese Excellent Traditional Culture into Primary School Moral Education. In Curriculum and Teaching Methodology (Vol. 6, Issue 7). DOI: 10.23977/curtm.2023.060704

Yefremtseva, T. N., Musagulova, R. E., Takanova, O. V., Zaitsev, A. A., & Sergeeva, N. (2021). Rethinking the intercultural communicative competence evaluation in higher education. In SHS Web of Conferences (Vol. 127, p. 2001). EDP Sciences. https://doi.org/DOI: 10.1051/shsconf/202112702001

Yi, H., Liu, T., & Lan, G. (2024). The key artificial intelligence technologies in early childhood education: a review [Review of The key artificial intelligence technologies in early childhood education: a review]. Artificial Intelligence Review, 57(1). Springer Science+Business Media. DOI: 10.1007/s10462-023-10637-7

Yim, I. H. Y., & Su, J. (2024). Artificial intelligence (AI) learning tools in K-12 education: A scoping review [Review of Artificial intelligence (AI) learning tools in K-12 education: A scoping review]. Journal of Computers in Education. Springer Science+Business Media. https://doi.org/DOI: 10.1007/s40692-023-00304-9

Yu, X. (2021). Research on the Strategy of Multi Ethnic Culture Blending in School Field Based on Internet of Things. In Journal of Physics Conference Series (Vol. 1744, Issue 4, p. 42022). IOP Publishing. https://doi.org/DOI: 10.1088/1742-6596/1744/4/042022

Yundayani, A., Suseno, M., & Herlina, E. (2023). A Duolingo-based English Language Skills Assessment: Through the Eyes of Vocational Students. In Jurnal Ilmu Pendidikan (JIP) STKIP Kusuma Negara (Vol. 15, Issue 1, p. 9). https://doi.org/DOI: 10.37640/jip.v15i1.1683

Zhai, X., Chu, X., Chai, C. S., Jong, M. S., Starčič, A. I., Spector, M., Liu, J., Jing, Y., & Li, Y. (2021). A Review of Artificial Intelligence (AI) in Education from 2010 to 2020 [Review of A Review of Artificial Intelligence (AI) in Education from 2010 to 2020]. Complexity, 2021(1). Hindawi Publishing Corporation. DOI: 10.1155/2021/8812542

Zhang, K., & Aslan, A. B. (2021). AI technologies for education: Recent research & future directions. https://www.sciencedirect.com/science/article/pii/S2666920X21000199

Zhao, J., & Li, X. (2022). Research on the Mining of Intangible Cultural Heritage Digital Resources in the Manual Online Teaching System of Preschool Education. In Computational Intelligence and Neuroscience (Vol. 2022, p. 1). Hindawi Publishing Corporation. https://doi.org/DOI: 10.1155/2022/2136597

Zhao, Y. (2023). Globalization in Education. https://www.sciencedirect.com/ science/article/pii/B9780080970868921135

Zhu, J., & Ren, C. (2022). Analysis of the Effect of Artificial Intelligence on Role Cognition in the Education System. In *Occupational Therapy International* (Vol. 2022, p. 1). Hindawi Publishing Corporation., DOI: 10.1155/2022/1781662

Chapter 9
Funding Models for AI in Education:
Ensuring Sustainability and Impact

Rahmawati Rahmawati
https://orcid.org/0000-0002-4783-7268
Universitas Muhammadiyah Palopo, Indonesia

Rismawati Sudirman
https://orcid.org/0000-0001-8046-6764
Universitas Muhammadiyah Palopo, Indonesia

Duriani Duriani
Universitas Muhammadiyah Palopo, Indonesia

Yunus Yunus
Universitas Muhammadiyah Palopo, Indonesia

ABSTRACT

This chapter examines various funding strategies crucial for the sustainable incorporation of Artificial Intelligence (AI) in education. While AI revolutionizes education via adaptive systems, data analytics, and personalized learning tools, sustainable financing continues to be a significant obstacle. The study examines conventional funding sources including government grants and philanthropy, alongside innovative forms such as venture capital, social impact bonds, and subscription-based frameworks. Case studies demonstrate both successful and unsuccessful AI applications, emphasizing lessons about stakeholder participation, equity, and quantifiable impact. Focus is directed towards synchronizing financial strategies with educational objectives, utilizing data to illustrate value, and establishing partnerships for sustained viability. The results support the implementation of innovative, inclusive,

DOI: 10.4018/979-8-3373-5781-2.ch009

and performance-oriented funding mechanisms to guarantee that AI technologies improve educational outcomes broadly.

INTRODUCTION TO AI IN EDUCATION

The Rise of AI in Educational Settings

Artificial Intelligence (AI) has swiftly revolutionized numerous sectors, including education. The use of AI technology in educational environments has transformed the processes of teaching and learning, enhancing personalization, efficiency, and accessibility (Ayeni et al., 2024). Artificial intelligence comprises many technologies, such as machine learning, natural language processing, and data analytics, which combined empower instructors to customize their methodologies to address the unique requirements of pupils.

A prominent trend in AI within education is the advancement of adaptive learning systems (Kabudi et al., 2021). These systems employ algorithms to assess student performance in real-time, facilitating tailored learning experiences that adapt to individual strengths and limitations. Platforms such as DreamBox and Knewton offer personalized mathematics training tailored to an individual student's learning speed, hence increasing engagement and enhancing results. This transition to individualized learning is not merely a fad; it signifies a fundamental alteration in the delivery and consumption of educational content.

A significant advancement is the implementation of AI-powered chatbots and virtual assistants. These tools augment student support by delivering immediate responses to inquiries, streamlining administrative work, and giving tutoring assistance beyond conventional classroom hours (Lin et al., 2023). Georgia State University has deployed an AI chatbot to assist students with financial aid, leading to enhanced retention rates. These applications highlight AI's capacity to optimize operations and improve the student experience.

Contemporary trends underscore the increasing focus on data analytics within the educational sector. Institutions are progressively utilizing big data to get insights into student behavior, learning patterns, and institutional efficacy (Kizilcec2024). Utilizing this data enables educators to make informed decisions that enhance instructional methodologies and optimize resource allocation. Furthermore, predictive analytics can detect at-risk kids promptly, facilitating timely interventions that can profoundly influence student progress.

Notwithstanding these gains, the extensive implementation of AI in education encounters obstacles, especially concerning financing. Numerous creative AI initiatives encounter difficulties in obtaining the requisite financial backing to expand

and maintain their operations. As educational institutions endeavor to incorporate AI technology, comprehending the financial landscape is essential (Wang & Cheng, 2021). This book seeks to examine diverse funding approaches that might guarantee the sustainability and efficacy of AI efforts in education, facilitating the connection between invention and execution. By tackling these funding obstacles, we can realize the complete promise of AI in revolutionizing educational experiences for learners globally.

Importance of Funding for AI Initiatives

The effective implementation of Artificial Intelligence (AI) in educational environments is heavily dependent on sufficient financing. Financial resources are crucial for the development, implementation, and expansion of AI technologies that improve educational experiences (Schiff, 2022). Insufficient finance can hinder the realization of even the most innovative concepts, hence constraining the potential advantages of AI in education.

Funding is essential at multiple phases of technology adoption. It primarily facilitates research and development, enabling institutions to investigate novel AI applications customized for their particular educational environments (Schiff, 2022). This stage frequently necessitates considerable effort to implement pilot programs, collect data, and enhance algorithms. Following the development of a technology, financial resources are essential for the training of educators, the incorporation of AI tools into current curricula, and the establishment of infrastructure to support these advancements. Ultimately, sustained financial backing is essential for the maintenance and enhancement of AI systems, which are perpetually advancing.

Multiple case studies demonstrate the transformative effect of funding on AI projects within education. A prominent example is Carnegie Learning, a firm that integrates artificial intelligence with cognitive science to deliver customized mathematics tuition. Carnegie Learning developed its MATHia software, which adapts to individual student needs in real-time, with early investment from startup capital and government funds (Tariq, 2025). The initiative has exhibited substantial enhancements in student performance, especially in marginalized neighborhoods, illustrating how focused investment can result in favorable educational outcomes.

A notable example is the implementation of AI in the advising system at Georgia State University (GSU). GSU obtained money to create an AI-powered chatbot called Pounce, intended to aid students with inquiries regarding admissions, financial assistance, and course selection (Aytaç, 2024). The deployment of Pounce has resulted in enhanced student engagement and elevated retention rates, especially among first-generation college students. This effort highlights the significance of funding in both the development of AI technologies and their effective integration into the student experience.

The collaboration between the University of Southern California and the AI firm Knewton exemplifies how joint funding might improve educational activities (Marques-Cobeta, 2024). They collaboratively created individualized learning pathways that have markedly enhanced student performance across multiple courses. This partnership underscores the capacity of collaborative finance methods to stimulate innovation and effect significant transformation in education.

In conclusion, sufficient financing is essential for the effective implementation of AI technology in education. An analysis of successful case studies reveals that investment in AI initiatives promotes technological progress and substantially improves educational achievements, thereby ensuring the realization of AI's transformational potential in global classrooms.

UNDERSTANDING THE LANDSCAPE OF EDUCATIONAL FUNDING

Traditional Funding Sources

Effectively navigating educational finance is crucial for the successful execution of AI efforts in education (Norton2025). Conventional funding sources, encompassing government grants, public financing, private donations, and charitable contributions, are crucial in facilitating educational institutions and their technology implementation initiatives.

Government funds are a crucial source of funding for educational efforts, especially for those focused on incorporating technology into classrooms (Okoye et al. 2023). Numerous federal and state initiatives designate financial resources explicitly for educational innovation, encompassing the incorporation of AI. The U.S. Department of Education provides grants via programs such as the Education Innovation and Research (EIR) initiative, which facilitates the development and expansion of evidence-based educational approaches. These funds frequently focus on marginalized communities, seeking to enhance equity in educational access and results. Securing government funding is competitive and necessitates a stringent application process, potentially presenting difficulties for smaller institutions or businesses.

Public financing is essential in bolstering educational endeavors. Numerous school districts depend on state and local financing to execute technology initiatives. This funding frequently depends on budget allocations that emphasize instructional technology, which may vary according to economic situations and political priorities (Favero & Kagalwala, 2025). Consequently, whereas public funding might furnish significant resources for AI initiatives, its inconsistency may engender doubt regarding long-term planning and sustainability.

Alongside government sources, private donations and philanthropic contributions have gained significance in the educational funding arena. Numerous foundations and affluent individuals acknowledge the capacity of AI to revolutionize education and are prepared to finance novel initiatives. Entities such as the Bill & Melinda Gates Foundation and the Chan Zuckerberg Initiative have allocated substantial funding to promote technology-based educational programs. These charitable donations can furnish essential financing for pilot initiatives, research, and development, enabling educators to explore AI solutions that may not yet demonstrate established efficacy (Canfield, 2023).

Nevertheless, dependence on private contributions may sometimes pose difficulties. Philanthropic support frequently entails certain expectations and achievements that may not consistently correspond with the institution's overarching objectives (Maclean et al. 2021). The competitive landscape for obtaining private funding can create resource inequities among institutions, particularly disadvantaging those with less visibility or established networks.

In summary, conventional financial sources, such as government grants, public financing, and private contributions, are essential for sustaining AI projects in education. Comprehending the complexities of these funding channels is crucial for educators and administrators aiming to initiate and maintain creative AI projects. By properly utilizing these traditional sources, educational institutions can establish a robust foundation for the successful integration of AI technology, hence improving learning experiences and outcomes for students.

Emerging Funding Models

As educational funding advances, new models are gaining prominence, especially for efforts that integrate Artificial Intelligence (AI) in education (Yadav and Shrawankar, 2025). Among these methods, venture capital in ed-tech and crowdfunding/community-driven initiatives are significant for their capacity to offer creative funding alternatives that can improve the sustainability and effect of AI projects.

Venture capital (VC) has emerged as a prominent force in the educational technology sector, especially for businesses concentrating on AI-driven solutions. Investors are increasingly acknowledging the transformative potential of AI in education and are prepared to allocate significant cash to innovative ventures. These investments empower organizations to innovate advanced technology, perform market analysis, and expand their operations swiftly (Sergi & Popkova, 2022). Companies such as Coursera and Duolingo have secured substantial venture capital funding, enabling them to broaden their platforms and engage millions of learners globally. This influx of finance accelerates technological improvements and stimulates competitiveness, hence fostering innovation in the ed-tech sector.

Nevertheless, although venture capital might offer significant resources, it frequently entails elevated expectations for swift growth and profitability. This pressure may result in an emphasis on immediate benefits instead of enduring educational outcomes (Jeon & Maula, 2022). Moreover, the competitive landscape of obtaining venture capital funding can provide obstacles for smaller firms or projects lacking the visibility or connections of larger entities. Consequently, although venture capital serves as a significant funding source, it is imperative for stakeholders to reconcile the quest for financial support with a dedication to substantive educational results.

Crowdfunding and community-driven initiatives signify a burgeoning funding paradigm that has attained prominence in recent years. Platforms such as Kickstarter and GoFundMe enable educators and innovators to solicit financial backing directly from the community (Escudero et al. 2025). This concept enables individuals to articulate their ambitions for AI in education and connect with prospective advocates dedicated to enhancing educational experiences. Effective crowdfunding campaigns can yield both financial resources and a community of advocates committed to the project's success.

Furthermore, community-driven initiatives frequently prioritize collaboration and collective ownership, cultivating a feeling of accountability among stakeholders (Ahmad and Islam 2024). Local schools may initiate crowdfunding campaigns to create AI-enhanced educational tools customized to their specific need, involving parents, alumni, and local companies in the endeavor. This grassroots methodology can yield more sustainable financial options, as community people are more inclined to endorse programs that directly affect their local educational settings.

In conclusion, innovative funding mechanisms like venture capital and crowdfunding are transforming the educational funding landscape. By utilizing these innovative strategies, educators and entrepreneurs can obtain the resources required to implement AI programs efficiently. It is essential to reconcile financial goals with a dedication to cultivating significant educational experiences, guaranteeing that the incorporation of AI in education results in sustainable and impactful benefits for all students.

Challenges in Securing Funding

Although multiple funding sources are available to facilitate AI projects in education, certain hurdles may obstruct the effective procurement of essential financial resources (Al-Zahrani & Alasmari, 2025). Two significant challenges are the fierce rivalry for few resources and the discordance of funding priorities among stakeholders.

The rivalry for educational funding has escalated in recent years, propelled by a growing desire for new solutions that meet varied educational requirements. As numerous institutions and organizations endeavor to adopt AI technologies, they frequently compete for the same financial resources (Thompson et al., 2022). The competition is especially intense among startups in the ed-tech industry, where many companies are vying for venture financing or grants. Consequently, numerous promising initiatives may have challenges in attaining awareness or reputation within a saturated marketplace, complicating the acquisition of necessary finance for development and implementation.

Moreover, conventional funding sources, including government grants, can exhibit constraints in both scope and accessibility. Financial limitations at federal, state, and municipal levels may result in diminished funding for educational programs, compelling institutions to vie not just against each other but also with other sectors considered of greater priority (Jayabalan et al. 2021). This context can provide substantial obstacles for AI initiatives, especially those aimed at marginalized communities or novel methodologies lacking established success.

A significant problem in obtaining funding for AI initiatives in education is the discordance of funding objectives among diverse stakeholders. Financial backers, such as governmental bodies, philanthropic entities, and private investors, frequently possess distinct agendas or ambitions that may not correspond with the aims of educational institutions or the requirements of students (Audretsch & Belitski, 2022). For example, whereas a funding agency may emphasize programs that yield instant quantifiable results, educators may favor long-term developmental objectives that necessitate time to materialize.

This disconnection might result in frustration for educators and entrepreneurs pursuing funding for AI programs that may not align with established funding structures. The focus on quantitative measurements may obscure the qualitative advantages of AI in education, like the enhancement of creativity, critical thinking, and social-emotional learning (Sethi and Jain 2024). Consequently, projects with substantial potential may be disregarded only due to their misalignment with the particular metrics preferred by financiers.

In conclusion, the obstacles to obtaining funding for AI efforts in education are complex, involving fierce competition for scarce resources and a misalignment of financial priorities. To surmount these challenges, it is imperative for educators, legislators, and financiers to participate in transparent discourse and cooperation, guaranteeing that funding plans correspond with the dynamic requirements of educational institutions and the varied demographics they serve. By tackling these problems, stakeholders may establish a more conducive funding landscape that promotes innovation and amplifies the influence of AI technology in education.

EVALUATING AI PROJECTS IN EDUCATION

Criteria for Assessing AI Initiatives

As educational institutions progressively implement Artificial Intelligence (AI) technology, it is crucial to create explicit criteria for assessing the efficacy and feasibility of these projects (Okunlaya et al., 2022). Two essential factors for evaluating AI initiatives in education are their effect on learning outcomes and their scalability and durability.

The effect on learning outcomes is arguably the most critical factor for assessing AI programs. Educational stakeholders, comprising educators, administrators, and financiers, must evaluate the efficacy of a particular AI initiative in improving student learning and engagement. This assessment entails analyzing both quantitative and qualitative variables (Alotaibi & Alshehri, 2023). Quantitative metrics may consist of standardized test scores, graduation rates, and retention rates, whereas qualitative metrics could include student and teacher feedback, classroom observations, and case studies. Successful AI projects must exhibit a positive relationship with enhanced learning outcomes, indicating their significant contribution to student achievement. An AI-driven personalized learning platform must demonstrate that students utilizing the system get superior academic achievement relative to their non-using counterparts.

Furthermore, the assessment method must take into account the varied requirements of learners. AI initiatives must be structured to promote fairness and inclusivity, guaranteeing that all students, including individuals with impairments and those from marginalized communities, derive advantages from the technology (Hooda et al. 2022). This emphasis on inclusivity not only improves learning results but also corresponds with overarching educational objectives of equity and access.

Scalability and sustainability are both critical factors in evaluating AI ventures. An effective AI project must not only exhibit success in a confined context but also have the capacity for wider applicability across various educational environments (Merhi, 2023). Scalability denotes the capacity to broaden the initiative to engage a bigger audience without sacrificing quality. A pilot AI program demonstrating favorable results in one school should be assessed for its applicability to other schools with diverse demographics and resources.

Sustainability, conversely, pertains to the enduring feasibility of the AI endeavor. This encompasses elements of sustained finance, institutional backing, and the ability for continual enhancement (Olawade et al. 2024). An effort dependent exclusively on temporary grants or one-time funding may encounter difficulties in sustaining its impact over time. Consequently, it is essential to evaluate whether the initiative had a definitive strategy for obtaining sustained resources, including collaborations with local enterprises or community organizations, to guarantee its ongoing success.

In conclusion, assessing AI projects in education necessitates a holistic approach that accounts for their effects on learning outcomes as well as their scalability and sustainability. By utilizing these criteria, educational stakeholders can make informed decisions regarding which AI projects to endorse, thereby promoting innovations that improve educational experiences and outcomes for all learners. This assessment procedure is essential for guaranteeing the appropriate integration of AI technologies in educational environments, resulting in significant and enduring enhancements in teaching and learning.

Metrics for Success

Assessing the efficacy of AI initiatives in education necessitates a comprehensive set of measurements that can yield insights into their effectiveness and impact (Halagatti et al. 2023). Key performance indicators (KPIs) and longitudinal studies are critical elements of this evaluation approach, enabling stakeholders to evaluate the efficacy of AI projects over time and across many contexts.

Key performance indicators (KPIs) are measurable metrics that businesses utilize to assess the effectiveness of particular activities in relation to established objectives. In the realm of AI in education, KPIs may include diverse indicators customized for various facets of learning and instruction (Rompho, 2024).

Typical KPIs may encompass enhancements in student grades, course completion rates, engagement metrics (such as time allocated on learning platforms), and satisfaction ratings from both students and educators. An AI-driven tutoring system may monitor the quantity of sessions completed by students and link these statistics with later academic results to assess the system's efficacy.

Moreover, KPIs can be employed to evaluate the operational efficacy of AI activities. Metrics include cost per student served, response speed in AI-driven support systems, and user retention rate can yield significant insights into the efficacy of the technology (Dua2025). By defining explicit KPIs, educational institutions can set standards that enable continuous monitoring and enhancement, ensuring that AI initiatives remain congruent with educational objectives.

Longitudinal studies and data analysis are essential for comprehending the enduring effects of AI initiatives on educational results. In contrast to short-term assessments that may reflect immediate impacts, longitudinal studies monitor the same cohort of students over an extended duration, facilitating a more thorough comprehension of how AI technologies affect learning trajectories (Salmela-Aro et al. 2021). This methodology can uncover trends and patterns that may not be apparent in brief assessments, such as the enduring advantages of tailored learning pathways or the prolonged engagement of students with AI tools.

Data analysis is essential for the formulation of KPIs and the implementation of longitudinal studies. Utilizing big data, educational institutions can discern relationships between AI utilization and student achievement, revealing insights that guide future decision-making (Han et al., 2024). Data analysis may indicate that kids utilizing AI-driven resources routinely surpass their peers, leading instructors to broaden access to these tools.

In conclusion, the establishment of effective performance measures is essential for assessing AI initiatives in education. Utilizing key performance metrics and performing longitudinal studies enables stakeholders to acquire significant insights into the efficacy and influence of AI efforts. These criteria assist in evaluating current initiatives and guide future investments and developments, ultimately guaranteeing that AI technologies significantly enhance educational experiences and outcomes for all learners.

Case Studies of Funded AI Projects

Examining case studies of financed AI projects in education yields significant insights into both effective and ineffective implementations, uncovering lessons learned and best practices that can inform future endeavors (Demartini et al., 2024). These examples demonstrate the intricacies of incorporating AI technology into educational environments and underscore the elements that influence their success or failure.

A notable case study is the deployment of the AI-driven platform, Carnegie Learning, which emphasizes individualized mathematics instruction. This effort secured substantial money from governmental grants and private investors, enabling the development of an adaptive learning system that customizes training to meet individual student requirements. The technology employs real-time data to modify material and deliver customized feedback, leading to significant enhancements in student performance. Institutions implementing Carnegie Learning observed elevated mathematics results and enhanced student engagement (Khazanchi et al. 2025). This research highlights the necessity of integrating technology with curriculum standards and providing educators with sufficient training to effectively use AI tools into their instructional methods.

The deployment of the AI-driven tool, Knewton, encountered obstacles that eventually constrained its effectiveness. Knewton, despite obtaining significant venture capital investment and being initially acclaimed as an innovative solution for individualized learning, encountered difficulties in attaining widespread classroom acceptance. Educators' feedback revealed that the platform was intricate and not user-friendly, resulting in irritation for both teachers and pupils. This scenario highlights the imperative of engaging educators in the development process to guarantee that AI technologies are user-friendly and address the genuine wants of users (Zainuddin, 2024). Moreover, it underscores the significance of continuous support and training to ensure seamless integration into current teaching methodologies.

A significant initiative is the Georgia State University chatbot, Pounce, which aids students with administrative questions and academic guidance (Halmo, 2025). Pounce has markedly enhanced student engagement and retention rates, financed by a blend of institutional resources and philanthropic donations. The project illustrates the efficacy of AI in improving student assistance services. Essential insights from this program encompass the significance of tackling particular challenges within the student experience and the necessity of ongoing evaluation and refinement informed by user feedback.

In conclusion, examining case studies of financed AI initiatives in education uncovers essential insights into the determinants of success or failure. Successful programs generally synchronize technology with educational objectives, include educators in the planning phase, and offer continuous support and training. Conversely, projects that neglect these factors may falter in realizing their intended impact. By analyzing both successful and unsuccessful initiatives, stakeholders may formulate best practices that improve the efficacy of AI in education, guaranteeing that future projects are both innovative and sustainable.

STRATEGIES FOR SUSTAINABLE FUNDING

Building Partnerships and Collaborations

Establishing strategic alliances and collaborations is crucial for securing sustained funding for AI efforts in education. Collaborating with educational institutions, technology firms, and other stakeholders can establish a strong support network that improves the feasibility of AI initiatives and guarantees their sustained success (Bowser et al. 2024).

An excellent strategy is to cultivate collaborations between educational institutions and technology firms. Through collaboration, educational institutions can utilize the expertise and resources of technology companies to create and execute AI-driven solutions customized to their particular requirements (Zamiri & Esmaeili, 2024). Partnerships can enable the collaborative development of instructional tools that integrate effortlessly into current curricula, ensuring that the technology is both innovative and practical. Such cooperation may also result in joint financial opportunities, as technology firms can be inclined to invest in initiatives that correspond with their corporate social responsibility objectives or have potential for market expansion.

Furthermore, involving educational institutions in the development process facilitates a deeper comprehension of the distinct issues encountered by educators and students. This information can inform the development of AI tools that are more efficient and pertinent, ultimately resulting in enhanced learning outcomes (Heilporn et al. 2021). A collaboration between a university and a technology firm might yield an AI platform designed to target certain learning deficiencies recognized by instructors, thereby assuring the technology fulfills a significant role in the classroom.

Establishing consortiums for collaborative funding is an additional strategic method for obtaining resources for AI activities. Consortiums can amalgamate various educational institutions, organizations, and stakeholders to consolidate their resources and skills, addressing shared difficulties and seeking collective funding opportunities (Charlwood and Guenole 2022). This collaborative concept promotes the financial feasibility of individual initiatives while fostering a sense of community and shared responsibility among participants.

Furthermore, consortiums can augment the legitimacy of funding offers. When many institutions collaborate on a united project, they can exhibit a greater effect and a dedication to cooperation, enhancing the appeal of their applications to prospective funders (Van et al. 2021). A consortium dedicated to creating AI solutions for STEM education might propose a detailed plan illustrating how the program will advantage a varied array of students across the involved institutions.

Moreover, consortiums can promote the exchange of knowledge and exemplary practices among members, enabling institutions to benefit from each other's experiences and achievements. This collaborative setting may result in more inventive solutions and an increased probability of securing sustained funding.

In conclusion, establishing partnerships and collaborations is an essential method for obtaining sustained funding for AI efforts in education. By collaborating with educational institutions and technology firms to establish consortiums for collective funding, stakeholders can augment the efficacy and scope of AI initiatives. This collaborative method promotes innovation and guarantees efficient resource utilization, resulting in significant and enduring enhancements in educational performance.

Innovative Funding Approaches

Educational institutions are pursuing sustainable finance for AI efforts, leading to the emergence of novel funding strategies as viable options (Okunlaya et al., 2022). Social impact bonds, outcome-based funding, subscription models, and pay-for-success frameworks are increasingly popular, providing innovative financing methods for educational projects while ensuring accountability and demonstrable results.

Social impact bonds (SIBs) constitute an innovative funding mechanism that harmonizes the interests of investors, service providers, and educational institutions (Millner & Meyer, 2022). In a SIB arrangement, private investors supply initial funding to finance educational projects, including AI initiatives designed to enhance student results. The government or a philanthropic entity commits to reimbursing these funders with a return on investment solely if the program achieves specified success measures, such as elevated graduation rates or improved learning outcomes. This concept incentivizes good program execution while transferring financial risk from educational institutions, enabling them to concentrate on providing quality education without the encumbrance of upfront expenses. By linking funding to quantifiable results, Social Impact Bonds promote ongoing enhancement and accountability, guaranteeing that resources are allocated to initiatives that genuinely effect change.

Outcome-based funding is an innovative strategy that prioritizes results in the distribution of financial resources. This strategy enables educational institutions to obtain money contingent upon their capacity to attain designated outcomes, such as enhanced student engagement or elevated test scores. Outcome-based funding promotes the adoption of evidence-based strategies and the ongoing evaluation of their efficacy by associating financial support with performance (Dixon, 2021). This methodology can be very advantageous for AI projects, as it encourages the utilization of data analytics to monitor advancement and implement educated modifications to programs. Institutions that effectively exhibit favorable results might obtain sustained support, promoting a culture of accountability and quality.

Subscription models and pay-for-success frameworks are increasingly prevalent in the education sector. In a subscription approach, educational institutions or districts remit a periodic charge for access to AI tools and services, facilitating predictable budgeting and continuous support. This method can reduce the entry barriers for educational institutions, allowing them to explore AI technology without substantial initial investments (Wang & Cheng, 2021). Moreover, subscription models frequently provide continuous training and support, guaranteeing that instructors can proficiently use AI products in their instructional methodologies.

Pay-for-success schemes, akin to outcome-based funding, link financial assistance to the attainment of designated objectives. This approach stipulates that financing is dependent on the successful achievement of predetermined outcomes, fostering a results-driven mentality among educators and administrators (Waymack et al., 2024). This strategy can incentivize universities to use breakthrough AI systems that exhibit distinct advantages for student learning and engagement.

In conclusion, novel finance mechanisms such as social impact bonds, outcome-based financing, subscription models, and pay-for-success frameworks present viable possibilities for obtaining sustainable funding for AI efforts in education. By synchronizing financial resources with quantifiable results and promoting accountability, these models can augment the efficacy and influence of AI technology, ultimately resulting in enhanced educational experiences for all learners. Adopting these new solutions can facilitate a more sustainable and efficient integration of AI in education.

Leveraging Data and Evidence

In the pursuit of sustainable financing for AI initiatives in education, utilizing data and proof is essential for attracting investors and showcasing the impact of these projects (Pancholi and Shukla 2025). Through the application of comprehensive data analytics, educational institutions may make educated decisions and articulate the significance of their AI initiatives to prospective sponsors.

Attracting investors with data commences with the formulation of a definitive structure for the collection and analysis of pertinent metrics. Educational institutions must ascertain key performance indicators (KPIs) that embody the objectives of their AI initiatives (Milić et al. 2024). These KPIs may encompass indicators such as student engagement levels, enhancements in learning outcomes, and general satisfaction rates among students and educators. By carefully collecting and evaluating this data, organizations can construct persuasive narratives that underscore the efficacy of their AI programs.

An institution utilizing an AI-driven personalized learning platform may monitor student performance data longitudinally, revealing substantial enhancements in test scores and engagement relative to conventional teaching approaches. Presenting this data to prospective investors can effectively demonstrate the project's success and its scaling possibilities. Investors are more inclined to endorse programs substantiated by robust proof of impact, since they require assurance that their financial contributions will yield significant educational results (Busch et al. 2021).

Exhibiting impact using analytics is crucial for securing financing and maintaining stakeholder support.

Through the ongoing assessment and scrutiny of AI projects, educational institutions can pinpoint areas for enhancement and modify their plans accordingly. This iterative data-driven decision-making process cultivates a culture of responsibility and openness, essential for sustaining investor confidence.

Furthermore, employing analytics enables institutions to perform longitudinal studies that evaluate the enduring impacts of AI projects on student learning (Shoaib et al. 2024). By monitoring cohorts of students who have utilized AI tools over multiple years, schools can obtain insights on the enduring advantages of these technologies. This longitudinal data can be especially compelling when pursuing financial support from philanthropic entities or governmental bodies that emphasize evidence-based methodologies.

Furthermore, institutions can utilize data to generate visualizations and reports that successfully convey their findings to varied audiences. Utilizing engaging infographics, dashboards, and success narratives can effectively communicate intricate information in an accessible style, facilitating potential investors' understanding of the data's value.

In conclusion, utilizing data and evidence is an effective way for obtaining sustained funding for AI initiatives in education. Educational institutions may recruit funders and demonstrate impact through analytics by utilizing data to craft compelling narratives that underscore the efficacy and promise of their AI initiatives. This data-driven methodology not only improves accountability but also cultivates a culture of ongoing enhancement, ultimately resulting in more effective and lasting AI programs that benefit both learners and instructors.

FUTURE DIRECTIONS AND RECOMMENDATIONS

Trends Shaping the Future of AI Funding in Education

The evolving environment of AI funding in education is giving rise to various trends that may influence its future. The influence of policy and regulatory modifications, along with the effects of worldwide occurrences on financial accessibility, is notably substantial (Schiff2022). Comprehending these tendencies is crucial for stakeholders aiming to adeptly manage the intricacies of financing AI ventures.

Policy and regulatory modifications significantly influence the accessibility and distribution of financing for AI in education. Governments globally are progressively acknowledging the significance of technology in improving educational results and are initiating legislation that facilitate the incorporation of AI in schools

(Timotheou et al. 2023). Initiatives designed to enhance digital literacy and ensure fair access to technology can result in augmented funding prospects for AI projects. As regulations progress, they may create frameworks that encourage educational institutions to embrace novel technology, thus cultivating a more conducive climate for AI financing.

Moreover, regulatory modifications can affect the categories of data that may be gathered and the manner in which it is utilized, especially regarding student privacy and data security. As rules tighten, educational institutions must assure compliance while successfully utilizing data to illustrate the benefit of their AI activities (Han et al., 2024). This equilibrium will be essential for sustaining trust among stakeholders, including as parents, students, and financiers, and will influence how institutions navigate funding applications and collaborations.

The influence of worldwide occurrences, notably the COVID-19 pandemic, has significantly impacted the availability of financing for AI in education. The transition to remote learning during the pandemic underscored the pressing demand for technological solutions, resulting in a significant increase in financing for educational technology efforts (Treve, 2021). Governments and philanthropic entities augmented financial assistance to facilitate institutions' adaptation to novel learning environments. As the current crisis abates, there exists a possibility of budget reduction, necessitating that educational institutions push for sustained investment in AI technologies that improve learning.

Furthermore, worldwide occurrences can alter financing priorities, as evidenced during economic recessions or public health emergencies. Stakeholders must stay adaptable and receptive to these changes, modifying their funding methods to correspond with new objectives (Apollo & Mbah, 2021). For example, programs aimed at mental health assistance or addressing learning disparities intensified by the pandemic may garner increased attention and financing.

The future of AI funding in education will be influenced by legislative and regulatory modifications, together with the effects of global events on financial accessibility. Educational institutions must be cognizant of these developments and actively collaborate with policymakers and financiers to promote sustainable investment in AI initiatives. By matching their initiatives with shifting objectives and showcasing their capacity to tackle urgent educational issues, stakeholders can obtain the requisite resources to improve learning results and guarantee the sustained success of AI in education.

Recommendations for Stakeholders

As the incorporation of Artificial Intelligence (AI) in education progresses, it is imperative for educators, policymakers, and financiers to interact efficiently to optimize the efficacy of AI efforts (Schiff2022). This section provides specific advice for each stakeholder group, highlighting tactics for goal alignment and securing sustainable funding.

For Instructors: Educators are essential for the effective integration of AI technologies in the classroom. To enhance effectiveness, they must actively participate in the creation and selection of AI tools that correspond with their educational objectives (Dimitriadou & Lanitis, 2023). This participation guarantees that the selected technologies meet particular educational requirements and improve student engagement. Furthermore, educators must emphasize continuous professional development to enhance their digital literacy and comprehension of AI applications. By mastering AI tools, educators can seamlessly incorporate them into their pedagogical methods and promote their sustained application.

Collaboration among educators is crucial. Establishing professional learning networks can enhance the exchange of best practices and ideas for AI adoption (Vičič et al. 2024). These communities can function as forums for educators to exchange issues, triumphs, and techniques for effectively utilizing AI to enhance learning outcomes.

Policymakers should cultivate a conducive climate for AI in education by formulating explicit regulations that encourage equitable access to technology and financial resources. This entails promoting enhanced investment in educational technology and ensuring that funding is allocated to initiatives that have quantifiable benefit (Ticona et al. 2025). Policymakers should endeavor to optimize legislative frameworks that may obstruct the implementation of AI technologies, especially concerning data privacy and security.

Moreover, interacting with educational stakeholders, such as educators and administrators, is essential for comprehending the practical issues they encounter. Policymakers ought to solicit feedback from these groups during the formulation of policies and funding programs to guarantee that initiatives are pertinent and efficacious (Li et al., 2022).

For Funders: Funding entities, such as governmental bodies and philanthropic organizations, have to emphasize financial support for initiatives that exhibit a distinct alignment with educational objectives and quantifiable results (Hassan et al. 2022). Formulating criteria that prioritize evidence-based approaches can facilitate the allocation of resources to initiatives with the highest potential for effect.

Moreover, financiers ought to promote cooperation among educational entities, technology firms, and community organizations. By endorsing consortiums and partnerships, donors can enable the sharing of resources and experience, resulting in more inventive solutions to complex educational challenges (Mariani et al., 2022).

Ultimately, financiers ought to maintain adaptability and responsiveness to evolving demands and trends in education. By modifying their funding strategies to correspond with the changing scenario, they can guarantee that their investments persist in fostering significant progress in AI technology and education.

In conclusion, adhering to these principles will enable educators, policymakers, and funders to collaborate effectively, aligning their objectives to enhance the efficacy of AI projects in education. By fostering collaboration, ongoing education, and adherence to evidence-based methodologies, stakeholders may establish a sustainable financial framework that improves educational results and equips students for success in a progressively digital environment.

CONCLUSION

The effective incorporation of Artificial Intelligence (AI) in education depends on both technological advancement and the sustainability and strategic coherence of funding models. This paper has illustrated that diverse financing mechanisms—spanning conventional government grants and philanthropic contributions to novel models like social impact bonds, outcome-based funding, and subscription frameworks—can facilitate AI initiatives at multiple stages of development and implementation.

The efficacy of these approaches hinges on their capacity to synchronize financial resources with educational objectives and quantifiable results. Case studies indicate that effective AI initiatives are supported by stakeholder collaboration, instructor involvement, and a well-defined evaluation framework based on data and impact indicators. In contrast, unsuccessful programs frequently exhibited deficiencies in alignment, usability, or sustainable funding strategies.

Furthermore, collaborations among educational institutions, private investors, and technology providers are essential for expanding solutions and tackling inequalities in access and uptake. Inclusivity, ethical design, and sustained support must be fundamental to all funding methods.

In summary, sustainable and impact-driven funding structures are crucial to optimize the transformative capabilities of AI in education. Educators, legislators, and funders must collaborate to create frameworks that emphasize equity, transparency, and scalability. By doing so, they can guarantee that AI technologies not only improve educational outcomes but also promote creativity, resilience, and accessibility in global learning environments. The future of artificial intelligence in education relies not only on the technologies developed but also on the methods and beneficiaries of its financing.

REFERENCES

Ahmad, I., & Islam, M. R. (2024). Empowerment and participation: Key strategies for inclusive development. In Building Strong Communities: Ethical Approaches to Inclusive Development (pp. 47-68). Emerald Publishing Limited. [HTML]

Al-Zahrani, A. M., & Alasmari, T. M. (2025). A comprehensive analysis of AI adoption, implementation strategies, and challenges in higher education across the Middle East and North Africa (MENA) region. [HTML]. *Education and Information Technologies*, *30*(8), 11339–11389. DOI: 10.1007/s10639-024-13300-y

Alotaibi, N. S. & Alshehri, A. H. (2023). Prospers and obstacles in using artificial intelligence in Saudi Arabia higher education institutions—The potential of AI-based learning outcomes. Sustainability. mdpi.com

Apollo, A. & Mbah, M. F. (2021). Challenges and opportunities for climate change education (Cce) in East Africa: A critical review. Climate. mdpi.com

Audretsch, D. B. & Belitski, M. (2022). A strategic alignment framework for the entrepreneurial university. Industry and Innovation. tandfonline.com

Ayeni, O. O., Al Hamad, N. M., Chisom, O. N., Osawaru, B., & Adewusi, O. E. (2024). AI in education: A review of personalized learning and educational technology. [researchgate.net]. *GSC Advanced Research and Reviews*, *18*(2), 261–271. DOI: 10.30574/gscarr.2024.18.2.0062

Aytaç, Z. (2024). Using artificial intelligence tools in higher education. In *Innovation in the University 4.0 System based on Smart Technologies* (pp. 164–175). Chapman and Hall/CRC. [HTML]

Bowser, G., Ho, S. S., Ziebell, A., & Lazendic-Galloway, J. (2024). Networking and collaborating: The role of partnerships across sectors to achieve educational goals in sustainability. [springer.com]. *Sustainable Earth Reviews*, *7*(1), 17. DOI: 10.1186/s42055-024-00080-z

Busch, T., Bruce-Clark, P., Derwall, J., Eccles, R., Hebb, T., Hoepner, A., Klein, C., Krueger, P., Paetzold, F., Scholtens, B., & Weber, O. (2021). Impact investments: A call for (re) orientation. [springer.com]. *SN Business & Economics*, *1*(2), 1–13. DOI: 10.1007/s43546-020-00033-6

Canfield, M. (2023). The ideology of innovation: Philanthropy and racial capitalism in global food governance. The Journal of Peasant Studies. tandfonline.com

Charlwood, A., & Guenole, N. (2022). Can HR adapt to the paradoxes of artificial intelligence? [wiley.com]. *Human Resource Management Journal*, *32*(4), 729–742. DOI: 10.1111/1748-8583.12433

Demartini, C. G., Sciascia, L., Bosso, A., & Manuri, F. (2024). Artificial intelligence bringing improvements to adaptive learning in education: A case study. Sustainability. mdpi.com

Dimitriadou, E. & Lanitis, A. (2023). A critical evaluation, challenges, and future perspectives of using artificial intelligence and emerging technologies in smart classrooms. Smart Learning Environments. springer.com

Dixon, R. (2021). Performance management in social impact bonds: how an outcomes-based approach shapes hybrid partnerships. International Journal of Public Sector Management. emerald.com

Dua, G. K. (2025). Enhancing Organizational Performance Through Process Performance Measurement and KPIs in AI-Based Digital Transformation. Perspectives on Digital Transformation in Contemporary Business, 241-268. [HTML]

Escudero, S. B., Anglin, A. H., Allison, T. H., & Wolfe, M. T. (2025). Crowdfunding: A Theory-Centered Review and Roadmap of the Multidisciplinary Literature. [sagepub.com]. *Journal of Management*, •••, 01492063251328267. DOI: 10.1177/01492063251328267

Favero, N., & Kagalwala, A. (2025). The politics of school funding: How state political ideology is associated with the allocation of revenue to school districts. [HTML]. *Educational Policy*, *39*(3), 693–722. DOI: 10.1177/08959048241258724

Gardner, A., Smith, A. L., Steventon, A., Coughlan, E., & Oldfield, M. (2022). Ethical funding for trustworthy AI: Proposals to address the responsibilities of funders to ensure that projects adhere to trustworthy AI practice. [springer.com]. *AI and Ethics*, *2*(2), 1–15. DOI: 10.1007/s43681-021-00069-w PMID: 34790951

Halagatti, M., Gadag, S., Mahantshetti, S., Hiremath, C. V., Tharkude, D., & Banakar, V. (2023). Artificial intelligence: the new tool of disruption in educational performance assessment. In *Smart analytics, artificial intelligence and sustainable performance management in a global digitalised economy* (pp. 261–287). Emerald Publishing Limited. [HTML] DOI: 10.1108/S1569-37592023000110A014

Halmo, H. (2025). Human-Centered, Tech-Enabled: Scaling Academic Advising in Higher Education Through Predictive Analytics and Organizational Change an Innovation Study. [HTML]

Han, X., Xiao, S., Sheng, J., & Zhang, G. (2024). Enhancing efficiency and decision-making in higher education through intelligent commercial integration: Leveraging artificial intelligence. [HTML]. *Journal of the Knowledge Economy*, *16*(1), 1546–1582. DOI: 10.1007/s13132-024-01868-2

Hassan, E., Groot, W., & Volante, L. (2022). Education funding and learning outcomes in Sub-Saharan Africa: A review of reviews. [sciencedirect.com]. *International Journal of Educational Research Open*, *3*, 100181. DOI: 10.1016/j.ijedro.2022.100181

Heilporn, G., Lakhal, S., & Bélisle, M. (2021). An examination of teachers' strategies to foster student engagement in blended learning in higher education. [springer.com]. *International Journal of Educational Technology in Higher Education*, *18*(1), 25. DOI: 10.1186/s41239-021-00260-3 PMID: 34805484

Hooda, M., Rana, C., Dahiya, O., Rizwan, A., & Hossain, M. S. (2022). Artificial intelligence for assessment and feedback to enhance student success in higher education. [wiley.com]. *Mathematical Problems in Engineering*, *2022*(1), 5215722. DOI: 10.1155/2022/5215722

Jayabalan, J., Dorasamy, M., & Raman, M. (2021). Reshaping higher educational institutions through frugal open innovation. [mdpi.com]. *Journal of Open Innovation*, *7*(2), 145. DOI: 10.3390/joitmc7020145

Jeon, E. & Maula, M. (2022). Progress toward understanding tensions in corporate venture capital: A systematic review. Journal of Business Venturing. sciencedirect.com

Kabudi, T., Pappas, I., & Olsen, D. H. (2021). AI-enabled adaptive learning systems: A systematic mapping of the literature. Computers and education [sciencedirect.com]. *Artificial Intelligence*, *2*, 100017.

Khazanchi, R., Di Mitri, D., & Drachsler, H. (2025). The Effect of AI-Based Systems on Mathematics Achievement in Rural Context: A Quantitative Study. [wiley.com]. *Journal of Computer Assisted Learning*, *41*(1), e13098. DOI: 10.1111/jcal.13098

Kizilcec, R. F. (2024). To advance AI use in education, focus on understanding educators. [springer.com]. *International Journal of Artificial Intelligence in Education*, *34*(1), 12–19. DOI: 10.1007/s40593-023-00351-4 PMID: 37359103

Li, L., Taeihagh, A., & Tan, S. Y. (2022). What factors drive policy transfer in smart city development? Insights from a Delphi study. Sustainable Cities and Society. sciencedirect.com

Lin, C. C., Huang, A. Y. Q., & Yang, S. J. H. (2023). A review of ai-driven conversational chatbots implementation methodologies and challenges (1999–2022). Sustainability. mdpi.com

Maclean, M., Harvey, C., Yang, R., & Mueller, F. (2021). Elite philanthropy in the United States and United Kingdom in the new age of inequalities. [wiley.com]. *International Journal of Management Reviews*, *23*(3), 330–352. DOI: 10.1111/ijmr.12247

Mariani, L., Trivellato, B., Martini, M., & Marafioti, E. (2022). Achieving sustainable development goals through collaborative innovation: Evidence from four European initiatives. Journal of Business Ethics. springer.com

Marques-Cobeta, N. (2024). Artificial Intelligence in Education: Unveiling Opportunities and Challenges. Innovation and Technologies for the Digital Transformation of Education: European and Latin American Perspectives, 33-42. [HTML]

Merhi, M. I. (2023). An evaluation of the critical success factors impacting artificial intelligence implementation. [HTML]. *International Journal of Information Management*, *69*, 102545. DOI: 10.1016/j.ijinfomgt.2022.102545

Milić, T., Tomić, B., Marinković, S., & Jeremić, V. (2024). ESPRIT adventure: Assessing hybrid fuzzy-crisp rule-based AI method effectiveness in teaching key performance indicators. [sciencedirect.com]. *International Journal of Management Education*, *22*(3), 101022. DOI: 10.1016/j.ijme.2024.101022

Millner, R. & Meyer, M. (2022). Collaborative governance in Social Impact Bonds: aligning interests within divergent accountabilities?. Public Management Review. tandfonline.com

Norton, J. (2025). Navigating the AI Policy Landscape: AI in Community College Education. In Navigating AI in Academic Libraries: Implications for Academic Research (pp. 109-130). IGI Global. [HTML]

Okoye, K., Hussein, H., Arrona-Palacios, A., Quintero, H. N., Ortega, L. O. P., Sanchez, A. L., Ortiz, E. A., Escamilla, J., & Hosseini, S. (2023). Impact of digital technologies upon teaching and learning in higher education in Latin America: An outlook on the reach, barriers, and bottlenecks. [springer.com]. *Education and Information Technologies*, *28*(2), 2291–2360. DOI: 10.1007/s10639-022-11214-1 PMID: 35992366

Okunlaya, R. O., Syed Abdullah, N., & Alias, R. A. (2022). Artificial intelligence (AI) library services innovative conceptual framework for the digital transformation of university education. [HTML]. *Library Hi Tech*, *40*(6), 1869–1892. DOI: 10.1108/LHT-07-2021-0242

Olawade, D. B., Wada, O. Z., David-Olawade, A. C., Fapohunda, O., Ige, A. O., & Ling, J. (2024). Artificial intelligence potential for net zero sustainability: Current evidence and prospects. Next sustainability, 4, 100041. sciencedirect.com

Pancholi, K., & Shukla, P. (2025). Harnessing AI for Sustainability: Innovations, Policies, and Investment Paradigms. In Diversity, AI, and Sustainability for Financial Growth (pp. 97-124). IGI Global Scientific Publishing. [HTML]

Rompho, N. (2024). Do objectives and key results solve organizational performance measurement issues? [HTML]. *Benchmarking*, *31*(3), 669–682. DOI: 10.1108/BIJ-07-2022-0464

Salmela-Aro, K., Tang, X., Symonds, J., & Upadyaya, K. (2021). Student engagement in adolescence: A scoping review of longitudinal studies 2010–2020. [wiley.com]. *Journal of Research on Adolescence*, *31*(2), 256–272. DOI: 10.1111/jora.12619 PMID: 33991151

Schiff, D. (2022). Education for AI, not AI for education: The role of education and ethics in national AI policy strategies. [springer.com]. *International Journal of Artificial Intelligence in Education*, *32*(3), 527–563. DOI: 10.1007/s40593-021-00270-2

Sergi, B. S. & Popkova, E. G. (2022). Towards a 'wide'role for venture capital in OECD countries' industry 4.0. Heliyon. cell.com

Sethi, S. S., & Jain, K. (2024). AI technologies for social emotional learning: Recent research and future directions. [emerald.com]. *Journal of Research in Innovative Teaching & Learning*, *17*(2), 213–225. DOI: 10.1108/JRIT-03-2024-0073

Shoaib, M., Sayed, N., Singh, J., Shafi, J., Khan, S., & Ali, F. (2024). AI student success predictor: Enhancing personalized learning in campus management systems. [HTML]. *Computers in Human Behavior*, *158*, 108301. DOI: 10.1016/j.chb.2024.108301

Tariq, M. U. (2025). *Advancing Inquiry-Based Learning Through Generative AI-Enabled Assessments*. Educational Assessments in the Age of Generative AI. [HTML] DOI: 10.4018/979-8-3693-6351-5.ch007

Thompson, F., Rongen, F., Cowburn, I., & Till, K. (2022). The impacts of sports schools on holistic athlete development: a mixed methods systematic review. Sports medicine. springer.com

Ticona Machaca, A., Cano Ccoa, D. M., Gutiérrez Castillo, F. H., Quispe Gomez, F., Arroyo Beltrán, M., Zirena Cano, M. G., Sánchez-Chávez-Arroyo, V., Manrique Chavez, C. P., Romualdo Rosario, A., Adauto-Medina, W. A., & Montes Salcedo, M. (2025). Public Policy for Human Capital: Fostering Sustainable Equity in Disadvantaged Communities. [mdpi.com]. *Sustainability (Basel)*, *17*(2), 535. DOI: 10.3390/su17020535

Timotheou, S., Miliou, O., Dimitriadis, Y., Sobrino, S. V., Giannoutsou, N., Cachia, R., Monés, A. M., & Ioannou, A. (2023). Impacts of digital technologies on education and factors influencing schools' digital capacity and transformation: A literature review. [springer.com]. *Education and Information Technologies*, *28*(6), 6695–6726. DOI: 10.1007/s10639-022-11431-8 PMID: 36465416

Treve, M. (2021). What COVID-19 has introduced into education: Challenges facing higher education institutions (HEIs). Higher Education Pedagogies. tandfonline.com

Van der Graaf, P., Blank, L., Holding, E., & Goyder, E. (2021). What makes a 'successful' collaborative research project between public health practitioners and academics? A mixed-methods review of funding applications submitted to a local intervention evaluation scheme. [springer.com]. *Health Research Policy and Systems*, *19*(1), 1–13. DOI: 10.1186/s12961-020-00671-0 PMID: 33472643

Vičič Krabonja, M., Kustec, S., Skrbinjek, V., Aberšek, B., & Flogie, A. (2024). Innovative professional learning communities and sustainable education practices through digital transformation. [mdpi.com]. *Sustainability (Basel)*, *16*(14), 6250. DOI: 10.3390/su16146250

Wang, T. & Cheng, E. C. K. (2021). An investigation of barriers to Hong Kong K-12 schools incorporating Artificial Intelligence in education. Computers and Education: Artificial Intelligence. sciencedirect.com

Waymack, N., Groom-Thomas, L., Loeb, S., & Bendheim, K. (2024). Outcomes-Based Contracting in Tutoring: Insights and Recommendations. studentsupportaccelerator.org

Yadav, U., & Shrawankar, U. (2025). Artificial Intelligence Across Industries: A Comprehensive Review With a Focus on Education. AI Applications and Strategies in Teacher Education, 275-320. [HTML]

Zainuddin, Z. (2024). Integrating ease of use and affordable gamification-based instruction into a remote learning environment. Asia Pacific Education Review. springer.com

Zamiri, M. & Esmaeili, A. (2024). Methods and technologies for supporting knowledge sharing within learning communities: A systematic literature review. Administrative Sciences. mdpi.com

Chapter 10
Bridging the Gap:
The Role of Public-Private Partnerships in Educational Technology

Mulyadi Mulyadi
https://orcid.org/0009-0001-8246-2158
Universitas Islam Makassar, Indonesia

Andi Asrifan
https://orcid.org/0000-0002-9934-6129
Universitas Negeri Makassar, Indonesia

ABSTRACT

This study examines the crucial function of public-private partnerships (PPPs) in promoting educational technology to mitigate gaps in access, innovation, and quality. Given the issues in education stemming from the digital divide, antiquated infrastructure, and constrained resources, public-private partnerships present a collaborative framework to address these deficiencies. The paper emphasizes different PPP models—contractual agreements, joint ventures, and strategic alliances—and presents successful case studies in K-12 education, higher education, and marginalized populations. Essential elements for successful relationships are trust cultivation, objective congruence, and ongoing assessment. The document analyzes new developments such as AI-driven education and virtual reality, suggesting regulatory frameworks and stakeholder collaboration to guarantee sustainability and effectiveness. Ultimately, public-private partnerships are positioned as key instruments for redefining education in a digital era.

DOI: 10.4018/979-8-3373-5781-2.ch010

INTRODUCTION TO EDUCATIONAL TECHNOLOGY

Definition and Importance

Educational technology, commonly known as EdTech, includes many tools, resources, and methodologies aimed at improving teaching and learning experiences (Dexter, 2023). It encompasses a range of classic classroom instruments, including projectors and whiteboards, as well as sophisticated digital platforms such as learning management systems (LMS), interactive software, and mobile applications. The principal objective of educational technology is to enhance learning efficacy and improve educational results by utilizing new solutions that address the varied demands of students and educators.

In contemporary education, technology is essential in revolutionizing conventional teaching methods. It facilitates personalized learning experiences, permitting educators to customize their teaching strategies to address specific student requirements (Haleem et al., 2022). Adaptive learning technology may evaluate a student's progress in real-time and modify the curriculum accordingly, ensuring that each learner receives the suitable amount of challenge and assistance. This personalization enhances engagement and motivation, resulting in superior academic performance.

Furthermore, educational technology dismantles geographical obstacles, granting access to quality education for kids in isolated or disadvantaged regions. Online courses, virtual classrooms, and digital resources democratize education, enabling learners from varied backgrounds to engage with experienced educators and access extensive knowledge (Alomar, 2025). This accessibility is essential in tackling the persistent issues of the digital divide, where inequities in technological access can profoundly affect educational equity.

The incorporation of technology in education fosters collaboration and communication between students and educators. Instruments including discussion forums, collaborative documents, and video conferencing platforms facilitate learners' collaboration on projects, idea exchange, and substantive debates, irrespective of their geographical location (Vahed & Rodriguez, 2021). This collaborative setting fosters the development of crucial skills, like cooperation, critical thinking, and digital literacy, which are vital for success in the 21st-century workforce.

Moreover, the application of data analytics in educational technology facilitates informed decision-making. Educators can evaluate student performance data to discern trends, assess the efficacy of instructional tactics, and implement requisite modifications to improve learning outcomes (Hooda et al., 2022). This data-centric methodology promotes a culture of ongoing enhancement inside educational establishments.

In conclusion, educational technology serves as a significant catalyst for transformation in contemporary education. Its capacity to customize learning, enhance accessibility, promote collaboration, and utilize data analytics highlights its importance in reconciling conventional educational methods with the requirements of a swiftly changing world. In examining the role of public-private partnerships in enhancing educational technology, it is crucial to acknowledge the fundamental significance of these advances in determining the future of education.

Historical Context

The progression of educational technology has been a dynamic process characterized by pivotal milestones that have altered the realm of teaching and learning (Makda, 2025). Since the inception of formal education, technology has consistently transformed the methods of knowledge dissemination and acquisition.

The origins of instructional technology can be traced to the advent of the printing press in the 15th century, which transformed access to knowledge. Textbooks became widely accessible, facilitating standardized curriculum and promoting a more homogeneous educational experience (Alnahdi et al., 2024). This signified the transition from oral traditions to written methods of information transmission.

The advent of audiovisual devices, like film projectors and overhead transparencies, significantly improved the educational experience in the 20th century (Dar et al., 2022). These tools enabled educators to convey knowledge in more captivating manners, accommodating diverse learning styles. The 1960s and 1970s witnessed the advent of programmed instruction and computer-assisted learning, utilizing early computers to deliver personalized educational experiences. Despite being primitive by contemporary standards, these innovations established the foundation for subsequent advancements.

The emergence of personal computers in the 1980s signified a crucial turning point in educational technology (Campbell-Kelly et al., 2023). Educational institutions commenced the incorporation of computers into classrooms, enabling students to interact with software that enhanced learning in disciplines such as mathematics and language arts. This period witnessed the emergence of the internet, which would ultimately transform education by offering unparalleled access to knowledge and resources.

The 1990s and early 2000s marked the advent of online education. The advent of learning management systems (LMS) has empowered educators to design and administer courses online, hence enhancing the flexibility and accessibility of education (Camilleri & Camilleri). Institutions commenced the provision of distance learning programs, enabling students to obtain education from any location globally.

This transition was essential in broadening educational prospects, especially for non-traditional students.

With technological advancements, the 2010s seen the emergence of mobile learning and the widespread availability of educational applications. Smartphones and tablets become pervasive, enabling students to access educational resources while mobile (Andersson, 2022). The concept of blended learning arose, integrating traditional face-to-face instruction with online elements, thereby augmenting the educational experience.

We are currently in the front of a new epoch in educational technology, defined by artificial intelligence, virtual reality, and customized learning platforms. These technologies are transforming educators' methodologies and students' interactions with learning resources.

The historical backdrop of educational technology demonstrates an ongoing progress propelled by breakthroughs in tools and approaches. Comprehending this trajectory is crucial as we examine the function of public-private partnerships in advancing the incorporation of technology in education, guaranteeing that these innovations are adeptly utilized to enhance learning outcomes for all pupils.

Challenges in Education

Notwithstanding the considerable progress in educational technology, some problems remain that obstruct its successful implementation and fair access (Dritsas & Trigka, 2025). These obstacles encompass access and equality concerns, the digital divide, and opposition to transformation within conventional educational systems.

Access and equity concerns persist as important topics in conversations regarding educational technology. Although technology can improve learning experiences, unequal access may intensify existing discrepancies. Students from economically disadvantaged backgrounds or inadequately supported educational institutions may be deprived of essential technology, stable internet access, and technical assistance to effectively utilize digital learning materials (Mhlanga, 2024). This disparity may result in a scenario where only a limited cohort of pupils reaps the benefits of technological progress, while others remain disadvantaged. Consequently, addressing access and equity is essential for enabling all students to leverage the advantages of instructional technology.

The digital divide, denoting the disparity between individuals with access to contemporary information and communication technology and those without, constitutes a substantial obstacle in education. This divide is characterized not just by access to devices and internet connectivity but also by the skills and knowledge necessary for efficient technology utilization. A significant number of students, especially in rural or economically challenged regions, are positioned on the unfavorable side of this split. The absence of digital literacy may hinder their complete engagement in the digital learning environment, exacerbating educational inequalities (Memon and Memon 2025). Addressing this gap necessitates coordinated efforts by governments, educational institutions, and private sector collaborators to furnish resources, training, and infrastructure.

A notable obstacle is the opposition to reform inside conventional educational systems. Numerous instructors and administrators are familiar with traditional teaching approaches and may exhibit reluctance to embrace new technologies. This reluctance may arise from various circumstances, such as insufficient training, apprehension regarding the unfamiliar, or doubts about the efficacy of technology in enhancing educational results. Moreover, certain stakeholders may emphasize standardized testing and conventional success indicators, perceiving technology as a distraction rather than an augmentation. Surmounting this opposition necessitates a transformation in perspective, wherein technology is regarded as an invaluable instrument that may enhance and augment conventional pedagogical methods.

In conclusion, whereas educational technology has substantial potential for enhancing learning outcomes, considerable difficulties require resolution. Access and equity challenges, the digital divide, and reluctance to change within educational systems are significant obstacles that must be addressed. Public-private partnerships are essential in tackling these difficulties, promoting collaboration among stakeholders to guarantee that all students may benefit from the transformative capabilities of educational technology. By addressing these disparities, we may establish a more equitable and efficient educational environment for future generations.

UNDERSTANDING PUBLIC-PRIVATE PARTNERSHIPS (PPPs)

Definition and Characteristics of PPPs

Public-private partnerships (PPPs) are cooperative arrangements between governmental bodies and private sector firms designed to provide public services or infrastructure projects (Joudyian et al. 2021). In the realm of educational technology, public-private partnerships (PPPs) function as a strategic framework to harness the advantages of both sectors to improve educational outcomes and accessibility. These collaborations facilitate the aggregation of resources, experience, and innovation, potentially resulting in more effective solutions to the difficulties encountered in education.

A fundamental attribute of PPPs is their collective accountability. In contrast to conventional procurement procedures, where the public sector alone oversees the project, Public-Private Partnerships (PPPs) entail a collaborative approach in which both sides participate in planning, financing, and execution. This collective duty cultivates a sense of ownership and accountability, as both public and private stakeholders collaborate towards shared objectives. Furthermore, PPPs typically involve a long-term obligation, facilitating ongoing collaboration and the capacity to adjust to evolving requirements over time.

A key characteristic of PPPs is the congruence of interests between the public and private sectors. The public sector endeavors to enhance educational quality and accessibility, whereas the private sector strives for a return on investment (Sehl et al., 2024). This alignment can result in new solutions that may not be feasible within the limitations of conventional public funding sources. Private enterprises can provide advanced technology and specialized knowledge to the collaboration, whereas public institutions can offer critical insights into the distinct requirements of the educational landscape.

The advantages of public-private partnerships in educational technology are numerous (Casprini & Palumbo, 2022). Initially, they can improve resource efficiency by utilizing private sector investment to augment governmental spending. This may lead to the creation of novel technology, infrastructure, and educational initiatives that would otherwise be financially impractical for public institutions alone. Moreover, PPPs can expedite the swift execution of novel solutions, as private partners typically possess the agility and competence to rapidly deploy new technology.

Another notable benefit of PPPs is their capacity to stimulate innovation. Public-private partnerships (PPPs) can foster innovative teaching and learning methodologies by integrating the creative resources of private enterprises with the educational proficiency of public institutions (Deppeler et al. 2022). Collaborations may yield the development of interactive learning platforms, data-driven evaluation instruments, or individualized educational settings that address varied student requirements.

In conclusion, public-private partnerships serve as a potent instrument for advancing educational technology efforts. By delineating explicit duties and responsibilities, harmonizing interests, and utilizing the capabilities of both sectors, public-private partnerships can foster innovation, enhance resource efficiency, and eventually yield improved educational outcomes. In examining the function of PPPs in education, it is crucial to acknowledge their capacity to reconcile conventional educational methods with the requirements of a technology-oriented society.

Types of PPP Models

Public-private partnerships (PPPs) can assume diverse configurations, each designed to address certain requirements and goals within the educational sector (Alrasheed et al. 2024). Comprehending the many forms of PPP models is crucial for stakeholders seeking to utilize these partnerships efficiently. The three principal forms are contractual arrangements, joint ventures, and strategic alliances, each presenting distinct attributes and advantages.

Contractual agreements represent a prevalent form of public-private partnerships in the education sector. This strategy involves the public sector formalizing a contract with a private business to furnish certain services or execute specific projects. This may encompass the creation of instructional software, the delivery of training for educators, or the provision of technology infrastructure. Contractual agreements are generally marked by explicitly delineated roles, obligations, and performance criteria, so assuring accountability for both parties (Aben et al. 2021). This paradigm enables public institutions to obtain specialized expertise and resources from the private sector while retaining monitoring and control over educational outcomes.

Joint Ventures signify a more cohesive mode of collaboration between public and private organizations (Kraus et al. 2021). In this concept, both parties establish a new, co-owned organization to undertake specific educational objectives. A university may collaborate with a technology firm to create a research center dedicated to the advancement of novel instructional technologies. Joint ventures facilitate collaborative investment and risk-sharing, enabling the pursuit of more ambitious initiatives that may be unattainable for either side independently. This paradigm promotes enhanced collaboration, with both parties providing resources, skills, and networks, thereby advancing innovation in educational technology.

Strategic Alliances are a significant category of Public-Private Partnerships (PPP), defined by a flexible and collaborative interaction between public and private organizations (Kim, 2023). In contrast to joint ventures, strategic alliances do not entail the establishment of a new company; rather, they emphasize collaboration to attain shared objectives. A school district may collaborate with a private technology company to test a new digital learning platform, exchanging insights and feedback during the process. This strategy prioritizes collaboration and knowledge exchange, enabling both parties to swiftly adjust to evolving situations and educational requirements. Strategic alliances can promote the sharing of best practices and resources, so improving the overall efficacy of educational programs.

In conclusion, comprehending the diverse sorts of PPP models—contractual agreements, joint ventures, and strategic alliances—empowers stakeholders to identify the most suitable method for their particular educational technology projects. Each model presents unique benefits, and the selection of partnership structure must correspond with the project's objectives, available resources, and intended results. By adeptly utilizing these PPP models, educational institutions can augment their ability to innovate and increase student learning experiences.

The Role of Stakeholders

Public-private partnerships (PPPs) in educational technology encompass a variety of stakeholders, each contributing significantly to the efficacy of these collaborations (Upadhyay et al. 2025). The principal stakeholders comprise governmental bodies, business enterprises, and educational institutions along with communities. Comprehending the functions and contributions of each stakeholder is crucial for cultivating productive collaborations that improve educational results.

Government agencies constitute the foundation of public-private collaborations in education. They are accountable for establishing policies, laws, and standards that direct the incorporation of technology in educational institutions. Government organizations can foster a conducive atmosphere for public-private partnerships (PPPs) by supplying financing, resources, and infrastructure. Moreover, they are important in recognizing educational requirements and priorities, guaranteeing that collaborations correspond with overarching educational objectives (Imran2023). By collaborating with private entities, government agencies can utilize external expertise and innovation while ensuring responsibility and monitoring. Moreover, they can provide access to data and research that informs decision-making, aiding in the assessment of the efficacy of technology projects.

Private sector companies are key catalysts for innovation and technological progress in educational collaborations (Rossoni et al. 2024). These companies provide specific expertise, research proficiency, and advanced technologies that can substantially improve the educational experience. Through collaboration with public institutions, private sector partners can create customized solutions that tackle unique difficulties encountered by schools and educators. Their participation frequently encompasses delivering training, technical assistance, and continuous maintenance for educational devices. Furthermore, private enterprises can facilitate the expansion of effective projects by disseminating best practices and resources across various educational settings. The congruence of their corporate objectives with educational results can foster mutually advantageous connections that promote ongoing enhancement.

Educational institutions and communities are crucial to public-private partnerships, as they are the ultimate beneficiaries of the technologies and services offered (Tarchiani & Grey, 2025). Educational institutions must proactively participate in the partnership process to ensure their specific needs and difficulties are adequately addressed. Educators and administrators are essential in articulating these demands and offering feedback on the efficacy of deployed technologies. Moreover, community engagement is crucial for cultivating a supportive atmosphere for educational endeavors. Involving parents, local organizations, and community leaders can improve the significance and longevity of technology programs. Engaging all stakeholders in the decision-making process enables educational institutions to foster a sense of ownership and dedication to the partnership's success.

The efficacy of public-private partnerships in educational technology relies on the active engagement and cooperation of government entities, private sector firms, and educational institutions and communities. Every stakeholder contributes unique insights, resources, and skills, fostering a synergistic impact that can result in new solutions and enhanced educational outcomes. By cultivating robust partnerships among various stakeholders, PPPs can effectively reconcile traditional educational practices with the requirements of a technology-driven future.

CASE STUDIES OF SUCCESSFUL PPPS IN EDUCATIONAL TECHNOLOGY

Case Study 1: Technology Integration in K-12 Schools

A noteworthy instance of an effective public-private partnership (PPP) in educational technology is the collaboration between a major school district and a leading technology firm focused on incorporating technology into K-12 classrooms (Upadhyay et al. 2025). This collaboration model aims to improve teaching and learning by integrating digital tools and resources, thereby improving the educational experience for both students and educators.

The collaboration commenced with an extensive needs assessment performed by the school system, which pinpointed critical areas where technology could markedly enhance student engagement and learning outcomes. The technology firm collaborated with the district to supply both hardware, including tablets and interactive whiteboards, and software solutions customized to the curriculum (Mogas et al. 2022). This encompassed adaptive learning platforms that facilitated tailored learning experiences, allowing instructors to address the varied requirements of their pupils.

An essential element of this relationship was the focus on professional development for educators. The technology firm collaborated with educators to deliver training sessions and continuous assistance, ensuring teachers felt assured in incorporating technology into their teaching methodologies (Alenezi, 2023). This collaborative strategy developed an innovative culture within the school district, prompting educators to explore novel instructional methodologies and resources.

The influence of this PPP on student learning outcomes was substantial. Data gathered across multiple school years indicated significant enhancements in student involvement, motivation, and academic achievement. Students engaged more actively in their learning by employing technology to investigate concepts, collaborate with colleagues, and access extensive online resources (Alam & Mohanty, 2023). The adaptive learning platforms facilitated customized instruction, contributing to the reduction of achievement disparities among students with diverse ability levels. Educators indicated heightened satisfaction with their pedagogical methods, as they utilized technology to foster more dynamic and participatory learning settings.

Furthermore, the collaboration developed a sense of community among stakeholders. Parents and community people increased their engagement in the educational process, observing the beneficial transformations resulting from technological integration (Brenton & Slawinski, 2023). The collaboration also exemplified a framework for other districts, demonstrating the capacity of public-private partnerships to effect significant transformation in education.

The case of technology integration in K-12 classrooms illustrates the efficacy of public-private collaborations in improving educational performance. This partnership, via the amalgamation of resources, talent, and a unified vision for enhancement, not only revolutionized classrooms but also favorably influenced student learning experiences. This case study emphasizes the significance of strategic alliances in tackling the issues encountered by educational institutions and demonstrates the potential of technology to effect revolutionary change in contemporary education.

Case Study 2: Higher Education Collaborations

An exemplary instance of an effective public-private partnership (PPP) in higher education is the collaboration between a prestigious institution and a distinguished technology company to create innovative educational programs designed to improve student learning and employability (Khallaf et al., 2022). This collaboration aimed to develop a series of online courses and degree programs that utilized the newest technological breakthroughs, offering students flexible and accessible educational possibilities.

The collaboration commenced with a mutual objective: to connect academic expertise with industry requirements. The university acknowledged the necessity of providing students with pertinent skills to prepare them for employment, while the technology firm aimed to broaden its influence and presence in the educational sector (Putjorn and Putjorn 2023). They collaboratively created a series of online courses that integrated advanced technologies including artificial intelligence, data analytics, and cloud computing. These courses were crafted to be interactive and engaging, employing multimedia tools and practical tasks to enrich the learning experience.

A notable result of this collaboration was the creation of a distinctive internship program that matched students with industry executives. This effort provided students with practical exposure on actual projects, hence improving their employability upon graduation (Chan et al. 2024). The initiative helped both students and the technology industry by supplying innovative ideas and insights from emerging talent.

The insights gained from this PPP were numerous. The significance of connecting educational curriculum with industry requirements became apparent (Casprini & Palumbo, 2022). The collaboration engaged industry professionals in the curriculum creation process, ensuring its relevance and currency. The collaboration underscored the importance of adaptability in program implementation. The online model enabled students to learn at their own pace, supporting various schedules and learning styles.

Scalability emerged as another crucial learning from this collaboration. The success of the inaugural programs motivated the institution and technology firm to pursue additional collaborations, broadening the course offerings and increasing audience reach. Utilizing the technology firm's resources and experience, the institution rapidly and efficiently expanded its services, drawing students from diverse backgrounds and regions (Shan & Wang, 2024).

The partnership between the institution and the technology company illustrates the possibilities of public-private collaborations in higher education. This PPP improved educational outcomes and cultivated a culture of continuous improvement by creating new programs that meet industry demands and offering students significant practical experiences. This collaboration highlights the significance of strategic partnerships in meeting the dynamic needs of the workforce and equipping students for success in a swiftly transforming environment.

Case Study 3: Non-Profit and For-Profit Collaborations

An exemplary instance of an effective public-private partnership (PPP) in educational technology is the collaboration of a non-profit organization dedicated to educational equity and a for-profit technology firm (Ali et al. 2024). This collaboration sought to address educational disparities in marginalized groups by facilitating access to premium digital learning resources and professional development for instructors.

The effort commenced with the non-profit's objective to rectify the inequities in educational access encountered by low-income children. The firm acknowledged technology's capacity to enhance learning experiences and pursued a for-profit partner proficient in creating educational software and platforms (Patil, 2023). They together developed an extensive program that encompassed the distribution of devices, internet connectivity, and a range of digital learning tools customized to the distinct requirements of the targeted populations.

A major aspect of this relationship was the execution of training programs for educators. The technology firm offered professional development programs that enabled instructors to proficiently incorporate digital resources into their classrooms. This training was crucial for improving teaching methodologies and cultivating a culture of innovation in educational institutions (Alenezi, 2023). The alliance sought to enable teachers to maximize student benefits from the introduced technology.

The influence of this PPP on marginalized populations was significant. Students acquired access to an abundance of instructional tools that were once inaccessible, including interactive classes, online exams, and customized learning pathways. Consequently, there was a significant enhancement in student engagement, motivation, and academic achievement. The program enhanced community involvement, with parents and local organizations actively supporting the initiative and lobbying for sustained investment in educational technology (Lansing et al. 2023).

The cooperation prioritized long-term sustainability. To guarantee the program's benefits would persist beyond the first implementation phase, both partners pledged to continuous support and assessment (Ho et al., 2023). The non-profit organization developed a methodology for impact assessment, consistently gathering data on student performance and program efficacy. This data-centric methodology enabled stakeholders to pinpoint areas for enhancement and implement requisite modifications to the program.

Additionally, the team aimed to develop a reproducible model that could be adopted and executed in other marginalized areas. The non-profit and for-profit organizations sought to inspire analogous collaborations nationwide by documenting best practices and disseminating insights acquired from their relationship (Mariani et al., 2022).

In conclusion, the collaboration between non-profit and for-profit entities shows the capacity of public-private partnerships to address educational disparities in marginalized communities. This public-private partnership, through the amalgamation of resources, skills, and a collective dedication to equity, not only improved access to technology but also promoted enduring sustainability and impact. This case study underscores the significance of collaboration in mitigating educational gaps and guaranteeing that all students can thrive in a technology-centric environment.

BEST PRACTICES FOR EFFECTIVE PPPs IN EDUCATIONAL TECHNOLOGY

Building Trust and Communication

In the domain of public-private partnerships (PPPs) within educational technology, fostering trust and instituting transparent communication channels are essential for the success of collaborative endeavors (Sanni, 2025). Effective communication not only enables the interchange of ideas and resources but also cultivates a robust foundation of trust among stakeholders. This trust is crucial for surmounting obstacles, aligning objectives, and guaranteeing that all parties are dedicated to attaining common goals.

Effective communication channels are essential for ensuring that all stakeholders—government agencies, private sector partners, educational institutions, and community members—are informed and engaged during the partnership process (Jun & Kim, 2021). Consistent updates, transparent reporting, and open communication foster an environment conducive to the prompt and collaborative resolution of concerns.

Employing several communication channels, including newsletters, webinars, and social media, can improve outreach and guarantee that all stakeholders receive relevant information. Furthermore, designating specific points of contact inside each business can enhance communication and enable prompt responses to requests or issues.

To promote collaboration, it is crucial to establish chances for stakeholders to engage substantively. Collaborative workshops, brainstorming sessions, and collaborative planning meetings foster rapport and promote the exchange of ideas and best practices (Gray et al., 2024). These interactions enable stakeholders to cultivate a mutual comprehension of the partnership's aims and objectives, while also acknowledging the distinct capabilities and contributions of each entity. Participating in team-building activities can enhance connections and foster a culture of collaboration.

An additional successful method for promoting collaboration is to define explicit roles and duties from the beginning. By specifying distinct responsibilities and expectations for each stakeholder, the partnership can reduce misunderstandings and ensure alignment among all stakeholders in their endeavors (Ali and Haapasalo 2023). This transparency also facilitates stakeholder accountability, since all parties comprehend their roles in the partnership's success.

Furthermore, engaging stakeholders in the decision-making process can augment buy-in and dedication to the collaboration. When stakeholders perceive that their opinions are acknowledged and their viewpoints are esteemed, they are more inclined to dedicate time and resources to the partnership (MacLeod et al. 2022). Establishing advisory committees or stakeholder forums can facilitate continuous input and feedback, ensuring that the partnership adapts to the changing demands of the educational environment.

In summary, cultivating trust and creating efficient communication channels are essential elements of successful public-private collaborations in educational technology. By emphasizing effective communication, promoting teamwork, and engaging stakeholders in decision-making, partnerships can establish a robust framework for attaining shared objectives. These best practices not only augment the efficacy of PPPs but also guarantee that the advantages of educational technology are accessible to all students, ultimately reconciling traditional educational methodologies with the exigencies of a swiftly evolving environment.

Aligning Goals and Objectives

Aligning goals and objectives is essential for the success of public-private partnerships (PPPs) in educational technology (Almarri & Boussabaine, 2025). When all stakeholders possess a unified vision and explicitly articulated goals, they may collaborate effectively to attain reciprocal advantages. This alignment is crucial for cultivating ownership, commitment, and accountability among stakeholders, hence resulting in more effective collaborations.

To guarantee reciprocal advantages for all parties, it is essential to involve stakeholders in the goal-setting process from the beginning. This encompasses governmental authorities, commercial sector collaborators, educational establishments, and community leaders. Incorporating multiple viewpoints enables the partnership to discern common interests and priorities that align with all stakeholders. For instance, although a technological firm may concentrate on market expansion, educational institutions may emphasize enhanced student results (Ozdemir et al. 2023). Identifying shared objectives, such as improving digital literacy or expanding access to technology, facilitates a cooperative strategy that advantages all stakeholders.

Moreover, setting explicit and attainable objectives facilitates the development of a strategic framework for the collaboration. These objectives must be specific, measurable, achievable, relevant, and time-bound (SMART) (Do et al. 2024). A collaboration may aim to enhance student involvement in digital learning by 30% during a single academic year. By establishing explicit objectives, stakeholders may monitor advancement and make data-informed decisions to adjust tactics as necessary.

Establishing quantifiable objectives is essential for assessing the efficacy of the collaboration. By defining key performance indicators (KPIs) linked with the partnership's aims, stakeholders can evaluate the effectiveness of their actions (Aguilera et al. 2024). These KPIs may encompass indicators including student performance data, technology utilization rates, teacher satisfaction surveys, and community participation levels. Consistent collection and analysis of this data enables stakeholders to discern accomplishments and areas needing enhancement, promoting a culture of ongoing assessment and adaptation.

Furthermore, establishing a feedback loop is crucial for stakeholders to exchange thoughts and experiences during the relationship (Tobin et al., 2022). This iterative procedure allows the collaboration to stay adaptable to evolving requirements and problems. If data reveals that a specific technology is underutilized, stakeholders might jointly investigate remedies, including more training or modifications to the implementation approach.

In conclusion, the alignment of goals and objectives is a crucial best practice for productive public-private collaborations in educational technology. By guaranteeing reciprocal advantages for all stakeholders and establishing quantifiable objectives, partnerships can promote collaboration, accountability, and ongoing enhancement. This alignment promotes the efficacy of educational efforts and reinforces the commitment of all stakeholders to create significant and sustainable impacts on student learning and educational equity. By means of strategic alignment, public-private partnerships can effectively connect conventional educational methodologies with the creative opportunities presented by technology.

Evaluating and Sustaining Partnerships

Assessing and maintaining public-private partnerships (PPPs) in educational technology is crucial for guaranteeing that these collaborations consistently yield significant results over time. Effective evaluation necessitates the establishment of success criteria, whereas sustainability demands a dedication to ongoing development and adaptation to evolving conditions (Chugh et al. 2023).

Metrics for Success

To evaluate the efficacy of a PPP, it is essential to establish explicit success indicators that correspond with the partnership's aims and objectives (Akomea-Frimpong et al., 2022). These measurements may be quantitative or qualitative, offering a holistic perspective on the partnership's impact. Quantitative metrics may encompass student performance indicators, including test scores, graduation rates, and technology utilization statistics. A collaboration designed to enhance digital literacy may monitor the proportion of students adept in technology-related competencies over a designated timeframe.

Qualitative metrics carry equal significance, as they encapsulate the experiences and perspectives of stakeholders engaged in the collaboration. Surveys and focus groups can be employed to collect feedback from educators, students, and parents concerning the efficacy of the adopted technology and its influence on the learning environment (Chiu, 2024). This feedback offers essential insights into successful areas and suggestions for enhancement.

Consistent evaluation of these measures enables stakeholders to assess the partnership's efficacy and make informed decisions regarding future trajectories (Khan et al. 2023). Creating a schedule for evaluations—such as mid-year and end-of-year assessments—ensures that stakeholders remain involved and proactive in tackling any emerging difficulties.

Continuous Improvement and Adaptation

Maintaining a successful PPP necessitates a dedication to ongoing enhancement and adaptability. The educational landscape is ever transforming, shaped by technology progress, evolving student requirements, and altering educational regulations (Huang & Yanan, 2024). To maintain relevance and efficacy, partnerships must be prepared to modify their tactics and methodologies in response to these alterations.

An excellent technique for promoting continuous improvement is the implementation of regular communication and feedback systems among stakeholders (Martínez-Peláez et al. 2023). This may encompass regular meetings, workshops, and collaborative planning sessions that promote open discourse regarding achievements, obstacles, and new trends. By cultivating a culture of transparency and collaboration, stakeholders may collectively pinpoint areas for improvement and devise innovative strategies to address them.

Moreover, professional development opportunities for educators can significantly contribute to the maintenance of partnerships. Continuous training ensures that educators possess the most current skills and knowledge to properly integrate technology into their classrooms (Akram et al. 2022). This investment in professional development not only improves the efficacy of the collaboration but also fosters a more engaged and motivated teaching workforce.

In conclusion, assessing and maintaining public-private partnerships in educational technology necessitates the establishment of explicit success criteria and a dedication to ongoing enhancement and adaptation. By consistently evaluating the partnership's effects and promoting a culture of collaboration and professional growth, stakeholders may guarantee that their initiatives stay effective and pertinent. This dedication to assessment and modification ultimately enhances the partnership's capacity to connect conventional educational methods with the transformative possibilities of technology, resulting in better outcomes for students and communities.

FUTURE DIRECTIONS AND POLICY RECOMMENDATIONS

Emerging Trends in Educational Technology

The evolving environment of educational technology is affecting the future of learning through various developing trends. Among these themes, artificial intelligence (AI) and personalized learning, along with virtual and augmented reality (VR/AR), emerge as revolutionary elements capable of substantially improving educational experiences (Cheung et al. 2021). Comprehending these patterns is essential for stakeholders engaged in public-private partnerships (PPPs) in education, since they offer avenues for innovation and enhancement.

AI and Personalized Learning

Artificial intelligence is swiftly emerging as a fundamental element of educational technology, providing the capacity to develop highly individualized learning experiences for pupils (Lagos-Castillo et al. 2025). AI-driven platforms may assess individual student data, encompassing learning styles, strengths, and places for enhancement, to customize educational content and instructional methodologies. This degree of customisation allows educators to offer tailored assistance, guaranteeing that each student obtains the necessary tools and guidance for success.

AI can enable adaptive learning systems that modify task difficulty according to real-time evaluations of student performance. This not only maintains student engagement but also mitigates irritation or boredom by presenting challenges at an appropriate level. Moreover, AI can aid instructors in the early identification of at-risk pupils, facilitating prompt interventions and support.

Integrating AI into educational projects via public-private partnerships offers a chance to utilize advanced technology to improve learning results (Salla et al. 2025). Policymakers ought to devise frameworks that promote collaboration between educational institutions and technology firms to develop AI-driven solutions targeting specific educational difficulties.

Virtual and Augmented Reality in Education

Virtual and augmented reality technologies are developing as potent instruments for augmenting educational experiences. Virtual Reality (VR) and Augmented Reality (AR) can establish immersive educational environments that captivate pupils in ways that conventional techniques cannot (Kuhail et al., 2022). For instance, virtual reality can immerse students in historical events, scientific explorations, or intricate mathematical ideas, enabling them to engage in a tactile, interactive learning experience.

These technologies are especially advantageous in disciplines such as science, engineering, and the arts, where experiential learning is crucial. Virtual reality (VR) and augmented reality (AR) can improve critical thinking, problem-solving abilities, and creativity in pupils by mimicking real-world settings (Alkhabra et al. 2023).

The use of VR and AR into educational programs for PPPs presents intriguing opportunities for collaboration. Technology firms may collaborate with educational institutions to create tailored content that conforms to curriculum standards, so ensuring the effective utilization of these tools in classrooms (Zhao et al., 2024).

In conclusion, the future of educational technology is influenced by rising trends, including AI-driven personalized learning and VR/AR applications. Public-private partnerships possess a distinct opportunity to leverage these advances to enhance educational results. Policymakers must emphasize the establishment of supportive frameworks that foster collaboration between educational institutions and technology suppliers, guaranteeing that all students reap the benefits of these transformational innovations. By adopting these trends, stakeholders may collaboratively cultivate a more engaging, effective, and fair educational environment.

Policy Frameworks for Supporting PPPs

To optimize the efficacy of public-private partnerships (PPPs) in educational technology, it is imperative to create strong legislative frameworks that promote collaboration between governmental bodies and private sector entities (Vogel et al. 2022). Such frameworks can offer explicit principles, support systems, and incentives that promote the establishment and durability of good partnerships. This section delineates essential proposals for governmental policies and incentives designed to promote private sector engagement in educational technology initiatives.

Recommendations for Government Policies

Initially, governments ought to formulate detailed policies delineating the duties and obligations of stakeholders engaged in public-private partnerships (PPPs). This entails the establishment of explicit criteria for partnership development, project execution, and assessment. Governments can alleviate risks and uncertainties that frequently discourage private sector involvement by offering a standardized framework. Policies must prioritize transparency and accountability, guaranteeing that all stakeholders are held accountable for their contributions and results (Olasehinde-Williams et al. 2023).

Secondly, governments ought to prioritize the deployment of financing and resources for educational technology initiatives that incorporate public-private partnerships (PPPs). This may encompass subsidies, matching funding, or strategic investments in technological infrastructure for educational institutions in underprivileged regions. Governments can stimulate private sector investment in educational initiatives, especially in resource-limited areas, by offering financial assistance (Wang et al. 2023).

Third, it is essential for governments to foster collaboration between educational institutions and private sector partners via networking events, conferences, and forums (Bowser et al. 2024). These initiatives can promote knowledge exchange and optimal practices, assisting stakeholders in recognizing possible collaboration possibilities and aligning their objectives efficiently.

Incentives for Private Sector Involvement

Governments should contemplate the use of various incentives to promote private sector involvement in educational technology. Tax credits or deductions for corporations that participate in educational programs can serve as a significant incentive (Qadir et al. 2024). These financial incentives can mitigate the expenses related to the research, development, and deployment of educational technology, rendering public-private partnerships more appealing for enterprises.

Furthermore, governments can implement award programs that emphasize effective collaborations and their impact on educational enhancement. By demonstrating exceptional collaborations, governments can motivate private enterprises to engage in similar projects, promoting a culture of creativity and dedication to educational equity (Zhang et al., 2024).

Moreover, establishing an efficient procedure for private enterprises to engage in public procurement can increase involvement (Manta & Mansi, 2024). Streamlining the bidding process and minimizing regulatory obstacles can facilitate commercial engagement with educational institutions, ultimately fostering more productive relationships.

In conclusion, the establishment of supportive policy frameworks is crucial for promoting public-private partnerships in educational technology. Governments can foster a collaborative atmosphere by establishing explicit norms, prioritizing funding, and providing incentives for private sector participation. These initiatives will not only improve the efficacy of educational technology but also guarantee that all students have access to the tools and opportunities necessary for success in a progressively digital landscape.

The Path Forward

Public-private partnerships (PPPs) provide significant potential to revolutionize education, especially in the domain of educational technology (Galikhanov et al. 2021). By utilizing the capabilities and resources of both public and private sectors, these alliances can tackle significant difficulties confronting educational institutions today. Public-private partnerships can significantly influence the future of education by improving technological access in marginalized populations and promoting creative learning experiences.

The incorporation of technology in education has transitioned from a luxury to an essential requirement. As the requirements of the 21st-century workforce change, it is imperative for educational institutions to provide students with the skills and knowledge critical for success in a digital environment. Public-private partnerships provide a strategic method for accomplishing this objective by promoting the creation of innovative educational tools and resources that can captivate students and improve learning outcomes (Bhimavarapu2025). Furthermore, these collaborations can connect conventional educational methods with the creative opportunities presented by technology, guaranteeing that all students receive high-quality education.

Nonetheless, actualizing the complete potential of PPPs necessitates a collaborative endeavor from all stakeholders within the education system. Educators, administrators, legislators, and business sector leaders must unite to promote collaboration and cultivate an environment that encourages innovation (Thawesaengskulthai et al. 2024). This call to action entails pushing for supportive policy frameworks and financial possibilities, as well as engaging in the development and implementation of educational technology programs.

Stakeholders must emphasize transparent communication and trust cultivation to establish robust relationships. Through the exchange of insights, resources, and best practices, they can cooperatively tackle the distinct issues encountered in various educational environments (Charalambous et al. 2021). Moreover, stakeholders must engage in continuous assessment and modification of programs to guarantee their effectiveness and relevance in a swiftly evolving environment.

Moreover, it is essential to involve communities and families in the partnering process. Their participation can offer significant insights and assistance, guaranteeing that educational programs are customized to the distinct requirements of pupils and their communities (Wiedermann et al. 2023). By cultivating a sense of ownership and collaboration, stakeholders may establish a more inclusive and adaptive educational environment.

In conclusion, the future of public-private collaborations in educational technology is promising. By leveraging the collective talents of all stakeholders, these collaborations can effectuate significant change and enhance educational results for kids worldwide. The moment to act is now; collectively, we can create a future in which every kid has the opportunity to thrive in an ever-evolving digital landscape.

CONCLUSION

Public-private partnerships (PPPs) have become essential tools in revolutionizing educational technology and tackling systemic issues related to access, innovation, and sustainability. This article has illustrated how public-private partnerships (PPPs)—via mechanisms such as contractual agreements, joint ventures, and strategic alliances—can effectively amalgamate the strengths of government, industry, and educational institutions. These collaborations significantly reduce the digital divide, promote innovation in pedagogy, and provide fair access to technology-enhanced education in many contexts.

The case studies demonstrate the tangible advantages of public-private partnerships (PPPs) in K-12 education, higher education, and marginalized areas, highlighting enhancements in digital literacy, student involvement, and educational results. Successful partnerships are founded on mutual trust, effective communication, aligned objectives, and strong evaluation systems.

Moreover, as emerging technologies such as artificial intelligence and virtual/augmented reality transform educational experiences, public-private partnerships offer the infrastructure and flexibility required for scaling execution. Realizing the full potential of these partnerships necessitates supportive legislative frameworks, targeted incentives for private sector involvement, and inclusive stakeholder engagement.

In summary, PPPs signify more than fiscal cooperation; they serve as strategic instruments for comprehensive educational transformation. By promoting innovation, distributing risk, and integrating varied skills, public-private partnerships can enhance education and equip learners for the challenges of a swiftly changing digital landscape. As the future of education becomes progressively technology-oriented, the significance of public-private partnerships (PPPs) will be crucial in developing inclusive, adaptive, and future-ready educational systems. Stakeholders must collaborate and act decisively to leverage this potential for the advantage of all learners.

REFERENCES

Aben, T. A., van der Valk, W., Roehrich, J. K., & Selviaridis, K. (2021). Managing information asymmetry in public–private relationships undergoing a digital transformation: The role of contractual and relational governance. [emerald.com]. *International Journal of Operations & Production Management*, *41*(7), 1145–1191. DOI: 10.1108/IJOPM-09-2020-0675

Aguilera, R. V., De Massis, A., Fini, R., & Vismara, S. (2024). Organizational goals, outcomes, and the assessment of performance: Reconceptualizing success in management studies. [wiley.com]. *Journal of Management Studies*, *61*(1), 1–36. DOI: 10.1111/joms.12994

Akomea-Frimpong, I., Jin, X., & Osei-Kyei, R. (2022). Mapping studies on sustainability in the performance measurement of public-private partnership projects: A systematic review. Sustainability. mdpi.com

Akram, H., Abdelrady, A. H., Al-Adwan, A. S., & Ramzan, M. (2022). Teachers' perceptions of technology integration in teaching-learning practices: A systematic review. [frontiersin.org]. *Frontiers in Psychology*, *13*, 920317. DOI: 10.3389/fpsyg.2022.920317 PMID: 35734463

Alam, A., & Mohanty, A. (2023). Educational technology: Exploring the convergence of technology and pedagogy through mobility, interactivity, AI, and learning tools. Cogent Engineering. tandfonline.com

Alenezi, M. (2023). Digital learning and digital institution in higher education. Education Sciences. mdpi.com

Ali, F., & Haapasalo, H. (2023). Development levels of stakeholder relationships in collaborative projects: Challenges and preconditions. [emerald.com]. *International Journal of Managing Projects in Business*, *16*(8), 58–76. DOI: 10.1108/IJMPB-03-2022-0066

Ali, S., Bhutta, S. M., Ahmad, S., Ansari, A. N., Ahmed, A., & Qadir, Y. (2024). PROTOCOL: Effectiveness of public-private partnerships on educational access and quality of primary and secondary schooling in low-and middle-income countries: A systematic review. [wiley.com]. *Campbell Systematic Reviews*, *20*(2), e1385. DOI: 10.1002/cl2.1385 PMID: 38444642

Alkhabra, Y. A., Ibrahem, U. M., & Alkhabra, S. A. (2023). Augmented reality technology in enhancing learning retention and critical thinking according to STEAM program. [nature.com]. *Humanities & Social Sciences Communications*, *10*(1), 1–10. DOI: 10.1057/s41599-023-01650-w

Almarri, K., & Boussabaine, H. (2025). Critical success factors for public–private partnerships in smart city infrastructure projects. [HTML]. *Construction Innovation*, *25*(2), 224–247. DOI: 10.1108/CI-04-2022-0072

Alnahdi, G. H., Alwadei, A., & Alharbi, N. (2024). Enhancing special education programs' curricula for students with intellectual disabilities in saudi arabia: A call for personalized approaches and inclusive practices. [HTML]. *Research in Developmental Disabilities*, *151*, 104785. DOI: 10.1016/j.ridd.2024.104785 PMID: 38941691

Alomar, M. (2025). Inclusivity and diversity on massive open online course platforms: a multicultural evaluation of NovoEd. Journal for Multicultural Education. emerald.com

Alrasheed, K. A., Albader, H. B., Khalafallah, A. M., Gerges, M., & Alkandari, F. A. (2024). Framework for PPP partner selection in K-12 educational facility procurement. [sciencedirect.com]. *Journal of Engineering Research*, *12*(3), 369–378. DOI: 10.1016/j.jer.2023.11.025

Andersson, C. (2022). Smartphones and online search: shifting frames in the everyday life of young people. Information and learning sciences. emerald.com

Bhimavarapu, U. (2025). Exploring Public-Private Partnership Models in Higher Education Through Regression Approach. In Public Private Partnerships for Social Development and Impact (pp. 321-338). IGI Global Scientific Publishing. [HTML] DOI: 10.4018/979-8-3373-3471-4.ch013

Bowser, G., Ho, S. S., Ziebell, A., & Lazendic-Galloway, J. (2024). Networking and collaborating: The role of partnerships across sectors to achieve educational goals in sustainability. [springer.com]. *Sustainable Earth Reviews*, *7*(1), 17. DOI: 10.1186/s42055-024-00080-z

Brenton, J., & Slawinski, N. (2023). Collaborating for community regeneration: Facilitating partnerships in, through, and for place. [HTML]. *Journal of Business Ethics*, *184*(4), 815–834. DOI: 10.1007/s10551-023-05365-5

Camilleri, M. A. & Camilleri, A. C. (). The acceptance of learning management systems and video conferencing technologies: Lessons learned from COVID-19. Technology. springer.com

Campbell-Kelly, M., Aspray, W. F., Yost, J. R., Tinn, H., & Díaz, G. C. (2023). *Computer: A history of the information machine*. Routledge. [HTML] DOI: 10.4324/9781003263272

Casprini, E. & Palumbo, R. (2022). Reaping the benefits of digital transformation through Public-Private Partnership: A service ecosystem view applied to healthcare. Global Public Policy and Governance. springer.com

Chan, K., Serban, F. C., Tse, M., & Ho, A. (2024). Impact of collaboration with ICT industry partners on secondary students' knowledge, attitudes, and IT competence. [HTML]. *Education and Information Technologies*, *29*(5), 5259–5282. DOI: 10.1007/s10639-023-12036-5

Charalambous, C. Y., Praetorius, A. K., Sammons, P., Walkowiak, T., Jentsch, A., & Kyriakides, L. (2021). Working more collaboratively to better understand teaching and its quality: Challenges faced and possible solutions. [HTML]. *Studies in Educational Evaluation*, *71*, 101092. DOI: 10.1016/j.stueduc.2021.101092

Cheung, S. K., Kwok, L. F., Phusavat, K., & Yang, H. H. (2021). Shaping the future learning environments with smart elements: Challenges and opportunities. [springer.com]. *International Journal of Educational Technology in Higher Education*, *18*(1), 1–9. DOI: 10.1186/s41239-021-00254-1 PMID: 34778521

Chiu, T. K. F. (2024). The impact of Generative AI (GenAI) on practices, policies and research direction in education: A case of ChatGPT and Midjourney. Interactive Learning Environments. tandfonline.com

Chugh, R., Turnbull, D., Cowling, M. A., Vanderburg, R., & Vanderburg, M. A. (2023). Implementing educational technology in Higher Education Institutions: A review of technologies, stakeholder perceptions, frameworks and metrics. [springer.com]. *Education and Information Technologies*, *28*(12), 16403–16429. DOI: 10.1007/s10639-023-11846-x

Dar, M. A., Kudare, R., Dar, Y. A., Ali, I., & Mohammed, S. (2022). Role Of Projected And Non-Projected Teaching Aids In Teaching Learning Process. [researchgate.net]. *Journal of Positive School Psychology*, *6*(10), 1725–1743.

Deppeler, J., Corrigan, D., Macaulay, L., & Aikens, K. (2022). Innovation and risk in an innovative learning environment: A Private Public Partnership in Australia. [HTML]. *European Educational Research Journal*, *21*(4), 602–626. DOI: 10.1177/14749041211030400

Dexter, S. (2023). Developing faculty EdTech instructional decision-making competence with principles for the integration of EdTech. Educational technology research and development. springer.com

Do, N. X. B., An, T. S., & Krauss, C. (2024, May). SMART-goal-buddy: Goal-setting oriented adaptive learning paths. In International workshop on learning technology for education challenges (pp. 319-331). Cham: Springer Nature Switzerland. [HTML]

Dritsas, E. & Trigka, M. (2025). Methodological and Technological Advancements in E-Learning. Information. mdpi.com

Galikhanov, M. F., Barabanova, S. V., Elizarov, D. V., & Suntsova, M. S. (2021). Public-private partnership within the context of digital transformation: increasingly larger role of educational institutions. In Educating Engineers for Future Industrial Revolutions: Proceedings of the 23rd International Conference on Interactive Collaborative Learning (ICL2020), Volume 2 23 (pp. 339-349). Springer International Publishing. [HTML] DOI: 10.1007/978-3-030-68201-9_34

Gray, E. K., Fahy, F., McArdle, R., & Rohse, M. (2024). Co-creating a community visioning methodology for energy transitions: Principles, practices, and reflections. Energy Research & Social Science. sciencedirect.com

Haleem, A., Javaid, M., Qadri, M. A., & Suman, R. (2022). Understanding the role of digital technologies in education: A review. Sustainable operations and computers, 3, 275-285. sciencedirect.com

Ho, S. S., Bowser, G., Templer, P., & Green, S. A. (2023). Learning for sustainability: partnerships for the goals. Sustainable Earth Reviews. springer.com

Hooda, M., Rana, C., Dahiya, O., & Rizwan…, A. (2022). Artificial intelligence for assessment and feedback to enhance student success in higher education. Mathematical …. wiley.com

Huang, Z. & Yanan, S. (2024). The Transforming Landscape of higher Education: Trends and challenges. Economic Sciences. economic-sciences.com

Imran, A. (2023). Why addressing digital inequality should be a priority. [wiley.com]. *The Electronic Journal on Information Systems in Developing Countries*, *89*(3), e12255. DOI: 10.1002/isd2.12255

Joudyian, N., Doshmangir, L., Mahdavi, M., Tabrizi, J. S., & Gordeev, V. S. (2021). Public-private partnerships in primary health care: A scoping review. [springer.com]. *BMC Health Services Research*, *21*(1), 1–18. DOI: 10.1186/s12913-020-05979-9 PMID: 33397388

Jun, H. & Kim, M. (2021). From stakeholder communication to engagement for the sustainable development goals (SDGs): A case study of LG electronics. Sustainability. mdpi.com

Khallaf, R., Kang, K., Hastak, M., & Othman, K. (2022). Public–Private Partnerships for Higher Education Institutions in the United States. Buildings. mdpi.com

Khan, S. M., Shafi, I., Butt, W. H., Diez, I. D. L. T., Flores, M. A. L., Galán, J. C., & Ashraf, I. (2023). A systematic review of disaster management systems: Approaches, challenges, and future directions. [mdpi.com]. *Land (Basel), 12*(8), 1514. DOI: 10.3390/land12081514

Kim, M. J. (2023). Toward coherence: A space sector public-private partnership typology. Space Policy. sciencedirect.com

Kraus, S., McDowell, W., Ribeiro-Soriano, D. E., & Rodríguez-García, M. (2021). The role of innovation and knowledge for entrepreneurship and regional development. [tandfonline.com]. *Entrepreneurship and Regional Development, 33*(3-4), 175–184. DOI: 10.1080/22797254.2021.1872929

Kuhail, M. A., ElSayary, A., Farooq, S., & Alghamdi, A. (2022). Exploring immersive learning experiences: A survey. Informatics. mdpi.com

Lagos-Castillo, A., Chiappe, A., Ramirez-Montoya, M. S., & Rodríguez, D. F. B. (2025). Mapping the Intelligent Classroom: Examining the Emergence of Personalized Learning Solutions in the Digital Age. Contemporary Educational Technology, 17(1). ed.gov

Lansing, A. E., Romero, N. J., Siantz, E., Silva, V., Center, K., Casteel, D., & Gilmer, T. (2023). Building trust: Leadership reflections on community empowerment and engagement in a large urban initiative. [springer.com]. *BMC Public Health, 23*(1), 1252. DOI: 10.1186/s12889-023-15860-z PMID: 37380973

MacLeod, C. J., Brandt, A. J., Collins, K., & Dicks, L. V. (2022). Giving stakeholders a voice in governance: Biodiversity priorities for New Zealand's agriculture. [wiley.com]. *People and Nature, 4*(2), 330–350. DOI: 10.1002/pan3.10285

Makda, F. (2025). Digital education: Mapping the landscape of virtual teaching in higher education–a bibliometric review. Education and Information Technologies. springer.com

Manta, O. & Mansi, E. (2024). The impact of globalization on innovative public procurement: challenges and opportunities. Administrative sciences. mdpi.com

Mariani, L., Trivellato, B., Martini, M., & Marafioti, E. (2022). Achieving sustainable development goals through collaborative innovation: Evidence from four European initiatives. Journal of Business Ethics. springer.com

Martínez-Peláez, R., Ochoa-Brust, A., Rivera, S., Félix, V. G., Ostos, R., Brito, H., Félix, R. A., & Mena, L. J. (2023). Role of digital transformation for achieving sustainability: Mediated role of stakeholders, key capabilities, and technology. [mdpi.com]. *Sustainability (Basel), 15*(14), 11221. DOI: 10.3390/su151411221

Memon, F. N., & Memon, S. N. (2025). Digital Divide and Equity in Education: Bridging Gaps to Ensure Inclusive Learning. In Impact of Digitalization on Education and Social Sustainability (pp. 107-130). IGI Global. [HTML]

Mhlanga, D. (2024). Digital transformation of education, the limitations and prospects of introducing the fourth industrial revolution asynchronous online learning in emerging markets. Discover education. springer.com

Mogas, J., Palau, R., Fuentes, M., & Cebrián, G. (2022). Smart schools on the way: How school principals from Catalonia approach the future of education within the fourth industrial revolution. [springer.com]. *Learning Environments Research, 25*(3), 875–893. DOI: 10.1007/s10984-021-09398-3

Olasehinde-Williams, G., Özkan, O., & Akadiri, S. S. (2023). Effects of climate policy uncertainty on sustainable investment: A dynamic analysis for the US. [HTML]. *Environmental Science and Pollution Research International, 30*(19), 55326–55339. DOI: 10.1007/s11356-023-26257-1 PMID: 36892691

Ozdemir, S., de Arroyabe, J. C. F., Sena, V., & Gupta, S. (2023). Stakeholder diversity and collaborative innovation: Integrating the resource-based view with stakeholder theory. [sciencedirect.com]. *Journal of Business Research, 164*, 113955. DOI: 10.1016/j.jbusres.2023.113955

Patil, L. (2023). The business of development: The institutional rationales of technology corporations in educational development. International Journal of Educational Development. sciencedirect.com

Putjorn, T., & Putjorn, P. (2023, October). Augmented imagination: Exploring generative AI from the perspectives of young learners. In 2023 15th International Conference on Information Technology and Electrical Engineering (ICITEE) (pp. 353-358). IEEE. [HTML]

Qadir, S. A., Ahmad, F., Al-Wahedi, A. M. A., Iqbal, A., & Ali, A. (2024). Navigating the complex realities of electric vehicle adoption: A comprehensive study of government strategies, policies, and incentives. [sciencedirect.com]. *Energy Strategy Reviews, 53*, 101379. DOI: 10.1016/j.esr.2024.101379

Rossoni, A. L., de Vasconcellos, E. P. G., & de Castilho Rossoni, R. L. (2024). Barriers and facilitators of university-industry collaboration for research, development and innovation: A systematic review. [springer.com]. *Management Review Quarterly*, *74*(3), 1841–1877. DOI: 10.1007/s11301-023-00349-1

Salla, S., Pasumarthy, A., Tadikonda, D., Parsha, T., & Mandal, S. K. (2025). Private AI in Education: Critical Challenges and Aspects of Enhancement Strategies. In Sustainable Development Using Private AI (pp. 109-131). CRC Press. [HTML]

Sanni, M. A. (2025). Entrepreneurship and Innovation in Enhancing Public-Private Partnership Effectiveness for Unlocking Economic Potential. In Public Private Partnership Dynamics for Economic Development (pp. 213-242). IGI Global Scientific Publishing. [HTML] DOI: 10.4018/979-8-3693-9153-2.ch011

Sehl, A., Cornia, A., & Nielsen, R. K. (2024). … do funding models and organizational legacy shape news organizations' social media strategies? A comparison of public service and private sector news media in six…. [HTML]. *Digital Journalism (Abingdon, England)*, *12*(9), 1377–1396. DOI: 10.1080/21670811.2021.1968920

Shan, Z., & Wang, Y. (2024). Strategic talent development in the knowledge economy: A comparative analysis of global practices. [HTML]. *Journal of the Knowledge Economy*, *15*(4), 19570–19596. DOI: 10.1007/s13132-024-01933-w

Tarchiani, V. & Grey, S. (2025). Bridging the communication gap in agrometeorological services: Enhancing the uptake and effectiveness for users in developing countries. Climate Services. sciencedirect.com

Thawesaengskulthai, N., Chatmarathong, A., & Koiwanit, J. (2024). Impact and policy supporting Thailand innovation driven enterprise: Orchestrating university innovation and entrepreneurship ecosystem with public and private stakeholders. [springer.com]. *Journal of Innovation and Entrepreneurship*, *13*(1), 16. DOI: 10.1186/s13731-024-00371-x

Tobin, R., Crawford, G., Hallett, J., Maycock, B. R., & Lobo, R. (2022). Critical factors that affect the functioning of a research and evaluation capacity building partnership: A causal loop diagram. Plos one. plos.org

Upadhyay, P., Kumar, A., & Mukerji, M. (2025). Evolving role of public-private stakeholders in technology mediated teaching. Digital Policy [HTML]. *Regulation & Governance*, *27*(1), 56–73. DOI: 10.1108/DPRG-09-2023-0130

Vahed, A., & Rodriguez, K. (2021). Enriching students' engaged learning experiences through the collaborative online international learning project. [HTML]. *Innovations in Education and Teaching International*, *58*(5), 596–605. DOI: 10.1080/14703297.2020.1792331

Vogel, R., Göbel, M., Grewe-Salfeld, M., Herbert, B., Matsuo, Y., & Weber, C. (2022). Cross-sector partnerships: Mapping the field and advancing an institutional approach. [wiley.com]. *International Journal of Management Reviews*, *24*(3), 394–414. DOI: 10.1111/ijmr.12283

Wang, F., Wong, W. K., Wang, Z., Albasher, G., Alsultan, N., & Fatemah, A. (2023). Emerging pathways to sustainable economic development: An interdisciplinary exploration of resource efficiency, technological innovation, and ecosystem resilience in resource-rich regions. [HTML]. *Resources Policy*, *85*, 103747. DOI: 10.1016/j.resourpol.2023.103747

Wiedermann, C. J., Barbieri, V., Plagg, B., Marino, P., Piccoliori, G., & Engl, A. (2023, May). Fortifying the foundations: a comprehensive approach to enhancing mental health support in educational policies amidst crises. In Healthcare (Vol. 11, No. 10, p. 1423). MDPI. mdpi.com DOI: 10.3390/healthcare11101423

Zhang, S., Sun, Z., Fan, Z., & Weng, S. (2024). Transforming talent development: A reflective analysis of the innovative government-school cooperation model under the paradigm of knowledge innovation. [HTML]. *Journal of the Knowledge Economy*.

Zhao, Y., Zhao, M., & Shi, F. (2024). Integrating moral education and educational information technology: A strategic approach to enhance rural teacher training in universities. [HTML]. *Journal of the Knowledge Economy*.

Chapter 11
Building a Culture of Accountability: Best Practices for Credential Management in Educational Institutions

Deby Rita Karundeng
https://orcid.org/0009-0002-8476-2549
Universitas Gorontalo, Indonesia

Ilyas Lamuda
Universitas Gorontalo, Indonesia

Mohamad Afan Suyanto
https://orcid.org/0000-0001-7440-4006
Universitas Gorontalo, Indonesia

Meimoon Ibrahim
https://orcid.org/0000-0002-3549-6646
Universitas Gorontalo, Indonesia

ABSTRACT

Accountability is crucial to credential management in educational institutions. Credential rules and technology must ensure correctness, transparency, and security as credentials increasingly affect academic integrity, employment chances, and institutional reputation. The chapter covers leadership commitment, role clarity, regulatory compliance, and stakeholder involvement. It emphasizes using technology like credential management systems, data encryption, and system interoperability to improve efficiency and prevent fraud. Case studies and best practices demonstrate

DOI: 10.4018/979-8-3373-5781-2.ch011

how continual development and responsive feedback loops sustain accountability. The chapter concludes by recognizing blockchain and micro-credentialing trends and encouraging institutions to innovate ethically. These findings offer a complete paradigm for improving institutional trust and academic credential management

UNDERSTANDING ACCOUNTABILITY IN CREDENTIAL MANAGEMENT

Defining Accountability

Accountability in education denotes the obligation of educational institutions to fulfill predetermined criteria of performance and integrity in their operations (Aburizaizah, 2022). This idea includes various actions, such as the administration of academic qualifications. In credential management, accountability denotes that institutions must not only confer credentials but also guarantee their authenticity, accuracy, and relevance. This obligation encompasses the preservation of transparent procedures that sustain the integrity of the educational system.

The significance of accountability in credential management is paramount. Educational institutions confer degrees, certificates, and licenses, signifying the knowledge and abilities attained by pupils (Varadarajan et al. 2023). These credentials are essential in the job market, as employers utilize them to evaluate the qualifications of prospective candidates. When institutions neglect accountability, they jeopardize the integrity of their credentials, resulting in diminished trust from students, employers, and the wider community.

Furthermore, accountability in credential management entails protection against fraud and misrepresentation. Occurrences of credential fraud can significantly impact both the persons implicated and the institution's reputation (Eaton and Carmichael 2023). An instance in which an institution inadvertently acknowledges a counterfeit degree may result in legal consequences and a deterioration of public trust. Consequently, establishing rigorous procedures and policies that guarantee the legitimacy of credentials is vital for upholding accountability.

Moreover, accountability cultivates a culture of ongoing enhancement inside educational institutions. By instituting explicit norms and expectations for credential management, institutions may consistently evaluate their procedures and pinpoint areas for improvement (Girmanová et al., 2022). This proactive strategy enhances operational efficiency and guarantees that children obtain the excellent education they merit.

In conclusion, delineating accountability within credential management is essential for educational institutions. It entails the obligation to furnish precise and authentic credentials while preserving the integrity of the educational system. Accountability is crucial not only for compliance but also for fostering trust, improving institutional reputation, and ultimately aiding students in their future success. In the following chapters, we will examine how institutions can successfully create and sustain a culture of responsibility in credential management.

The Role of Credentials in Education

Credentials demonstrate educational success and competence. Educational credentials include degrees, certifications, and licenses (Ewell et al., 2023). Each certificate validates a learner's knowledge and skills, affecting career paths and prospects.

Degrees, awarded by universities and colleges, are the most widely recognised credential (Laryea et al-2021). Associate, bachelor's, master's, and doctoral degrees are available. Each level indicates a distinct level of knowledge and competence, which might effect career advancement. For example, many professional tasks require a bachelor's degree, whereas specialized or academic employment may require a master's or doctoral degree.

Courses or training programs that focus on certain skills or knowledge lead to certificates (Blažič, 2022). These certificates are becoming more popular since they let people improve their skills without a degree. Certificates are especially useful in fast-changing areas like technology and healthcare, where constant learning is needed to compete. They demonstrate particular knowledge and boost resumes.

In regulated fields like medical, law, and engineering, licenses are essential (Gershuni et al.2023). A license usually requires passing tough exams and completing educational and experiential requirements. Licenses prove a professional's competence and safeguard the public by enforcing ethical norms.

Credentials affect educational institutions as well as individuals. Credentials boost the institution's credibility because graduates' employment and career success often determine its programs' value (Varadarajan et al.2023). Credentialing standards that are high create a culture of accountability that attracts students and businesses.

Finally, certifications validate abilities and knowledge and affect career chances in education. Effective credential management helps educational institutions retain quality, comply, and develop a strong reputation in a competitive environment. As we discuss accountability in credential management, it becomes evident that knowing credentials is essential to promoting education quality.

Current Challenges in Credential Management

Credential management in educational institutions encounters various issues that may compromise the integrity of the educational system (Ayub et al., 2021). As institutions endeavor to maintain accountability, they must traverse an environment replete with challenges such as credential fraud, mismanagement, and the intricacies of technological integration. Comprehending these problems is essential for formulating effective solutions to improve accountability in credential management.

Credential fraud is a critical issue that has grown increasingly sophisticated in recent years. Fraudulent actions encompass the issuance of counterfeit certificates and degrees as well as the alteration of academic records (Eaton and Carmichael 2023). A prominent case involved a collective that managed a bogus diploma mill, distributing degrees without necessitating the completion of any coursework by students. This not only deceived employers but also diminished the value of legitimate degrees and certificates, inflicting considerable damage on universities that maintain stringent academic standards. These instances underscore the necessity for stringent verification procedures and diligent supervision to avert the spread of counterfeit credentials.

The mismanagement of credentials constitutes a considerable challenge. This may arise from deficient record-keeping processes, absence of standardized procedures, or poor training for personnel engaged in credential management (Singo & Makgahlela, 2024). An institution may encounter difficulties in preserving precise records of student accomplishments, resulting in inconsistencies in transcripts and diplomas. Such errors can result in significant repercussions, including legal penalties and a deterioration of trust among students and employers. Institutions must emphasize the formulation of explicit regulations and efficient mechanisms to manage credentials effectively, guaranteeing that all records are precise and current.

The swift progression of technology offers both advantages and obstacles in credential management. Although technology can optimize procedures and improve security, it simultaneously poses issues with data privacy and cybersecurity. Institutions must manage the intricacies of deploying new technology while protecting sensitive student data (Shandilya et al. 2024). Cyberattacks on educational institutions have increased, with hackers aiming to exploit weaknesses in credential management systems. This requires a proactive strategy for cybersecurity, encompassing routine audits and employee training on optimal data protection practices.

ESTABLISHING A FRAMEWORK FOR CREDENTIAL MANAGEMENT

Developing Policies and Procedures

Implementing a comprehensive framework for credential management is crucial for educational institutions seeking to maintain accountability and safeguard the integrity of their credentialing processes (Ramasamy & Khan, 2024). Robust policies and processes are the foundation of this framework, directing institutions in the methodical and transparent management of credentials.

Essential elements of effective credential management rules encompass clarity, consistency, and compliance (Iatrellis et al., 2024). Initially, policies must explicitly delineate the categories of credentials provided, the standards for their issue, and the procedures for verification. This clarity eradicates uncertainty and guarantees that all stakeholders—students, instructors, and administrative personnel—comprehend their roles and duties in credentialing. Uniformity is vital; policies must be consistently implemented throughout all programs and agencies to uphold fairness and integrity. Finally, schools must guarantee that their policies adhere to applicable laws and regulations, including those pertaining to data privacy and academic standards. This adherence safeguards the institution legally while simultaneously augmenting its credibility.

Institutions should undertake a collaborative process involving essential stakeholders in the development of these policies. This encompasses faculty members, administrative personnel, legal consultants, and students. By integrating varied perspectives, organizations can formulate inclusive policies that cater to the needs and concerns of all stakeholders (Chan, 2023). Moreover, periodic evaluations and revisions of these policies are crucial to accommodate evolving rules and developing best practices in credential management.

Following the establishment of policies, the subsequent step is to formulate and execute procedures that operationalize these policies. Effective procedures must delineate sequential steps for credential issue, verification, and maintenance (Rani et al., 2024). Institutions should establish explicit protocols for the generation of transcripts, the conferral of degrees, and the investigation of fake credentials. These protocols must provide means for reporting discrepancies or concerns, so facilitating rapid resolution of issues.

Training is an essential component in executing these procedures (Díaz-Rodríguez et al. 2023). Personnel engaged in credential management must undergo extensive training to comprehend the relevant regulations, processes, and technologies. This training must encompass both the technical sides of credential management and the ethical implications related to data integrity and student privacy.

Roles and Responsibilities

Efficient credential administration in educational institutions depends on well-defined roles and duties among diverse stakeholders (Iatrellis et al., 2024). Identifying these stakeholders and defining their specific roles is essential for creating a unified framework that fosters accountability and integrity in the credentialing process.

The principal stakeholders in credential management comprise teachers, administrative personnel, students, and external organizations, including employers and accrediting agencies (Reddy et al. 2024). Each group is essential in guaranteeing the effective and transparent execution of processes related to credential issue, verification, and maintenance.

Faculty members frequently lead in credential management. They are tasked with evaluating student performance, ascertaining eligibility for degrees and certifications, and maintaining academic standards. Faculty must possess a comprehensive understanding of the institution's credentialing rules and procedures, as they are integral to the evaluation process (Venkatesh and Rajavelu, 2025). Furthermore, faculty members may participate in the formulation of curriculum and assessment strategies that conform to the institution's credentialing criteria, so guaranteeing that the credentials conferred appropriately represent the skills and knowledge attained by students.

Administrative personnel are essential to the operational facets of credential management (Ayub et al., 2021). Their duties encompass maintaining precise records, processing credential applications, and supervising the issuance of diplomas and transcripts. Administrative staff must oversee adherence to legal and regulatory obligations, protecting the organization from potential liabilities. Training for administrative personnel is crucial, as it provides them with the expertise and competencies required to manage credentialing operations efficiently and to handle sensitive student information with diligence.

Students have a significant part in the credential management process. They are accountable for comprehending the prerequisites for acquiring their certifications and assuring compliance with these standards. Students must proactively consult academic advisors and professors to resolve any ambiguities concerning their advancement toward graduation or certification (Suárez & Beatty, 2022). Additionally, students can offer significant feedback on the certification process, assisting schools in pinpointing areas for enhancement.

Finally, external stakeholders, like employers and accrediting organizations, significantly influence the impression and credibility of credentials. Employers depend on the authenticity of academic qualifications during recruitment, whereas accrediting organizations evaluate institutions to confirm compliance with defined criteria (Bohlens, 2025). Interacting with external stakeholders can furnish institutions with insights into industry expectations and assist them in preserving the relevance of their credentialing methods.

In conclusion, explicitly delineating the roles and duties of stakeholders in credential management is vital for cultivating a culture of accountability inside educational institutions. By clarifying the roles of teachers, administrative staff, students, and external groups, institutions can provide a unified and efficient structure that maintains the integrity of the credentialing process. We will investigate how collaboration among stakeholders in credential management might augment accountability and boost outcomes for all parties involved.

Compliance and Regulatory Considerations

In credential management, adherence to applicable laws and regulations is essential for educational institutions. These frameworks not only safeguard the integrity of the credentialing process but also shield institutions from legal liability and augment their credibility. Comprehending the compliance landscape is crucial for formulating efficient credential management rules (Salama & Hinton, 2023).

Numerous essential statutes and regulations regulate credential administration inside educational institutions. The Family Educational Rights and Privacy Act (FERPA) is a United States statute that safeguards the confidentiality of student education records (Rights & Act, 2021). FERPA confers upon students the right to examine their records and mandates that institutions secure consent before to sharing personally identifiable information. Adherence to FERPA is essential for preserving student confidence and protecting sensitive information.

The Higher Education Act (HEA) is a significant legislation that delineates the criteria for federal student aid programs and requires institutions to maintain precise records of student enrollment and academic progress (Johnson et al., 2023). Adherence to the HEA guarantees that universities maintain the requisite criteria for federal funding and accreditation. Furthermore, universities must comply with state-specific rules and accrediting criteria, which might differ markedly among jurisdictions.

To adeptly traverse this intricate regulatory framework, educational institutions must implement best practices to ensure compliance (Sato et al. 2023). Institutions must implement a thorough compliance structure that encompasses routine audits and evaluations of their credential management procedures. These audits must assess compliance with applicable rules and regulations, identify potential risk areas, and provide corrective measures as needed.

Training and professional development for personnel engaged in credential management are essential (Thornhill-Miller et al., 2023). Institutions must offer continuous education on compliance mandates, data privacy, and ethical considerations.

This training guarantees that professors and administrative personnel are prepared to manage sensitive material judiciously and comprehend the legal ramifications of their conduct.

Furthermore, institutions ought to establish comprehensive data management systems that ensure adherence to record-keeping and reporting obligations (Chittoor2025). These systems must incorporate functionalities for the secure storage of student records, the tracking of credential issuance, and the management of access to sensitive information. By utilizing technology, institutions can improve their capacity to adhere to regulations and reduce the danger of data breaches.

Ultimately, cultivating a culture of accountability within the organization is vital for compliance. Leadership must underscore the significance of complying with rules and regulations, fostering transparent dialogue around compliance-related issues (Nandan2024). By fostering an atmosphere that encourages staff and students to identify potential issues, institutions can proactively tackle compliance challenges.

In conclusion, adherence to pertinent laws and regulations is essential for effective credential administration in educational institutions. By comprehending the regulatory framework and adopting best practices, schools may maintain the integrity of their credentialing processes, safeguard student privacy, and bolster their overall credibility. This book will examine the integration of compliance procedures into a comprehensive framework for accountability in credential management.

IMPLEMENTING TECHNOLOGY SOLUTIONS

Choosing the Right Credential Management System

In the contemporary digital era, choosing a suitable credential management system (CMS) is essential for educational institutions seeking to improve accountability and optimize their credentialing procedures (Ayub et al., 2021). An appropriately selected CMS may markedly enhance the efficiency of academic record management, mitigate fraud risk, and guarantee adherence to regulatory standards. The selection process necessitates meticulous evaluation of diverse parameters to guarantee that the system fulfills the institution's particular requirements.

A key criterion for assessing credential management software is usability. The system must provide an intuitive interface that facilitates navigation for both staff and students. An intuitive design minimizes the learning curve and promotes user adoption (Almaiah et al., 2022). The system must provide comprehensive training resources and customer assistance to enable users to optimize the software's functionalities.

Security aspects are another vital concern. Due to the sensitive nature of student data, the CMS must implement robust security measures, including data encryption, access controls, and routine security audits (Vashishth et al., 2024). Institutions ought to seek systems that adhere to data protection standards, such as FERPA, and that provide features like two-factor authentication to prevent illegal access.

Integration capabilities are crucial. The selected CMS must interact effortlessly with current institutional systems, including learning management systems (LMS), student information systems (SIS), and financial aid platforms (Alalawi et al., 2025). This interface guarantees seamless data transfer between systems, minimizing mistake risk and enhancing overall operational efficiency.

Scalability constitutes a significant criteria. As institutions develop and progress, their requirements for credential management may alter. A scalable CMS may manage growing data volumes and enhanced functionality without necessitating a complete system redesign (Cappelli & Di Marzo Serugendo, 2025). Institutions must evaluate their prospective requirements and choose a CMS that can accommodate such adaptations.

This example demonstrates the effective deployment of technological solutions, namely a mid-sized institution that adopted a new credential management system to resolve inefficiencies and enhance data security (Kioskli et al. 2025). Before implementation, the university encountered difficulties with manual record-keeping, resulting in frequent inaccuracies in transcripts and delays in diploma issuance. Upon assessing various CMS alternatives according to the specified criteria, the university selected a cloud-based solution that provided comprehensive security features and effortless connection with their current SIS.

Following deployment, the university observed a substantial drop in processing times for credential requests and a notable reduction in errors (Oyedokun et al. 2025). Moreover, the system's reporting functionalities enabled administrators to oversee adherence to regulatory standards with greater efficacy. This instance emphasizes the significance of selecting an appropriate CMS and illustrates how a deliberate deployment can enhance results for both the school and its students.

In conclusion, choosing an appropriate credential management system is essential for educational institutions seeking to improve accountability and efficiency in their credentialing procedures. By assessing prospective systems based on essential criteria and analyzing successful case studies, institutions can make educated decisions that align with their long-term objectives. We will investigate how technology solutions in credential management can be effectively employed to promote a culture of accountability in educational institutions.

Data Security and Privacy

In the digital realm of education, safeguarding student data is of utmost significance (Hakimi et al. 2021). Educational institutions handle a substantial amount of sensitive information, encompassing personal identity data, academic records, and financial information. Unauthorized access or mismanagement of sensitive data may result in significant implications, such as identity theft, fraud, and legal ramifications. Consequently, guaranteeing strong data security and privacy is crucial for preserving the integrity of credential management systems and cultivating confidence among students and stakeholders.

The significance of safeguarding student data beyond mere adherence to legislation like the Family Educational Rights and Privacy Act (FERPA). Institutions must acknowledge that protecting personal information is both a legal requirement and a moral commitment (Prinsloo and Kaliisa 2022). Students confide sensitive information to their institutions, anticipating it would be managed with diligence and respect. A violation of this trust can harm an institution's reputation and diminish the confidence of its students and the community.

To effectively safeguard student data in credential management systems, schools must use best practices that include both technical and organizational strategies (Azem et al. 2025). Primarily, the establishment of robust access controls is essential. This entails specifying the individuals authorized to access sensitive data and the conditions governing such access. Role-based access controls (RBAC) facilitate the restriction of student record access and modification to authorized workers, hence reducing the likelihood of unauthorized access.

Data encryption constitutes an essential safeguard. Encrypting sensitive data both at rest and in transit safeguards it against potential breaches (Shaik & Natarajan, 2022). Data interception is rendered ineffective by encryption, which makes the information incomprehensible without the corresponding decryption key. Institutions must employ secure communication protocols, such as HTTPS, to protect data exchanged across the internet.

Regular security audits and assessments are crucial for identifying weaknesses in the credential management system (Ali et al. 2024). Institutions must do regular assessments to evaluate the efficacy of their security protocols and guarantee adherence to data protection requirements. This proactive strategy enables institutions to mitigate potential vulnerabilities prior to exploitation.

Moreover, cultivating a culture of data security awareness among personnel and students is essential. Institutions ought to deliver training on data privacy protocols, underscoring the significance of protecting personal information (Prinsloo and Kaliisa 2022). Instructing staff about phishing assaults, password management, and secure data handling techniques can markedly diminish the likelihood of human error resulting in data breaches.

Ultimately, developing a thorough incident response plan is essential for managing data breaches if they arise. This strategy must delineate the actions to be executed in the occurrence of a breach, encompassing notification protocols for impacted persons and regulatory authorities. A well-defined and efficient response strategy can alleviate the consequences of a data breach and exhibit the institution's dedication to accountability and transparency (Cheng & Wang, 2022).

In conclusion, safeguarding student data is a crucial element of credential administration within educational institutions. By adopting optimal data security procedures and cultivating a culture of awareness, institutions may protect sensitive information, adhere to legal obligations, and preserve the trust of their students and stakeholders. In our ongoing examination of technological options for credential management, prioritizing data security and privacy will be essential for cultivating a culture of accountability.

Integrating Systems for Efficiency

The integration of diverse systems is crucial for improving operational efficiency and assuring data accuracy in credential management (Pop et al., 2023). Educational institutions frequently employ several platforms, including Student Information Systems (SIS), Learning Management Systems (LMS), and financial aid systems. The integration of these systems facilitates uninterrupted data transfer, minimizes redundancy, and enhances the comprehensive management of student credentials.

An effective option for integrating credential management with current systems is to utilize an Application Programming Interface (API) approach (Gupta et al. 2024). APIs provide connection between disparate software applications, allowing for real-time data sharing. For example, upon a student's completion of a course in a Learning Management System (LMS), the completion data can be automatically synchronized with the Student Information System (SIS), so guaranteeing that academic records remain up-to-date. This not only reduces the likelihood of errors linked to human data entry but also optimizes operations like transcript generation and degree audits.

Another option entails employing a centralized data repository (Aldoseri et al., 2023). By integrating all student data into a singular database, universities may provide a cohesive perspective of student qualifications. This repository is accessible to multiple departments, facilitating more effective management of academic records and minimizing the potential for discrepancies. Centralized data management streamlines reporting and ensures compliance with regulatory mandates, enabling institutions to effortlessly produce precise reports derived from extensive data.

The implementation of data integration technologies can significantly improve the efficiency of credential management (Olanrewaju et al. 2022). These solutions can automate data synchronization between systems, guaranteeing that updates made in one platform are mirrored across all pertinent systems. For instance, when a student's status transitions—from enrolled to graduated—the integration tool can immediately revise all related information, including financial aid eligibility and alumni status.

A cohesive strategy for data management offers significant advantages (Liu et al., 2021). Primarily, system integration enhances data precision. The interconnection of all systems substantially diminishes the chance of errors stemming from duplicate entries or obsolete information. This precision is essential for upholding the integrity of academic qualifications and assuring adherence to regulatory norms.

Moreover, a cohesive strategy improves operational efficiency. Staff members can access extensive student records via a unified platform, minimizing the time required to navigate several systems (Habib et al. 2021). This efficiency liberates resources and enables staff to concentrate on more strategic activities, like student involvement and support.

Furthermore, the integration of credential management systems enhances interdepartmental collaboration. When all stakeholders—academic advisors, registrars, financial aid personnel, and faculty—have access to same data, communication enhances, and choices can be made more jointly (Salomon-Fernández2022). This comprehensive perspective on student credentials promotes a more unified strategy for student achievement.

In conclusion, the integration of credential management with existing systems is vital for improving efficiency and accuracy in educational institutions. Institutions can establish a cohesive data management strategy through the utilization of API integration, centralized data repositories, and data integration tools. The resultant advantages—augmented data precision, operational efficacy, and greater collaboration—are essential for cultivating a culture of accountability in credential management. The focus on integration will remain paramount in developing effective credentialing frameworks as we pursue technological solutions.

FOSTERING A CULTURE OF ACCOUNTABILITY

Leadership Commitment

The dedication of institutional leadership is essential for cultivating a culture of accountability in educational institutions, especially regarding credential management (Mgaiwa, 2021). Leaders establish the organizational atmosphere, and their conduct and perspectives toward accountability can profoundly affect the behavior of faculty, staff, and students. When leaders emphasize accountability, they foster an environment that values integrity and transparency, so augmenting the institution's credibility and the legitimacy of its credentials.

Institutional leadership's fundamental responsibility in fostering accountability is to delineate explicit expectations and norms around credential management (Gershuni et al. 2023). Leaders must emphasize the significance of precise record-keeping, ethical conduct, and adherence to regulations. By explicitly conveying these expectations, leaders establish a framework that enables professors and staff to function effectively, ensuring that all individuals comprehend their duties in upholding the integrity of the credentialing process.

Furthermore, leaders must exemplify accountability by their activities (Bøe et al. 2022). This entails transparency in decision-making processes, recognition of errors, and accountability for results. For instance, if a mistake arises in the credentialing process, leaders ought to confront it transparently, examine the underlying causes, and enact remedial actions. This not only underscores the significance of accountability but also fosters a culture in which employees feel empowered to report difficulties and pursue enhancements without fear of retaliation.

To enhance accountability, leaders may establish regular training and professional development initiatives centered on ethical practices and compliance in credential management (Faizuddin et al., 2022). By investing in employee development, leaders demonstrate their commitment to responsibility and anticipate that their teams will maintain these standards. Training sessions may encompass subjects such as data security, regulatory compliance, and optimal credential management procedures, thereby giving personnel with the requisite knowledge and abilities to execute their responsibilities proficiently.

A further technique for cultivating a culture of accountability is to implement systems for feedback and transparent communication. Leaders ought to promote the sharing of views and concerns among professors and staff pertaining to credential management processes. Establishing avenues for anonymous reporting can assist in identifying possible issues without jeopardizing individuals (Vian et al., 2022). Consistently requesting feedback illustrates that leadership appreciates contributions from all organizational tiers and is dedicated to ongoing enhancement.

Ultimately, acknowledging and incentivizing accountability among academics and staff helps strengthen the intended culture. Leaders ought to acknowledge accomplishments pertaining to ethical practices, compliance, and proficient credential management. By recognizing individuals and teams that demonstrate accountability, executives foster a sense of pride and drive inside the organization (Matahela & van Rensburg, 2022).

In summary, institutional leadership is essential in cultivating a culture of accountability in credential management. By establishing explicit expectations, exemplifying accountability via their conduct, investing in training, promoting open communication, and acknowledging accomplishments, leaders can cultivate an environment where accountability is embedded in the institution's procedures. The dedication of leadership will continue to be fundamental in establishing a culture of responsibility as we investigate optimal techniques in credential management.

Training and Professional Development

Training and professional development are vital elements in cultivating a culture of accountability in educational institutions, especially with credential management methods (Geletu & Mihiretie, 2023). As the educational landscape transforms, the intricacies of managing student credentials also increase. Institutions must guarantee that their personnel possess the requisite knowledge and abilities to adeptly address these difficulties.

The significance of educating personnel on credential management techniques is paramount (Love et al., 2021). Primarily, thorough training programs guarantee that staff comprehend the institution's policies and procedures for credentialing. This encompasses an understanding of regulatory mandates, data security measures, and optimal methods for ensuring precise record-keeping. When personnel are proficient in these domains, they are more inclined to comply with established standards, thereby diminishing the likelihood of errors and augmenting the integrity of the credentialing process.

Furthermore, training cultivates a sense of ownership and accountability among employees. When employees acknowledge their essential role in credential management, they are more inclined to regard their responsibilities with seriousness (Dimitriou, 2022). This sense of accountability promotes the institution and instills confidence in students and stakeholders over the legitimacy of the credentials awarded.

Establishing a continual learning environment is vital for maintaining a culture of accountability. Educational institutions ought to facilitate continuous professional development opportunities that enable workers to remain abreast of industry trends, technical innovations, and regulatory changes (Mlambo et al., 2021). This can be accomplished through several techniques, such as workshops, online courses, and involvement in professional organizations pertinent to credential management.

Moreover, cultivating a culture of perpetual learning necessitates promoting collaboration and the exchange of knowledge among employees. Institutions may implement mentorship programs in which seasoned employees instruct fresher staff on optimal credential management methods (Smithwick et al. 2023). This collaborative method not only improves individual skills but also fortifies the team's overall competence.

Moreover, institutions must to consistently assess the efficacy of their training programs and solicit feedback from personnel. Through the evaluation of training programs, leadership may pinpoint areas for enhancement and guarantee that the material remains pertinent and stimulating (Ahsan, 2025). This continuous assessment method exemplifies a dedication to employee growth and underscores the significance of accountability in credential oversight.

Ultimately, acknowledging and compensating employees who participate in training and professional development can enhance a culture of accountability. Institutions may commemorate accomplishments with awards, recognitions during meetings, or opportunities for professional progress. This acknowledgment not only inspires individuals to engage in lifelong learning but also conveys to the entire organization that responsibility and professional development are esteemed.

In conclusion, training and professional development are essential for cultivating a culture of accountability in credential management. By emphasizing comprehensive training programs and fostering a continuous learning environment, educational institutions can enable their staff to maintain the highest standards of honesty and quality in handling student credentials. The ongoing examination of optimal credential management systems will prioritize training and professional development as fundamental to fostering a culture of accountability.

Engaging Students and Stakeholders

Involving students and external stakeholders in the credentialing process is essential for cultivating a culture of accountability inside educational institutions (Kayyali2024). By engaging these groups, schools may improve transparency, foster confidence, and guarantee that the credentials conferred accurately represent the genuine competencies and accomplishments of students.

An effective technique for engaging students in the credentialing process is to offer them opportunities for input and feedback (Tereshchenko et al. 2024). Institutions may establish advisory committees comprising student representatives to express their perspectives on credentialing rules and processes. This engagement not only empowers students but also guarantees that their viewpoints are taken into account when formulating or amending systems pertaining to credential management. Furthermore, colleges may administer surveys or convene focus groups to collect student input regarding their experiences with credentialing, including the transparency of standards and the efficacy of the application process. By prioritizing student feedback, schools exhibit their dedication to accountability and responsiveness.

An alternative method is to instruct pupils on the significance of their qualifications and the procedures required to get them. Institutions may provide workshops or instructional sessions that elucidate credentialing requirements, the need of upholding academic integrity, and the consequences of credential fraud. By cultivating a profound comprehension among students, institutions can motivate them to assume responsibility for their academic pursuits and engage actively in upholding the integrity of the credentialing process (Singh et al. 2022).

Establishing collaborations with external stakeholders, including employers, industry representatives, and certifying organizations, is as essential (Valk and Kratovitš 2021). These collaborations can yield significant insights on the skills and abilities most pertinent in the job market, ensuring that the credentials conferred by the school correspond with industry standards. Involving employers in conversations regarding the requisite competencies for graduates might assist universities in enhancing their programs and certifying methodologies.

Moreover, partnering with accrediting organizations promotes accountability by guaranteeing that schools adhere to defined criteria of quality and integrity in credential administration. Consistent communication and collaboration with external stakeholders can assist institutions in remaining updated about best practices and developing trends in credentialing (Varadarajan et al. 2023).

Furthermore, institutions can utilize these collaborations to establish internship and job placement chances for students, so augmenting their employability and offering practical experience (Adeosun et al., 2022). Students are more inclined to appreciate the integrity of the credentialing process when they recognize the direct correlation between their qualifications and employment opportunities.

In conclusion, including students and external stakeholders is crucial for cultivating a culture of accountability in credential management. By engaging students in decision-making and fostering collaborations with companies and accrediting organizations, educational institutions may augment transparency, enhance the pertinence of their credentials, and ultimately facilitate student success. In our ongoing examination of optimal credential management procedures, prioritizing engagement will be essential in fostering a culture of responsibility that serves all stakeholders.

ASSESSING AND IMPROVING CREDENTIAL MANAGEMENT PRACTICES

Measuring Accountability and Effectiveness

Assessing accountability and efficacy in credential management methods is crucial for educational institutions dedicated to upholding high standards and safeguarding the integrity of the credentials they confer (Kooli & Abadli, 2022). Defining key performance indicators (KPIs) and utilizing diverse assessment tools and methodologies enables institutions to review their credentialing processes, pinpoint areas for enhancement, and guarantee compliance with accountability targets.

Key Performance Indicators (KPIs) for credential management must include both quantitative and qualitative measurements (Bashir et al. 2023). Quantitative KPIs give measurable data that can be readily monitored over time. Prevalent quantitative metrics encompass:

- Accuracy Rate of Issued Credentials: This indicator quantifies the proportion of credentials issued error-free, indicating the institution's proficiency in maintaining precise records.
- Credential Request Processing Time: This KPI measures the average duration required to process requests for transcripts, diplomas, or certificates, reflecting the efficiency of the credentialing procedure.
- Compliance Rate with Regulatory Standards: This assesses the institution's conformity to applicable laws and regulations, ensuring that credentialing methods align with external mandates.

Conversely, qualitative KPIs emphasize the experiences and perspectives of stakeholders engaged in the credentialing process. Surveys and feedback systems can be employed to evaluate:

- Student Satisfaction: Collecting student feedback regarding their experiences with the credentialing process can reveal areas requiring enhancement.
- Faculty and Staff Engagement: Assessing faculty perceptions of the credential management system can uncover potential deficiencies in training or support.

Institutions can utilize many techniques and methodologies to successfully evaluate these KPIs (Bashir et al. 2023). An successful strategy involves performing regular audits of credential management methods. These audits verify adherence to set regulations, discover inconsistencies in data, and evaluate the overall efficacy of the credentialing process. Through comprehensive examination of procedures, institutions can identify areas needing attention and formulate specific improvement plans.

Data analytics solutions can significantly contribute to the evaluation of credential management. Through the examination of data trends—such as the incidence of credential requests, prevalent application problems, and processing durations—institutions can make educated judgments on process improvements and resource distribution (Kamyab et al. 2023). Evaluating against industry standards and best practices is an effective assessment strategy (Ouakka et al., 2022). By juxtaposing their credential management methods with those of comparable institutions or esteemed leaders in the domain, educational institutions can discern deficiencies in their processes and implement effective strategies utilized by others.

Ultimately, the creation of a feedback loop is essential for ongoing enhancement. Institutions must to consistently seek feedback from stakeholders, including as students, professors, and employers, concerning their experiences with the credentialing process (Cheng et al. 2024). This feedback can guide modifications to policies and practices, ensuring the institution remains attuned to the needs of its community.

In conclusion, assessing accountability and efficacy in credential management is essential for educational institutions striving to maintain high standards. Institutions can improve their credentialing procedures and fulfill the requirements of their students and stakeholders by identifying key performance indicators, employing diverse assessment tools and methods, and committing to continual development.

Continuous Improvement Strategies

Strategies for continuous improvement are essential for educational institutions aiming to refine their credential management processes (Kooli & Abadli, 2022). By establishing feedback loops and analyzing successful case studies, institutions may cultivate a culture of accountability and responsiveness that ultimately advantages students, faculty, and stakeholders.

Implementing Feedback Loops for Ongoing Improvement

Feedback loops are crucial for establishing a dynamic system of ongoing enhancement in credential management (Charles and Hill 2025). These loops entail the methodical collection, analysis, and implementation of input from diverse stakeholders, including students, professors, and administrative personnel. By instituting regular feedback mechanisms, institutions can acquire critical insights into the efficacy of their credentialing procedures and pinpoint areas for improvement.

A proficient approach of establishing feedback loops is via surveys and focus groups. Institutions may perform regular surveys to evaluate stakeholder satisfaction about credential management processes, encompassing the clarity of requirements, the efficiency of request processing, and the overall experience. Focus groups yield profound qualitative insights, enabling participants to articulate specific difficulties and propose viable solutions (Lim, 2024). This information can facilitate informed modifications to policies and procedures, guaranteeing their continued relevance and efficacy.

Furthermore, institutions may establish suggestion boxes or digital platforms that allow stakeholders to anonymously provide input or report concerns regarding credential management. This method promotes transparent communication and can reveal issues that may not be immediately evident through official surveys.

Case Studies of Institutions That Have Successfully Improved Their Practices

Numerous institutions have effectively executed continuous improvement techniques in their credential management procedures, leading to increased accountability and efficiency.

A significant instance is a large community college that had difficulties with prolonged processing times for transcript requests (McKinney et al. 2022). To resolve this issue, the college implemented feedback mechanisms through questionnaires administered to students and staff. The findings indicated that numerous students were uninformed about the necessary procedures for acquiring transcripts, resulting in confusion and delays. In response, the college overhauled its communication strategy, establishing explicit standards and teaching resources for students. Furthermore, they optimized the processing system by implementing a new credential management software that interfaced with their current student information system. Consequently, the college markedly decreased transcript processing durations and enhanced student satisfaction.

A university aimed to improve the precision of its credentialing procedures. The university established a thorough audit system encompassing routine examinations of academic records and credential granting (Samson et al. 2024). They also instituted a feedback mechanism with faculty members, prompting them to identify anomalies or issues. This proactive strategy enabled the university to swiftly identify and resolve errors, resulting in a significant enhancement in the precision of issued credentials. The institution's dedication to ongoing enhancement not only bolstered its image but also cultivated increased confidence among students and employers.

In conclusion, ongoing enhancement techniques are vital for optimizing credential management processes at educational institutions. By establishing feedback loops and analyzing successful case studies, institutions may foster a responsive and accountable climate that serves all stakeholders. The ongoing examination of optimal credential management processes will prioritize continual improvement as a fundamental element in cultivating a culture of accountability and excellence in education.

Future Trends in Credential Management

Educational institutions are adapting to the changing dynamics of credential management, with several developing trends and technologies influencing the future of credential issuance, verification, and valuation (Salama & Hinton, 2023). Comprehending these tendencies is essential for institutions seeking to maintain competitiveness and accountability in a swiftly evolving educational landscape.

A notable trend is the growing adoption of blockchain technology for credential management. Blockchain provides a decentralized and secure mechanism for the storage and verification of academic credentials. Through the implementation of blockchain technology, institutions can establish immutable records of degrees and certificates that can be readily confirmed by employers and other educational entities (Rama et al. 2021). This technology strengthens the security and integrity of credentials while streamlining the verification process, hence alleviating the administrative strain on institutions. As an increasing number of enterprises embrace blockchain technology, it is poised to establish itself as a standard in credential management, offering a dependable way to mitigate credential fraud.

A notable trend is the proliferation of digital badges and micro-credentials. These digital representations of abilities and accomplishments enable institutions to acknowledge and authenticate particular competencies outside conventional degree programs. With the labor market prioritizing skills over formal degrees, universities are implementing micro-credentialing to offer students a more adaptable and customized learning experience (Alenezi et al., 2024). Digital badges can be disseminated on social media platforms and professional networks, augmenting students' visibility to prospective employers. This trend signifies a transition to competency-based education, emphasizing students' capabilities over mere completion of tasks.

Furthermore, data analytics is becoming essential to credential management. Institutions are utilizing data analytics tools to obtain insights on student performance, credentialing patterns, and labor market requirements. Through the analysis of this data, universities can more effectively match their programs with industry requirements, so ensuring the credentials they provide stay pertinent and desirable (Varadarajan et al. 2023). Moreover, data-driven decision-making enables institutions to pinpoint areas for enhancement in their credential management procedures, thereby improving overall efficiency and accountability.

Institutions must use emerging trends and technologies to prepare for the future of education and credential management (Varadarajan et al. 2023). This entails investing in essential infrastructure, educating personnel on new systems, and cultivating a culture of innovation. Institutions must collaborate with industry partners and stakeholders to achieve alignment with market demands and best practices.

Furthermore, institutions must emphasize data security and privacy while integrating new technology. The growing dependence on digital platforms for credential administration necessitates the protection of student information (Aldboush & Ferdous, 2023). Institutions must adopt stringent security protocols and remain cognizant of regulatory obligations to safeguard sensitive information.

In conclusion, the future of credential management is influenced by rising developments including blockchain technology, digital badges, and data analytics. By anticipating these changes and adopting innovation, educational institutions can improve their credentialing procedures, maintain accountability, and more effectively meet the demands of their students and the workforce. The ongoing examination of optimal credential management practices will prioritize future trends, which are essential for cultivating a culture of accountability and excellence in education.

CONCLUSION

Establishing a culture of accountability in credential management is a critical imperative for educational institutions navigating an increasingly complex academic and professional landscape. As credentials represent more than mere documentation—symbolizing academic achievement, professional competence, and institutional credibility—their integrity must be preserved through deliberate, strategic, and ethical practices.

This chapter has emphasized the multifaceted nature of credential management, beginning with the foundational importance of defining accountability. It has explored the essential role of clear policies, defined responsibilities, regulatory compliance, and robust technological systems. Together, these elements ensure that credentials are issued, verified, and maintained with the highest standards of accuracy, transparency, and security. Moreover, the proactive engagement of stakeholders—including faculty, administrators, students, employers, and accrediting bodies—reinforces collective responsibility and enhances institutional trust.

The integration of technological solutions such as credential management systems, blockchain, and data analytics has emerged as both a necessity and an opportunity. These innovations not only streamline operations and enhance security but also pave the way for future-oriented practices like digital badges and micro-credentials that reflect evolving workforce demands.

However, technology alone is insufficient without committed leadership and a sustained investment in professional development. Training, ethical awareness, and continuous feedback loops are vital for maintaining quality and adapting to change. Institutions that cultivate a responsive, transparent, and accountable environment will be better positioned to uphold their academic mission and societal role.

In conclusion, credential management should not be viewed as an isolated administrative task but as a strategic pillar of institutional integrity and excellence. By embedding accountability into every aspect of credentialing—from policy formation to system integration—educational institutions can ensure that their credentials remain credible, respected, and aligned with the needs of learners and the broader world. This holistic approach is essential for building lasting trust and supporting student success in a dynamic global landscape.

REFERENCES

Aburizaizah, S. J. (2022). The role of quality assurance in Saudi higher education institutions. International Journal of Educational Research Open. sciencedirect.com

Adeosun, O. T., Shittu, A. I., & Owolabi, T. J. (2022). University internship systems and preparation of young people for world of work in the 4th industrial revolution. Rajagiri Management Journal. emerald.com

Ahsan, M. J. (2025). Cultivating a culture of learning: The role of leadership in fostering lifelong development. [HTML]. *The Learning Organization*, *32*(2), 282–306. DOI: 10.1108/TLO-03-2024-0099

Alalawi, K., Athauda, R., Chiong, R., & Renner, I. (2025). Evaluating the student performance prediction and action framework through a learning analytics intervention study. [springer.com]. *Education and Information Technologies*, *30*(3), 2887–2916. DOI: 10.1007/s10639-024-12923-5

Aldboush, H. H. H. & Ferdous, M. (2023). Building trust in fintech: an analysis of ethical and privacy considerations in the intersection of big data, AI, and customer trust. International Journal of Financial Studies. mdpi.com

Aldoseri, A., Al-Khalifa, K. N., & Hamouda, A. M. (2023). Re-thinking data strategy and integration for artificial intelligence: concepts, opportunities, and challenges. Applied Sciences. mdpi.com

Alenezi, M., Akour, M., & Alfawzan, L. (2024). Evolving Microcredential Strategies for Enhancing Employability: Employer and Student Perspectives. Education Sciences. mdpi.com

Ali, T., Al-Khalidi, M., & Al-Zaidi, R. (2024). Information security risk assessment methods in cloud computing: Comprehensive review. [tandfonline.com]. *Journal of Computer Information Systems*, •••, 1–28. DOI: 10.1080/08874417.2024.2329985

Almaiah, M. A., Alfaisal, R., Salloum, S. A., Hajjej, F., Shishakly, R., Lutfi, A., Alrawad, M., Al Mulhem, A., Alkhdour, T., & Al-Maroof, R. S. (2022). Measuring institutions' adoption of artificial intelligence applications in online learning environments: Integrating the innovation diffusion theory with technology adoption rate. [mdpi.com]. *Electronics (Basel)*, *11*(20), 3291. DOI: 10.3390/electronics11203291

Ayub Khan, A., Laghari, A. A., Shaikh, A. A., Bourouis, S., Mamlouk, A. M., & Alshazly, H. (2021). Educational blockchain: A secure degree attestation and verification traceability architecture for higher education commission. [mdpi.com]. *Applied Sciences (Basel, Switzerland)*, *11*(22), 10917. DOI: 10.3390/app112210917

Azem Qashou, A. M., Bahar, N., & Mohamed, H. (2025). Qualitative Exploration of Data Security Risks in Mobile Cloud Computing for Higher Education. [wiley.com]. *Security and Privacy*, *8*(2), e70001. DOI: 10.1002/spy2.70001

Bashir, H., Araci, Z. C., Obaideen, K., & Alsyouf, I. (2023). An approach for analyzing and visualizing the relationships among key performance indicators for creating sustainable campuses in higher education institutions. [sciencedirect.com]. *Environmental and Sustainability Indicators*, *19*, 100267. DOI: 10.1016/j.indic.2023.100267

Blažič, B. J. (2022). Changing the landscape of cybersecurity education in the EU: Will the new approach produce the required cybersecurity skills?. Education and information technologies. springer.com

Bøe, M., Heikka, J., Kettukangas, T., & Hognestad, K. (2022). Pedagogical leadership in activities with children–A shadowing study of early childhood teachers in Norway and Finland. [sciencedirect.com]. *Teaching and Teacher Education*, *117*, 103787. DOI: 10.1016/j.tate.2022.103787

Bohlens, C. (2025). Corruption in Accreditation at HEIs: When Corruption Erodes Trust in Higher Learning. In Navigating Quality Assurance and Accreditation in Global Higher Education (pp. 165-192). IGI Global Scientific Publishing. [HTML]

Cappelli, M. A. & Di Marzo Serugendo, G. (2025). Ontology-Based Customisation Management System for Driver-Vehicle Interfaces: A Preventive Approach to Incident Reduction and Legal Accountability in …. Applied Sciences. mdpi.com

Chan, C. K. Y. (2023). A comprehensive AI policy education framework for university teaching and learning. [springer.com]. *International Journal of Educational Technology in Higher Education*, *20*(1), 38. DOI: 10.1186/s41239-023-00408-3

Charles, T., & Hill, C. (2025). Micro-Credentials and AI in Higher Education: Transforming Professional Development. In Prompt Engineering and Generative AI Applications for Teaching and Learning (pp. 1-14). IGI Global Scientific Publishing. [HTML]

Cheng, E. C. K. & Wang, T. (2022). Institutional strategies for cybersecurity in higher education institutions. Information. mdpi.com

Cheng, J. K., Yong, I. S. C., Ch'ng, C. K., & Lim, H. T. (2024). Micro-credentials in Malaysian higher education: A comprehensive case study approach. [HTML]. *Education and Information Technologies*, •••, 1–25.

Chittoor, D. S.Dorai Surendar Chittoor. (2025). Implementing data lineage frameworks in financial institutions: A systematic analysis of compliance, efficiency, and risk management. [journalijsra.com]. *International Journal of Science and Research Archive*, *14*(1), 353–361. DOI: 10.30574/ijsra.2025.14.1.0062

Díaz-Rodríguez, N., Del Ser, J., Coeckelbergh, M., de Prado, M. L., Herrera-Viedma, E., & Herrera, F. (2023). Connecting the dots in trustworthy Artificial Intelligence: From AI principles, ethics, and key requirements to responsible AI systems and regulation. [sciencedirect.com]. *Information Fusion*, *99*, 101896. DOI: 10.1016/j.inffus.2023.101896

Dimitriou, C. K. (2022). The critical role that national culture and ethical leadership play in fostering employee commitment to service quality in the hotel industry. Research in Hospitality Management. tandfonline.com

Eaton, S. E., & Carmichael, J. J. (2023). Fake degrees and credential fraud, contract cheating, and paper mills: Overview and historical perspectives. Fake Degrees and Fraudulent Credentials in Higher Education, 1-22. [HTML]

Ewell, P., Van Noy, M., & Gaston, P. L. (2023). Credentials: Understand the problems. Identify the opportunities. Create the solutions.. [HTML]

Faizuddin, A., Azizan, N. A., Othman, A., & Ismail, S. N. (2022). Continuous professional development programmes for school principals in the 21st century: Lessons learned from educational leadership practices. Frontiers in Education. frontiersin.org

Geletu, G. M., & Mihiretie, D. M. (2023). Professional accountability and responsibility of learning communities of practice in professional development versus curriculum practice in classrooms: Possibilities and pathways. [sciencedirect.com]. *International Journal of Educational Research Open*, *4*, 100223. DOI: 10.1016/j.ijedro.2022.100223

Gershuni, O., Orr, J. M., Vogel, A., Park, K., Leider, J. P., Resnick, B. A., & Czabanowska, K. (2023). A systematic review on professional regulation and credentialing of public health workforce. [mdpi.com]. *International Journal of Environmental Research and Public Health*, *20*(5), 4101. DOI: 10.3390/ijerph20054101 PMID: 36901111

Girmanová, L., Šolc, M., Blaško, P., & Petrík, J. (2022). Quality management system in education: Application of quality management models in educational organization—case study from the Slovak Republic. Standards. mdpi.com

Gupta, A., Panda, M., & Gupta, A. (2024). Advancing API Security: A Comprehensive Evaluation of Authentication Mechanisms and Their Implications for Cybersecurity. International Journal of Global Innovations and Solutions (IJGIS). pubpub.org

Habib, M. N., Jamal, W., Khalil, U., & Khan, Z. (2021). Transforming universities in interactive digital platform: Case of city university of science and information technology. [springer.com]. *Education and Information Technologies*, *26*(1), 517–541. DOI: 10.1007/s10639-020-10237-w PMID: 32837236

Hakimi, L., Eynon, R., & Murphy, V. A. (2021). The ethics of using digital trace data in education: A thematic review of the research landscape. [sagepub.com]. *Review of Educational Research*, *91*(5), 671–717. DOI: 10.3102/00346543211020116

Iatrellis, O., Samaras, N., & Kokkinos, K. (2024). Towards a capability maturity model for Micro-credential providers in European higher education. Trends in Higher Education. mdpi.com

Johnson, S. D., Kuykendall, J. A., & Winkle-Wagner, R. (2023). Financing the dream: The impact of financial aid on graduate education for underrepresented minority students. In *Standing on the Outside Looking* (pp. 45–62). Routledge. [HTML] DOI: 10.4324/9781003447085-4

Kamyab, H., Khademi, T., Chelliapan, S., SaberiKamarposhti, M., Rezania, S., Yusuf, M., Farajnezhad, M., Abbas, M., Hun Jeon, B., & Ahn, Y. (2023). The latest innovative avenues for the utilization of artificial Intelligence and big data analytics in water resource management. [sciencedirect.com]. *Results in Engineering*, *20*, 101566. DOI: 10.1016/j.rineng.2023.101566

Kayyali, M. (2024). Exploring Accreditation Standards and Processes. In Quality Assurance and Accreditation in Higher Education: Issues, Models, and Best Practices (pp. 1-60). Cham: Springer Nature Switzerland. [HTML] DOI: 10.1007/978-3-031-66623-0_1

Kioskli, K., Grigoriou, E., Islam, S., Yiorkas, A. M., Christofi, L., & Mouratidis, H. (2025). A risk and conformity assessment framework to ensure security and resilience of healthcare systems and medical supply chain. [springer.com]. *International Journal of Information Security*, *24*(2), 1–28. DOI: 10.1007/s10207-025-01009-z

Kooli, C. & Abadli, R. (2022). Could education quality audit enhance human resources management processes of the higher education institutions?. Vision. sagepub.com

Laryea, K., Paepcke, A., Mirzaei, K., & Stevens, M. L. (2021). Ambiguous credentials: How learners use and make sense of Massively Open Online Courses. [tandfonline.com]. *The Journal of Higher Education, 92*(4), 596–622. DOI: 10.1080/00221546.2020.1851571

Lim, W. M. (2024). What is qualitative research? An overview and guidelines. Australasian Marketing Journal. sagepub.com

Liu, T. L., Song, Q. J., & Qi, Y. (2021). An integrated approach to evaluating the coupling coordination degree between low-carbon development and air quality in Chinese cities. Advances in Climate Change Research. sciencedirect.com

Love, E. A., Degen, S. C., Craig, J. E., & Helmers, R. A. (2021). Activating the hospital incident command system response in a community specialty practice: the Mayo clinic experience. WMJ. wmjonline.org

Matahela, V. E. & van Rensburg, G. H. (2022). Motivation as a facilitator of self-leadership in nurse academics. Heliyon. cell.com

McKinney, L., Burridge, A. B., Lee, M. M., Bourdeau, G. V., & Miller-Waters, M. (2022). Incentivizing full-time enrollment at community colleges: What influences students' decision to take more courses? [HTML]. *Community College Review, 50*(2), 144–170. DOI: 10.1177/00915521211061416

Mgaiwa, S. J. (2021). Leadership initiatives in response to institutional quality assurance challenges in Tanzania's private universities. Journal of Further and Higher Education. academia.edu

Mlambo, M., Silén, C., & McGrath, C. (2021). Lifelong learning and nurses' continuing professional development, a metasynthesis of the literature. BMC nursing. springer.com

Nandan Prasad, A. (2024). Regulatory Compliance and Risk Management. In Introduction to Data Governance for Machine Learning Systems: Fundamental Principles, Critical Practices, and Future Trends (pp. 485-624). Berkeley, CA: Apress. [HTML] DOI: 10.1007/979-8-8688-1023-7_8

Olanrewaju, O. I., Enegbuma, W. I., Donn, M., & Chileshe, N. (2022). Building information modelling and green building certification systems: A systematic literature review and gap spotting. [HTML]. *Sustainable Cities and Society, 81*, 103865. DOI: 10.1016/j.scs.2022.103865

Ouakka, S., Verlinden, O., & Kouroussis, G. (2022). Railway ground vibration and mitigation measures: benchmarking of best practices. Railway Engineering Science. springer.com

Oyedokun, T. O., Nair, R., Stempien, J., Moulton, K., Mondal, P., & Trivedi, S. V. (2025). Reducing emergency department return visits for ultrasound imaging: A quality improvement initiative. [HTML]. *Canadian Journal of Emergency Medical Care, 27*(6), 1–7. DOI: 10.1007/s43678-025-00880-y PMID: 40053311

Pop, G. I., Titu, A. M., & Pop, A. B. (2023). Enhancing aerospace industry efficiency and sustainability: Process integration and quality management in the context of Industry 4.0. Sustainability. mdpi.com

Prinsloo, P., & Kaliisa, R. (2022). Data privacy on the African continent: Opportunities, challenges and implications for learning analytics. [wiley.com]. *British Journal of Educational Technology, 53*(4), 894–913. DOI: 10.1111/bjet.13226

Rama Reddy, T., Prasad Reddy, P. V. G. D., Srinivas, R., Raghavendran, C. V., Lalitha, R. V. S., & Annapurna, B. (2021). Proposing a reliable method of securing and verifying the credentials of graduates through blockchain. [springer.com]. *EURASIP Journal on Information Security, 2021*(1), 1–9. DOI: 10.1186/s13635-021-00122-5

Ramasamy, L. K., & Khan, F. (2024). *Blockchain-Based Certification System: Ensuring Trust in Educational Credentials*. Blockchain for Global Education. [HTML]

Rani, P., Sachan, R. K., & Kukreja, S. (2024). Educert-chain: A secure and notarized educational certificate authentication and verification system using permissioned blockchain. [HTML]. *Cluster Computing, 27*(7), 10169–10196. DOI: 10.1007/s10586-024-04469-5

Reddy, J. S., Sharma, R., & Gupta, N. (2024). The accreditation paradigm: A comparative analysis of accreditations for management programmes. [HTML]. *International Journal of Educational Management, 38*(1), 73–95. DOI: 10.1108/IJEM-05-2023-0250

Rights, F. E., & Act, P. (2021). Family Educational Rights and Privacy Act. URL https://studentprivacy. ed. gov/ferpa. amazonaws.com

Salama, R. & Hinton, T. (2023). Online higher education: Current landscape and future trends. Journal of Further and Higher Education. tandfonline.com

Salomon-Fernández, Y. (2022). Using shared governance to advance completion and transfer. [HTML]. *New Directions for Community Colleges, 2022*(198), 161–170. DOI: 10.1002/cc.20518

Samson, A. A. C., Abarquez, J. K. S. L., Llave, J. N. J., Sing, J. A. P., & Estrella, N. E. (2024, December). BEYOND THE ARCH: a web and mobile alumni record verification system for the University of Santo Tomas Office of the Registrar. In International Conference on Green Energy, Computing and Intelligent Technology 2024 (GEn-CITy 2024) (Vol. 2024, pp. 56-65). IET. [HTML]

Sato, S. N., Condes Moreno, E., Rubio-Zarapuz, A., Dalamitros, A. A., Yañez-Sepulveda, R., Tornero-Aguilera, J. F., & Clemente-Suárez, V. J. (2023). Navigating the new normal: Adapting online and distance learning in the post-pandemic era. [mdpi.com]. *Education Sciences*, *14*(1), 19. DOI: 10.3390/educsci14010019

Shaik, V. & Natarajan, K. (2022). Flexible and cost-effective cryptographic encryption algorithm for securing unencrypted database files at rest and in transit. Methodsx. sciencedirect.com

Shandilya, S. K., Datta, A., Kartik, Y., & Nagar, A. (2024). Navigating the regulatory landscape. In Digital Resilience: Navigating Disruption and Safeguarding Data Privacy (pp. 127-240). Cham: Springer Nature Switzerland. [HTML] DOI: 10.1007/978-3-031-53290-0_3

Singh, J., Evans, E., Reed, A., Karch, L., Qualey, K., Singh, L., & Wiersma, H. (2022). Online, hybrid, and face-to-face learning through the eyes of faculty, students, administrators, and instructional designers: Lessons learned and directions for the post-vaccine and post-pandemic/COVID-19 world. [sagepub.com]. *Journal of Educational Technology Systems*, *50*(3), 301–326. DOI: 10.1177/00472395211063754

Singo, G. & Makgahlela, L. (2024). Records management practices to support administrative operations at the University of Venda in South Africa. Journal of the South African Society of Archivists. ajol.info

Smithwick, J., Nance, J., Covington-Kolb, S., Rodriguez, A., & Young, M. (2023). "Community health workers bring value and deserve to be valued too:" Key considerations in improving CHW career advancement opportunities. [frontiersin.org]. *Frontiers in Public Health*, *11*, 1036481. DOI: 10.3389/fpubh.2023.1036481 PMID: 36969656

Suárez, E. & Beatty, C. C. (2022). Advising in science education: Critiquing where we have been, moving toward an equitable and holistic advising approach. Science Education. wiley.com

Tereshchenko, E., Salmela, E., Melkko, E., Phang, S. K., & Happonen, A. (2024). Emerging best strategies and capabilities for university–industry cooperation: Opportunities for MSMEs and universities to improve collaboration. A literature review 2000–2023. [springer.com]. *Journal of Innovation and Entrepreneurship*, *13*(1), 28. DOI: 10.1186/s13731-024-00386-4

Thornhill-Miller, B., Camarda, A., Mercier, M., Burkhardt, J. M., Morisseau, T., Bourgeois-Bougrine, S., Vinchon, F., El Hayek, S., Augereau-Landais, M., Mourey, F., Feybesse, C., Sundquist, D., & Lubart, T. (2023). Creativity, critical thinking, communication, and collaboration: Assessment, certification, and promotion of 21st century skills for the future of work and education. [mdpi.com]. *Journal of Intelligence*, *11*(3), 54. DOI: 10.3390/jintelligence11030054 PMID: 36976147

Valk, A., & Kratovitš, M. (2021). We collaborate with everyone, but with some more than others: Evidence of stakeholder collaboration among internal security professional higher education institutions. [springer.com]. *Empirical Research in Vocational Education and Training*, *13*(1), 4. DOI: 10.1186/s40461-021-00110-6

Varadarajan, S., Koh, J. H. L., & Daniel, B. K. (2023). A systematic review of the opportunities and challenges of micro-credentials for multiple stakeholders: Learners, employers, higher education institutions and government. [springer.com]. *International Journal of Educational Technology in Higher Education*, *20*(1), 13. DOI: 10.1186/s41239-023-00381-x PMID: 36874535

Vashishth, T. K., Sharma, V., Sharma, K. K., Kumar, B., Chaudhary, S., & Panwar, R. (2024). Security and Privacy Considerations in Cloud-Based Data Processing Solutions for Sensitive Data. In Developments Towards Next Generation Intelligent Systems for Sustainable Development (pp. 35-61). IGI Global. [HTML] DOI: 10.4018/979-8-3693-5643-2.ch002

Venkatesh, R., & Rajavelu, S. (2025). Effective Strategies for Involving Faculty and Staff in Every Stage of the Accreditation Journey to Achieve Excellence. In Global Perspectives on Quality Management and Accreditation in Higher Education (pp. 351-386). IGI Global Scientific Publishing. [HTML] DOI: 10.4018/979-8-3693-9481-6.ch015

Vian, T., Agnew, B., & McInnes, K. (2022). Whistleblowing as an anti-corruption strategy in health and pharmaceutical organizations in low-and middle-income countries: a scoping review. Global health action. tandfonline.com

Chapter 12
Language and Digital Rights:
Fostering Communication Skills for Responsible Online Engagement

Harmita Sari
https://orcid.org/0000-0002-7324-0764
Universitas Muhammadiyah Palopo, Indonesia

A. Nurhayati A. Nurhayati
Universitas Muhammadiyah Palopo, Indonesia

Sulaeman Sulaeman
https://orcid.org/0009-0000-7579-5408
Universitas Muhammadiyah Palopo, Indonesia

Hadi Pajarianto
Universitas Muhammadiyah Palopo, Indonesia

Andi Asrifan
https://orcid.org/0000-0002-9934-6129
Universitas Negeri Makassar, Indonesia

ABSTRACT

This chapter examines the convergence of language, digital rights, and communication competencies to foster responsible online participation. As digital communication advances, so do the linguistic practices and ethical considerations that influence interactions on global platforms. The research emphasizes the significance of

DOI: 10.4018/979-8-3373-5781-2.ch012

language in constructing digital identities, promoting inclusivity, and maneuvering through varied cultural situations. It also analyzes the importance of digital rights—encompassing freedom of expression, privacy, and data protection—and underscores the necessity for ethical communication practices. Proposed strategies include multilingual inclusiveness, proficient writing, empathic communication, and media literacy to enable users to navigate digital settings responsibly. The study promotes digital citizenship education and the safeguarding of linguistic diversity as vital elements for fostering equitable and inclusive digital environments through multidisciplinary perspectives.

INTRODUCTION: UNDERSTANDING LANGUAGE IN THE DIGITAL AGE

The Evolution of Language in Digital Communication

The emergence of digital communication has significantly altered the utilization and comprehension of language. Historically, language has developed through diverse means, ranging from oral traditions to written writings (Verčič et al., 2024). The advent of the internet represented a pivotal moment, facilitating immediate contact over extensive distances. In the nascent phase of the internet, communication was predominantly textual, exemplified by emails, forums, and chat rooms. These platforms created a distinctive digital vernacular, wherein conciseness and clarity became essential owing to character constraints and the necessity for swift communication.

With technological advancement, the intricacy and depth of online language also evolved. The advent of social media platforms such as Facebook, Twitter, and Instagram has facilitated novel modes of expression, enabling users to concurrently exchange thoughts, photographs, and videos (Bhandari & Bimo, 2022). This multimodal approach has resulted in a more dynamic language that integrates text with visual elements, creating a hybrid communication style. Emojis, GIFs, and memes have become essential components of internet communication, enabling users to express emotions and concepts concisely and innovatively. The influence of these digital technologies has been substantial, as they allow users to articulate themselves in manners that conventional words may not fully convey.

Furthermore, social media has democratized language utilization, empowering various people and promoting linguistic diversity. Individuals from diverse cultural and linguistic origins enhance a dynamic digital lexicon by integrating slang, dialects, and even new languages (Bonotti & Willoughby, 2022). This linguistic advancement illustrates the worldwide character of the internet, where language transcends geographical limitations. This evolution also poses issues, as the swift pace of change may result in misunderstandings and miscommunications, especially among individuals from diverse language origins.

The influence of social media on language development encompasses not only vocabulary alterations but also affects language structure and grammar (Sato et al. 2025). The casual character of online communication frequently results in the use of non-standard grammar and spelling, inciting discussions over the consequences for literacy and language education. Critics assert that this trend could undermine conventional language skills, but advocates maintain that it demonstrates the flexibility of language in adapting to new settings.

The growth of language in digital communication is marked by a combination of historical influences and modern advances. In navigating this changing environment, it is essential to cultivate communication skills that enhance understanding and respect for linguistic diversity, so assuring responsible participation in an increasingly interconnected globe.

Language Diversity and Inclusivity

The internet functions as a worldwide platform that surpasses geographical limitations, facilitating unparalleled multicultural connections (Kumar, 2023). Language variety and inclusivity are vital elements of the digital landscape, facilitating communication among individuals from diverse language origins. Multilingualism in digital environments is essential, reflecting the diverse human experience and facilitating equitable access to information and discourse.

The significance of multilingualism in digital communication is paramount. The proficiency in nearly 7,000 languages enables individuals to interact with various cultures, exchange ideas, and partake in global dialogues (Pimienta et al. 2023). Multilingual systems enable users to communicate honestly, maintaining cultural subtleties that are frequently diminished in translation. Moreover, multilingualism fosters innovation and problem-solving by incorporating many perspectives and methodologies into talks, hence enhancing the quality of online interactions.

Nonetheless, despite the advantages of multilingualism, language obstacles continue to exist in digital communication, frequently obstructing substantive interaction. Numerous online platforms predominantly function in prevalent languages, such as English, which may marginalize non-native speakers and restrict their engagement (Higgins et al. 2023). This linguistic inequality can result in information asymmetry, wherein certain groups possess access to resources and knowledge, while others remain sidelined. To tackle these problems, it is imperative to advocate for inclusive practices that emphasize linguistic accessibility.

An effective technique for surmounting language barriers is the adoption of multilingual interfaces and content. Websites and applications that provide language options allow users to access and interact with content in their chosen language (Kreienbrinck et al. 2025). Furthermore, utilizing translation tools and services can enhance communication among speakers of diverse languages, hence simplifying the exchange of ideas and collaboration on projects. It is essential to acknowledge that automatic translations may fail to convey linguistic nuances, necessitating the involvement of human translators for more intricate interactions.

Furthermore, cultivating a culture of inclusion necessitates the active engagement of both individuals and organizations (Shrivastava et al. 2024). Promoting the sharing of content in users' native languages, advancing language learning efforts, and establishing secure environments for multilingual discourse can substantially improve inclusivity in digital communication.

In conclusion, respecting linguistic variety and inclusivity in digital environments is essential for promoting responsible participation and guaranteeing that all perspectives are acknowledged. By emphasizing multilingualism and mitigating language barriers, we may cultivate a more fair digital landscape that embodies the diversity of our global community and enables individuals to connect, collaborate, and communicate proficiently.

The Role of Language in Shaping Online Identities

In the contemporary interconnected world, language is crucial in building online identities and impacting personal branding. As individuals construct their digital identities across several platforms, the language they select has a crucial role in their self-presentation to others (Karhunen et al. 2023). This deliberate or inadvertent use of language not only mirrors individual values and views but also influences how others perceive and interact with them.

Language serves as a potent instrument for personal branding, enabling individuals to express their unique narratives and cultivate a distinctive voice in the digital realm. The selection of vocabulary, tone, and style can communicate professionalism, inventiveness, or accessibility, contingent upon the target audience (Golombek & Johnson, 2021). A professional on LinkedIn may employ a formal tone, utilizing industry-specific terminology to establish credibility and knowledge. Conversely, the same individual may employ a more informal and accessible linguistic style on sites such as Instagram or TikTok to engage a younger demographic. This adaptability illustrates the malleability of language and its ability to influence perceptions and cultivate connections.

Furthermore, the selection of language can profoundly influence community development in digital environments. Communities frequently coalesce around common interests, ideals, or cultural backgrounds, with the language employed within these groups acting as a unifying element (Tao & Gao, 2022). Niche communities may cultivate unique lexicons or slang, fostering a sense of belonging among their members. This language cohesiveness cultivates a collective identity, strengthening group dynamics and promoting engagement. The utilization of exclusive or specialized language can estrange newcomers, establishing hurdles to entrance that impede community expansion.

The impact of language on online identities is exacerbated by the internet's global character. The interaction of persons from varied linguistic and cultural origins can result in the formation of hybrid identities through language amalgamation. Bilingual or multilingual individuals frequently traverse diverse linguistic environments, enabling them to connect with different communities while concurrently exhibiting their cultural history (Jain, 2022). This linguistic adaptability enhances the digital environment, fostering cross-cultural comprehension and cooperation.

It is crucial to acknowledge the potential issues associated with language use in digital environments. Miscommunication may arise when individuals misinterpret cultural references or idiomatic language, resulting in conflicts or exclusion (Kosimova et al. 2024). Consequently, cultivating an understanding of linguistic diversity and advocating for inclusive communication practices is essential for establishing polite and helpful online communities.

In conclusion, language is essential in constructing online identities and impacting personal branding. Comprehending the influence of language on community development and personal expression enables us to cultivate a more inclusive digital landscape that appreciates varied perspectives and encourages responsible participation.

DIGITAL RIGHTS AND RESPONSIBILITIES

Defining Digital Rights

In the digital age, the notion of digital rights has arisen as a crucial component of human rights dialogue. Digital rights denote the privileges individuals own concerning their engagement with digital technology, platforms, and information (Custers, 2022). These rights are crucial for enabling persons to traverse the digital realm securely, autonomously, and ethically, facilitating self-expression, information access, and engagement in online communities without apprehension of censorship or discrimination. The importance of digital rights resides in their capacity to safeguard users from exploitation, encourage equitable access to information, and cultivate a culture of respect and accountability in online engagements.

The fundamental tenet of digital rights is the principle of freedom of expression, enabling individuals to articulate their thoughts, opinions, and ideas without apprehension of censorship or retribution. This right is essential for promoting free discourse and the dissemination of information in digital environments (Garenne et al. 2021). Moreover, digital rights include the right to privacy, safeguarding persons from unlawful surveillance and data acquisition. As personal data is increasingly commercialized, it is essential to implement strong privacy rules to preserve trust in digital platforms and protect individual autonomy.

Significant international frameworks and agreements have been instituted to delineate and safeguard digital rights. The Universal Declaration of Human Rights (UDHR), ratified by the United Nations in 1948, is a fundamental text. Article 19 of the UDHR underscores the right to freedom of thought and expression, encompassing digital communication (Mallén2021). This fundamental value has been bolstered by successive international treaties and declarations, including the International Covenant on Civil and Political Rights (ICCPR), which further emphasizes the significance of safeguarding free expression in the digital domain.

In recent years, numerous groups and alliances have arisen to champion digital rights globally. The Internet Governance Forum (IGF), created by the United Nations, functions as a forum for stakeholders to deliberate on and tackle issues pertaining to internet governance, including digital rights (Haggart & Keller, 2021). The Council of Europe's Convention on Cybercrime delineates strategies to address cybercrime while upholding human rights, emphasizing the necessity for a balanced approach to digital security and personal liberties.

Regional activities are essential in advancing digital rights (Grover, 2022). The African Union's Agenda 2063 underscores the significance of information and communication technology in advancing human rights and sustainable development throughout the continent.

In summary, delineating digital rights is crucial for protecting personal liberties and fostering responsible participation in the digital era. Comprehending the importance of these rights and the international institutions that uphold them enables individuals to more effectively navigate online environments, advocate for their rights, and foster a more fair digital landscape.

The Balance Between Freedom of Expression and Responsibility

The interplay between freedom of expression and accountability is a fundamental element of digital rights discussions, especially as online platforms have emerged as primary arenas for public conversation (Caruso, 2024). The right to free speech is fundamental in democratic countries; yet, it is crucial to recognize that this freedom is not unlimited and must be weighed against the obligation to prevent harm, especially with hate speech.

Hate speech denotes any discourse that provokes violence, prejudice, or animosity towards persons or groups based on characteristics such as race, religion, gender, or sexual orientation. The difficulty resides in differentiating hate speech from free speech (Marques, 2023). Proponents of free expression contend that all views, including those deemed objectionable, need to be permitted to foster open discourse. They argue that censorship may result in a slippery slope that suppresses valid conversation. In contrast, adversaries argue that hate speech constitutes a direct menace to social unity and may incite actual violence and discrimination. This distinction requires a thorough analysis of how civilizations delineate and govern speech.

Numerous case studies exemplify the intricacies associated with censorship and infringements on digital rights. A notable instance is the influence of social media during the 2016 U.S. presidential election. Platforms like as Facebook and Twitter encountered significant attention for permitting the dissemination of hate speech and misinformation. Consequently, these companies established content moderation rules designed to eliminate dangerous content and identify misinformation (Dubois & Reepschlager, 2024). Although these measures aimed to safeguard users and uphold community standards, they also elicited apprehensions regarding censorship and the possible stifling of legitimate political discourse, underscoring the challenges of controlling speech without violating individual rights.

A notable instance is the utilization of social media in Myanmar, where hate speech directed against the Rohingya minority incited violence and ethnic cleansing. The inability of platforms to adequately monitor and combat hate speech in this context elicited global condemnation and highlighted the pressing necessity for responsible administration of digital environments (Schissler, 2024). The repercussions of inaction were catastrophic, demonstrating how unrestrained hate speech can result in significant human rights abuses.

Ultimately, attaining equilibrium between freedom of expression and accountability necessitates continuous discourse among stakeholders, including governments, civil society, and technology firms. Formulating explicit criteria that distinguish free speech from hate speech is crucial for cultivating a robust digital environment (Gelber2021). By fostering a culture of respect and accountability, we can establish an online environment that upholds the right to free expression while safeguarding individuals from harm, so ensuring that digital spaces remain secure and inclusive for all users.

Ethical Communication in Digital Spaces

In a time characterized by swift digital communication, promoting ethical interactions in online environments is crucial for cultivating a courteous and inclusive atmosphere. The internet's anonymity and distance can occasionally precipitate a decline in civility, leading to detrimental behaviors such as trolling, harassment, and the dissemination of misinformation (Dwivedi et al. 2023). To foster a constructive digital environment, it is essential to implement protocols for polite online engagement and to underscore the need of empathy in communication.

A fundamental principle for courteous online conversations is to engage in active listening. This is not merely listening to others but also endeavoring to comprehend their viewpoints and experiences. Interacting with multiple perspectives cultivates an inclusive culture and prompts individuals to contemplate the intricacies of different topics (Markey et al. 2021). By recognizing and appreciating diverse perspectives, individuals can enhance the complexity and respectfulness of debate.

A crucial principle is to be cognizant of language utilization. Language possesses considerable significance, and the selection of words can profoundly affect the tone of a dialogue. Eschewing provocative or disparaging language fosters a courteous environment, enabling arguments to remain constructive rather than descending into personal attacks (Ryan et al. 2023). Moreover, use inclusive language that honors individuals' identities and experiences is essential for cultivating a sense of belonging within digital groups.

Empathy is essential in ethical communication. It entails acknowledging and affirming the feelings and experiences of others, which is especially crucial in online encounters where non-verbal signals may be lacking. Engaging in empathy enables individuals to behave with deliberation instead of impulsivity, fostering a more compassionate attitude towards disputes and confrontations (Addimando2024). By acknowledging the emotions and viewpoints of others, individuals can foster a conducive atmosphere that promotes candid and sincere communication.

Furthermore, ethical communication in digital environments necessitates accountability. Individuals must assume accountability for their statements and behaviors, recognizing that online conduct can yield tangible repercussions (Kim & Wang, 2023). This entails a readiness to apologize for errors and to assimilate recommendations for improvement. Fostering a culture of accountability cultivates trust among community members and underscores the significance of polite interactions.

Ultimately, fostering digital literacy is crucial for ethical communication. Users must possess the ability to critically assess information, identify reputable sources, and participate in informed discourse (Korte et al. 2024). Digital literacy enables individuals to traverse online environments safely and fosters a more informed and respectful community.

In summary, ethical communication in digital environments is essential for promoting responsible interaction and safeguarding digital rights. By following protocols for polite engagement, fostering empathy, and enhancing accountability and digital literacy, we may establish a more inclusive and supportive online atmosphere that appreciates varied perspectives and promotes constructive discourse.

DEVELOPING COMMUNICATION SKILLS FOR ONLINE ENGAGEMENT

Effective Writing for Digital Platforms

In the rapidly evolving digital environment, proficient writing is crucial for effective communication. Formulating clear and succinct communications is essential, given that attention spans are frequently constrained and people are overwhelmed with information (Ciampa et al. 2023). Writers must prioritize clarity to properly engage audiences, ensuring their words are comprehensible and accessible.

A core component of effective digital writing is conciseness. Users value succinct communications that deliver critical information without superfluous detail (Mounir, 2025). This can be accomplished by use clear language and eschewing jargon that may perplex the audience. Utilizing bullet points or numbered lists helps deconstruct intricate information into manageable segments, facilitating readers' rapid comprehension of essential concepts. Furthermore, use active voice instead of passive speech improves clarity and renders writing more captivating. A more direct formulation might be, “The team completed the report,” rather than stating, “The report was completed by the team.”

An essential element of proficient writing is the significance of tone and style in digital communication. Tone denotes the writer's disposition towards the subject and the audience, whereas style comprises the comprehensive methodology and organization of the writing (Dingus & Black, 2021). The tone may change considerably based on the platform and the target audience. A formal tone is acceptable for professional emails or academic essays, whilst a relaxed tone may be appropriate for social media posts or personal blogs. Comprehending the context and audience is essential for determining the suitable tone, as it can profoundly influence the reception of the message.

Furthermore, integrating storytelling components might augment the efficacy of digital communication. Personal anecdotes or relatable instances can engage readers and foster an emotional connection, enhancing the memorability of the information (Yang et al. 2022). This narrative technique humanizes the content, cultivating a sense of authenticity that resonates with consumers.

Visual components are essential for proficient writing on digital platforms. Integrating visuals, infographics, or videos can augment written content and improve comprehension. Visuals can enhance text by rendering it more attractive and easier to comprehend (Romero & Bobkina, 2021). It is crucial to ensure that any graphics employed are pertinent and reinforce the message rather than detract from it.

In conclusion, cultivating proficient writing skills for digital platforms is essential for promoting successful online engagement. By formulating clear and succinct messages, being cognizant of tone and style, and integrating storytelling and images, individuals can enhance their communication efficacy in the digital domain. These abilities promote communication clarity and foster greater connections with audiences, so fostering responsible and meaningful online interactions.

Navigating Digital Discourse

Mastering digital communication is a crucial competency in the contemporary interconnected landscape, where online dialogues can profoundly impact public perception and societal interactions. Comprehending the distinct dynamics of online discourse is essential for effective involvement, as the digital landscape frequently contrasts significantly with conventional face-to-face communication (Sharma et al. 2024). The anonymity and immediacy of online platforms can foster both productive dialogues and confrontational interactions, necessitating that individuals engage in these talks with caution and purpose.

The key characteristic of online debates is the swift dissemination and consumption of information. In this context, people frequently respond rapidly to postings and comments, potentially resulting in misunderstandings or heightened confrontations (Abbas et al. 2022). Consequently, it is essential to cultivate patience and invest time in comprehending others' perspectives before to reacting. Participating in active listening—by meticulously reading statements or posing clarifying inquiries—can foster a more courteous and informed discourse.

A vital element of internet conversation is the existence of varied opinions. Digital platforms unite individuals from diverse origins, cultures, and experiences, enhancing discourse while also presenting opportunities for discord. Embracing this diversity necessitates an open mind and a readiness to contemplate perspectives that diverge from one's own. Recognizing the legitimacy of others' experiences cultivates a more inclusive atmosphere and promotes productive discourse (Markey et al. 2021).

To participate effectively in online discussions, it is crucial to utilize tactics that foster positive dialogue. An excellent tactic is to concentrate on topics rather than resorting to personal assaults. In the event of conflicts, it is essential to focus on the issue rather than engaging in ad hominem attacks that may exacerbate tensions

(Weinstein et al. 2022). By structuring arguments based on concepts and evidence, individuals can enhance the rationality and productivity of discourse.

Furthermore, employing "I" sentences can facilitate the articulation of personal emotions and viewpoints without appearing accusatory (He & Huang, 2025). For instance, rather than stating, "You are incorrect regarding this matter," one could articulate, "I perceive it differently due to…" This method reduces defensiveness and facilitates collaborative examination of divergent perspectives.

Moreover, acknowledging the significance of tone in written communication is essential. In the absence of non-verbal clues, written communication is susceptible to misinterpretation (Aqil & Jameel). To prevent this risk, individuals should pursue clarity and positivity in their language, eschewing sarcasm or too strong rhetoric that may be construed as hostile.

Ultimately, recognizing the appropriate moment to withdraw is a crucial element of managing digital communication. Not all discussions yield productivity, and identifying when a conversation has turned unconstructive helps conserve time and emotional resources. It is entirely appropriate to disengage from conversations that deteriorate into animosity or fail to promote reciprocal comprehension.

In conclusion, managing digital discourse necessitates comprehension of the distinct dynamics of online discussions and the implementation of tactics for constructive interaction. By cultivating patience, embracing diversity, addressing pertinent concerns, employing "I" statements, sustaining a positive tone, and recognizing the appropriate moments to disconnect, individuals can foster meaningful and courteous online conversations that encourage responsible engagement in digital environments.

Utilizing Multimedia for Enhanced Communication

In the digital era, efficient communication increasingly depends on multimedia components, such as graphics, videos, and music, to transmit messages in a more engaging and memorable manner. As audiences are overwhelmed with information, the capacity to seize attention and articulate intricate concepts concisely is essential (Roux et al. 2024). The use of multimedia promotes comprehension and caters to various learning styles, hence increasing material accessibility for a wider audience.

Visuals significantly enhance communication. Infographics, charts, and illustrations can elucidate intricate data and render information more comprehensible. An infographic highlighting crucial statistics can communicate a message more effectively than an extensive textual presentation (Lee et al., 2022). Visuals facilitate the segmentation of text, enhancing the aesthetic appeal of content and improving navigability. It is crucial to include high-quality, pertinent pictures that are properly attributed to prevent copyright infringement difficulties.

Videos have emerged as a progressively favored medium for communication, providing a dynamic method to captivate people. They can offer a more personalized experience, enabling artists to express emotions and tone that textual material may lack (Schellewald). Tutorial films can elucidate processes or concepts clearly, whereas storytelling videos can elicit emotional responses that resonate with the audience. Best practices for producing engaging video content encompass brevity, clarity of language, and high production quality. Captions and transcripts must be supplied to improve accessibility for those with hearing impairments and to assist non-native speakers.

Audio content, including podcasts and voiceovers, serves as a potent medium for communication. Audio facilitates storytelling and discourse that can be accessed while in transit, rendering it a practical choice for occupied listeners (Privitera et al., 2024). In the production of audio information, articulateness and captivating presentation are essential. Furthermore, the inclusion of sound effects or background music can augment the auditory experience, provided it does not detract from the primary message.

Creating compelling multimedia content necessitates consideration of the target audience and their preferences. Conducting audience research can yield insights into the content formats that resonate most effectively (Ye et al. 2021). Moreover, utilizing a uniform style and branding across various multimedia formats reinforces identity and cultivates trust with the audience.

Another optimal strategy is to promote engagement. Integrating calls to action, such as encouraging viewers to remark, share, or engage in debates, enhances engagement and cultivates a feeling of community surrounding the information (Lansing et al. 2023). Furthermore, examining audience comments and engagement metrics can guide future content development, facilitating ongoing enhancement.

In conclusion, employing multimedia for improved communication is essential in the digital realm. By adeptly integrating graphics, videos, and audio, communicators can transmit content in a more engaging and accessible manner. Following best practices in content creation promotes comprehension and cultivates a more participatory and inclusive online atmosphere, hence encouraging responsible and significant interaction.

PROTECTING YOUR DIGITAL IDENTITY AND PRIVACY

Understanding Digital Footprints

In the contemporary digital environment, comprehending digital footprints is essential for safeguarding one's online identity and privacy. A digital footprint denotes the data trail individuals create when utilizing the internet. This encompasses social media postings, comments, emails, internet purchases, search history, and website visits. Digital footprints are categorized into two types: active and passive. Active footprints refer to those intentionally generated by humans, such as social media postings or the completion of online forms (Allmann & Radu, 2023). Conversely, passive footprints are amassed without explicit user input, including tracking cookies and analytics data that websites compile regarding visitors.

The ramifications of digital footprints are substantial. Every online behavior contributes to an individual's digital profile, accessible by numerous entities, including employers, advertisers, and potentially harmful individuals. This data may be utilized for targeted advertising, background investigations, and, in certain instances, identity theft (Kapustina2021). Furthermore, digital footprints can influence personal reputation; unethical or unprofessional content may resurface and harm possibilities in school and employment. Consequently, individuals must recognize the information they disseminate online and the possible repercussions of their digital conduct.

To properly manage and monitor one's online presence, various tools and tactics may be utilized. Initially, individuals ought to perform systematic evaluations of their digital footprint. This can be accomplished by querying one's name on multiple search engines to ascertain the publicly accessible information (Allmann & Radu, 2023). By comprehending what others may discover, individuals might undertake proactive measures to mitigate any undesirable or detrimental content.

Privacy settings on social networking platforms are essential for managing digital traces. Users ought to examine and modify their privacy settings to regulate access to their posts and personal information. Restricting the visibility of personal information can markedly diminish the likelihood of undesired disclosure (Gillespie, 2022). Moreover, users ought to exercise caution when accepting friend requests or connections from unfamiliar persons, as this may result in possible privacy violations.

An additional successful technique is to employ technologies specifically developed for monitoring online presence. Services such as Google Alerts can inform individuals when their name is used online, enabling them to monitor their digital footprint (Alanzi, 2021). Moreover, reputation management solutions facilitate the monitoring and administration of online evaluations and mentions, offering insights into one's digital perception.

In conclusion, comprehending digital footprints is crucial for safeguarding online identity and privacy. By understanding the components of a digital footprint and its ramifications, individuals can implement proactive strategies to efficiently manage and oversee their online presence. Employing privacy settings, performing frequent audits, and utilizing monitoring tools are essential measures for preserving a favorable digital identity and protecting personal information in a progressively networked environment.

Privacy Rights and Data Protection

In a time where personal information is always gathered and scrutinized, comprehending privacy rights and data security is crucial for preserving digital identities. Privacy rules and regulations have been established to safeguard individuals from unlawful access to their personal data and to guarantee that corporations manage this information properly (Beduschi, 2021). These regulations differ by location yet adhere to shared principles designed to improve user privacy and foster openness.

The General Data Protection Regulation (GDPR), implemented by the European Union in 2018, is a significant piece of legislation in this domain. The GDPR establishes rigorous regulations for the collecting, processing, and storage of data, empowering individuals with more control over their personal information (Almeida et al., 2022). Essential provisions encompass the right to access personal data, the right to rectify erroneous information, and the right to erasure, frequently referred to as the "right to be forgotten." Entities who do not adhere to the GDPR incur significant penalties, underscoring the criticality of data protection.

In the United States, privacy legislation is more fragmented, comprising diverse restrictions at both federal and state levels. The California Consumer Privacy Act (CCPA) exemplifies a significant framework, granting California individuals rights akin to those delineated by the GDPR. The CCPA permits individuals to ascertain what personal data is gathered, the entities to whom it is transferred, and to decline the sale of their information (Mulgund et al. 2021). Although a comprehensive federal privacy law is absent, these state-level measures indicate an increasing acknowledgment of the necessity for stringent data protection.

To protect personal information online, individuals might implement many measures. Primarily, it is essential to be cognizant of the information disseminated on digital media. Individuals should refrain from revealing sensitive personal information, such as residential addresses or financial data, unless it is imperative (Javaid et al., 2023). Furthermore, users ought to examine the privacy settings on social media and other internet accounts, ensuring that access to their profiles and posts is restricted to trusted contacts exclusively.

Employing robust, distinctive passwords for many accounts is an essential practice. Password managers facilitate the generation and storage of intricate passwords, hence diminishing the likelihood of unwanted access (Tian, 2025). Implementing two-factor authentication (2FA) enhances security by necessitating users to confirm their identification via an additional way, such as a text message or authentication application.

Moreover, consumers must exercise caution when utilizing public Wi-Fi networks, as they may be susceptible to data breaches. Employing Virtual Private Networks (VPNs) can encrypt internet data, offering an extra degree of security when viewing sensitive information on public networks.

In summary, comprehending privacy rights and data protection is essential in the digital era. By understanding pertinent laws and regulations and employing effective ways to secure personal information, individuals can proactively protect their digital identities. This awareness empowers users and fosters a culture of respect for privacy rights in online environments, ultimately promoting responsible engagement in the digital realm.

Responsible Sharing and Content Creation

The digital landscape has facilitated the effortless dissemination of information and material, altering interpersonal interactions and communication. Nonetheless, this convenience entails an ethical need to disseminate information judiciously and honor the rights of content creators (Szymkowiak et al. 2021). Responsible sharing and content production are vital elements of digital citizenship, guaranteeing that individuals participate in online environments with integrity and respect for intellectual property.

The ethics of information sharing entail comprehending the potential consequences of content dissemination. Prior to disseminating articles, photographs, or videos, persons must to evaluate the accuracy and credibility of the material. Disseminating disinformation can result in confusion, sustain erroneous narratives, and undermine trust in online sources (Shahbazi & Bunker, 2024). Consequently, it is imperative to authenticate information and consult reliable sources prior to disseminating content. This technique improves the quality of online debate and cultivates a culture of accountability among users.

An additional crucial element of responsible sharing is honoring the privacy of others. Obtaining consent is crucial when disseminating anything that contains personal information or photos of individuals. Disseminating another individual's content without authorization may violate their privacy rights and result in possible legal repercussions (Murdoch, 2021). Furthermore, persons must consider the context in which they disseminate content, ensuring it accurately reflects the original intent without distortion or misrepresentation.

The significance of ethical content creation and dissemination is further emphasized by copyright, plagiarism, and intellectual property problems. Copyright law safeguards the rights of authors by conferring exclusive authority over the utilization and dissemination of their original works. This encompasses textual material, visuals, audio, and video content (Quintais et al. 2023). Utilizing copyrighted content without authorization exposes persons to the danger of infringing upon these rights, potentially leading to legal consequences.

Plagiarism, the act of representing another individual's work or ideas as one's own, constitutes a significant ethical issue in digital content creation. It compromises the individual's integrity and disregards the original creator's efforts (Mulenga & Shilongo, 2024). To prevent plagiarism, individuals must consistently offer appropriate attribution when utilizing another person's ideas or information, whether through direct quotations, paraphrasing, or citing sources.

To address these difficulties proficiently, individuals must acquaint themselves with copyright legislation and optimal procedures for content creation. This encompasses comprehension of fair use, which permits restricted utilization of copyrighted content under particular conditions, including commentary, criticism, or instructional objectives (Thorn et al., 2023). Moreover, employing Creative Commons licenses enables authors to legally disseminate their work while delineating the conditions for its utilization by others.

In summary, responsible dissemination and content generation are essential for ethical participation in the digital realm. By acknowledging the ethics of information dissemination, honoring intellectual property rights, and complying with copyright rules, individuals can foster a respectful and reliable online environment. This dedication to ethical practices not only bolsters personal credibility but also cultivates a culture of respect and accountability in digital interactions.

PROMOTING RESPONSIBLE ONLINE ENGAGEMENT

Building a Culture of Respect and Inclusion

In a progressively interconnected digital landscape, cultivating a culture of respect and inclusiveness is vital for establishing healthy online communities. As varied groups of persons converge in different digital environments, it is essential to adopt techniques that foster inclusion and guarantee that all viewpoints are acknowledged and esteemed (Sumo et al. 2021). Establishing such a culture not only improves user experience but also fosters the overall welfare of online communities.

An excellent technique for cultivating inclusive online communities is to implement explicit community norms that encourage respectful conduct. These guidelines must delineate appropriate behavior, underscore the significance of empathy, and forbid hate speech, harassment, and discrimination. Establishing explicit expectations increases the likelihood of community members participating in constructive interactions (Zamiri & Esmaeili, 2024). Moreover, moderators are important in upholding these principles, guaranteeing that any infractions are rectified swiftly and equitably. This proactive strategy fosters an atmosphere in which individuals feel secure and valued.

A crucial technique is to promote diverse representation in online environments. This can be accomplished by advocating for information and opinions from marginalized groups, so assuring a diverse array of viewpoints in debates (Carpenter et al. 2021). Platforms may also facilitate events, webinars, or forums that emphasize the experiences and contributions of various populations. By amplifying these voices, online communities can cultivate a sense of belonging and affirm the experiences of all members.

Education is essential for fostering respect and inclusivity in online environments. Digital citizenship education provides individuals with the knowledge and skills required to navigate the digital environment ethically. This education should encompass subjects such as digital etiquette, the significance of empathy, and the consequences of one's words and deeds in online environments (Yingsoon et al. 2025). Integrating digital citizenship into educational curricula enables schools and organizations to equip individuals for deliberate and polite online engagement.

Furthermore, integrating talks regarding the ethical ramifications of digital conduct helps elevate understanding of the repercussions of online activities. When individuals comprehend the potential consequences of their actions on others, they are more inclined to adopt courteous and inclusive behaviors (Newman et al. 2021). Workshops, training sessions, and community forums can function as venues for these talks, promoting dialogue and contemplation among participants.

Alongside formal schooling, peer-led activities can foster a culture of respect and inclusiveness. Promoting community members to assume leadership positions in advocating for beneficial behavior fosters a sense of ownership and accountability within the community (Chang et al. 2021). Mentorship programs and peer support networks can enable individuals to advocate for inclusivity and respect, thereby strengthening these principles.

In summary, fostering a culture of respect and inclusiveness within online communities necessitates deliberate initiatives and a dedication to digital citizenship education. By instituting explicit norms, advocating for diverse representation, and cultivating educational efforts, we may develop environments where all persons feel esteemed and empowered to participate. This dedication to inclusivity not only improves the quality of online interactions but also fosters the emergence of responsible digital citizens who champion a more equitable and courteous digital environment.

Advocacy for Digital Rights

Advocacy for digital rights is essential in the contemporary interconnected world, when concerns such as privacy, freedom of expression, and access to information are increasingly jeopardized. Individuals and groups can significantly contribute to the promotion and protection of human rights by participating in advocacy movements aimed at influencing policy, raising awareness, and empowering communities (Pangrazio and Sefton-Green 2021). This chapter examines how individuals might engage in digital rights movements and underscores effective advocacy initiatives that have achieved substantial influence.

Engaging in digital rights advocacy commences with education and awareness. Individuals ought to acquaint themselves with critical concerns impacting digital rights, including data privacy, internet censorship, and monitoring. Various groups, such the Electronic Frontier Foundation (EFF) and Access Now, offer materials, articles, and updates on contemporary digital rights problems (Wilson-Menzfeld et al. 2023). By remaining educated, advocates can participate in substantive discussions and contribute to initiatives that align with their principles.

An effective method to promote digital rights is to engage in grassroots movements. Grassroots activism typically entails organizing local communities to enhance awareness and advocate for change (Walker2022). This may encompass the organization of events, workshops, or instructional sessions to enlighten others regarding digital rights issues. Furthermore, individuals may utilize social media channels to enhance their voices, disseminate materials, and engage with like-minded advocates. Hashtags such as #DigitalRights and #PrivacyMatters can enhance awareness and promote community involvement.

An alternative approach for activism is to endorse or affiliate with established groups dedicated to digital rights. Numerous organizations actively endeavor to shape policy and legislation concerning technology and privacy. Individuals can enhance broader initiatives to safeguard digital rights by volunteering, giving, or engaging in campaigns coordinated by these organizations. Advocacy campaigns typically encompass petitions, letter-writing efforts, and public protests, all necessitating grassroots support for efficacy (Sanders & Scanlon, 2021).

Case examples of effective lobbying campaigns demonstrate the efficacy of collective action in advancing digital rights. A prominent instance is the opposition against the Stop Online Piracy Act (SOPA) in the United States in 2012 (Khobragade et al. 2021). This legislation sought to address online piracy but elicited apprehensions of possible censorship and the violation of free expression. A combination of internet firms, civil society organizations, and activists united to contest the bill, resulting in extensive protests and a synchronized blackout of prominent websites. The effort effectively compelled legislators to reevaluate the proposal, ultimately leading to its retraction.

The European Union's General Data Protection Regulation (GDPR), which was implemented in 2018, is another significant campaign. Advocacy organizations significantly influenced the formulation of the GDPR, advocating for enhanced safeguards for individual data privacy (Almeida et al., 2022). The rule has established a global benchmark for data protection, prompting analogous attempts in other locations.

In conclusion, the promotion of digital rights is vital for fostering responsible online participation. Individuals may engage by acquiring knowledge, participating in grassroots initiatives, and endorsing established groups. Successful case studies illustrate the efficacy of collective action in shaping policy and safeguarding digital rights. Through active advocacy, individuals may foster a more equal and just digital environment that honors the rights of all users.

The Future of Language and Digital Rights

As technology advances, the realm of digital communication is seeing substantial changes. Emerging developments in digital communication are transforming individual interactions, information sharing, and the assertion of rights online (Grewal et al., 2022). Comprehending these tendencies is essential for anticipating the issues that await in the domain of language and digital rights.

A significant trend is the emergence of artificial intelligence (AI) and machine learning in digital communication. AI technologies are progressively employed to analyze language, automate content generation, and enhance communication via chatbots and virtual assistants. Although these developments may improve efficiency and accessibility, they also provoke worries over the possibility for bias in language processing and the ethical ramifications of AI-generated material (Sarker, 2022). As AI systems increasingly integrate into our communication patterns, it is crucial to design them with justice and inclusivity, reflecting multiple perspectives and preventing the perpetuation of damaging stereotypes.

A notable trend is the increasing significance of multimodal communication. As platforms increasingly emphasize visual and audio material, individual expression is developing (Cheng et al. 2023). The utilization of videos, podcasts, and interactive media is more common, facilitating enhanced storytelling and interaction. This transition also presents problems with accessibility and diversity. Ensuring multimedia information is accessible to those with impairments and adapting various linguistic origins is essential for promoting equitable communication.

The emergence of decentralized communication platforms is influencing the future of digital rights. Technologies like blockchain facilitate peer-to-peer interactions devoid of centralized oversight, permitting consumers to retain enhanced control over their data and privacy (Huang, 2024). Although these advancements offer potential for improving digital rights, they simultaneously pose issues regarding regulation and accountability. As decentralized platforms proliferate, it is imperative to develop frameworks that safeguard consumers while fostering innovation.

The continuous discussion around privacy and data protection continues to be a significant issue. As individuals become awareness of their digital footprints and the ramifications of data collecting, there is an increasing desire for enhanced privacy safeguards and improved transparency from enterprises (Mühlhoff, 2023). Advocacy for digital rights will remain essential in influencing regulations that protect individual rights in the digital realm.

To address the problems of the future digital landscape, individuals must emphasize digital literacy and critical thinking abilities. As misinformation and deception proliferate, the capacity to identify reputable sources and participate in informed discourse will be essential (Yu et al., 2024). Educational programs that focus on digital citizenship, ethical communication, and responsible technology use will enable individuals to adeptly traverse the complexity of the digital realm.

In conclusion, the future of language and digital rights is influenced by growing developments in digital communication that offer both opportunities and challenges. By adopting technical innovations, promoting diversity, and emphasizing digital literacy, individuals can foster a more equal and accountable digital environment. Advancing a culture of respect and accountability is crucial for safeguarding digital rights for all users in a constantly changing online landscape.

CONCLUSION

In the digital era, language functions as a mechanism for communication, a means of identity formation, a vehicle for rights assertion, and a foundation for constructing inclusive online communities. This paper has highlighted the essential significance of language awareness and ethical communication in navigating intricate digital environments. As technology advances and online platforms increasingly influence public debate, the imperative to cultivate courteous, knowledgeable, and inclusive communication intensifies.

Digital rights, including freedom of expression, privacy, and access to information, necessitate comprehension and safeguarding through responsible engagement and education. Individuals must possess essential digital literacy abilities, encompassing the capacity to evaluate information, employ inclusive language, and engage constructively in many online environments. Advocating for multilingualism, acknowledging the complexities of digital identity, and supporting fair platform policies are essential for enabling all users to engage meaningfully in digital discourse.

Ethical communication techniques, grounded in empathy, accountability, and cultural awareness, establish the basis for polite digital interaction. Furthermore, cultivating awareness of one's digital footprint and comprehending the duties associated with information creation and dissemination are essential for upholding personal integrity and safeguarding the rights of others.

In conclusion, equipping users with communication skills rooted on language diversity and digital rights is vital for fostering a more equitable and inclusive digital landscape. Integrating these principles into education, legislation, and platform design may cultivate a culture of responsible digital citizenship that promotes democratic values and respects the voices of all participants in the global online community.

REFERENCES

Abbas, A. F., Jusoh, A., Mas'od, A., Alsharif, A. H., & Ali, J. (2022). Bibliometrix analysis of information sharing in social media. *Cogent Business & Management, 9*(1), 2016556. DOI: 10.1080/23311975.2021.2016556

Addimando, F. (2024). Emotional Intelligence in Negotiation. In Negotiation Neuroscience: The Brain Science Behind Business Deals (pp. 61-76). Cham: Springer Nature Switzerland. DOI: 10.1007/978-3-031-69754-8_3

Alanzi, T. (2021). A review of mobile applications available in the app and google play stores used during the COVID-19 outbreak. *Journal of Multidisciplinary Healthcare*, •••, 45–57.

Allmann, K., & Radu, R. (2023). Digital footprints as barriers to accessing e-government services. *Global Policy, 14*(1), 84–94.

Almeida, D., Shmarko, K., & Lomas, E. (2022). The ethics of facial recognition technologies, surveillance, and accountability in an age of artificial intelligence: A comparative analysis of US, EU, and UK regulatory frameworks. *AI and Ethics, 2*(3), 377–387.

Aqil, Z., & Jameel, A. (2023). Mitigating Communication Obstacles Presented by Non-Verbal Factors. In Panjwani, D., Sahrish, F., & Akhlaq, N. (Eds.), *Crucial Communication: Improving Conversations at Workplace* (pp. 9–16).

Beduschi, A. (2021). Rethinking digital identity for post-COVID-19 societies: Data privacy and human rights considerations. *Data & Policy, 3*, e15. DOI: 10.1017/dap.2021.15

Bhandari, A., & Bimo, S. (2022). Why's everyone on TikTok now? The algorithmized self and the future of self-making on social media. *Social Media + Society, 8*(1), 20563051221086241.

Bonotti, M., & Willoughby, L. (2022). Citizenship, language tests, and political participation. *Nations and Nationalism, 28*(2), 449–464.

Carpenter, J. P., Trust, T., Kimmons, R., & Krutka, D. G. (2021). Sharing and self-promoting: An analysis of educator tweeting at the onset of the COVID-19 pandemic. *Computers and Education Open, 2*, 100038. DOI: 10.1016/j.caeo.2021.100038

Caruso, C. (2024). Towards the Institutions of Freedom: The European Public Discourse in the Digital Era. *German Law Journal, 26*(1), 114–137.

Chang, J., Shelly, S., Busz, M., Stoicescu, C., Iryawan, A. R., Madybaeva, D., de Boer, Y., & Guise, A. (2021). Peer driven or driven peers? A rapid review of peer involvement of people who use drugs in HIV and harm reduction services in low- and middle-income countries. *Harm Reduction Journal, 18*(1), 1–13. DOI: 10.1186/s12954-021-00461-z PMID: 33536033

Cheng, X., He, H., & Jiang, Y. (2023, July). Analysis of User Participatory Design and Gamification in Modern Media. In International Conference on Human-Computer Interaction (pp. 78-93). Cham: Springer Nature Switzerland. DOI: 10.1007/978-3-031-35699-5_7

Ciampa, K., Wolfe, Z. M., & Bronstein, B. (2023). ChatGPT in education: Transforming digital literacy practices. *Journal of Adolescent & Adult Literacy*, *67*(3), 186–195. DOI: 10.1002/jaal.1310

Custers, B. (2022). New digital rights: Imagining additional fundamental rights for the digital era. *Computer Law & Security Review*, *44*, 105636.

Dingus, R., & Black, H. G. (2021). Choose your words carefully: An exercise to introduce artificial intelligence to the marketing classroom using tone analysis. *Marketing Education Review*, *31*(2), 64–69. DOI: 10.1080/10528008.2020.1843361

Dubois, E., & Reepschlager, A. (2024). How harassment and hate speech policies have changed over time: Comparing Facebook, Twitter and Reddit (2005–2020). *Policy and Internet*, *16*(3), 523–542.

Dwivedi, Y. K., Kshetri, N., Hughes, L., Rana, N. P., Baabdullah, A. M., Kar, A. K., Koohang, A., Ribeiro-Navarrete, S., Belei, N., Balakrishnan, J., Basu, S., Behl, A., Davies, G. H., Dutot, V., Dwivedi, R., Evans, L., Felix, R., Foster-Fletcher, R., Giannakis, M., & Yan, M. (2023). Exploring the darkverse: A multi-perspective analysis of the negative societal impacts of the metaverse. *Information Systems Frontiers*, *25*(5), 2071–2114. DOI: 10.1007/s10796-023-10400-x PMID: 37361890

Garenne, D., Haines, M. C., Romantseva, E. F., Freemont, P., Strychalski, E. A., & Noireaux, V. (2021). Cell-free gene expression. *Nature Reviews. Methods Primers*, *1*(1), 49. DOI: 10.1038/s43586-021-00046-x

Gelber, K. (2021). Differentiating hate speech: A systemic discrimination approach. *Critical Review of International Social and Political Philosophy*, *24*(4), 393–414. DOI: 10.1080/13698230.2019.1576006

Gillespie, T. (2022). Do not recommend? Reduction as a form of content moderation. *Social Media + Society*, *8*(3), 20563051221117552.

Golombek, P. R., & Johnson, K. E. (2021). Recurrent restorying through language teacher narrative inquiry. *System, 102*, 102601. DOI: 10.1016/j.system.2021.102601

Grewal, D., Herhausen, D., Ludwig, S., & Ordenes, F. V. (2022). The future of digital communication research: Considering dynamics and multimodality. *Journal of Retailing*, *98*(2), 224–240.

Grover, R. (2022). The geopolitics of digital rights activism: Evaluating civil society's role in the promises of multistakeholder internet governance. *Telecommunications Policy*, *46*(10), 102437. DOI: 10.1016/j.telpol.2022.102437

Haggart, B., & Keller, C. I. (2021). Democratic legitimacy in global platform governance. *Telecommunications Policy*, *45*(6), 102152.

He, R., & Huang, X. (2025). Conceptualizing gossip as a counterdiscourse: Alternative ways of publicly alleging sexual misconduct in an online groupie community. *International Journal of Cultural Studies*, *28*(2), 425–441. DOI: 10.1177/13678779241280291

Higgins, N., Ferri, D., & Donnellan, K. (2023). Enhancing access to digital culture for vulnerable groups: the role of public authorities in breaking down barriers. *International Journal for the Semiotics of Law-Revue internationale de Sémiotique juridique, 36*(5), 2087-2114.

Huang, T. (2024). Decentralized social networks and the future of free speech online. *Computer Law & Security Review*, *55*, 106059.

Jain, R. (2022). Translingual-identity-as-pedagogy: Problematizing monolingually oriented "native-nonnative" identity constructions through critical dialogues in EAP classrooms. *TESOL Journal*, *13*(3), e666. DOI: 10.1002/tesj.666

Javaid, M., Haleem, A., Singh, R. P., & Suman, R. (2023). Towards insighting cybersecurity for healthcare domains: A comprehensive review of recent practices and trends. *Cyber Security and Applications*, *1*, 100016.

Kapustina, L. V. (2021). Digital footprint analysis to develop a personal digital competency-based profile. In *Current Achievements, Challenges and Digital Chances of Knowledge Based Economy* (pp. 591–596). Springer International Publishing.

Karhunen, P., Kankaanranta, A., & Räisänen, T. (2023). Towards a Richer understanding of language and identity in the MNC: Constructing cosmopolitan identities through "English". *MIR. Management International Review*, *63*(3), 507–530. DOI: 10.1007/s11575-023-00504-6

Khobragade, J. W., Kumar, A., Binti Abd Aziz, S. N., & Maurya, D. (2021). The anti-maritime piracy law in india and malaysia: An analytical study. *Journal of International Maritime Safety, Environmental Affairs, and Shipping*, *5*(4), 208–219. DOI: 10.1080/25725084.2021.2006462

Kim, D., & Wang, Z. (2023). The ethics of virtuality: Navigating the complexities of human-like virtual influencers in the social media marketing realm. *Frontiers in Communication*, *8*, 1205610.

Korte, S. M., Cheung, W. M. Y., Maasilta, M., Kong, S. C., Keskitalo, P., Wang, L., Lau, C. M., Lee, J. C. K., & Gu, M. M. (2024). Enhancing artificial intelligence literacy through cross-cultural online workshops. *Computers and Education Open*, *6*, 100164. DOI: 10.1016/j.caeo.2024.100164

Kosimova, M., Qambarova, A., & Salimova, D. (2024, November). The Problems of Intercultural Communication of English Language. In *Conference Proceedings: Fostering Your Research Spirit* (pp. 390-393).

Kreienbrinck, A., Hanft-Robert, S., Forray, A. I., Nozewu, A., & Mösko, M. (2025). Usability of technological tools to overcome language barriers in healthcare–a scoping review. *Archives of Public Health = Archives Belges de Santé Publique*, *83*(1), 52. DOI: 10.1186/s13690-025-01543-1 PMID: 40001263

Kumar, R. (2023). English language and digital literacy: Navigating the information age. *Journal of International English Research Studies (JIERS)*, *1*(2), 25-31. ISSN: 3048-5231

Lansing, A. E., Romero, N. J., Siantz, E., Silva, V., Center, K., Casteel, D., & Gilmer, T. (2023). Building trust: Leadership reflections on community empowerment and engagement in a large urban initiative. *BMC Public Health*, *23*(1), 1252. DOI: 10.1186/s12889-023-15860-z PMID: 37380973

Lee, S., Kim, J., & Sung, Y. H. (2022). When infographics work better: The interplay between temporal frame and message format in e-health communication. *Psychology & Health*, *37*(7), 917–931. DOI: 10.1080/08870446.2021.1912342 PMID: 33886402

Mallén, I. B. (2021). Freedom as the Essential Basis for Communication Rights. *The Handbook of Communication Rights, Law, and Ethics: Seeking Universality, Equality, Freedom and Dignity*, 7-19. DOI: 10.1002/9781119719564.ch1

Markey, K., O'Brien, B., Kouta, C., Okantey, C., & O'Donnell, C. (2021). Embracing classroom cultural diversity: Innovations for nurturing inclusive intercultural learning and culturally responsive teaching. *Teaching and Learning in Nursing*, *16*(3), 258–262. DOI: 10.1016/j.teln.2021.01.008

Marques, T. (2023). The expression of hate in hate speech. *Journal of Applied Philosophy*, *40*(5), 769–787.

Mounir, A. S. (2025). The Lingopragmatic Role of Punctuation Marks in Digital Advertising: A Comparative Case Study in Belarus, Egypt, and the UK.

Mühlhoff, R. (2023). Predictive privacy: Collective data protection in the context of artificial intelligence and big data. *Big Data & Society*, *10*(1), 20539517231166886.

Mulenga, R. & Shilongo, H. (2024). Academic integrity in higher education: Understanding and addressing plagiarism. Acta Pedagogia Asiana.

Mulgund, P., Mulgund, B. P., Sharman, R., & Singh, R. (2021). The implications of the California Consumer Privacy Act (CCPA) on healthcare organizations: Lessons learned from early compliance experiences. *Health Policy and Technology*, *10*(3), 100543. DOI: 10.1016/j.hlpt.2021.100543

Murdoch, B. (2021). Privacy and artificial intelligence: Challenges for protecting health information in a new era. *BMC Medical Ethics*, *22*(1), 122.

Newman, P. A., Guta, A., & Black, T. (2021). Ethical considerations for qualitative research methods during the COVID-19 pandemic and other emergency situations: Navigating the virtual field. *International Journal of Qualitative Methods*, *20*, 16094069211047823. DOI: 10.1177/16094069211047823

Pangrazio, L., & Sefton-Green, J. (2021). Digital rights, digital citizenship and digital literacy: What's the difference?. *Journal of new approaches in educational research, 10*(1), 15-27.

Pimienta, D., Blanco, Á., & de Oliveira, G. M. (2023). The method behind the unprecedented production of indicators of the presence of languages in the Internet. *Frontiers in Research Metrics and Analytics*, *8*, 1149347. DOI: 10.3389/frma.2023.1149347 PMID: 37273659

Privitera, A. G., Fontana, F., & Geronazzo, M. (2024). The Role of Audio in Immersive Storytelling: A Systematic Review in Cultural Heritage. *Multimedia Tools and Applications*, *84*(16), 16105–16143.

Quintais, J. P., De Gregorio, G., & Magalhães, J. C. (2023). How platforms govern users' copyright-protected content: Exploring the power of private ordering and its implications. *Computer Law & Security Review*, *48*, 105792. DOI: 10.1016/j.clsr.2023.105792

Romero, E. D., & Bobkina, J. (2021). Exploring critical and visual literacy needs in digital learning environments: The use of memes in the EFL/ESL university classroom. *Thinking Skills and Creativity*.

Roux, A. T., Wannenburg, E., & Manetje, T. V. (2024). The Environment and Features of Digital Place-Based Media at Minibus Taxi Ranks as Nontraditional Advertising Media. *Advances in Human-Computer Interaction, 2024*(1), 3984159. DOI: 10.1155/2024/3984159

Ryan, L., Coyne, R., Heary, C., Birney, S., Crotty, M., Dunne, R., Conlan, O., & Walsh, J. C. (2023). Weight stigma experienced by patients with obesity in healthcare settings: A qualitative evidence synthesis. *Obesity Reviews, 24*(10), e13606. DOI: 10.1111/obr.13606 PMID: 37533183

Sanders, C. K., & Scanlon, E. (2021). The digital divide is a human rights issue: Advancing social inclusion through social work advocacy. *Journal of Human Rights and Social Work, 6*(2), 130–143.

Sarker, I. H. (2022). AI-based modeling: Techniques, applications and research issues towards automation, intelligent and smart systems. *SN Computer Science, 3*(2), 158.

Sato, M., Thorne, S. L., Michel, M., Alexopoulou, T., & Hellermann, J. (2025). Language, people, classrooms, world: Blending disparate theories for united language education practices. [wiley.com]. *Modern Language Journal, 109*(S1), 15–38. DOI: 10.1111/modl.12976

Schellewald, A. (2023). Understanding the popularity and affordances of TikTok through user experiences. *Media Culture & Society, 45*(8), 1568–1582.

Schissler, M. (2024). Beyond Hate Speech and Misinformation: Facebook and the Rohingya Genocide in Myanmar. *Journal of Genocide Research, 27*(3), 445–470.

Shahbazi, M., & Bunker, D. (2024). Social media trust: Fighting misinformation in the time of crisis. *International Journal of Information Management, 77*, 102780.

Sharma, P., Akgun, M., & Li, Q. (2024). Understanding student interaction and cognitive engagement in online discussions using social network and discourse analyses. *Educational Technology Research and Development, 72*(5), 2631–2654. DOI: 10.1007/s11423-023-10261-w

Shrivastava, A., Anand, G., & Shrivastava, A. (2024). A study on principles, processes and practice for building an inclusive diversity culture. In Organization, Purpose, and Values (pp. 359-370). Routledge. DOI: 10.4324/9781003501374-26

Sumo, J. N., Staffileno, B. A., Warner, K., Arrieta, M., & Salinas, I. (2021). The development of an online diversity and inclusion community: Promoting a culture of inclusion within a college of nursing. *Journal of Professional Nursing*, *37*(1), 18–23. DOI: 10.1016/j.profnurs.2020.10.002 PMID: 33674090

Szymkowiak, A., Melović, B., Dabić, M., Jeganathan, K., & Kundi, G. S. (2021). Information technology and Gen Z: The role of teachers, the internet, and technology in the education of young people. *Technology in Society*, *65*, 101565. DOI: 10.1016/j.techsoc.2021.101565

Tao, J., & Gao, X. A. (2022). Teaching and learning languages online: Challenges and responses. *System*, *107*, 102819.

Thorn, P., La Sala, L., Hetrick, S., Rice, S., Lamblin, M., & Robinson, J. (2023). Motivations and perceived harms and benefits of online communication about self-harm: An interview study with young people. *Digital Health*, *9*, 20552076231176689.

Tian, X. (2025). Unraveling the dynamics of password manager adoption: A deeper dive into critical factors. *Information and Computer Security*, *33*(1), 117–139. DOI: 10.1108/ICS-09-2023-0156

Verčič, A. T., Verčič, D., Čož, S., & Špoljarić, A. (2024). A systematic review of digital internal communication. *Public Relations Review*.

Walker, R. T. (2022). Grassroots Communication. In *The Palgrave Encyclopedia of Interest Groups, Lobbying and Public Affairs* (pp. 599–604). Springer International Publishing. DOI: 10.1007/978-3-030-44556-0_196

Weinstein, N., Itzchakov, G., & Legate, N. (2022). The motivational value of listening during intimate and difficult conversations. *Social and Personality Psychology Compass*, *16*(2), e12651. DOI: 10.1111/spc3.12651

Wilson-Menzfeld, G., Gates, J. R., Moreland, M., Raw, H., & Johnson, A. (2023). Learning digital skills online: Empowering older adults through one-to-one, online digital training provision. *Frontiers in Psychology*, *14*, 1122277. DOI: 10.3389/fpsyg.2023.1122277 PMID: 37213359

Yang, Y. T. C., Chen, Y. C., & Hung, H. T. (2022). Digital storytelling as an interdisciplinary project to improve students' English speaking and creative thinking. *Computer Assisted Language Learning*, *35*(4), 840–862. DOI: 10.1080/09588221.2020.1750431

Ye, G., Hudders, L., De Jans, S., & De Veirman, M. (2021). The value of influencer marketing for business: A bibliometric analysis and managerial implications. *Journal of Advertising*, *50*(2), 160–178. DOI: 10.1080/00913367.2020.1857888

Yingsoon, G. Y., Chua, N. A., Suyan, Z., Yiming, C., Haiyan, Z., & Xiaoyao, T. (2025). Empowering Digital Citizens: Navigating AI Ethics, Engagement, and Privacy in the Era of Advanced Education. In *Digital Citizenship and the Future of AI Engagement, Ethics, and Privacy* (pp. 79-110). IGI Global Scientific Publishing.

Yu, J., Bekerian, D. A., & Osback, C. (2024). Navigating the Digital Landscape: Challenges and Barriers to Effective Information Use on the Internet. *Encyclopedia*, *4*(4), 1665–1680.

Zamiri, M., & Esmaeili, A. (2024). Methods and technologies for supporting knowledge sharing within learning communities: A systematic literature review. *Administrative Sciences*, *14*(1), 17.

Chapter 13
Empowering Citizens:
Integrating Digital Citizenship Skills into Public Policy and Governance

Robby Hunawa
https://orcid.org/0009-0009-9863-6093
Universitas Gorontalo, Indonesia

Robby Waluyo Amu
Universitas Gorontalo, Indonesia

Zumiyati Sanu Ibrahim
IAIN Gorontalo, Indonesia

Sri Rahayu Amri
Universitas Muhammadiyah Palopo, Indonesia

ABSTRACT

This chapter examines the incorporation of digital citizenship competencies into public policy and governance, highlighting the necessity for responsible, ethical, and informed digital participation. It emphasizes essential elements—digital literacy, online safety, and digital collaboration—and their influence on civic engagement and democratic procedures. This chapter illustrates how governments, educational institutions, and communities may cultivate a culture of engaged digital citizenship through policy analysis, case studies, and pedagogical strategies. It addresses obstacles including misinformation, institutional opposition, and the digital divide, while promoting inclusive access, lifelong learning, and secure digital environments. The chapter analyzes emerging technology and changing civic behaviors, presenting a vision for policies that equip citizens for the future. Integrating digital competencies

DOI: 10.4018/979-8-3373-5781-2.ch013

into public frameworks can enhance civic participation, socioeconomic justice, and democratic robustness in a more digital society.

INTRODUCTION: UNDERSTANDING DIGITAL CITIZENSHIP

Definition and Importance

Digital citizenship denotes the responsible and acceptable utilization of technology and the internet by persons in their everyday activities. It includes many skills, behaviors, and attitudes that allow humans to maneuver the digital environment efficiently and ethically (Milenkova & Lendzhova, 2021). As technology advances and infiltrates many facets of our existence, comprehending digital citizenship has become progressively vital. It transcends the mere utilization of gadgets or information access; it encompasses being an informed, active, and responsible participant in the digital realm.

In contemporary culture, digital citizenship is crucial in determining how individuals communicate, obtain information, and participate in their communities. The internet has revolutionized communication, facilitating immediate links worldwide (Attaran, 2023). This connectedness promotes collaboration, idea exchange, and joint problem-solving. Nonetheless, it also poses obstacles, including misinformation, cyberbullying, and privacy issues. Consequently, digital citizenship is essential for empowering individuals with the competencies required to address these difficulties while optimizing the advantages of digital technologies.

Digital citizenship is crucial not only for individual users but also has profound ramifications for society at large (Harrison & Polizzi, 2022). Informed and responsible digital citizens foster a healthier online ecosystem by encouraging respectful dialogue and mitigating the dissemination of harmful content. They possess superior skills to distinguish trustworthy information from falsehoods, therefore improving the overall quality of public conversation. This talent is especially crucial at a time when social media platforms significantly shape public opinion and affect political results.

Furthermore, digital citizenship is intricately associated with civic engagement. Individuals with robust digital competencies are more inclined to engage in democratic activities, including voting, advocacy, and community organization (Peart et al., 2024). They can utilize technology to garner support for initiatives, engage with political representatives, and ensure governmental accountability. Thus, digital citizenship enables individuals to participate actively in governance and public policy, cultivating a more engaged and educated populace.

In exploring the incorporation of digital citizenship skills into public policy and governance, it is crucial to acknowledge that the cultivation of these abilities is not exclusively the obligation of individuals (Milenkova & Lendzhova, 2021). Educational institutions, governmental bodies, and community organizations must cooperate to foster an atmosphere that enhances digital literacy and encourages responsible online conduct. By emphasizing digital citizenship, we can enable individuals to flourish in the digital era and make constructive contributions to society.

Key Components of Digital Citizenship

Digital citizenship includes numerous critical elements for responsible and effective digital use (Sarwatay et al.2021). Digital literacy, online safety and security, and digital communication and collaboration allow citizens to use technology and collaborate.

Digital literacy is the capacity to find, assess, and use digital information. Beyond fundamental computer abilities, it involves critical thinking, information processing, and identifying trustworthy sources. Digital literacy is essential for making informed decisions and participating carefully in conversations in an information-rich world (Panda and Kaur, 2024). Digital literacy helps people grasp difficult topics, participate in civic life, and contribute to informed public conversation.

Digital citizenship includes online safety and security (Stellmann & Song, 2024). Cyber hazards have increased as people undertake personal, financial, and professional activities online. Phishing schemes, identity theft, and cyberbullying are online safety risks. Citizens must know how to preserve their privacy and personal data. They should use secure passwords, avoid exchanging sensitive data, and understand their digital footprints. Individuals and groups can avoid digital misuse by prioritizing online safety.

Digital communication and collaboration are vital for digital interaction (Mena-Guacas et al., 2023). Citizens must learn to communicate effectively and respectfully online as digital platforms grow. Understanding tone and context in writing and empathy and respect in digital conversations are important. Social media, video conferencing, and shared online workplaces aid teamwork and problem-solving. Digital collaboration skills let citizens participate in community projects, activism, and public discourse.

These digital citizenship principles constitute a framework that helps people succeed in the digital age. By increasing digital literacy, online safety, and communication and collaboration, we can make citizens more aware, engaged, and responsible (Milenkova & Lendzhova, 2021). As we integrate these abilities into public policy and governance, stakeholders must recognize their importance and work together to promote digital citizenship in our communities.

The Impact of Digital Citizenship on Civic Engagement

Digital citizenship profoundly impacts civic participation by providing individuals with the requisite skills and knowledge to partake in democratic processes actively (Gupta et al., 2021). In the contemporary interconnected world, digital competencies augment participation by equipping citizens with diverse tools to engage with their communities, advocate for reform, and ensure governmental accountability.

Digital skills primarily enhance engagement by enabling access to information. Individuals with digital literacy can efficiently locate and assess information pertaining to local, national, and global matters (Lybeck et al., 2024). This capability enables people to make informed choices, participate in dialogues, and champion issues of significance to them. Moreover, social media platforms and online forums enable citizens to express their views, galvanize support, and raise awareness on urgent matters. Consequently, individuals can engage in public discourse and affect governmental decisions in previously inconceivable manners.

Case studies of effective digital engagement projects underscore the transformative capacity of digital citizenship in civic involvement. The "#BlackLivesMatter" campaign illustrates the capacity of digital media to galvanize grassroots activism. Activists utilized social media to illuminate systematic racism and police brutality, orchestrating protests and advocacy campaigns that attracted global attention. The movement's capacity to attract a varied audience and promote discourse on social justice demonstrates how digital citizenship can enable individuals to instigate change within their communities (He, 2024).

A prominent instance is the "Participatory Budgeting" effort in numerous places globally, when individuals employ digital tools to impact local government expenditures. In cities such as Porto Alegre, Brazil, and New York City, inhabitants can suggest and vote on budget distributions for community initiatives via online platforms. This process increases openness and accountability while fostering a sense of ownership among individuals through their active participation in community development.

Furthermore, the emergence of e-government initiatives illustrates the influence of digital citizenship on civic participation (Tran & Le, 2024). Governments are progressively offering online venues for citizens to access services, make criticism, and participate in policy discussions. Platforms such as "We the People" in the United States enable citizens to formulate and endorse petitions, so directly impacting governmental actions. These initiatives underscore the necessity of incorporating digital citizenship competencies into public policy, since they enable citizens to interact with their government more efficiently.

THE INTERSECTION OF DIGITAL CITIZENSHIP AND PUBLIC POLICY

Current Public Policy Landscape

The existing public policy framework for digital citizenship is varied and dynamic, illustrating the increasing acknowledgment of the significance of digital competencies in contemporary society (Pangrazio & Sefton-Green, 2021). Diverse countries and organizations have enacted regulations to foster digital literacy, online safety, and responsible internet usage. These policies frequently emphasize education, technological accessibility, and safeguarding citizens' rights in the digital domain.

Numerous countries have integrated digital citizenship into their educational curricula, acknowledging the imperative to provide pupils with the competencies required to navigate the digital realm. Initiatives like the International Society for Technology in Education (ISTE) standards offer frameworks for incorporating digital citizenship into educational activities (Simon, 2025). Moreover, government initiatives frequently seek to improve digital literacy within marginalized communities, guaranteeing fair access to technology and resources. These initiatives are essential for bridging the digital divide and cultivating an informed populace.

Nonetheless, despite these gains, considerable deficiencies remain in the existing public policy framework for digital citizenship (Wang & Si, 2024). A significant disparity exists in the application of policies across various regions and educational institutions. Some regions possess strong digital citizenship programs, whilst others lack thorough methodologies, resulting in differences in residents' digital literacy levels. This inconsistency can intensify existing disparities, as individuals lacking access to quality digital education are disadvantaged in an increasingly digital society.

A significant deficiency is the inadequate emphasis on internet safety and security in current policies. Despite several initiatives advocating for digital literacy, they frequently neglect the significance of educating citizens regarding online risks and protective strategies (El-Kady et al., 2023). As cyber risks evolve in complexity, public policies must encompass the necessity for thorough online safety education. This encompasses not just educating citizens about potential threats but also providing them with practical skills to safeguard their personal information and navigate the digital environment securely.

Moreover, there is little emphasis on cultivating digital citizenship among adults and older generations, who may not have experienced equivalent access to technology during their developmental years. Public policies frequently emphasize youth education, overlooking the necessity for continuous digital skills training across all age demographics (Eynon, 2021). This oversight constrains the possibility for enhanced civic engagement and involvement in democratic processes.

The Role of Government in Promoting Digital Citizenship

Governments are essential in advancing digital citizenship by executing initiatives that include digital skills in public services and cultivating partnerships with educational institutions (AbdulKareem & Oladimeji, 2024). As the digital ecosystem evolves, it is imperative for public policy to adapt and guarantee that citizens possess the requisite abilities to navigate this environment efficiently.

A key strategy for incorporating digital skills into public services is the establishment of extensive digital literacy programs. Governments can establish projects that include training sessions, workshops, and online resources designed to improve residents' digital abilities (Chohan & Hu, 2022). These programs must be tailored to meet the varied requirements of different demographics, encompassing children, adults, and elders. Community centers and libraries can function as centers for digital literacy instruction, providing courses on fundamental computer skills, internet navigation, and online safety. By ensuring the accessibility of these resources, governments can enable individuals to participate more actively in the digital realm and utilize online services efficiently.

Furthermore, governments may establish rules mandating that public service employees receive training in the ideals of digital citizenship (AbdulKareem and Oladimeji 2024). This training guarantees that public officials are adept in technology usage and comprehend the significance of promoting digital citizenship among the communities they serve. Public agency personnel can be trained to aid individuals in using digital resources, navigating online platforms, and comprehending their rights in the digital realm. This method improves the user experience and fosters a culture of digital citizenship in public services.

Partnerships between governmental entities and educational institutions are essential for advancing digital citizenship (Tokovska et al., 2023). Through collaboration with schools, colleges, and vocational training institutions, governments can create curriculum that integrate digital citizenship competencies into established educational frameworks. Joint endeavors can facilitate the development of specialized courses concentrating on digital literacy, online safety, and responsible internet usage. These programs may be customized for various age groups, guaranteeing that pupils receive age-appropriate guidance in navigating the digital realm.

Furthermore, governments can endorse after-school activities and community initiatives that prioritize digital citizenship. By supplying financial support and resources for these initiatives, they can facilitate the connection between formal education and practical application. Partnerships with non-profit organizations and technology firms can augment these initiatives by providing expertise, resources, and mentorship opportunities (Brzustewicz et al. 2021).

In conclusion, the government's role in fostering digital citizenship is crucial for empowering citizens with the skills required to succeed in the digital era. Governments may cultivate a more informed and active populace by employing initiatives that incorporate digital competencies into public services and promoting partnerships with educational institutions. This proactive strategy augments individual competencies and fortifies the structure of democracy by promoting active engagement in civic affairs.

Policy Frameworks for Digital Citizenship

With the increasing significance of digital citizenship, some nations have established policy frameworks that exemplify best practices for fostering digital skills and responsible internet usage among their populations (Yue, 2022). These frameworks not only tackle the necessity for digital literacy but also underscore the importance of online safety, civic participation, and equal access to technology. By analyzing these best practices, we may formulate helpful recommendations for creating effective policies that promote digital citizenship.

Finland's National Curriculum Framework exemplifies a successful policy model by incorporating digital citizenship into the education system across all levels (Niemelä et al. 2021). This framework underscores the significance of imparting critical thinking, media literacy, and online safety to students from a young age. Finnish educators are urged to integrate digital citizenship across all disciplines, promoting a comprehensive awareness of responsible online conduct. This method not only provides students with vital skills but also fosters a culture of digital accountability within the educational setting.

The United Kingdom's Digital Strategy serves as another exemplary model, aiming to enhance digital skills among the populace. The approach encompasses efforts that offer training for adults, especially in marginalized communities, guaranteeing that all individuals have access to digital literacy resources (Wang & Si, 2024). The UK government partners with the corporate sector to improve digital skills training and foster lifelong learning possibilities. This collaborative method illustrates the efficacy of alliances in broadening access to digital citizenship education.

Several recommendations can be derived from these best practices to formulate effective policies for digital citizenship (Milenkova & Lendzhova, 2021). Policymakers should prioritize incorporating digital citizenship into current school programs. This can be accomplished by partnering with educators to develop age-appropriate resources and training programs catering to various student demographics' distinct requirements.

Secondly, governments ought to prioritize the cultivation of collaborations among public institutions, private entities, and non-profit organizations to augment the scope and efficacy of digital citizenship initiatives (Djatmiko et al., 2025). By leveraging resources and knowledge from many sectors, these alliances can produce comprehensive programs that fulfill the diverse needs of citizens.

Third, governments must guarantee that digital citizenship activities are inclusive and equitable, addressing vulnerable communities that may lack access to technology and digital skills training (Memon & Memon, 2025). This may entail financing community-oriented initiatives, creating digital literacy centers, and granting scholarships for digital skills education.

Continuous assessment and modification of policies are crucial to maintain their efficacy in a swiftly evolving digital environment. Policymakers must develop metrics to evaluate the effectiveness of digital citizenship projects and implement data-informed modifications as necessary (Kaluarachchi, 2022).

In conclusion, by analyzing successful policy frameworks globally and applying these ideas, governments can formulate effective policies that foster digital citizenship. These initiatives will enable citizens to traverse the digital realm responsibly, participate in civic affairs, and foster a more informed and resilient society.

EDUCATIONAL STRATEGIES FOR DIGITAL CITIZENSHIP

Curriculum Development

Incorporating digital citizenship into educational curricula is essential for equipping students to adeptly and ethically manage the intricacies of the digital realm (Yingsoon et al., 2025). As technology becomes more integrated into daily life, educational institutions must prioritize the cultivation of digital skills that enable students to participate wisely and ethically in online settings. This integration can be accomplished through a holistic strategy that includes the infusion of digital citizenship concepts into current disciplines and the creation of specialized courses centered on digital skills.

To effectively include digital citizenship into educational curricula, educators must first define essential characteristics that students need to cultivate. These qualities encompass digital literacy, internet safety, critical thinking, and responsible communication. By integrating these concepts into disciplines such as language arts, social studies, and science, educators can cultivate a comprehensive learning experience that underscores the significance of digital citizenship in diverse circumstances (Milenkova & Lendzhova, 2021). Language arts classrooms may include talks on source credibility and the effects of disinformation, whilst social studies might examine the influence of social media on public opinion and civic participation.

Moreover, age-appropriate digital skills training is crucial for guaranteeing that pupils get the requisite competences at every developmental phase. Younger kids may benefit from basic teachings on online safety, including the identification of secure websites and the significance of privacy (Martin et al., 2023). As kids proceed to middle and high school, courses may incorporate more sophisticated subjects, like digital ethics, online collaboration, and the consequences of digital footprints. This stratified method enables educators to enhance students' pre-existing knowledge and skills, cultivating a more profound comprehension of digital citizenship as they develop.

Alongside incorporating digital citizenship into current curricula, educational institutions can contemplate providing specialized courses centered on digital competencies (Bal & Akcil, 2024). These courses offer students the ability to engage in experiential learning activities, including the creation of digital content, participation in online discussions, and collaboration on projects with peers. Through active participation in these activities, students can cultivate practical skills while contemplating the ethical ramifications of their digital behaviors.

Furthermore, professional development for educators is essential to guarantee that teachers possess confidence in imparting digital citizenship knowledge. Equipping educators with training and tools will facilitate the successful instruction of digital skills and promote a culture of digital responsibility in their classrooms (Wiyono et al. 2024).

In conclusion, incorporating digital citizenship into educational curricula is vital for providing students with the necessary abilities to succeed in the digital era. By implementing a holistic strategy that encompasses age-appropriate training and specialized courses, educational institutions may enable students to safely traverse the digital terrain, cultivating a generation of knowledgeable and active digital citizens. This core effort will augment individual competencies and foster a more resilient and participatory society.

Community Education and Outreach

Community education and outreach are essential for fostering digital citizenship by providing individuals with the skills and information required to navigate the digital environment ethically (Liu, 2025). As technology advances, it is imperative to provide chances for citizens of all ages to improve their digital literacy, comprehend online safety, and participate actively in civic life. Workshops, seminars, and collaborations with community organizations are useful techniques for promoting digital citizenship in communities.

Workshops and seminars may be conducted to focus on particular elements of digital citizenship, offering practical learning experiences for attendees (Alenezi & Alfaleh, 2024). These lessons may encompass several subjects, such as internet safety, digital privacy, social media etiquette, and the critical assessment of information sources. Community centers, libraries, and local government offices can conduct programs that instruct participants on identifying phishing schemes, safeguarding personal information, and responsibly navigating social media platforms. These courses provide practical, real-world scenarios that enable students to apply their lessons instantly, thereby boosting their confidence in utilizing technology.

Moreover, these instructional events can be customized to address the varied requirements of distinct demographic groups. Workshops tailored for elders may concentrate on fundamental computer skills and online safety, whilst those intended for younger audiences could highlight digital creativity and appropriate online communication. Community education efforts can promote inclusion and guarantee that all citizens acquire basic digital skills by addressing the distinct problems encountered by diverse groups (Memon & Memon, 2025).

Collaborations with community organizations are essential for enhancing the scope and efficacy of digital citizenship activities (Ramiro & Mazur, 2024). Partnering with local non-profits, technology firms, and educational organizations can yield essential resources, expertise, and assistance for community engagement initiatives. A collaboration with a local institution could facilitate the establishment of a mentorship program in which students aid community members in enhancing their digital competencies. This improves the community and offers them practical experience and a sense of civic duty.

Furthermore, community organizations can enhance outreach by pinpointing specific needs within their populations and customizing programs accordingly (Caldwell et al., 2021). By utilizing their established networks and ties, these organizations may efficiently advocate for workshops and seminars, guaranteeing that digital citizenship education reaches the individuals who may derive the greatest advantage.

In conclusion, community education and outreach are vital elements in advancing digital citizenship. By conducting workshops and seminars tailored to varied audiences and cultivating collaborations with community organizations, we may establish a conducive atmosphere for residents to enhance their digital abilities (Lo, 2024). These initiatives will enable citizens to engage responsibly in the digital realm, augmenting their capacity to partake in civic life and foster a more informed and interconnected society. By means of collaborative projects, we may establish a foundation for a digitally literate community, promoting a culture of responsible online conduct and active participation.

Assessing Digital Citizenship Skills

Evaluating digital citizenship competencies is crucial for comprehending the efficacy of educational programs and ensuring learners are prepared to responsibly navigate the digital environment (Bal & Akcil, 2024). The assessment of digital citizenship competences can be conducted using many techniques and approaches, allowing educators and community leaders to gauge progress and pinpoint areas for enhancement. Moreover, the ongoing enhancement of digital literacy programs is essential for adjusting to the swiftly evolving digital landscape.

A proficient approach to evaluating digital citizenship competencies is the implementation of standardized exams and surveys. These instruments can assess participants' comprehension and grasp of essential concepts, including online safety, digital ethics, and information literacy (Myoung & Liou, 2022). Pre- and post-assessments can be conducted prior to and following workshops or training sessions to evaluate the enhancement of participants' competencies. Surveys can also collect input on participants' trust in utilizing digital tools and their capacity to engage properly online. This quantitative data offers significant insights into the efficacy of educational programs and identifies particular areas that may necessitate additional focus.

Alongside standardized assessments, qualitative procedures like interviews and focus groups might be utilized to get a more profound comprehension of participants' perspectives and issues concerning digital citizenship (Carter et al., 2021). These discussions might elucidate individuals' perceptions of their digital competencies and the obstacles encountered in their application. By integrating qualitative feedback, educators can customize their programs to more effectively address the requirements of their audiences.

A novel method for evaluating digital citizenship competencies is the implementation of digital portfolios. Participants may construct portfolios that exhibit their digital initiatives, online engagements, and thoughts on their educational experiences (Afrilyasanti et al., 2025). This method facilitates a thorough assessment of individual competencies while promoting self-reflection and personal development. Educators may evaluate these portfolios to gauge students' comprehension of digital citizenship principles and offer constructive criticism.

The ongoing enhancement of digital literacy programs is crucial for maintaining their relevance and efficacy. Consistently analyzing evaluation data and participant comments allows educators and program leaders to discern strengths and problems in their programs (Chiu, 2024). Based on these assessments, modifications can be implemented to improve the content, distribution methods, and overall framework of digital citizenship programs. This iterative process cultivates a culture of perpetual learning and adaptation, guaranteeing that educational programs stay aligned with the changing digital context.

In conclusion, evaluating digital citizenship competencies through a blend of quantitative and qualitative approaches is essential for comprehending the effects of educational programs. Through the use of standardized exams, qualitative feedback, and new methods such as digital portfolios, instructors can proficiently measure participants' competencies. Moreover, dedicating efforts to the ongoing enhancement of digital literacy programs guarantees that these initiatives stay pertinent and efficient, ultimately enabling individuals to traverse the digital realm responsibly and participate meaningfully in civic life.

TECHNOLOGY AND TOOLS FOR EMPOWERING CITIZENS

Digital Platforms for Civic Engagement

In a progressively digitized society, technology is crucial in augmenting civic engagement by equipping citizens with tools and platforms for active participation in governance and community efforts (Kangana et al., 2024). These digital platforms enable communication, collaboration, and information dissemination, empowering individuals to express their views, campaign for reform, and interact with their governments. A review of current digital tools and platforms, accompanied by case studies of effective technology deployment, underscores the transformative capacity of technology in civic involvement.

A plethora of digital tools has arisen to enhance civic engagement, encompassing social media platforms and specialized civic technology applications. Social media platforms such as Twitter and Facebook enable individuals to express their opinions, get support for initiatives, and engage with similar-minded peers (Nyhan et al., 2023). Hashtags and trending topics can enhance visibility and elevate awareness of significant issues, facilitating citizen participation in public discourse. Moreover, websites such as Change.org facilitate the creation and signing of petitions, empowering users to advocate for policy modifications and ensure accountability among decision-makers.

In recent years, dedicated civic tech platforms have gained prominence (Gritsenko & Indukaev, 2021). Platforms such as "Nextdoor" promote community engagement by linking residents and encouraging discourse on local matters. Likewise, "SeeClickFix" enables residents to report communal issues, such as potholes or malfunctioning streetlights, directly to municipal authorities. This bilateral contact not only improves governmental responsiveness but also motivates residents to actively participate in the upkeep of their communities.

Case studies of successful technology implementation demonstrate the efficacy of these digital platforms in enhancing civic engagement. A prominent instance is the "Participatory Budgeting" project in New York City, wherein residents can propose and vote on the allocation of a segment of the city's budget. Citizens utilize an online platform to join in conversations, submit project proposals, and vote on funding choices. This project has led to heightened civic engagement, especially among traditionally marginalized groups, and has cultivated a sense of ownership among individuals concerning local governance.

A notable example is the "We the People" platform initiated by the White House, enabling citizens to formulate and endorse petitions to present issues directly to the federal government. Utilizing this digital technology, citizens can promote policy modifications and obtain replies from government authorities, hence improving openness and accountability in governance (Androutsopoulou et al., 2024).

In summary, digital platforms for civic participation have transformed citizen interactions with their governments and communities. These platforms facilitate communication, collaboration, and advocacy, so enabling citizens to engage actively in civic life. The effective execution of programs such as Participatory Budgeting and We the People illustrates technology's capacity to improve democratic processes and cultivate a more involved populace (Leclercq & Rijshouwer, 2022). As we investigate the convergence of technology and civic engagement, it is essential to guarantee that these tools are accessible and inclusive, allowing all citizens to participate in the democratic process.

Promoting Access to Technology

Facilitating access to technology is essential for empowering individuals and cultivating digital citizenship (Gonzalez-Mohino et al., 2023). The digital divide—the disparity between individuals with easy access to digital technologies and those without—presents considerable obstacles to equal engagement in civic life. Bridging this difference is crucial for enabling all individuals to participate effectively in the digital realm, access information, and employ online resources for civic engagement.

The digital gap manifests in multiple dimensions, encompassing inequalities in internet access, device availability, and digital literacy competencies. Underserved communities, especially low-income households, rural regions, and disadvantaged groups, frequently encounter substantial obstacles to technology access (Raihan et al., 2024). In the absence of dependable internet connections and requisite gadgets, residents in these regions may encounter difficulties in participating in online education, accessing government services, or engaging in civic activities. The absence of access can perpetuate disparities and obstruct civic participation, ultimately jeopardizing the democratic process.

Numerous projects have arisen to mitigate the digital divide by enhancing technological access in marginalized populations. An effective strategy is the creation of community technology centers that offer complimentary or affordable access to computers and the internet (Almalki et al., 2023). These institutes frequently provide training programs to improve digital literacy, assisting individuals in acquiring the skills necessary to navigate the digital environment. Organizations such as the Technology Access Foundation in Washington State have effectively established community-oriented initiatives that offer technology access and training to kids and families in marginalized regions.

A notable endeavor is the enhancement of public Wi-Fi networks in both urban and rural regions. Communities can establish free Wi-Fi zones in public areas like parks, libraries, and community centers by collaborating with local governments and business enterprises (Ribeiro et al., 2022). These initiatives not only enhance internet accessibility but also promote community engagement, collaboration, and participation in local events. Cities such as San Francisco and New York have enacted programs to bridge the digital divide and provide fair access to technology.

Moreover, initiatives that offer subsidized gadgets and internet services to economically disadvantaged families are essential for enhancing technological access (Horrigan et al., 2024). Programs such as the Federal Communications Commission's Lifeline initiative provide discounts on telecommunication and internet services for qualifying households, facilitating greater access to the digital realm. Organizations such as PCs for People refurbish and distribute computers to economically disadvantaged families, facilitating their access to vital online resources.

In conclusion, mitigating the digital gap is crucial for enhancing technological access and empowering individuals. Implementing activities that enhance access to devices, internet connectivity, and digital literacy training in marginalized groups helps cultivate a more inclusive digital environment. These initiatives not only augment individual competencies but also bolster civic participation, guaranteeing that all individuals can engage actively in the democratic process and contribute to their communities. In our pursuit of a more equal society, it is essential to emphasize projects that close the digital gap and enhance access to technology for everyone.

Ensuring Security and Privacy

Ensuring security and privacy in the digital era is essential for empowering citizens and cultivating trust in online platforms (Asimakopoulos et al., 2025). As individuals increasingly utilize technology for civic engagement, it is imperative to adopt best practices for online safety and formulate comprehensive government rules to safeguard citizens' data. By emphasizing security and privacy, we may establish a more secure digital landscape that fosters active participation and responsible technology utilization.

Optimal online safety practices include many strategies individuals might implement to safeguard themselves while traversing the digital environment. A crucial practice is employing robust, distinct passwords for several accounts. Citizens ought to be urged to formulate intricate passwords comprising a combination of letters, numbers, and special characters and employ password managers to secure these credentials (Zaidi et al., 2024). Furthermore, activating two-factor authentication (2FA) provides an additional security layer, necessitating users to confirm their identity by a secondary way, such as a text message or authentication application.

A vital component of online safety is the recognition of phishing scams and harmful software. Citizens ought to be instructed on identifying dubious emails, messages, and connections, along with the significance of refraining from disclosing personal information to unverified sources (Prabhu et al., 2022). Regular workshops and community seminars may be conducted to deliver practical training on recognizing online risks and implementing safe surfing practices.

Alongside individual practices, governmental rules are essential for safeguarding individuals' data and maintaining online security. Governments must implement explicit legislation that require data protection protocols for entities that gather and retain personal information. The General Data Protection Regulation (GDPR) in the European Union establishes rigorous protocols for data management, enhancing individual autonomy over personal information and mandating enterprises to use comprehensive security measures (Niebel, 2021).

Moreover, governments have to advocate for transparency in data gathering methodologies, guaranteeing that citizens are apprised of the utilization and dissemination of their data (Park & Gil-Garcia, 2022). Policies mandating enterprises to secure explicit consent from users prior to data collection might enable citizens to make informed choices regarding their online engagements. Furthermore, governments may conduct frequent audits and evaluations of data security protocols in both public and commercial sectors to guarantee adherence to existing standards.

Public awareness programs are crucial for informing citizens about their rights about data privacy and security (Rizi & Seno, 2022). By supplying tools and information on personal data protection, governments can enable individuals to actively preserve their online presence.

In conclusion, safeguarding security and privacy is essential for cultivating a secure digital environment that enables citizens to participate in civic life. We can foster trust in digital platforms and promote responsible technology utilization by advocating for optimal online safety practices and enacting stringent governmental rules to safeguard citizens' data. In the digital age, prioritizing security and privacy will empower citizens to engage completely and confidently in the democratic process, thereby reinforcing societal cohesion.

FUTURE DIRECTIONS AND CHALLENGES

Emerging Trends in Digital Citizenship

As we anticipate the future, various emerging trends are influencing the realm of digital citizenship, notably the effects of artificial intelligence (AI) and automation, along with the changing function of social media in civic participation (Al et al., 2023). Comprehending these tendencies is crucial for modifying educational programs and public policies that enable citizens in a swiftly evolving digital landscape.

The emergence of artificial intelligence and automation offers both prospects and obstacles for digital citizenship. AI can improve the accessibility of information and services, facilitating citizen engagement with their governments and communities (Al-Besher & Kumar, 2022). AI-driven chatbots can offer immediate support for accessing public services, responding to inquiries, and navigating intricate procedures. This technology can optimize interactions and enhance user experiences, ultimately promoting increased civic engagement.

The growing dependence on AI poses problems over privacy, bias, and misinformation. Algorithms influence the information individuals receive, posing a risk of generating echo chambers and reinforcing preexisting biases (Figà Talamanca & Arfini, 2022). Citizens must cultivate critical digital literacy skills to address these challenges, allowing them to differentiate credible information from deceptive content. Educational initiatives must emphasize the significance of comprehending AI's implications and the necessity for responsible technology use in civic engagement.

A notable trend is the changing function of social media in civic participation. Social media platforms have emerged as potent instruments for mobilizing citizens, fostering discussions, and enhancing awareness of social and political issues (Choi et al., 2021). Movements like Black Lives Matter and climate activism have gained traction via social media, illustrating its capacity to facilitate collective action and shape public discourse. The swift dissemination of misinformation and polarization on these platforms presents a considerable obstacle to informed civic engagement.

Individuals must possess the skills to engage critically and responsibly to leverage social media's benefits while minimizing its dangers. Digital citizenship education must encompass instruction on source evaluation, bias recognition, and the effects of online conduct on public discourse (Kozyreva et al., 2023). By cultivating a culture of respectful and informed interaction, we can enable citizens to utilize social media as a means for constructive discourse and civic involvement.

In summary, the future of digital citizenship will be influenced by emerging trends, including artificial intelligence and the changing dynamics of social media. These developments offer opportunities for improving civic engagement, but they also pose challenges that require resolution through thorough education and policy initiatives. By providing citizens with the skills to navigate this intricate environment, we can encourage responsible digital citizenship and cultivate a more engaged and informed society. As we move forward, it is imperative to embrace these trends while remaining vigilant about their implications, ensuring that all individuals have the tools they need to participate meaningfully in the democratic process.

Challenges to Implementing Digital Citizenship Skills

Notwithstanding the increasing acknowledgment of the significance of digital citizenship, numerous obstacles impede the successful integration of digital citizenship competencies in educational settings and society at large (Tadlaoui-Brahmi et al., 2022). Two major impediments are institutional opposition to change and the widespread problem of disinformation, both of which can hinder initiatives aimed at promoting responsible digital engagement.

Institutional resistance to change significantly hinders the incorporation of digital citizenship into curricula and public policy. Numerous educational institutions function within conventional frameworks that emphasize standardized testing and traditional teaching techniques, allowing minimal scope for new strategies in digital literacy. Educators may experience apprehension regarding the implementation of new curricula or the incorporation of technology into their pedagogical methods, especially in the absence of sufficient training and resources (Ngao et al., 2022). This aversion may arise from a fear of the unfamiliar or a conviction that digital competencies are subordinate to fundamental academic disciplines.

To tackle this difficulty, it is imperative to cultivate a culture of transparency and flexibility inside educational institutions. Professional development programs must be instituted to provide educators with the requisite knowledge and resources to teach digital citizenship proficiently (ElSayary, 2023). By offering continuous assistance and resources, institutions can enhance educators' confidence in their capacity to incorporate digital skills into their classes. Furthermore, leadership in educational institutions and organizations must emphasize digital citizenship as an essential element of education, promoting its integration into curricula and acknowledging its significance in equipping students for the contemporary landscape.

A notable concern is the spread of misinformation and its harmful impact on public debate (Komendantova et al., 2023). In an age where information disseminates swiftly via social media and other platforms, individuals frequently encounter inaccurate or erroneous content. This climate can undermine faith in credible information sources and generate misunderstanding over essential problems, ultimately obstructing informed democratic participation. Misinformation can polarize societies, hindering members' ability to engage in productive conversation and work on solutions to common concerns.

To mitigate the impact of disinformation, digital citizenship education must prioritize critical thinking and media literacy competencies. Citizens ought to be educated in source evaluation, bias recognition, and the differentiation of credible information from unreliable content. Educational programs must to integrate real-world scenarios that assist individuals in navigating the intricacies of the digital information domain (Panda and Kaur 2024). Moreover, collaborations with media organizations and fact-checking agencies can furnish essential resources and assistance for the dissemination of accurate information.

In conclusion, the implementation of digital citizenship skills encounters substantial obstacles, such as institutional reluctance to change and the widespread problem of misinformation. By cultivating a culture of adaptation and emphasizing professional development for educators, institutions can more effectively incorporate digital citizenship into their frameworks. Concurrently, providing citizens with critical thinking and media literacy skills will enable them to traverse the digital realm responsibly. Confronting these difficulties is crucial for cultivating an informed and active citizenry, so enhancing democratic processes and nurturing a more resilient society.

Vision for the Future

In contemplating the future of digital citizenship, it is imperative to set enduring objectives that emphasize the incorporation of digital competencies into governance and civic participation (Asimakopoulos et al., 2025). These objectives should emphasize the development of an informed, engaged, and responsible citizenry adept at navigating the intricacies of the digital realm while actively participating in democratic processes. Realizing this objective necessitates a cooperative endeavor among all stakeholders, including government officials, educators, and citizens.

A key long-term objective for digital citizenship in governance is to design extensive policies that enhance digital literacy throughout all societal sectors (Tokovska et al., 2023). This entails incorporating digital citizenship education into school curricula from an early age, ensuring that children acquire the requisite skills for responsible engagement in the digital realm. Furthermore, governments ought to establish programs that offer continuous digital skills training for adults, with a particular focus on marginalized areas. By cultivating a culture of perpetual education, we can enable citizens to adjust to technological progress and engage substantively in civic affairs.

A primary objective is to improve transparency and accountability in government by utilizing digital tools. Governments ought to utilize technology to establish platforms that promote transparent communication between citizens and public officials (Aguerre & Bonina, 2024). This encompasses using online platforms for public discourse, deploying e-government technologies that facilitate information access, and promoting citizen input on policy decisions. By emphasizing transparency, governments can foster confidence with their constituents and promote more civic involvement.

A call to action is essential for all stakeholders to actualize this vision. Governments should prioritize digital citizenship in public policy and invest in infrastructure that facilitates access to technology and digital literacy initiatives (Chohan & Hu, 2022). This entails partnering with educational institutions and community organizations to create extensive training programs that cater to individuals' varied requirements.

Educators are essential to this vision by incorporating digital citizenship into their pedagogical methods and promoting a culture of critical thinking and responsible online conduct among students (Althibyani & Al-Zahrani, 2023). Professional development opportunities must be offered to furnish educators with the knowledge and tools essential for effectively teaching digital citizenship.

Citizens also play a vital role in this vision. They should actively cultivate their digital competencies and participate in civic affairs. Citizens can foster a more informed and involved society by participating in community activities, advocating for digital literacy initiatives, and ensuring governmental accountability for transparency and responsiveness (Gardner et al., 2021).

In conclusion, the future vision for digital citizenship in governance relies on the establishment of enduring objectives that emphasize education, transparency, and active engagement. By promoting collaboration among government, educators, and citizens, we may cultivate a society in which individuals are equipped to navigate the digital realm responsibly and participate meaningfully in democratic processes. This collaborative endeavor will ultimately fortify the foundations of democracy and cultivate a more resilient and knowledgeable populace.

CONCLUSION

In a more digital landscape, the incorporation of digital citizenship into public policy and governance is both essential and imperative. This chapter has highlighted the complex dimensions of digital citizenship, including digital literacy, online safety, ethical involvement, and collaborative participation. These qualities are crucial for enabling individuals to engage ethically in the digital landscape and to participate effectively in civic life.

The chapter emphasized that cultivating digital citizenship necessitates a collaborative endeavor; governments, educators, and communities must unite to formulate inclusive legislation, execute effective educational initiatives, and advocate for equal technological access. Case studies like participatory budgeting and civic technology platforms demonstrate the transformative power of digital tools when linked with objectives of citizen involvement. Simultaneously, obstacles such as misinformation, institutional slowness, and the digital gap must be proactively confronted to prevent the worsening of existing imbalances.

Future-oriented policy must include the changing digital landscape, encompassing the ethical ramifications of artificial intelligence, the influential capacity of social media, and the significance of data privacy and security. An anticipatory and inclusive strategy—anchored on education, accessibility, and transparency—will guarantee that all citizens, irrespective of age or background, possess the requisite skills for active engagement in democracy.

In summary, integrating digital citizenship into public governance strengthens human agency as well as the resilience and integrity of democratic communities. Equitable and responsive governance can be completely achieved through informed, empowered, and engaged digital citizens.

REFERENCES

AbdulKareem, A. K., & Oladimeji, K. A. (2024). Cultivating the digital citizen: trust, digital literacy and e-government adoption. Transforming Government: People. *Process and Policy*, *18*(2), 270–286.

Afrilyasanti, R., Suhartoyo, E., & Widiati, U. (2025). Researching the use of e-portfolios to promote students thinking in digital age: A qualitative action study. *Interactive Technology and Smart Education*, *22*(1), 25–42. DOI: 10.1108/ITSE-08-2023-0167

Aguerre, C. & Bonina, C. (2024). Open government, civic tech and digital platforms in Latin America: A governance study of Montevideo's urban app 'Por Mi Barrio'. Information Systems Journal.

Al-Besher, A. & Kumar, K. (2022). Use of artificial intelligence to enhance e-government services. Measurement: sensors.

Al Husseiny, F. A., Saab, J. M., Abdallah, M. H., & Wehbe, N. H. (2023). Digital citizenship and digital literacy: An evolving trend. In *Innovations in digital instruction through virtual environments* (pp. 205–220). IGI Global. DOI: 10.4018/978-1-6684-7015-2.ch012

Alenezi, N. & Alfaleh, M. (2024). Enhancing digital citizenship education in Saudi Arabian elementary schools: designing effective activities for curriculum integration. Frontiers in Education.

Almalki, F. A., Alsamhi, S. H., Sahal, R., Hassan, J., Hawbani, A., Rajput, N. S., Saif, A., Morgan, J., & Breslin, J. (2023). Green IoT for eco-friendly and sustainable smart cities: Future directions and opportunities. *Mobile Networks and Applications*, *28*(1), 178–202. DOI: 10.1007/s11036-021-01790-w

Althibyani, H. A. & Al-Zahrani, A. M. (2023). Investigating the effect of students' knowledge, beliefs, and digital citizenship skills on the prevention of cybercrime. Sustainability.

Androutsopoulou, M., Askounis, D., Carayannis, E. G., & Zotas, N. (2024). Leveraging AI for Enhanced eGovernment: Optimizing the Use of Open Governmental Data.. *Journal of the Knowledge Economy*, 1–36. DOI: 10.1007/s13132-024-02317-w

Asimakopoulos, G., Antonopoulou, H., Giotopoulos, K., & Halkiopoulos, C. (2025). Impact of Information and Communication Technologies on Democratic Processes and Citizen Participation. *Societies (Basel, Switzerland)*, *15*(2), 40. DOI: 10.3390/soc15020040

Attaran, M. (2023). The impact of 5G on the evolution of intelligent automation and industry digitization. *Journal of Ambient Intelligence and Humanized Computing*, *14*(5), 5977–5993. DOI: 10.1007/s12652-020-02521-x PMID: 33643481

Bal, E. & Akcil, U. (2024). The implementation of a sustainable online course for the development of digital citizenship skills in higher education. Sustainability.

Brzustewicz, P., Escher, I., Hermes, J., & Ulkuniemi, P. (2021). Value creation in company–NGO collaboration in corporate volunteering. *Journal of Business and Industrial Marketing*, *36*(8), 1504–1519. DOI: 10.1108/JBIM-01-2020-0057

Caldwell, C. H., Thomas, D., Hoelscher, H., Williams, H., Mason, Z.II, Valerio-Shewmaker, M. A., & Panapasa, S. V. (2021). Tailoring recruitment and outreach strategies for underrepresented students in public health pipeline programs. *Pedagogy in Health Promotion*, *7*(1, suppl), 36S–43S. DOI: 10.1177/23733799211047517

Carter, S. M., Shih, P., Williams, J., Degeling, C., & Mooney-Somers, J. (2021). Conducting qualitative research online: Challenges and solutions. *Patient*, *14*(6), 711–718. DOI: 10.1007/s40271-021-00528-w PMID: 34114170

Chiu, T. K. F. (2024). The impact of Generative AI (GenAI) on practices, policies and research direction in education: A case of ChatGPT and Midjourney. Interactive Learning Environments.

Chohan, S. R. & Hu, G. (2022). Strengthening digital inclusion through e-government: Cohesive ICT training programs to intensify digital competency. Information technology for development.

Choi, D. H., Nah, S., & Chung, D. S. (2021). Social media as a civic mobilizer: Community storytelling network, social media, and civic engagement in South Korea.. *Journal of Broadcasting & Electronic Media*, *65*(1), 46–65. DOI: 10.1080/08838151.2021.1897818

Djatmiko, G. H., Sinaga, O., & Pawirosumarto, S. (2025). Digital Transformation and Social Inclusion in Public Services: A Qualitative Analysis of E-Government Adoption for Marginalized Communities in Sustainable …. Sustainability.

El-Kady, A. H., Halim, S., El-Halwagi, M. M., & Khan, F. (2023). Analysis of safety and security challenges and opportunities related to cyber-physical systems. *Process Safety and Environmental Protection*, *173*, 384–413. DOI: 10.1016/j.psep.2023.03.012

ElSayary, A. (2023). The impact of a professional upskilling training programme on developing teachers' digital competence. *Journal of Computer Assisted Learning*, *39*(4), 1154–1166. DOI: 10.1111/jcal.12788

Eynon, R. (2021). Becoming digitally literate: Reinstating an educational lens to digital skills policies for adults. British educational research journal.

Figà Talamanca, G. & Arfini, S. (2022). Through the newsfeed glass: Rethinking filter bubbles and echo chambers. Philosophy & Technology.

Gardner, C. J., Thierry, A., Rowlandson, W., & Steinberger, J. K. (2021). From publications to public actions: The role of universities in facilitating academic advocacy and activism in the climate and ecological emergency. *Frontiers in Sustainability*, *2*, 679019. DOI: 10.3389/frsus.2021.679019

Gonzalez-Mohino, M., Rodriguez-Domenech, M. Á., Callejas-Albiñana, A. I., & Castillo-Canalejo, A. (2023). Empowering critical thinking: The role of digital tools in citizen participation. [springer.com]. *Journal of New Approaches in Educational Research*, *12*(2), 258–275. DOI: 10.7821/naer.2023.7.1385

Gritsenko, D. & Indukaev, A. (2021). Digitalising city governance in Russia: The case of the 'active citizen'platform. Europe-Asia Studies.

Gupta, S., Mishra, O. N., & Kumar, S. (2021). Citizen empowerment and adoption of E-governance services: The role of online citizen skills, awareness, and engagement.. *International Journal of Electronic Governance*, *13*(4), 386–407. DOI: 10.1504/IJEG.2021.121237

Harrison, T. & Polizzi, G. (2022). (In) civility and adolescents' moral decision making online: Drawing on moral theory to advance digital citizenship education. Education and Information Technologies.

He, R. (2024). Let's keep boys out: promoting exclusion as a means to actualize feminist digital citizenship in China. Citizenship Studies.

Horrigan, J. B., Whitacre, B. E., & Galperin, H. (2024). Understanding uptake in demand-side broadband subsidy programs: The affordable connectivity program case.. *Telecommunications Policy*, *48*(8), 102812. DOI: 10.1016/j.telpol.2024.102812

Kaluarachchi, Y. (2022). Implementing data-driven smart city applications for future cities. Smart Cities.

Kangana, N., Kankanamge, N., De Silva, C., Goonetilleke, A., Mahamood, R., & Ranasinghe, D. (2024). Bridging Community Engagement and Technological Innovation for Creating Smart and Resilient Cities: A Systematic Literature Review. *Smart Cities*, *7*(6), 3823–3852. DOI: 10.3390/smartcities7060147

Komendantova, N., Erokhin, D., & Albano, T. (2023). Misinformation and its impact on contested policy issues: the example of migration discourses. Societies.

Kozyreva, A., Wineburg, S., Lewandowsky, S., & Hertwig, R. (2023). Critical ignoring as a core competence for digital citizens. *Current Directions in Psychological Science*, *32*(1), 81–88. DOI: 10.1177/09637214221121570 PMID: 37994317

Leclercq, E. M. & Rijshouwer, E. A. (2022). Enabling citizens' Right to the Smart City through the co-creation of digital platforms. Urban Transformations.

Liu, Y. (2025). The Digital Horizon: Opportunities for Developing Social Capital and Advancing Digital Citizenship. In Digital Citizenship and Building a Responsible Online Presence (pp. 43-76). IGI Global Scientific Publishing.

Lo, N. P. K. (2024). The confluence of digital literacy and eco-consciousness: harmonizing digital skills with sustainable practices in education. Platforms.

Lybeck, R., Koiranen, I., & Koivula, A. (2024). From digital divide to digital capital: The role of education and digital skills in social media participation. *Universal Access in the Information Society*, *23*(4), 1657–1669. DOI: 10.1007/s10209-022-00961-0

Martin, F., Bacak, J., Polly, D., Wang, W., & Ahlgrim-Delzell, L. (2023). Teacher and school concerns and actions on elementary school children digital safety. TechTrends.

Memon, F. N., & Memon, S. N. (2025). Digital Divide and Equity in Education: Bridging Gaps to Ensure Inclusive Learning. In Impact of Digitalization on Education and Social Sustainability (pp. 107-130). IGI Global.

Mena-Guacas, A. F., Meza-Morales, J. A., Fernández, E., & López-Meneses, E. (2023). Digital collaboration in higher education: A study of digital skills and collaborative attitudes in students from diverse universities. *Education Sciences*, *14*(1), 36. DOI: 10.3390/educsci14010036

Milenkova, V. & Lendzhova, V. (2021). Digital citizenship and digital literacy in the conditions of social crisis. Computers.

Myoung, E., & Liou, P. Y. (2022). Systematic review of empirical studies on international large-scale assessments of civic and citizenship education. *Scandinavian Journal of Educational Research*, *66*(7), 1269–1291. DOI: 10.1080/00313831.2022.2131903

Ngao, A. I., Sang, G., & Kihwele, J. E. (2022). Understanding teacher educators' perceptions and practices about ICT integration in teacher education program. Education Sciences.

Niebel, C. (2021). The impact of the general data protection regulation on innovation and the global political economy.. *Computer Law & Security Review*, *40*, 105523. DOI: 10.1016/j.clsr.2020.105523

Niemelä, P., Pears, A., Dagienė, V., & Laanpere, M. (2021, August). Computational thinking–Forces shaping curriculum and policy in Finland, Sweden and the Baltic countries. In *Open Conference on Computers in Education* (pp. 131-143). Cham: Springer International Publishing.

Nyhan, B., Settle, J., Thorson, E., Wojcieszak, M., Barberá, P., Chen, A. Y., Allcott, H., Brown, T., Crespo-Tenorio, A., Dimmery, D., Freelon, D., Gentzkow, M., González-Bailón, S., Guess, A. M., Kennedy, E., Kim, Y. M., Lazer, D., Malhotra, N., Moehler, D., & Tucker, J. A. (2023). Like-minded sources on Facebook are prevalent but not polarizing. *Nature, 620*(7972), 137–144. DOI: 10.1038/s41586-023-06297-w PMID: 37500978

Panda, S., & Kaur, N. (2024). Empowered minds: Navigating digital seas with emerging information literacy framework. In *Examining information literacy in academic libraries* (pp. 48–82). IGI Global. DOI: 10.4018/979-8-3693-1143-1.ch004

Pangrazio, L., & Sefton-Green, J. (2021). Digital rights, digital citizenship and digital literacy: What's the difference?. Journal of new approaches in educational research, 10(1), 15-27.

Park, S., & Gil-Garcia, J. R. (2022). Open data innovation: Visualizations and process redesign as a way to bridge the transparency-accountability gap.. *Government Information Quarterly, 39*(1), 101456. DOI: 10.1016/j.giq.2020.101456

Peart, M., Higgins, S., Gutiérrez-Esteban, P., & Cubo Delgado, S. (2024). Digital and socio-civic skills development and young people's perceptions of digital citizenship in the UK. *Education, Citizenship and Social Justice, 19*(3), 463–475. DOI: 10.1177/17461979231170232

Prabhu Kavin, B., Karki, S., Hemalatha, S., Singh, D., Vijayalakshmi, R., Thangamani, M., Haleem, S. L. A., Jose, D., Tirth, V., Kshirsagar, P. R., & Adigo, A. G. (2022). Machine learning-based secure data acquisition for fake accounts detection in future mobile communication networks. *Wireless Communications and Mobile Computing, 2022*(1), 6356152. DOI: 10.1155/2022/6356152

Raihan, M. M., Subroto, S., Chowdhury, N., Koch, K., Ruttan, E., & Turin, T. C. (2024). Dimensions and barriers for digital (in) equity and digital divide: A systematic integrative review. Digital Transformation and Society.

Ramiro Troitiño, D., & Mazur, V. (2024). Digital Social Initiatives: Europe Connecting Citizens with Social Transformation. In E-Governance in the European Union: Strategies, Tools, and Implementation (pp. 71-85). Cham: Springer Nature Switzerland.

Ribeiro, M., Nunes, N., Nisi, V., & Schöning, J. (2022). Passive wi-fi monitoring in the wild: A long-term study across multiple location typologies. *Personal and Ubiquitous Computing*, *26*(3), 505–519. DOI: 10.1007/s00779-020-01441-z PMID: 32958999

Rizi, M. H. P., & Seno, S. A. H. (2022). A systematic review of technologies and solutions to improve security and privacy protection of citizens in the smart city. *Internet of Things : Engineering Cyber Physical Human Systems*.

Sarwatay, D., Raman, U., & Ramasubramanian, S. (2021). Media literacy, social connectedness, and digital citizenship in India: Mapping stakeholders on how parents and young people navigate a social world. *Frontiers in Human Dynamics*, *3*, 601239. DOI: 10.3389/fhumd.2021.601239

Simon, N. (2025). Towards Technological Literacy: Fostering Digital Citizenship and Sustainable Development Education in Next-Generation Teaching. Digital Citizenship and Building a Responsible Online.

Stellmann, E., & Song, L. (2024). Essential elements of digital citizenship: Insights from the literature. *TechTrends*, *68*(4), 749–760. DOI: 10.1007/s11528-024-00985-8

Tadlaoui-Brahmi, A., Çuko, K., & Alvarez, L. (2022). Digital citizenship in primary education: A systematic literature review describing how it is implemented. *Social Sciences & Humanities Open*, *6*(1), 100348. DOI: 10.1016/j.ssaho.2022.100348

Tokovska, M., Ferreira, V. N., Vallušova, A., & Seberíni, A. (2023). E-Government—The inclusive way for the future of digital citizenship. Societies.

Tran Pham, T. K., & Le Hoang Thuy To Nguyen, Q. (2024). Impact of e-government on citizen engagement: The role of government reputation and digital divide. Journal of Information. *Communication and Ethics in Society*, *22*(4), 419–433. DOI: 10.1108/JICES-08-2023-0109

Wang, C. & Si, L. (2024). The intersection of public policy and public access: Digital inclusion, digital literacy education, and libraries. Sustainability.

Wiyono, B. B., Imron, A., Rahma, L., Arifah, N., Azhari, R., Sibula, I., & Maharmawan, M. (2024). Elevating teachers' professional digital competence: Synergies of principals' instructional e-supervision, technology leadership and digital culture for educational excellence in digital-savvy era. *Education Sciences*, *14*(3), 266. DOI: 10.3390/educsci14030266

Yingsoon, G. Y., Chua, N. A., Suyan, Z., Yiming, C., Haiyan, Z., & Xiaoyao, T. (2025). Empowering Digital Citizens: Navigating AI Ethics, Engagement, and Privacy in the Era of Advanced Education. In Digital Citizenship and the Future of AI Engagement, Ethics, and Privacy (pp. 79-110). IGI Global Scientific Publishing.

Yue, A. (2022). From digital literacy to digital citizenship: Policies, assessment frameworks and programs for young people in the Asia Pacific. *Media Asia*.

Zaidi, T., Garai, S., & Biradar, T. V. (2024). Exploring the landscape of password managers for individual users through innovative solution. In Information Technology Security: Modern Trends and Challenges (pp. 69-99). Singapore: Springer Nature Singapore. DOI: 10.1007/978-981-97-0407-1_4

Chapter 14
Technology Literacy in Empowering University Students' Extrinsic Motivation in Language Learning

M Asia
https://orcid.org/0009-0004-7371-7106
Universitas Negeri Makassar, Indonesia

Abd Rahim
Universitas Negeri Makassar, Indonesia

Andi Hamsiah
Universitas Bosowa, Indonesia

ABSTRACT

Technology capabilities, relevant learning objectives, and how technology motivates students are misaligned. This necessitates a more integrated, flexible, and relevant approach to students' needs and situations. This research investigates how technological literacy affects language learners' extrinsic motivation. 102 students participated in the quantitative descriptive study. Extrinsic motivation is high for 72.5% of technology literacy. Awards, recognition, and practical results motivate most students to use technology instruction to improve their Indonesian language skills. They were more excited by interactive learning resources (61.8%, Purple). After employing language learning technologies, students felt confident explaining topics. This suggests that technological literacy increases extrinsic language learning

DOI: 10.4018/979-8-3373-5781-2.ch014

motivation, especially in digital education. Online platforms, apps, and interactive software make language learning more fun

INTRODUCTION

Within the framework of language instruction, extrinsic motivation is quite important in maintaining student involvement and dedication over the learning process. Unlike intrinsic motivation, which results from personal interest or the fun of learning itself, extrinsic motivation is driven by outside benefits, including grades, recognition, or future career prospects (Ramazani & Talebi, 2024). In controlled learning environments where students might not first feel a natural connection to the target language, these concrete rewards can be especially effective (Rosmayanti, 2024). For many students, particularly in settings where language learning is required, extrinsic motivators are crucial instruments to inspire and preserve their involvement and effort in the classroom (Takaloo et al., 2017).

Moreover, extrinsic drive might function as a link towards evolving intrinsic motivation throughout time. For example, many students start to see the personal and pragmatic benefits of learning a new language as they strive for excellent test results or satisfying curriculum requirements. This insight might inspire more self-confidence, a feeling of accomplishment, and finally a greater respect of the language and its cultural background. In this sense, extrinsic motivation lays the groundwork for more sustainable, self-directed learning practices, which are essential for long-term success in language education; it does more than just propel temporary effort (Ramalingam & Jiar, 2022). Under this kind of motivation, the focus is on outside incentives—that is, awards, accolades, or results that might be precisely counted. Students often need more help to overcome obstacles in their path of language acquisition (Takaloo et al., 2017). These difficulties could be a lack of confidence, difficulty understanding the subject, or limitations in always practising the language. Thanks to developments in electronic technology, new chances to assist students' extrinsic motivation have opened themselves (Amiryousefi et al., 2024; Imran et al., 2022; Sasabone et al., 2023).

Technology-based applications, tools, and devices abound that are meant to captivate students by offering engaging and entertaining elements (Kurniawati et al., 2023). Duolingo, for example, offers a gamified learning experience using a reward system comprising of badges, points, and daily reminders encouraging students to keep using their language abilities (Fattah et al., 2023). Using this function, a healthy competitive environment is generated, thereby inspiring students to reach their learning goals. Many other programs, such as Grammarly, use artificial intelligence to offer quick comments on grammar and writing style mistakes (Han et al., 2024).

Students can see their development over time by using features like general scores or progress analysis, therefore enabling them to feel that their efforts are being valued and acknowledged. Reminders sent to students in the form of consistent alerts showing their achievements or tips for improving their performance help them to keep their interest in the learning process. The usage of technology not only makes students excited about studying but also gives them incentives that inspire them to keep developing inside the curriculum (Liu, 2024; Sujarwo et al., 2020), Still, it's important to make sure that technology is used wisely and in balance so that this extrinsic incentive can also help the students become more intrinsically motivated to pick up the language. Technological literacy is the capacity of a human to understand, use effectively, and assess technology in a variety of contexts (Asdar et al., 2024; Wahid et al., 2025). Particularly in the sector of education, which includes the acquisition of linguistic abilities, literacy in technology has evolved into a critical talent in this age of digitalisation (Prior et al., 2016).

This capacity enables students to maximize technology as a learning tool, therefore improving their understanding of the topic and increasing their involvement in the whole learning process.

Regarding language acquisition, technology presents a great potential to assist students in their extrinsic motivation (Campillo-Ferrer et al., 2020). Gamification, virtual prizes, and automated feedback are examples of components that are frequently included in language learning apps and platforms that have been developed with innovation in mind (Pujolà & Appel, 2020). Students are provided with tangible incentives, such as earning badges, points, or acknowledgment for their learning progress, through the use of these features, which in turn encourages them to maintain their dedication to the acquisition of knowledge.

It is not enough for students to only use technology passively; they must also be able to understand how the technology runs, evaluate how successful it is, and apply it critically if technological literacy is to be included in language instruction (Ramazani & Talebi, 2024). This becomes a more and more crucial issue in a classroom atmosphere going more and more digital, where technology is not only a tool but also a necessary part of the learning process. High degrees of technical literacy help students to feel more confident and independent in their use of technology to achieve their learning goals. This then makes learning a language more interesting, efficient, and relevant to the demands of the here and now.

LITERATURE REVIEW

Language Learning Through Technology

The development of core competencies in a target language, which includes listening, speaking, reading, and writing, is the goal of language learning (Sasabone et al., 2022), which is a dynamic and diversified process that focuses on the acquisition of these competencies (Sujarwo et al., 2023). These capabilities make it possible to communicate effectively in a large number of different situations. The accumulation of vocabulary and grammar rules by rote repetition or simple memorization is not the only goal; there are other aspects to consider as well (Saputra, 2022). As an alternative, it is a comprehensive trip that integrates the development of linguistic proficiency and communicative competence. This trip is designed to prepare learners to use the language in a fluid and contextual manner in situations that are based on real-life situations (Sujarwo et al., 2024).

Supported by a wide range of materials and strategies tailored to the particular needs of the person learning a language, the road to become fluent in a language often includes using a variety of formal and informal learning approaches. Learning that is regarded formal usually occurs in settings that are organized, including classrooms or language courses, where experienced teachers lead students through curricula that are methodically scheduled (Imran et al., 2022). This method underlines the need of phonology, grammar, and syntax as well as the methodical application of language skills. Unlike formal education, which occurs in conventional environments, informal learning occurs outside of such settings through regular interactions, media consumption, or immerse events such travel or contact with native speakers. The natural acquisition of language is encouraged by these tactics in many different ways, one of which is by providing students with opportunities to experience the practical and real-world applications of language.

Technology has made substantial improvements in language acquisition by enhancing the accessibility and personalization of the learning process (Imran & Sulviana, 2022). Various digital platforms allow students to learn anytime and anywhere, according to their specific needs. This technology also enables the personalization of learning (Asia et al., 2024), offering students the option to pick their own speed and learning style (Muhammadiah et al., 2022). By way of illustration, students who want additional time to comprehend the subject matter can repeat the lesson without feeling any pressure, whilst students who can learn more quickly can effortlessly go to the subsequent level.

On the other hand, the degree of technical literacy that students possess is a significant factor in determining how effectively technology can enhance language acquisition. The students may have difficulty when it comes to exploiting the potential of technology to its maximum extent if they do not have proper technological literacy (Alavi et al., 2016). It is possible, for instance, that children will be unable to operate software or applications correctly, will struggle to comprehend particular functions, or may even have feelings of being overwhelmed by the numerous alternatives that are accessible.

This condition emphasizes the significance of acquiring technical literacy as an essential component of the process of language acquisition. When students have a strong command of literacy, they are not only able to use technology, but they are also able to make efficient use of the more advanced capabilities of technology to develop their language skills (Hadad et al., 2023). In the other way, should kids lack adequate reading ability, the technology meant to help them may turn into a barrier impeding their educational process. Thus, it is essential to equip students with the appropriate tools and instruction so that they may maximize the use of technology in their learning process.

The integration of information and communication technology (ICT) has caused major changes in language education (Warni et al., 2018). ICT makes it easier for teachers and students to gain access to a wide variety of authentic resources, which in turn increases the level of interaction (Asia et al., 2024) and engagement that occurs during the learning process (Redmond et al., 2018). Through the use of technology, the breadth of language instruction has been increased, and students are now engaged in a variety of interactive activities. The most recent developments in educational technology have brought about a revolution in the resources available for learning and instruction. In today's world, both teachers and students are dependent on a wide variety of electronic resources, both within and outside of the classroom.

Integration Technology Literacy

The practice of adding technological skills into educational settings to assist and reinforce learning is referred to as integrating technology literacy. It is becoming increasingly important for students to acquire technological literacy, which encompasses the skills necessary to comprehend, utilize, and efficiently assess technology (Özdere, 2023). The incorporation of technology into the learning process serves not only as a tool but also as an essential component that is aimed to improve the overall experience of the learner. For example, students who are literate in technology can make use of a variety of digital platforms, including language analysis software, online communication tools, and learning programs (Choukaier, 2024). This applies to language learning as well. Students can access interactive digital learning materials, receive immediate feedback, and autonomously monitor their progress thanks to this technology. Personalized learning, in which students can study according to their particular learning style, requirements, and speed, is supported by this progress.

Nevertheless, a deliberate strategy is necessary to successfully integrate technological literacy efforts. Ensuring that students not only have access to suitable technology but also acquire the skills required to make successful use of it is vital. Students must thus get continuous training and coaching so they may maximize technology as a learning tool instead of a source of entertainment. Teachers too must have a high-tech literacy while leading pupils through the process of grasping the possibilities of technology (Creely, 2024). If technology is applied correctly, learning might become something more interesting, dynamic, and relevant for the demands of the times. An key component of this integration is building a learning environment that supports the acquisition of abilities relevant in the twenty-first century, such as critical thinking, creativity, and cooperation. It is insufficient to only apply fresh technologies (Gumelar et al., 2022).

Educators also need to have a strong understanding of technology to guarantee that technology is utilized in the most effective manner possible in the classroom (Valtonen et al., 2018). They are not only responsible for teaching the topic but also for assisting students in exploring and exploiting the potential of technology in the learning process. This additional responsibility falls under their purview as educators. When teachers have a comprehensive understanding of the many digital tools available, they are better able to guide students in the use of technology in ways that effectively support their learning (Prior et al., 2016).

The role of instructors is extremely significant in the process of developing an educational setting that is both dynamic and engaging. Teachers who have a strong understanding of technology can make use of a variety of interactive digital platforms, such as learning programs, simulation software, or online collaboration tools, to boost student engagement (Nedungadi et al., 2023). Because of this, the process of learning will become more enjoyable, pertinent, and in line with the requirements of the generation that is constantly changing. Technology has the potential to create chances for learning that is more flexible and immersive, providing students with the option to study in a manner that is tailored to their individual preferences and speed

When it comes to incorporating technology into the educational process, however, it is not enough to simply accept new technology or use the most recent gear (Souza et al., 2021). Rather, the emphasis should be on creating an environment that supports the evolution of skills pertinent in the twenty-first century, such critical thinking, creativity, and teamwork. Technology not only lets students learn the knowledge required to grasp it, but it also helps them develop the skills needed to address world challenges, interact with others, and employ creativity (Gomez et al., 2022). In this particular situation, teachers serve as facilitators, guiding students through the process of including technology into their education and also helping them to understand how carefully and crucially technology might be used. By means of this approach, technology becomes not just a tool but also a part of a learning environment enabling students to be ready for a future marked by challenges and changes.

Extrinsic Motivation

Since its major influence on the learning process, motivation has long been regarded as the basic element of educational psychology. It serves as the impetus for students' involvement, tenacity, and effort towards meeting their academic goals (Ramalingam & Jiar, 2022). Whether internal or extrinsic, motivation affects the degree of effort students are ready to commit to their learning, therefore determining their academic performance, attitude towards education, and general success. In educational psychology, motivation is judged essential since it determines both the degree and the quality of learning. Motivated students are more likely to participate fully in the curriculum, study problems outside of surface-level inquiry, and take ownership of their educational route (Wannas & Alshaye, 2024). On the other hand, pupils without drive could have trouble focusing, show little enthusiasm in the topic, and might not be able to keep on in the face of challenges. From early childhood education to higher education, motivation is important in many different settings for education. Two theories of motivation—Self-Determination Theory (Deci & Ryan, 2000) and Expectancy-Value Theory (Deci & Ryan, 2000) and Expectancy-Value Theory (Eccles & Wigfield, 2002), offer important new perspectives on the several elements—spanning intrinsic interests, personal objectives, external rewards, and social influences—that affect students' motivation. Developing effective strategies to increase motivation and create an environment that supports major learning depends on an awareness of these qualities. An essential component of educational research, motivation helps teachers to improve their support for the academic activities of their pupils. Teachers can help students overcome challenges, interact more successfully with their tools, and finally achieve improved academic performance by helping them develop motivation (Attwell et al., 2024).

Unlike intrinsic drive, extrinsic motivation is driven by outside factors including rewards, praise, or avoidance of punishment. While extrinsic motivation comes from outside rewards, intrinsic motivation comes from inside and results from personal interest or enjoyment of the work. Depending on the degree of internalization inside a person's self-concept, the extrinsic drive can be divided into four kinds rather than being a monolithic force. The categories are external control, introjected control, identifiable control, and integrated control (Ramalingam & Jiar, 2022).

External Regulation

This is the fundamental form of extrinsic motivation. In external regulation, the individual is motivated chiefly by external incentives or sanctions. With little or no internalizing the underlying impulses, they engage in an activity hoping for a benefit or avoiding a negative outcome. A student might study assiduously to get good marks or to avoid the fallout from failing. External stimuli mostly control the impulse instead of personal principles or interests.

Regulated Intrusiveness

When people internalize specific outside cues while still motivated by pressure or guilt, they engage in introspection. This kind of drive results from a wish to avoid negative emotions, such as guilt or anxiety, not from a real intrinsic need. Notwithstanding their lack of interest in the topic, a student may study because of remorse about unmet expectations or fear of failing their parents. The incentive is still largely external, but it has been internalized to the degree that the person feels responsible for their behaviors.

Recognized Control

By now, the person has absorbed the importance of the action. Though they may not enjoy the activity itself, they still recognise its importance in helping to reach a more general goal. A student could study a difficult topic not out of fun but rather because it is important for their future career or personal goals. Though lacking inherent satisfaction, the action fits their values.

Integrated Regulation

Integrated regulation constitutes the pinnacle of extrinsic incentive. At this juncture, the activity is wholly assimilated into the individual's identity and personal principles. The person participates in the activity as it aligns with their overarching objectives, identity, or convictions. A student may engage in a demanding subject due to their passion for it and its significance to their identity or future goals. Despite being influenced by external objectives, the motivation is profoundly internalized, rendering it nearly indistinguishable from intrinsic motivation. As such, the four types of extrinsic motivation differ in their fit with a person's inherent goals and values.

More internalization of motivation corresponds with more chances of maintaining long-term involvement and endurance despite outside challenges. Extrinsic motivation is the drive to study that comes from outside sources, including credit for success, grades, or prizes. This motivation is frequently related to practical goals in the context of language learning. For example, the desire to enhance language skills to promote work chances, gain recognized certification, or get good grades are all examples of things that fall under this category. Students can maintain their interest in the learning process with the assistance of this drive, even if their motivation does not originate only from an innate desire to achieve knowledge (Liu et al., 2018).

There is a significant contribution that technology makes to the process of supporting and promoting this extrinsic motivation. As a result of technological advancements, numerous educational platforms are now in a position to provide rapid benefits and results that can be easily measured. One example of a gamification system that is available in language learning programs is Duolingo. This system allows students to earn badges, points, and alerts of achievements that are displayed immediately. Students will have a genuine feeling of accomplishment as a result of this feature, which serves as a drive for them to continue their education (Gea et al., 2024).

Students are also able to monitor their progress in real-time with the use of technology, which can be accomplished through the use of progress charts, scores, or automatic feedback. As a result of the quick gratification and the sense of recognition that these features provide for the efforts that have been made, students are encouraged to continue working toward reaching their educational objectives. Therefore, technology is not only a tool for learning, but it is also a mechanism that can be used to inspire students in an extrinsic manner by providing a reward system that is both measurable and physically felt.

Review of Previous Studies on AI in Language Learning

Digital literacy is crucial in enhancing students' educational experience in online or hybrid English for Specific Purposes (ESP) lessons. Integrating digital tools and interactive learning platforms enhances student engagement with the instructional material. This engagement, then, enhances their motivation, as students see a greater connection to pertinent material and innovative learning methods. Moreover, digital literacy enhances students' technical competencies, which are vital in the professional realm, equipping them to utilize technology in specific linguistic and communicative contexts as required by the business. Consequently, digital literacy not only improves the educational experience but also equips students with skills applicable in the professional environment (Kirovska-Simjanoska, 2022). This research enhances the comprehension of the impact of curiosity and excessive technology usage on digital literacy abilities, which are essential for addressing the difficulties of the Industrial Revolution 4.0 era (Hendriyani et al., 2023). It is possible for technology to serve as an efficient instrument for encouraging young people to read and for enhancing their comprehension of digital literacy requirements (Gea et al., 2024).

Problem Statements of Study

1. How do language learners perceive the role of technology literacy in enhancing their extrinsic motivation to learn a language?
2. How do students perceive the impact of their technology literacy on their ability to utilize digital resources for language learning?

METHOD

Research Design

This study aims to thoroughly investigate the conditions or phenomena connected to technological literacy and its influence on students' extrinsic motivation in language learning. This study focuses on gathering data that can provide an overview of how technological literacy teaching can boost students' extrinsic motivation to learn Indonesian. The research methodology employs a survey to gather data regarding the extent of students' extrinsic motivation in technological literacy teaching. Utilization of descriptive statistics to encapsulate main trends and patterns within the data (Arkkelin, 2014; Leavy, 2017). Data were obtained from Indonesian students' proficiency assessments utilizing a 5-point Likert Scale questionnaire. Data from the 5-point Likert Scale questionnaire revealed students' perceptions regarding technological literacy and its influence on students' extrinsic motivation in language learning. The data analysis techniques employed in this study included percentage, mean, and theme analysis (Creswell, 2013).

Participants

The participants of this study comprised 102 undergraduate students enrolled in the Regional Language and Literature Education Study Program at Universitas Negeri Makassar. The selected students participated in a program that combines language acquisition with technology, rendering them an optimal group for investigating the influence of technological literacy on their motivation. The cohort comprised students with diverse levels of technological experience, facilitating a comprehensive analysis of how technology-based instruction may affect their extrinsic motivation in language acquisition. The students, hailing from varied backgrounds, offered significant perspectives on the influence of technology on their participation in language learning activities. The selection of this particular program guaranteed that the participants were actively engaged in language learning, rendering their experiences and feedback significantly pertinent to the research aims.

Research Instruments

Extrinsic motivation was examined at both the beginning and conclusion of the trial to track any changes over time. This allowed for an assessment of whether the technological literacy teaching had a demonstrable influence on the student's motivation. The research instrument employed in this study enabled the acquisition of quantitative data, yielding significant insights into the impact of technology literacy education on students' extrinsic motivation. This data-driven methodology facilitated a more profound comprehension of the influence of technology-mediated learning on students' language acquisition behaviors in higher education. The findings offer practical implications for enhancing teaching practices in the digital era, demonstrating that technology integration in education can elevate students' external motivation and augment the efficacy of the language learning process.

Data Collection and Analysis

Data were gathered over a two-month duration. Extrinsic motivation was evaluated at the study's commencement and conclusion to gauge advancement. Surveys assessing engagement and confidence were conducted monthly. The data obtained from these instruments were evaluated utilizing descriptive statistics, including frequencies, means, and standard deviations, to present a comprehensive overview of the students' technology literacy and extrinsic incentive levels. Furthermore, correlational analysis may be employed to investigate the relationship between technological literacy and extrinsic motivation, thereby assessing whether elevated levels of technological literacy correlate with enhanced extrinsic motivation in language learning. The research tools facilitated the collection of both quantitative data, yielding a thorough comprehension of the impact of technology literacy teaching on extrinsic motivation in language learning among university students.

FINDINGS AND DISCUSSION

Students feel motivated to learn languages by using various learning technologies.

Figure 1. Students' external motivation in technology literacy instruction

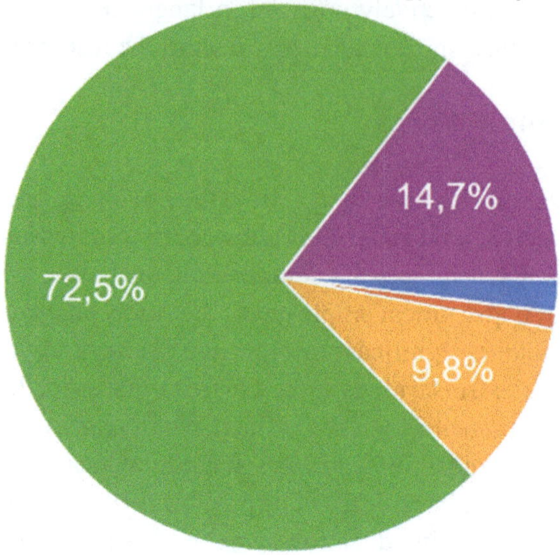

Figure 1 illustrates that 72.5% of students exhibit a high degree of external motivation in technology literacy instruction, indicating that external rewards or recognition significantly influence their engagement with the subject. 14.7% (purple) indicates that a limited proportion of students exhibit a moderate degree of external motivation, implying a degree of dependence on external influences, albeit less pronounced than that of the majority of 9.8% (orange) signifies that a smaller cohort has a less degree of external motivation, suggesting negligible impact from external variables on their technology literacy acquisition.

this statistic underscores the prevalence of external incentives among students in technological literacy teaching, indicating that prizes or external recognition serve as effective catalysts for engagement for the majority of learners.

External motivation data for students to improve their Indonesian language skills to be more confident in communicating using learning technology.

Figure 2. Students' confidence in communicating using learning technology

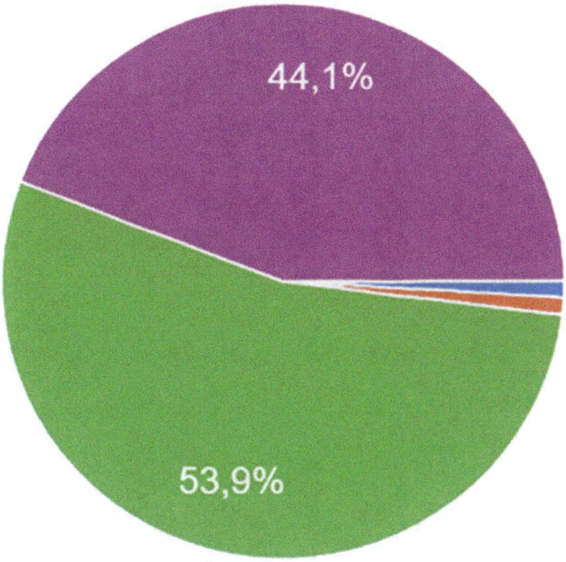

Based on Figure 2 which describes the data on external motivation of students to improve their Indonesian language skills to be more confident in communicating using learning technology, it shows that 61.8% (Purple) means that the majority of students show quite high external motivation. This shows that most students are motivated by external factors, such as awards, recognition, or practical results, to improve their Indonesian language skills using learning technology. There are 37.3% (Green) means that some students have lower external motivation. This group seems to be less dependent on external factors to encourage them to utilize learning technology for Indonesian language skills. Although students' degree of motivation varies, this statistic indicates that outside inspiration is crucial in motivating them to use learning technologies to raise their language competency.

When the learning content is interesting and interactive, students become more eager about picking Indonesian.

Figure 3. Students' enthusiasm for learning through technology

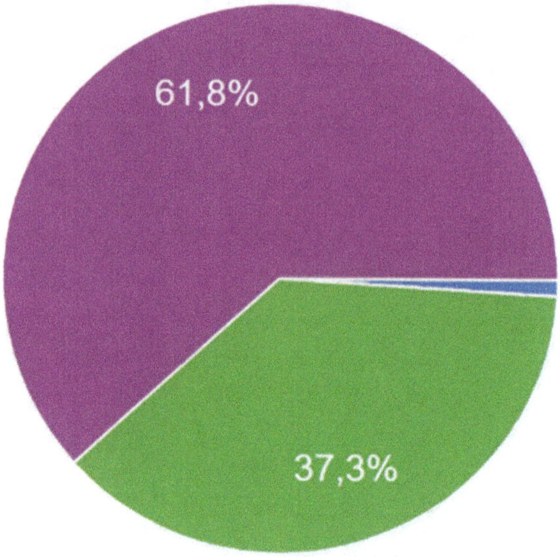

Figure 3 demonstrates the effect of engaging and interactive educational resources on students' motivation to learn Indonesian. There were 61.8% (Purple) indicates that a majority of students demonstrate elevated enthusiasm when the learning materials are engaging and participatory. This suggests that compelling content markedly enhances students' motivation and readiness to engage in language learning. There were 37.3% (Green): A smaller yet significant segment of students exhibits enthusiasm, albeit to a lesser degree than the majority. This group may gain from enhanced customization or modification of the materials.

The data underscores the significance of developing engaging and interactive educational materials to enhance student enthusiasm in their language acquisition process.

Students' mastery of Indonesian makes them feel able to convey ideas clearly and precisely after implementing language learning technology.

Figure 4. Language learning technology on students' proficiency in Indonesian

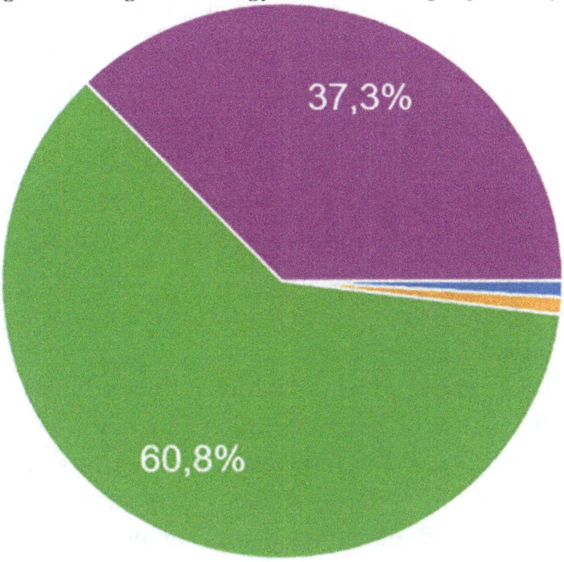

Figure 4 illustrates the impact of language learning technology on students' proficiency in Indonesian, emphasizing their capacity to articulate concepts effectively and accurately. 61.8% (Purple) indicates that the majority of students felt assured and competent in articulating concepts clearly and accurately following the use of language learning technologies. This indicates that technology significantly contributes to improving students' linguistic accuracy and articulation. 37.3% of students (Green) exhibit gains in their communication skills, but to a lesser extent than the majority. This suggests potential for enhanced optimization in the implementation of technology to meet varied learner requirements.

This study emphasises how well language learning technologies help students to acquire Indonesian and express themselves with accuracy and confidence.

In technology literacy instruction, students displayed more external motivation, meaning that their participation was much influenced by outside factors as incentives, recognition, or prizes. Whether as official recognition of their achievements or as symbolic awards like badges or diplomas, their obvious drive was shown in their readiness to use learning technology when outside incentives were provided. These data validate that external rewards enhance student participation and further motivate them to remain engaged in the learning process. In the realm of technology-driven education, this approach gains significance due to the numerous platforms and applications that provide reward systems to enhance user motivation.

Nonetheless, the efficacy of this method necessitates uniformity in the delivery of rewards. Effectively structured rewards that align with students' requirements can optimize the advantages of technology-enhanced learning (Wang, 2021). Furthermore, it is crucial to guarantee that the awards are inclusive and accessible to all students, preventing any feelings of marginalization or diminished motivation. Consequently, our findings emphasize the significance of external incentives in technology literacy education and highlight the necessity for educational institutions and instructors to develop learning programs that systematically incorporate these reward components. This seeks to establish a more captivating and dynamic educational atmosphere that fosters optimal student involvement in the contemporary digital age (Souza et al., 2021).

Students exhibited significant external motivation in their learning, mostly influenced by variables such as prizes, recognition, or tangible consequences attained through technology utilization. This motive underscores the significance of external forces as a primary catalyst for fostering student engagement. Incentives like badges, awards, or official acknowledgment of accomplishments have proven beneficial in motivating the majority of students to engage more actively in the learning process. Still, the statistics also revealed differences in student needs. Although most students are driven by outside variables, some groups call for distinct approaches. These strategies could help students to pursue learning for personal goals or improve their natural motivation using a feeling of personal satisfaction or self-accomplishment. The personalization of learning technology is crucial for meeting the demands of students who are not entirely motivated by external influences (Ramalingam & Jiar, 2022).

Although external rewards are important, it is essential to adopt a balanced learning strategy that combines external incentives with the cultivation of intrinsic desire to effectively engage all students. Personalization in technology applications, such as customizing learning tools or platforms to individual interests and needs, can effectively ensure that all students, irrespective of their external motivation levels, remain actively involved in the learning process.

Most students showed high enthusiasm for learning Indonesian, especially when the material presented was interesting and interactive. This indicates that the design of learning materials focused on active student engagement can positively influence their motivation. Interactive resources—group discussions, technology-driven assessments, creative projects—help to create a more dynamic and interesting learning environment, therefore encouraging ideal student involvement. This study emphasises how important teachers are in providing their students with both practical and interesting learning tools. Students who participate actively in the learning process—a participatory approach—have shown great success in raising their attention, emotional commitment, and drive to understand the given material.

Therefore, the production of engaging and interactive resources serves not only as a teaching tool but also as a means of creating a welcoming and inspiring classroom. This technique is gaining significance in the contemporary learning landscape, as technology may be employed to foster a more dynamic and impactful educational experience for students (Sun & Shi, 2024).

After the adoption of learning technology, the majority of students said that they felt more competent to articulate their thoughts clearly and precisely. This suggests a significant, positive impact of using technology on improving students' communication abilities, especially in the framework of studying Indonesian. Many students battled to properly arrange and express their ideas before technology arrived; yet, the availability of many technology-based learning tools and applications now gives them a lot of resources to improve their language abilities (Ata et al., 2021). Many of the features of educational technology help students to participate in more dynamic learning. Using tools that help students participate in group conversations, improve their points of view, and get quick comments helps them to engage in online cooperation.

Moreover, technology gives students the chance to consider and change the messages they want to transmit—text, images, music, or video—so helping them to choose the best media for their intended use. Technology's integration into education helps to raise student participation in the learning process (Tawafak et al., 2023). They rely not just on the material the teacher provides but also have access to a wealth of extra knowledge on reliable digital channels. This helps students to widen their horizons, improve their vocabulary, and polish their written or spoken skills in a more creative and joyful way. Students have many tools to methodically organise and express their ideas from technologies such word processing applications, online learning platforms, and language learning programs.

Moreover, educational technology substantially influences students' self-assurance. As students enhance their technological proficiency for articulating ideas, their confidence in communication increases (Gunuç & Babacan, 2017). This is also intimately connected to enhancing critical thinking abilities, as students are prompted to engage in more analytical thought when selecting pertinent information and the most effective means of articulating their ideas. This self-confidence affects their capacity for daily contacts, therefore transcending the classroom. One can say that the use of learning technologies is rather important for improving the accuracy, clarity, and confidence of students on learning the Indonesian language. Technology lets kids improve their creative ability, language proficiency, and clear communication skills (Ortikov & Akbarovich, 2024). Consequently, the integration of technology in education emphasizes not only the dissemination of knowledge but also the cultivation of students' competencies to navigate communication obstacles in an increasingly digital landscape.

SOLUTIONS AND RECOMMENDATIONS

Give students who are actively engaged in technology-based learning regular, clear incentives. Certificates, in-class awards, or other prizes meant to raise student drive are among the rewards available. Provide technology-driven challenges or contests meant to improve student involvement and inspire success. Using visual elements, tests, simulations, and movies will help to improve instructional materials by increasing student interaction with the topic. By incorporating gamification features or fostering healthy competition to sustain student attention and engagement. Offer training or tutorials for students to optimize their use of learning technology, particularly for those who feel inadequately supported by current technological tools. While external motivation is significant, it is crucial to cultivate students' intrinsic motivation by rendering learning more meaningful and pertinent to their lives. Facilitate chances for students to investigate subjects of personal interest and observe the tangible effects of technology in daily life. Facilitate autonomous exploration of themes and learning materials for students, utilizing digital resources or individual projects to enhance their sense of responsibility and autonomy in learning.

FUTURE RESEARCH DIRECTIONS

Examining the interaction between intrinsic and extrinsic motivation in technology-based learning calls for knowledge of how both kinds of motivation could interact and enhance one another to increase student participation and performance. In particular, in technology-enhanced environments, motivation in learning is crucial in determining students' involvement with the subject, their endurance through challenges, and their accomplishment of educational goals. These two kinds of drives have a complex interaction. Particularly in cases when students lack natural drive or knowledge of the technology, extrinsic benefits could first inspire them to use tools based on technology. Studies show that depending too much on outside rewards could compromise natural drive, sometimes known as the over-justification effect. When students get continuous praise for small accomplishments, for example, their focus could shift from learning for personal growth to learning only for the reward.

CONCLUSION

Particularly in digital learning, technological literacy increases extrinsic drive in language acquisition. Applications, online platforms, and interactive software make language learning be more interesting. These technologies can motivate students to keep learning and reach their objectives with their interesting material and outside incentives, including badges, points, and progress acknowledgement. Still, the success of this method depends on students technological literacy. Excellent, technologically literate students can learn better by using technology. Students who have little technological literacy could find it difficult to access, use, and maximise technologies. Teachers and institutions have therefore to provide technological literacy training and make technologies simply accessible and intelligible to their students. Furthermore, it is essential to have the help of schools and instructors. Teachers with technological literacy can assist their pupils in learning using technology. Educational institutions need appropriate technological infrastructure if they are to improve language acquisition via technology. More study is required to ascertain how effectively to include technological literacy into language acquisition and how it might be applied in many educational environments. This clarifies how best technology might increase extrinsic drive and language acquisition.

REFERENCES

Alavi, S. M., Borzabadi, D., & Dashtestani, R. (2016). Computer Literacy in Learning Academic English: Iranian EAP Students' and Instructors' Attitudes and Perspectives. *Teaching English with Technology, 16*(4), 56–77.

Amiryousefi, M., Daliranfirouz, E., Geld, R., & Nejad Ansari, D. (2024). Gamification and the Duality of Extrinsic and Intrinsic Motivation. *Journal of English Language Teaching and Learning, 16*(33). Advance online publication. DOI: 10.22034/elt.2024.60736.2615

Arkkelin, D. (2014). *Using SPSS to Understand Research and Data Analysis*. Psychology Curricular Materials.

Asdar, A., Hamsiah, A., Sujarwo, S., Lutfin, N., & Sukmawati, S. (2024). Integrative Approach for Reading Comprehension Espousing Information Communication Technology Literacy. [IJERE]. *International Journal of Evaluation and Research in Education, 13*(6), 4384. DOI: 10.11591/ijere.v13i6.29461

Ata, R., Yıldırım, K., İpek, P., & Ataş, U. C. (2021). Technology Integration of Turkish Elementary School: Teaching Literacy Skills in the Post-COVID-19 Era. *The European Educational Researcher, 4*(2), 193–207. DOI: 10.31757/euer.424

Attwell, G., Sl, P., Bekiaridis, G., & Karadog, A. (2024). *AI and Education: Agency, Motivation, Literacy and Democracy*. the European Union. https://www.researchgate.net/profile/Angela-Karadog/publication/385812674_AI_and_Education_Agency_Motivation_Literacy_and_Democracy/links/6736114168de5e5a3075d9bb/AI-and-Education-Agency-Motivation-Literacy-and-Democracy.pdf

Campillo-Ferrer, J.-M., Miralles-Martínez, P., & Sánchez-Ibáñez, R. (2020). Gamification in Higher Education: Impact on Student Motivation and the Acquisition of Social and Civic Key Competencies. *Sustainability (Basel), 12*(12), 4822. DOI: 10.3390/su12124822

Choukaier, D. (2024). Integrating AI In English Language Pedagogy: Innovations And Outcomes In Teaching English As Second /Foreign Language. *Educational Administration: Theory and Practice, 30*(5), 3811–3822. https://doi.org/Doi: DOI: 10.53555/kuey.v30i5.3538

Creely, E. (2024). Exploring the Role of Generative AI in Enhancing Language Learning: Opportunities and Challenges. *International Journal of Changes in Education, 1*(3), 158–167. DOI: 10.47852/bonviewIJCE42022495

Creswell, J. W. (2013). *Educational research: Planning, conducting, and evaluating quantitative and qualitative research* (Fourth Indian edition). PHI Learning Private Limited.

Fattah, H. A., Vadivel, B., Shaban, A. A., & Shanmugam, K. (2023). Enhancing English Language Education: The Impact of AI Integration in the Classroom. *The Journal of Humanistic Education and Development*, *5*(6), 116–123. DOI: 10.22161/jhed.5.6.15

Gea, N. S., Gulo, U. B. M., Bawamenewi, A., & Gulo, W. M. (2024). Motivating the Younger Generation in Reading: Integrating Technology in Understanding Digital Literacy. *International Journal of Educatio Elementaria and Psychologia*, *1*(3), 135–145. DOI: 10.70177/ijeep.v1i3.998

Gomez, F. C.Jr, Trespalacios, J., Hsu, Y.-C., & Yang, D. (2022). Exploring Teachers' Technology Integration Self-Efficacy through the 2017 ISTE Standards. *TechTrends*, *66*(2), 159–171. DOI: 10.1007/s11528-021-00639-z PMID: 34378007

Gumelar, G., Martadi, M., Rosalinda, I., Yudhaningrum, L., & Warju, W. (2022). *Computer Self-Efficacy, Task Value, Digital Literacy, Online Learning Perceptions on Indonesian University Students' Learning Satisfaction:* 1st World Conference on Social and Humanities Research (W-SHARE 2021), Makassar, Indonesia. DOI: 10.2991/assehr.k.220402.021

Gunuç, S., & Babacan, N. (2017). Technology integration in English language teaching and learning. Positioning English for Specific Purposes in an English Language Teaching Context. *The Journal Of Teaching English For Specific And Academic Purposes*, *5*(2), 349–358. DOI: 10.22190/JTESAP1702349G

Hadad, S., Watted, A., & Blau, I. (2023). Cultural background in digital literacy of elementary and middle school students: Self-appraisal versus actual performance. *Journal of Computer Assisted Learning*, *39*(5), 1591–1606. DOI: 10.1111/jcal.12820

Han, A., Zhou, X., Cai, Z., Han, S., Ko, R., Corrigan, S., & Peppler, K. A. (2024). Teachers, Parents, and Students' perspectives on Integrating Generative AI into Elementary Literacy Education. *Proceedings of the CHI Conference on Human Factors in Computing Systems*, 1–17. DOI: 10.1145/3613904.3642438

Hendriyani, Y., Anwar, M., Hidayat, H., Sabrina, E., Pardjono, P., & Saari, E. M. (2023). Factor Analysis of the Relationship of Curiosity and Device Addiction Through Motivation to Digital Literacy in the Context of Smart Learning. *Jurnal Pendidikan Vokasi*, *13*(3), 320–333. DOI: 10.21831/jpv.v13i3.62720

Imran, M. C., Khaliq Bashar, Budiarti Putri Uleng, Nina Ariani, Sukmawati, Suharti Siradjuddin, Sujarwo, & Irman. (2022). The Impact of Computer Assisted Language Learning (CALL) Technology on Indonesian Learners' Speaking Skills. *IJOLEH : International Journal of Education and Humanities, 1*(2), 183–189. DOI: 10.56314/ijoleh.v1i2.83

Kirovska-Simjanoska, D. (2022). Digital Literacy as a Tool for Fostering Engagement and Motivation in Online/Hybrid Esp Classes. *Journal of Teaching English for Specific and Academic Purposes, 10*(3), 533–546. DOI: 10.22190/JTESAP2203533K

Kurniawati, M. P., Mustakim, A., & Hudha, M. N. (2023). Peningkatan Motivasi dan Hasil Belajar Fisika Dengan Penggunaan Teknologi Dalam Pembelajaran dan Pendekatan Berdiferensiasi Pada Peserta Didik Kelas X – 1 SMA Negeri 6 Kediri Tahun Pelajaran 2022/2023. *Jurnal Pembelajaran, Bimbingan, dan Pengelolaan Pendidikan, 3*(6), 484–499. DOI: 10.17977/um065v3i62023p484-499

Leavy, P. (2017). *Research design: Quantitative, qualitative, mixed methods, arts-based and community-based participatory research approaches*. The Guilford Press.

Liu, K.-P., Tai, S.-J. D., & Liu, C.-C. (2018). Enhancing Language Learning Through Creation: The Effect of Digital Storytelling on Student Learning Motivation and Performance in a School English Course. *Educational Technology Research and Development, 66*(4), 913–935. DOI: 10.1007/s11423-018-9592-z

Liu, W. (2024). The Integration of ChatGPT in Language Education: Exploring Contexts, Assessing Impacts, and Unpacking Implications. In *In AI in Language Teaching, Learning, and Assessment* (pp. 1–21). IGI Global. https://www.igi-global.com/chapter/the-integration-of-chatgpt-in-language-education/339086

Mohseni Takaloo, N. (2017). English Literature Department, Payame Noor University, Tehran, Iran, Ahmadi, M. R., & English Language Department, Shahid Beheshti University, Tehran, Iran. The Effect of Learners' Motivation on Their Reading Comprehension Skill: A Literature Review. *International Journal of Research in English Education, 2*(3), 10–21. DOI: 10.18869/acadpub.ijree.2.3.10

Muhammadiah, M., Turibius Rahmat, S., Fatmawati, E., Bintoro Johan, A., & Jacob Pattiasina, P. (2022). How Teacher Creativity Brings to Indonesian Language Teaching Innovations in The Multimedia Era. *Nazhruna: Jurnal Pendidikan Islam, 5*(1), 169–172. DOI: 10.31538/nzh.v5i1.2003

Nedungadi, P., Devenport, K., Sutcliffe, R., & Raman, R. (2023). Towards a Digital Learning Ecology to Address the Grand Challenge in Adult Literacy. *Interactive Learning Environments, 31*(1), 383–396. DOI: 10.1080/10494820.2020.1789668

Ortikov, U., & Akbarovich, B. D. (2024). New Trends. In *Integrating Digital Literacies In Language Teaching*. Science Promotion.

Özdere, M. (2023). The Integration of Artificial Intelligence in English Education: Opportunities and Challenges. [LET Journal]. *Language Education & Technology, 3*(2), 137–172.

Prior, D. D., Mazanov, J., Meacheam, D., Heaslip, G., & Hanson, J. (2016). Attitude, digital literacy and self efficacy: Flow-on effects for online learning behavior. *The Internet and Higher Education, 29*, 91–97. DOI: 10.1016/j.iheduc.2016.01.001

Pujolà, J.-T., & Appel, C. (2020). Gamification for Technology-Enhanced Language Teaching and Learning. In Kruk, M., & Peterson, M. (Eds.), (pp. 93–111). Advances in Educational Technologies and Instructional Design. IGI Global., DOI: 10.4018/978-1-7998-2591-3.ch005

Ramalingam, K., & Jiar, Y. K. (2022). Influence of Intrinsic and Extrinsic Motivation in Learning Among Primary School Students. *Central Asia and The Caucasus, 23*(1). Advance online publication. DOI: 10.37178/ca-c.23.1.186

Ramazani, A., & Talebi, Z. (2024). A Consideration of the Roles of Preservice Teachers' Information Literacy, Digital Literacy, and Ict Self-Efficacy in Teaching. [TEJ]. *Technology of Education Journal, 18*(1). Advance online publication. DOI: 10.22061/tej.2024.10254.2979

Redmond, P., Heffernan, A., Abawi, L., Brown, A., & Henderson, R. (2018). An Online Engagement Framework for Higher Education. *Online Learning : the Official Journal of the Online Learning Consortium, 22*(1). Advance online publication. DOI: 10.24059/olj.v22i1.1175

Rosmayanti, V. (2024). Addressing English Language Anxiety in High School Students. *EDULEC : Education, Language, and Culture Journal, 4*(3), 351–361. DOI: 10.56314/edulec.v4i3.275

Saputra, W. A.Wongso Adi Saputra. (2022). Analyzing Context in English as Lingua Franca (ELF): A Discourse Analysis in an Indonesian Higher Education Institution (HEI). [IJOLEH]. *International Journal of Education and Humanities, 1*(1), 18–29. DOI: 10.56314/ijoleh.v1i1.36

Sasabone, L. (2023). Applying Google Classroom As An Instructional Technology Media In Improving Students' Reading For English For Specific Purposes (ESP). *EDULEC : Education. Language And Culture Journal, 3*(1), 110–119. DOI: 10.56314/edulec.v3i1.123

Sasabone, L., Limbong, S., Pongpalilu, F., Soepriadi, & Jubhari. (2022). Utilizing WhatsApp As An Educational Technology Tool In Improving Students' Speaking For ESP Instruction. *EDULEC : Education, Language, and Culture Journal, 2*(2). https://doi.org/DOI: 10.56314/edulec.v2i2

Souza, R. D., Parveen, R., Chupradit, S., Velasco, L. G., Tabuena, A. C., Pentang, J. T., & Ventayen, R. J. M. (2021). Language Teachers' Pedagogical Orientations in Integrating Technology in the Online Classroom: Its Effect on Students Motivation and Engagement. *Turkish Journal of Computer and Mathematics Education, 12*. https://papers.ssrn.com/sol3/papers.cfm?abstract_id=3844678

Sujarwo, Abdul Hakim Yassi, & Abbas, Herawaty, & Harlinah sahib. (2024). An Interactive-Based E-Module of Translation Technology of Blended and Online Learning to Improve Autonomous Learning. [TSRJ]. *The Seyreport Journal, 19*(06), 193–209. DOI: 10.5281/ZENODO.11547317

Sujarwo, S., Asdar, A., Sabillah, B. M., Sukmawati, S., Akhiruddin, A., & Muh. Syata, W. (2023). Innovation In English Language Learning Model Based Digital Literacy To Construct Young Learners' Character. *Ethical Lingua. Journal of Language Teaching and Literature, 10*(2). Advance online publication. DOI: 10.30605/25409190.640

Sujarwo, S., Sukmawati, S., Asdar, A., Siradjuddin, S., & Ariani, N. (2020). University Students' Perception on the Verbal Interaction through WhatsApp Chat Group. *Al-Ta Lim Journal, 27*(3), 250–257. DOI: 10.15548/jt.v27i3.633

Sulviana, Muhammad Chairil Imran & Sulviana. (2022). Using BBC Web-Based Learning Courses to Improve Vocational High School (VHS) Students' Speaking Skill. *EDULEC : Education, Language, and Culture Journal, 2*(1), 94–100. DOI: 10.56314/edulec.v2i1.34

Sun, W., & Shi, H. (2024). Fostering Success in Online English Education: Exploring the Effects of ICT Literacy, Online Learning Self-Efficacy, and Motivation on Deep Learning. *Education and Information Technologies, 29*(18), 24899–24920. DOI: 10.1007/s10639-024-12827-4

Tawafak, R. M., Al-Obaydi, L. H., Klimova, B., & Pikhart, M. (2023). Technology Integration of Using Digital Gameplay for Enhancing Efl College Students' Behavior Intention. *Contemporary Educational Technology, 15*(4), ep452. DOI: 10.30935/cedtech/13454

Valtonen, T., Kukkonen, J., Kontkanen, S., Mäkitalo-Siegl, K., & Sointu, E. (2018). Differences in pre-service teachers' knowledge and readiness to use ICT in education. *Journal of Computer Assisted Learning, 34*(2), 174–182. DOI: 10.1111/jcal.12225

Wahid, A., Afni, N., & Sujarwo, S. (2025). Promoting Learners' Autonomy through Metacognitive, Higher-Order Thinking Skills and Digital Literacy of Indonesian Private Universities. *Educational Process International Journal, 16*(1). Advance online publication. DOI: 10.22521/edupij.2025.16.204

Wang, Y. (2021). In-Service Teachers' Perceptions of Technology Integration and Practices in a Japanese University Context. *The JALT CALL Journal, 17*(1), 45–71. DOI: 10.29140/jaltcall.v17n1.377

Wannas, A. S., & Alshaye, R. A. (2024). Integration of Intrinsic and Extrinsic Motivation in Second Language Acquisition: Magnetism as a Proposed Theory. *World Journal of English Language, 14*(4), 76. DOI: 10.5430/wjel.v14n4p76

Warni, S., Aziz, T. A., & Febriawan, D. (2018). The Use of Technology in English as a Foreign Language Learning Outside the Classroom: An Insight into Learner Autonomy. *LLT Journal: A Journal on Language and Language Teaching, 21*(2), 148–156. DOI: 10.24071/llt.v21i2.1259

Compilation of References

7. principles on responsible AI use in education. (2024). https://www.weforum.org/agenda/2024/01/ai-guidance-school-responsible-use-in-education/

A Policy Agenda for Responsible Progress in Artificial Intelligence. (n.d.). Retrieved December 30, 2024, from https://storage.googleapis.com/gweb-uniblog-publish-prod/documents/A_Policy_Agenda_for_Responsible_Progress_in_Artificial_Intelligence.pdf

Abadi, T. & Mebratie, A. D. (2021). Cost of treating maternal complications and associated factors in Mekelle General Hospital, northern Ethiopia. Risk management and healthcare policy. tandfonline.com

Abbas, A. F., Jusoh, A., Mas'od, A., Alsharif, A. H., & Ali, J. (2022). Bibliometrix analysis of information sharing in social media. *Cogent Business & Management*, *9*(1), 2016556. DOI: 10.1080/23311975.2021.2016556

Abdeen, F. N., Fernando, T., Kulatunga, U., Hettige, S., & Ranasinghe, K. A. (2021). Challenges in multi-agency collaboration in disaster management: A Sri Lankan perspective. [sciencedirect.com]. *International Journal of Disaster Risk Reduction*, *62*, 102399. DOI: 10.1016/j.ijdrr.2021.102399

Abdi, A. W., Ridha, S., Yunus, M., Kamil, P. A., Safiah, I., & Gadeng, A. N. (2021). Assessing the Effectiveness of Geography-based Online Learning During the Covid-19 Pandemic in Higher Education. In Geosfera Indonesia (Vol. 6, Issue 3, p. 319). https://doi.org/DOI: 10.19184/geosi.v6i3.25811

Abdul, R. K., Muhammad, I. H., & Zakki, Ah. F., M. Yunus, A. B., Muhaemin, M., & Arifuddin, A. (2024). Exploring The Rationality of Religious-Rational Islamic Thinkers Towards The Compatibility of The Islamic Education System (Vol. 13, Issue 2, p. 187). https://jurnal.uin-antasari.ac.id/index.php/jtjik/article/view/13638

AbdulKareem, A. K., & Oladimeji, K. A. (2024). Cultivating the digital citizen: trust, digital literacy and e-government adoption. Transforming Government: People. *Process and Policy*, *18*(2), 270–286.

Abdurrahman, A. B. S. (2020). the Application of «Nemo» Artificial Intelligence in Arabic Language Learning in the 4.0 Revolution Era At Al-Khalifah Islamic Boarding School Cibubur. learning, 6(1).

Aben, T. A., van der Valk, W., Roehrich, J. K., & Selviaridis, K. (2021). Managing information asymmetry in public–private relationships undergoing a digital transformation: The role of contractual and relational governance. [emerald.com]. *International Journal of Operations & Production Management*, *41*(7), 1145–1191. DOI: 10.1108/IJOPM-09-2020-0675

Aburizaizah, S. J. (2022). The role of quality assurance in Saudi higher education institutions. International Journal of Educational Research Open. sciencedirect.com

Addimando, F. (2024). Emotional Intelligence in Negotiation. In Negotiation Neuroscience: The Brain Science Behind Business Deals (pp. 61-76). Cham: Springer Nature Switzerland. DOI: 10.1007/978-3-031-69754-8_3

Adeosun, O. T., Shittu, A. I., & Owolabi, T. J. (2022). University internship systems and preparation of young people for world of work in the 4th industrial revolution. Rajagiri Management Journal. emerald.com

Adewumi, A. (2022). Built heritage and planning laws in Africa: the Nigerian Experience. In Built Heritage (Vol. 6, Issue 1). Springer Nature. https://doi.org/DOI: 10.1186/s43238-022-00052-2

Afrilyasanti, R., Suhartoyo, E., & Widiati, U. (2025). Researching the use of e-portfolios to promote students thinking in digital age: A qualitative action study. *Interactive Technology and Smart Education*, *22*(1), 25–42. DOI: 10.1108/ITSE-08-2023-0167

Afzal, A., Khan, S., Daud, S., Ahmad, Z., & Butt, A. (2023). Addressing the Digital Divide: Access and Use of Technology in Education. In journal of social sciences review (Vol. 3, Issue 2, p. 883). https://doi.org/DOI: 10.54183/jssr.v3i2.326

Aguerre, C. & Bonina, C. (2024). Open government, civic tech and digital platforms in Latin America: A governance study of Montevideo's urban app 'Por Mi Barrio'. Information Systems Journal.

Aguilera, R. V., De Massis, A., Fini, R., & Vismara, S. (2024). Organizational goals, outcomes, and the assessment of performance: Reconceptualizing success in management studies. [wiley.com]. *Journal of Management Studies*, *61*(1), 1–36. DOI: 10.1111/joms.12994

Ahmad, I., & Islam, M. R. (2024). Empowerment and participation: Key strategies for inclusive development. In Building Strong Communities: Ethical Approaches to Inclusive Development (pp. 47-68). Emerald Publishing Limited. [HTML]

Ahmad, S., Umirzakova, S., Mujtaba, G., Amin, M., & Whangbo, T. K. (2023). Education 5.0: Requirements, Enabling Technologies, and Future Directions. In arXiv (Cornell University). Cornell University. https://doi.org//arxiv.2307.15846DOI: 10.48550

Ahmadi, M. J., Fadil, M., & Miri, M. A. (2021). Feedback loops in teacher professional development: A qualitative study in Herat Province of Afghanistan. Cogent Education. tandfonline.com

Ahmed, I., Asif, M., Alhelou, H. H., & Khalid, M. (2024). A review on enhancing energy efficiency and adaptability through system integration for smart buildings. [HTML]. *Journal of Building Engineering*.

Ahsan, M. J. (2025). Cultivating a culture of learning: The role of leadership in fostering lifelong development. [HTML]. *The Learning Organization*, *32*(2), 282–306. DOI: 10.1108/TLO-03-2024-0099

Ahuja, A., & Sah, A. (2021). Artificial Intelligence in Education: Future Prospects and Challenges. *International Journal of Educational Technology*, *15*(3), 101–115.

Akdim, K., Casaló, L. V., & Flavián, C. (2022). The role of utilitarian and hedonic aspects in the continuance intention to use social mobile apps. [sciencedirect.com]. *Journal of Retailing and Consumer Services*, *66*, 102888. DOI: 10.1016/j.jretconser.2021.102888

Akgün, S., & Greenhow, C. (2021). Artificial intelligence in education: Addressing ethical challenges in K-12 settings [Review of Artificial intelligence in education: Addressing ethical challenges in K-12 settings]. AI and Ethics, 2(3), 431. Springer Nature. https://doi.org/DOI: 10.1007/s43681-021-00096-7

Akinwalere, S. N., & Ivanov, V. (2022). Artificial Intelligence in Higher Education: Challenges and Opportunities. *Border Crossing*, *12*(1), 1–15. Advance online publication. DOI: 10.33182/bc.v12i1.2015

Akomea-Frimpong, I., Jin, X., & Osei-Kyei, R. (2022). Mapping studies on sustainability in the performance measurement of public-private partnership projects: A systematic review. Sustainability. mdpi.com

Akram, H., Abdelrady, A. H., Al-Adwan, A. S., & Ramzan, M. (2022). Teachers' perceptions of technology integration in teaching-learning practices: A systematic review. [frontiersin.org]. *Frontiers in Psychology, 13*, 920317. DOI: 10.3389/fpsyg.2022.920317 PMID: 35734463

Al Husseiny, F. A., Saab, J. M., Abdallah, M. H., & Wehbe, N. H. (2023). Digital citizenship and digital literacy: An evolving trend. In *Innovations in digital instruction through virtual environments* (pp. 205–220). IGI Global. DOI: 10.4018/978-1-6684-7015-2.ch012

Al-Adwan, A. S., Albelbisi, N. A., Hujran, O., Al-Rahmi, W. M., & Alkhalifah, A. (2021). Developing a holistic success model for sustainable e-learning: A structural equation modeling approach. [mdpi.com]. *Sustainability (Basel), 13*(16), 9453. DOI: 10.3390/su13169453

Alalawi, K., Athauda, R., Chiong, R., & Renner, I. (2025). Evaluating the student performance prediction and action framework through a learning analytics intervention study. [springer.com]. *Education and Information Technologies, 30*(3), 2887–2916. DOI: 10.1007/s10639-024-12923-5

Alam, A., & Mohanty, A. (2023). Educational technology: Exploring the convergence of technology and pedagogy through mobility, interactivity, AI, and learning tools. Cogent Engineering. tandfonline.com

Alam, A., & Mohanty, A. (2023, January). From bricks to clicks: The potential of big data analytics for revolutionizing the information landscape in higher education sector. In International Conference on Data Management, Analytics & Innovation (pp. 721-732). Singapore: Springer Nature Singapore. [HTML] DOI: 10.1007/978-981-99-1414-2_51

Alami, H., Rivard, L., Lehoux, P., Hoffman, S. J., Cadeddu, S. B. M., Savoldelli, M., Samri, M., Ahmed, M. A. A., Fleet, R., & Fortin, J. (2020). Artificial intelligence in health care: laying the Foundation for Responsible, sustainable, and inclusive innovation in low- and middle-income countries. In Globalization and Health (Vol. 16, Issue 1). BioMed Central. https://doi.org/DOI: 10.1186/s12992-020-00584-1

Alamleh, H. (2020). Private and Secure Students' Data Sharing in Educational Systems (Vol. 71, p. 158). https://doi.org/DOI: 10.1109/econf51404.2020.9385450

Alanzi, T. (2021). A review of mobile applications available in the app and google play stores used during the COVID-19 outbreak. *Journal of Multidisciplinary Healthcare*, •••, 45–57.

Alasadi, E. A., & Baiz, C. R. (2023). Generative AI in education and research: Opportunities, concerns, and solutions. *Journal of Chemical Education*, *100*(8), 2965–2971. DOI: 10.1021/acs.jchemed.3c00323

Alavi, S. M., Borzabadi, D., & Dashtestani, R. (2016). Computer Literacy in Learning Academic English: Iranian EAP Students' and Instructors' Attitudes and Perspectives. *Teaching English with Technology*, *16*(4), 56–77.

Al-Besher, A. & Kumar, K. (2022). Use of artificial intelligence to enhance e-government services. Measurement: sensors.

Aldboush, H. H. H. & Ferdous, M. (2023). Building trust in fintech: an analysis of ethical and privacy considerations in the intersection of big data, AI, and customer trust. International Journal of Financial Studies. mdpi.com

Aldosari, S. A. M. (2020). The Future of Higher Education in the Light of Artificial Intelligence Transformations. *International Journal of Higher Education*, *9*(3), 145. Advance online publication. DOI: 10.5430/ijhe.v9n3p145

Aldoseri, A., Al-Khalifa, K. N., & Hamouda, A. M. (2023). Re-thinking data strategy and integration for artificial intelligence: concepts, opportunities, and challenges. Applied Sciences. mdpi.com

Alenezi, M. (2023). Digital learning and digital institution in higher education. Education Sciences. mdpi.com

Alenezi, M., Akour, M., & Alfawzan, L. (2024). Evolving Microcredential Strategies for Enhancing Employability: Employer and Student Perspectives. Education Sciences. mdpi.com

Alenezi, N. & Alfaleh, M. (2024). Enhancing digital citizenship education in Saudi Arabian elementary schools: designing effective activities for curriculum integration. Frontiers in Education.

Al-Ghonmein, A. M., & Al-Moghrabi, K. G. (2024). The potential of ChatGPT technology in education: advantages, obstacles and future growth. IAES International Journal of Artificial Intelligence (IJ-AI), 13(2), 1206-1213.

Alharbi, L. A. (2023). A Systematic Literature Review on AI Algorithms and Techniques Adopted by e-Learning Platforms for Psychological and Emotional States. In International Journal of Advanced Computer Science and Applications (Vol. 14, Issue 2). Science and Information Organization. . 2023.0140254DOI: 10.14569/IJACSA.2023.0140254

Aliabadi, R., Singh, A., & Wilson, J. E. (2023). Transdisciplinary AI Education: The Confluence of Curricular and Community Needs in the Instruction of Artificial Intelligence. In Lecture notes on data engineering and communications technologies (p. 137). Springer International Publishing. DOI: 10.1007/978-981-99-7947-9_11

Ali, F., & Haapasalo, H. (2023). Development levels of stakeholder relationships in collaborative projects: Challenges and preconditions. [emerald.com]. *International Journal of Managing Projects in Business*, *16*(8), 58–76. DOI: 10.1108/IJMPB-03-2022-0066

Ali, S., Bhutta, S. M., Ahmad, S., Ansari, A. N., Ahmed, A., & Qadir, Y. (2024). PROTOCOL: Effectiveness of public-private partnerships on educational access and quality of primary and secondary schooling in low-and middle-income countries: A systematic review. [wiley.com]. *Campbell Systematic Reviews*, *20*(2), e1385. DOI: 10.1002/cl2.1385 PMID: 38444642

Ali, T., Al-Khalidi, M., & Al-Zaidi, R. (2024). Information security risk assessment methods in cloud computing: Comprehensive review. [tandfonline.com]. *Journal of Computer Information Systems*, •••, 1–28. DOI: 10.1080/08874417.2024.2329985

Alkhabra, Y. A., Ibrahem, U. M., & Alkhabra, S. A. (2023). Augmented reality technology in enhancing learning retention and critical thinking according to STEAM program. [nature.com]. *Humanities & Social Sciences Communications*, *10*(1), 1–10. DOI: 10.1057/s41599-023-01650-w

Allmann, K., & Radu, R. (2023). Digital footprints as barriers to accessing e-government services. *Global Policy*, *14*(1), 84–94.

Almaiah, M. A., Alfaisal, R., Salloum, S. A., Hajjej, F., Shishakly, R., Lutfi, A., Alrawad, M., Al Mulhem, A., Alkhdour, T., & Al-Maroof, R. S. (2022). Measuring institutions' adoption of artificial intelligence applications in online learning environments: Integrating the innovation diffusion theory with technology adoption rate. [mdpi.com]. *Electronics (Basel)*, *11*(20), 3291. DOI: 10.3390/electronics11203291

Almalki, F. A., Alsamhi, S. H., Sahal, R., Hassan, J., Hawbani, A., Rajput, N. S., Saif, A., Morgan, J., & Breslin, J. (2023). Green IoT for eco-friendly and sustainable smart cities: Future directions and opportunities. *Mobile Networks and Applications*, *28*(1), 178–202. DOI: 10.1007/s11036-021-01790-w

Almarri, K., & Boussabaine, H. (2025). Critical success factors for public–private partnerships in smart city infrastructure projects. [HTML]. *Construction Innovation*, *25*(2), 224–247. DOI: 10.1108/CI-04-2022-0072

Almeida, D., Shmarko, K., & Lomas, E. (2022). The ethics of facial recognition technologies, surveillance, and accountability in an age of artificial intelligence: A comparative analysis of US, EU, and UK regulatory frameworks. *AI and Ethics*, *2*(3), 377–387.

Alnahdi, G. H., Alwadei, A., & Alharbi, N. (2024). Enhancing special education programs' curricula for students with intellectual disabilities in saudi arabia: A call for personalized approaches and inclusive practices. [HTML]. *Research in Developmental Disabilities*, *151*, 104785. DOI: 10.1016/j.ridd.2024.104785 PMID: 38941691

Alomar, M. (2025). Inclusivity and diversity on massive open online course platforms: a multicultural evaluation of NovoEd. Journal for Multicultural Education. emerald.com

Alotaibi, N. S. & Alshehri, A. H. (2023). Prospers and obstacles in using artificial intelligence in Saudi Arabia higher education institutions—The potential of AI-based learning outcomes. Sustainability. mdpi.com

Alrasheed, K. A., Albader, H. B., Khalafallah, A. M., Gerges, M., & Alkandari, F. A. (2024). Framework for PPP partner selection in K-12 educational facility procurement. [sciencedirect.com]. *Journal of Engineering Research*, *12*(3), 369–378. DOI: 10.1016/j.jer.2023.11.025

Althibyani, H. A. & Al-Zahrani, A. M. (2023). Investigating the effect of students' knowledge, beliefs, and digital citizenship skills on the prevention of cybercrime. Sustainability.

Al-Zahrani, A. M., & Alasmari, T. M. (2025). A comprehensive analysis of AI adoption, implementation strategies, and challenges in higher education across the Middle East and North Africa (MENA) region. [HTML]. *Education and Information Technologies*, *30*(8), 11339–11389. DOI: 10.1007/s10639-024-13300-y

Amiryousefi, M., Daliranfirouz, E., Geld, R., & Nejad Ansari, D. (2024). Gamification and the Duality of Extrinsic and Intrinsic Motivation. *Journal of English Language Teaching and Learning*, *16*(33). Advance online publication. DOI: 10.22034/elt.2024.60736.2615

Andersson, C. (2022). Smartphones and online search: shifting frames in the everyday life of young people. Information and learning sciences. emerald.com

Androutsopoulou, M., Askounis, D., Carayannis, E. G., & Zotas, N. (2024). Leveraging AI for Enhanced eGovernment: Optimizing the Use of Open Governmental Data.. *Journal of the Knowledge Economy*, 1–36. DOI: 10.1007/s13132-024-02317-w

Angrist, N., Evans, D. K., Filmer, D., Glennerster, R., Rogers, H., & Sabarwal, S. (2024). How to improve education outcomes most efficiently? A review of the evidence using a unified metric [Review of How to improve education outcomes most efficiently? A review of the evidence using a unified metric]. Journal of Development Economics, 172, 103382. Elsevier BV. DOI: 10.1016/j.jdeveco.2024.103382

Anyanwu, E. C., Maduka, C. P., Ayo-Farai, O., Okongwu, C. C., & Daraojimba, A. I. (2024). Maternal and child health policy: A global review of current practices and future directions. [semanticscholar.org]. *World Journal of Advanced Research and Reviews, 21*(2), 1770–1781. DOI: 10.30574/wjarr.2024.21.2.0306

Apollo, A. & Mbah, M. F. (2021). Challenges and opportunities for climate change education (Cce) in East Africa: A critical review. Climate. mdpi.com

Apriliani, D. (2024). *Penggunaan Artificial Intelligence dalam Pembelajaran Bahasa Indonesia*. DIKBASTRA: Jurnal Pendidikan Bahasa dan Sastra 7(1), DOI: 10.22437/dikbastra.v7i1.33262

Aqil, Z., & Jameel, A. (2023). Mitigating Communication Obstacles Presented by Non-Verbal Factors. In Panjwani, D., Sahrish, F., & Akhlaq, N. (Eds.), *Crucial Communication: Improving Conversations at Workplace* (pp. 9–16).

Ardiansyah. (2022). VIRTUAL SYNCHRONOUS LEARNING AKUNTANSI MANUFAKTUR DALAM MENDORONG EFEKTIVITAS PEMBELAJARAN: Virtual Synchronous Learning of Manufacturing Accounting In Supporting Learning Effectiveness. Jurnal Teknodik, 49–68. https://doi.org/10.32550/teknodik.vi.871

Arkkelin, D. (2014). *Using SPSS to Understand Research and Data Analysis*. Psychology Curricular Materials.

Armanda, L. (2022). *Multimodal Large Language Models for Inclusive Collaboration Learning Tasks*. Proceedings of the 2022 Conference of the North American Chapter of the Association for Computational Linguistics: Human Language Technologies: Student Research Workshop, https://doi.org/ srw.26DOI: 10.18653/v1/2022.naacl

Artificial Intelligence and the Future of Teaching and Learning. (2023). https://tech.ed.gov/files/2023/05/ai-future-of-teaching-and-learning-report.pdf

Artificial Intelligence and the Future of Teaching and Learning. (n.d.). Retrieved December 31, 2024, from https://www2.ed.gov/documents/ai-report/ai-report.pdf

Artificial Intelligence in Higher Education: Applications, Promise and Perils, and Ethical Questions. (2019). https://er.educause.edu/articles/2019/8/artificial-intelligence-in-higher-education-applications-promise-and-perils-and-ethical-questions

Aruah, D. E., Henshaw, Y., & Walsh-Childers, K. (2023). Tweets that matter: Exploring the solutions to maternal mortality in the United States discussed by advocacy organizations on twitter. [mdpi.com]. *International Journal of Environmental Research and Public Health*, *20*(9), 5617. DOI: 10.3390/ijerph20095617 PMID: 37174137

Asdar, A., Hamsiah, A., Sujarwo, S., Lutfin, N., & Sukmawati, S. (2024). Integrative Approach for Reading Comprehension Espousing Information Communication Technology Literacy. [IJERE]. *International Journal of Evaluation and Research in Education*, *13*(6), 4384. DOI: 10.11591/ijere.v13i6.29461

Asimakopoulos, G., Antonopoulou, H., Giotopoulos, K., & Halkiopoulos, C. (2025). Impact of Information and Communication Technologies on Democratic Processes and Citizen Participation. *Societies (Basel, Switzerland)*, *15*(2), 40. DOI: 10.3390/soc15020040

Aslantekin Özçoban, F., Ergün, S., & Erkal Aksoy, Y. (2022). Effects of health literacy education on adaptation to pregnancy, self-efficacy, fear of childbirth and health literacy in Turkish pregnant women: A randomized, controlled trial. [HTML]. *Health & Social Care in the Community*, *30*(2), e537–e549. DOI: 10.1111/hsc.13690 PMID: 34957621

Aswani, R. S., Sajith, S., & Bhat, M. Y. (2021). Realigning India's Vietnam policy through cooperative sustainable development: A geostrategic counterbalancing to China in Indo-Pacific. *East Asia (Piscataway, N.J.)*, 1–19. PMID: 34276182

Ata, R., Yıldırım, K., İpek, P., & Ataş, U. C. (2021). Technology Integration of Turkish Elementary School: Teaching Literacy Skills in the Post-COVID-19 Era. *The European Educational Researcher*, *4*(2), 193–207. DOI: 10.31757/euer.424

Atifnigar, H., Israr, S. W., Khanjar, I., & Hameed, S. A. B. A. (2023). Impacts of Culture on Classroom Participation Among Undergraduate EFL Learners in Afghanistan. In European Journal of Theoretical and Applied Sciences (Vol. 1, Issue 2, p. 291). https://doi.org/DOI: 10.59324/ejtas.2023.1(2).25

Atkinson, J., Hastie, R., Walker, S., Lindquist, A., & Tong, S. (2023). Telehealth in antenatal care: recent insights and advances. BMC medicine. springer.com

Attaran, M. (2023). The impact of 5G on the evolution of intelligent automation and industry digitization. *Journal of Ambient Intelligence and Humanized Computing*, *14*(5), 5977–5993. DOI: 10.1007/s12652-020-02521-x PMID: 33643481

Attwell, G., Sl, P., Bekiaridis, G., & Karadog, A. (2024). *AI and Education: Agency, Motivation, Literacy and Democracy*. the European Union. https://www.researchgate.net/profile/Angela-Karadog/publication/385812674_AI_and_Education_Agency_Motivation_Literacy_and_Democracy/links/6736114168de5e5a3075d9bb/AI-and-Education-Agency-Motivation-Literacy-and-Democracy.pdf

Audretsch, D. B. & Belitski, M. (2022). A strategic alignment framework for the entrepreneurial university. Industry and Innovation. tandfonline.com

Ayele, A. A., Tefera, Y. G., & East, L. (2021). Ethiopia's commitment towards achieving sustainable development goal on reduction of maternal mortality: There is a long way to go. Women's Health. sagepub.com

Ayeni, O. O., Al Hamad, N. M., Chisom, O. N., Osawaru, B., & Adewusi, O. E. (2024). AI in education: A review of personalized learning and educational technology. [researchgate.net]. *GSC Advanced Research and Reviews*, *18*(2), 261–271. DOI: 10.30574/gscarr.2024.18.2.0062

Aytaç, Z. (2024). Using artificial intelligence tools in higher education. In *Innovation in the University 4.0 System based on Smart Technologies* (pp. 164–175). Chapman and Hall/CRC. [HTML]

Ayub Khan, A., Laghari, A. A., Shaikh, A. A., Bourouis, S., Mamlouk, A. M., & Alshazly, H. (2021). Educational blockchain: A secure degree attestation and verification traceability architecture for higher education commission. [mdpi.com]. *Applied Sciences (Basel, Switzerland)*, *11*(22), 10917. DOI: 10.3390/app112210917

Azem Qashou, A. M., Bahar, N., & Mohamed, H. (2025). Qualitative Exploration of Data Security Risks in Mobile Cloud Computing for Higher Education. [wiley.com]. *Security and Privacy*, *8*(2), e70001. DOI: 10.1002/spy2.70001

Babu, S., Park, N., Woodland, G., Garcia, N., Page, W., & Page, R. (2024). Maternal health applications: Qualitative findings of user needs. [sagepub.com]. *Digital Health*, *10*, 20552076241285422. DOI: 10.1177/20552076241285422 PMID: 39347510

Bahja, M., Kuhail, M. A., & Hammad, R. (2021). Embracing Technological Change in Higher Education. In *IntechOpen eBooks*. IntechOpen., DOI: 10.5772/intechopen.100431

Bal, E. & Akcil, U. (2024). The implementation of a sustainable online course for the development of digital citizenship skills in higher education. Sustainability.

Balta, N. (2023). Embracing the Future: AI's Transformative Potential in Educational Research. In The European Educational Researcher (Vol. 6, Issue 2, p. 1). https://doi.org/DOI: 10.31757/euer.624

Banwo, B. O., Khalifa, M., & Seashore Louis, K. (2022). Exploring trust: Culturally responsive and positive school leadership. [HTML]. *Journal of Educational Administration*, *60*(3), 323–339. DOI: 10.1108/JEA-03-2021-0065

Bashir, H., Araci, Z. C., Obaideen, K., & Alsyouf, I. (2023). An approach for analyzing and visualizing the relationships among key performance indicators for creating sustainable campuses in higher education institutions. [sciencedirect.com]. *Environmental and Sustainability Indicators*, *19*, 100267. DOI: 10.1016/j.indic.2023.100267

Batani, J. & Maharaj, M. S. (2022). Towards data-driven models for diverging emerging technologies for maternal, neonatal and child health services in Sub-Saharan Africa: a systematic review. Global Health Journal. sciencedirect.com

Becker, H., & Park, Y. (2019). Sustainability Education and AI Integration in Global Learning Systems. *Journal of Sustainability Education*, *23*(2), 46–59.

Bedenkov, A., Moreno, C., Agustin, L., Jain, N., Newman, A., Feng, L., & Kostello, G. (2021). Customer centricity in medical affairs needs human-centric artificial intelligence. [springer.com]. *Pharmaceutical Medicine*, *35*(1), 21–29. DOI: 10.1007/s40290-020-00378-1 PMID: 33464482

Beduschi, A. (2021). Rethinking digital identity for post-COVID-19 societies: Data privacy and human rights considerations. *Data & Policy*, *3*, e15. DOI: 10.1017/dap.2021.15

Benboujja, F., Hartnick, E., Zablah, E., Hersh, C., Callans, K., Villamor, P., Yager, P. H., & Hartnick, C. J. (2024). Overcoming language barriers in pediatric care: a multilingual, AI-driven curriculum for global healthcare education. In *Frontiers in Public Health* (Vol. 12). Frontiers Media., DOI: 10.3389/fpubh.2024.1337395

Berendt, B., Littlejohn, A., & Blakemore, M. (2020). AI in education: Learner choice and fundamental rights. *Learning, Media and Technology*, *45*(3), 312–324. DOI: 10.1080/17439884.2020.1786399

Bhandari, A., & Bimo, S. (2022). Why's everyone on TikTok now? The algorithmized self and the future of self-making on social media. *Social Media + Society*, *8*(1), 20563051221086241.

Bhardwaj, V., Zhang, S., Tan, Y. Q., & Pandey, V. (2025). Redefining learning: student-centered strategies for academic and personal growth. Frontiers in Education. frontiersin.org

Bhimavarapu, U. (2025). Exploring Public-Private Partnership Models in Higher Education Through Regression Approach. In Public Private Partnerships for Social Development and Impact (pp. 321-338). IGI Global Scientific Publishing. [HTML] DOI: 10.4018/979-8-3373-3471-4.ch013

Bhimdiwala, A., Neri, R. C., & Gomez, L. M. (2022). Advancing the design and implementation of artificial intelligence in education through continuous improvement. [springer.com]. *International Journal of Artificial Intelligence in Education, 32*(3), 1–27. DOI: 10.1007/s40593-021-00278-8

Bhuiyan, M. I. & Haque, M. A. (2024). NGOs' initiatives and grassroots approach for accessing to health care services for the slum people in Dhaka. Frontiers in Health Services. frontiersin.org

Bhutoria, A. (2022). Personalized education and artificial intelligence in the United States, China, and India: A systematic review using a human-in-the-loop model. *Computers and Education: Artificial Intelligence, 3*, 100068. DOI: 10.1016/j.caeai.2022.100068

Bilal, W., Mohanan, P., Rahmat, Z. S., Ahmed Gangat, S., Islam, Z., Essar, M. Y., Aborode, A. T., & Onyeaka, H. (2022). Improving access to maternal care in Africa through telemedicine and digital health. [HTML]. *The International Journal of Health Planning and Management, 37*(4), 2494–2500. DOI: 10.1002/hpm.3498 PMID: 35570361

Bittencourt, I. I., Cukurova, M., Müldner, K., Luckin, R., & Millán, E. (2020). Artificial Intelligence in Education. In Lecture notes in computer science. Springer Science+Business Media. https://doi.org/DOI: 10.1007/978-3-030-52237-7

Bizimana, B. (2018). Revolutionizing Education through Information Communication Technology: Progress and Challenges in Rwanda. In SSRN Electronic Journal. RELX Group (Netherlands). https://papers.ssrn.com/sol3/papers.cfm?abstract_id=3178209 DOI: 10.15580/GJER.2018.2.031018038

Blackwell, C. K., Lauricella, A. R., Wartella, E., Robb, M., & Schomburg, R. (2023). Adoption and use of technology in early education: The interplay of extrinsic barriers and teacher attitudes. https://www.sciencedirect.com/science/article/ pii/S0360131513001917

Blažič, B. J. (2022). Changing the landscape of cybersecurity education in the EU: Will the new approach produce the required cybersecurity skills?. Education and information technologies. springer.com

Bøe, M., Heikka, J., Kettukangas, T., & Hognestad, K. (2022). Pedagogical leadership in activities with children–A shadowing study of early childhood teachers in Norway and Finland. [sciencedirect.com]. *Teaching and Teacher Education, 117*, 103787. DOI: 10.1016/j.tate.2022.103787

Bohlens, C. (2025). Corruption in Accreditation at HEIs: When Corruption Erodes Trust in Higher Learning. In Navigating Quality Assurance and Accreditation in Global Higher Education (pp. 165-192). IGI Global Scientific Publishing. [HTML]

Bonotti, M., & Willoughby, L. (2022). Citizenship, language tests, and political participation. *Nations and Nationalism, 28*(2), 449–464.

Botes, M., & Townsend, B. (2023). Bridging the regulatory gaps created by Smart and Connected technologies in South Africa. In South African Journal of Bioethics and Law (Vol. 16, Issue 2, p. 36). Health and Medical Publishing Group. https://doi.org/DOI: 10.7196/SAJBL.2023.v16i2.201

Bowser, G., Ho, S. S., Ziebell, A., & Lazendic-Galloway, J. (2024). Networking and collaborating: The role of partnerships across sectors to achieve educational goals in sustainability. [springer.com]. *Sustainable Earth Reviews, 7*(1), 17. DOI: 10.1186/s42055-024-00080-z

Bozkurt, A., Karadeniz, A., Baneres, D., Guerrero-Roldán, A. E., & Rodríguez, M. E. (2021). Artificial intelligence and reflections from educational landscape: A review of AI studies in half a century. *Sustainability (Basel), 13*(2), 800. DOI: 10.3390/su13020800

Brandenberger, J. W. (2023). Investigating personal development outcomes in service learning: Theory and research. Research on service learning. [HTML]

Brenton, J., & Slawinski, N. (2023). Collaborating for community regeneration: Facilitating partnerships in, through, and for place. [HTML]. *Journal of Business Ethics, 184*(4), 815–834. DOI: 10.1007/s10551-023-05365-5

Brinson, A. K., Jahnke, H. R., Rubin-Miller, L., Henrich, N., Challa, B., Moss, C., Shah, N., & Peahl, A. (2023). Trajectories of digital prenatal service utilization and pregnancy outcomes: A multitrajectory analysis. [sciencedirect.com]. *Mayo Clinic Proceedings. Digital Health, 1*(1), 13–24. DOI: 10.1016/j.mcpdig.2022.12.001 PMID: 40207144

Brzustewicz, P., Escher, I., Hermes, J., & Ulkuniemi, P. (2021). Value creation in company–NGO collaboration in corporate volunteering. *Journal of Business and Industrial Marketing, 36*(8), 1504–1519. DOI: 10.1108/JBIM-01-2020-0057

Buckley, R. P., Arner, D. W., Zetzsche, D. A., & Weber, R. H. (2019). The road to RegTech: the (astonishing) example of the European Union. In Journal of Banking Regulation (Vol. 21, Issue 1, p. 26). Palgrave Macmillan. https://doi.org/DOI: 10.1057/s41261-019-00104-1

Bulathwela, S., Pérez-Ortiz, M., Holloway, C., & Shawe-Taylor, J. (2021). Could AI Democratise Education? Socio-Technical Imaginaries of an EdTech Revolution. In arXiv (Cornell University). Cornell University. https://doi.org/DOI: 10.48550/arXiv.2112

Bulut, O., & Beiting-Parrish, M. (2024). The Rise of Artificial Intelligence in Educational Measurement: Opportunities and Ethical Challenges. In Chinese/English Journal of Educational Measurement and Evaluation (Vol. 5, Issue 3). https://doi.org/DOI: 10.59863/MIQL7785

Bulut, O., Gorgun, G., & Yildirim-Erbasli, S. N. (2025). The impact of frequency and stakes of formative assessment on student achievement in higher education: A learning analytics study. [wiley.com]. *Journal of Computer Assisted Learning*, *41*(1), e13087.

Busch, T., Bruce-Clark, P., Derwall, J., Eccles, R., Hebb, T., Hoepner, A., Klein, C., Krueger, P., Paetzold, F., Scholtens, B., & Weber, O. (2021). Impact investments: A call for (re) orientation. [springer.com]. *SN Business & Economics*, *1*(2), 1–13. DOI: 10.1007/s43546-020-00033-6

Butcher, C. J. T. & Hussain, W. (2022). Digital healthcare: the future. Future healthcare journal. sciencedirect.com

Caldwell, C. H., Thomas, D., Hoelscher, H., Williams, H., Mason, Z.II, Valerio-Shewmaker, M. A., & Panapasa, S. V. (2021). Tailoring recruitment and outreach strategies for underrepresented students in public health pipeline programs. *Pedagogy in Health Promotion*, *7*(1, suppl), 36S–43S. DOI: 10.1177/23733799211047517

Camilleri, M. A. & Camilleri, A. C. (). The acceptance of learning management systems and video conferencing technologies: Lessons learned from COVID-19. Technology. springer.com

Camilleri, P. (2018). Robot-proof: Higher education in the age of artificial intelligence. *Journal of Education for Teaching*, *44*(4), 519–520. DOI: 10.1080/02607476.2018.1500792

Campbell-Kelly, M., Aspray, W. F., Yost, J. R., Tinn, H., & Díaz, G. C. (2023). *Computer: A history of the information machine*. Routledge. [HTML] DOI: 10.4324/9781003263272

Campillo-Ferrer, J.-M., Miralles-Martínez, P., & Sánchez-Ibáñez, R. (2020). Gamification in Higher Education: Impact on Student Motivation and the Acquisition of Social and Civic Key Competencies. *Sustainability (Basel)*, *12*(12), 4822. DOI: 10.3390/su12124822

Canfield, M. (2023). The ideology of innovation: Philanthropy and racial capitalism in global food governance. The Journal of Peasant Studies. tandfonline.com

Cantor, A. G., Jungbauer, R. M., Totten, A. M., Tilden, E. L., Holmes, R., Ahmed, A., Wagner, J., Hermesch, A. C., & McDonagh, M. S. (2022). Telehealth strategies for the delivery of maternal health care: A rapid review. [HTML]. *Annals of Internal Medicine*, *175*(9), 1285–1297. DOI: 10.7326/M22-0737 PMID: 35878405

Canty, L. (2022). The lived experience of severe maternal morbidity among Black women. Nursing Inquiry. wiley.com

Cappelli, M. A. & Di Marzo Serugendo, G. (2025). Ontology-Based Customisation Management System for Driver-Vehicle Interfaces: A Preventive Approach to Incident Reduction and Legal Accountability in .... Applied Sciences. mdpi.com

Carpenter, J. P., Trust, T., Kimmons, R., & Krutka, D. G. (2021). Sharing and self-promoting: An analysis of educator tweeting at the onset of the COVID-19 pandemic. *Computers and Education Open*, *2*, 100038. DOI: 10.1016/j.caeo.2021.100038

Carter, S. M., Shih, P., Williams, J., Degeling, C., & Mooney-Somers, J. (2021). Conducting qualitative research online: Challenges and solutions. *Patient*, *14*(6), 711–718. DOI: 10.1007/s40271-021-00528-w PMID: 34114170

Caruso, C. (2024). Towards the Institutions of Freedom: The European Public Discourse in the Digital Era. *German Law Journal*, *26*(1), 114–137.

Casprini, E. & Palumbo, R. (2022). Reaping the benefits of digital transformation through Public-Private Partnership: A service ecosystem view applied to healthcare. Global Public Policy and Governance. springer.com

Castro, A., Siegel-Hawley, G., Bridges, K., & Williams, S. E. (2024). Drawn into policy: A systematic review of school rezoning rationales, processes, and outcomes. [HTML]. *Review of Educational Research*, *94*(4), 539–583. DOI: 10.3102/00346543231195816

Cath, C. (2018). Artificial intelligence and the 'good society': The US, EU, and UK approach. *Science and Engineering Ethics*, *24*, 505–528. PMID: 28353045

Çelik, İ. (2022). Towards Intelligent-TPACK: An empirical study on teachers' professional knowledge to ethically integrate artificial intelligence (AI)-based tools into education. In Computers in Human Behavior (Vol. 138, p. 107468). Elsevier BV. https://doi.org/DOI: 10.1016/j.chb.2022.107468

Çetin, E. (2021). Digital storytelling in teacher education and its effect on the digital literacy of pre-service teachers. [HTML]. *Thinking Skills and Creativity*.

Chan, C. K. Y. (2023). A comprehensive AI policy education framework for university teaching and learning. [springer.com]. *International Journal of Educational Technology in Higher Education*, *20*(1), 38. DOI: 10.1186/s41239-023-00408-3

Chan, C. K. Y., & Tsi, L. H. Y. (2023). The AI Revolution in Education: Will AI Replace or Assist Teachers in Higher Education? In arXiv (Cornell University). Cornell University. https://doi.org/DOI: 10.48550/arXiv.2305

Chandra, M. J. A., Fernando, Z. J., & Wahyuni, P. M. (2023). The New Navigation of Education: Opportunities and Challenges for Artificial Intelligence (AI) Lecturers in Indonesia. In *Proceeding of the International Conference on Innovation in Open and Distance Learning* (Vol. 4, pp. 939-957).

Chang, J., Shelly, S., Busz, M., Stoicescu, C., Iryawan, A. R., Madybaeva, D., de Boer, Y., & Guise, A. (2021). Peer driven or driven peers? A rapid review of peer involvement of people who use drugs in HIV and harm reduction services in low- and middle-income countries. *Harm Reduction Journal*, *18*(1), 1–13. DOI: 10.1186/s12954-021-00461-z PMID: 33536033

Chang, S., Cheong, M., & Oliveira, E. (2024). Digital Environment and AI in International Education: The Gaps and Implications. In *International Higher Education*. Boston College Center for International Higher Education., DOI: 10.6017/895b9e0d.2b6eeadd

Chan, K., Serban, F. C., Tse, M., & Ho, A. (2024). Impact of collaboration with ICT industry partners on secondary students' knowledge, attitudes, and IT competence. [HTML]. *Education and Information Technologies*, *29*(5), 5259–5282. DOI: 10.1007/s10639-023-12036-5

Charalambous, C. Y., Praetorius, A. K., Sammons, P., Walkowiak, T., Jentsch, A., & Kyriakides, L. (2021). Working more collaboratively to better understand teaching and its quality: Challenges faced and possible solutions. [HTML]. *Studies in Educational Evaluation*, *71*, 101092. DOI: 10.1016/j.stueduc.2021.101092

Charles, T., & Hill, C. (2025). Micro-Credentials and AI in Higher Education: Transforming Professional Development. In Prompt Engineering and Generative AI Applications for Teaching and Learning (pp. 1-14). IGI Global Scientific Publishing. [HTML]

Charlwood, A., & Guenole, N. (2022). Can HR adapt to the paradoxes of artificial intelligence? [wiley.com]. *Human Resource Management Journal*, *32*(4), 729–742. DOI: 10.1111/1748-8583.12433

Chen, Z. (2023). Ethics and discrimination in artificial intelligence-enabled recruitment practices. In Humanities and Social Sciences Communications (Vol. 10, Issue 1). Palgrave Macmillan. https://doi.org/DOI: 10.1057/s41599-023-02079-x

Chen, C. Y. (2022). Immersive virtual reality to train preservice teachers in managing students' challenging behaviours: A pilot study. [HTML]. *British Journal of Educational Technology*, *53*(4), 998–1024. DOI: 10.1111/bjet.13181

Cheng, E. C. K. & Wang, T. (2022). Institutional strategies for cybersecurity in higher education institutions. Information. mdpi.com

Cheng, X., He, H., & Jiang, Y. (2023, July). Analysis of User Participatory Design and Gamification in Modern Media. In International Conference on Human-Computer Interaction (pp. 78-93). Cham: Springer Nature Switzerland. DOI: 10.1007/978-3-031-35699-5_7

Cheng, J. K., Yong, I. S. C., Ch'ng, C. K., & Lim, H. T. (2024). Micro-credentials in Malaysian higher education: A comprehensive case study approach. [HTML]. *Education and Information Technologies*, •••, 1–25.

Cheung, S. K., Kwok, L. F., Phusavat, K., & Yang, H. H. (2021). Shaping the future learning environments with smart elements: Challenges and opportunities. [springer.com]. *International Journal of Educational Technology in Higher Education*, *18*(1), 1–9. DOI: 10.1186/s41239-021-00254-1 PMID: 34778521

Chittoor, D. S.Dorai Surendar Chittoor. (2025). Implementing data lineage frameworks in financial institutions: A systematic analysis of compliance, efficiency, and risk management. [journalijsra.com]. *International Journal of Science and Research Archive*, *14*(1), 353–361. DOI: 10.30574/ijsra.2025.14.1.0062

Chiu, T. K. F. (2024). The impact of Generative AI (GenAI) on practices, policies and research direction in education: A case of ChatGPT and Midjourney. Interactive Learning Environments.

Chiu, T. K. F. (2024). The impact of Generative AI (GenAI) on practices, policies and research direction in education: A case of ChatGPT and Midjourney. Interactive Learning Environments. tandfonline.com

Chiu, T. K. F., Xia, Q., Zhou, X., Chai, C. S., & Cheng, M. (2023). Systematic Literature Review on Opportunities, Challenges, And Future Research Recommendations of Artificial Intelligence in Education. *Computers and Education: Artificial Intelligence*, *4*, 100118. DOI: 10.1016/j.caeai.2022.100118

Chiu, T. K., Moorhouse, B. L., Chai, C. S., & Ismailov, M. (2024). Teacher support and student motivation to learn with Artificial Intelligence (AI) based chatbot. *Interactive Learning Environments*, *32*(7), 3240–3256.

Chohan, S. R. & Hu, G. (2022). Strengthening digital inclusion through e-government: Cohesive ICT training programs to intensify digital competency. Information technology for development.

Choi, D. H., Nah, S., & Chung, D. S. (2021). Social media as a civic mobilizer: Community storytelling network, social media, and civic engagement in South Korea.. *Journal of Broadcasting & Electronic Media*, *65*(1), 46–65. DOI: 10.1080/08838151.2021.1897818

Cholilah, M., & Tatuwo, A. G. P., Komariah, Rosdiana, S. P., & Fatirul, A. N. (2023). Pengembangan Kurikulum Merdeka Dalam Satuan Pendidikan Serta Implementasi Kurikulum Merdeka Pada Pembelajaran Abad 21. *Sanskara Pendidikan Dan Pengajaran*, *1*(02), 56–67. DOI: 10.58812/spp.v1i02.110

Choukaier, D. (2024). Integrating AI In English Language Pedagogy: Innovations And Outcomes In Teaching English As Second /Foreign Language. *Educational Administration: Theory and Practice*, *30*(5), 3811–3822. https://doi.org/Doi: DOI: 10.53555/kuey.v30i5.3538

Chugh, R., Turnbull, D., Cowling, M. A., Vanderburg, R., & Vanderburg, M. A. (2023). Implementing educational technology in Higher Education Institutions: A review of technologies, stakeholder perceptions, frameworks and metrics. [springer.com]. *Education and Information Technologies*, *28*(12), 16403–16429. DOI: 10.1007/s10639-023-11846-x

Ciampa, K., Wolfe, Z. M., & Bronstein, B. (2023). ChatGPT in education: Transforming digital literacy practices. *Journal of Adolescent & Adult Literacy*, *67*(3), 186–195. DOI: 10.1002/jaal.1310

Ciampa, K., Wolfe, Z., & Hensley, M. (2024). From entry to transformation: Exploring AI integration in teachers' K–12 assessment practices. *Technology, Pedagogy and Education*, •••, 1–20. DOI: 10.1080/1475939X.2024.2413378

Collins, T. A., Heidelburg, K., & Scott, M. N. (2020). Using Technology to Teach Cultural Competence. In *Innovations in higher education teaching and learning* (p. 219). Emerald Publishing Limited., DOI: 10.1108/S2055-364120200000028021

Correa, V., & Tulbert, B. (2023). Teaching Culturally Diverse Students. https://www.tandfonline.com/doi/abs/10.1080/1045988X.1991.10871070

Cotton, D. R., Cotton, P. A., & Shipway, J. R. (2024). Chatting and cheating: Ensuring academic integrity in the era of ChatGPT. *Innovations in Education and Teaching International*, *61*(2), 228–239. DOI: 10.1080/14703297.2023.2190148

Coulton, C., Richter, F. G. C., Cho, Y., Park, J., Jeon, J., & Fischer, R. L. (2023). Making the case for lead safe housing: Downstream effects of lead exposure on outcomes for children and youth. [HTML]. *Health & Place*, *84*, 103118. DOI: 10.1016/j.healthplace.2023.103118 PMID: 37839260

Creely, E. (2024). Exploring the Role of Generative AI in Enhancing Language Learning: Opportunities and Challenges. *International Journal of Changes in Education*, *1*(3), 158–167. DOI: 10.47852/bonviewIJCE42022495

Crepinsek, M., Bell, R., Graham, I., & Coutts, R. (2023). A global review of the inferred meaning of woman centred care within midwifery professional standards. [HTML]. *Women and Birth; Journal of the Australian College of Midwives*, *36*(1), e99–e105. DOI: 10.1016/j.wombi.2022.05.001 PMID: 35550121

Creswell, J. W. (2013). *Educational research: Planning, conducting, and evaluating quantitative and qualitative research* (Fourth Indian edition). PHI Learning Private Limited.

Crompton, H., & Burke, D. (2023). Artificial intelligence in higher education: the state of the field. In International Journal of Educational Technology in Higher Education (Vol. 20, Issue 1). Springer Nature. https://doi.org/DOI: 10.1186/s41239-023-00392-8

Crossley, S., & Baybutt, M. (2024). Access to healthcare: Underserved communities. [tandfonline.com]. *International Journal of Health Promotion and Education*, *62*(5), 341–342. DOI: 10.1080/14635240.2024.2403238

Cui, W., Xue, Z., & Thai, K.-P. (2019). Performance comparison of an AI-based Adaptive Learning System in China. In arXiv (Cornell University). Cornell University. https://doi.org/DOI: 10.48550/arxiv.1901.10268

Cunningham-Nelson, S., Boles, W., Trouton, L., & Margerison, E. (2019). A review of chatbots in education: practical steps forward. In 30th annual conference for the australasian association for engineering education (AAEE 2019): educators becoming agents of change: innovate, integrate, motivate (pp. 299-306). Engineers Australia.

Custers, B. (2022). New digital rights: Imagining additional fundamental rights for the digital era. *Computer Law & Security Review*, *44*, 105636.

Dakulagi, V., Yeap, K. H., Nisar, H., Dakulagi, R., Basavaraj, G. N., & Galindo, M. V. (2025). An overview of techniques and best practices to create intuitive and user-friendly human-machine interfaces. Artificial Intelligence and Multimodal Signal Processing in Human-Machine Interaction, 63-77. [HTML]

Dangol, A., Newman, M., Wolfe, R., Lee, J. H., Kientz, J. A., Yip, J., & Pitt, C. (2024). Mediating Culture: Cultivating Socio-cultural Understanding of AI in Children through Participatory Design. In *Designing Interactive Systems Conference* (p. 1805). https://doi.org/DOI: 10.1145/3643834.3661515

Dar, M. A., Kudare, R., Dar, Y. A., Ali, I., & Mohammed, S. (2022). Role Of Projected And Non-Projected Teaching Aids In Teaching Learning Process. [researchgate.net]. *Journal of Positive School Psychology*, *6*(10), 1725–1743.

Datta, S. D., Islam, M., Sobuz, Md. H. R., Ahmed, S., & Kar, M. (2024). Artificial intelligence and machine learning applications in the project lifecycle of the construction industry: A comprehensive review [Review of Artificial intelligence and machine learning applications in the project lifecycle of the construction industry: A comprehensive review]. Heliyon, 10(5). Elsevier BV. https://doi.org/. 2024. e26888DOI: 10.1016/j.heliyon

Dawadi, S., Goshtasbpour, F., & Kukulska-Hulme, A. (2024). Equitable Access to Higher Education Learning and Assessment: Perspectives from Low-Resource Contexts. In Journal of Interactive Media in Education (Vol. 2024, Issue 1). Ubiquity Press. https://doi.org/DOI: 10.5334/jime.832

De, P. & Pradhan, M. R. (2023). Effectiveness of mobile technology and utilization of maternal and neonatal healthcare in low and middle-income countries (LMICs): a systematic review. BMC Women's Health. springer.com

Deepa, N., Devi, T., Gayathri, N., & Kumar, S. R. (2022). Decentralized healthcare management system using blockchain to secure sensitive medical data for users. Blockchain security in cloud computing, 265-282. [HTML]

Dehouche, N. (2021). Plagiarism in the age of massive Generative Pre-trained Transformers (GPT-3). *Ethics in Science and Environmental Politics*, *21*, 17–23. Advance online publication. DOI: 10.3354/esep00195

Demartini, C. G., Sciascia, L., Bosso, A., & Manuri, F. (2024). Artificial intelligence bringing improvements to adaptive learning in education: A case study. Sustainability. mdpi.com

Deppeler, J., Corrigan, D., Macaulay, L., & Aikens, K. (2022). Innovation and risk in an innovative learning environment: A Private Public Partnership in Australia. [HTML]. *European Educational Research Journal*, *21*(4), 602–626. DOI: 10.1177/14749041211030400

DeSa, S., Gebremeskel, A. T., Omonaiye, O., & Yaya, S. (2022). Barriers and facilitators to access mental health services among refugee women in high-income countries: a systematic review. Systematic reviews. springer.com

Dexter, S. (2023). Developing faculty EdTech instructional decision-making competence with principles for the integration of EdTech. Educational technology research and development. springer.com

Di Vaio, A., Palladino, R., Hassan, R., & Escobar, O. (2020). Artificial intelligence and business models in the sustainable development goals perspective: A systematic literature review. *Journal of Business Research*, *121*, 283–314. DOI: 10.1016/j.jbusres.2020.08.019

Díaz-Rodríguez, N., Del Ser, J., Coeckelbergh, M., de Prado, M. L., Herrera-Viedma, E., & Herrera, F. (2023). Connecting the dots in trustworthy Artificial Intelligence: From AI principles, ethics, and key requirements to responsible AI systems and regulation. [sciencedirect.com]. *Information Fusion*, *99*, 101896. DOI: 10.1016/j.inffus.2023.101896

Dimitriadou, E. & Lanitis, A. (2023). A critical evaluation, challenges, and future perspectives of using artificial intelligence and emerging technologies in smart classrooms. Smart Learning Environments. springer.com

Dimitriou, C. K. (2022). The critical role that national culture and ethical leadership play in fostering employee commitment to service quality in the hotel industry. Research in Hospitality Management. tandfonline.com

Dingus, R., & Black, H. G. (2021). Choose your words carefully: An exercise to introduce artificial intelligence to the marketing classroom using tone analysis. *Marketing Education Review*, *31*(2), 64–69. DOI: 10.1080/10528008.2020.1843361

Dixon, R. (2021). Performance management in social impact bonds: how an outcomes-based approach shapes hybrid partnerships. International Journal of Public Sector Management. emerald.com

Djatmiko, G. H., Sinaga, O., & Pawirosumarto, S. (2025). Digital Transformation and Social Inclusion in Public Services: A Qualitative Analysis of E-Government Adoption for Marginalized Communities in Sustainable …. Sustainability.

Do, N. X. B., An, T. S., & Krauss, C. (2024, May). SMART-goal-buddy: Goal-setting oriented adaptive learning paths. In International workshop on learning technology for education challenges (pp. 319-331). Cham: Springer Nature Switzerland. [HTML]

Domoff, V. Ill., Pratt, Y. P., Drefs, M., & Wick, M. (2023). Challenging Definitions of Student Success Through Indigenous Involvement: An Opportunity to Inform School Psychology Practice. In Canadian Journal of School Psychology (Vol. 38, Issue 3, p. 191). SAGE Publishing. https://doi.org/DOI: 10.1177/08295735221149225

Dritsas, E. & Trigka, M. (2025). Methodological and Technological Advancements in E-Learning. Information. mdpi.com

Dua, G. K. (2025). Enhancing Organizational Performance Through Process Performance Measurement and KPIs in AI-Based Digital Transformation. Perspectives on Digital Transformation in Contemporary Business, 241-268. [HTML]

Dubois, E., & Reepschlager, A. (2024). How harassment and hate speech policies have changed over time: Comparing Facebook, Twitter and Reddit (2005–2020). *Policy and Internet*, *16*(3), 523–542.

Dudek, C. M., Reddy, L. A., & Kettler, R. J. (2023). One size does not fit all: A concurrent analysis of the framework for teaching and the Classroom Strategies Assessment System. [HTML]. *Educational Assessment, Evaluation and Accountability*, *35*(3), 353–386. DOI: 10.1007/s11092-023-09405-6

Durall, E., & Kapros, E. (2020). Co-design for a competency self-assessment chatbot and survey in science education. In Learning and Collaboration Technologies. Human and Technology Ecosystems: 7th International Conference, LCT 2020, Held as Part of the 22nd HCI International Conference, HCII 2020, Copenhagen, Denmark, July 19–24, 2020 [Springer International Publishing.]. *Proceedings*, *22*(Part II), 13–24.

Dutta, D., & Pal, S. K. (2022). Interpretation of black box for short-term predictions of pre-monsoon cumulonimbus cloud events over Kolkata.

Dwivedi, Y. K., Kshetri, N., Hughes, L., Rana, N. P., Baabdullah, A. M., Kar, A. K., Koohang, A., Ribeiro-Navarrete, S., Belei, N., Balakrishnan, J., Basu, S., Behl, A., Davies, G. H., Dutot, V., Dwivedi, R., Evans, L., Felix, R., Foster-Fletcher, R., Giannakis, M., & Yan, M. (2023). Exploring the darkverse: A multi-perspective analysis of the negative societal impacts of the metaverse. *Information Systems Frontiers*, *25*(5), 2071–2114. DOI: 10.1007/s10796-023-10400-x PMID: 37361890

Eaton, S. E., & Carmichael, J. J. (2023). Fake degrees and credential fraud, contract cheating, and paper mills: Overview and historical perspectives. Fake Degrees and Fraudulent Credentials in Higher Education, 1-22. [HTML]

Ebadpour, Z., Nikghadam-Hojjati, S., & Barata, J. (2024, June). Human-Centric Principles for Computational Systems Supporting Collaborative Creativity. In Doctoral Conference on Computing, Electrical and Industrial Systems (pp. 61-81). Cham: Springer Nature Switzerland. [HTML] DOI: 10.1007/978-3-031-63851-0_4

Eguchi, A., Okada, H., & Muto, Y. (2021). Contextualizing AI Education for K-12 Students to Enhance Their Learning of AI Literacy Through Culturally Responsive Approaches. In KI - Künstliche Intelligenz (Vol. 35, Issue 2, p. 153). Springer Science+Business Media. https://doi.org/DOI: 10.1007/s13218-021-00737-3

El Kotni, M. (2021). Midwifery in cross-cultural perspectives. In *The Routledge Handbook of Anthropology and Reproduction* (pp. 454–467). Routledge. [HTML] DOI: 10.4324/9781003216452-36

El-Afifi, M. I., Sedhom, B. E., Eladl, A. A., & Padmanaban, S. (2024). Survey of technologies, techniques, and applications for big data analytics in smart energy hub. [sciencedirect.com]. *Energy Strategy Reviews*, *56*, 101582. DOI: 10.1016/j.esr.2024.101582

El-Kady, A. H., Halim, S., El-Halwagi, M. M., & Khan, F. (2023). Analysis of safety and security challenges and opportunities related to cyber-physical systems. *Process Safety and Environmental Protection*, *173*, 384–413. DOI: 10.1016/j.psep.2023.03.012

ElSayary, A. (2023). The impact of a professional upskilling training programme on developing teachers' digital competence. *Journal of Computer Assisted Learning*, *39*(4), 1154–1166. DOI: 10.1111/jcal.12788

Ertel, W. (2024). *Introduction to artificial intelligence*. Springer Nature., DOI: 10.1007/978-3-658-43102-0

Escudero, S. B., Anglin, A. H., Allison, T. H., & Wolfe, M. T. (2025). Crowdfunding: A Theory-Centered Review and Roadmap of the Multidisciplinary Literature. [sagepub.com]. *Journal of Management*, •••, 01492063251328267. DOI: 10.1177/01492063251328267

Ethics of AI in Education. Towards a Community-Wide Framework. In International Journal of Artificial Intelligence in Education (Vol. 32, Issue 3, p. 504). Springer Science+Business Media. https://doi.org/DOI: 10.1007/s40593-021-00239-1

Ethics of Artificial Intelligence. (2024). https://www.unesco.org/en/artificial-intelligence/recommendation-ethics

Etri, W. (2021). Intercultural sensitivity and its effects on ELT curricula – Teacher insights. In Higher Education Evaluation and Development (Vol. 16, Issue 1, p. 32). Emerald Publishing Limited. https://doi.org/DOI: 10.1108/HEED-03-2021-0027

Ewell, P., Van Noy, M., & Gaston, P. L. (2023). Credentials: Understand the problems. Identify the opportunities. Create the solutions.. [HTML]

Eynon, R. (2021). Becoming digitally literate: Reinstating an educational lens to digital skills policies for adults. British educational research journal.

Ezeamuzie, N. O., & Ezeamuzie, M. N. (2024). Multidimensional Framing of Environments Beyond Blocks and Texts in K–12 Programming. In *Review of Educational Research*. SAGE Publishing., DOI: 10.3102/00346543231216958

Faizuddin, A., Azizan, N. A., Othman, A., & Ismail, S. N. (2022). Continuous professional development programmes for school principals in the 21st century: Lessons learned from educational leadership practices. Frontiers in Education. frontiersin.org

Fan, K. & Zhao, Y. (2022). Mobile health technology: a novel tool in chronic disease management. Intelligent Medicine. sciencedirect.com

Fattah, H. A., Vadivel, B., Shaban, A. A., & Shanmugam, K. (2023). Enhancing English Language Education: The Impact of AI Integration in the Classroom. *The Journal of Humanistic Education and Development*, *5*(6), 116–123. DOI: 10.22161/jhed.5.6.15

Favero, N., & Kagalwala, A. (2025). The politics of school funding: How state political ideology is associated with the allocation of revenue to school districts. [HTML]. *Educational Policy*, *39*(3), 693–722. DOI: 10.1177/08959048241258724

Felix, J. R. B., & Webb, L. (2024). Use of artificial intelligence in education delivery and assessment. https://doi.org/DOI: 10.58248/PN712

Ferguson, B., Baldwin, A., Harvey, C., & Henderson, A. (2025). Navigating Quality and Innovation: Actor-Network Theory and Hybrid Assemblages in Midwifery Practice, Implications of Maternity Early Warning Tools and Artificial Intelligence. [wiley.com]. *Nursing Inquiry*, *32*(2), e70001. DOI: 10.1111/nin.70001 PMID: 40025864

Feroz, A. K., & Stines, A. (2024). Utilization of AI, big data, and internet of things (IoT) in sustainable innovation and their role in the emergence of novel business models. *Issues in Information Systems*, *25*(1).

Ferrara, E. (2023). Fairness And Bias in Artificial Intelligence: A Brief Survey of Sources, Impacts, And Mitigation Strategies. In arXiv (Cornell University). Cornell University. https://doi.org/DOI: 10.48550/arXiv.2304

Figà Talamanca, G. & Arfini, S. (2022). Through the newsfeed glass: Rethinking filter bubbles and echo chambers. Philosophy & Technology.

Finlay, J. (2020). *An introduction to artificial intelligence*. Crc Press., DOI: 10.1201/9781003072485

Firdaus, M. R., Irawan, R. R., Mahardika, C. H. Y., Gaol, P. L., & Prinaryanto, B. A. (2024). Tantangan teknologi artificial intelligence pada kegiatan pembelajaran mahasiswa. *Indonesian Journal of Education and Development Research*, *2*(1), 379–384.

Fischer, G., Klemmer, S. R., & Grudin, J. (2019). The Role of AI in Education: Insights and Prospects. *Journal of Educational Technology & Society*, *22*(4), 40–50.

Fischer, H. E., Boone, W. J., & Neumann, K. (2023). Quantitative research designs and approaches. In *Handbook of research on science education* (pp. 28–59). Routledge. [HTML] DOI: 10.4324/9780367855758-3

Fitrianto, I., Setyawan, C. E., & Saleh, M. (2024). Utilizing Artificial Intelligence for Personalized Arabic Language Learning Plans. International Journal of Post Axial: Futuristic Teaching and Learning, 30-40.

Franco D'Souza, R., Mathew, M., Mishra, V., & Surapaneni, K. M. (2024). Twelve tips for addressing ethical concerns in the implementation of artificial intelligence in medical education. [tandfonline.com]. *Medical Education Online*, *29*(1), 2330250. DOI: 10.1080/10872981.2024.2330250 PMID: 38566608

Gabriel, F., Marrone, R., Van Sebille, Y., Kovanovic, V., & de Laat, M. (2022). Digital education strategies around the world: Practices and policies. *Irish Educational Studies*, *41*(1), 85–106. DOI: 10.1080/03323315.2021.2022513

Gagné, J. C. D. (2023). The State of Artificial Intelligence in Nursing Education: Past, Present, and Future Directions. In International Journal of Environmental Research and Public Health (Vol. 20, Issue 6, p. 4884). Multidisciplinary Digital Publishing Institute. https://doi.org/DOI: 10.3390/ijerph20064884

Galikhanov, M. F., Barabanova, S. V., Elizarov, D. V., & Suntsova, M. S. (2021). Public-private partnership within the context of digital transformation: increasingly larger role of educational institutions. In Educating Engineers for Future Industrial Revolutions: Proceedings of the 23rd International Conference on Interactive Collaborative Learning (ICL2020), Volume 2 23 (pp. 339-349). Springer International Publishing. [HTML] DOI: 10.1007/978-3-030-68201-9_34

Gaol, F. L., & Prasolova-Førland, E. (2021). Special section editorial: The frontiers of augmented and mixed reality in all levels of education. In Education and Information Technologies (Vol. 27, Issue 1, p. 611). Springer Science+Business Media. https://doi.org/DOI: 10.1007/s10639-021-10746-2

Gardner, A., Smith, A. L., Steventon, A., Coughlan, E., & Oldfield, M. (2022). Ethical funding for trustworthy AI: Proposals to address the responsibilities of funders to ensure that projects adhere to trustworthy AI practice. [springer.com]. *AI and Ethics*, *2*(2), 1–15. DOI: 10.1007/s43681-021-00069-w PMID: 34790951

Gardner, C. J., Thierry, A., Rowlandson, W., & Steinberger, J. K. (2021). From publications to public actions: The role of universities in facilitating academic advocacy and activism in the climate and ecological emergency. *Frontiers in Sustainability*, *2*, 679019. DOI: 10.3389/frsus.2021.679019

Garenne, D., Haines, M. C., Romantseva, E. F., Freemont, P., Strychalski, E. A., & Noireaux, V. (2021). Cell-free gene expression. *Nature Reviews. Methods Primers*, *1*(1), 49. DOI: 10.1038/s43586-021-00046-x

Garnham, A. (2017). *Artificial intelligence: An introduction*. Routledge., DOI: 10.4324/9780203704394

Gaskins, N. R. (2022). Interrogating Algorithmic Bias: From Speculative Fiction to Liberatory Design. In TechTrends (Vol. 67, Issue 3, p. 417). Springer Science+Business Media. https://doi.org/DOI: 10.1007/s11528-022-00783-0

Gasser, U. (2023). An EU landmark for AI governance. In Science (Vol. 380, Issue 6651, p. 1203). American Association for the Advancement of Science. https://doi.org/DOI: 10.1126/science.adj1627

Gea, N. S., Gulo, U. B. M., Bawamenewi, A., & Gulo, W. M. (2024). Motivating the Younger Generation in Reading: Integrating Technology in Understanding Digital Literacy. *International Journal of Educatio Elementaria and Psychologia, 1*(3), 135–145. DOI: 10.70177/ijeep.v1i3.998

Gelber, K. (2021). Differentiating hate speech: A systemic discrimination approach. *Critical Review of International Social and Political Philosophy, 24*(4), 393–414. DOI: 10.1080/13698230.2019.1576006

Geletu, G. M., & Mihiretie, D. M. (2023). Professional accountability and responsibility of learning communities of practice in professional development versus curriculum practice in classrooms: Possibilities and pathways. [sciencedirect.com]. *International Journal of Educational Research Open, 4*, 100223. DOI: 10.1016/j.ijedro.2022.100223

Generative Artificial Intelligence for Education and Pedagogy. (2024). https://teaching.cornell.edu/generative-artificial-intelligence/cu-committee-report-generative-artificial-intelligence-education

Gentili, P. L. (2022). Photochromic and luminescent materials for the development of Chemical Artificial Intelligence. In *Dyes and Pigments* (Vol. 205, p. 110547). Elsevier BV., DOI: 10.1016/j.dyepig.2022.110547

George, B. & Wooden, O. (2023). Managing the strategic transformation of higher education through artificial intelligence. Administrative Sciences. mdpi.com

Gershuni, O., Orr, J. M., Vogel, A., Park, K., Leider, J. P., Resnick, B. A., & Czabanowska, K. (2023). A systematic review on professional regulation and credentialing of public health workforce. [mdpi.com]. *International Journal of Environmental Research and Public Health, 20*(5), 4101. DOI: 10.3390/ijerph20054101 PMID: 36901111

Gesualdo, F., Daverio, M., Palazzani, L., Dimitriou, D., Diez-Domingo, J., Fons-Martinez, J., Jackson, S., Vignally, P., Rizzo, C., & Tozzi, A. E. (2021). Digital tools in the informed consent process: A systematic review. [springer.com]. *BMC Medical Ethics, 22*(1), 1–10. DOI: 10.1186/s12910-021-00585-8 PMID: 33639926

Getachew, E., Adebeta, T., Muzazu, S. G., Charlie, L., Said, B., Tesfahunei, H. A., Wanjiru, C. L., Acam, J., Kajogoo, V. D., Solomon, S., Atim, M. G., & Manyazewal, T. (2023). Digital health in the era of COVID-19: Reshaping the next generation of healthcare. [frontiersin.org]. *Frontiers in Public Health, 11*, 942703. DOI: 10.3389/fpubh.2023.942703 PMID: 36875401

Gevaert, C., Carman, M., Rosman, B., Georgiadou, Y., & Soden, R. (2021). Fairness and accountability of AI in disaster risk management: Opportunities and challenges [Review of Fairness and accountability of AI in disaster risk management: Opportunities and challenges]. Patterns, 2(11), 100363. Elsevier BV. https://doi.org/DOI: 10.1016/j.patter.2021.100363

Ge, X., Xu, C., Misaki, D., Markus, H. R., & Tsai, J. L. (2024). *How Culture Shapes What People Want From AI.*, DOI: 10.1145/3613904.3642660

Ghamrawi, N., Shal, T., & Ghamrawi, N. A. (2024). Exploring the impact of AI on teacher leadership: Regressing or expanding? [springer.com]. *Education and Information Technologies*, *29*(7), 8415–8433. DOI: 10.1007/s10639-023-12174-w

Ghosh, M., & Thirugnanam, A. (2021). Introduction to Artificial Intelligence. In: Srinivasa, K.G., G. M., S., Sekhar, S.R.M. (eds) Artificial Intelligence for Information Management: A Healthcare Perspective. Studies in Big Data, vol 88. Springer, Singapore. https://doi.org/DOI: 10.1007/978-981-16-0415-7_2

Giannakos, M., Azevedo, R., Brusilovsky, P., Cukurova, M., Dimitriadis, Y., Hernandez-Leo, D., Järvelä, S., Mavrikis, M., & Rienties, B. (2024). The promise and challenges of generative AI in education. *Behaviour & Information Technology*, •••, 1–27. DOI: 10.1080/0144929X.2024.2394886

Gillespie, T. (2022). Do not recommend? Reduction as a form of content moderation. *Social Media + Society*, *8*(3), 20563051221117552.

Gillie, M., Ali, D., Vadlamuri, D., & Carstarphen, K. J. (2022). Telehealth literacy as a social determinant of health: A novel screening tool to support vulnerable patient equity. [sagepub.com]. *Journal of Alzheimer's Disease Reports*, *6*(1), 67–72. DOI: 10.3233/ADR-210024 PMID: 35360275

Girmanová, L., Šolc, M., Blaško, P., & Petrík, J. (2022). Quality management system in education: Application of quality management models in educational organization—case study from the Slovak Republic. Standards. mdpi.com

Gligorea, I., Cioca, M., Oancea, R., Gorski, A.-T., Gorski, H., & Tudorache, P. (2023). Adaptive Learning Using Artificial Intelligence in e-Learning: A Literature Review [Review of Adaptive Learning Using Artificial Intelligence in e-Learning: A Literature Review]. Education Sciences, 13(12), 1216. Multidisciplinary Digital Publishing Institute. https://doi.org/DOI: 10.3390/educsci13121216

Golombek, P. R., & Johnson, K. E. (2021). Recurrent restorying through language teacher narrative inquiry. *System*, *102*, 102601. DOI: 10.1016/j.system.2021.102601

Gomez, F. C.Jr, Trespalacios, J., Hsu, Y.-C., & Yang, D. (2022). Exploring Teachers' Technology Integration Self-Efficacy through the 2017 ISTE Standards. *TechTrends*, *66*(2), 159–171. DOI: 10.1007/s11528-021-00639-z PMID: 34378007

Gomez-Roas, M. V., Davis, K. D. M., Leziak, K., Jackson, J., Williams, B. R., Feinglass, J. M., Grobman, W. A., & Yee, L. M. (2022). Postpartum during a pandemic: Challenges of low-income individuals with healthcare interactions during COVID-19. [plos.org]. *PLoS One*, *17*(5), e0268698. DOI: 10.1371/journal.pone.0268698 PMID: 35609090

Gonzalez-Mohino, M., Rodriguez-Domenech, M. Á., Callejas-Albiñana, A. I., & Castillo-Canalejo, A. (2023). Empowering critical thinking: The role of digital tools in citizen participation. [springer.com]. *Journal of New Approaches in Educational Research*, *12*(2), 258–275. DOI: 10.7821/naer.2023.7.1385

Gonzalez-Nucamendi, A., Noguez, J., Neri, L., Robledo-Rella, V., & García-Castelán, R. M. G. (2023, October). Predictive analytics study to determine undergraduate students at risk of dropout. [). Frontiers Media SA. frontiersin.org]. *Frontiers in Education*, *8*, 1244686. DOI: 10.3389/feduc.2023.1244686

Goode, K., Kim, H. M., & Deng, M. (2023). Examining Singapore's AI Progress. https://doi.org/DOI: 10.51593/2021CA014

Grabowicz, P. A., Perello, N., & Zick, Y. (2023). Towards an AI Accountability Policy. In arXiv (Cornell University). Cornell University. https://doi.org/DOI: 10.48550/arXiv.2307

Graesser, A. C. (2016). Conversations with AutoTutor Help Students Learn. *International Journal of Artificial Intelligence in Education*, *26*(1), 124–132. Advance online publication. DOI: 10.1007/s40593-015-0086-4

Gray, E. K., Fahy, F., McArdle, R., & Rohse, M. (2024). Co-creating a community visioning methodology for energy transitions: Principles, practices, and reflections. Energy Research & Social Science. sciencedirect.com

Grecu, Y. V. (2023). Differentiated instruction: Curriculum and resources provide a roadmap to help English teachers meet students' needs. [HTML]. *Teaching and Teacher Education*, *125*, 104064. DOI: 10.1016/j.tate.2023.104064

Grewal, D., Herhausen, D., Ludwig, S., & Ordenes, F. V. (2022). The future of digital communication research: Considering dynamics and multimodality. *Journal of Retailing*, *98*(2), 224–240.

Gritsenko, D. & Indukaev, A. (2021). Digitalising city governance in Russia: The case of the 'active citizen'platform. Europe-Asia Studies.

Grover, R. (2022). The geopolitics of digital rights activism: Evaluating civil society's role in the promises of multistakeholder internet governance. *Telecommunications Policy*, *46*(10), 102437. DOI: 10.1016/j.telpol.2022.102437

Guan, C., Mou, J., & Jiang, Z. (2020). Artificial intelligence innovation in education: A twenty-year data-driven historical analysis. In International Journal of Innovation Studies (Vol. 4, Issue 4, p. 134). Elsevier BV. DOI: 10.1016/j.ijis.2020.09.001

Gumelar, G., Martadi, M., Rosalinda, I., Yudhaningrum, L., & Warju, W. (2022). *Computer Self-Efficacy, Task Value, Digital Literacy, Online Learning Perceptions on Indonesian University Students' Learning Satisfaction:* 1st World Conference on Social and Humanities Research (W-SHARE 2021), Makassar, Indonesia. DOI: 10.2991/assehr.k.220402.021

Gunawan, K. D. H., Liliasari, L., Kaniawati, I., & Setiawan, W. (2021). Implementation of competency enhancement program for science teachers assisted by artificial intelligence in designing HOTS-based integrated science learning. *Jurnal Penelitian Dan Pembelajaran IPA*, *7*(1), 55–65. DOI: 10.30870/jppi.v7i1.8655

Gunuç, S., & Babacan, N. (2017). Technology integration in English language teaching and learning. Positioning English for Specific Purposes in an English Language Teaching Context. *The Journal Of Teaching English For Specific And Academic Purposes*, *5*(2), 349–358. DOI: 10.22190/JTESAP1702349G

Guo, L. (2021). Research on the Main Strategies of Using Computer Technology to Inherit Traditional Culture. In Journal of Physics Conference Series (Vol. 1915, Issue 3, p. 32089). IOP Publishing. https://doi.org/DOI: 10.1088/1742-6596/1915/3/032089

Gupta, A., Panda, M., & Gupta, A. (2024). Advancing API Security: A Comprehensive Evaluation of Authentication Mechanisms and Their Implications for Cybersecurity. International Journal of Global Innovations and Solutions (IJGIS). pubpub.org

Gupta, S., Mishra, O. N., & Kumar, S. (2021). Citizen empowerment and adoption of E-governance services: The role of online citizen skills, awareness, and engagement.. *International Journal of Electronic Governance*, *13*(4), 386–407. DOI: 10.1504/IJEG.2021.121237

Gurjar, N., & Bai, H. (2023). Assessing culturally inclusive instructional design in online learning. In Educational Technology Research and Development (Vol. 71, Issue 3, p. 1253). Springer Science+Business Media. DOI: 10.1007/s11423-023-10226-z

Habib, M. N., Jamal, W., Khalil, U., & Khan, Z. (2021). Transforming universities in interactive digital platform: Case of city university of science and information technology. [springer.com]. *Education and Information Technologies*, *26*(1), 517–541. DOI: 10.1007/s10639-020-10237-w PMID: 32837236

Hadad, S., Watted, A., & Blau, I. (2023). Cultural background in digital literacy of elementary and middle school students: Self-appraisal versus actual performance. *Journal of Computer Assisted Learning*, *39*(5), 1591–1606. DOI: 10.1111/jcal.12820

Hadley, E. (2022). Prioritizing Policies for Furthering Responsible Artificial Intelligence in the United States. In arXiv (Cornell University). Cornell University. https://doi.org/DOI: 10.48550/arXiv.2212

Haggart, B., & Keller, C. I. (2021). Democratic legitimacy in global platform governance. *Telecommunications Policy*, *45*(6), 102152.

Hailikari, T., Virtanen, V., Vesalainen, M., & Postareff, L. (2022). Student perspectives on how different elements of constructive alignment support active learning. [sagepub.com]. *Active Learning in Higher Education*, *23*(3), 217–231. DOI: 10.1177/1469787421989160

Hakimi, L., Eynon, R., & Murphy, V. A. (2021). The ethics of using digital trace data in education: A thematic review of the research landscape. [sagepub.com]. *Review of Educational Research*, *91*(5), 671–717. DOI: 10.3102/00346543211020116

Halagatti, M., Gadag, S., Mahantshetti, S., Hiremath, C. V., Tharkude, D., & Banakar, V. (2023). Artificial intelligence: the new tool of disruption in educational performance assessment. In *Smart analytics, artificial intelligence and sustainable performance management in a global digitalised economy* (pp. 261–287). Emerald Publishing Limited. [HTML] DOI: 10.1108/S1569-37592023000110A014

Haleem, A., Javaid, M., Qadri, M. A., & Suman, R. (2022). Understanding the role of digital technologies in education: A review. Sustainable operations and computers, 3, 275-285. sciencedirect.com

Halmo, H. (2025). Human-Centered, Tech-Enabled: Scaling Academic Advising in Higher Education Through Predictive Analytics and Organizational Change an Innovation Study. [HTML]

Han, A., Zhou, X., Cai, Z., Han, S., Ko, R., Corrigan, S., & Peppler, K. A. (2024). Teachers, Parents, and Students' perspectives on Integrating Generative AI into Elementary Literacy Education. *Proceedings of the CHI Conference on Human Factors in Computing Systems*, 1–17. DOI: 10.1145/3613904.3642438

Hanna, M., Pantanowitz, L., Jackson, B., Palmer, O., Visweswaran, S., Pantanowitz, J., & Rashidi, H. (2024). Ethical and Bias considerations in artificial intelligence (AI)/machine learning. [sciencedirect.com]. *Modern Pathology*, •••, 100686. PMID: 39694331

Hannon, S., Newnham, E., Hannon, K., Wuytack, F., Johnson, L., McEvoy, E., & Daly, D. (2022). Positive postpartum well-being: What works for women. [wiley.com]. *Health Expectations*, *25*(6), 2971–2981. DOI: 10.1111/hex.13605 PMID: 36321376

Han, X., Xiao, S., Sheng, J., & Zhang, G. (2024). Enhancing efficiency and decision-making in higher education through intelligent commercial integration: Leveraging artificial intelligence. [HTML]. *Journal of the Knowledge Economy*, *16*(1), 1546–1582. DOI: 10.1007/s13132-024-01868-2

Haristiani, N. (2019). *Artificial Intelligence (AI) Chatbot as Language Learning Medium: An inquiry*. Journal of Physics: Conference Series, Volume 1387, International Conference on Education, Science and Technology 2019, Padang, Indonesia, https://doi.org/DOI: 10.1088/1742 6596/1387/1/012020

Harrison, T. & Polizzi, G. (2022). (In) civility and adolescents' moral decision making online: Drawing on moral theory to advance digital citizenship education. Education and Information Technologies.

Harrison, J. H.Jr, Gilbertson, J. R., Hanna, M. G., Olson, N. H., Seheult, J. N., Sorace, J. M., & Stram, M. N. (2021). Introduction to artificial intelligence and machine learning for pathology. *Archives of Pathology & Laboratory Medicine*, *145*(10), 1228–1254. DOI: 10.5858/arpa.2020-0541-CP PMID: 33493264

Hassan, E., Groot, W., & Volante, L. (2022). Education funding and learning outcomes in Sub-Saharan Africa: A review of reviews. [sciencedirect.com]. *International Journal of Educational Research Open*, *3*, 100181. DOI: 10.1016/j.ijedro.2022.100181

Hassani, H. & Silva, E. S. (2023). The role of ChatGPT in data science: how ai-assisted conversational interfaces are revolutionizing the field. Big data and cognitive computing. mdpi.com

He, R. (2024). Let's keep boys out: promoting exclusion as a means to actualize feminist digital citizenship in China. Citizenship Studies.

Heilporn, G., Lakhal, S., & Bélisle, M. (2021). An examination of teachers' strategies to foster student engagement in blended learning in higher education. [springer.com]. *International Journal of Educational Technology in Higher Education*, *18*(1), 25. DOI: 10.1186/s41239-021-00260-3 PMID: 34805484

Helmiatin, H., Hidayat, A., & Kahar, M. R. (2024). Investigating the adoption of AI in higher education: A study of public universities in Indonesia. *Cogent Education, 11*(1), 2380175. Advance online publication. DOI: 10.1080/2331186X.2024.2380175

Hendriyani, Y., Anwar, M., Hidayat, H., Sabrina, E., Pardjono, P., & Saari, E. M. (2023). Factor Analysis of the Relationship of Curiosity and Device Addiction Through Motivation to Digital Literacy in the Context of Smart Learning. *Jurnal Pendidikan Vokasi, 13*(3), 320–333. DOI: 10.21831/jpv.v13i3.62720

Hennessy, S., D'Angelo, S., McIntyre, N., Koomar, S., Kreimeia, A., Cao, L., Brugha, M., & Zubairi, A. (2022). Technology use for teacher professional development in low-and middle-income countries: A systematic review. [sciencedirect.com]. *Computers and Education Open, 3*, 100080. DOI: 10.1016/j.caeo.2022.100080

He, R., & Huang, X. (2025). Conceptualizing gossip as a counterdiscourse: Alternative ways of publicly alleging sexual misconduct in an online groupie community. *International Journal of Cultural Studies, 28*(2), 425–441. DOI: 10.1177/13678779241280291

Hershcovich, D., Frank, S., Lent, H., de Lhoneux, M., Abdou, M., Brandl, S., Bugliarello, E., Piqueras, L. C., Chalkidis, I., Cui, R., Fierro, C., Margatina, K., Rust, P., & Søgaard, A. (2022). Challenges and Strategies in Cross-Cultural NLP. In *Proceedings of the 60th Annual Meeting of the Association for Computational Linguistics* (Volume 1: Long Papers). https://doi.org/DOI: 10.18653/v1/2022.acl-long.482

Higgins, N., Ferri, D., & Donnellan, K. (2023). Enhancing access to digital culture for vulnerable groups: the role of public authorities in breaking down barriers. *International Journal for the Semiotics of Law-Revue internationale de Sémiotique juridique, 36*(5), 2087-2114.

Hill, J., Ford, R., & Fareras, I. (2015). Real Conversations with Artificial Intelligence: A Comparison Between Human–Human Online Conversations and Human Chatbot Conversations. *Computers in Human Behavior, 49*, 245–250. Advance online publication. DOI: 10.1016/j.chb.2015.02.026

Ho, S. S., Bowser, G., Templer, P., & Green, S. A. (2023). Learning for sustainability: partnerships for the goals. Sustainable Earth Reviews. springer.com

Hod, M., Divakar, H., Kihara, A. B., & Geary, M. (2023). The femtech revolution—A new approach to pregnancy management: Digital transformation of maternity care—The hybrid e-health perinatal clinic addressing the unmet needs of low-and middle-income countries. [wiley.com]. *International Journal of Gynaecology and Obstetrics: the Official Organ of the International Federation of Gynaecology and Obstetrics, 163*(1), 4–10. DOI: 10.1002/ijgo.15032 PMID: 37554042

Holmes, W. (2020). Artificial intelligence in education. In *Encyclopedia of education and information technologies* (pp. 88–103). Springer International Publishing., DOI: 10.1007/978-3-030-10576-1_107

Holmes, W., Bialik, M., & Fadel, C. (2019). *Artificial intelligence in education promises and implications for teaching and learning*. Center for Curriculum Redesign.

Holmes, W., Bialik, M., & Fadel, C. (2019). *Artificial intelligence in education: Promises and implications for teaching and learning*. Center for Curriculum Redesign.

Holroyd, C. (2023). Technological innovation and building a 'super smart' society: Japan's vision of society 5.0. https://www.tandfonline.com/doi/full/10.1080/17516234.2020.1749340

Holroyd, C. (2022). Technological innovation and building a 'super smart' society: Japan's vision of society 5.0. *Journal of Asian Public Policy, 15*(1), 18–31. DOI: 10.1080/17516234.2020.1749340

Hong, J., & Kim, K. (2025). Impact of AIoT education program on digital and AI literacy of elementary school students. *Education and Information Technologies, 30*(1), 107–130. DOI: 10.1007/s10639-024-12758-0

Hooda, M., Rana, C., Dahiya, O., & Rizwan…, A. (2022). Artificial intelligence for assessment and feedback to enhance student success in higher education. Mathematical …. wiley.com

Hooda, M., Rana, C., Dahiya, O., Rizwan, A., & Hossain, M. S. (2022). Artificial intelligence for assessment and feedback to enhance student success in higher education. [wiley.com]. *Mathematical Problems in Engineering, 2022*(1), 5215722. DOI: 10.1155/2022/5215722

Horrigan, J. B., Whitacre, B. E., & Galperin, H. (2024). Understanding uptake in demand-side broadband subsidy programs: The affordable connectivity program case.. *Telecommunications Policy, 48*(8), 102812. DOI: 10.1016/j.telpol.2024.102812

Hsieh, Y.-Z., Lin, S.-S., Luo, Y.-C., Jeng, Y.-L., Tan, S.-W., Chen, C.-R., & Chiang, P.-Y. (2020). ARCS-Assisted Teaching Robots Based on Anticipatory Computing and Emotional Big Data for Improving Sustainable Learning Efficiency and Motivation. *Sustainability (Basel), 12*(14), 5605. Advance online publication. DOI: 10.3390/su12145605

Huang, L. (2023). Ethics of Artificial Intelligence in Education: Student Privacy and Data Protection. In Science Insights Education Frontiers (Vol. 16, Issue 2, p. 2577). https://doi.org/DOI: 10.15354/sief.23.re202

Huang, Z. & Yanan, S. (2024). The Transforming Landscape of higher Education: Trends and challenges. Economic Sciences. economic-sciences.com

Huang, T. (2024). Decentralized social networks and the future of free speech online. *Computer Law & Security Review*, *55*, 106059.

Hu, C. (2022). A Comparative Study of Cultural and Traditional Education in Primary and Secondary Schools in Developed Countries Based on the MOPSO-CD-DNN Model. In *Computational Intelligence and Neuroscience* (Vol. 2022, p. 1). Hindawi Publishing Corporation., DOI: 10.1155/2022/3973763

Hwang, Y., & Lim, C. (2024). Development of instructional design principles for using ICT in resource-limited learning environments: a case of Bangladesh. In Asia Pacific Education Review (Vol. 25, Issue 5, p. 1465). Springer Science+Business Media. https://doi.org/DOI: 10.1007/s12564-024-09996-9

Hyrynsalmi, S. M. (2024). Challenges and opportunities: Implementing diversity and inclusion in software engineering university level education in Finland. In *Journal of Systems and Software* (p. 112239). Elsevier BV., DOI: 10.1016/j.jss.2024.112239

Iakovlev, I., Kremleva, E. S., & Guzanov, R. (2023). Enterprise automation using artificial intelligence: Methods, technologies and prospects. In *E3S Web of Conferences* (Vol. 460, p. 4007). EDP Sciences., DOI: 10.1051/e3sconf/202346004007

Iatrellis, O., Samaras, N., & Kokkinos, K. (2024). Towards a capability maturity model for Micro-credential providers in European higher education. Trends in Higher Education. mdpi.com

Idrus, F., Ramli, L. N., & Habib, N. J. (2023). Exploring Preservice Teachers' Experiences of Implementing Culturally Responsive Teaching in the ESL Classrooms. In Theory and Practice in Language Studies (Vol. 13, Issue 3, p. 766). Academy Publication. https://doi.org/DOI: 10.17507/tpls.1303.26

Imran, M. C., Khaliq Bashar, Budiarti Putri Uleng, Nina Ariani, Sukmawati, Suharti Siradjuddin, Sujarwo, & Irman. (2022). The Impact of Computer Assisted Language Learning (CALL) Technology on Indonesian Learners' Speaking Skills. *IJOLEH : International Journal of Education and Humanities, 1*(2), 183–189. DOI: 10.56314/ijoleh.v1i2.83

Imran, A. (2023). Why addressing digital inequality should be a priority. [wiley.com]. *The Electronic Journal on Information Systems in Developing Countries, 89*(3), e12255. DOI: 10.1002/isd2.12255

Indrajaya, A. N. (n.d.). Critical reflections on flourishing businesses through collaborative online international learning in the context of the UN Sustainable Development Goals.

Iqbal, M., Nasir, J., Supriyadi, A., Nurhayati, S., Hafidzah, H., Pernando, Y., & Purtiningrum, S. W. (2024). *Konsep Kecerdasan Buatan* (Vol. CV). Gita Lentera.

Jacques, P. (2020). *Sustainability: The basics*. Routledge. DOI: 10.4324/9780429346613

Jain, R. (2022). Translingual-identity-as-pedagogy: Problematizing monolingually oriented "native-nonnative" identity constructions through critical dialogues in EAP classrooms. *TESOL Journal, 13*(3), e666. DOI: 10.1002/tesj.666

Jakob, J. C. (2023). Exploring the Use of Flipped Classroom in Influencing Listening Comprehension of Civil Engineering Students. [Indonesian Journal of English Teaching]. *IJET, 12*(1), 48–56. DOI: 10.15642/ijet2.2023.12.1.48-56

Jakob, J. C., Sari, H. F. A., Wuarlela, M., Persulessy, S. I., Saptenno, S., Nussy, H., & Salawaney, V. S. (2024). How Does Technology-Assisted Language Learning (TALL) Influence Elementary School Students Learning? *IDEAS: Journal on English Language Teaching and Learning. Linguistics and Literature, 12*(2), 1633–1646. DOI: 10.24256/ideas.v12i2.5860

Javaid, M., Haleem, A., Singh, R. P., & Suman, R. (2023). Towards insighting cybersecurity for healthcare domains: A comprehensive review of recent practices and trends. *Cyber Security and Applications, 1*, 100016.

Jayabalan, J., Dorasamy, M., & Raman, M. (2021). Reshaping higher educational institutions through frugal open innovation. [mdpi.com]. *Journal of Open Innovation, 7*(2), 145. DOI: 10.3390/joitmc7020145

Jegan, R. & Nimi, W. S. (2024). On the development of low power wearable devices for assessment of physiological vital parameters: a systematic review. Journal of Public Health. springer.com

Jeon, E. & Maula, M. (2022). Progress toward understanding tensions in corporate venture capital: A systematic review. Journal of Business Venturing. sciencedirect.com

Jin, L., Zhai, X., Wang, K., Zhang, K., Wu, D., Nazir, A., Jiang, J., & Liao, W. H. (2024). Big data, machine learning, and digital twin assisted additive manufacturing: A review. [sciencedirect.com]. *Materials & Design*, *244*, 113086. DOI: 10.1016/j.matdes.2024.113086

Johnson, S. D., Kuykendall, J. A., & Winkle-Wagner, R. (2023). Financing the dream: The impact of financial aid on graduate education for underrepresented minority students. In *Standing on the Outside Looking* (pp. 45–62). Routledge. [HTML] DOI: 10.4324/9781003447085-4

Joudyian, N., Doshmangir, L., Mahdavi, M., Tabrizi, J. S., & Gordeev, V. S. (2021). Public-private partnerships in primary health care: A scoping review. [springer.com]. *BMC Health Services Research*, *21*(1), 1–18. DOI: 10.1186/s12913-020-05979-9 PMID: 33397388

JOYCE. J., & Harris, L. A. (2018). Artificial Intelligence (AI) and Education. https://digital.library.unt.edu/ark:/67531/metadc1228526/m2/1/high_res_d/IF10937_2018Aug01.pdf

Jun, H. & Kim, M. (2021). From stakeholder communication to engagement for the sustainable development goals (SDGs): A case study of LG electronics. Sustainability. mdpi.com

Juwika, A. (2023). Peran Artificial Intelligence dalam Meningkatkan Efisiensi dan Efektifitas Sistem Pendidikan. *COMSERVA: Jurnal Penelitian Dan Pengabdian Masyarakat*, *2*(12), 3181–3187. Advance online publication. DOI: 10.59141/comserva.v2i12.731

Kabudi, T., Pappas, I., & Olsen, D. H. (2021). AI-enabled adaptive learning systems: A systematic mapping of the literature. Computers and education [sciencedirect.com]. *Artificial Intelligence*, *2*, 100017.

Kallunki, V., Katajavuori, N., Kinnunen, P., Anttila, H., Tuononen, T., Haarala-Muhonen, A., Pyörälä, E., & Myyry, L. (2023). Comparison of voluntary and forced digital leaps in higher education – Teachers' experiences of the added value of using digital tools in teaching and learning. In Education and Information Technologies (Vol. 28, Issue 8, p. 10005). Springer Science+Business Media. https://doi.org/DOI: 10.1007/s10639-022-11559-7

Kalogirou, S. A. (2007). Introduction to artificial intelligence technology. *Artificial intelligence in energy and renewable energy systems*, 1-46.

Kaluarachchi, Y. (2022). Implementing data-driven smart city applications for future cities. Smart Cities.

Kamalov, F., Calonge, D. S., & Gurrib, I. (2023). New Era of Artificial Intelligence in Education: Towards a Sustainable Multifaceted Revolution. In Sustainability (Vol. 15, Issue 16, p. 12451). Multidisciplinary Digital Publishing Institute. https://doi.org/DOI: 10.3390/su151612451

Kamila, J. T., Nurnazhiifa, K., Sati, L., & Setiawati, R. (2022). Pengembangan guru dalam menghadapi tantangan kebijakan pendidikan di era revolusi industri 4.0. *Jurnal Pendidikan Tambusai*, *6*(2), 10013–10018.

Kamyab, H., Khademi, T., Chelliapan, S., SaberiKamarposhti, M., Rezania, S., Yusuf, M., Farajnezhad, M., Abbas, M., Hun Jeon, B., & Ahn, Y. (2023). The latest innovative avenues for the utilization of artificial Intelligence and big data analytics in water resource management. [sciencedirect.com]. *Results in Engineering*, *20*, 101566. DOI: 10.1016/j.rineng.2023.101566

Kangana, N., Kankanamge, N., De Silva, C., Goonetilleke, A., Mahamood, R., & Ranasinghe, D. (2024). Bridging Community Engagement and Technological Innovation for Creating Smart and Resilient Cities: A Systematic Literature Review. [mdpi.com]. *Smart Cities*, *7*(6), 3823–3852. DOI: 10.3390/smartcities7060147

Kapustina, L. V. (2021). Digital footprint analysis to develop a personal digital competency-based profile. In *Current Achievements, Challenges and Digital Chances of Knowledge Based Economy* (pp. 591–596). Springer International Publishing.

Karhunen, P., Kankaanranta, A., & Räisänen, T. (2023). Towards a Richer understanding of language and identity in the MNC: Constructing cosmopolitan identities through "English". *MIR. Management International Review*, *63*(3), 507–530. DOI: 10.1007/s11575-023-00504-6

Kayyali, M. (2024). Exploring Accreditation Standards and Processes. In Quality Assurance and Accreditation in Higher Education: Issues, Models, and Best Practices (pp. 1-60). Cham: Springer Nature Switzerland. [HTML] DOI: 10.1007/978-3-031-66623-0_1

Kazimzade, G., Patzer, Y., & Pinkwart, N. (2019). Artificial Intelligence in Education Meets Inclusive Educational Technology—The Technical State-of-the-Art and Possible Directions. In *Perspectives on rethinking and reforming education* (p. 61). Springer Nature., DOI: 10.1007/978-981-13-8161-4_4

Kerimbayev, N., Umirzakova, Z., Shadiev, R., & Jotsov, V. (2023). A student-centered approach using modern technologies in distance learning: a systematic review of the literature [Review of A student-centered approach using modern technologies in distance learning: a systematic review of the literature]. Smart Learning Environments, 10(1). Springer Nature. DOI: 10.1186/s40561-023-00280-8

Keshta, I. & Odeh, A. (2021). Security and privacy of electronic health records: Concerns and challenges. Egyptian Informatics Journal. sciencedirect.com

Khallaf, R., Kang, K., Hastak, M., & Othman, K. (2022). Public–Private Partnerships for Higher Education Institutions in the United States. Buildings. mdpi.com

Khan, R. A., Jawaid, M., Khan, A. R., & Sajjad, M. (2023). ChatGPT - Reshaping medical education and clinical management. In Pakistan Journal of Medical Sciences (Vol. 39, Issue 2). Professional Medical Publications. https://doi.org/DOI: 10.12669/pjms.39.2.7653

Khang, A., Ragimova, N. A., Hajimahmud, V. A., & Alyar, A. V. (2022). Advanced technologies and data management in the smart healthcare system. In *AI-Centric Smart City Ecosystems* (pp. 261–270). CRC Press. [HTML] DOI: 10.1201/9781003252542-16

Khan, I., Ahmad, A. R., Jabeur, N., & Mahdi, M. N. (2021). An Artificial Intelligence Approach To Monitor Student Performance and Devise Preventive Measures. *Smart Learning Environments*, *8*(1), 17. Advance online publication. DOI: 10.1186/s40561-021-00161-y

Khan, S. M., Shafi, I., Butt, W. H., Diez, I. D. L. T., Flores, M. A. L., Galán, J. C., & Ashraf, I. (2023). A systematic review of disaster management systems: Approaches, challenges, and future directions. [mdpi.com]. *Land (Basel)*, *12*(8), 1514. DOI: 10.3390/land12081514

Khazanchi, R., Di Mitri, D., & Drachsler, H. (2025). The Effect of AI-Based Systems on Mathematics Achievement in Rural Context: A Quantitative Study. [wiley.com]. *Journal of Computer Assisted Learning*, *41*(1), e13098. DOI: 10.1111/jcal.13098

Khobragade, J. W., Kumar, A., Binti Abd Aziz, S. N., & Maurya, D. (2021). The anti-maritime piracy law in india and malaysia: An analytical study. *Journal of International Maritime Safety, Environmental Affairs, and Shipping*, *5*(4), 208–219. DOI: 10.1080/25725084.2021.2006462

Khosravi, H., Shum, S. B., Chen, G., Conati, C., Tsai, Y., Kay, J., Knight, S., Martínez-Maldonado, R., Sadiq, S., & Gašević, D. (2022). Explainable Artificial Intelligence in education. In *Computers and Education Artificial Intelligence* (Vol. 3, p. 100074). Elsevier BV., DOI: 10.1016/j.caeai.2022.100074

Kieslich, K., Keller, B., & Starke, C. (2022). Artificial intelligence ethics by design. Evaluating public perception on the importance of ethical design principles of artificial intelligence. In Big Data & Society (Vol. 9, Issue 1). SAGE Publishing. https://doi.org/DOI: 10.1177/20539517221092956

Kim, J., Lee, H.-K., & Cho, Y. H. (2022). Learning design to support student-AI collaboration: perspectives of leading teachers for AI in education. In Education and Information Technologies (Vol. 27, Issue 5, p. 6069). Springer Science+Business Media. https://doi.org/DOI: 10.1007/s10639-021-10831-6

Kim, M. J. (2023). Toward coherence: A space sector public-private partnership typology. Space Policy. sciencedirect.com

Kim, D., & Wang, Z. (2023). The ethics of virtuality: Navigating the complexities of human-like virtual influencers in the social media marketing realm. *Frontiers in Communication*, *8*, 1205610.

Kim, H. S., Kim, N. Y., & Cha, Y. (2021). Is it beneficial to use AI chatbots to improve learners' speaking performance? *Journal of Asia TEFL*, *18*(1), 161–178. DOI: 10.18823/asiatefl.2021.18.1.10.161

Kim, S., Jang, Y., Kim, W., Choi, S., Jung, H., Kim, S., & Kim, H. (2021). Why and What to Teach: AI Curriculum for Elementary School. *Proceedings of the AAAI Conference on Artificial Intelligence*, *35*(17), 15569–15576. Advance online publication. DOI: 10.1609/aaai.v35i17.17833

Kioskli, K., Grigoriou, E., Islam, S., Yiorkas, A. M., Christofi, L., & Mouratidis, H. (2025). A risk and conformity assessment framework to ensure security and resilience of healthcare systems and medical supply chain. [springer.com]. *International Journal of Information Security*, *24*(2), 1–28. DOI: 10.1007/s10207-025-01009-z

Kirovska-Simjanoska, D. (2022). Digital Literacy as a Tool for Fostering Engagement and Motivation in Online/Hybrid Esp Classes. *Journal of Teaching English for Specific and Academic Purposes*, *10*(3), 533–546. DOI: 10.22190/JTESAP2203533K

Kissler, K., Thumm, E. B., Smith, D. C., Anderson, J. L., Wood, R. E., Johnson, R., Roberts, M., Carmitchel-Fifer, A., Patterson, N., Amura, C. R., Barton, A. J., & Jones, J. (2024). Perinatal telehealth: Meeting patients where they are. [wiley.com]. *Journal of Midwifery & Women's Health*, *69*(1), 9–16. DOI: 10.1111/jmwh.13560 PMID: 37641584

Kizilcec, R. F. (2024). To advance AI use in education, focus on understanding educators. [springer.com]. *International Journal of Artificial Intelligence in Education*, *34*(1), 12–19. DOI: 10.1007/s40593-023-00351-4 PMID: 37359103

Komendantova, N., Erokhin, D., & Albano, T. (2023). Misinformation and its impact on contested policy issues: the example of migration discourses. Societies.

Kooli, C. & Abadli, R. (2022). Could education quality audit enhance human resources management processes of the higher education institutions?. Vision. sagepub.com

Korte, S. M., Cheung, W. M. Y., Maasilta, M., Kong, S. C., Keskitalo, P., Wang, L., Lau, C. M., Lee, J. C. K., & Gu, M. M. (2024). Enhancing artificial intelligence literacy through cross-cultural online workshops. *Computers and Education Open*, *6*, 100164. DOI: 10.1016/j.caeo.2024.100164

Kosimova, M., Qambarova, A., & Salimova, D. (2024, November). The Problems of Intercultural Communication of English Language. In *Conference Proceedings: Fostering Your Research Spirit* (pp. 390-393).

Kozyreva, A., Wineburg, S., Lewandowsky, S., & Hertwig, R. (2023). Critical ignoring as a core competence for digital citizens. *Current Directions in Psychological Science*, *32*(1), 81–88. DOI: 10.1177/09637214221121570 PMID: 37994317

Kraus, S., McDowell, W., Ribeiro-Soriano, D. E., & Rodríguez-García, M. (2021). The role of innovation and knowledge for entrepreneurship and regional development. [tandfonline.com]. *Entrepreneurship and Regional Development*, *33*(3-4), 175–184. DOI: 10.1080/22797254.2021.1872929

Kreienbrinck, A., Hanft-Robert, S., Forray, A. I., Nozewu, A., & Mösko, M. (2025). Usability of technological tools to overcome language barriers in healthcare–a scoping review. *Archives of Public Health = Archives Belges de Santé Publique*, *83*(1), 52. DOI: 10.1186/s13690-025-01543-1 PMID: 40001263

Krutka, D. G., Smits, R. M., & Willhelm, T. A. (2021). Don't be evil: Should we use Google in schools?. TechTrends. springer.com

Kuhail, M. A., ElSayary, A., Farooq, S., & Alghamdi, A. (2022). Exploring immersive learning experiences: A survey. Informatics. mdpi.com

Kumar, R. (2023). English language and digital literacy: Navigating the information age. *Journal of International English Research Studies (JIERS), 1*(2), 25-31. ISSN: 3048-5231

Kuppan, N., Padman, M., Mahadeva, M., Srinivasan, S., & Devarajan, R. (2024). A comprehensive review of sustainable bioremediation techniques: Eco friendly solutions for waste and pollution management. Waste Management Bulletin. sciencedirect.com

Kurniawati, M. P., Mustakim, A., & Hudha, M. N. (2023). Peningkatan Motivasi dan Hasil Belajar Fisika Dengan Penggunaan Teknologi Dalam Pembelajaran dan Pendekatan Berdiferensiasi Pada Peserta Didik Kelas X – 1 SMA Negeri 6 Kediri Tahun Pelajaran 2022/2023. *Jurnal Pembelajaran, Bimbingan, dan Pengelolaan Pendidikan, 3*(6), 484–499. DOI: 10.17977/um065v3i62023p484-499

Lagos-Castillo, A., Chiappe, A., Ramirez-Montoya, M. S., & Rodríguez, D. F. B. (2025). Mapping the Intelligent Classroom: Examining the Emergence of Personalized Learning Solutions in the Digital Age. Contemporary Educational Technology, 17(1). ed.gov

Lai, Y.-H. (2023). Multi-ethnic computational thinking and cultural respect in unmanned aerial vehicle-assisted culturally responsive teaching. In *Frontiers in Psychology* (Vol. 14). Frontiers Media., DOI: 10.3389/fpsyg.2023.1098812

Lamptey, D., McIsaac, J. D., MacQuarrie, M., Cummings, R., Rossiter, M. D., Janus, M., & Turner, J. (2024). Relationship between Childhood Disability or Developmental Delay and COVID-19 Pandemic Impacts on Families across the Canadian Maritime Provinces. In Journal of Child and Family Studies (Vol. 33, Issue 2, p. 458). Springer Science+Business Media. DOI: 10.1007/s10826-023-02779-7

Lansing, A. E., Romero, N. J., Siantz, E., Silva, V., Center, K., Casteel, D., & Gilmer, T. (2023). Building trust: Leadership reflections on community empowerment and engagement in a large urban initiative. [springer.com]. *BMC Public Health, 23*(1), 1252. DOI: 10.1186/s12889-023-15860-z PMID: 37380973

Laryea, K., Paepcke, A., Mirzaei, K., & Stevens, M. L. (2021). Ambiguous credentials: How learners use and make sense of Massively Open Online Courses. [tandfonline.com]. *The Journal of Higher Education, 92*(4), 596–622. DOI: 10.1080/00221546.2020.1851571

Le, A. V., & Metzger, W. (2024). Assessing the impact and challenges of AI-based language models on the education sector: A proposal for new assessment strategies and design. *Journal of Teaching in Travel & Tourism, 24*(2), 167–178. DOI: 10.1080/15313220.2024.2311907

Leavy, P. (2017). *Research design: Quantitative, qualitative, mixed methods, arts-based and community-based participatory research approaches*. The Guilford Press.

Leclercq, E. M. & Rijshouwer, E. A. (2022). Enabling citizens' Right to the Smart City through the co-creation of digital platforms. Urban Transformations.

Lee, H. Y., Lin, C. J., Wang, W. S., Chang, W. C., & Huang, Y. M. (2023). Precision education via timely intervention in K-12 computer programming course to enhance programming skill and affective-domain learning objectives. [springer.com]. *International Journal of STEM Education, 10*(1), 52. DOI: 10.1186/s40594-023-00444-5

Lee, S., Kim, J., & Sung, Y. H. (2022). When infographics work better: The interplay between temporal frame and message format in e-health communication. *Psychology & Health, 37*(7), 917–931. DOI: 10.1080/08870446.2021.1912342 PMID: 33886402

Lee, V. V., Vijayakumar, S., Ng, W. Y., Lau, N. Y., Leong, Q. Y., Ooi, D. S. Q., Su, L. L., Lee, Y. S., Chan, S.-Y., Blasiak, A., & Ho, D. (2023). Personalization and localization as key expectations of digital health intervention in women pre- to post-pregnancy. [nature.com]. *NPJ Digital Medicine*, *6*(1), 183. DOI: 10.1038/s41746-023-00924-6 PMID: 37775533

Legislation and Ethics. (2020). https://www.educause.edu/ecar/research-publications/the-evolving-landscape-of-data-privacy-in-higher-education/legislation-and-ethics

Levin, M. (2022). Technological approach to mind everywhere: an experimentally-grounded framework for understanding diverse bodies and minds. Frontiers in systems neuroscience. frontiersin.org

Li, L., Taeihagh, A., & Tan, S. Y. (2022). What factors drive policy transfer in smart city development? Insights from a Delphi study. Sustainable Cities and Society. sciencedirect.com

Liang, W. (2020). *Development Trend and Thinking of Artificial Intelligence in Education. In 2022 International Wireless Communications and Mobile Computing*. IWCMC., DOI: 10.1109/IWCMC48107.2020.9148078

Li, C., & Xing, W. (2021). Natural language generation using deep learning to support MOOC learners. *International Journal of Artificial Intelligence in Education, 31*(2), 186–214. DOI: 10.1007/s40593-020-00235-x

Lievens, E., & Verdoodt, V. (2017). Looking for needles in a haystack: Key issues affecting children's rights in the General Data Protection Regulation. In Computer Law & Security Review (Vol. 34, Issue 2, p. 269). Elsevier BV. https://doi.org/DOI: 10.1016/j.clsr.2017.09.007

Lim, W. M. (2024). What is qualitative research? An overview and guidelines. Australasian Marketing Journal. sagepub.com

Lin, C. C., Huang, A. Y. Q., & Yang, S. J. H. (2023). A review of ai-driven conversational chatbots implementation methodologies and challenges (1999–2022). Sustainability. mdpi.com

Lin, M. P. C., & Chang, D. (2020). Enhancing post-secondary writers' writing skills with a chatbot. *Journal of Educational Technology & Society*, *23*(1), 78–92.

Liriwati, F. Y. (2023). Transformasi Kurikulum; Kecerdasan Buatan untuk Membangun Pendidikan yang Relevan di Masa Depan. *IHSAN: Jurnal Pendidikan Islam*, *1*(2), 62–71. DOI: 10.61104/ihsan.v1i2.61

Liu, M. (2023). Exploring the Application of Artificial Intelligence in Foreign Language Teaching: Challenges and Future Development. In SHS Web of Conferences (Vol. 168, p. 3025). EDP Sciences. DOI: 10.1051/shsconf/202316803025

Liu, T. L., Song, Q. J., & Qi, Y. (2021). An integrated approach to evaluating the coupling coordination degree between low-carbon development and air quality in Chinese cities. Advances in Climate Change Research. sciencedirect.com

Liu, W. (2024). The Integration of ChatGPT in Language Education: Exploring Contexts, Assessing Impacts, and Unpacking Implications. In *In AI in Language Teaching, Learning, and Assessment* (pp. 1–21). IGI Global. https://www.igi-global.com/chapter/the-integration-of-chatgpt-in-language-education/339086

Liu, Y. (2025). The Digital Horizon: Opportunities for Developing Social Capital and Advancing Digital Citizenship. In Digital Citizenship and Building a Responsible Online Presence (pp. 43-76). IGI Global Scientific Publishing.

Liu, B. F., Shi, D., Lim, J. R., Islam, K., Edwards, A. L., & Seeger, M. (2022). When crises hit home: How US higher education leaders navigate values during uncertain times. [springer.com]. *Journal of Business Ethics*, *179*(2), 353–368. DOI: 10.1007/s10551-021-04820-5 PMID: 34002104

Liu, K.-P., Tai, S.-J. D., & Liu, C.-C. (2018). Enhancing Language Learning Through Creation: The Effect of Digital Storytelling on Student Learning Motivation and Performance in a School English Course. *Educational Technology Research and Development*, *66*(4), 913–935. DOI: 10.1007/s11423-018-9592-z

Liu, Z., & Yushchik, E. (2024). Exploring the prospects of using artificial intelligence in education. *Cogent Education*, *11*(1), 2353464. Advance online publication. DOI: 10.1080/2331186X.2024.2353464

Lo, N. P. K. (2024). The confluence of digital literacy and eco-consciousness: harmonizing digital skills with sustainable practices in education. Platforms.

Louie, B., Björling, E. A., Kuo, A. C., & Alves-Oliveira, P. (2022). Designing for culturally responsive social robots: An application of a participatory framework. In *Frontiers in Robotics and AI* (Vol. 9). Frontiers Media., DOI: 10.3389/frobt.2022.983408

Love, E. A., Degen, S. C., Craig, J. E., & Helmers, R. A. (2021). Activating the hospital incident command system response in a community specialty practice: the Mayo clinic experience. WMJ. wmjonline.org

Luan, H., Géczy, P., Lai, H., Gobert, J. D., Yang, S. J. H., Ogata, H., Baltes, J., Guerra, R. da S., Li, P., & Tsai, C. (2020). *Challenges and Future Directions of Big Data and Artificial Intelligence in Education* [Review of Challenges and Future Directions of Big Data and Artificial Intelligence in Education]. Frontiers Media., DOI: 10.3389/fpsyg.2020.580820

Luckin, R., & Holmes, W. (2016). Intelligence Unleashed: An argument for AI in Education. https://oro.open.ac.uk/50104/

Luckin, R., & Holmes, W. (2016). *Intelligence Unleashed: An argument for AI in Education*. UCL Knowledge Lab, University College London, https://www.researchgate.net/publication/299561597_Intelligence_Unleashed_An_argument_for_AI_in_Education

Luckin, R., Holmes, W., Griffiths, M., & Forcier, L. B. (2016). *Intelligence Unleashed: An Argument for AI in Education*. Pearson Education.

Lukita, C., Lutfiani, N., Salam, R., Pangilinan, G. A., Rafika, A. S., & Ahsanitaqwim, R. (2024, August). Technology Integration in Cultural Heritage Preservation Enhancing Community Engagement and Effectiveness. In 2024 3rd International Conference on Creative Communication and Innovative Technology (ICCIT) (pp. 1-5). IEEE. [HTML] DOI: 10.1109/ICCIT62134.2024.10701088

Luo, S. (2022). The Optimization of Civic Education with the Assistance of Artificial Intelligence Devices. In *Wireless Communications and Mobile Computing* (Vol. 2022, p. 1). Wiley., DOI: 10.1155/2022/4144654

Luo, Z., & Zhang, X. (2024). AI in education risk assessment mechanism analysis. *Applied Economics*, •••, 1–13. DOI: 10.1080/00036846.2024.2321835

Lybeck, R., Koiranen, I., & Koivula, A. (2024). From digital divide to digital capital: The role of education and digital skills in social media participation. *Universal Access in the Information Society*, *23*(4), 1657–1669. DOI: 10.1007/s10209-022-00961-0

Lytras, M. D. (2024). Transformative learning for future higher education: The artificial intelligence-enabled learning revolution 2035. In *Digital Transformation in Higher Education, Part B* (pp. 231–241). Emerald Publishing Limited.

Maclean, M., Harvey, C., Yang, R., & Mueller, F. (2021). Elite philanthropy in the United States and United Kingdom in the new age of inequalities. [wiley.com]. *International Journal of Management Reviews, 23*(3), 330–352. DOI: 10.1111/ijmr.12247

MacLeod, C. J., Brandt, A. J., Collins, K., & Dicks, L. V. (2022). Giving stakeholders a voice in governance: Biodiversity priorities for New Zealand's agriculture. [wiley.com]. *People and Nature, 4*(2), 330–350. DOI: 10.1002/pan3.10285

Madden, S. K., Ahuja, K. D., Blewitt, C., Hill, B., Hills, A. P., & Skouteris, H. (2023). Understanding the pathway between work and health outcomes for women during the preconception, pregnancy, and postpartum periods through the framing of maternal obesity. [wiley.com]. *Obesity Reviews, 24*(12), e13637. DOI: 10.1111/obr.13637 PMID: 37655832

Mageira, K., Pittou, D., Papasalouros, A., Kotis, K., Zangogianni, P., & Daradoumis, A. (2022). Educational AI Chatbots for Content and Language Integrated Learning. *Applied Sciences (Basel, Switzerland), 12*(7), 3239. Advance online publication. DOI: 10.3390/app12073239

Maghsudi, S., Lan, A., Xu, J., & van der Schaar, M. (2021). Personalized Education in the Artificial Intelligence Era: What to Expect Next. In IEEE Signal Processing Magazine (Vol. 38, Issue 3, p. 37). Institute of Electrical and Electronics Engineers. https://doi.org/DOI: 10.1109/MSP.2021.3055032

Mak, K.-K., Wong, Y.-H., & Pichika, M. R. (2024). Artificial intelligence in drug discovery and development. In *Drug discovery and evaluation: Safety and pharmacokinetic assays* (pp. 1461–1498). DOI: 10.1007/978-3-031-35529-5_92

Makda, F. (2025). Digital education: Mapping the landscape of virtual teaching in higher education–a bibliometric review. Education and Information Technologies. springer.com

Malia, A. (2024). New opportunities for sustainable development in the tourism sector with the use of disruptive digital technologies. In *Sustainable Tourism, Part A* (pp. 67–86). Emerald Publishing Limited. DOI: 10.1108/978-1-83797-979-020241005

Mallén, I. B. (2021). Freedom as the Essential Basis for Communication Rights. *The Handbook of Communication Rights, Law, and Ethics: Seeking Universality, Equality, Freedom and Dignity*, 7-19. DOI: 10.1002/9781119719564.ch1

Mani, N. S., Cawley, M., Henley, A., Triumph, T., & Williams, J. M. (2021). Creating a data science framework: A model for academic research libraries. [tandfonline.com]. *Journal of Library Administration, 61*(3), 281–300. DOI: 10.1080/01930826.2021.1883366

Manongga, D., Rahardja, U., Sembiring, I., Lutfiani, N., & Yadila, A. B. (2022). Dampak Kecerdasan Buatan Bagi Pendidikan. *ADI: Bisnis Digital Interdisiplin Jurnal, 3*(2), 41–55. Advance online publication. DOI: 10.34306/abdi.v3i2.792

Manta, O. & Mansi, E. (2024). The impact of globalization on innovative public procurement: challenges and opportunities. Administrative sciences. mdpi.com

Mantula, F., Chamisa, J. A., Nunu, W. N., & Nyanhongo, P. S. (2023). Women's Perspectives on Cultural Sensitivity of Midwives During Intrapartum Care at a Maternity Ward in a National Referral Hospital in Zimbabwe. [sagepub.com]. *SAGE Open Nursing, 9*, 23779608231160476. DOI: 10.1177/23779608231160476 PMID: 36875792

Mariani, L., Trivellato, B., Martini, M., & Marafioti, E. (2022). Achieving sustainable development goals through collaborative innovation: Evidence from four European initiatives. Journal of Business Ethics. springer.com

Markey, K., O'Brien, B., Kouta, C., Okantey, C., & O'Donnell, C. (2021). Embracing classroom cultural diversity: Innovations for nurturing inclusive intercultural learning and culturally responsive teaching. *Teaching and Learning in Nursing, 16*(3), 258–262. DOI: 10.1016/j.teln.2021.01.008

Marques-Cobeta, N. (2024). Artificial Intelligence in Education: Unveiling Opportunities and Challenges. Innovation and Technologies for the Digital Transformation of Education: European and Latin American Perspectives, 33-42. [HTML]

Marques, T. (2023). The expression of hate in hate speech. *Journal of Applied Philosophy, 40*(5), 769–787.

Marras, M., Boratto, L., Ramos, G., & Fenu, G. (2022). Equality of learning opportunity via individual fairness in personalized recommendations. [springer.com]. *International Journal of Artificial Intelligence in Education, 32*(3), 636–684. DOI: 10.1007/s40593-021-00271-1

Martin, F., Bacak, J., Polly, D., Wang, W., & Ahlgrim-Delzell, L. (2023). Teacher and school concerns and actions on elementary school children digital safety. TechTrends.

Martínez-Peláez, R., Ochoa-Brust, A., Rivera, S., Félix, V. G., Ostos, R., Brito, H., Félix, R. A., & Mena, L. J. (2023). Role of digital transformation for achieving sustainability: Mediated role of stakeholders, key capabilities, and technology. [mdpi.com]. *Sustainability (Basel), 15*(14), 11221. DOI: 10.3390/su151411221

Maslov, I., Nikou, S., & Hansen, P. (2021). Exploring user experience of learning management system. [emerald.com]. *The International Journal of Information and Learning Technology, 38*(4), 344–363. DOI: 10.1108/IJILT-03-2021-0046

Matahela, V. E. & van Rensburg, G. H. (2022). Motivation as a facilitator of self-leadership in nurse academics. Heliyon. cell.com

Matli, W., & Wamba, S. F. (2023). Work from anywhere: inequalities in technology infrastructure distribution for digit workers. In Digital Transformation and Society (Vol. 2, Issue 2, p. 149). https://doi.org/DOI: 10.1108/DTS-08-2022-0042

Ma, X., & Jiang, C. (2023; Vol. 14). On the Ethical Risks of Artificial Intelligence Applications in Education and Its Avoidance Strategies. In Journal of Education Humanities and Social Sciences., DOI: 10.54097/ehss.v14i.8868

McCoy, H. C., Allison, M. K., Hernandez, M., Ali, M. M., Stokes, M., Bogulski, C. A., & Eswaran, H. (2024). Assessment of pregnancy-related telehealth interventions in the United States: A 10-year scoping review. [HTML]. *Telemedicine Journal and e-Health, 30*(1), 36–46. PMID: 37256707

McKinney, L., Burridge, A. B., Lee, M. M., Bourdeau, G. V., & Miller-Waters, M. (2022). Incentivizing full-time enrollment at community colleges: What influences students' decision to take more courses? [HTML]. *Community College Review, 50*(2), 144–170. DOI: 10.1177/00915521211061416

Memon, F. N., & Memon, S. N. (2025). Digital Divide and Equity in Education: Bridging Gaps to Ensure Inclusive Learning. In Impact of Digitalization on Education and Social Sustainability (pp. 107-130). IGI Global.

Memon, F. N., & Memon, S. N. (2025). Digital Divide and Equity in Education: Bridging Gaps to Ensure Inclusive Learning. In Impact of Digitalization on Education and Social Sustainability (pp. 107-130). IGI Global. [HTML]

Mena-Guacas, A. F., Meza-Morales, J. A., Fernández, E., & López-Meneses, E. (2023). Digital collaboration in higher education: A study of digital skills and collaborative attitudes in students from diverse universities. *Education Sciences, 14*(1), 36. DOI: 10.3390/educsci14010036

Merhi, M. I. (2023). An evaluation of the critical success factors impacting artificial intelligence implementation. [HTML]. *International Journal of Information Management, 69*, 102545. DOI: 10.1016/j.ijinfomgt.2022.102545

Mészáros, J., Minari, J., & Huys, I. (2022). The future regulation of artificial intelligence systems in healthcare services and medical research in the European Union. In *Frontiers in Genetics* (Vol. 13). Frontiers Media., DOI: 10.3389/fgene.2022.927721

Mgaiwa, S. J. (2021). Leadership initiatives in response to institutional quality assurance challenges in Tanzania's private universities. Journal of Further and Higher Education. academia.edu

Mhlanga, D. (2024). Digital transformation of education, the limitations and prospects of introducing the fourth industrial revolution asynchronous online learning in emerging markets. Discover education. springer.com

Mhlanga, D. (2023). Open AI in Education, the Responsible and Ethical Use of ChatGPT Towards Lifelong Learning. In *FinTech and Artificial Intelligence for Sustainable Development*. Sustainable Development Goals Series. Palgrave Macmillan., DOI: 10.1007/978-3-031-37776-1_17

Milenkova, V. & Lendzhova, V. (2021). Digital citizenship and digital literacy in the conditions of social crisis. Computers.

Milić, T., Tomić, B., Marinković, S., & Jeremić, V. (2024). ESPRIT adventure: Assessing hybrid fuzzy-crisp rule-based AI method effectiveness in teaching key performance indicators. [sciencedirect.com]. *International Journal of Management Education, 22*(3), 101022. DOI: 10.1016/j.ijme.2024.101022

Millikin, C. C. (2023). Future-Proof your Instructional Design with Universal Design for Learning and Translanguaging. In Literacy Information and Computer Education Journal (Vol. 14, Issue 1, p. 3709). DOI: 10.20533/licej.2040.2589.2023.0488

Millner, R. & Meyer, M. (2022). Collaborative governance in Social Impact Bonds: aligning interests within divergent accountabilities?. Public Management Review. tandfonline.com

Milne, E., & Wotherspoon, T. (2023). 'Success is different in our eyes': reconciling definitions of educational success among Indigenous families and education systems in Alberta, Canada. In Critical Studies in Education (Vol. 64, Issue 5, p. 428). Taylor & Francis. https://doi.org/DOI: 10.1080/17508487.2023.2173266

Mintz, Y., & Brodie, R. (2019). Introduction to artificial intelligence in medicine. *Minimally Invasive Therapy & Allied Technologies, 28*(2), 73–81. DOI: 10.1080/13645706.2019.1575882 PMID: 30810430

Mishra, P., & Koehler, M. J. (2006). Technological pedagogical content knowledge: A framework for teacher knowledge. *Teachers College Record, 108*(6), 1017–1054. DOI: 10.1111/j.1467-9620.2006.00684.x

Mlambo, M., Silén, C., & McGrath, C. (2021). Lifelong learning and nurses' continuing professional development, a metasynthesis of the literature. BMC nursing. springer.com

Mogas, J., Palau, R., Fuentes, M., & Cebrián, G. (2022). Smart schools on the way: How school principals from Catalonia approach the future of education within the fourth industrial revolution. [springer.com]. *Learning Environments Research, 25*(3), 875–893. DOI: 10.1007/s10984-021-09398-3

Mohammed, P., & Watson, E. (2019). Towards Inclusive Education in the Age of Artificial Intelligence: Perspectives, Challenges, and Opportunities. In Perspectives on rethinking and reforming education (p. 17). Springer Nature. https://doi.org/DOI: 10.1007/978-981-13-8161-4_2

Mohseni Takaloo, N. (2017). English Literature Department, Payame Noor University, Tehran, Iran, Ahmadi, M. R., & English Language Department, Shahid Beheshti University, Tehran, Iran. The Effect of Learners' Motivation on Their Reading Comprehension Skill: A Literature Review. *International Journal of Research in English Education, 2*(3), 10–21. DOI: 10.18869/acadpub.ijree.2.3.10

Moise, I. K., Ivanova, N., Wilson, C., Wilson, S., Halwindi, H., & Spika, V. M. (2023). Lessons from digital technology-enabled health interventions implemented during the coronavirus pandemic to improve maternal and birth outcomes: A global scoping review. [springer.com]. *BMC Pregnancy and Childbirth, 23*(1), 195. DOI: 10.1186/s12884-023-05454-3 PMID: 36941565

Moore, A., Nguyen, A., Rivas, S., Bany-Mohammed, A., Majeika, J., & Martinez, L. (2021). A qualitative examination of the impacts of financial stress on college students' well-being: Insights from a large, private institution. [sagepub.com]. *SAGE Open Medicine, 9*, 20503121211018122. DOI: 10.1177/20503121211018122 PMID: 34094560

Moulaei, K., Sheikhtaheri, A., Ghafaripour, Z., & Bahaadinbeigy, K. (2021). The development and usability assessment of an mhealth application to encourage self-care in pregnant women against COVID-19. [wiley.com]. *Journal of Healthcare Engineering, 2021*(1), 9968451. DOI: 10.1155/2021/9968451 PMID: 34336175

Mounir, A. S. (2025). The Lingopragmatic Role of Punctuation Marks in Digital Advertising: A Comparative Case Study in Belarus, Egypt, and the UK.

Mozer, M. C., Wiseheart, M., & Novikoff, T. P. (2019, February 19). Artificial intelligence to support human instruction. In Proceedings of the National Academy of Sciences (Vol. 116, Issue 10, p. 3953). National Academy of Sciences. https://doi.org/DOI: 10.1073/pnas.1900370116

Mpofu, S., & Chasokela, D. (2025). Data-Informed Decision-Making: Using Analytics to Drive Strategic Management in Higher Education. In Building Organizational Capacity and Strategic Management in Academia (pp. 103-138). IGI Global Scientific Publishing. [HTML]

Muarif, J. A., Jihad, F. A., Alfadli, M. I., & Setiabudi, D. I. (2023). Hubungan perkembangan teknologi AI terhadap pembelajaran mahasiswa. Jurnal Pendidikan. *SEROJA*, *2*(2), 53–60.

Mufid, Z., & Musafa, M. (2022). Implementasi penggunaan Internet of Things (IoT) di dunia pendidikan selama masa pendemi COVID-19. *Jurnal Konseling Pendidikan Islam*, *3*(2), 439–446.

Muhammadiah, M., Turibius Rahmat, S., Fatmawati, E., Bintoro Johan, A., & Jacob Pattiasina, P. (2022). How Teacher Creativity Brings to Indonesian Language Teaching Innovations in The Multimedia Era. *Nazhruna: Jurnal Pendidikan Islam*, *5*(1), 169–172. DOI: 10.31538/nzh.v5i1.2003

Mühlhoff, R. (2023). Predictive privacy: Collective data protection in the context of artificial intelligence and big data. *Big Data & Society*, *10*(1), 20539517231166886.

Mulenga, R. & Shilongo, H. (2024). Academic integrity in higher education: Understanding and addressing plagiarism. Acta Pedagogia Asiana.

Mulgund, P., Mulgund, B. P., Sharman, R., & Singh, R. (2021). The implications of the California Consumer Privacy Act (CCPA) on healthcare organizations: Lessons learned from early compliance experiences. *Health Policy and Technology*, *10*(3), 100543. DOI: 10.1016/j.hlpt.2021.100543

Müllensiefen, D., Elvers, P., & Frieler, K. (2022). Musical development during adolescence: Perceptual skills, cognitive resources, and musical training. [wiley.com]. *Annals of the New York Academy of Sciences*, *1518*(1), 264–281. DOI: 10.1111/nyas.14911 PMID: 36251356

Murdoch, B. (2021). Privacy and artificial intelligence: Challenges for protecting health information in a new era. *BMC Medical Ethics*, *22*(1), 122.

Muthmainnah, N., Rahmayanti, V. A., & Faizin, M. (2024). *Modernitas Alat Pendidikan Dalam Perspektif Artificial Intelligence Fenomena Kemajuan Zaman Pendidik Abad 21*. Pedagogi. *Jurnal Ilmu Pendidikan, 24*(1), 46–55. Advance online publication. DOI: 10.24036/pedagogi.v24i1.1937

Myoung, E., & Liou, P. Y. (2022). Systematic review of empirical studies on international large-scale assessments of civic and citizenship education. *Scandinavian Journal of Educational Research, 66*(7), 1269–1291. DOI: 10.1080/00313831.2022.2131903

Nadeem, M. (2024). Distributed leadership in educational contexts: A catalyst for school improvement. Social Sciences & Humanities Open. sciencedirect.com

Nandan Prasad, A. (2024). Regulatory Compliance and Risk Management. In Introduction to Data Governance for Machine Learning Systems: Fundamental Principles, Critical Practices, and Future Trends (pp. 485-624). Berkeley, CA: Apress. [HTML] DOI: 10.1007/979-8-8688-1023-7_8

Nayze, L. S. A.. (2021). Smartpathk: A Platform for Teaching Glomerulopathies Using Machine Learning. *BMC Medical Education, 21*(1), 248. Advance online publication. DOI: 10.1186/s12909-021-02680-1 PMID: 33926437

Nazer, L., Zatarah, R., Waldrip, S., Ke, J. X. C., Moukheiber, M., Khanna, A. K., Hicklen, R. S., Moukheiber, L., Moukheiber, D., Ma, H., & Mathur, P. (2023). Bias in artificial intelligence algorithms and recommendations for mitigation [Review of Bias in artificial intelligence algorithms and recommendations for mitigation]. PLOS Digital Health, 2(6). Public Library of Science. DOI: 10.1371/journal.pdig.0000278

Ndasauka, Y. (2024). Historical Origins of Technology in Africa. In African Mind, Culture, and Technology: Philosophical Perspectives (pp. 17-36). Cham: Springer Nature Switzerland. [HTML] DOI: 10.1007/978-3-031-62979-2_2

Nedungadi, P., Devenport, K., Sutcliffe, R., & Raman, R. (2023). Towards a Digital Learning Ecology to Address the Grand Challenge in Adult Literacy. *Interactive Learning Environments, 31*(1), 383–396. DOI: 10.1080/10494820.2020.1789668

Nelson, G. A., & Holschuh, C. (2021). Evaluation of telehealth use in prenatal care for patient and provider satisfaction: A step toward reducing barriers to care. [HTML]. *The Journal for Nurse Practitioners, 17*(4), 481–484. DOI: 10.1016/j.nurpra.2020.12.026

Newman, P. A., Guta, A., & Black, T. (2021). Ethical considerations for qualitative research methods during the COVID-19 pandemic and other emergency situations: Navigating the virtual field. *International Journal of Qualitative Methods, 20*, 16094069211047823. DOI: 10.1177/16094069211047823

Nezami, M. R., de Bruijne, M. L., Hertogh, M. J., & Bakker, H. L. (2022). Collaboration and data sharing in inter-organizational infrastructure construction projects. [mdpi.com]. *Sustainability (Basel), 14*(24), 16835. DOI: 10.3390/su142416835

Ngao, A. I., Sang, G., & Kihwele, J. E. (2022). Understanding teacher educators' perceptions and practices about ICT integration in teacher education program. Education Sciences.

Nguyen, A., Ngo, H. N., Hong, Y., Dang, B., & Nguyen, B. P. T. (2023). Ethical principles for artificial intelligence in education. [springer.com]. *Education and Information Technologies*, *28*(4), 4221–4241. DOI: 10.1007/s10639-022-11316-w PMID: 36254344

Niebel, C. (2021). The impact of the general data protection regulation on innovation and the global political economy.. *Computer Law & Security Review*, *40*, 105523. DOI: 10.1016/j.clsr.2020.105523

Niemelä, P., Pears, A., Dagienė, V., & Laanpere, M. (2021, August). Computational thinking–Forces shaping curriculum and policy in Finland, Sweden and the Baltic countries. In *Open Conference on Computers in Education* (pp. 131-143). Cham: Springer International Publishing.

Nimbarte, N. (2024). Quantitative analysis of urban transformation using remote sensing data and machine learning approach. *Communications on Applied Nonlinear Analysis*, *31*(2s), 388–401. DOI: 10.52783/cana.v31.656

Norris, P. (2001). *Digital divide: Civic engagement, information poverty, and the internet worldwide*. Cambridge University Press. DOI: 10.1017/CBO9781139164887

Norton, J. (2025). Navigating the AI Policy Landscape: AI in Community College Education. In Navigating AI in Academic Libraries: Implications for Academic Research (pp. 109-130). IGI Global. [HTML]

Nurhuda, H. (2022). *Masalah-masalah Pendidikan Nasional; Faktor-Faktor dan Solusi yang Ditawarkan*. Jurnal Pemikiran dan Pendidikan 5(2), https://doi.org/ https://doi.org/10.51476/dirasah.v5i2.406

Nurlaily, S., Ahmad, M., Syarif, S., & Idris, I. (2021). Effectiveness of Augmented Reality (AR) based learning media on increasing the physical examination system of pregnant women urinary system. Gaceta Sanitaria. sciencedirect.com

NXP Ethical Framework for Artificial Intelligence. (2020). https://www.nxp.com/docs/en/white-paper/AI-ETHICAL-FRAMEWORK-WP.pdf

Nyhan, B., Settle, J., Thorson, E., Wojcieszak, M., Barberá, P., Chen, A. Y., Allcott, H., Brown, T., Crespo-Tenorio, A., Dimmery, D., Freelon, D., Gentzkow, M., González-Bailón, S., Guess, A. M., Kennedy, E., Kim, Y. M., Lazer, D., Malhotra, N., Moehler, D., & Tucker, J. A. (2023). Like-minded sources on Facebook are prevalent but not polarizing. *Nature*, *620*(7972), 137–144. DOI: 10.1038/s41586-023-06297-w PMID: 37500978

O'neil, C. (2017). *Weapons of math destruction: How big data increases inequality and threatens democracy*. Crown.

Ober, T. M., Lehman, B., Gooch, R., Oluwalana, O., Solyst, J., Phelps, G., & Hamilton, L. S. (2023). Culturally Responsive Personalized Learning: Recommendations for a Working Definition and Framework. In ETS Research Report Series (Vol. 2023, Issue 1, p. 1). Wiley. DOI: 10.1002/ets2.12372

Ohyver, D. A., Junaidi, S., & Adawiyah, R. (2024). *Buku Ajar Kecerdasan Buatan*. PT. Sonpedia Publishing Indonesia.

Okoye, K., Hussein, H., Arrona-Palacios, A., Quintero, H. N., Ortega, L. O. P., Sanchez, A. L., Ortiz, E. A., Escamilla, J., & Hosseini, S. (2023). Impact of digital technologies upon teaching and learning in higher education in Latin America: An outlook on the reach, barriers, and bottlenecks. [springer.com]. *Education and Information Technologies*, *28*(2), 2291–2360. DOI: 10.1007/s10639-022-11214-1 PMID: 35992366

Okunlaya, R. O., Syed Abdullah, N., & Alias, R. A. (2022). Artificial intelligence (AI) library services innovative conceptual framework for the digital transformation of university education. [HTML]. *Library Hi Tech*, *40*(6), 1869–1892. DOI: 10.1108/LHT-07-2021-0242

Olanrewaju, O. I., Enegbuma, W. I., Donn, M., & Chileshe, N. (2022). Building information modelling and green building certification systems: A systematic literature review and gap spotting. [HTML]. *Sustainable Cities and Society*, *81*, 103865. DOI: 10.1016/j.scs.2022.103865

Olasehinde-Williams, G., Özkan, O., & Akadiri, S. S. (2023). Effects of climate policy uncertainty on sustainable investment: A dynamic analysis for the US. [HTML]. *Environmental Science and Pollution Research International*, *30*(19), 55326–55339. DOI: 10.1007/s11356-023-26257-1 PMID: 36892691

Olawade, D. B., Wada, O. Z., David-Olawade, A. C., Fapohunda, O., Ige, A. O., & Ling, J. (2024). Artificial intelligence potential for net zero sustainability: Current evidence and prospects. Next sustainability, 4, 100041. sciencedirect.com

Onesi-Ozigagun, O., Ololade, Y. J., Eyo-Udo, N. L., & Ogundipe, D. O. (2024). REVOLUTIONIZING EDUCATION THROUGH AI: A COMPREHENSIVE REVIEW OF ENHANCING LEARNING EXPERIENCES [Review of] ENHANCING LEARNING EXPERIENCES]. International Journal of Applied Research in Social Sciences, 6(4), 589. Fair East Publishers. https://doi.org/DOI: 10.51594/ijarss.v6i4.1011

Ortikov, U., & Akbarovich, B. D. (2024). New Trends. In *Integrating Digital Literacies In Language Teaching*. Science Promotion.

Ortiz Juarez-Paz, A. V., Doherty, E. F., Storch, S. L., Kallis, R. B., & Kleinman, S. B. (2023). "Anyone else? Is this normal?": Anonymously seeking information on the Ovia Pregnancy App. [HTML]. *Atlantic Journal of Communication, 31*(1), 30–51. DOI: 10.1080/15456870.2021.1984238

Ouakka, S., Verlinden, O., & Kouroussis, G. (2022). Railway ground vibration and mitigation measures: benchmarking of best practices. Railway Engineering Science. springer.com

Oyedokun, T. O., Nair, R., Stempien, J., Moulton, K., Mondal, P., & Trivedi, S. V. (2025). Reducing emergency department return visits for ultrasound imaging: A quality improvement initiative. [HTML]. *Canadian Journal of Emergency Medical Care, 27*(6), 1–7. DOI: 10.1007/s43678-025-00880-y PMID: 40053311

Ozdemir, S., de Arroyabe, J. C. F., Sena, V., & Gupta, S. (2023). Stakeholder diversity and collaborative innovation: Integrating the resource-based view with stakeholder theory. [sciencedirect.com]. *Journal of Business Research, 164*, 113955. DOI: 10.1016/j.jbusres.2023.113955

Özdere, M. (2023). The Integration of Artificial Intelligence in English Education: Opportunities and Challenges. [LET Journal]. *Language Education & Technology, 3*(2), 137–172.

Pabubung, M. R. (2021a). 'Human Dignity' dalam Pemikiran Yohanes Paulus II dan Relevansi untuk Dunia Masa Kini. [Journal of Theology]. *Jurnal Teknologi, 10*(1), 49–70. http://dx.doi.org/10.24071/jt.v10i1.2905

Pabubung, M. R. (2021b). Epistemologi kecerdasan buatan (AI) dan pentingnya ilmu etika dalam pendidikan interdisipliner. *Jurnal Filsafat Indonesia, 4*(2), 152–159. DOI: 10.23887/jfi.v4i2.34734

Pancholi, K., & Shukla, P. (2025). Harnessing AI for Sustainability: Innovations, Policies, and Investment Paradigms. In Diversity, AI, and Sustainability for Financial Growth (pp. 97-124). IGI Global Scientific Publishing. [HTML]

Panda, S., & Kaur, N. (2024). Empowered minds: Navigating digital seas with emerging information literacy framework. In *Examining information literacy in academic libraries* (pp. 48–82). IGI Global. DOI: 10.4018/979-8-3693-1143-1.ch004

Pangrazio, L., & Sefton-Green, J. (2021). Digital rights, digital citizenship and digital literacy: What's the difference?. *Journal of new approaches in educational research, 10*(1), 15-27.

Park, S., & Gil-Garcia, J. R. (2022). Open data innovation: Visualizations and process redesign as a way to bridge the transparency-accountability gap.. *Government Information Quarterly*, *39*(1), 101456. DOI: 10.1016/j.giq.2020.101456

Patil, L. (2023). The business of development: The institutional rationales of technology corporations in educational development. International Journal of Educational Development. sciencedirect.com

Paunov, C., Planes-Satorra, S., & Ravelli, G. (2019). Review of national policy initiatives in support of digital and AI-driven innovation. In OECD science, technology and industry policy papers. https://doi.org/DOI: 10.1787/23074957

Peart, M., Higgins, S., Gutiérrez-Esteban, P., & Cubo Delgado, S. (2024). Digital and socio-civic skills development and young people's perceptions of digital citizenship in the UK. *Education, Citizenship and Social Justice*, *19*(3), 463–475. DOI: 10.1177/17461979231170232

Pedro, F., Subosa, M., Rivas, A., & Valverde, P. (2019). Artificial intelligence in education: Challenges and opportunities for sustainable development.

Pedro, F., Subosa, M., Rivas, A., & Valverde, P. (2019). *Artificial intelligence in education: Challenges and opportunities for sustainable development*. Working papers on education policy, 7. UNESCO. https://unesdoc.unesco.org/ark:/48223/pf0000366994?posInSet=7&queryId=N-EXPLORE-cff47795-58ac-43ec-9f45-b1acf2920b16

Perrotta, C., & Selwyn, N. (2019). Deep learning goes to school: Toward a relational understanding of AI in education. *Learning, Media and Technology*, *45*(3), 251–269. DOI: 10.1080/17439884.2020.1686017

Persulessy, S. I., Nikijuluw, R. P. V., & Jakob, J. C. (2024). Utilizing Artificial Intelligence in Language Learning: What About Engineering Students' Perception? *Journal of English Education Program*, *5*(1). Advance online publication. DOI: 10.26418/jeep.v5i1.71159

Piaget, J. (1976). *The grasp of consciousness: Action and concept in the young child*. Harvard University Press.

Pimienta, D., Blanco, Á., & de Oliveira, G. M. (2023). The method behind the unprecedented production of indicators of the presence of languages in the Internet. *Frontiers in Research Metrics and Analytics*, *8*, 1149347. DOI: 10.3389/frma.2023.1149347 PMID: 37273659

Pineiro-Villaverde, G., & García-Álvarez, M. T. (2020). Sustainable consumption and production: Exploring the links with resources productivity in the EU-28. *Sustainability (Basel)*, *12*(21), 8760. DOI: 10.3390/su12218760

Plant, R. (2011). An introduction to artificial intelligence. In *32nd Aerospace Sciences Meeting and Exhibit* (p. 294).

Pop, G. I., Titu, A. M., & Pop, A. B. (2023). Enhancing aerospace industry efficiency and sustainability: Process integration and quality management in the context of Industry 4.0. Sustainability. mdpi.com

Popenici, S. A. D., & Kerr, S. (2017). Exploring the impact of artificial intelligence on teaching and learning in higher education. *Research in Learning Technology*, *25*, 1–13. DOI: 10.25304/rlt.v25.1941 PMID: 30595727

Popescu, C. R. G., & González, A. L. (2024). Exploring the synergies between environmental social governance and AI for business sustainability: Tackling climate adaptation, mitigating climate change efforts, and pursuing climate justice. In *Intersecting Environmental Social Governance and AI for Business Sustainability* (pp. 1–41). IGI Global. DOI: 10.4018/979-8-3693-1151-6.ch001

Porayska-Pomsta, K. (2024). From Algorithm Worship to the Art of Human Learning: Insights from 50-year journey of AI in Education. In arXiv (Cornell University). Cornell University. https://doi.org/DOI: 10.48550/arXiv.2403

Prabhakar, P., Pati, P. B., & Parida, S. (2025). Navigating Legal and Ethical Dimensions in AI, IoT, and Cloud Solutions for Women's Safety. In Developing AI, IoT and Cloud Computing-based Tools and Applications for Women's Safety (pp. 155-191). Chapman and Hall/CRC. [HTML]

Prabhu Kavin, B., Karki, S., Hemalatha, S., Singh, D., Vijayalakshmi, R., Thangamani, M., Haleem, S. L. A., Jose, D., Tirth, V., Kshirsagar, P. R., & Adigo, A. G. (2022). Machine learning-based secure data acquisition for fake accounts detection in future mobile communication networks. *Wireless Communications and Mobile Computing*, *2022*(1), 6356152. DOI: 10.1155/2022/6356152

Pratiwi, H. (2024). *Buku ajar kecerdasan buatan: disertai praktik baik pemanfaatannya*. Asadel Liamsindo Teknologi.

Prinsloo, P., & Kaliisa, R. (2022). Data privacy on the African continent: Opportunities, challenges and implications for learning analytics. [wiley.com]. *British Journal of Educational Technology, 53*(4), 894–913. DOI: 10.1111/bjet.13226

Prior, D. D., Mazanov, J., Meacheam, D., Heaslip, G., & Hanson, J. (2016). Attitude, digital literacy and self efficacy: Flow-on effects for online learning behavior. *The Internet and Higher Education, 29*, 91–97. DOI: 10.1016/j.iheduc.2016.01.001

Privitera, A. G., Fontana, F., & Geronazzo, M. (2024). The Role of Audio in Immersive Storytelling: A Systematic Review in Cultural Heritage. *Multimedia Tools and Applications, 84*(16), 16105–16143.

Pujolà, J.-T., & Appel, C. (2020). Gamification for Technology-Enhanced Language Teaching and Learning. In Kruk, M., & Peterson, M. (Eds.), (pp. 93–111). Advances in Educational Technologies and Instructional Design. IGI Global., DOI: 10.4018/978-1-7998-2591-3.ch005

Pulimamidi, R. (2024). To enhance customer (or patient) experience based on IoT analytical study through technology (IT) transformation for E-healthcare. Measurement: Sensors. sciencedirect.com

Putjorn, T., & Putjorn, P. (2023, October). Augmented imagination: Exploring generative AI from the perspectives of young learners. In 2023 15th International Conference on Information Technology and Electrical Engineering (ICITEE) (pp. 353-358). IEEE. [HTML]

Qadir, J. (2023, May). Engineering education in the era of ChatGPT: Promise and pitfalls of generative AI for education. In *2023 IEEE Global Engineering Education Conference (EDUCON)* (pp. 1-9). IEEE. https://doi.org/DOI: 10.1109/EDUCON54358.2023.10125121

Qadir, S. A., Ahmad, F., Al-Wahedi, A. M. A., Iqbal, A., & Ali, A. (2024). Navigating the complex realities of electric vehicle adoption: A comprehensive study of government strategies, policies, and incentives. [sciencedirect.com]. *Energy Strategy Reviews, 53*, 101379. DOI: 10.1016/j.esr.2024.101379

Qaffas, A. A., Kaabi, K., Shadiev, R., & Essalmi, F. (2020). Towards an optimal personalization strategy in MOOCs. In Smart Learning Environments (Vol. 7, Issue 1). Springer Nature. https://doi.org/DOI: 10.1186/s40561-020-0117-y

Quintais, J. P., De Gregorio, G., & Magalhães, J. C. (2023). How platforms govern users' copyright-protected content: Exploring the power of private ordering and its implications. *Computer Law & Security Review, 48*, 105792. DOI: 10.1016/j.clsr.2023.105792

Rachmi, . (2024). Transformasi Pendidikan di Era Digital Tantangan dan Peluang. *Journal of International Multidisciplinary Research*, *2*(2). Advance online publication. DOI: 10.62504/6y4qb169

Radanliev, P., Roure, D. D., Walton, R., Kleek, M. V., Montalvo, R. M., Maddox, L., Santos, O., Burnap, P., & Anthi, E. (2020). Artificial intelligence and machine learning in dynamic cyber risk analytics at the edge. In SN Applied Sciences (Vol. 2, Issue 11). Springer Nature. https://doi.org/DOI: 10.1007/s42452-020-03559-4

Rahm, L. (2024). 'Help!? My students created an evil AI': On the irony of speculative methods and design fiction. *Learning, Media and Technology*, •••, 1–15. DOI: 10.1080/17439884.2024.2367707

Raihan, M. M., Subroto, S., Chowdhury, N., Koch, K., Ruttan, E., & Turin, T. C. (2024). Dimensions and barriers for digital (in) equity and digital divide: A systematic integrative review. Digital Transformation and Society.

Raj, M., Silva, L. Q., & Khan, N. (2024). Building an inclusive health care system requires offering culturally inclusive foods in health care environments. Journal of the Academy of Nutrition and Dietetics. sciencedirect.com

Rajaram, K., & Rajaram, K. (2021). Learning interventions: collaborative learning, critical thinking and assessing participation real-time. Evidence-Based Teaching for the 21st Century Classroom and Beyond: Innovation-Driven Learning Strategies, 77-120. [HTML]

Rakuasa, H., Faris, D. A., & Hidayatullah, M. (2024). Transforming Education in the Age of Artificial Intelligence: Challenges and Opportunities in Indonesia, A Literature Review. [JEI]. *Journal Education Innovation*, *2*(1), 180–186.

Rama Reddy, T., Prasad Reddy, P. V. G. D., Srinivas, R., Raghavendran, C. V., Lalitha, R. V. S., & Annapurna, B. (2021). Proposing a reliable method of securing and verifying the credentials of graduates through blockchain. [springer.com]. *EURASIP Journal on Information Security*, *2021*(1), 1–9. DOI: 10.1186/s13635-021-00122-5

Ramalingam, K., & Jiar, Y. K. (2022). Influence of Intrinsic and Extrinsic Motivation in Learning Among Primary School Students. *Central Asia and The Caucasus*, *23*(1). Advance online publication. DOI: 10.37178/ca-c.23.1.186

Ramasamy, L. K., & Khan, F. (2024). *Blockchain-Based Certification System: Ensuring Trust in Educational Credentials*. Blockchain for Global Education. [HTML]

Ramazani, A., & Talebi, Z. (2024). A Consideration of the Roles of Preservice Teachers' Information Literacy, Digital Literacy, and Ict Self-Efficacy in Teaching. [TEJ]. *Technology of Education Journal*, *18*(1). Advance online publication. DOI: 10.22061/tej.2024.10254.2979

Ramiro Troitiño, D., & Mazur, V. (2024). Digital Social Initiatives: Europe Connecting Citizens with Social Transformation. In E-Governance in the European Union: Strategies, Tools, and Implementation (pp. 71-85). Cham: Springer Nature Switzerland.

Rana, R., Bhambri, P., & Kautish, S. (2024). Responsible digital technologies: Shaping sustainable practices. In *Digital technologies to implement the UN Sustainable Development Goals* (pp. 399–411). Springer Nature Switzerland. DOI: 10.1007/978-3-031-68427-2_20

Rani, P., Sachan, R. K., & Kukreja, S. (2024). Educert-chain: A secure and notarized educational certificate authentication and verification system using permissioned blockchain. [HTML]. *Cluster Computing*, *27*(7), 10169–10196. DOI: 10.1007/s10586-024-04469-5

Reddy, J. S., Sharma, R., & Gupta, N. (2024). The accreditation paradigm: A comparative analysis of accreditations for management programmes. [HTML]. *International Journal of Educational Management*, *38*(1), 73–95. DOI: 10.1108/IJEM-05-2023-0250

Redmond, P., Heffernan, A., Abawi, L., Brown, A., & Henderson, R. (2018). An Online Engagement Framework for Higher Education. *Online Learning : the Official Journal of the Online Learning Consortium*, *22*(1). Advance online publication. DOI: 10.24059/olj.v22i1.1175

Rejeb, A. (2022). The Learning Situation in the Computer-Oriented Centers for Children in Tunisia, Interchangeability, and Interdependence: Contexts, Challenges and Experience's Building Ethnographic Approach. In Education and human development. https://doi.org/DOI: 10.5772/intechopen.101736

Renz, A., Krishnaraja, S., & Gronau, E. (2020). Demystification of Artificial Intelligence in Education – How much AI is really in the Educational Technology? [iJAI]. *International Journal of Learning Analytics and Artificial Intelligence for Education*, *2*(1), 14–30. DOI: 10.3991/ijai.v2i1.12675

Reyer van der Vlies. (2020). Trustworthy artificial intelligence (AI) in education: Promises and challenges. https://www.oecd-ilibrary.org/education/trustworthy-artificial-intelligence-ai-in-education_a6c90fa9-en;jsessionid=dy2TD8yZnRd3pW9wSCpMWEPG.ip-10-240-5-70

Ribeiro, M., Nunes, N., Nisi, V., & Schöning, J. (2022). Passive wi-fi monitoring in the wild: A long-term study across multiple location typologies. *Personal and Ubiquitous Computing*, *26*(3), 505–519. DOI: 10.1007/s00779-020-01441-z PMID: 32958999

Rifky, S. (2024). Dampak Penggunaan Artificial Intelligence Bagi Pendidikan Tinggi. *Indonesian Journal of Multidisciplinary on Social and Technology*, *2*(1), 37–42. DOI: 10.31004/ijmst.v2i1.287

Rifky, S. (2024). Professionalism Of Educators In Learning Development. *International Journal of Teaching Learning*, *2*(2). https://injotel.org/index.php/12/article/view/93

Rights, F. E., & Act, P. (2021). Family Educational Rights and Privacy Act. URL https://studentprivacy. ed. gov/ferpa. amazonaws.com

Rizi, M. H. P., & Seno, S. A. H. (2022). A systematic review of technologies and solutions to improve security and privacy protection of citizens in the smart city. *Internet of Things : Engineering Cyber Physical Human Systems.*

Rizkianti, A., Saptarini, I., & Rachmalina, R. (2021). Perceived barriers in accessing health care and the risk of pregnancy complications in Indonesia. [tandfonline.com]. *International Journal of Women's Health*, *13*, 761–772. DOI: 10.2147/IJWH.S310850 PMID: 34429661

Roberts, J. M., Heider, D., Bergman, L., & Thornburg, K. L. (2022). Vision for improving pregnancy health: innovation and the future of pregnancy research. Reproductive Sciences. springer.com

Rogers, E. M. (2003). *Diffusion of innovations* (5th ed.). Free Press.

Romero, E. D., & Bobkina, J. (2021). Exploring critical and visual literacy needs in digital learning environments: The use of memes in the EFL/ESL university classroom. *Thinking Skills and Creativity*.

Rompho, N. (2024). Do objectives and key results solve organizational performance measurement issues? [HTML]. *Benchmarking*, *31*(3), 669–682. DOI: 10.1108/BIJ-07-2022-0464

Ronsumbre, S., Rukmawati, T., Sumarsono, A., & Waremra, R. S. (2023). Pembelajaran digital dengan kecerdasan buatan (AI): Korelasi AI terhadap motivasi belajar siswa. *Jurnal Educatio Fkip Unma*, *9*(3), 1464–1474.

Rooein, D. (2019). Data-Driven Edu Chatbots. Conference: Companion The 2019 World Wide Web Conference, DOI: 10.1145/3308560.3314191

Rosid, M. A. (2022). Buku Ajar Kecerdasan Buatan/Artificial Intelegent (AI). *Umsida Press*, 1-197.

Rosmayanti, V. (2024). Addressing English Language Anxiety in High School Students. *EDULEC : Education, Language, and Culture Journal*, *4*(3), 351–361. DOI: 10.56314/edulec.v4i3.275

Rossoni, A. L., de Vasconcellos, E. P. G., & de Castilho Rossoni, R. L. (2024). Barriers and facilitators of university-industry collaboration for research, development and innovation: A systematic review. [springer.com]. *Management Review Quarterly*, *74*(3), 1841–1877. DOI: 10.1007/s11301-023-00349-1

Roux, A. T., Wannenburg, E., & Manetje, T. V. (2024). The Environment and Features of Digital Place-Based Media at Minibus Taxi Ranks as Nontraditional Advertising Media. *Advances in Human-Computer Interaction*, *2024*(1), 3984159. DOI: 10.1155/2024/3984159

Ryan, L., Coyne, R., Heary, C., Birney, S., Crotty, M., Dunne, R., Conlan, O., & Walsh, J. C. (2023). Weight stigma experienced by patients with obesity in healthcare settings: A qualitative evidence synthesis. *Obesity Reviews*, *24*(10), e13606. DOI: 10.1111/obr.13606 PMID: 37533183

Sabella, B., Rhomadhona, H., & Arrahimi, A. R. (2023). Pelatihan pembuatan game sederhana sebagai media pembelajaran untuk pengajar smp berbasis artificial intelegent. Jurnal Widya Laksmi. *Jurnal Pengabdian Kepada Masyarakat*, *3*(2), 69–76.

Safii, M., & Amanda, A. (2023). Optimisasi Algoritma MOOSRA Pada Seleksi Penerima Beasiswa KIP Kuliah. [Jurnal Sains Manajemen Informatika dan Komputer]. *Jurnal SAINTIKOM*, *22*(2), 555–561.

Sajja, P. S., & Sajja, P. S. (2021). Introduction to artificial intelligence. *Illustrated Computational Intelligence: Examples and Applications*, 1-25. https://doi.org/DOI: 10.1007/978-981-15-9589-9_1

Salama, R. & Hinton, T. (2023). Online higher education: Current landscape and future trends. Journal of Further and Higher Education. tandfonline.com

Salas-Pilco, S. Z., Xiao, K., & Oshima, J. (2022). Artificial Intelligence and New Technologies in Inclusive Education for Minority Students: A Systematic Review [Review of Artificial Intelligence and New Technologies in Inclusive Education for Minority Students: A Systematic Review]. Sustainability, 14(20), 13572. Multidisciplinary Digital Publishing Institute. DOI: 10.3390/su142013572

Salazar, D., & Guillaumier, C. (2024). *7. The Global Conservatoire*. In Open Book Publishers., DOI: 10.11647/obp.0353.07

Salem, I. (2024). Integrating Artificial Intelligence in Personalized Learning: A Future-Oriented Approach to Enhance Student Engagement and Achievement. *International Journal of Post Axial*, *2*(2). Advance online publication. DOI: 10.59944/postaxial.v2i2.299

Salla, S., Pasumarthy, A., Tadikonda, D., Parsha, T., & Mandal, S. K. (2025). Private AI in Education: Critical Challenges and Aspects of Enhancement Strategies. In Sustainable Development Using Private AI (pp. 109-131). CRC Press. [HTML]

Salmela-Aro, K., Tang, X., Symonds, J., & Upadyaya, K. (2021). Student engagement in adolescence: A scoping review of longitudinal studies 2010–2020. [wiley.com]. *Journal of Research on Adolescence*, *31*(2), 256–272. DOI: 10.1111/jora.12619 PMID: 33991151

Salomon-Fernández, Y. (2022). Using shared governance to advance completion and transfer. [HTML]. *New Directions for Community Colleges*, *2022*(198), 161–170. DOI: 10.1002/cc.20518

Salsabilla, K. A. Z., Hadi, T. D. F., Pratiwi, W., & Mukaromah, S. (2023, November). Pengaruh penggunaan kecerdasan buatan terhadap mahasiswa di perguruan tinggi. In Prosiding Seminar Nasional Teknologi Dan Sistem Informasi (Vol. 3, No. 1, pp. 168-175). DOI: 10.33005/sitasi.v3i1.371

Samıer, E. A., & ElKaleh, E. S. (2023). Culturally Sensitive Research Methods for Educational Administration and Leadership. In *Routledge eBooks*. Informa., DOI: 10.4324/9781003130666

Samson, A. A. C., Abarquez, J. K. S. L., Llave, J. N. J., Sing, J. A. P., & Estrella, N. E. (2024, December). BEYOND THE ARCH: a web and mobile alumni record verification system for the University of Santo Tomas Office of the Registrar. In International Conference on Green Energy, Computing and Intelligent Technology 2024 (GEn-CITy 2024) (Vol. 2024, pp. 56-65). IET. [HTML]

Sanders, C. K. & Scanlon, E. (2021). The digital divide is a human rights issue: Advancing social inclusion through social work advocacy. Journal of human rights and social work. springer.com

Sanders, C. K., & Scanlon, E. (2021). The digital divide is a human rights issue: Advancing social inclusion through social work advocacy. *Journal of Human Rights and Social Work*, *6*(2), 130–143.

Sandoval, J. C. B., de Santana, V. F., Berger, S., Thomas, L., & Hobson, S. (2023). Responsible and Inclusive Technology Framework: A Formative Framework to Promote Societal Considerations in Information Technology Contexts. In arXiv (Cornell University). Cornell University. https://doi.org/. 11565DOI: 10.48550/arxiv.2302

Sanni, M. A. (2025). Entrepreneurship and Innovation in Enhancing Public-Private Partnership Effectiveness for Unlocking Economic Potential. In Public Private Partnership Dynamics for Economic Development (pp. 213-242). IGI Global Scientific Publishing. [HTML] DOI: 10.4018/979-8-3693-9153-2.ch011

Saputra, W. A.Wongso Adi Saputra. (2022). Analyzing Context in English as Lingua Franca (ELF): A Discourse Analysis in an Indonesian Higher Education Institution (HEI). [IJOLEH]. *International Journal of Education and Humanities, 1*(1), 18–29. DOI: 10.56314/ijoleh.v1i1.36

Sarker, I. H. (2022). AI-based modeling: Techniques, applications and research issues towards automation, intelligent and smart systems. *SN Computer Science, 3*(2), 158.

Sarwatay, D., Raman, U., & Ramasubramanian, S. (2021). Media literacy, social connectedness, and digital citizenship in India: Mapping stakeholders on how parents and young people navigate a social world. *Frontiers in Human Dynamics, 3*, 601239. DOI: 10.3389/fhumd.2021.601239

Sasabone, L., Limbong, S., Pongpalilu, F., Soepriadi, & Jubhari. (2022). Utilizing WhatsApp As An Educational Technology Tool In Improving Students' Speaking For ESP Instruction. *EDULEC : Education, Language, and Culture Journal, 2*(2). https://doi.org/DOI: 10.56314/edulec.v2i2

Sasabone, L. (2023). Applying Google Classroom As An Instructional Technology Media In Improving Students' Reading For English For Specific Purposes (ESP). *EDULEC : Education. Language And Culture Journal, 3*(1), 110–119. DOI: 10.56314/edulec.v3i1.123

Sato, M., Thorne, S. L., Michel, M., Alexopoulou, T., & Hellermann, J. (2025). Language, people, classrooms, world: Blending disparate theories for united language education practices. [wiley.com]. *Modern Language Journal, 109*(S1), 15–38. DOI: 10.1111/modl.12976

Sato, S. N., Condes Moreno, E., Rubio-Zarapuz, A., Dalamitros, A. A., Yañez-Sepulveda, R., Tornero-Aguilera, J. F., & Clemente-Suárez, V. J. (2023). Navigating the new normal: Adapting online and distance learning in the post-pandemic era. [mdpi.com]. *Education Sciences, 14*(1), 19. DOI: 10.3390/educsci14010019

Saxena, S., & Parivara, S. A. (2025). Leveraging Data Analytics for Enhanced Academic Outcomes: Strategies and Applications. In Impacts of AI on Students and Teachers in Education 5.0 (pp. 349-380). IGI Global Scientific Publishing. [HTML]

Schellewald, A. (2023). Understanding the popularity and affordances of TikTok through user experiences. *Media Culture & Society*, *45*(8), 1568–1582.

Schiff, D., Rakova, B., Ayesh, A., Fanti, A., & Lennon, M. (2021). Explaining the Principles to Practices Gap in AI. In IEEE Technology and Society Magazine (Vol. 40, Issue 2, p. 81). Institute of Electrical and Electronics Engineers. https://doi.org/ DOI: 10.1109/MTS.2021.3056286

Schiff, D. (2022). Education for AI, not AI for education: The role of education and ethics in national AI policy strategies. [springer.com]. *International Journal of Artificial Intelligence in Education*, *32*(3), 527–563. DOI: 10.1007/s40593-021-00270-2

Schissler, M. (2024). Beyond Hate Speech and Misinformation: Facebook and the Rohingya Genocide in Myanmar. *Journal of Genocide Research*, *27*(3), 445–470.

Sehgal, G. (2023). Refocusing Indian education system in the perspective of ancient Indian education system. In World Journal of Advanced Research and Reviews (Vol. 19, Issue 2, p. 861). GSC Online Press. https://doi.org/DOI: 10.30574/wjarr.2023.19.2.1673

Sehl, A., Cornia, A., & Nielsen, R. K. (2024). … do funding models and organizational legacy shape news organizations' social media strategies? A comparison of public service and private sector news media in six…. [HTML]. *Digital Journalism (Abingdon, England)*, *12*(9), 1377–1396. DOI: 10.1080/21670811.2021.1968920

Selwyn, N. (2019). Should Robots Replace Teachers? AI and the Future of Education. *British Journal of Educational Technology*, *50*(5), 2126–2136.

Selwyn, N. (2019). Should robots replace teachers? AI in education. *Learning, Media and Technology*, *44*(1), 1–17. DOI: 10.1080/17439884.2018.1532015

Sematlane, M. (2022). The universal language of sustaining quality peace and resilience: Enhancing learning and harmony across cultures. In *Handbook of Research on Teaching in Multicultural and Multilingual Contexts* (pp. 143–169). IGI Global. DOI: 10.4018/978-1-6684-5034-5.ch009

Sergi, B. S. & Popkova, E. G. (2022). Towards a 'wide'role for venture capital in OECD countries' industry 4.0. Heliyon. cell.com

Sethi, S. S., & Jain, K. (2024). AI technologies for social emotional learning: Recent research and future directions. [emerald.com]. *Journal of Research in Innovative Teaching & Learning*, *17*(2), 213–225. DOI: 10.1108/JRIT-03-2024-0073

Shahbazi, M., & Bunker, D. (2024). Social media trust: Fighting misinformation in the time of crisis. *International Journal of Information Management*, *77*, 102780.

Shaik, V. & Natarajan, K. (2022). Flexible and cost-effective cryptographic encryption algorithm for securing unencrypted database files at rest and in transit. Methodsx. sciencedirect.com

Shams, R. A., Zowghi, D., & Bano, M. (2023). Challenges and Solutions in AI for All. In arXiv (Cornell University). Cornell University. https://doi.org/DOI: 10.48550/ arXiv.2307

Shandilya, S. K., Datta, A., Kartik, Y., & Nagar, A. (2024). Navigating the regulatory landscape. In Digital Resilience: Navigating Disruption and Safeguarding Data Privacy (pp. 127-240). Cham: Springer Nature Switzerland. [HTML] DOI: 10.1007/978-3-031-53290-0_3

Shan, Z., & Wang, Y. (2024). Strategic talent development in the knowledge economy: A comparative analysis of global practices. [HTML]. *Journal of the Knowledge Economy*, *15*(4), 19570–19596. DOI: 10.1007/s13132-024-01933-w

Sharif, H. & Atif, A. (2024). The evolving classroom: How learning analytics is shaping the future of education and feedback mechanisms. Education Sciences. mdpi.com

Sharma, B. P. (2024). Role of advanced cybersecurity frameworks in safeguarding data integrity and consumer trust in digital commerce and enterprise systems. researchgate.net

Sharma, K., & Giannakos, M. (2020). Multimodal data capabilities for learning: What can multimodal data tell us about learning? *British Journal of Educational Technology*, *51*(5), 1450–1484. DOI: 10.1111/bjet.12993

Sharma, P., Akgun, M., & Li, Q. (2024). Understanding student interaction and cognitive engagement in online discussions using social network and discourse analyses. *Educational Technology Research and Development*, *72*(5), 2631–2654. DOI: 10.1007/s11423-023-10261-w

Shiddiq, A. B. (2020). The Application of «Nemo» Artificial Intelegence in Arabic Language Learning in the 4.0 Revolution Era At Al-Khalifah Islamic Boarding School Cibubur. *IJLECR International Journal of Language Education and Cultural Review*, *6*(1), 58–61. DOI: 10.21009/IJLECR.061.07

Shikuku, D. N., Bar-Zeev, S., Ladur, A. N., Allott, H., Mwaura, C., Nandikove, P., Uyara, A., Tallam, E., Ndirangu, E., Waweru, L., Nyaga, L., Bashir, I., Bedwell, C., & Ameh, C. (2024). Experiences, barriers and perspectives of midwifery educators, mentors and students implementing the updated emergency obstetric and newborn care-enhanced pre-service midwifery curriculum in Kenya: A nested qualitative study. [springer.com]. *BMC Medical Education, 24*(1), 950. DOI: 10.1186/s12909-024-05872-7 PMID: 39217305

Shoaib, M., Sayed, N., Singh, J., Shafi, J., Khan, S., & Ali, F. (2024). AI student success predictor: Enhancing personalized learning in campus management systems. [HTML]. *Computers in Human Behavior, 158*, 108301. DOI: 10.1016/j.chb.2024.108301

Shrivastava, A., Anand, G., & Shrivastava, A. (2024). A study on principles, processes and practice for building an inclusive diversity culture. In Organization, Purpose, and Values (pp. 359-370). Routledge. DOI: 10.4324/9781003501374-26

Simon, N. (2025). Towards Technological Literacy: Fostering Digital Citizenship and Sustainable Development Education in Next-Generation Teaching. Digital Citizenship and Building a Responsible Online.

Singh, K. & Walters, M. R. (2024). Use of mHealth in promoting maternal and child health in "BIMARU" states of India "A health system strengthening strategy": Systematic literature review. PLOS Digital Health. plos.org

Singh, J., Evans, E., Reed, A., Karch, L., Qualey, K., Singh, L., & Wiersma, H. (2022). Online, hybrid, and face-to-face learning through the eyes of faculty, students, administrators, and instructional designers: Lessons learned and directions for the post-vaccine and post-pandemic/COVID-19 world. [sagepub.com]. *Journal of Educational Technology Systems, 50*(3), 301–326. DOI: 10.1177/00472395211063754

Singh, S. (Eds.). (2023). *Data-driven intelligent business sustainability*. IGI Global. DOI: 10.4018/979-8-3693-0049-7

Singo, G. & Makgahlela, L. (2024). Records management practices to support administrative operations at the University of Venda in South Africa. Journal of the South African Society of Archivists. ajol.info

Sir Michel Barber. (2021). *Gravity assist: Propelling higher education towards a brighter future – Digital teaching and learning review*. https://blobofsproduks.blob.core.windows.net/files/Gravity%20assist/Gravity-assist-DTL-finalforweb.pdf

Smith, E. (2023). Challenges Encountered in the Implementation of Online Distance Learning in African Countries. In International Journal of Online and Distance Learning (Vol. 4, Issue 1, p. 1). https://doi.org/DOI: 10.47604/ijodl.1998

Smith, M., & Neupane, S. (2023). Artificial intelligence and human development. https://idl-bnc-idrc.dspacedirect.org/handle/10625/56949?show=full

Smithwick, J., Nance, J., Covington-Kolb, S., Rodriguez, A., & Young, M. (2023). "Community health workers bring value and deserve to be valued too:" Key considerations in improving CHW career advancement opportunities. [frontiersin.org]. *Frontiers in Public Health*, *11*, 1036481. DOI: 10.3389/fpubh.2023.1036481 PMID: 36969656

Smuha, N. A. (2020). Trustworthy Artificial Intelligence in Education: Pitfalls and Pathways. In SSRN Electronic Journal. RELX Group (Netherlands). https://doi.org/DOI: 10.2139/ssrn.3742421

Soegiarto, I. (2023). *Inovasi Pembelajaran Berbasis Teknologi Artificial Intelligences (AI) pada Sekolah Kedinasan di Era Revolusi Industri 4.0 dan Society 5.0.* Innovative. *Journal of Social Science Research*, *3*(5). https://j-innovative.org/index.php/Innovative/article/view/6132/4308

Song, C., Shin, S. Y., & Shin, K. S. (2024). Implementing the dynamic feedback-driven learning optimization framework: a machine learning approach to personalize educational pathways. Applied Sciences. mdpi.com

Son, T. H., Weedon, Z., Yigitcanlar, T., Sanchez, T., Corchado, J. M., & Mehmood, R. (2023). Algorithmic urban planning for smart and sustainable development: Systematic review of the literature. *Sustainable Cities and Society*, *94*, 104562. DOI: 10.1016/j.scs.2023.104562

Sopiansyah, D., Masruroh, S., Zaqiah, Q. Y., & Erihadiana, M. (2022). Konsep dan implementasi kurikulum MBKM (merdeka belajar kampus merdeka). *Reslaj: Religion Education Social Laa Roiba Journal*, *4*(1), 34–41. DOI: 10.47467/reslaj.v4i1.458

Soubra, L., Al-Ghouti, M. A., Abu-Dieyeh, M., Crovella, S., & Abou-Saleh, H. (2022). Impacts on student learning and skills and implementation challenges of two student-centered learning methods applied in online education. [mdpi.com]. *Sustainability (Basel)*, *14*(15), 9625. DOI: 10.3390/su14159625

Souza, R. D., Parveen, R., Chupradit, S., Velasco, L. G., Tabuena, A. C., Pentang, J. T., & Ventayen, R. J. M. (2021). Language Teachers' Pedagogical Orientations in Integrating Technology in the Online Classroom: Its Effect on Students Motivation and Engagement. *Turkish Journal of Computer and Mathematics Education, 12*. https://papers.ssrn.com/sol3/papers.cfm?abstract_id=3844678

Srivastava, S. (2023). The evolution of education: Navigating 21st-century challenges. *International Journal for Multidisciplinary Research*, *5*(5), 1–9.

Stellmann, E., & Song, L. (2024). Essential elements of digital citizenship: Insights from the literature. *TechTrends*, *68*(4), 749–760. DOI: 10.1007/s11528-024-00985-8

Stelwagen, M., van Kempen, A., Westmaas, A., Vet, E., & Scheele, F. (2021). Parents' experiences with a model of integrated maternity and neonatal care designed to empower parents. [sciencedirect.com]. *Journal of Obstetric, Gynecologic, and Neonatal Nursing : JOGNN*, *50*(2), 181–192. DOI: 10.1016/j.jogn.2020.11.001 PMID: 33428875

Stover, J., Avadhanula, L., & Sood, S. (2024). A review of strategies and levels of community engagement in strengths-based and needs-based health communication interventions. Frontiers in Public Health. frontiersin.org

Strazdins, L. (2024). Action: Time to Change?. The Unequal Hour: How Time Is Shaping Health. [HTML]

Suárez, E. & Beatty, C. C. (2022). Advising in science education: Critiquing where we have been, moving toward an equitable and holistic advising approach. Science Education. wiley.com

Sui, J. (2023). Confucius Influence on Primary Education--- Research Based on Eastsouthern Asian Countries. In Lecture Notes in Education Psychology and Public Media (Vol. 2, Issue 1, p. 1049). https://doi.org/DOI: 10.54254/2753-7048/2/2022657

Su, J., & Yang, W. (2023). Unlocking the power of ChatGPT: A framework for applying generative AI in education. *ECNU Review of Education*, *6*(3), 355–366. DOI: 10.1177/20965311231168423

Sujarwo, Abdul Hakim Yassi, & Abbas, Herawaty, & Harlinah sahib. (2024). An Interactive-Based E-Module of Translation Technology of Blended and Online Learning to Improve Autonomous Learning. [TSRJ]. *The Seyreport Journal*, *19*(06), 193–209. DOI: 10.5281/ZENODO.11547317

Sujarwo, S., Asdar, A., Sabillah, B. M., Sukmawati, S., Akhiruddin, A., & Muh. Syata, W. (2023). Innovation In English Language Learning Model Based Digital Literacy To Construct Young Learners' Character. *Ethical Lingua. Journal of Language Teaching and Literature, 10*(2). Advance online publication. DOI: 10.30605/25409190.640

Sujarwo, S., Sukmawati, S., Asdar, A., Siradjuddin, S., & Ariani, N. (2020). University Students' Perception on the Verbal Interaction through WhatsApp Chat Group. *Al-Ta Lim Journal, 27*(3), 250–257. DOI: 10.15548/jt.v27i3.633

Sullamo, A. E., Mekonnen, E. A., & Mihirete, D. M. (2023). Teacher educators' views vis-à-vis their practices on facilitating learning to teach. In Pedagogical Research (Vol. 8, Issue 4). Lectito Journals. https://doi.org/DOI: 10.29333/pr/13477

Sulviana, Muhammad Chairil Imran & Sulviana. (2022). Using BBC Web-Based Learning Courses to Improve Vocational High School (VHS) Students' Speaking Skill. *EDULEC : Education, Language, and Culture Journal, 2*(1), 94–100. DOI: 10.56314/edulec.v2i1.34

Sumo, J. N., Staffileno, B. A., Warner, K., Arrieta, M., & Salinas, I. (2021). The development of an online diversity and inclusion community: Promoting a culture of inclusion within a college of nursing. *Journal of Professional Nursing, 37*(1), 18–23. DOI: 10.1016/j.profnurs.2020.10.002 PMID: 33674090

Sun, W., & Shi, H. (2024). Fostering Success in Online English Education: Exploring the Effects of ICT Literacy, Online Learning Self-Efficacy, and Motivation on Deep Learning. *Education and Information Technologies, 29*(18), 24899–24920. DOI: 10.1007/s10639-024-12827-4

Supriyadi, S., & Nasution, Z. (2024). Teknologi Artificial Intelligence (AI) dan Literasi Digital Mahasiswa terhadap Hasil Belajar Mata Kuliah Evaluasi Pembelajaran: Artificial Intelligence, Literasi Digital, Evaluasi Pembelajaran. Jurnal Teknodik, 113-118.

Supriyadi, S. M., & Maesyaroh, S. (2023). The Effect of Parenting Patterns and Digital Literacy on Social-Emotional Development in Early Children. *Jurnal Ilmiah Profesi Pendidikan, 8*(1b), 859–867. Advance online publication. DOI: 10.29303/jipp.v8i1b.1202

Supriya, Y., Bhulakshmi, D., Bhattacharya, S., Gadekallu, T. R., Vyas, P., Kaluri, R., Sumathy, S., Koppu, S., Brown, D. J., & Mahmud, M. (2024). Industry 5.0 in smart education: Concepts, applications, challenges, opportunities, and future directions. *IEEE Access : Practical Innovations, Open Solutions, 12*, 81938–81967. DOI: 10.1109/ACCESS.2024.3401473

Syanurdin, S. (2020, October). Pembelajaran Bahasa Indonesia Berbasis Digital dalam Membina Karakter Siswa. In Seminar Nasional Pendidikan Bahasa dan Sastra (pp. 44-51).

Syarafudin, H. M., & Ikawati, H. D. (2020). Faktor-faktor yang mempengaruhi profesionalisme guru. Jurnal Cahaya Mandalika ISSN 2721-4796 (online), 1(2), 47-51.

Szymkowiak, A., Melović, B., Dabić, M., Jeganathan, K., & Kundi, G. S. (2021). Information technology and Gen Z: The role of teachers, the internet, and technology in the education of young people. *Technology in Society*, *65*, 101565. DOI: 10.1016/j.techsoc.2021.101565

Taddeo, M., & Floridi, L. (2018). How AI can be a force for good. In Science (Vol. 361, Issue 6404, p. 751). American Association for the Advancement of Science. https://doi.org/DOI: 10.1126/science.aat5991

Tadlaoui-Brahmi, A., Çuko, K., & Alvarez, L. (2022). Digital citizenship in primary education: A systematic literature review describing how it is implemented. *Social Sciences & Humanities Open*, *6*(1), 100348. DOI: 10.1016/j.ssaho.2022.100348

Taherdoost, H. (2022). What are different research approaches? Comprehensive review of qualitative, quantitative, and mixed method research, their applications, types, and limitations. [hal.science]. *Journal of Management Science & Engineering Research*, *5*(1), 53–63. DOI: 10.30564/jmser.v5i1.4538

Tandiono, R. (2024). Gamifying online learning: An evaluation of Kahoot's effectiveness in promoting student engagement. [HTML]. *Education and Information Technologies*, *29*(18), 24005–24022. DOI: 10.1007/s10639-024-12800-1

Tanjga, M. (2023). E-learning and the Use of AI: A Review of Current Practices and Future Directions [Review of E-learning and the Use of AI: A Review of Current Practices and Future Directions]. https://doi.org/DOI: 10.32388/AP0208

Tanveer, M., Hassan, S., & Bhaumik, A. (2020). Academic Policy Regarding Sustainability and Artificial Intelligence (AI). In Sustainability (Vol. 12, Issue 22, p. 9435). Multidisciplinary Digital Publishing Institute. https://doi.org/DOI: 10.3390/su12229435

Tao, J., & Gao, X. A. (2022). Teaching and learning languages online: Challenges and responses. *System*, *107*, 102819.

Tarchiani, V. & Grey, S. (2025). Bridging the communication gap in agrometeorological services: Enhancing the uptake and effectiveness for users in developing countries. Climate Services. sciencedirect.com

Tariq, M. U. (2025). *Advancing Inquiry-Based Learning Through Generative AI-Enabled Assessments*. Educational Assessments in the Age of Generative AI. [HTML] DOI: 10.4018/979-8-3693-6351-5.ch007

Tautz, D., Sprenger, D. A., & Schwaninger, A. (2021). Evaluation of four digital tools and their perceived impact on active learning, repetition and feedback in a large university class. [HTML]. *Computers & Education*, *175*, 104338. DOI: 10.1016/j.compedu.2021.104338

Tawafak, R. M., Al-Obaydi, L. H., Klimova, B., & Pikhart, M. (2023). Technology Integration of Using Digital Gameplay for Enhancing Efl College Students' Behavior Intention. *Contemporary Educational Technology*, *15*(4), ep452. DOI: 10.30935/cedtech/13454

Tereshchenko, E., Salmela, E., Melkko, E., Phang, S. K., & Happonen, A. (2024). Emerging best strategies and capabilities for university–industry cooperation: Opportunities for MSMEs and universities to improve collaboration. A literature review 2000–2023. [springer.com]. *Journal of Innovation and Entrepreneurship*, *13*(1), 28. DOI: 10.1186/s13731-024-00386-4

Thawesaengskulthai, N., Chatmarathong, A., & Koiwanit, J. (2024). Impact and policy supporting Thailand innovation driven enterprise: Orchestrating university innovation and entrepreneurship ecosystem with public and private stakeholders. [springer.com]. *Journal of Innovation and Entrepreneurship*, *13*(1), 16. DOI: 10.1186/s13731-024-00371-x

The Impact of Artificial Intelligence on Learning. (2018). https://publications.jrc.ec.europa.eu/repository/bitstream/JRC113226/jrc113226_jrcb4_the_impact_of_artificial_intelligence_on_learning_final_2.pdf

Theodorio, A. O. (2024). Examining the support required by educators for successful technology integration in teacher professional development program. Cogent Education. tandfonline.com

Thompson, F., Rongen, F., Cowburn, I., & Till, K. (2022). The impacts of sports schools on holistic athlete development: a mixed methods systematic review. Sports medicine. springer.com

Thornhill-Miller, B., Camarda, A., Mercier, M., Burkhardt, J. M., Morisseau, T., Bourgeois-Bougrine, S., Vinchon, F., El Hayek, S., Augereau-Landais, M., Mourey, F., Feybesse, C., Sundquist, D., & Lubart, T. (2023). Creativity, critical thinking, communication, and collaboration: Assessment, certification, and promotion of 21st century skills for the future of work and education. [mdpi.com]. *Journal of Intelligence*, *11*(3), 54. DOI: 10.3390/jintelligence11030054 PMID: 36976147

Thorn, P., La Sala, L., Hetrick, S., Rice, S., Lamblin, M., & Robinson, J. (2023). Motivations and perceived harms and benefits of online communication about self-harm: An interview study with young people. *Digital Health, 9*, 20552076231176689.

Tian, X. (2025). Unraveling the dynamics of password manager adoption: A deeper dive into critical factors. *Information and Computer Security, 33*(1), 117–139. DOI: 10.1108/ICS-09-2023-0156

Ticona Machaca, A., Cano Ccoa, D. M., Gutiérrez Castillo, F. H., Quispe Gomez, F., Arroyo Beltrán, M., Zirena Cano, M. G., Sánchez-Chávez-Arroyo, V., Manrique Chavez, C. P., Romualdo Rosario, A., Adauto-Medina, W. A., & Montes Salcedo, M. (2025). Public Policy for Human Capital: Fostering Sustainable Equity in Disadvantaged Communities. [mdpi.com]. *Sustainability (Basel), 17*(2), 535. DOI: 10.3390/su17020535

Timotheou, S., Miliou, O., Dimitriadis, Y., Sobrino, S. V., Giannoutsou, N., Cachia, R., Monés, A. M., & Ioannou, A. (2023). Impacts of digital technologies on education and factors influencing schools' digital capacity and transformation: A literature review. [springer.com]. *Education and Information Technologies, 28*(6), 6695–6726. DOI: 10.1007/s10639-022-11431-8 PMID: 36465416

Tjahyanti, L. P. A. S., Saputra, P. S., & Santo Gitakarma, M. (2022). Peran artificial intelligence (AI) untuk mendukung pembelajaran di masa pandemi Covid-19. Komteks, 1(1).

Tobin, R., Crawford, G., Hallett, J., Maycock, B. R., & Lobo, R. (2022). Critical factors that affect the functioning of a research and evaluation capacity building partnership: A causal loop diagram. Plos one. plos.org

Tokovska, M., Ferreira, V. N., Vallušova, A., & Seberíni, A. (2023). E-Government—The inclusive way for the future of digital citizenship. Societies.

Toyokawa, Y., Horikoshi, I., Majumdar, R., & Ogata, H. (2023). Challenges and opportunities of AI in inclusive education: a case study of data-enhanced active reading in Japan. In Smart Learning Environments (Vol. 10, Issue 1). Springer Nature. https://doi.org/DOI: 10.1186/s40561-023-00286-2

Tran Pham, T. K., & Le Hoang Thuy To Nguyen, Q. (2024). Impact of e-government on citizen engagement: The role of government reputation and digital divide. Journal of Information. *Communication and Ethics in Society, 22*(4), 419–433. DOI: 10.1108/JICES-08-2023-0109

Treve, M. (2021). What COVID-19 has introduced into education: Challenges facing higher education institutions (HEIs). Higher Education Pedagogies. tandfonline.com

Tsai, C., Ma, Y., Chang, Y., & Lai, Y.-H. (2022). Integrating Multiculturalism Into Artificial Intelligence-Assisted Programming Lessons: Examining Inter-Ethnicity Differences in Learning Expectancy, Motivation, and Effectiveness. In Frontiers in Psychology (Vol. 13). Frontiers Media. https://doi.org/. 868698DOI: 10.3389/fpsyg.2022

U.S. Department of Education. (n.d.). Artificial Intelligence and the Future of Teaching and Learning (PDF). Retrieved December 30, 2024, from https://www2.ed.gov/documents/ai-report/ai-report.pdf

Umer, R., Susnjak, T., Mathrani, A., & Suriadi, L. (2023). Current stance on predictive analytics in higher education: Opportunities, challenges and future directions. [HTML]. *Interactive Learning Environments*, *31*(6), 3503–3528. DOI: 10.1080/10494820.2021.1933542

UNESCO. (2015). *Incheon Declaration and Framework for Action for the implementation of SDG 4*. UNESCO.

UNESCO. (2018). *ICT in Education: A Tool for Achieving SDG 4*. UNESCO.

UNESCO. (2019). *AI for education: Policy, challenges, and opportunities*. UNESCO.

UNESCO. (2019). *Education for sustainable development goals: Learning objectives*. https://www.unesco.org/en/articles/education-sustainable-development-goals-learning-objectives

UNESCO. (2020). *AI in education: A strategic overview*. UNESCO.

United Nations. (2015). *Transforming our world: The 2030 agenda for sustainable development*. United Nations. https://sdgs.un.org/2030agenda

Upadhyay, P., Kumar, A., & Mukerji, M. (2025). Evolving role of public-private stakeholders in technology mediated teaching. Digital Policy [HTML]. *Regulation & Governance*, *27*(1), 56–73. DOI: 10.1108/DPRG-09-2023-0130

Utina, S. S., Chusniyah, T., Inseachiangmai, J., Zahra, G. A., & Pambudi, K. S. (2024). A comparative study of artificial intelligence in education psychology: The cases of Indonesia and Thailand. *Bulletin of Social Informatics Theory and Application*, *8*(1), 70–85. DOI: 10.31763/businta.v8i1.663

Vahed, A., & Rodriguez, K. (2021). Enriching students' engaged learning experiences through the collaborative online international learning project. [HTML]. *Innovations in Education and Teaching International*, *58*(5), 596–605. DOI: 10.1080/14703297.2020.1792331

Vaishya, R., Scarlat, M. M., Bhadani, J. S., & Vaish, A. (2024). Ethics in orthopaedic surgery practice: balancing patient care and technological advances. International Orthopaedics. springer.com

Valk, A., & Kratovitš, M. (2021). We collaborate with everyone, but with some more than others: Evidence of stakeholder collaboration among internal security professional higher education institutions. [springer.com]. *Empirical Research in Vocational Education and Training*, *13*(1), 4. DOI: 10.1186/s40461-021-00110-6

Valtonen, T., Kukkonen, J., Kontkanen, S., Mäkitalo-Siegl, K., & Sointu, E. (2018). Differences in pre-service teachers' knowledge and readiness to use ICT in education. *Journal of Computer Assisted Learning*, *34*(2), 174–182. DOI: 10.1111/jcal.12225

Van Baarle, E., Hartman, L., Rooijakkers, S., Wallenburg, I., Weenink, J. W., Bal, R., & Widdershoven, G. (2022). Fostering a just culture in healthcare organizations: Experiences in practice. [springer.com]. *BMC Health Services Research*, *22*(1), 1035. DOI: 10.1186/s12913-022-08418-z PMID: 35964117

Van der Graaf, P., Blank, L., Holding, E., & Goyder, E. (2021). What makes a 'successful' collaborative research project between public health practitioners and academics? A mixed-methods review of funding applications submitted to a local intervention evaluation scheme. [springer.com]. *Health Research Policy and Systems*, *19*(1), 1–13. DOI: 10.1186/s12961-020-00671-0 PMID: 33472643

Varadarajan, S., Koh, J. H. L., & Daniel, B. K. (2023). A systematic review of the opportunities and challenges of micro-credentials for multiple stakeholders: Learners, employers, higher education institutions and government. [springer.com]. *International Journal of Educational Technology in Higher Education*, *20*(1), 13. DOI: 10.1186/s41239-023-00381-x PMID: 36874535

Vashishth, T. K., Sharma, V., Sharma, K. K., Kumar, B., Chaudhary, S., & Panwar, R. (2024). Security and Privacy Considerations in Cloud-Based Data Processing Solutions for Sensitive Data. In Developments Towards Next Generation Intelligent Systems for Sustainable Development (pp. 35-61). IGI Global. [HTML] DOI: 10.4018/979-8-3693-5643-2.ch002

Vashishth, T. K., Sharma, V., Sharma, K. K., Kumar, B., Panwar, R., & Chaudhary, S. (2024). AI-driven learning analytics for personalized feedback and assessment in higher education. In *Using traditional design methods to enhance AI-driven decision making* (pp. 206–230). IGI Global Scientific Publishing. [HTML] DOI: 10.4018/979-8-3693-0639-0.ch009

Vassilakopoulou, P., & Hustad, E. (2021). Bridging Digital Divides: a Literature Review and Research Agenda for Information Systems Research [Review of Bridging Digital Divides: a Literature Review and Research Agenda for Information Systems Research]. Information Systems Frontiers, 25(3), 955. Springer Science+Business Media. https://doi.org/DOI: 10.1007/s10796-020-10096-3

Vázquez-Cano, E., Mengual-Andrés, S., & López-Meneses, E. (2021). Chatbot To Improve Learning Punctuation in Spanish and To Enhance Open and Flexible Learning Environments. *International Journal of Educational Technology in Higher Education, 18*(33), 33. Advance online publication. DOI: 10.1186/s41239-021-00269-8

Venkatesh, R., & Rajavelu, S. (2025). Effective Strategies for Involving Faculty and Staff in Every Stage of the Accreditation Journey to Achieve Excellence. In Global Perspectives on Quality Management and Accreditation in Higher Education (pp. 351-386). IGI Global Scientific Publishing. [HTML] DOI: 10.4018/979-8-3693-9481-6.ch015

Verčič, A. T., Verčič, D., Čož, S., & Špoljarić, A. (2024). A systematic review of digital internal communication. *Public Relations Review*.

Vian, T., Agnew, B., & McInnes, K. (2022). Whistleblowing as an anti-corruption strategy in health and pharmaceutical organizations in low-and middle-income countries: a scoping review. Global health action. tandfonline.com

Vičič Krabonja, M., Kustec, S., Skrbinjek, V., Aberšek, B., & Flogie, A. (2024). Innovative professional learning communities and sustainable education practices through digital transformation. [mdpi.com]. *Sustainability (Basel), 16*(14), 6250. DOI: 10.3390/su16146250

Vincent-Lancrin, S., & Van der Vlies, R. (2020). Trustworthy artificial intelligence (AI) in education: Promises and challenges. OECD education working papers, (218), 0_1-17.

Viswanadham, N. (2021). Ecosystem model for healthcare platform. Sādhanā. springer.com

Vogel, R., Göbel, M., Grewe-Salfeld, M., Herbert, B., Matsuo, Y., & Weber, C. (2022). Cross-sector partnerships: Mapping the field and advancing an institutional approach. [wiley.com]. *International Journal of Management Reviews, 24*(3), 394–414. DOI: 10.1111/ijmr.12283

Vygotsky, L. S. (1978). *Mind in society: The development of higher psychological processes*. Harvard University Press.

Wahid, A., Afni, N., & Sujarwo, S. (2025). Promoting Learners' Autonomy through Metacognitive, Higher-Order Thinking Skills and Digital Literacy of Indonesian Private Universities. *Educational Process International Journal, 16*(1). Advance online publication. DOI: 10.22521/edupij.2025.16.204

Wakelin, K. J., McAra-Couper, J., Fleming, T., & Erlam, G. D. (2023). Communication technology practices used by midwives with pregnant women/people in Aotearoa New Zealand to ensure quality maternal and newborn care. Midwifery. sciencedirect.com

Wakiyama, T., Lenzen, M., Faturay, F., Geschke, A., Malik, A., Fry, J., & Nansai, K. (2019). Responsibility for food loss from a regional supply-chain perspective. *Resources, Conservation and Recycling, 146*, 373–383. DOI: 10.1016/j.resconrec.2019.04.003

Walker, R. T. (2022). Grassroots Communication. In *The Palgrave Encyclopedia of Interest Groups, Lobbying and Public Affairs* (pp. 599–604). Springer International Publishing. DOI: 10.1007/978-3-030-44556-0_196

Wang, C. & Si, L. (2024). The intersection of public policy and public access: Digital inclusion, digital literacy education, and libraries. Sustainability.

Wang, R., Standfield, B., Dou, C., Law, A. C., & Kong, Z. J. (2023). Real-time process monitoring and closed-loop control on laser power via a customized laser powder bed fusion platform. Additive Manufacturing. sciencedirect.com

Wang, T. & Cheng, E. C. K. (2021). An investigation of barriers to Hong Kong K-12 schools incorporating Artificial Intelligence in education. Computers and Education: Artificial Intelligence. sciencedirect.com

Wang, Y. (2020). When artificial intelligence meets educational leaders' data-informed decision-making: A cautionary tale. In Studies In Educational Evaluation (Vol. 69, p. 100872). Elsevier BV. https://doi.org/. 2020.100872DOI: 10.1016/j.stueduc

Wang, F., Wong, W. K., Wang, Z., Albasher, G., Alsultan, N., & Fatemah, A. (2023). Emerging pathways to sustainable economic development: An interdisciplinary exploration of resource efficiency, technological innovation, and ecosystem resilience in resource-rich regions. [HTML]. *Resources Policy, 85*, 103747. DOI: 10.1016/j.resourpol.2023.103747

Wang, V. (2025). *Ethics and Equity in AI-Driven Education.* AI Integration Into Andragogical Education. [HTML] DOI: 10.4018/979-8-3373-0502-8.ch010

Wang, X., & Zhang, W. (2022). Improvement of Students' Autonomous Learning Behavior by Optimizing Foreign Language Blended Learning Mode. In Open, S. A. G. E. (Ed.), *Issue 1). SAGE Publishing* (Vol. 12)., DOI: 10.1177/21582440211071108

Wang, Y. (2020). When artificial intelligence meets educational leaders' data-informed decision-making: A cautionary tale. In *Studies In Educational Evaluation* (Vol. 69, p. 100872). Elsevier BV., DOI: 10.1016/j.stueduc.2020.100872

Wang, Y. (2021). In-Service Teachers' Perceptions of Technology Integration and Practices in a Japanese University Context. *The JALT CALL Journal*, *17*(1), 45–71. DOI: 10.29140/jaltcall.v17n1.377

Wang, Y., Fu, E. Y., Zhai, X., Yang, C., & Pei, F. (2024). Introduction of Artificial Intelligence. In Huang, X., & Tam, W. C. (Eds.), *Intelligent Building Fire Safety and Smart Firefighting. Digital Innovations in Architecture, Engineering and Construction*. Springer., DOI: 10.1007/978-3-031-48161-1_4

Wannas, A. S., & Alshaye, R. A. (2024). Integration of Intrinsic and Extrinsic Motivation in Second Language Acquisition: Magnetism as a Proposed Theory. *World Journal of English Language*, *14*(4), 76. DOI: 10.5430/wjel.v14n4p76

Warni, S., Aziz, T. A., & Febriawan, D. (2018). The Use of Technology in English as a Foreign Language Learning Outside the Classroom: An Insight into Learner Autonomy. *LLT Journal: A Journal on Language and Language Teaching, 21*(2), 148–156. DOI: 10.24071/llt.v21i2.1259

Waymack, N., Groom-Thomas, L., Loeb, S., & Bendheim, K. (2024). Outcomes-Based Contracting in Tutoring: Insights and Recommendations. studentsupportaccelerator.org

Weber, F., Wambsganss, T., & Söllner, M. (2025). Enhancing legal writing skills: The impact of formative feedback in a hybrid intelligence learning environment. British Journal of Educational Technology, 56(2), 650-677. wiley.com

Weber, R. H. (2019). Socio-ethical values and legal rules on automated platforms: The quest for a symbiotic relationship. In *Computer Law & Security Review* (Vol. 36, p. 105380). Elsevier BV., DOI: 10.1016/j.clsr.2019.105380

Weinstein, N., Itzchakov, G., & Legate, N. (2022). The motivational value of listening during intimate and difficult conversations. *Social and Personality Psychology Compass*, *16*(2), e12651. DOI: 10.1111/spc3.12651

Wellner, G., & Levin, I. (2023). Ihde meets Papert: Combining postphenomenology and constructionism for a future agenda of philosophy of education in the era of digital technologies. *Learning, Media and Technology*, *49*(4), 656–669. DOI: 10.1080/17439884.2023.2251388

Welukar, J. N., & Bajoria, G. P. (2021). Artificial Intelligence in Cyber Security - A Review [Review of Artificial Intelligence in Cyber Security - A Review]. International Journal of Scientific Research in Science and Technology, 488. Technoscience Academy. https://doi.org/DOI: 10.32628/IJSRST218675

West, D. M. (2018). *Artificial intelligence: The implications for education*. Brookings Institution.

Widdows, D. (2024). *Natural Language, AI, and Quantum Computing 2024: Research*. Research Ingredients and Directions in QNLP, http://arxiv.org/abs/2403.19758

Wiedermann, C. J., Barbieri, V., Plagg, B., Marino, P., Piccoliori, G., & Engl, A. (2023, May). Fortifying the foundations: a comprehensive approach to enhancing mental health support in educational policies amidst crises. In Healthcare (Vol. 11, No. 10, p. 1423). MDPI. mdpi.com DOI: 10.3390/healthcare11101423

Wilson-Menzfeld, G., Gates, J. R., Moreland, M., Raw, H., & Johnson, A. (2023). Learning digital skills online: Empowering older adults through one-to-one, online digital training provision. *Frontiers in Psychology*, *14*, 1122277. DOI: 10.3389/fpsyg.2023.1122277 PMID: 37213359

Winkler, R., & Soellner, M. (2018). Rainer Winkler dan Matthias Söllner. (2018). *Unleashing the Potential of Chatbots in Education: A State-Of-The-Art Analysis. Proceedings - Academy of Management*, *2018*(1), 15903. Advance online publication. DOI: 10.5465/AMBPP.2018.15903abstract

Winston, P. H. (1984). *Artificial intelligence*. Addison-Wesley Longman Publishing Co., Inc.

Wiyono, B. B., Imron, A., Rahma, L., Arifah, N., Azhari, R., Sibula, I., & Maharmawan, M. (2024). Elevating teachers' professional digital competence: Synergies of principals' instructional e-supervision, technology leadership and digital culture for educational excellence in digital-savvy era. *Education Sciences*, *14*(3), 266. DOI: 10.3390/educsci14030266

Wong, P. (2020). Cultural Differences as Excuses? Human Rights and Cultural Values in Global Ethics and Governance of AI. In Philosophy & Technology (Vol. 33, Issue 4, p. 705). Springer Nature (Netherlands). DOI: 10.1007/s13347-020-00413-8

Woolf, B. P., Arroyo, I., & Zualkernan, I. (2011). *Education Technology for the Developing World.*, DOI: 10.1109/GHTC.2011.69

World Commission on Environment and Development (WCED). (1987). *Our common future*. Oxford University Press.

Wu, H., Liu, J., & Liang, B. (2024). AI-driven supply chain transformation in Industry 5.0: Enhancing resilience and sustainability. *Journal of the Knowledge Economy*, *16*(1), 1–43. DOI: 10.1007/s13132-024-01999-6

Xia, Q., Chiu, T. K. F., Lee, M., Sanusi, I. T., Dai, Y., & Chai, C. S. (2022). A self-determination Theory (SDT) Design Approach for Inclusive and Diverse Artificial Intelligence (AI) Education. *Computers & Education*, *189*, 104582. Advance online publication. DOI: 10.1016/j.compedu.2022.104582

Xiuzhi, F., & Yongtao, X. (2023). Excellent Traditional Culture Entering College Campus: Mechanism Innovation and Practical Strategies. In SHS Web of Conferences (Vol. 168, p. 1016). EDP Sciences. https://doi.org/DOI: 10.1051/shsconf/202316801016

Xu, S. (2023). Retracted: Design and Implementation of Intelligent Teaching System Based on Artificial Intelligence and Computer Technology. *Security and Communication Networks*, *2023*, 1. Advance online publication. DOI: 10.1155/2023/9854971

Yadav, S. (2025). Leveraging AI to Enhance Teaching and Learning in Education: The Role of Artificial Intelligence in Modernizing Classroom Practices. In Optimizing Research Techniques and Learning Strategies With Digital Technologies (pp. 211-238). IGI Global Scientific Publishing. [HTML]

Yadav, U., & Shrawankar, U. (2025). Artificial Intelligence Across Industries: A Comprehensive Review With a Focus on Education. AI Applications and Strategies in Teacher Education, 275-320. [HTML]

Yahya, M., & Hidayat, A. (2023, July). Implementasi Artificial Intelligence (AI) di bidang pendidikan kejuruan pada era revolusi industri 4.0. In Seminar Nasional Dies Natalis 62 (Vol. 1, pp. 190-199).

Yam, K. C., Tan, T. C. Y., Jackson, J. C., Shariff, A., & Gray, K. (2023). Cultural Differences in People's Reactions and Applications of Robots, Algorithms, and Artificial Intelligence. In Management and Organization Review (Vol. 19, Issue 5, p. 859). Cambridge University Press. https://doi.org/DOI: 10.1017/mor.2023.21

Yang, Y. T. C., Chen, Y. C., & Hung, H. T. (2022). Digital storytelling as an interdisciplinary project to improve students' English speaking and creative thinking. *Computer Assisted Language Learning*, *35*(4), 840–862. DOI: 10.1080/09588221.2020.1750431

Ye, Z., & Hu, D.-Y. (2023). Research on the Strategy of Integrating Chinese Excellent Traditional Culture into Primary School Moral Education. In Curriculum and Teaching Methodology (Vol. 6, Issue 7). DOI: 10.23977/curtm.2023.060704

Yee, G. A. (2022). Midwives in Egypt, Mesopotamia, and Ancient Israel: An Intersectional Investigation. [HTML]. *Biblical Theology Bulletin*, *52*(3), 146–159. DOI: 10.1177/01461079221102970

Yefremtseva, T. N., Musagulova, R. E., Takanova, O. V., Zaitsev, A. A., & Sergeeva, N. (2021). Rethinking the intercultural communicative competence evaluation in higher education. In SHS Web of Conferences (Vol. 127, p. 2001). EDP Sciences. https://doi.org/DOI: 10.1051/shsconf/202112702001

Ye, G., Hudders, L., De Jans, S., & De Veirman, M. (2021). The value of influencer marketing for business: A bibliometric analysis and managerial implications. *Journal of Advertising*, *50*(2), 160–178. DOI: 10.1080/00913367.2020.1857888

Yi, H., Liu, T., & Lan, G. (2024). The key artificial intelligence technologies in early childhood education: a review [Review of The key artificial intelligence technologies in early childhood education: a review]. Artificial Intelligence Review, 57(1). Springer Science+Business Media. DOI: 10.1007/s10462-023-10637-7

Yim, I. H. Y., & Su, J. (2024). Artificial intelligence (AI) learning tools in K-12 education: A scoping review [Review of Artificial intelligence (AI) learning tools in K-12 education: A scoping review]. Journal of Computers in Education. Springer Science+Business Media. https://doi.org/DOI: 10.1007/s40692-023-00304-9

Yingsoon, G. Y., Chua, N. A., Suyan, Z., Yiming, C., Haiyan, Z., & Xiaoyao, T. (2025). Empowering Digital Citizens: Navigating AI Ethics, Engagement, and Privacy in the Era of Advanced Education. In *Digital Citizenship and the Future of AI Engagement, Ethics, and Privacy* (pp. 79-110). IGI Global Scientific Publishing.

Yoon, M., Lee, J., & Jo, I. H. (2021). Video learning analytics: Investigating behavioral patterns and learner clusters in video-based online learning. [HTML]. *The Internet and Higher Education*, *50*, 100806. DOI: 10.1016/j.iheduc.2021.100806

Yu, J., Kreijkes, P., & Salmela-Aro, K. (2022). Students' growth mindset: Relation to teacher beliefs, teaching practices, and school climate. Learning and Instruction. sciencedirect.com

Yu, X. (2021). Research on the Strategy of Multi Ethnic Culture Blending in School Field Based on Internet of Things. In Journal of Physics Conference Series (Vol. 1744, Issue 4, p. 42022). IOP Publishing. https://doi.org/DOI: 10.1088/1742-6596/1744/4/042022

Yue, A. (2022). From digital literacy to digital citizenship: Policies, assessment frameworks and programs for young people in the Asia Pacific. *Media Asia.*

Yu, J., Bekerian, D. A., & Osback, C. (2024). Navigating the Digital Landscape: Challenges and Barriers to Effective Information Use on the Internet. *Encyclopedia, 4*(4), 1665–1680.

Yundayani, A., Suseno, M., & Herlina, E. (2023). A Duolingo-based English Language Skills Assessment: Through the Eyes of Vocational Students. In Jurnal Ilmu Pendidikan (JIP) STKIP Kusuma Negara (Vol. 15, Issue 1, p. 9). https://doi.org/ DOI: 10.37640/jip.v15i1.1683

Zaidi, T., Garai, S., & Biradar, T. V. (2024). Exploring the landscape of password managers for individual users through innovative solution. In Information Technology Security: Modern Trends and Challenges (pp. 69-99). Singapore: Springer Nature Singapore. DOI: 10.1007/978-981-97-0407-1_4

Zainuddin, Z. (2024). Integrating ease of use and affordable gamification-based instruction into a remote learning environment. Asia Pacific Education Review. springer.com

Zamiri, M. & Esmaeili, A. (2024). Methods and technologies for supporting knowledge sharing within learning communities: A systematic literature review. Administrative Sciences. mdpi.com

Zamiri, M. & Esmaeili, A. (2024). Strategies, methods, and supports for developing skills within learning communities: A systematic review of the literature. Administrative Sciences. mdpi.com

Zamiri, M., & Esmaeili, A. (2024). Methods and technologies for supporting knowledge sharing within learning communities: A systematic literature review. *Administrative Sciences, 14*(1), 17.

Zawacki-Richter, O., Marín, V. I., Bond, M., & Gouverneur, F. (2019). Systematic Review of Research on Artificial Intelligence Applications in Higher Education-Where Are the Educators? *International Journal of Educational Technology in Higher Education, 16*(39), 39. Advance online publication. DOI: 10.1186/s41239-019-0171-0

Zebua, R. S. Y., Khairunnisa, K., Hartatik, H., Pariyadi, P., Wahyuningtyas, D. P., Thantawi, A. M., ... & Kharisma, L. P. I. (2023). *Fenomena Artificial Intelligence (Ai).* PT. Sonpedia Publishing Indonesia.

Zhai, X., Chu, X., Chai, C. S., Jong, M. S., Starčič, A. I., Spector, M., Liu, J., Jing, Y., & Li, Y. (2021). A Review of Artificial Intelligence (AI) in Education from 2010 to 2020 [Review of A Review of Artificial Intelligence (AI) in Education from 2010 to 2020]. Complexity, 2021(1). Hindawi Publishing Corporation. DOI: 10.1155/2021/8812542

Zhang, K., & Aslan, A. B. (2021). AI technologies for education: Recent research & future directions. https://www.sciencedirect.com/science/article/pii/S2666920X21000199

Zhang, K., & Aslan, A. B. (2023). AI technologies for education: Recent research & future directions. https://www.sciencedirect.com/science/article/pii/S2666920X21000199

Zhang, L., Pan, Y., Wu, X., & Skibniewski, M. J. (2021). Introduction to Artificial Intelligence. In *Artificial Intelligence in Construction Engineering and Management. Lecture Notes in Civil Engineering* (Vol. 163). Springer., DOI: 10.1007/978-981-16-2842-9_1

Zhang, S., Sun, Z., Fan, Z., & Weng, S. (2024). Transforming talent development: A reflective analysis of the innovative government-school cooperation model under the paradigm of knowledge innovation. [HTML]. *Journal of the Knowledge Economy*.

Zhang, Y., Pei, H., Zhen, S., Li, Q., & Liang, F. (2023). Chat Generative Pre-Trained Transformer (ChatGPT) Usage in Healthcare. *Gastroenterology & Endoscopy*, *1*(3), 139–143. Advance online publication. DOI: 10.1016/j.gande.2023.07.002

Zhang, Y., Ruan, H., Fan, Z., & Roychoudhury, A. (2024, September). AutoCodeRover: Autonomous program improvement. In *Proceedings of the 33rd ACM SIGSOFT International Symposium on Software Testing and Analysis* (pp. 1592-1604). doi:DOI: 10.48550/arXiv.2404.0542

Zhao, J., & Li, X. (2022). Research on the Mining of Intangible Cultural Heritage Digital Resources in the Manual Online Teaching System of Preschool Education. In Computational Intelligence and Neuroscience (Vol. 2022, p. 1). Hindawi Publishing Corporation. https://doi.org/DOI: 10.1155/2022/2136597

Zhao, Y. (2023). Globalization in Education. https://www.sciencedirect.com/ science/article/pii/B9780080970868921135

Zhao, Y., Zhao, M., & Shi, F. (2024). Integrating moral education and educational information technology: A strategic approach to enhance rural teacher training in universities. [HTML]. *Journal of the Knowledge Economy*.

Zhu, J., & Ren, C. (2022). Analysis of the Effect of Artificial Intelligence on Role Cognition in the Education System. In *Occupational Therapy International* (Vol. 2022, p. 1). Hindawi Publishing Corporation., DOI: 10.1155/2022/1781662

About the Contributors

Andi Asrifan, S.Pd, M.Pd, a distinguished figure in the realm of education, particularly in English Language Education, has made significant contributions through his extensive research, teaching, and leadership roles. As the Head of the Institute for Cooperation and International Affairs at Universitas Muhammadiyah Sidenreng Rappang and now a lecturer in Universitas Negeri Makassar (UNM), Dr. Asrifan's academic journey is marked by a rich tapestry of achievements, including a Doctor of Education in English Language Education. His work spans various facets of education, language, and technology, reflecting the diverse topics covered in his publications and research endeavors. These include, but are not limited to, the impact of the COVID-19 pandemic on educational practices, methodologies in English as a Foreign Language (EFL) classrooms, and the integration of technology in teaching and learning processes. Dr. Asrifan's commitment to advancing educational standards and practices is further evidenced by his active participation in international conferences, webinars, and workshops across countries like India, the Philippines, and Pakistan. These events, organized by various institutions and associations, underscore his role as a global educator and thought leader. His dedication to professional development is also highlighted through his involvement in numerous courses and certifications in personal branding, public speaking, and literacy teaching. Moreover, Dr. Asrifan's leadership extends beyond academia into organizational and educational development, where he has served in various capacities, including as an external examiner for Ph.D. dissertations and a reviewer for scientific journals. His accolades, memberships in professional organizations, and roles as an ambassador for international associations speak volumes of his influence and commitment to fostering educational excellence and sustainable development goals globally.

***

Maslan Abdin is a civics lecturer at Ambon State Polytechnic in the Civil Engineering Department and teaches Pancasila Education, Civics Education and Anti-Corruption Education courses in the Construction Project Management (D4), Civil Engineering (D3) and Road and Bridge Construction Engineering (D4) study programs.

Nihla Afdaliah earned her Bachelor's degree in English Education from Universitas Negeri Makassar in 2014 and a Master's degree in 2017 from the same field and institution. She has taught at several universities as an adjunct lecturer and, since 2019, has served as a civil servant under the Ministry of Religious Affairs at Sekolah Tinggi Agama Islam Negeri (STAIN) Majene. Her academic interests include English education, language pedagogy, etc.

Asia M, M. Pd, is an Indonesian Language Education and literature lecturer from the State University Makassar, Indonesia. She has over 24 years of academic experience and is currently an associate professor. Her current research interest includes students' learning and development at various levels and areas of education and literature. Her publication topics include reading comprehension, technology in language learning, and Indonesian language skills

Andi Hamsiah, M. Pd is a master's degree in Indonesian language education from the State University Makassar, Indonesia. With over 15 years of experience, he currently holds the position of Associate Professor and Vice Dean of the Faculty of Education and Literatures at Bosowa University. She is currently focused on researching students' learning and development across different educational levels and sectors. She publishes on reading comprehension, learning media, students' interest and motivation, and speaking and writing skills

Robby Hunawa was born in Jayapura on July 18, 1973. He completed his primary education at SD XXI Manado, followed by SMP II Manado, and graduated from SMA Kabila Gorontalo in 1993. He pursued higher education at Hasanuddin University, earning a degree in International Relations from the Faculty of Social and Political Sciences in 1999. Since 2001, he has served as a lecturer at Gorontalo University, where he held various administrative positions, including Assistant Dean for Student Affairs from 2002 to 2003, Assistant Dean for Academic Affairs from 2003 to 2004, and Dean from 2004 to 2011. From 2011 to 2014, he was appointed to the Human Resource Development Division at the Duluwo Limo Lo Pohalaa Education Foundation and has been the Chair of the Supervisory Board of the DLP Gorontalo Education Foundation since 2014. He holds the academic rank of Lector, classified as III.C. Robby completed his Master's degree at Sam Ratulangi University from 2009 to 2012 and his Doctorate at Gorontalo State University from

2016 to 2021. In addition to his academic career, he is actively involved in social and political activities, serving as a member of the Bone Bolango Regional House of Representatives from 2014 to 2024, Vice Chair of the Gorontalo Province DPD KNPI in 2003, and as a key figure in various initiatives for regional development.

Rajiv Iyer is currently an Associate Professor in Computer Science and Engineering at Amity University, Mumbai. With a Ph.D. in the domain of Internet of Things, he has had a distinguished career spanning 14 years in academia. He is a registered Patent Agent (IN/PA3625). He is certified educator for AWS, Celonis. He is Google Facilitator for Machine Learning and Kaggle BIPOC program mentor/advisor.

Juvrianto Chrissunday Jakob is an English lecturer at the Civil Engineering Department of Ambon State Polytechnic, Indonesia. His study interests focus on Teaching English as a Foreign Language (TEFL), Technology in Language Learning, Discourse Analysis, and English for Specific Purposes (ESP). He finished his master's degree from Universitas Negeri Makassar, Indonesia, in the English Education Department. He also serves as a tutor, a language instructor, and a reviewer in some local and international journals.

Jasmine Kaur completed her Bachelor's degree in Mathematics (Hons.) from Miranda House, University of Delhi, followed by Master of Science, Master of Philosophy, and Doctorate degrees from the Department of Operational Research, University of Delhi. Her academic focus includes Operations, Decision Sciences, and Data Analytics, with specialized research in Software Reliability and Security. She has authored publications in prestigious international journals and books. Dr. Kaur is an Assistant Professor in Christ University and brings over 2 years of teaching experience, having previously served as a faculty member at USME, Delhi Technological University, and SSCBS, University of Delhi.

Mulyadi, an academic professional with a significant background in educational management, has cultivated an extensive career in teaching and research. Born on November 4, 1973, in Bone, he pursued his higher education at Universitas Muslim Indonesia (UMI), earning his bachelor's degree in Ushuluddin in 1997. He furthered his education by obtaining a master's degree in Educational Management from PPS UNM in 2002 and a doctorate in Educational Science from the same institution in 2018. Over the years, Dr. Mulyadi has actively contributed to the academic community through teaching various subjects in educational foundations, evaluation, and counseling at Universitas Islam Makassar. His professional development includes participating in numerous workshops, seminars, and training sessions, both as a participant and a contributor, enhancing his expertise in educational methodologies and Islamic education. In addition to his academic duties, he has played a pivotal role in organizational activities, including serving as a secretary for the Nahdlatul Ulama in Makassar and contributing to educational development programs at various levels. His research interests are diverse, encompassing the evaluation of teacher performance post-certification, the development of educational models for marginalized communities, and the social-emotional development of early childhood education.

Mustafa, S.Pd.I., M.Pd.I., was born on November 28, 1985, in Manuba, Barru Regency. He began his education at SD Negeri No. 13 Manuba and continued his studies at various Islamic educational institutions in Barru, including Madrasah Tsanawiyah DDI Siddo, Madrasah I'dadiyah Pesantren DDI Mangkoso, and Madrasah Aliyah Pesantren DDI Takkalasi. He completed his undergraduate degree in Arabic Language Education at UIN Alauddin Makassar in 2008, followed by a Master's degree in Islamic Studies with a concentration in Arabic Language Education (PBA) in 2012. Currently, he is pursuing a Doctorate in the same field at UIN Alauddin Makassar. Since 2013, Mustafa has been a lecturer in Arabic Language Education at IAIN Palopo. He also served as the Secretary of the Arabic Language Education Program at the Faculty of Tarbiyah and Teacher Training (FTIK) IAIN Palopo for two terms: 2019-2023 and 2023-2027. His academic career is complemented by his extensive work in curriculum development and educational publications, reflecting his passion for improving the quality of Arabic language education. Mustafa is also a prolific author, having written and contributed to numerous books and academic works. His publications include books on Arabic language teaching, curriculum development, and practical applications for education and business. Notable works include "Catatan Seorang Pendidik" (2020), "Dinamika Pembelajaran Bahasa Arab" (2021), and "Bahasa Arab Komunikatif Berbasis Kosakata Kontemporer untuk Ekonomi dan Bisnis" (2024). His contributions continue to inspire and guide both students and fellow educators in the field of Arabic language education.

Hadi Pajarianto is a distinguished academic in the field of Islamic Education, with a profound focus on research related to religious moderation, tolerance, and local wisdom. Since 2011, he has successfully secured numerous research grants from prestigious institutions such as the Ministry of Education and Culture, LPDP, and Johns Hopkins Bloomberg School of Public Health. His dedication to education is further exemplified by his participation in the Training of Trainers (TOT) for National Values Enhancement organized by LEMHANNAS in 2022. Prof. Pajarianto's professional journey includes roles as a high school teacher and a lecturer since 2004. He has held significant positions such as Head of Quality Assurance Unit and Head of Research and Community Service at AKBIDM Palopo, as well as

Vice Director for Student Affairs and Finance. Currently, he serves as Vice Rector II for Resources, Assets, and Business at Universitas Muhammadiyah Palopo. His academic credentials include a Bachelor's degree in Islamic Education from STAIN Palopo (2004), a Master's, and a Doctorate in Education from UIN Alauddin Makassar (2013, 2016). Prof. Pajarianto is renowned for his skills in teaching, research, community service, and higher education management. His motto, "Give One Hundred Percent or Not at All," reflects his commitment to excellence in all his endeavors.

Sri Ananda Pertiwi pursued her academic journey by enrolling in the English Education Department at Muhammadiyah University of Makassar in 2010, from which she graduated in 2014. Subsequently, she advanced her studies at the Postgraduate Program of State University of Makassar, specializing in English Education, and obtained her Master's degree in 2017. Currently, she serves as a lecturer in the English Education Department at Musamus University in South Papua. Her academic interests are primarily focused on language teaching, with a particular emphasis on Teaching English as a Foreign Language (TEFL) and Teaching Young Learners (TYL).

Alfan Putra was born in Luwu, South Sulawesi, on October 21, 1988. He earned his bachelor's degree in Arabic Language from Ain Shams University, Cairo, in 2011, and continued his studies at the master's level in Arabic Literature and Language at the Arab League University/Alecso Institute of Arab Research & Studies, Cairo. His professional journey began in 2009 as a translator at Saudisoft Co. Ltd in Giza, Egypt. In 2011, he participated in Indonesia's Hajj Mission, serving in Jeddah and Arafah. Upon returning to Indonesia, he joined Pondok Pesantren Nurul Jadid Bua in 2019. In 2023, he began his academic career as a lecturer in Arabic Language Education at Institut Agama Islam Negeri (IAIN) Palopo. The author has also been active in organizational roles, including serving as Coordinator for Foreign Language Development at KKS Egypt (2007–2008) and Chairman of the Forum Kajian Bahasa Arab Indonesia Mesir (FKIBAR) in Cairo (2014–2016). With a strong background in Arabic language and education, he is dedicated to advancing the dissemination of knowledge in Indonesia.

Rismawati Sudirman is a distinguished academic and consultant with a robust focus on sustainability reporting. She currently holds the position of lecturer and Head of the Quality Assurance Institute at Universitas Muhammadiyah Palopo, where she has been pivotal in ensuring the quality of university processes and outputs since February 2020. Additionally, she serves as an Assurer for Sustainability Reporting at the National Center for Sustainability Reporting in Jakarta, specializing in the evaluation of sustainability reports for mining companies across Indonesia. Her academic qualifications are extensive, comprising a Bachelor's degree in Economics and Accounting, a Master's degree in Accounting Science, and a Doctorate in Accounting from Universitas Brawijaya, Malang. Rismawati is also a certified specialist in sustainability reporting, risk management, and tax planning, holding several prestigious certifications including Certified Sustainability Reporting Specialist (CSRS) and Certified Risk Management Practitioner (CRMP). In her professional capacity, she has provided consultancy services in financial management and tax compliance for companies such as PT. Reski Barito Timur and PT. Helay Raya. Furthermore, she has authored multiple publications on taxation and management, contributing significantly to the academic community. Her interests in reading, writing, and travel reflect her commitment to lifelong learning and professional growth in her field.

Sulaeman, born on November 17, 1974, in Barugae, is a distinguished academic specializing in Islamic Education. He holds the position of permanent lecturer in the Islamic Education Study Program at the Faculty of Islamic Studies, Universitas Muhammadiyah Makassar (Unismuh Makassar). Dr. Sulaeman earned his Bachelor's degree in Islamic Education from Unismuh Makassar in 2006, followed by a Master's degree and a Doctorate in Education and Teaching from UIN Alauddin Makassar, which he completed in 2013 and 2020, respectively. His scholarly contributions are significant, with a focus on innovative pedagogical approaches and educational methodologies. Among his notable publications are his 2023 work on innovations in Al-Islam and Kemuhammadiyahan learning, and his 2024 research addressing the enhancement of educational services for families of Indonesian migrant workers, as well as the improvement of human resource competencies through edutourism. Dr. Sulaeman is also actively involved in the publication of foundational educational texts, including "Perkembangan Peserta Didik" and "Dasar-Dasar Ilmu Pendidikan." His research and teaching endeavors not only advance academic discourse but also foster the development of essential soft skills among students, in alignment with the Merdeka Belajar Kampus Merdeka initiative.

Index

A

B

C

D

E

F

G

H

I

L

M

O

P

Q

R

S

T

www.ingramcontent.com/pod-product-compliance
Lightning Source LLC
LaVergne TN
LVHW062213200926
848484LV00006B/1380